CHILD
PSYCHOLOGY

CHILD
PSYCHOLOGY

a developmental perspective

WILLIAM J. MEYER

JEROME B. DUSEK

Syracuse University

D. C. HEATH AND COMPANY   Lexington, Massachusetts   Toronto

To Diane and Joan, and our children Beth,
David, Eric, and David.

PREFACE

OUR AIM in *Child Psychology* is to present a general survey of child growth and development solidly based on psychological theory and instructive in the practical aspects of child development. The text accordingly provides an empirical and conceptual background for those who wish to continue their studies in the field as well as for those who desire basic knowledge useful to parents, teachers and others who interact daily with children. Through the integration of disparate areas of inquiry, the complexities involved in child development and the implicit coherence of the process are illustrated.

In keeping with our objectives, we have chosen a topical format rather than a stage or eclectic (stage/topical) format. The stage format is not conducive to an understanding of developmental continuities because it leaves the child age-fragmented and obscures the emergent nature of child development across stages. The eclectic format disrupts the learning process because of the constant changes of orientation. To achieve a sense of continuity, therefore, material has to be reintroduced and repeated throughout. We believe that a topical format, with each area woven around the central underlying theme of the text, avoids the problems of these alternative approaches and provides both a coherent view of development within an area and a sense of development across areas.

A second decision based on our goals involves the choice of a theme around which the various content areas (chapters) could be integrated. Our biases led to a cognitive-developmental, or active-organism, view. This approach provides a mechanism for demonstrating the continuity of development across the content areas, so that the essence of development is communicated both within and between the areas in which it occurs. A chapter on evolution and the biological antecedents of behavior is included to prepare the way for understanding the empirical facts and conceptual tenets of the cognitive-developmental view.

Other chapters follow a traditional organization and discuss the areas of perception, cognition, models of development, physical and motor development, and adolescent development. The boldface terms found in each chapter are defined in the Glossary.

Our emphasis on the cognitive-developmental approach does not mean that we have omitted the large body of information gleaned from learning-theory investigations of development. Conceptual consistency dictates that topics related to learning be discussed throughout the text rather than in a separate chapter entitled "Learning." Hence, such concepts as classical, instrumental, or operant conditioning are discussed in the context of specific topics—for example, assessment of the sensory capacities of infants, socialization processes, and acquired fears.

The third consequence of our objectives is an extensive discussion of models of development (Chapter 2). This material provides a broad philosophical overview of pertinent developmental theories and gives students a foundation for understanding the diverse theories of, among others, Piaget, Bruner, Freud, Bandura, and Chomsky.

In each chapter we have tried to maintain a balance between a scientific approach to the study of children and a concern for practical applications. The scientific approach is presented through the discussion of specific studies and experiments that are described in sufficient detail to provide students with a degree of knowledge about how and why research is done. These research topics have been chosen for their potential interest to students. The material is designed to lead to an understanding of development itself and the various possible theoretical positions. Thus, students interested in pursuing a career in child development, or in related areas such as clinical or school psychology, education, or social work, will gain a firm scientific background.

Students interested in the practical aspects of child development will find that we have related scientific findings to various applied problems encountered by parents, teachers, or others who relate to children on a daily basis. For example, a discussion of the theoretical foundations of and research on child-rearing techniques is followed by a discussion of the influence of alternative child-rearing techniques on other aspects of the child's behavior, such as moral development, prosocial behavior, and future parenting techniques. However, we have eschewed a how-to-approach. Instead, the material we present suggests alternative strategies that may be used in child-rearing and provides students with a knowledge base for evaluating these strategies.

We hope that, on balance, what we have achieved will communicate our conviction that the scientific study of children sheds light on the everyday aspects of children's behavior. If we have succeeded, the student will be able to share our excitement about children and the study of their development.

Acknowledgments

A number of individuals provided constructive criticism for various sections of the book. In particular, we appreciate the help received from Paula Menyuk, Jeff Travis, and James Bryant, each of whom ably reviewed materials for us. A special thanks goes to Aletha Huston and John Wright who extensively reviewed the entire enterprise.

Kathie Kelly-McNeil and Karen Starr were especially helpful in all phases of preparing the manuscript. We genuinely appreciate their efforts.

William J. Meyer
Jerome B. Dusek

CONTENTS

CHILD

PSYCHOLOGY

CHAPTER 1

(Top: Elizabeth Hamlin/Stock, Boston; bottom: Joel Gordon)

INTRODUCTION

INTENDED AS a brief historical overview of the field of child development, this chapter presents several major themes in the study of human development (which will be elaborated in subsequent chapters) and explores the relationship between theory and research as each relates to practical questions about child development. We believe this overview helps explain why psychologists find the study of child development exciting.

A Brief History of Child Development

Child psychology is an important subfield of developmental psychology, an area, in general, concerned with the study of changes in behavior throughout the life span of the organism, human or animal. Most of the research and theorizing in developmental psychology has been in the area of child development. Although occasionally drawing on research conducted with nonhuman subjects, we emphasize the processes related to change in human behavior during infancy and early childhood. Among the most interesting and informative historical accounts, the works of Kessen (1965), Stevenson (1968), and Sears (1975) capture the important philosophical and social influences which have shaped the field and which we shall present here in a brief history of child psychology.

G. STANLEY HALL. Although philosophers have always speculated about the nature of the child and the underlying causes of development, and parents and other adults have recorded much "common sense" knowledge about children, it was not until the late 1800s, when the monumental work of Charles Darwin was adapted to psychology by G. Stanley Hall, that the study of child development became a legitimate field of scientific inquiry for psychologists. Darwin set the stage with his *Origin of Species* (1859) and, later, *Descent of Man* (1897). These landmark works proposed that the observation of the human infant might provide insight into the evolution of human beings. A major result of this thesis was the publication of a large number of baby biographies, which provided the first data on various aspects of child growth, noting the gross changes that occur, such as size of vocabulary and changes in physical growth, and providing information on personality development. Unfortunately, these biographies were undoubtedly biased (that is, parents tended to see what they wished to see in their children's behavior), reflected change at irregular intervals over time, were limited in scope, and lacked generalizability. Moreover, because the information contained in them was purely descriptive and observational, the baby biographies raised questions about the processes underlying child development without providing any answers. For example, although many biographers described the course of growth of motor development, they could provide no information to explain why the sequences occurred. Despite this difficulty, these biographies did supply valuable information about developmental patterns and raised a number of interesting questions about developmental processes, many of which are still of great interest.

G. Stanley Hall, often called the "founder" of developmental psychology, was strongly influenced by Darwin's evolutionary theory. He believed that "**ontogeny** recapitulates **phylogeny**," that is, that the development of the individual (ontogeny) mirrors the development of the species (phylogeny). Among his ac-

Baby biographies kept by parents are an important source of normative-descriptive data about child development. (Peter Vandermark)

complishments, Hall introduced the questionnaire method to the study of child psychology. By asking children to answer specific questions or, more commonly, by requesting parents to fill out questionnaires, Hall was able to collect data systematically from large groups of children in order to study changes in interest patterns, wishes, and a variety of social behaviors. The questionnaire method, much refined, is still in wide use.

Hall was also among the first to study children in the laboratory. His early experiments with children were little more than demonstrations that children possessed essentially the same psychological processes demonstrable in both lower animals and human adults (Stevenson, 1968). Systematic research on the *processes* underlying development of these abilities was nearly nonexistent. The intent in these experiments was not to study children as a unique group of subjects but rather to demonstrate that children, like adults, could learn, had memory and perceptual abilities, and possessed the various psychological processes assumed to be the basis of adult psychological functioning. Although this research was not aimed at explaining developmental changes in learning, memory, or other processes, it did reveal that children behaved differently from adults. As a result, the information gained from these experiments helped invalidate the conception of children as miniature adults and promoted the study of the child's psychological development as a legitimate field of interest in its own right.

NATURE/NURTURE.   Perhaps the most significant issue raised during the early history of child psychology was whether *the child is best conceived as a product of nature (heredity) or nurture (environment)* (Kessen, 1965). Although philosophers had written extensively on this issue for centuries, it reached its high point on the issue of the inheritance of intelligence. Is intelligence primarily a result of the genetic material of the organism (nature) or is it largely due to the environmental influences under which the organism lives (nurture)? With the development of intelligence tests, this issue became a heated controversy. The initial research to develop a measure of intelligence was undertaken in France by Alfred Binet and Theophile Simon (1916), who devised a test to distinguish slow learners from normal learners so that the former might be placed in special-education classes. The work of Binet and Simon represented the first systematic and objective study of individual differences in children. Lewis Terman, an American who studied with Binet, translated the Binet test into English. The introduction of the IQ concept (IQ = mental age/chronological age × 100) resulted in a number of studies that fueled the fires of the nature-nurture controversy with respect to intelligence. This controversy is still very much at the heart of a number of issues in the study of child psychology, including personality disorders and sex-typed behaviors, as well as intelligence (Jensen, 1969). Although a great deal of research is concerned with the nature-nurture issue, nearly seventy-five years later, the issue remains unsettled.

SIGMUND FREUD.   It was also during this period, from the late 1800s to the early 1900s, that Sigmund Freud (1930) was formulating his theory of psychosexual development. Freud was trained as a physiologist and was actively engaged in medical research when he entered the world of the practicing physician. Through his experiences with patients exhibiting hysterical symptoms (e.g., an arm that is paralyzed because of psychic and not physical disorders) and his study with Charcot, who refined and taught hypnosis, Freud became convinced that experiences in early childhood were crucial for a thorough understanding of adult behavior. From his work in these areas, psychoanalytic theory (Freud, 1935) developed. At the invitation of G. S. Hall, Freud visited Clark University in 1908 to deliver a series of lectures detailing his theories of infantile sexuality and the importance of early childhood experiences. Although Hall felt that Freud would be introducing challenging and exciting ideas to the United States, American psychologists almost completely rejected Freud's concepts because of their lack of experimental rigor and because of the seemingly preposterous idea of infantile sexuality. Furthermore, American psychology at that time explained development by the learning-theory principles of reinforcement. Therefore, many of Freud's concepts, such as id, ego, and superego, which are unobservable, were not viewed as legitimate ways to explain behavior. Although initially ignored, he was later to become the man who, beyond any others, has had the greatest impact on the development of child psychology. His emphasis on the importance of early childhood experiences for long-term personality development and his theory that child development occurred in a sequence of stages—the first "stage" theory to be offered—have had a profound influence on the field. Research into child-rearing techniques, morality, and the development of personality all owe their origin to the impetus Freud's theorizing provided.

ARNOLD GESELL.   Another major figure in child psychology at this time was Arnold Gesell, who held an M.D. degree as well as a Ph.D. degree in psychology. Gesell's primary interest was developmental pathology and, as such, he was a forceful proponent of the maturational view, much in the same manner as G. S. Hall and, to a slightly lesser extent, Freud. In order to obtain information about pathological development, Gesell (e.g., 1928; 1948) studied large numbers of children and published numerous volumes that described the normal and abnormal development of children in great detail. He gave accounts of the motor, language, social, and personal as well as general physical development from birth through adolescence, along with age norms intended as a guide for comparative purposes. Hence, these data are called **normative**. Gesell's work gave the full flavor of the maturational view of development.

In order to obtain valid data about children's physical and social development, several large-scale longitudinal (repeated testing of the same people) research projects were instituted during the early 1900s and remain ongoing today. The Berkeley Growth Studies (Bayley, 1935; Jones & Bayley, 1950; Jones & Mussen, 1958), initiated in 1928, and the Fels Research Institute (Kagan & Moss, 1962) study, started in 1930, provided abundant data on many aspects of child development and child rearing. In the Fels study, for example, extensive measures were taken on personality development, sexuality, parent-child relations, and social development. The Berkeley growth studies have yielded extensive information on physical growth and IQ development. The participants are now full-grown adults with their own children, who are also being studied. Because of the nature of longitudinal research (see Chapter 2), these studies are able to provide considerable information about developmental trends from infancy and early childhood into adulthood, including further insights into intellectual, social, and marital development.

Normative data, information on the average development in different age groups, such as Gesell's or that from the large-scale longitudinal studies, like the observational data from baby biographies, provided important background information about child development. Such information is necessary in order to identify issues in need of investigation. For example, how do variations in child-rearing techniques affect personality development? What is the role of physical development? What are the advantages and disadvantages of being an early or late maturer? Normative data, however, are rarely capable of providing definitive answers to research questions or to hypotheses derived from alternative theories about various aspects of development, because they are aimed at descriptions and not processes.

One aspect of developmental psychology is the study and exploration of sex differences in developmental processes. (Left: Shirley Zeiberg/Taurus Photos; right: Chester Higgins, Jr./Rapho)

As a result, psychologists slowly shifted their research away from natural settings and into the laboratory. It was believed that the greater degree of control over extraneous variables and the ability to manipulate variables would allow the identification of causes of development. As McCall (1977) has noted, however, the advantages of laboratory research may be outweighed by the disadvantages that result from not studying behavioral change as it naturally occurs. However this question may be resolved, psychologists have learned much from laboratory research that they would not have learned otherwise.

JEAN PIAGET.   During these early years in the study of children, while most psychologists were concerned primarily with describing the child's physical and social development, Jean Piaget (e.g., 1926, 1929, 1952) conducted research and formulated a theory about the child's cognitive development. Piaget, a trained biologist, is concerned with the adaptive functions of behavior and, in the tradition of Freud,

Hall, and Gesell, tends toward a maturational theory. His primary impact on child psychology has come from a comprehensive theory of stages in the growth of cognitive processes. Like Freud, Piaget postulated unobservable internal mechanisms (for example, **assimilation**) that were assumed to be responsible for the course of cognitive development. Also like Freud, Piaget's writings were at first ignored by American psychologists, gaining popularity only in the late 1950s and early 1960s. Today, Piaget's theory and research are the basis of a large number of experiments published in child psychology.

BEHAVIORISM.   The maturational theories remained the sole attempts at a relatively coherent and complete statement of child development for a number of years. In 1913, however, John B. Watson, drawing on the philosophical movement known as **logical positivism**, ushered in the era of **behaviorism**, most often associated with the learning theorists. The logical positivists were interested in the philosophy of science, the study of how science should operate (Pepper, 1942; Stevens, 1939), and formulated a number of concepts, including the assertion that science should deal only with observable and objectively measurable events. For Watson this meant overt behavior. His theories about development subsequently led him to formulate the theory of behaviorism, the view that psychology should concern itself only with overt behavior and with the principles governing how it is learned and modified.

In general, behaviorism gradually encompassed all major areas of psychology, including child psychology, as a reaction to the less observable concepts of psychoanalytic theory, and the extreme maturational (biological) views of Hall or Gesell. Watson, as a radical advocate for an environmental (nurture) view of psychological development, argued that the only legitimate object of study was observable behavior. Moreover, he strongly believed that the experimental approach, epitomized by laboratory research and objectively definable terms and procedures, was the only legitimate method of scientific study. Watson viewed **introspection** (looking into one's own thoughts and feelings), clinical case studies, theories without a basis in empirical data, and other nonexperimental techniques and strategies as unproductive means of investigating behavior because they are nonobjective and not readily verifiable. He believed that the basic principles of learning, such as reward and punishment techniques, could be applied to such problems as child rearing much more successfully than Freudian notions such as the unconscious or the id, ego, and superego. His famous experiments on a baby's learning (conditioning) of fear (Watson & Rayner, 1920) were among his initial attempts to demonstrate that development, in this case of the emotions, could be readily explained without reference to other than observable events such as stimuli and responses. The contemporary work of B. F. Skinner (1971) lies very much within the behavioristic tradition. Like Watson, Skinner is a strong advocate of the learning-theory approach to human development.

Partly as a result of Watson's influence, a great deal of systematic, experimental research on child development was done in the laboratory. The primary focus of this research was on obtaining solutions to problems in education, pediatrics, child care, and, most importantly, child rearing (Stevenson, 1968). At this point, Freud's concepts were being systematically investigated by American psychologists and had found their way into the American home through newspapers and popular magazines. As a result, parents wanted to know the "right" way to raise their children. Research into such questions as the effects of breast versus bottle feeding, demand versus scheduled feeding, and early versus late toilet training was carried out within the behavioristic as well as Freudian frameworks from the early to mid-1900s. The lack of definitive answers to these questions is evident in the cyclical nature of the advice given to parents. For example, strong advice to breast feed a child was quickly followed by equally strong advice to bottle feed. Similarly, advice to toilet train early was soon followed by advice to toilet train late. As more and more research was conducted the evidence became more and more contradictory. The problems are still unresolved and even today research on these questions continues.

Quite probably the inability of research to answer these questions clearly resulted, at least in part, from the investigator's single-minded attention to the child's behavior and development to the exclusion of the characteristics of the parents. Current researchers focus not only on the child but also on parental characteristics and, more importantly, on the characteristics of the parent-child interaction. Mary Ainsworth (1973), for example, has investigated child-rearing techniques and parent-infant interaction patterns in the development of attachment. Elder's (1962, 1963) research on the relation between adolescent strivings for independence and parental child-rearing techniques is another important example of research in this area. As a result of improvements in research strategy, much better indications of the effects of particular child-rearing techniques are being obtained.

Another hindrance to providing parents and educators with specific and clear answers to questions about child rearing and education is the fact that conflicting theoretical areas would sometimes yield identical predictions and it was difficult, at best, to conduct "critical" experiments showing which theory might be the better.

On the one hand, proponents of behaviorism argued that only observable behaviors should be studied, primarily through rigorous experimental techniques, with no recourse to unobservable internal mechanisms for explaining development. On the other hand, those favoring the **organismic approach** argued as legitimate for study mechanisms that are not directly observable (for example, personality components, such as the ego, or aspects of intellectual functioning, such as cognitive structures) and initiated more flexible as well as varied approachs to experimentation. This conflict in part reflects a second major theme woven through all of child psychology: *Is the child best conceived as a bundle of S-R elements (the learning-theory approach) or as a set of integrated structures (the cognitive-developmental approach)* (Kessen, 1965)? Another fundamental theme is: *Is the child best con-*

ceived as an active explorer or passive receiver of environmental stimulation (Kessen, 1965)? These two issues, like the nature-nurture controversy, concern the nature of the organism.

Despite Watson's plea, it was not until the mid-1900s that the focus of research in child development turned from the normative-descriptive to the experimental approach, with an emphasis on the building and testing of theories. Behaviorists believed that the experimental approach could be used both to determine cause-effect relationships between environmental stimulation and the child's development and to gain insights into the psychological processes involved in development. As a result, much current research on childhood is focused on testing alternative theories about the processes of psychological development. That is, current research is basically process-oriented rather than normative-descriptive in nature. Many professional psychologists believe that by testing various theories of development we shall gain insights into the causes of development, both normal and abnormal, and thereby come to a reasonable understanding of the nature of the human organism. Developmental psychologists conduct research, whether in the laboratory or in naturalistic settings, in order to test theories. As theories develop, they may be used to make decisions about their practical applications to development. In this way, research that may at first seem unrelated to the "real world" problems of development makes a significant contribution to the welfare of children.

Two other major events in child psychology in the United States have occurred during the past quarter-century. First, there was a "rediscovery" of Piaget's theorizing. American psychologists, finding the behavioristic approach less satisfactory than they at first thought, that is, finding it incapable of explaining many aspects of development, began to apply the experimental approach to the study of Piagetian concepts. Today Piaget has a greater influence on the research and theorizing of American psychologists than any other single individual. Second, the research of the Russian psychologists (e.g., Luria, 1966), primarily psychophysiological in nature, has begun to exert a significant influence on American thinking about child development. This influence may be seen, for example, in research dealing with the **orienting reflex**. Both of these influences have greatly changed our views of children and development and have provided new insights into the complexities of human psychological functioning.

As this brief history of some of the highlights of the development of child psychology indicates, the field is a rapidly changing one. It is very difficult at this time to determine the immediate directions the field will take. However, it does seem clear that one major emphasis will be a strong theory-and-research effort outside the confines of strict learning theory.

This is not to say that research from a learning-theory perspective will come to a halt. Rather, the exciting developments stemming from research such as Piaget's are broadening our perspective on the child. As a result, developmental psychologists are asking new and exciting questions that they could not have asked previously.

The two different approaches, behavioristic and organismic, to studying children seem to complement each other and to present a more complete picture of children and their development than either alone.

Throughout this book we will contrast and juxtapose these two views in an attempt to answer the question, "What is the best way to represent the psychological makeup of the child and how shall we best represent the psychological processes of development?" This contrast will serve two purposes. First, it will provide an appropriately broad foundation for understanding current thinking and methods in research on child development. Second, it will allow us to present more information in answer to the issues posed above than either view alone. Although at times this may seem confusing, an understanding of child development requires familiarity with evidence from opposing views.

Why Study Child Development?

Certainly the reasons for studying child development are as numerous as the number of people in the field, or in your classroom, for that matter. However, there appear to be several overriding reasons for the historical interest in children and their development. One reason, as reflected in the writings of the baby biographers as well as in the normative-descriptive data such as those presented by Gesell, is to understand both normal and abnormal patterns of development in children. This is the very problem which Binet and Simon, Gesell, and many others attempted to resolve. Once norms of "normal" development are established, whether about physical development or psychological competencies, abnormal development may be more readily identified and, if needed, appropriate remedial procedures may be administered. The delineation of normal development also allows for large-scale planning for normal children, for example, in the development of educational curricula.

The work of Freud (e.g., 1930), Erikson (e.g., 1950), and others highlights a second major impetus behind the study of child development, namely, to gain a better understanding of adult behavior. The lifetime goals, self-concept, and personality characteristics of adults all become more understandable from a knowledge of the individual's childhood experiences.

Finally, the study of child development deserves scientific inquiry in its own right. Although many early philosophers regarded children as simply "little adults" and therefore of no greater interest than adults, this view of children began to change during the seventeenth century. People gradually began to be interested in studying children in their own right as providing unique information about human development. The primary interest of many child psychologists today is to explicate the laws of development during the childhood years; they have little interest in the practical application of research findings or developmental laws covering the life span of the individual. These scientists provide a theoretical foundation for explaining development, for asking questions about development, and for providing comprehensible data and techniques that others may use in the actual practice of child rearing.

The Study of Human Behavior

One of the major objectives in the study of children is to describe the course of development, the rates at which different behaviors change or mature over time. The early workers in the field developed an enormous amount of age-descriptive data encompassing such diverse behaviors as thumb-forefinger prehension, walking, talking, and a variety of perceptual behaviors, and they established the average age of the onset of pubescence. These data are frequently used to determine whether a child's growth rate is normal. The information provides important clues about the laws governing development and the environmental and biological variables that influence the course of development. Many principles emerged from the descriptive data and are found in modern developmental theories. There has been a renewed interest in descriptive research but with a greater stress laid on environmental contexts. This kind of ecological approach has been urged most recently by McCall (1977). As part of his case for moving away from solely experimental methods and returning to descriptive studies, McCall (1977, p. 337) states:

> We could learn much from a descriptive survey of the environmental and behavioral landscape before charting our experimental expeditions. Detailed multivariate longitudinal descriptive studies could reveal ages at which the variability of a behavior is greater (presumably when it is most plastic), patterns of correlated factors could suggest causal hypotheses, and the interrelationships among dependent variables, as well as their differential correlation with other factors might point out the most salient measurements as well as the number of independent manifestations of the behavior.

McCall claims here that new techniques for collecting detailed naturalistic data and new methods of data analysis will answer important conceptual questions about development. He also believes that the descriptive approach is crucial if the work of specialists in child development is to have a significant impact on social policy because psychologists' recommendations will have greater validity than in the past.

Another problem of interest in the study of human behavior is the influence of certain environmental events on children of different ages or developmental levels. A classic example, examined in detail in Chapter 3, involves systematically training one identical twin to perform some skill the other twin is not trained to do until some later time. Training can have very different effects on children at different age levels. For example, early training in roller skating taught one twin to skate. But the twin trained later learned the task as well and in less time. Such research provides clues about how children at different developmental levels cope with environmental demands, and may, therefore, reveal how they process information at different developmental levels.

We can ask somewhat more complex questions about the relationship between developmental level or age and some other characteristic(s) of the child. One characteristic that has received a great deal of attention is the sex of the child. Studies of the developmental patterns of males and females show some significant differences between the sexes, the most general finding being that females mature more rapidly than males. A more detailed description of sex differences and the interaction of sex and age changes is described in several other chapters.

A description of the research endeavors of developmental psychologists, in fact, encompasses every major area of psychology. However, the research of the developmentalists, unlike that of psychologists with other interests, asks questions about the effects of longer periods of time on behavioral change. Currently this work is being extended to cover a broader range of environmental circumstances in an effort to provide greater theoretical generality. These developmentalists are no less behaviorists than laboratory learning theorists nor is their work necessarily less precise (Bronfenbrenner, 1977).

The Scope
of the Book

The broad scope of issues subsumed in the study of child development and behavior requires a broad perspective of knowledge. In addition, to understand patterns of development fully we must know something about parental behaviors, environmental effects on developmental patterns, and biological effects on behavioral development. Thus, our objective is to provide a description of the fundamental knowledge and theories of child development upon which one can achieve a more profound understanding of the issues involved. Even if you discontinue the study of children after this course, you will have a knowledge base that will permit you to make informed decisions on a number of issues concerning children.

This book is organized into subject matter areas, for example, language development, cognitive development, perceptual processes, socialization, and so forth. Within each chapter, with the exception of those concerned almost exclusively with theory, an effort is made to explicate developmental changes that occur within each of the areas. In effect, this strategy divides up the study of the child into areas, as distinguished from stages or age levels. Our approach provides a means for more readily integrating various components (language, perception, socialization) of child development. An age approach, however, probably provides a somewhat better picture of the whole child at each developmental level. In our judgment, the latter approach often fails because the integration across aspects of development (language and socialization, for example) is very difficult to perceive, and even more difficult to explain, because of the lack of relevant data.

At the risk of being redundant, we would like to reiterate that the reader will find few hard incontrovertible facts in this book. We are in effect presenting the status of the field as of the moment, and this necessarily means that we have made some value judgments and that you will sometimes find conflicting conclusions on a particular subject (a clear symptom of this is shown in the effects of infant day-care on subsequent child development). It would seem more productive if the reader were to view these ambiguities as opportunities to think through the issues involved and try to arrive at some kind of conclusion based on the evidence presented. In many instances, we suspect, you will find that your conclusions are as valid as our own—or may be even better—and that you will have gained considerably from the process of thinking through complex issues.

SUMMARY

An examination of recent (the last 10 to 15 years) research concerned with child behavior and development reveals its historical antecedents, both theories and methods. Thus, the emphasis on organismic concepts involving biological variables and their adaptiveness to environmental demands is seen in Piaget's work as well as in the work of some scholars interested in socialization. The research literature also includes many studies of children's behavior from a more mechanistic or stimulus-response viewpoint that emphasizes laboratory studies. The material in this book is organized and viewed from fundamental organismic concepts and develops numerous themes around cognitive-developmental principles that seem most consistent with organismic theory.

The study of children can be viewed as a rewarding enterprise for its own sake, that is, to gain knowledge about one aspect of our world, indeed a very important one. Because of the importance placed upon children by most societies, the results of research also have potentially important implications for child-rearing practices and for educational programs, as well as a host of other services. All too often, however, our treatment of children is governed more by fads and uncritical beliefs than by empirical verification. It is our hope that the materials developed in this book will provide students with a more knowledgeable approach to evaluating programs for children and with a greater sensitivity to the principles of human development.

CHAPTER 2

(Top: Joel Gordon; bottom: Eric A. Roth/The Picture Cube)

DEVELOPMENTAL MODELS, THEORIES, AND RESEARCH

IN CHAPTER 1 we noted three basic questions that have been of historical concern to developmental psychologists:

1. Is the child best viewed as an active explorer or passive receiver of environmental stimulation?
2. Is the child best viewed as a product of heredity or of environment?
3. Is the child best conceived as a bundle of S-R elements or as a set of integrated structures?

Heated discussions of these issues were initiated by philosophers such as Plato, Aristotle, Rousseau, and Locke. What emerged from these debates were several models of how the human organism developed. Two of these, the learning theory and cognitive-developmental models, dominate current-day thinking about child development.

One purpose of this chapter is to discuss these models and their implications for understanding development because they will be encountered in various research contexts throughout this book. A second intent is to discuss the nature and role of theories in understanding child development. Theories about the child's growth to maturity are derived from models of development and help us not only to describe the course of development but also to understand why it occurs as it does. To appreciate fully the study of child development, we must understand the role, nature, and differences among developmental theories.

Finally, we shall discuss some basic aspects of research design and analysis used to investigate development. Unlike the philosophers, today's psychologists attempt to answer questions about the child's development by systematically collecting relevant information and not by debate and argument. The amount of research in the field has grown steadily. Research, done to answer questions based on theories of development, is evaluated by statistics. Hence, our discussion of the importance of research and statistics is intended to provide the background necessary for understanding much of the information presented in this book.

Models of Development

In this section we introduce the models that have been the most influential in the study of developmental psychology. As the term implies, *models* are representations of development. The most general models are philosophical systems that describe the nature of reality. The **mechanistic model**, for example, states that the universe may be viewed as functioning *as if* it were a machine. The model does not state that the universe actually is a machine, only that we can best conceive of it as operating as if it were a machine. One alternative to this model is the **organismic model**, which states that we may best view the universe as operating *as if* it were a living biological organism. As is true with the mechanistic model, the organismic model does not state the universe is a biological entity, only that it may function in a way similar to a biological organism (Reese & Overton, 1970; Overton & Reese, 1973).

These very general models give rise to successively more specific models, which we call theoretical models (Reese & Overton, 1970), or **theories**. Psychologists develop theories to explain the causes of behavior. Child psychologists are especially interested in explaining development during the early years of life.

Learning-Theory Model

The **learning-theory** approach to investigating and explaining development is based on the mechanistic model. In this model the universe is conceived as functioning *as if* it were a machine. The behavior of the machine depends upon its type and upon the forces exerted on it. For example, electricity, a force acting on a machine, causes the machine to work. But, the parts of the machine determine the work the machine does. Consider your toaster and your television. Electricity makes both of them work but their components determine the particular work that they do. The behavior of the machine, then, has two causes. One is the force applied to the machine, or **efficient cause**. The second type is the makeup of the machine and is called **material cause**. It causes the machine to carry out its specific functions, for example, toast bread or translate radio waves into a picture and sound. All behavior of the machine is a result of only these two causes. The machine cannot exhibit any purposive behavior. That is, it cannot do anything for which it was not designed and it cannot initiate behaviors by itself.

From this perspective, complexity is a summation of simple elements; complex machines are seen as combinations of simpler machines. To draw on our previous example, a television is no more than the sum of a number of simpler machines—tubes, receivers, tuners, and so forth. To understand the operation of the TV, we need only understand the simpler parts that make it up. Similar comments may be made about your toaster. It, too, is composed of simpler machines, each of which has a specific operation (material cause) and works only when some force (efficient cause) is applied to it. In either case, the machine is no more and no less than the sum of its individual parts. Furthermore, changes in the machine are of a quantitative nature—if we add more parts, the machine does more. Hence, change in the behavior of a machine is viewed as quantitative. As we add parts the machine becomes capable of doing more or working harder. Finally, prediction of the machine's behavior is possible from knowledge of the type of machine and the forces applied to it. If you apply electricity to your TV or toaster you expect (predict) a certain kind of behavior from the machine.

In psychology the mechanistic model is represented by the concept of the **reactive organism**, one whose behavior is determined by forces acting on it (efficient cause) and by its genetic makeup (material cause). In other words, humans are conceived as functioning *as if* they were machines, reacting to stimulation (internal or external forces) in a way predictable from a knowledge of the forces impinging on humans and from knowledge about their genetic makeup. The various learning-theory approaches to psychology and to child development stem from the mechanistic model. Although various learning theorists (e.g., Guthrie, 1935; Hull, 1943; Skinner, 1966, 1969; Spence, 1956; Tolman, 1932) may disagree about some of the specifics of how learning takes place and how learning principles can be applied to help us understand development, they can do research to resolve their disagreement. All learning theories, then, belong to the same family of theories.

The reactive-organism model assumes a *tabula rasa* ("blank slate"), or empty organism. In other words, all the individual is assumed to possess at birth are some basic reflexes, such as grasping or sucking, but no other psychological capabilities. More advanced psychological functioning and development, such as language learning or acquiring social behaviors, is assumed to be learned through the processes of reinforcement that occur in the course of living in and interacting with the environment. These environmental interactions "write" on the blank slate and determine the characteristics of the organism. Learning, the result of environmental interaction, is the process through which all psychological functions, be they simple or complex, are acquired. To return to the metaphor of the machine, the organism is capable of performing only those acts that have been stamped-in by the environment, much as a machine is capable of performing only those acts that it has been designed to perform. This model of the human organism is basically that presented by the British empiricists— John Locke, David Hume, James Mill, and John Stuart Mill—and still upheld by modern-day behaviorists.

The reactive-organism model has a number of implications for understanding human behavior and development. Motivation, or activation of behavior, is assumed to be due to forces impinging on the organism. Just as a machine is activated only when external forces are applied, for example, electricity or some other power source, human behavior is viewed as taking place only when some force is applied to the organism. This force may be a parental command, internal stimuli such as hunger pangs, or any environmental event that causes the organism to engage in some activity. Such forces are seen as the activators or efficient causes of behavior. The physical limits imposed by the genetic material of humans (material cause) limits the behaviors we can perform.

As a result of these assumptions about how the organism can be activated, learning theorists view the organism as being initially at rest; just as a machine remains idle until some power source is applied, the human organism is viewed as idle until some force pushes the organism into behaving. These basic assumptions lead much of learning-theory research to focus on the *setting conditions*, that is, the specific environmental cues and contexts under which a given type of behavior is likely to occur. This approach leads to an attempt to identify the motivational forces, both internal and external, that cause the organism to engage in specific behaviors.

In the mechanistic model, complex machines are viewed as reducible to simpler ones. In turn, by combining simple machines we can build machines that carry out more complex activities. The same concept applies to human behavior. Complex human behavior is seen as the summation of simpler behaviors. Hence, to understand a complex behavior we need only understand the simpler behaviors that make it up. As an example from psychology, consider the learning of sex-roles. According to learning theorists, sex-role learning begins with teaching the child simple sex-typed behaviors and continues by combining these into increasingly complex sex-typed behaviors that result in the person's behaving in a way we label masculine or feminine. The child is assumed to learn these sex-appropriate behaviors through reinforcemment. For example, parents teach their children sex-typed labels—boy and girl—and later more complex sex-typed play, attitudes and responsibilities that coalesce into a sex-role stereotype. The complex behavioral result is encompassed by the term "masculine" or "feminine."

One consequence of postulating that complex processes may be broken down into simpler ones is that complete prediction of behavior is, in principle, possible. In other words, we should be able to determine the exact conditions under which a simple behavior will occur if we know the forces acting on the person (efficient cause) and if we know the person's previous learning history. And the occurrence of complex behavior should be predictable from a knowledge of the factors that produce the simple behaviors that make it up. Of course, this requires knowing the specific environmental conditions surrounding the organism and the particular state of the organism at some given time. A corollary of these statements is that behavior can be quantified so that we should be able to predict the probability that it will occur. That is, we should be able to write equations that specify the causes of behavior and thereby predict the occurrence of that behavior under a given set of conditions. The most ambitious attempt to do this was carried out by Clark Hull (1943), who spent most of his professional years studying learning. He believed learning was a function of previously learned behavior, motivation to perform a given behavior, and a number of other variables. He expressed this in the equation

Both external stimuli, such as parental commands, and internal stimuli, such as hunger, cause the individual to initiate behavior. (Left: Peter Vandermark; right: Jean-Claude Lejeune)

$_sE_R = {_sH_R} \times D \times$ . . . , where $_sE_R$ was the probability of a response, $_sH_R$ was habit strength—a measure of previous learning—and D was drive, a measure of motivation. Hull believed that by putting appropriate values into this equation (for example, the number of previous practice trials for $_sH_R$ and hours of food deprivation for D) we could assess the likelihood (predict) a particular response would occur. More recent attempts at writing functional equations to predict behavior are found in various mathematical models that try to describe the numerous factors that affect learning (Atkinson, Bower & Crothers, 1965). Hypothetically, functional equations allow not only the prediction of behavior, when we know the values to put into the equation, but also "explain" the causes of the behavior, because they state the conditions under which the behavior occurs. This endeavor has been somewhat successful for simple tasks but has proven more difficult for complex ones.

The mechanistic model theorists explain development as simply a change over time from a simpler to a more complex form of behavior (Bijou & Baer, 1961; White, 1970). Therefore, "development" is a descriptive term that labels the phenomena to be explained by the theory. Mechanistic theories deal with two basic types of behavioral change. One is *ontogenetic* change and is represented by changes in behavior during the life-span of the individual organism. Ontogenetic behaviors are those that may be learned or taught to members of a species. The second type of behavior change that occurs in development is *phylogenetic*—behavioral changes that take place during the course of evolution. As organisms evolve, their increased or decreased capability to adapt to the environment reflects a form of developmental change.

From the mechanistic view, psychological development is represented by changes in behavior that occur over minutes, days, or years (Zigler, 1963). Development is explained by more or less complex extensions and refinements of simpler behaviors. Explanation of change in behavior proceeds by identifying variables that may be causes of the behavior or of changes in behavior. The approach to specifying the causes of development within the mechanistic model is limited to identifying either *material* or *efficient* causes (Overton & Reese, 1973). Material causes of behavior refer to their neurological, physiological, or genetic bases. Efficient causes are stimulus conditions that initiate behavior and are represented by manipulations of the **independent variables** in an experiment. Researchers manipulate variables that they believe represent causes of behavior in order to determine if the behavior changes in accordance with those variables. If the **dependent variable**, the behavior, for example, memory, changes as a function of the manipulation, for example, the amount of rehearsal time, it is assumed that the manipulated variable (rehearsal time) is a cause of the behavior (memory).

The mechanistic approach to psychology, then, uses learning theory to specify quantitative changes in behavior. In this manner, mechanistically oriented theorists attempt to describe how the "empty organism" is filled up during the course of development. According to learning theorists, the child responds with both **classical** and **instrumental** or **operant** types of responses (Bijou & Baer, 1961; White, 1970). In other words, the behavior of the child is controlled by eliciting stimuli (classical conditioning) or by stimuli that reinforce or strengthen an immediately previous response (instrumental or operant conditioning). Therefore, the task of the learning theorist is to analyze the child's environment to determine which stimuli elicit behavior and which stimuli reinforce behavior. Next, he must spell out how classical and instrumental or operant conditioning govern the child's learning of how to behave in his environment. This form of analysis is used to explain emotional development, language development, cultural differences in behavior, perceptual-motor development, and the like within a learning-theory framework. All behavior is considered to be acquired through one or another form of learning; very little innate behavior is attributed to the organism. Through the concepts of discrimination (learning to respond to a specific stimulus) and generalization (learning to respond to classes of similar stimuli) of responses, learning theorists attempt to explain the breadth and depth of human behavior. Hence, learning, viewed in terms of couplings between stimuli and responses as a result of reinforcement, is the concept used to account for the major aspects of development.

Although learning theory was the dominant force in psychology during the 1930s and early 1940s, a number of psychologists now criticize it severely. Among the criticisms is the belief that not all human behavior is learned. We shall discuss numerous examples of apparently unlearned (innate or emergent) behavior throughout this book. If some behavior is unlearned, then learning theorists find it difficult to explain that behavior. A second, and somewhat emotionally charged criticism that is often leveled against learning theorists is that they view humans as nothing but simple mechanical contrivances. This cricism is not necessarily negative, however. Keep in mind that the mechanistic model is an *as if* model. Learning theorists do not say that humans are nothing but machines, but rather that the analogy of a machine helps us understand human behavior. It is no more than an analogy. Nevertheless, these discontents led to a renewed interest in the applicability of other models to the problem of explaining development.

Cognitive-Developmental Model

The second model of the universe that has exerted a significant impact on psychological inquiry is the **organic model** (Overton & Reese, 1973; Reese & Overton, 1970). This model assumes the universe functions like a living organism and not like a machine. It is assumed as a given that change in the structure of the whole will occur and that this change is in the form or state of the universe and, therefore, is qualitative, not quantitative. As a result, change is conceived as occurring in a sequence of stages, each of which is qualitatively different from, and more complex than, the earlier stages and not directly reducible to them. A major interest is in the discovery of the rules of transition from one state (stage) to the next. In this model the *whole* is greater than the sum of its parts because it gives meaning to the parts; that is, unlike the mechanistic model, knowledge of the parts does not necessarily allow one to have knowledge of the whole. Finally, in this model the causes of behavior and its change are teleological, or purposeful, in nature (Reese & Overton, 1970; Overton & Reese, 1973). Change does not occur solely through efficient causes, although they may facilitate or hinder change. This is so because the model assumes the whole is active and in a state of continual transition. Hence, cause must be located in the whole. This is called **formal cause**. Formal cause, in conjunction with the concept of an active universe undergoing qualitative change, precludes a predictable, quantifiable universe because teleological causes do not allow complete predictability and qualitative changes cannot be rigorously quantified.

A common everyday example may help to clarify these points. Consider the chemical structure of water. Water is made up of hydrogen and oxygen, two parts of hydrogen to one part of oxygen. When we consider the properties of hydrogen and oxygen in isolation, it is clear that neither has the properties of water. When however, they are chemically united, the properties of water—for example, wetness—emerge. This is an instance in chemistry where the whole is greater than the sum of its parts. That is, the whole, hydrogen plus oxygen, is greater—has different properties—than either element taken individually. And the change is qualitative and due to the nature of the elements involved (formal cause). This change is not the same as the addition of parts to a machine because the new properties that emerge are not reducible to the simpler elements. In a machine, however, they are; a transistor operates the same way in a simple or a complex machine. An example involving multiple qualitative stages is the sequence of changes out of which a butterfly emerges—egg, caterpillar, cocoon, butterfly. These are qualitative changes of an irreversible sort (Reese & Overton, 1970). As these examples show, the whole gives meaning to the parts.

In psychology the organic model of the universe is translated into the **active-organism model** of human behavior (Reese & Overton, 1970; Overton & Reese, 1973). Humans are viewed as inherently and spontaneously active. They are a source of acts and not simply activated by efficient causes. Humans are seen as a source of behavior, as capable of generating novel behaviors, not simply as a repository of learned acts that are emitted in accordance with efficient causes. The various active-organism theories of development, for example, Piaget's (1952) theory of cognitive development and Freud's (1930, 1935) theory of personality formation, are based on the organic model. Like the various mechanistic theories, developmental theories derived from the organic model do have some basic differences. However, the commonalities underlying the theories place them into the same family. Each of the theories within the family shares with the others some common underlying principles regarding the nature of the human organism.

Within the organic model of development, change is accepted as a given. In other words, the organic model is developmental, a model of change (Overton & Reese, 1973). The nature of developmental change is qualitative (a change in kind) rather than quantitative (a change in amount). Change is from a less to a more complex stage of development. As a result, this model does not assume complete predictability of behavior; nor does it stress relating behavior to specific efficient causes. At each new level of development, new structural properties of the system emerge that are not directly reducible to the lower-level properties. As the organism grows, matures, and develops, it acquires new and qualitatively different modes of interacting with the environment because of structural changes, for example, in **cognitive structures**. These changes make prediction of behavior extremely difficult. The basic conception, according to Reese & Overton (1970, p. 126), is that "there is an organized structure, exhibiting certain functions, and that the structure changes in organization or form, with consequent changes in function. To many psychologists, especially those who have been called 'developmental psychologists' . . . it is also implied that the changes are unidirectional, irreversible, and directed toward certain end states or goals." Therefore, investigations based on the active-organism model emphasize the qualitative changes through which the human progresses during development. In our discussion of Piaget's theory of cognition we shall discuss various stages through which thinking processes develop. The infant thinks with actions; the adult can think with abstract symbols. These are qualitatively different ways of thinking and are the result of transitions from earlier to later stages of development. These changes, and more subtle ones that occur along the way, are revealed in behavior. The adult's thinking capabilities allow different kinds of behavior than the child's. Overt behavior, rather than being taken only as the result of development, also represents and indexes development because it reflects changes in the structure of the organism.

The cognitive-developmental view, then, conceives of development as a basic change taking place within the structure of either the intellect or the personality of the organism itself. The nature of this change is always toward greater complexities of development (Reese & Overton, 1970). This point of view has a number of implications that it will be helpful to review at this time.

CONTINUITY/DISCONTINUITY.   One issue is whether development occurs in a continuous or discontinuous manner. The active-organism theorists often conceive of development as progressing through a series of stages, each of which represents a qualitatively different mode of interaction with the environment. Piaget's (1952) theory of cognition, as we exemplified above, postulates a series of stages in the development of intellect. Each stage is more complex than the previous one and incorporates developmental advances from previous stages. Hence, although development may appear as a set of discontinuous stages, the stages represent high-

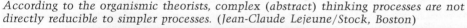

According to the organismic theorists, complex (abstract) thinking processes are not directly reducible to simpler processes. (Jean-Claude Lejeune/Stock, Boston)

lights of development and do not indicate genuine discontinuities. Development is viewed as a slow process of continuous change. Within each stage, the level of development is determined by the structures of the organism; that is, behavior indicates the structural development of the organism and is the method by which we know the stage of development of the organism. Structures, in turn, are assumed to be reflected in behavior. Hence, the logical sequence is that behavior is determined by structures which, in turn, reflect stages of development. Stages represent convenient markers for development but do not imply that development is discontinuous or steplike. Each stage is assumed to incorporate the competencies (structures) of the previous stages but is also assumed to be more than that. Hence, it is impossible to reduce a complex behavior to a set of simpler behaviors that make it up, as learning theorists attempt to do. The child is viewed as being capable of generating new and novel structures and, hence, behaviors, from mental combinations of existing structures. These new structures are not simple, direct combinations of existing elements but represent new, more complex modes of functioning. Recall our example of combining hydrogen and oxygen to obtain water. Again, neither hydrogen nor oxygen has the quality of wetness obtained through their combination. The change in the elements when they are combined is qualitative. A new property (wetness) emerges that is not directly reducible to the simpler elements. And the behavior of the combined elements is different from that of either element alone. The active-organism model assumes human behavior, intellect in particular, is also a result of qualitative changes. The properties of complex intellectual behavior are not reducible to the properties of the simpler intellectual behavior from which they emerge.

Each stage is presumed to have its own characteristics in addition to those of all preceding stages. For example, Piaget (1952) proposed that the intellectual competencies of each stage are incorporated into the competencies of the next stage. Thus, concrete operational thinking (Stage 3) is incorporated into formal operational thinking (the abstract thinking competencies of Stage 4). But abstract thinking is qualitatively different from concrete thinking. And formal operational thinking is not directly reducible to concrete thinking. Hence the whole, that is, the development of the organism at any given time, is greater than the sum of the parts.

COMPETENCE/PERFORMANCE.   A second important issue stemming from the active-organism model is the distinction between competence and performance. **Competence** may be defined as the organism's range of capabilities within some domain of behavior. **Performance** may be defined as the individual's actual behavior at some time in some given situation. Within the reactive-organism view, the individual's behavior, that is, his performance, indicates what the individual is capable of doing. This is not so for the organismic model. Behavior at any given time is typically assumed to reflect only performance and not the entire range of capabilities (competence). Performance is only an imperfect measure of competence. The behavior of the individual, then, only partly reflects the individual's competencies. As an example, consider language development. A 3-year-old may use a three- or four-word sentence to communicate to his parents or peers. However, is this the limit of the child's linguistic capabilities? Clearly, the answer is no. The child is certainly capable of producing longer strings of words. Even if we consider a larger sample of performance, we probably will not get an entirely accurate measure of the child's competence. The reason is that performance is affected by a number of factors, such as fatigue, situational demands, the particular measure of performance used, and the continual structural changes occurring in the child. Were we to alter these factors, performance would change. But it would probably never directly match competence. This is entirely obvious if we ask a child to imitate a string of nonsense words. The child may imitate them (performance) but we would not likely conclude that the child's competence reflects the ability to spontaneously generate nonsense words. Since competencies are assumed to change along with the individual's developmental level and since development is continually changing, competencies are continually changing.

It should now be possible to understand the meaning of the term "active organism." The organism is assumed to be in a state of continual change. This change is qualitative because the organism somehow "adds" to its experiences and develops new and different ways of reacting to the environment that are not directly reducible to specific environmental experiences and are not entirely explainable by efficient causes. In other words, the organism is seen as inherently and spontaneously active, as a source of behavior and changes in behavior; the organism takes an active part in changing its competencies, something no machine can do. These changes reflect qualitative differences in development. The 15-year-old, for example, is capable (competent) of producing different kinds of solutions to problems than the 5-year-old. Whether we say that the 15-year-old is ten times better or three times better at solving a problem as the 5-year-old is irrelevant. What is relevant is that the competencies, the level of functioning of the 15-year-old, are different from that of the 5-year-old.

One may well ask how these differences in competence come about and what the motivation behind this kind of change is. The basic cause of change within the organic model, as noted above, is teleological—directed toward some particular end state. Within the organic model two kinds of teleological causes are involved: formal cause and final cause. Formal cause refers to the organization of the individual, the psychological structures that constitute the organism. Since these structures are always aimed at increasingly more complex levels of functioning, formal cause is teleological in nature. It directs the organism to perform in more and more complex ways, toward increasingly higher levels of functioning.

Final cause refers to the individual's attempt to differentiate itself and the environment (Reese & Overton, 1970). In other words the individual and the environment have the relation of reciprocal action in which each member changes the other. This process of differentiation is considered to be necessary as a motivating condition (cause) for development. According to the active organism model, efficient causes (environmental interaction, or learning) are not the only ways in which change may occur.

These explanations of development are quite different from those of the reactive organism or the mechanistic model. As a result, cognitive-developmentalists ask different questions than do learning theorists about the nature of development. For example, cognitive-developmental theorists are primarily interested in the processes of development and less so its products (behaviors), which are of major interest to learning theorists. Reinforcing a child for behaving in a certain way may alter his behavior (a product), which for a learning theorist is development but for a cognitive psychologist may not be development because it may not result in structural change in the child. For example, we might show a 3-year-old two equal-size glasses filled with equal amounts of water. If we then pour the water from one glass into a dish and ask the child whether the dish or the other glass has more water or if they are the same, the child is very likely to say that one has more water than the other—the dish because it is wider or the glass because the water level is higher. In fact, we know that each contains the same amount of water. Using reinforcement principles we could teach the child to say that the glass and the dish each hold the same amount of water, but it is unlikely that the child will learn the general rule: if you have an amount of something and do not add to or subtract from it, the amount stays the same. What the child has learned is a specific response to a specific situation. Hence, reinforcement (efficient cause) can change performance without necessarily changing the structural characteristics of the child—the way he understands the world.

A word about the meaning of psychological structures is in order at this point. These structures are hypothetical constructs, concepts describing processes that are not directly observable (MacCorquodale & Meehl, 1948). Cognitive developmentalists do not say humans possess these structures, only that they act as if they do. These structures are not real and do not exist apart from the theory in which they are embedded. We cannot open up our heads and cut these structures out. Hence, when we speak of structural change we are speaking of a model of changes in the way in which the organism deals with the environment. Whether humans actually have structures or not is irrelevant to the utility of the concept as a tool for understanding human behavior.

Investigations demonstrating relationships between various areas of development are an important endeavor in cognitive-developmental theories. Considerable research effort has been aimed at demonstrating the relationships between intelligence and moral development (e.g., Kohlberg, 1969; 1973), cognitive and social development (e.g., Shantz, 1975), intelligence and language development, moral development and moral behavior (Hogan, 1973) and so forth. Such relationships are critical for the "wholism" on which the cognitive-developmental model is based (Overton & Reese, 1970).

From this model, prediction of behavior and explanation of behavior are separate issues. Prediction is, at best, tenuous because we cannot write functional equations relating behavior to specific efficient causes. Understanding or explaining behavior reflects our knowledge of the child's development across some particular age span. This is true even though we may not be able to delineate specifically how the environment and the characteristics and changes in the structures of the child interact to produce this particular behavior.

The two models discussed above have two distinct views of the human organism. As a result, they present two very different views of the nature of child development and they suggest different answers to questions about development. If we consider the three questions posed at the beginning of this chapter we find that learning theorists view the child as passive, a product of environment, and as a collection of S-R elements. The child is assumed to be born a blank slate. All development occurs because of environmental intervention (learning). Hence, the child is seen as a repository of learned behaviors (S-R elements). Development is due to learning combinations of simpler behaviors, making development quantitatively measurable.

Cognitive-developmental theorists view the child as an active explorer of the environment, as having some universally inherited characteristics (for example, Piaget's assimilation and accommodation mechanisms), and as having integrated cognitive structures. Development is seen as a qualitative change in the organism's structures that results from its active exploration of the environment.

As the reader progresses through this text the ways in which these two models have influenced research on child development will become obvious. In many instances we shall have occasion to discuss a research area, such as sex-role acquisition, from each of these two perspectives. By keeping in mind that the two views about development generate different research questions, the reader will quickly see that research based on each model significantly contributes to our understanding of the concept under investigation. Moreover, the different questions that each approach asks about the concept will become clearer. Hence we think it is important to become familiar with these two basic general models of development.

Role of Theory
in Child Development

Throughout the text we shall present various theories about child development. As we have noted, theories are derived from a more general model of the universe, serve a number of functions, and differ in their levels of specificity. For example, some, like Freud's theory of personality development, are very broad in scope, whereas most theories deal with relatively specific aspects of child development and are, therefore, more narrow in scope.

Definition and Function of Theories

A **theory** is simply a statement, or group of statements, that attempts to explain some event. In psychology that event is behavior. Our interest is in the child's behavior. In a sense, a theory is a model of why some particular behavior, as distinguished from some other behavior, occurs; or, to put it slightly differently, a theory describes the factors that produce or cause behavior. A combination of theories should give us a sound and reasonable picture of the factors underlying child behavior and development.

Theories serve several major functions. One function is *to integrate information about behavior*. However, a theory that is too broad or that has vaguely defined terms may incorporate a great deal of information but not be as adequate an explanation of behavior as a theory that is somewhat less broad and focused on more restricted ranges of behavior. Most theories tend to be relatively narrow in scope, dealing only with specific forms of behavior, for example, verbal learning or the effects of various child-rearing techniques on children's learning of dependency and aggression. How, then, can we hope to gain a comprehensive picture of the causes of the child's development? The obvious answer is that by picking and choosing theories for various aspects of the child's development, we can put together a more general picture. This is not a hard-and-fast approach however; there are some global theories, for example, Piaget's (1952) theory of intellectual development, that are quite adequate descriptions of very broad aspects of development, while some narrower theories are not very useful. Hence, simply being able to integrate a good deal of information is not necessarily a good criterion for the adequacy of a theory. Rather, the adequacy of a theory, broad or narrow, can be determined only by the results of experimentally testing hypotheses derived from it. That leads to the second function of theories: *to predict new events*.

By generating confirmable hypotheses, theories predict new events. That is, by closely examining a theory and deriving hypotheses from it, we should be able to predict that a certain behavior will occur given a certain set of circumstances. This behavior may be "new," in that it may not have been previously observed. Hence, theories predict when a specific event will occur, that is, what conditions (factors) will lead us to expect certain behaviors.

The final function of a theory is *to explain behavior or development*. To explain a behavior means that we can list its causes; that is, we can tell why the behavior occurs and list the conditions that will produce it. If a theory predicts that conditions x, y, and z should produce some particular behavior, and if we reproduce x, y, and z in an experiment and the predicted behavior occurs, we can argue that x, y, and z are the determinants (causes) of that behavior. Explaining behavior is simply the converse of predicting it and involves listing the conditions (causes) under which a behavior will occur. Hence, explanation involves stating the conditions that underlie the occurrence of some event. When we know these conditions we can explain the behavior.

When appropriate, we shall point out ways in which the theories of child development may be integrated. When this is not possible, it does not mean we are at a loss to explain behaviors. We may simply need an altered or new theory. This, in effect, is how science must proceed.

Theories are formulated and evaluated in the same way in all fields of science. Hence, theories about language development, mathematics, atomic particles, or personality development all have the same basic formulations. They all are attempts to explain why and how some behavior occurs. In all sciences theories are evaluated by research.

Relationship of Theory to Research

A critical feature of any theory is its testability. A theory that we cannot test is useless because we cannot ascertain its validity. But if a theory is testable and if hypotheses derived from it are supported by research, the theory gains in truth value. Each time a set of hypotheses from a particular theory is supported by research, we have more confidence that the theory is an accurate description of the factors underlying the behavior under investigation. On the contrary, if a theory generates hypotheses that are not supported by research, we lose confidence in that theory as an adequate explanation of behavior. In such cases we may either alter the theory or abandon it in favor of some alternative theory. Through research we also can test alternative theories of child development in order to ascertain which is the more accurate. Theory-guided research, then, is critical to our understanding of child development because it is the way we validate or invalidate theories about development.

Research in Child Development

Research serves a number of functions. One is to test hypotheses derived from a theory. If the research findings are in accord with the hypotheses, the theory gains in **truth value**, that is, in its validity as an adequate representation of how the child develops. If the research does not support the hypothesis, we may begin to doubt the theory or question the appropriateness of the research for testing the hypothesis. This function of research is also important in determining the *generalizability* of a theory, the degree to which the theory can explain behavior in more than one particular situation or with more than one sample of children.

A second function of research is to generate new **hypotheses** about behavior and development. Thus, research acts to help develop a theory and define its limits. Research may give rise to new constructs that relate to the particular theory or theories being tested. Hence, research aids theory development by suggesting how a theory may be refined. In this way, research is a critical tool for indicating directions in which theories should be changed.

A third function of research is to help explain and predict behavior. Through research we are able to determine the adequacy of theoretical statements as an explanation for some behavior. Other kinds of research allow us to derive predictions so that we are in a better position to determine the conditions necessary to bring about some bit of behavior.

As mentioned above, research is necessary to test competing theories of development. Theories are tested by accumulating evidence in support of them or by accumulating evidence indicating that an alternative theory is better. Without evidence from research it would be impossible to test alternative theories and, therefore, we would have no objective means of determining which of several theories is better or more useful.

Ethics in Research

Research not only tests theories and helps satisfy the curiosity of the researchers, but it can also make significant contributions to practical or applied issues. Knowledge gained from research has contributed, for example, to the development of school curricula, the formulation of new methods (for example, behavior modification) for treating mental illness and teaching autistic children, and to a better understanding of the impact of violence in movies and television on the child's developing social skills. These contributions benefit everyone in society, especially children.

One question of continual concern to psychologists is whether the benefits of research outweigh the risks to the subjects, children or adults, who participate in the research. In some instances this question is fairly easy to answer. No ethical psychologist would subject infants or young children to extreme food deprivation or painful punishment in order to assess its effects on adult personality. Nor would an ethical psychologist manipulate children's school grades in order to assess their academic self-concept. The more difficult ethical issues in research stem from much more subtle circumstances. The following list of questions will give you some idea of these more difficult ethical concerns. Does giving a child an IQ test, which is designed to continue until the child fails a number of items, alter the child's self-concept? Does asking a child about the types of discipline used by his parents affect his relationships with them? Is using behavior-modification techniques to teach a child not to fear snakes an appropriate way to investigate the utility of these procedures as a therapeutic tool? Every researcher must consider such ethical questions. All who do research are ethically bound to safeguard the rights and dignity of those who participate in an experiment. The responsibility includes not only a careful consideration of the effects on the subject but also of the effects on the subject's interaction with others, including peers, parents, siblings, and teachers.

To heighten researchers' sensitivity and to help them to deal with these problems, committees of the American Psychological Association have published a set of "Ethical Standards for Research with Human Subjects" (American Psychological Association, 1972). The Society for Research in Child Development (1973) has formulated a similar set of guidelines specifically directed to research with children. These guidelines were seen as necessary because children are less able than adults to evaluate the meaning of participating in research and because children are less experienced in judging their vulnerability, for example, to stress. The importance of these views about children is made apparent by the requirement that parents must give permission for a child to participate in an experiment and the child must also consent. The SRCD guidelines deal with three major issues: informed consent, peer review of research procedures, and confidentiality.

Informed consent means that the person giving consent has knowledge of all aspects of the research that might affect his willingness to participate. The researcher should inform the child, parent, or parent substitute (teacher, for example) of the nature and purposes of the research, the procedures to be used, and the use to be made of the information. All questions about the research should be answered in language the child, parent, or teacher can understand. The consent to participate may be withdrawn at any time, before or during the experiment. The child has the right to refuse participation even if others do give consent. Everyone who participates in the experiment, including those with whom the child is interacting (peers, teachers, parents), must be informed and give consent.

Several guidelines deal with peer review of research, that is, a review made by psychologists and others who are knowledgeable about research. Before the start of an experiment institutional peer-review committees screen both research procedures and procedures for obtaining informed consent. This screening helps to ensure the rights of the participants and to identify any problems in the procedures and suggest alterations and solutions. Peer reviews can be especially helpful in dealing with problems of potential psychological harm to participants by identifying them and suggesting alternative research strategies. Peer-review teams also monitor the use of deception in research. At times, researchers may have to use deception. For example, it would be impossible to study the effects of teachers' expectations (a teacher's expectations about a student's performance may influence his behavior) if the teachers were fully informed. By convincing the peer-review team of the need for deception or concealment, the researcher can be assured that the deception is justified. The guidelines state that after the experiment the investigator should explain the reason for the deception to the subjects as well as answer any other questions about the experiment.

Confidentiality is a third important area of concern. All information collected from subjects must be kept confidential. No individuals should be identified by name in written or verbal reports. Adequate steps should be taken to ensure that data files are kept protected.

Other guidelines require the researcher either to find new techniques of investigation if harm may come to the child or to abandon the research project. Still others point out that the researcher is responsible for the ethical conduct of assistants and students who help in the research and make clear that the researcher must honor any promises and commitments made to participants. Of course, these guidelines do not solve all the ethical problems in research and do not always make the job easier. Ethical judgments are typically subjective and, therefore, are always open to debate. Hence, it is the intent of the guidelines to foster thinking about ethical problems and provide some aids, such as the peer-review system, to ensure that researchers act in accordance with the highest integrity, honesty, and respect for the rights of participants. In the final analysis it is the responsibility of the individual researcher to act in an ethical manner.

Dimensions of Research

Psychological research projects may be classified in a number of ways (e.g., McCandless, 1970; Underwood, 1957). Table 2-1 lists four dimensions along which research projects may be classified and summarizes the major aspects of each dimension. Although these dimensions are not all-inclusive, they do serve to demonstrate the different focuses that a particular investigation may have. The end points of these four dimensions are not necessarily mutually exclusive either, since a single research project may concurrently focus on both ends of a single dimension.

Laboratory research is typically conducted in an artificially contrived situation and employs tasks that are unfamiliar to the subject. These procedures make it possible to gain control over a number of extraneous variables and allow for a purer

TABLE 2-1   Dimensions of Research

1. *Laboratory*	*vs.*	*Naturalistic*
Artificial situation		Natural environment
Controls extraneous variables		Loose control over extraneous variables
		Descriptive
2. *Manipulative*	*vs.*	*Nonmanipulative*
Cause-effect oriented		Discover relationships among variables—not cause-effect
Usually experimental		Usually correlational
3. *Theoretical*	*vs.*	*Atheoretical*
Test theories		Answer immediate questions of applied nature
Laboratory/manipulative		Naturalistic/observational
4. *Age change*	*vs.*	*Age difference*
Longitudinal		Cross-sectional
Growth oriented		Behavior difference oriented

SOURCE: Dusek J. *Adolescent development and behavior* (Palo Alto, Calif.: Science Research Associates, Inc., 1977).

and more sensitive measure of behavior. The artificially contrived situation eliminates distracting and extraneous influences on performance and the unfamiliar tasks allow measurements of behavior that are uncontaminated by previous learning because the tasks are equally novel to all those tested. Thus, in studies of classical conditioning, for example, the subject is not studied in his own living room but is more likely to be placed in a quiet chamber in order to obtain a sensitive measure of conditioning without the influence of extraneous and distracting stimuli.

Naturalistic observation is conducted "in the field" and usually entails simply observing and recording what people do under "real life" circumstances, for example, childrens' behavior in playgrounds, how people behave after witnessing an automobile accident. Such reactions would be extremely difficult to study in the laboratory, but they can be observed in the naturalistic setting. Other examples of observational research include assessments of social behaviors, the behaviors of street gangs, and surreptitious observations of individuals in any kind of a naturalistic situation.

Descriptive research is especially useful for studying development that cannot be studied in the laboratory because of ethical or practical concerns. One example is the study of parental disciplinary techniques on the child's social and emotional development. Use of the experimental method to investigate this interesting question would be both highly unethical and impractical. We would have to assign parents randomly to two groups, one of which punishes but uses no rewards and one of which rewards but uses no punishment. At various times we might obtain ratings of the children's social and emotional development and compare the ratings obtained for the two groups of children. If the measures for the two groups were different we could conclude that punishment affects social development. By observing the disciplinary techniques parents use and by relating these to ratings of the child's behavior, parental use of punishment can be related to the child's social development. Although the sample of parents is biased and despite the fact that no parents use only punishment, we can obtain a good deal of information from this approach. Psychologists are becoming increasingly interested in the use of descriptive research to supplement laboratory investigations (Bronfenbrenner, 1977; McCall, 1977). Their intent is to determine if the causes of development revealed through experimental manipulations are valid, that is, can be verified in observations of the daily interactions of children.

The second dimension is *manipulative* versus *nonmanipulative*. Manipulative research involves experimentally changing some variable in an attempt to determine whether or not it will produce differences in the behavior of the experimental subjects. The variable manipulated is called the *independent variable*. The variable that is measured is the *dependent variable*. The logic of the manipulative strategy is that subjects receiving one level (manipulation) of the independent variable should perform better (or worse) on the dependent variable than subjects receiving a different level of the treatment. For example, we might investigate the effects of different types of reinforcement on children's learning by reinforcing one group of children with candy and another group with praise for correct responses. The manipulation of the type of reinforcement is the independent variable and our measure of learning is the dependent variable. Many experiments involve more than one independent variable. If we used both boys and girls in the experiment on reinforcement, we would have two independent variables—type of reinforcement and sex of subject. We can then determine if the type of reinforcement influences learning, if the sex of subject influences learning, or if there is an interaction between the two independent variables, that is, if the two sexes react differently to the two types of reinforcement. In order to investigate some aspects of development, research must be done with three, four, or more independent variables. These studies allow the assessment of the independent contribution of each variable as well as the interactive influences of the variables on development.

Typically, manipulative research is conducted in the laboratory, although it may sometimes be carried out in naturalistic settings. In nonmanipulative research the experimenter simply observes and records the behavior of the subjects without performing any manipulations. This research is usually done in a naturalistic setting, although not necessarily so; some nonmanipulative research is quite precise and permits accurate identification of the ways in which a variable relates to behavior. Hence, cause-effect relationships may be determined. However, the two approaches often supplement each other. We might, for example, manipulate the amount of practice that children have in some particular situation and then assess their performance on a related task. In this way we can determine how much practice affects performance. On the other hand, we may go into naturalistic settings and find people who, in the normal course of events, have varying degrees of practice with some particular skill and assess their performance on some criterion task. In this case, we are not performing any particular manipulation. As noted above, observational research of this sort is often necessary because manipulations are not always ethical or practical. Although developmental research has a long history steeped in the observational-descriptive approach, the manipulative strategy has become more and more popular in the study of developmental phenomena. Much nonmanipulative research, especially questionnaire studies, is still being conducted but its inability to uncover cause-effect relationships has produced a decline in its use and has limited it to those areas in which manipulative research would be either impossible or a breach of professional ethics. The renewed interest in supplementing manipulative research with descriptive strategies has created a new place for this approach in the study of child development and will probably stimulate an increase in descriptive research (Bronfenbrenner, 1977; McCall, 1977).

The third dimension listed in Table 2-1 is *theoretical* versus *atheoretical*. A good deal of child development research is aimed at testing theories. Much research, however, is done with no interest in testing a particular theory, but is conducted simply to satisy the curiosity of the investigator, to describe some aspect of development, or to map out a new area of interest for which theory is lacking. These latter researches are atheoretical in the sense that no particular theory is tested by the research. Atheoretical research provides data that serve as a base for building a theory. In addition, atheoretical research is often conducted in order to answer questions of immediate practical concern; for example, much research on classroom behaviors and teaching methods has been atheoretical.

The fourth dimension on which developmental research projects may differ is *age change* versus *age difference*. Developmental researchers are typically interested in changes in behavior that occur with increases in age. Age-change research is the epitome of developmental research because it reflects growth curves for behavior by repeatedly testing the same group of subjects. Repeated measurements on a group of subjects as they mature allows for direct developmental assessments. Age-difference research reflects differences as a function of the different age groups of subjects under investigation. Because subjects at different age levels were born at different times and because they are tested only once, it is impossible to demonstrate growth trends in behavior. Nevertheless, a good deal of developmental research is of the age-difference sort. Growth trends derived from age-difference research must always be suspect when we wish to interpret them developmentally, although we do not deny that age-difference research yields much valuable information about development, particularly when there is no reason to suspect that important environmental events would cause differences in the psychological functioning of the various age groups.

These four dimensions represent a means of assessing the contribution of a research project to knowledge about development. For example, laboratory research that is manipulative, theoretical, and concerned with age-change should indicate something of theoretical interest about developmental changes in the effects of some variable on behavior. Naturalistic, correlational, and atheoretical research that involves several age groups may contribute to our understanding of age differences in the relationship(s) between two or more variables in the natural setting.

The dimensions of research presented in Table 2-1 do not represent mutually exclusive categories. Each of the four dimensions has intermediate categories. In addition, a particular research project may have components from each end of a single dimension. The value of these dimensions, then, lies in helping to describe the many types of developmental research. In the discussion that follows we shall describe the experimental designs of several types of research projects in terms of these dimensions.

Research Design in Child Psychology

Four research designs are commonly employed in developmental psychology. We shall discuss their limitations, advantages, and disadvantages and give examples of each kind.

Either observational or interview research is applicable to many areas of the child's development. (Judith Sedwick)

A **cross-sectional experiment** is defined as the systematic assessment of several groups of people at approximately the same time. It may be done in the laboratory or in a naturalistic setting. One major feature of the cross-sectional study is that all the groups of subjects are tested in a relatively short time span and are tested only once. A second feature is that manipulations of variables are usually involved, allowing the assessment of cause-effect relationships. As regards the dimensions listed in Table 2-1 the cross-sectional study is, in most instances, theoretical and manipulative. In developmental research it is also concerned with age differences, although only one age group need be involved. The major contribution of cross-sectional research to our understanding of child development lies in testing theories and providing data on the causes of behavior. Age differences in the effects of various manipulations may also be investigated.

A major advantage of the cross-sectional experiment is that it is relatively economical in time, money, and personnel. An experiment involving many hundreds of people might be conducted in just a few days, and a large amount of data can be collected for the effort expended.

The typical cross-sectional experiment is manipulative. In other words, the experimenter presumes that some particular independent variable is related to behavior in certain specifiable ways, and manipulates it in order to test whether it affects behavior in the predicted ways. Some subjects in the experiment will form the

experimental group—the subjects on which the manipulation is performed. The remainder of the subjects will form a **control group**, on whom no manipulation is performed. The behavior of all the subjects is measured on some task, their scores being the *dependent variable*. The particular manipulations performed define the treatment conditions and allow the experimenter to determine which particular treatments (manipulations of the independent variable) produce changes in the behavior of the subjects. In this way, cross-sectional experiments may enable us to make cause-effect statements relating particular manipulations to particular magnitudes of the dependent variable. Hence, experimental procedures of this sort are employed in order to test hypotheses derived from theories and to determine the causes underlying behavior.

Within the framework of developmental research one particular independent variable of interest is age. In many instances experimental treatments are assumed to affect subjects differently depending upon their age; that is, the interaction of age and treatment is of interest. Assessment of the differential effects of a manipulation on various age groups may yield insights into developmental processes. For example, Dusek (Dusek, Kermis, & Mergler, 1975; Dusek, Mergler, & Kermis, 1976) demonstrated that labeling of to-be-remembered information facilitated subsequent recall more for preadolescents (grades 4 and 6) than adolescents (grade 8). This research suggests that adolescents use more efficient methods of memorizing or coding information than do younger children.

A **longitudinal study** is the systematic study of the same group(s) of individuals at regular intervals over time. In other words, in a longitudinal study we have more than one measurement of the same individuals' behavior. Because the behaviors of the same group(s) of subjects are assessed at different times, the longitudinal study provides data about growth trends. Uniformity and diversity in patterns of growth over time may be delineated. For example, we can study growth in performance on IQ tests, problem-solving ability, or physical traits, and compare developmental (age change) trends with simple age differences. With respect to the four dimensions listed in Table 2-1 the longitudinal study is always an age-change study and may lie at either pole on the remaining three dimensions.

The longitudinal study has several additional advantages. First, it can be used to examine factors that influence behavior only over extended periods of time. In other words, the longitudinal study is ideal for investigating the influences of cultural factors that require the passage of time before their effects on behavior might be detectable. Second, longitudinal studies also demonstrate continuities and commonalities in behavior over time.

The use of longitudinal studies has some limitations and obstacles. They are expensive, requiring extensive time, money, and personnel. An investigator may have only a limited amount of time to devote to a longitudinal study, as well as a limited amount of money to keep track of subjects, establish and maintain testing procedures, and keep up the interest of the subjects.

Sample attrition can also be a severe problem in longitudinal studies, particularly when older people are involved. Subjects lose interest, move, or die. As a result, at each time of testing one is essentially dealing with a different sample and, therefore, the generality of the findings may be in question. Another drawback is that a longitudinal study is hard to replicate. Since replication is one way of ensuring that the results obtained are reliable, this limitation is very serious. Finally, introducing new testing procedures into an ongoing longitudinal study is often difficult. For example, we cannot conduct a longitudinal study on the growth of IQ using the Stanford-Binet IQ test and then change to the Wechsler Adult Intelligence Scale, because the two tests do not measure IQ in the same way. Therefore, our IQ scores would not be comparable from one testing to the next.

Combined longitudinal and cross-sectional designs are used to overcome some problems inherent in both the cross-sectional and longitudinal designs that sometimes make them inadequate for assessing developmental phenomena. In the traditional cross-sectional design, effects owing to age are confounded with effects owing to time of birth, which is called **cohort** (Schaie, 1965). In other words, because the subjects are of different ages at the same time (the test date), they must have been born in different years. Because they were born in different years, they may behave in ways that are different but irrelevant to age per se. What may appear in the results to be an age difference may, in reality, be a cohort (time of birth) difference. The two effects are perfectly **confounded**, and at times we can not logically conclude that one and not the other caused the results in the experiment. This phenomenon occurs perhaps most clearly when a significant cultural factor might influence development, as in the example of individuals of different age levels who happen to have been born pre- or post- World War II. Forty-year-olds might give very different test results from 20-year-olds quite apart from the age gap between the two groups because the 40-year-olds lived through a world war and that may cause them to perform differently than the younger group.

In the longitudinal study, age and time of measurement are perfectly confounded (Schaie, 1965). In other words, the age of the subjects is directly related to the time at which measurements are taken. If significant cultural events intervene between one testing and another, the age changes observed might or might not reflect differences owing to the particular time of measurement (that is, the intervening cultural events that occurred). Again, consider our 40-year-olds. Since they were born in, say, 1939 they have experienced one world war and two limited wars in which the United States was involved. One may well expect that a longitudinal measure of this group's attitude toward war may reflect current involvement in war quite apart from maturing psychological processes as roughly reflected by the age of the individual. As with the confoundings in the cross-sectional study, only rarely can this confounding be logically separated.

In the sense that we are using it, the term "confound" means that it is impossible for us to determine whether age differences or age changes are "real" or whether they are due to intervening cultural events. If no significant cultural factors intervene, the traditional designs present no difficulty. In our fast-paced, technological culture, however, this is unlikely. Hence, in a cross-sectional study it is very risky to make generalizations about age differences from one time of measurement to another. In a longitudinal design it is risky to make generalizations about age changes over time from one time of measurement to another. Clearly, because the cross-sectional and longitudinal studies involving the age variable are critical to developmental research, the ambiguities that result from their use are undesirable.

Since Schaie's (1965) original article, a great deal of discussion has focused on alternative research designs that might be used in order to separate age differences and age changes from effects owing to cohort and time-of-measurement influences. These procedures involve testing a cross-sectional sample several times. This design is illustrated in Table 2-2 for Dusek's study of the development of the self-concept in children and adolescents (grades 5–12). Each column of Table 2-2 is a cross-sectional study and each row is a longitudinal study. Differences between the columns are estimates of the influences of time of measurement, that is, differences owing to cultural change. Differences between the rows labeled 1959 through 1964 reflect cohort influences, which are due to different life experiences. By taking subsets of the total design we can answer questions about age changes and age differences independent of cohort and time-of-measurement influences. For example, the scores from the samples indexed by a * in Table 2-2 provide estimates of cohort and time-of-measurement effects and those indexed by a † provide estimates of age and time effects. By analyzing the data in this way, we obtain estimates that are unconfounded with the third variable in the overall design and gain a clearer picture of development than the cross-sectional and longitudinal studies.

TABLE 2-2   Combined Cross-Sectional and Longitudinal Design

	AGES		
TIME OF BIRTH	1975	1976	1977
1957	18	——	——
1958	17	18	——
1959	16	17	18
1960	15	16	17
1961	14	15	16
1962	13	14	15
1963	12*†	13*	14
1964	11*†	12*†	13
1965	——	11†	12
1966	——	——	11

*Estimates of cohort and time of measurement effects.
†Estimates of age and time effects.

A **case study** is a systematic assessment of a single individual at regular intervals over time. The case study, then, is a special case of the longitudinal approach. Typically the case study is naturalistic, correlational, and atheoretical. The case study approach has several advantages, including the fact that for the time and money invested the amount of data collected is large. The case study is also a very practical approach to therapy, where, in fact, it is most commonly found. Case studies also allow the examination of intraindividual change in behavior. By studying the stability of an individual's performance, some notion is gained about the stability of psychological traits. For example, case studies of the development of intelligence reveal wide variations in the tested IQ, leading to the conclusion that IQ test performance is not very stable (e.g., Honzik, Macfarlane, & Allen, 1948; Pinneau, 1961; Dearborn & Rathney, 1963).

Case studies do, however, have some disadvantages. First, the data are quite probably biased, because they represent growth and development for only one individual. As a result, the information may not lend itself to generalizations about other people and may not lead to general laws of development. A second problem with the case study is the difficulty of manipulating some variables and getting clearly interpretable results. For example, we may manipulate reinforcement contingencies and study their effects on the behavior of a single individual. Indeed, operant research (behavior modification) is often conducted in this fashion. However, organismic variables such as IQ, sex, and anxiety level cannot be manipulated in a case study. An individual cannot be both low and high anxious, or low and high IQ, or male and female.

Although case studies are popular and useful for illustrating many aspects of development, caution should be taken in generalizing the findings until a number of case studies show the same general trends of development. This is not to deny the importance of studying the individual but rather to emphasize the limitations of this approach for providing general laws of development.

Single-subject designs are employed by some psychologists (e.g., Skinner, 1953) who believe that performing a large number of manipulations on a single subject is the best way to discover the basic laws of learning. Hence, the single-subject design is manipulative. It is typically atheoretical, may be carried out either in the laboratory or a naturalistic setting, and usually is not concerned with age changes or age differences.

One type of single-subject design that has been used in a number of studies with children uses **behavior modification.** The typical procedure is first to obtain a base rate of occurrence of both the undesired behavior and the desired behavior. After a stable measure has been obtained, the experimenter reinforces the desired behavior and ignores the undesired behavior. This continues until the desired behavior is at a stable high rate, showing the effectiveness of reinforcement. Then, to demonstrate that the increase in desired behavior and decrease in undesired behavior are due to the reinforcement procedures, the experimenter withdraws the reinforcement, expecting the undesired behavior to return to its **base rate**. After the withdrawal of reinforcement demonstrates that no extraneous variable caused the changes in behavior, the reinforcement is reinstituted in order to bring the desired behavior back to a higher level and the undesired behavior to a lower level. Procedures such as these have been used to alter the aggressive behavior of children in the classroom, to help solve children's sleeping problems, and to investigate the role of reinforcement in explaining development.

Interview-survey research may be carried out in a variety of ways. A frequently used technique uses the survey-questionnaire approach. When the questionnaire asks children to state their views about some topic, for example, politics or morals, the questionnaire is called an **opinionnaire**, since the subjects are expected to respond by expressing their own feelings and opinions. When subjects are asked to respond to a questionnaire about themselves, it is often called an **inventory**. Children may, for example, be asked to describe their self-concept. A questionnaire given in person by an examiner is called an interview. When it is sent through the mail or is administered to a large group of people without the examiner necessarily being present it is often called a survey. Interviews and surveys usually are administered in the natural setting and most often are correlational in nature. They may have characteristics at either end of the other two dimensions.

This approach has a number of advantages that have made it very popular. First, a great deal of information may be collected from large numbers of children in a very short time. For example, one of the authors of this text and his assistants have administered as many as 1,200 questionnaires to large groups of adolescents in just several days. In that time approximately 400,000 pieces of data were collected.

The questionnaire method has the limitation of being normative and descriptive in nature. Hence, its use does not reveal cause-effect relationships. Issues such as whether subjects are lying or the interviewer is somehow biasing the subjects' responses, and the reliability of retrospective reports are other problems that enter into evaluating the utility of data collected by the questionnaire method.

Evaluating Research Results

The information resulting from any of these procedures for collecting data is evaluated in several ways. The use of statistical tests allows the investigator to evaluate whether or not the results support the hypothesis under investigation. Statistics are also used to summarize the information gathered in the research. A less formal evaluation is concerned with the **generalizability** of the information. This judgment rests on the nature of the tasks and procedures used in the research and on a knowledge of the characteristics of the sample of children, or others, who were the subjects.

After the researchers have collected the information from the subjects, they may use **descriptive statistics** to summarize it and **inferential statistics** to test whether the data support the hypotheses. The descriptive statistics most frequently encountered are the mean, the arithmetic average of a group of scores, and the correlation coefficient, a statistic indicating the degree of relationship between two measures (for example, school grades and IQ) taken on the same group of subjects. The **correlation coefficient** is denoted by r and may take any value from -1 to $+1$. Positive correlations indicate that people who score higher on one variable tend to score higher on the other variable. Negative correlations indicate that people who score high on one variable tend to score low on the other; those who score low on the first variable tend to score higher on the other. For example, school grades and IQ are positively correlated. Students who score high on IQ tests tend to get good grades in school, and students who score low on IQ tests do not score as high on school grades. A negative correlation exists between measures of test anxiety—the fear or nervousness that the child feels while taking a test—and test performance. Children who score high on measures of test anxiety tend to do less well on tests than children whose test-anxiety scores are lower. The size of the correlation reveals the degree of relationship. A correlation of $+.6$ shows as strong a relationship as a correlation of $-.6$. The only difference is the direction of the relationship.

If we have a number of measures on a group of people, we can compute the correlations among all the measures. For example, suppose we had five measures on a sample of 6-year-olds: height, weight, IQ, health status, and an achievement-test score. We could compute the correlations between all of the measures. This would produce ten correlations for our example. Through a technique called *factor analysis* (see Appendix) we can further analyze this set of correlations and derive several factors, clusters of variables that are highly correlated with each other but are not correlated with variables included in other clusters. In this manner we reduce the number of variables that must be dealt with, and this helps simplify the data and often makes them easier to understand.

As noted above, inferential statistics are used to test whether the results support the hypothesis. Suppose, for example, we hypothesize that teaching reading with method A is better than teaching it with method B, the one currently used at the school. We could test this hypothesis by teaching one group of first-graders to read with method A and a second group to read with the standard method, method B. The group receiving method A is called the *experimental group* because we give them the special treatment, reading method A. The group receiving no special treatment, in this case the standard reading program, is called the *control group*. At the end of the semester each group is given a reading test and scores of reading ability are obtained. We would use descriptive statistics to examine the mean performance of each group. Inferential statistics, on the other hand, would help determine whether the difference between the means was large enough to be attributed to the experimental manipulation—the two reading methods—or whether the difference was so small that it would have to be attributed to random, chance differences in the two groups' performance. In the latter case, we say that the data do not support the hypothesis—the reading methods are equally good for teaching reading. In the former case, we say that the data supported the hypothesis and method A is better than the standard method.

Evaluating the generalizability of research results requires information about the sample of children tested, the procedures used, and the tests or tasks employed. If the sample is chosen so that everyone in the group from which it is selected has an equal chance of being selected, the subjects make up a **random sample**. The characteristics of this sample will be highly similar to those of the larger group from which it was chosen. Two random samples drawn from the same larger group will also be highly similar to each other. Hence any difference between them at the end of an experiment must be due to the manipulations employed in the procedures. By using random instead of **biased samples**—samples selected for some specific characteristics—we may generalize the results to the larger group. Although psychologists use biased samples for some specific purposes, for example, to test issues related to a specific mental disorder, most research is conducted with random samples so the results can be generalized to the larger group, that is, so that we may assume that the performance of the children in the experiment will represent how each child in the larger group will perform. In this way it is possible to generate laws of development that are maximally generalizable.

Knowledge of the procedures used in an experiment is critical for replicating (reconducting) the experiment. To facilitate communication of the procedures, psychologists often use **operational definitions**, ways of defining concepts by stating the methods used to measure them. Use of these definitions ensures that any other person can know exactly what a concept means, for example, intelligence as measured by an IQ test or social reinforcement given by telling a child he did well on some task. By replicating the procedures used in the experiment and by defining concepts in the same way, psychologists can redo the experiment and thus check the reliability of the results. This is an important step in research because it allows greater confidence in the results of the experiment and in the laws of development that we derive from them.

Finding tasks that are suitable for use across a wide range of ages is an important problem in developmental research. This is necessary if psychologists are to investigate developmental change through longitudinal experiments and measure different age groups in a single experiment, the cross-sectional study. Obviously, some tasks are suitable only for a narrow age range because they are too difficult for younger children or too easy for older children. In these instances, psychologists try to devise tasks that measure similar processes in different age groups even though the tasks may be somewhat different.

SUMMARY

Two basic models, the mechanistic and organic, have guided psychologists' theorizing about human behavior, generally, and human development, specifically. In psychology the mechanistic model of development is related to the concept of the reactive organism which assumes human beings are able to respond to stimulation and react to stimuli with responses that are learned. This model views the human as operating as if he were a machine and is the basis of learning-theory approaches to development, which is defined as the learning of increasingly complex behaviors as a result of combining simpler behaviors.

The organic model of the universe is represented by the cognitive-developmental approach to development, which postulates that human development occurs in a sequence of stages representing qualitative changes in the structural aspects of the organism. This model views the organism as active, as an initiator of development because it seeks out stimulation from the environment.

Theories about developmental phenomena are derived from these more general and basic models. Theories serve three major functions: they allow us to integrate information about development, they attempt to specify the causes of behavior—the factors that lead to our acting the way we do, and they allow us to predict new behavior. Theories can never be judged true or false, only as more or less useful for describing development. The utility of a theory depends on the hypotheses derived from it. Research is then conducted to determine if these hypotheses are supported by data.

A variety of research techniques are available to test theories. Cross-sectional techniques, which are used to test children of different ages, provide information about age differences in development. Longitudinal studies are conducted by repeatedly testing the same group of subjects, thereby providing age-change information. Some sophisticated combined cross-sectional and longitudinal designs allow the simultaneous assessment of age change and age-difference aspects of development. These designs are especially useful if there is some reason to suspect that development of some characteristic may change with cultural shifts. In addition to being classifiable according to the type of design used, a research project may be described by a number of other dimensions: manipulative versus nonmanipulative, laboratory versus naturalistic, and theoretical versus atheoretical.

Since psychologists conduct research with children, they must confront a variety of important ethical considerations, which concern ensuring the rights of the child to refuse to participate and not be penalized for refusing, justifying the necessity to deceive the child about the nature of the experiment, disclosing the purposes and procedures to be used, and assuring that the value of the research will outweigh the harm or, if harm is likely, that the experiment will be either abandoned or changed to produce no harm to the child.

Statistics are tools used to analyze the data collected in a research project. Descriptive statistics, such as the mean, are used to summarize the information collected. An especially important descriptive statistic is the correlation coefficient, a measure of the degree of relatedness of two sets of measures taken on the same group of subjects. The greater the value of the coefficient, the stronger, more closely related, the variables are. The sign of the correlation coefficient indicates whether the relationship is positive (+) or negative (−). Inferential statistics are used to determine if the results of the experiment are due to the manipulations employed or are a result of chance fluctuations in the performance of the subjects.

Another important evaluation of research stems from considerations of the generalizability of the findings. Since psychologists are concerned primarily with discovering general laws of development, they use random samples of subjects so that the results can be assumed to apply to larger groups of children than those tested in the study. The use of operational definitions and provision of detailed descriptions of research procedures ensures the possibility of replicating the experiment and thereby testing the reliability of the findings. The greater the reliability, the greater our confidence in the laws derived from the study.

CHAPTER 3

(Susan Richter/Photo Researchers)

THE NATURE AND NURTURE OF HUMAN DEVELOPMENT

AT ONE TIME scientists generally believed that the same principles of inheritance governed both physical attributes and mental traits. Scholars such as Charles Darwin and Karl Pearson focused their interests on the relationship between inherited physical characteristics and their behavioral manifestations. The advent of behaviorism (Watson, 1924), however, saw the dismissal of the assumption that behavior is inherited in the same way as physical traits. Instead, it was assumed that behavior is determined only by environmental influences (learning). Today, research on inherited characteristics is called *behavioral genetics*. A bitter debate developed, and the schism between biology and psychology widened. In commenting on these events McClearn (1968, p. 9) observed: "This attitude came to be emotionally charged and, as a consequence, behavioral scientists in the past several decades not only did not encounter genetics during their training, they typically acquired a feeling of estrangement toward that subject matter. The enormous recent advances in genetics have therefore had but a limited impact upon psychology in general." He might well have added, "and upon developmental psychology in particular." Developmental psychology was particularly affected because it includes the study of biological predispositions, environmental influences, and the interaction of both variables. The biological basis of behavior has recently attracted particular interest because of the emergence of theoretical views advocating that certain behaviors, such as language, are an inevitable consequence of the physiological structure of human beings in interaction with a particular linguistic culture.

This chapter presents a highly abbreviated discussion of the essential principles of heredity and evolution and is particularly concerned with the implications of genetics and evolution for understanding human development and with the influence of heredity, evolution, and environment on the psychological development of children.

Origins of Behavior
and Development

The study of human development includes both **ontogeny** and **phylogeny**. Ontogeny is the study of behavioral changes in *individuals* over time, and phylogeny is the study of changes that occur in *populations* (species) over time. Studies of ontogenetic change involve shorter time periods (an individual's life span), whereas phylogeny is concerned with change over extended periods, often over many generations. Ontogenetic changes reflect the interaction between individuals and their environment. From careful observation of behavioral changes, we can formulate developmental principles that apply to all members of a species and describe what environmental events modify behavior. Some behaviors are rather insensitive to environmental variation (patterns of motor development), while others clearly reflect cultural variation (political attitudes). Phylogenetic changes, on the other hand, are more evolutionary in character and result in behaviors that are adaptive to the environment. For example, very young infants evidence numerous reflexes—like the palmar reflex—that probably have evolutionary significance. They will close their fingers around an object when that object causes stimulation of the palmar surface of the hand. This is significant because it does not involve thumb-forefinger prehension—that is, the thumb, uniquely employed by human beings, is not engaged in the grasping behavior. Some short time after birth, infants no longer respond reflexively to palmar stimulation, and thumb-forefinger prehension appears. Although thumb-forefinger prehension cannot be viewed as a predetermined evolutionary advance, it is nevertheless associated with high-level skills (language). The specific evolutionary significance of thumb-forefinger prehension can only be deduced from the behaviors it makes possible. Newborn babies also make reflexive swimming movements which subsequently disappear. This reflex is probably a residual behavior whose adaptive significance has long since been lost. It should be noted that both phylogeny and ontogeny involve behaviors that are adaptive to the environment within the limitations of the species or the individual.

Basic Genetic Mechanisms

Conception occurs when an ovum (egg cell) is penetrated by a sperm cell. The fertilized egg, called a **zygote**, contains the genetic material required for the development of the organism. Human beings have 23 pairs of **chromosomes**, 46 threadlike entities present in each cell. Along each chromosome are **genes**, each with a specific location, which carry the specific information for hereditary transmission; the gene's **deoxyribonucleic acid** (DNA) contains the genetic material which in turn directs the functions of **ribonucleic acid** (RNA). The molecular structure for

DNA was discovered by Watson and Crick (1953) and provides the explanation for how every cell in the body contains the same genetic pattern as the originally formed cell.

From the original cell formed at conception, development occurs by means of cell division. There are two kinds of structurally different cells: somatic, or body, cells that comprise the various organs and systems (digestive, respiratory), and sex cells, which are either sperm or ovum. The somatic cells divide to produce new cells in a process called **mitosis**, whereby each new somatic cell contains a pair of genes, one each contributed by the mother and father, and thus contains a full complement of 46 (23 pairs) chromosomes. The division of sex cells is called **meiosis**, a process in which each new sex cell contains only one-half of the chromosomes, or 23 chromosomes. Only after a new zygote is formed is the full complement of chromosomes restored.

Some of the simplest examples of the laws of heredity can be taken from Mendel's classic experiments in which he crossed tall plants with dwarfed plants. The gene for the tall plant (T) is *paired* with the gene from the small plant (t). The pair of genes are called **alleles**. Mendel noted that when he crossed plants that only produced tall plants with plants that only produced dwarfed plants, all the offspring were tall. The parental characteristic observed in the F_1 (first filial generation) was the tall feature, which was then assumed to be *dominant* over the dwarf trait, which is called *recessive*. Mendel then crossed two of the offspring plants, resulting in three tall plants and one dwarf plant. Remember that genetic structure consists of pairs and that one gene is dominant. In this simple case a tall plant may consist of the pairs TT or Tt, whereas the dwarf can only consist of the recessive pair tt. In two cases (TT,tt) the observable physical characteristic (called the phenotype) of the offspring (tall or dwarf) corresponds to the genetic structure (called the genotype). That is, in TT the plant not only appears tall but also contains both genes for tallness. In one instance the offspring is tall but also contains the recessive gene (Tt). The plants with TT and tt are called *homozygous* (common elements), but the plant Tt is called *heterozygous* (different elements). It should be noted that Mendel conducted his work under highly controlled environmental conditions. However, had one set of TT plants been grown in sand and another set, tt, in rich soil, the former TT plant might have appeared to be a tt plant.

Mendel's work showed that genes determine physical structures, that pairs of genes (alleles) are responsible for physical characteristics, that one gene is dominant over its pair, and that, with heterozygotic pairs, the dominant gene will be physically manifest. Mendel made other contributions that are extremely important in understanding the diversity of populations, among them, the facts that evolutionary changes have occurred in species and that, with the exception of identical twins, no two people have identical genetic structures. First, he identified the law of segregation which governs the separation of gene pairs to form sex cells. Thus, either the dominant or the recessive gene will be present in a particular sex cell (sperm or ovum). He then noted that the separation of these different gene pairs occurs randomly. Because of random separation it is unlikely that any one inherited characteristic will be consistently associated with another inherited characteristic. Through these processes, the combinations of genetic structures is practically infinite. One other principle operates among humans to alter the physical expression of the genes. This process is called **crossing-over** and occurs during meiosis. The process of crossing-over involves a pair of chromosomes that may overlap. At the point where the chromosomes make contact, an exchange of genes may take place. This means that the genetic characteristic of the chromosome is actually changed.

Sex-Linked Characteristics

We noted earlier that each bodily cell consists of 23 pairs of identical chromosomes. Actually that is true of only 22 pairs; the twenty-third pair (the sex chromosomes) differ for males and females. The female has two X chromosomes and the male has an X and a Y chromosome. Since the male carries both the X and Y, it is the father that determines the sex of the child; that is, if the successful sperm contains an X chromosome, then the child will be a female (the ovum only contains X chromosomes), whereas if it contains a Y chromosome, the child will be a male.

The sex chromosomes play another important role in determining the inherited characteristics of males and females. The one pair of chromosomes that determine sex also contain other genes. Because the chromosomal material for males and females is different, it follows that the essential genetic structure will be different and, therefore, the resulting characteristics and traits. The process in simple form is as follows:

1. The X chromosome is larger than the Y and contains more genes.
2. Males have only one X chromosome and, therefore, do not have a counteractive second chromosome (a single gene determines a trait, not a pair).
3. In males, a particular gene found on the X chromosome but not on the Y chromosome will determine the trait or characteristic of the offspring.
4. The process for females is different because each sex cell carries two X chromosomes and therefore paired genes; the recessive gene must occur on both chromosomes in order for the trait or characteristic to occur.

The most clearly defined sex-linked characteristics involve recessive genes that lead to negative physical manifestations: color blindness, hemophilia, anemia, albinism, and one form of muscular dystrophy. In addition, many authors have suggested that the increased susceptibility to disease and infant mortality among males is also a sex-linked (genetic) process.

Chromosomal Abnormalities

The most direct evidence for genetic effects on behavior comes from the study of genetic abnormalities. In some of these abnormalities, Down's syndrome (mongoloidism) for example, we can specifically identify the genetic malfunction. **Phenylketonuria** is a genetic abnormality that has received considerable attention in recent years largely because early identification permits successful treatment. Other genetic abnormalities that have been identified and well explained are Turner's syndrome, Kleinfelter's syndrome, and the XYY syndrome.

Individuals afflicted with *phenylketonuria* (*PKU*) fail to produce a liver enzyme that converts phenylalanine, an amino acid, into another amino acid, tyrosine. The failure of this metabolic step affects the liver, and the unmetabolized phenylpyruvic acid attacks the central nervous system, and causes cell damage and consequent mental retardation.

PKU is transmitted by a single somatic recessive gene. It occurs in approximately 6 out of every 10,000 births and does not differentiate between the sexes. Since the defective gene is recessive, it must be present in both the mother and father (see Figure 3-1 for a pedigree analysis). Fortunately, it is now possible to

FIGURE 3-1   The genetic transmission of phenylketonuria in the children of two heterozygous parents carrying the recessive allele for phenylketonuria (P is the dominant gene, p is the recessive gene).

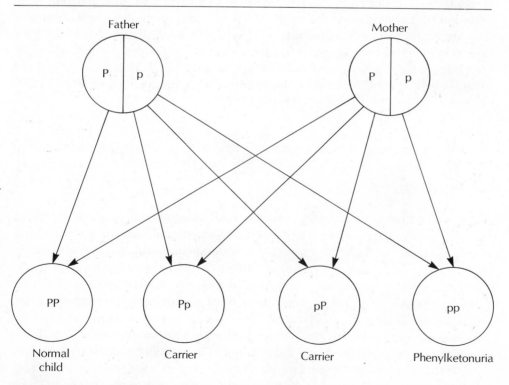

SOURCE: Hetherington, E. M., & Parke, R. D. *Child psychology: a contemporary viewpoint.* New York: McGraw-Hill, 1975, Figure 2-5 on p. 27.

identify PKU very early and to alleviate its devastating effects through a diet low in phenylalanine. It is also possible to identify carriers of the recessive gene. The technique involves giving suspected individuals an excessive amount of phenylalanine, which carriers metabolize at a slower rate than normal individuals. Advances in understanding genetic processes will allow parents to make more informed decisions concerning the risks of having children.

The sex-chromosome abnormalities result from the sex chromosomes' failure to divide normally. Because segregation of the genes does not occur during the initial meiotic division, a sperm cell can contain both X and Y chromosomes or no sex chromosomes at all. The fertilization of a normal ovum by an XY sperm produces a zygote with an extra X chromosome, XXY. This condition is called Kleinfelter's syndrome. When a sperm cell fails to produce sex chromosomes, the resulting zygote produces a female with only one X chromosome, XO. This condition is called Turner's syndrome. Both abnormalities result in incomplete sexual development and some degree of mental retardation. In Turner's syndrome, intellectual functioning involving spatial relationships appears to be more affected than verbal performance. A third abnormality due to sex chromosomes occurs when a YY sperm fertilizes a normal ovum producing an XYY male. The most apparent manifestation of this abnormality is height; XYY males are often over 6 feet. Typically they are below average intellectually. It has recently been suggested that the XYY male is more likely to be highly aggressive and to commit violent crimes. Although the evidence for this hypothesis is far from conclusive, individuals with any of the various forms of sex-chromosome abnormalities are more likely to experience psychological difficulties (Money & Ehrhardt, 1972).

Principles of Evolution

The study of human development includes both ontogeny, the study of change in the individual, and phylogeny, the study of the origins and changes of species, that is, evolution. A core principle of evolution is the spontaneous and frequent occurrence of gene **mutations**, which are not always lethal or nonadaptive. Obviously, when the mutation is lethal, the organism will not survive and the potential biological modification fails to come about. With a marginally adaptive mutation, the affected organism will also be unlikely to survive because it cannot adapt to the demands of its environment and is unlikely to reproduce. Occasionally, a mutation occurs that is neither biologically lethal nor environmentally maladaptive. Assuming that the mutant can reproduce (not all mutants can) a modified organism will come into being and presumably thrive. A viable mutant may or may not be superior or more advanced than the population norm for the species.

The evolutionary process has the important feature that the sorting of single chromosome sets is *random*. Random assortment has the effect of increasing variability within the species, thus providing greater adaptiveness to a broader range of environmental pressures.

Adaptiveness

Beyond the straightforward biological functions, one of the important principles of evolution is the ability of organisms (species) to adapt to the demands of the environment. We have already seen that the biology of reproduction is itself a manifestation of **adaptiveness**. For example, the pairing of lethal genes, presumably a random event, renders survival of the offspring impossible. This conception of adaptiveness joins together the genetic and behavioral components of evolution. The assignment of genetic and behavioral components to the theory is known as the *synthetic theory*. According to Simpson & Roe (1958, p. 21):

> An aspect of the synthetic theory especially pertinent here is that it again brings in behavior as a central element. It not only points the way to evolutionary, historical explanations of existing behavior patterns but also involves behavior as one of the factors that produce or guide evolution. Some phases of selection, as in zygote and embryo, are not directly behavioral, but aspects of breeding, care of young, and subsequent survival are preeminently so and are obviously crucial elements of selection.

This statement shows that genetic structure, consequent behaviors, and environmental demands are all related; a change in one component stimulates a change in each of the others. Species or genetic strains within species that are unable to adapt to environmental changes will be selected out and become extinct. Although these processes are more easily demonstrated among infrahuman species, the numerous examples that occur among humans make the concepts important in studying human development.

SELECTIVE MATING.   Evolution is largely a random process that generates considerable genetic variability. But evolution does not necessarily proceed in a direction that guarantees an improved breed. Yet it is plausible to claim that over eons of time a superior product did emerge, namely, the human being. To explain the formation of a superior product, we must look beyond randomness. One aspect of evolution that is not randomly selective is mating. Research has demonstrated that nonrandom mating occurs within populations. The genetic structures of parents are more likely to be correlated, which reduces the range of variability possible. Selective mating is successful only in so far as the environment remains constant, or relatively constant. This means that some individuals will be disadvantaged under these conditions and will serve as a safeguard in the event that the environment changes in ways that are compatible with their inheritance. Ideally, we might contend that society should strive for diverse environments wherein the entire range of genetic capability can function successfully. In the process of selective mating, or natural selection, two factors are operating: biological compatibility of the potential parents and a more socially oriented factor, sexual attractiveness. The latter variable is related to income, education, occupation, race, and an assortment of other variables. Because selective mating usually confounds environmental and genetic variables, it becomes very difficult to separate out each effect.

MUTATION.   Selective mating reduces genetic variation and, therefore, the adaptiveness of the population but not of any individual. Fortunately, a second process, mutation, functions to produce genetic heterogeneity and offsets the effects of selective mating. We do not understand the natural causes of mutation very well but we do know that X-rays, other forms of radiation, and extremes in temperature enhance the probability of mutation. We have already mentioned some of the known and obvious mutants that manifest themselves in various disease states, but it seems highly likely that the human population contains other, much less obvious mutant states. Since these mutations are unobservable, it cannot yet be determined where they may lead the human species over the next several millions of years.

Although most mutations are deleterious to survival and are also recessive (otherwise a broader array of mutations would be apparent), not all are negative. As environmental demands change, a small fraction of the mutants may be in a superior adaptive position. Because only a small fraction of individuals may possess the genes required for adaptation to the environmental change, it may take a very long time for the mutation to become part of the "normal" population. Under conditions of extreme environmental change, selective survival enhances the probability that mutants will reproduce. Extreme environmental change also takes considerable time, so that gradually the genetic structures of survivors become adaptive.

Unlearned Behavior

The theory of evolution derives from the principles of genetic transmission and assumes that adaptive behavior is a manifestation of an underlying genetically determined structure. These behaviors acquire their adaptiveness through evolution and are innately determined; that is, they are genetically programmed or unlearned behaviors. Scientists who study behavior in its natural situation and concentrate on its apparently unlearned components, are called **ethologists** and include Tinbergen (1951), Kuo (1932), Hess (1970), and Lorenz (1965, 1966), to mention but a few of the better-known investigators. They have made significant contributions to our understanding of the interaction of environmental demands and innate behavior patterns and have shown how environmental stimuli serve as signals for innate responses, and, further, how these responses are adaptive. Ethologists make their observations in naturalistic settings because of the broad range of stimuli present in nature as compared with the relatively few stimulus events in the laboratory. Through the sometimes tedious process of observing behavior in context, ethologists are able to piece together the signaling stimuli and the ensuing responses, and eventually to understand the adaptive purpose of the response. Hess (1970, pp. 31–32) views the contribution of the ethologists to developmental psychology as follows:

> [I]t would seem that the most significant contribution of ethology to the study of human development, in both phylogenetic and ontogenetic senses, is the recognition that man is a biological organism, and that he has an evolutionary history. The present-day members of the species of Man have an ancient repertoire of behaviors. From the ethological point of view, the human infant is not a completely naive being, but possesses a legacy of potential behavior patterns which at one time assured the survival of the organism even without the aid of social learning or customs. Some of these innate behavior patterns involve elements of sexual behavior, aggressive behavior, and innate social responses. Recognition of these as part of our heritage is important because, in terms of Man's evolutionary history, we are not at all far from the time when there were no widespread cultural influences upon behavior. Without our built-in behaviors, we, as a species, simply could not have managed to survive for a million years.

One of the older issues that concerns psychologists, but particularly ethologists, is whether some animal and human behaviors are instinctive or learned. Instinctive behaviors are inherited, and not learned, through either experience or imitation. The simplest human example might be the eye blink in response to an approaching stimulus. Human beings display many such reflexes which seem to be adaptive. The theoretical debate centers on more complex behavior such as aggression (Lorenz, 1966). It is in connection with these behavioral patterns that the old concept of instinct as an internal force—determined by the genes and independent of environmental (learning) stimulation—has been largely abandoned. Contemporary ethologists now accept some version of the view that heredity determines a preprogrammed physiological system that reacts to a broad range of environmental stimuli. These systems are adaptive but not independent of environmental stimulation; in other words, the environment interacts with genetic potential to produce the organization of each response system. In humans, the environment, perhaps because of its greater diversity relative to lower animals, has a greater impact on genetic potential and thus plays a more active role in determining action patterns.

CHARACTERISTICS OF UNLEARNED RESPONSES.   The key to understanding innate behavior, a very complex concept, is that its form is stereotyped and appears even though the organism has never had the opportunity to observe or otherwise encounter the stimuli that elicit the behavior. Behaviors meeting these criteria are called **Fixed Action Patterns** (FAP). Innate behavior patterns are as constant as the morphology of the species—the sequential development of the physiological features of the organism from conception through maturity. Since an organism could not survive if it indiscriminately responded to all the stimuli in its environment, it must respond only to a limited number. What determines which stimuli will elicit a FAP—learning or an innate mechanism? The answer, according to the ethologists, is that both learned and innate stimuli can elicit a particular response although the ethologists are interested in the stimuli that elicit innate responses. They refer to these eliciting stimuli as **sign stimuli**, or releasers. Sign stimuli function as releasers through a mechanism called the **Innate Releasing Mechanism** (IRM). Thus, rather than responding to all potential environmental stimuli, an organism responds only to the stimuli that correspond to a related innate releasing mechanism. Moreover, we have some reason to suspect that IRMs are activated only when the organism is in certain physiological states (hunger, fear, sexual arousal, and so forth). "The IRM is thought to operate as a receptor of key stimuli and by necessity adapted to the world as it exists, so that it will respond only to stimuli that unfailingly characterize a particular biological situation, and no other" (Hess, 1970, pp. 8–9).

Innate behaviors have three additional characteristics: universality, sequentiality, and species-specific adaptiveness. Although behaviors generally considered to be innate possess all three attributes, these criteria alone are insufficient to eliminate learning as a plausible alternative hypothesis.

Universality, as the term implies, requires that a FAP appears in all members of a species in order for it to qualify as an innate behavior. It may happen that a few members of a species do not display the behavior, perhaps because of some mutation or pathology. It would be difficult to ascertain whether some deviation in behavior resulted from a mutation or from learning but it seems reasonable that if only a few members of a species show the deviation, the cause is likely to be mutation. Universality as a criterion does not rule out the possibility of learning. Even though all members of a group exhibit a certain behavior, it may still be the result of a universal environmental influence. Given that all members of the species share a common morphology and physiology and, further, that they share the same general environment, then it would not be surprising to find that all members of the species behave in the same ways under the same conditions. Note that such a finding would not seriously harm the argument for innate mechanisms, for the ways in which the innate requirements of the organism (such as the need for sleep or warmth) are met may very well be learned. Organisms may well have innate requirements for survival, but behavior can take a number of forms in meeting these requirements for innateness.

To demonstrate how an apparently innate response is probably affected by learning, we have selected a classic experiment with ducklings by Eckhard Hess (1959). Other experiments have obtained similar results using dogs and birds. Hess's experiment was designed to test the apparently unlearned tendency of mallard ducklings to follow the mother duck. The experimental arrangement is shown in

FIGURE 3-2   The apparatus used in the study of imprinting consists primarily of a circular runway around which a decoy duck can be moved. In this drawing a duckling follows the decoy. The controls of the apparatus are in the foreground.

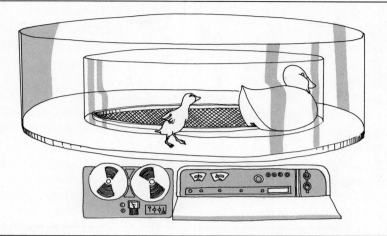

SOURCE: Hess, E. H. Imprinting: an effect of early experience. *Science*, 1959, *130*, 133–141.

Figure 3-2; a decoy mallard adult duck was attached to a rotating device and the ducklings were given an opportunity to follow the decoy. The speed of rotation and number of rotations of the decoy were recorded automatically and tape recorders provided calling sounds, both male and female, characteristic of the mature mallard duck. The ducklings were placed in the apparatus at various times after hatching, ranging from 1 to 4 hours to 29 to 32 hours. All the ducklings were first exposed to the male adult decoy, but in the testing condition the ducklings were placed between the male mallard model and a female mallard model, which differed from the male only by its coloration. Hess observed the animals to see which decoy they approached; he anticipated that the ducklings would turn toward the male mallard which had served as the model. The four test conditions represented a hierarchical order of difficulty: (1) both models stationary and silent; (2) both models stationary and calling; (3) the male stationary and the female calling; and, (4) the male stationary and silent and the female moving and calling. If the duckling responded to the male decoy on all four tests, it received a score of 100 percent.

Figure 3-3 shows the results of the most stringent analyses, namely, the percentage of ducklings that followed the model on all four criteria. There appears to be a "critical age" at which the impact of the initial experience was most effective—approximately 14 hours after hatching. The phenomenon just described suggests that the following behavior of mallard ducklings requires stimulation and lends support to the general belief that early infantile experiences are important to the subsequent development of the organism.

FIGURE 3-3 *Percentage of Animals in Each Age Group That Followed on Every Test Trial*

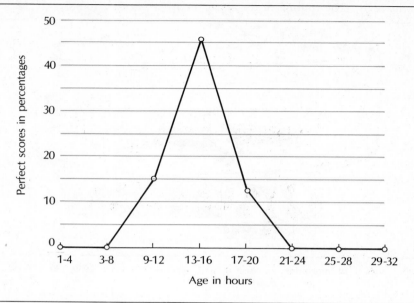

SOURCE: Hess, E. H. Imprinting: an effect of early experience. *Science,* 1959, *130,* 133–141.

The results of Hess's experiment show that behaviors that appear to be un-learned or instinctual in fact depend on specific stimulus events in the early life of the organism. Hess has referred to these behaviors as "instinctlike," but what is interesting about them is that their appearance depends not only on certain envi-ronmental events, but also on the timing of those events. If an environmental oppor-tunity presents itself too soon or too late, the strength of the response is weakened, and in extreme cases does not take place at all. A similar event may occur in human infants in formation of mother-child attachments (Bowlby, 1951, 1958).

Sequentiality as a requirement of innate behavior presents the same problems as those described for universality. For example, imagine a sequence of development such as might be found in the establishment of walking where the attainment of walking requires previously established patterns. On the face of it, such sequentiality suggests that the behavior is innate and biologically emergent. The *crucial* exper-iment would show that the environment does not somehow sequentially program the learning a child receives, thus giving the appearance of a built-in sequence. We shall explore this problem in greater detail in the discussion of Piaget's concept of cognitive development which relies on the assumption of universal sequences. In discussing such sequences, there is little debate about the more gross changes in behavior (a 9-month-old baby is not very apt to break the 4-minute mile, nor is a

6-year-old child very likely to solve simultaneous equations). The major dispute concerns the ordering of occurring stages in a fixed sequence.

Species-specific adaptiveness, or peculiar adaptiveness, is the final criterion for innate behavior. Behaviors that meet this criterion are uniquely used in coping with environmental demands and are essential to survival. Although innumerable examples of this phenomenon appear in studies of infrahuman organisms (see Hess, 1959), a particularly interesting series of research reports by Freedman (1961, 1964) suggests that the initial smiling responses of babies are (*a*) universal and (*b*) possess "peculiar adaptiveness" for they protect the baby from harm. (See Chapter 9 for the details of Freedman's work.) As with the criteria of universality and sequentiality, peculiar adaptiveness requires that all opportunities for learning are controlled, a condition that does not seem very likely to obtain with infant smiling. In animals that exhibit unusually complex behavioral sequences that probably cannot be learned in a short period of time, peculiar adaptiveness provides the strongest case, of the three criteria discussed, for the existence of unlearned behaviors.

In general it is easier with animals than with human beings to give examples of behavior that meets the criteria for innateness. The literature on unlearned behavior among human beings is far less conclusive in part because it is much more difficult to devise experimental situations that deprive organisms of opportunities to learn and because human beings are more responsive to variations in environmental demands.

In view of the difficulties in determining whether a behavior is innate and unlearned, we may well wonder whether any behavior meets the criteria. We shall now examine a few experiments with behaviors that apparently do meet these rigid criteria and thus are generally accepted as innate. One of the classic experiments was conducted by Carmichael (1926), who used amblystomas (salamanders) completely immersed in a solution containing chloretone, which immobilized the organisms completely without affecting their neuromuscular development. He immersed the amblystomas in the chloretone solution just before the time in their development when crude bodily movements would occur and he removed them from the solution at just the time when they would normally begin swimming. A control group of embryos were placed in common tap water and reared under approximately normal conditions. When the control group began swimming, the experimental subjects were removed from the chloretone, placed in normal tap water, and stimulated with an electric rod. Within approximately 30 minutes the salamanders exhibited normal swimming reactions. The interpretation of this experiment is that the swimming response could not have been learned but rather depended on innate growth processes. Incidentally, the generally accepted explanation of why it took the organism 30 minutes to swim is that it took approximately 30 minutes for the chloretone to wear off. Carmichael repeated the experiment using appropriate control groups to test for the effects of chloretone and found conclusive evidence that the 30-minute delay was caused by the chloretone.

A second classic experiment (Cruze, 1935) was performed on chicks. Cruze was interested in demonstrating that the pecking behavior of chicks is innate. Several studies had suggested that baby chicks exhibit rapid, accurate pecking from the time of hatching, even when reared in darkness. Cruze reared chicks in darkness, fed them by placing small food pellets in their mouths, and administered water with a medicine dropper. The experiment, summarized in Table 3-1, involved 8 different groups which varied in the amount of time reared in darkness: from 24 to 120 hours after hatching. Appropriate controls were maintained for testing conditions and motivation. The independent variables were the period of isolation and the amount of practice in pecking allowed in the test trials.

The results of the study are summarized in Figure 3-4, which shows that the initial pecking behavior was relatively inaccurate but improved rapidly with age. The most rapid improvement in pecking behavior occurred in the oldest chicks, that is, the Group E chicks who had been kept in isolation for 120 hours. Notice that Groups F, G, and H are not included in Figure 3-4. Note from Table 3-1 that these chicks remained in darkness between tests and thus had a much more limited number of practice pecks than the other groups. None of these groups attained a very high level of accuracy. Thus, the results of this experiment demonstrate that chicks have innate physiological mechanisms for pecking, but they require practice before they achieve a high level of proficiency.

Cruze's experiments are also relevant to the question of whether a behavior is innate or learned. To refer back to Figure 3-3, (the following behavior of mallard ducklings), you will note that some of the groups of ducklings showed only a weak following response, if any at all. Several studies, including the one by Cruze, have

TABLE 3-1   Experimental Conditions for the Eight Groups of Chicks in Cruze's Investigation

GROUP	NUMBER IN EACH GROUP	AGE WHEN TAKEN FROM DARK ROOM (HOURS)	NUMBER OF PECKS EACH TEST	METHOD OF SUBSEQUENT FEEDING
A	26	24	25	Natural
B	25	48	25	Natural
C	25	72	25	Natural
D	25	96	25	Natural
E	25	120	25	Natural
F	25	24	12	In dark 20 days
G	25	24	25	In dark 20 days
H	26	24	12 for 10 days, 25 for next 10	In dark 20 days

SOURCE: Cruze, W. W. Maturation and learning in chicks. *Journal of Comparative Psychology*, 1935, *19*, 371–409.

FIGURE 3-4   Curves representing the average number of missing errors of five groups of chicks deprived of pecking experience for the various periods of time indicated in the key.

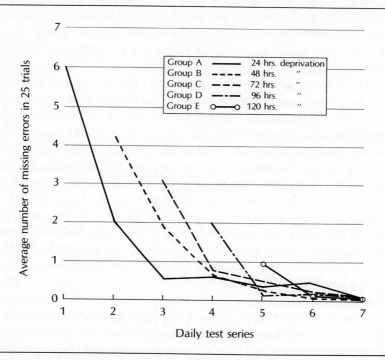

SOURCE: Cruze, W. W. Maturation and learning in chicks. *Journal of Comparative Psychology*, 1935, *19*, 371–409 (Fig. 1, p. 386).

found a **critical period** during development when certain external events must occur if a behavior is to become part of the organism's repertoire. Whether critical periods occur in human development is controversial. We have no hard evidence to support the idea. However, those who favor it concede that the span of time within which critical experiences must occur in order to have appropriate releasing effects on innately established readiness to respond is far broader for humans than it is for infrahuman organisms.

Studies of FAPs and IRMs, like those of physical maturation, build the case for innateness of some behaviors. Here we will analyze the implications of just a few experiments. Perhaps one of the most fascinating studies reported by Tinbergen, a leading investigator in this field, concerns reproduction in the stickleback fish. This study represents a classical ethological approach in that the observations of behavior were made in natural settings. The male stickleback selects a territory and builds a nest in which the female deposits eggs for fertilization by the male. When the male has completed nest building, he changes to the nuptial colors: his red underside becomes brighter, the back takes on a very bright bluish-green appearance, and a bright blue circle surrounds the eye. Until this point the female takes no part in any of this activity. Then, however, she develops a silvery gloss and her body becomes swollen by the eggs. When the male is ready to receive a female, he performs a dance in the area occupied by the females. Females who are ready to deposit eggs respond favorably to these signals from the male, whereas those females who are not ready to deposit eggs turn away in fear.

In interpreting the results of these observations, Tinbergen refers to the changes in the coloration of the male as the sign stimuli that trigger the IRMs referred to earlier. A similar process has been observed with herring gulls feeding their chicks. The female herring gull has a yellow spot on the bill and a red spot located at the end of the lower jaw. The newly hatched chick will beg for food by pecking at the tip of the parent's bill. In response to this stimulus the parent regurgitates food onto the ground and feeds it to the young. This study, according to Tinbergen, also shows the action of sign stimuli—the yellow bill and the red spot.

However interesting and informative these experiments are, they have been criticized for not providing conclusive evidence that the behaviors studied are innate (Munn, 1955). Munn argues that the research strategy used by Tinbergen and others permits the plausible alternative hypothesis that opportunities for observing the behaviors have occurred. The stickleback fish or the herring gull chicks may acquire these critical responses by observing what other members of the species do. Munn has argued that more convincing evidence for innateness requires a deprivation study and the demonstration that the behavior occurs without any opportunity to either observe or practice the behavior, as in the experiments with the salamander and the pecking behavior of chicks.

A second possible criticism of the ethological work concerns the significance attributed to the sign stimuli. Specifically, the question has been raised whether or not sign stimuli and IRMs have to be invoked to explain the behavior. Tinbergen has made an effort to answer this criticism by designing a series of experiments (in nonnaturalistic situations) in which if the presumed sign stimuli postulated by Tinbergen are responsible for the IRM, then changing some detail of these stimuli or removing them entirely should result in a failure of the IRM to occur. In general these experiments have been successful in demonstrating that the hypothesized sign stimuli are in fact responsible for the IRM. Figure 3-5 shows a series of herring gull models where the color of the spot on the lower jaw has been manipulated. The results of the experiment indicated that the chicks reacted to the red spot but only when it was located at the tip of the lower jaw. Tinbergen viewed this result as indicating that the sign stimuli do not occur singly but may well represent in many instances combinations of stimuli (in this case the color and location of the red spot). Thus, Tinbergen is probably correct in his interpretation of sign stimuli and IRMs, but it is not completely clear that the sign stimuli are innately determined; the crucial study, in which the herring gull chicks have no opportunity to associate the

FIGURE 3-5   Experiment with herring gull models shows that the begging response of the young depended on a spot on the beak, especially on a dark spot and on a red one.

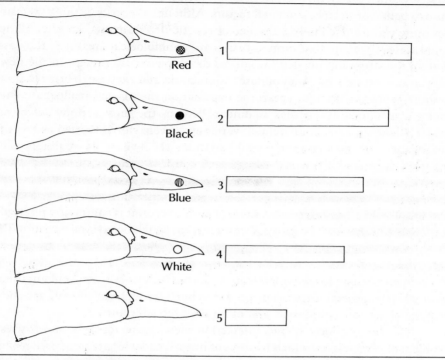

Red 1

Black 2

Blue 3

White 4

5

SOURCE: Adapted from Tinbergen, N. *The study of instinct.* Oxford: Clarendon Press, 1951, p. 30.

red spot with feeding, has not been conducted. We believe that, although such research is needed to determine conclusively whether sign stimuli are learned or innate, nevertheless, the enormous amount of research of this kind reported by the ethologists demonstrates convincingly that internal innate mechanisms interact with environmental stimuli in ways that are unique to species. In our judgment, this is an extremely important concept for understanding human development.

Genetics of Human Behavior

Before considering the data on the **heritability** of various human behaviors, we will first explore some of the fundamental conceptions of the relative roles of heredity and environment. These notions are remarkably simple but nonetheless frequently overlooked or misunderstood. One extreme position, for example, argues that all newborn babies possess basically the same genetic potential (*tabula rasa*), at least as regards the variables that will affect cognitive functioning. This view ascribes little or no significance to genetic characteristics; rather, it attributes nearly all differences in human behavior to environmental factors. Although theorists of this persuasion do not quite claim the complete absence of genetic determinants, for after all no one could seriously argue that human beings are nonbiological creatures, they assume that all the structures needed for normal development are present in the newborn baby and await only the "appropriate" stimulation and exercise to bring them forth. If these behaviors do not appear, the explanation then is "an inadequate environment"—an obviously circular argument. Perhaps the most serious defect of this model, however, is its additiveness: variation in behavior is viewed as the sum of hereditary traits plus environmental variations (H + E = B). A purely additive model is not plausible because it suggests that behavior can vary even though either factor can have a value of zero. It is logically consistent with the additive model that behavior can vary without any environmental contribution, or conversely, without any inherited base of behavior. A more plausible account is commonly referred to as the "interaction view": heredity × environment equals behavioral variation (H × E = B). According to this view, if either entry on the left-hand side of the equation is zero, then there can be no behavior, thus no variation. Thus, the more sensible position on human development would seem to be how heredity and environment interact. This general orientation has led to breakthroughs in treating genetic antecedents of mental retardation and other disease syndromes.

Despite the logic of the interaction view, there remains nevertheless the problem of determining which features of human behavior are primarily genetically determined. The purpose of this research is to increase our knowledge about genetic determinants in order to provide a basis for more intelligent environmental planning. For example, the evidence indicates that eye coloration is exclusively genetically determined, whereas height and weight, although also largely genetically determined, are apparently much more susceptible to environmental variation. (Greulich [1957] has shown that improved nutrition produces offspring who are taller and heavier than their parents.) Thus, human traits vary in their susceptibility to environmental effects. Stated differently, it seems apparent that some traits are more heritable than others.

The Heritability of Human Behavior

Research that is aimed at showing the interactive process at the human level in normal situations has proven very difficult to design and only recently has a relevant study been reported (Scarr & Weinberg, 1976). In order to test the interactive process, either the genetic structure or the environment must be manipulated. Genetic manipulations might involve creating mutations and testing for effects in diverse environments. Work of this kind is performed with animals in order to avoid ethical problems involved in the manipulation of human genetic structures. A second strategy for evaluating the interaction of heredity and environment involves depriving organisms of environmental stimuli and assessing the consequent changes in their behavior. This approach makes certain assumptions about the genetic potential of the organism. For example, we assume that a normal chimpanzee will acquire perceptual competence given a certain level of environmental stimulation and so we deprive the animal of all stimulus input having to do with form or environmental stimulation. As with genetic manipulation the deprivation strategy has been used with animals but cannot be used with human beings. In some instances, however, severe stimulus deprivation of a human being occurs in a natural setting and the consequences can be examined (some examples are described in the next chapter).

In this text we consider several instances when the development of some behavior appears to be largely controlled by heredity or at least some evolutionarily adaptive mechanism. In the next chapter, for example, we will examine the course of physical and motor development, introduce the concept of **maturation**, and present evidence that the rate and patterns of physical and motor development are genetically predetermined. Emotional development is another aspect of human development that appears to have strong genetic antecedents. Perceptual and cognitive development also involve genetic predispositions, although we are considerably less certain about the relative roles of heredity and environment. Two areas of human development and behavior whose heritabilities have received considerable attention from scientists are intelligence and personality.

Methods of Determining Heritability

Before we can fully understand the research dealing with the inheritance of behavior, we must examine some of the methods employed to estimate the degree to which a behavior or behavior pattern is genetically determined. Each procedure suffers to some degree from the same basic fault, specifically, the inability to cope with variations in environment. Thus, with perhaps one exception, people who hold an environmental view can always criticize this research on the grounds that commonalities in environment account for the data just as readily as *presumed* commonalities in genetic structure. To counter this criticism, we need evidence at the human level that drastic differences in environment do not produce significant differences in the performance of biologically related individuals, such as identical or fraternal twins. It is unfortunate from a scientific viewpoint that such cases that do exist do not occur randomly so that even under ideal conditions certain difficulties of interpretation present themselves.

POPULATION DISTRIBUTION.   One obvious approach in studying genetic effects is to administer a test to samples of people from two or more specified populations. The performance characteristics of the two, or more, defined populations are compared in terms of means and amount of variation. The concept underlying this approach is that identifiable groups of people come from different population gene pools; that is to say, the defined groups differ in the frequencies with which certain genes typically occur. The most obvious example of this research is on behavioral differences among races. What is less obvious, but has been pointed out clearly by Hirsch (1963), is that genes within, say, specific races may or may not be normally distributed. The assumption is made, nevertheless, that this distribution is normal within a population when only the differences between means are assessed. Little evidence exists for the assumption of a normal distribution, so that statistical comparisons based entirely on differences between means may be entirely inappropriate. Equally important, no such study has ever approached sampling an entire population of a specific identifiable group of people. Again let us use race as an example. A few studies have used national samples derived from single limited geographic regions (the Northeast, for example) or even a single city. Hence, only tentative inferences at the very best can be made about the *entire* population of both races. The data from these studies indicate that the white samples perform better than the black samples. Most of these differences occur on standard intelligence and achievement tests.

The plausible though dubious argument has been advanced that American blacks are not typical of blacks throughout the world (Eysenck, 1971), so that even a nationwide sample would not allow safe inferences about differences in the behavior of the races. Eysenck argues that blacks in the United States first arrived as slaves and that the blacks thought to be highly intelligent were also considered potential troublemakers and thus excluded from the slave population that reached the United States. A similar theme has been developed concerning the population of white immigrants of various ethnic origins. Thus, Eysenck suggests that during the period of high immigration many Europeans came to the United States because they were unable to succeed in their own countries. One might thus suspect that these people represented the less capable end of the distribution of talent in that country. No data are available to test Eysenck's genetic interpretations. If, however, we read accounts of the experiences encountered by blacks and other ethnic groups in this country, we might well make an equally plausible case for environmental factors as the major causes for average differences in performance.

Finally, there is the problem of differences in environment that are confounded with differences in populations. Comparisons between black and white populations assume roughly equivalent environments, which are probably impossible to find. We would have to find comparable environments, however, if we wished to attribute behavioral differences primarily to race and not to learning. Just as white subgroups differ among themselves in traditions and social expectations, so certainly must races. It is not known if these variations make any difference, but it is certain that such variations in environments do exist. This becomes apparent if we even try to compare middle-class blacks with middle-class whites; we would find it somewhat easier to obtain a sample of whites than blacks.

One very important study that attempts to attribute behavioral differences to (genetic) population differences will be examined later in some detail because of the care given to sample selection and to the interpretation of the data. First, however, a summary statement of population studies, no matter what their shortcomings, seems appropriate. Although we might examine any of several aspects of behavior, such as cognitive abilities, motor abilities, and personality variables, the general trend of the results indicates a greater overlap in the distribution of abilities between specifiable populations (blacks and whites) than differences between the population means. Even a single accurate generalization about the differences between the means is hard to come by because the results depend so extensively on the behavioral traits examined, the age of the children in question, and the methods of evaluation. It is true on most tests that the distributions of scores for whites and blacks overlap more than 50 percent, but most differences between the means tend to favor the white children. Again, keeping in mind all of the foregoing problems with this research, there is the additional problem that our intelligence tests are probably biased in favor of whites.

PEDIGREE ANALYSES.   As the term "pedigree" suggests, this approach to the study of genetics is similar to tracing one's family tree. Thus it is known that among several of the royal families of Europe, hemophilia is a distinct genetic possibility. The occurrence of hemophilia can be predicted in a particular offspring with some accuracy by tracing the history of his other genetic relatives. Perhaps the best known work in this field, however, concerns mental retardation and involves a family known as the Kallikaks. A mentally retarded woman gave birth to a child, and some 480 offspring have descended from that original union. As it turned out, the children tended to have a lower IQ than that of the general population and a greater incidence of general mental instability. A Kallikak male and a woman of apparently normal ability gave rise to a second strain of 496 offspring. In general this group of descendants was superior to the initial one. Again, it is impossible to determine what caused the initial level of retardation and to what degree environment rather than genetic differences contributed to the greater incidence of criminality and mental disease in the first family as compared with the second.

THE TWIN METHOD.   The twin method is a more precise technique for studying genetic determinants. It is the method required for obtaining the **heritability index** (h^2). This index estimates the degree to which differences among people on a trait is due to genetics or environment. Basically the method relies on the use of **monozygotic twins** (MZ) and **dizygotic** (DZ) **twins.** Monozygotic twins are commonly referred to as identical twins because they develop from a single ovum and a single

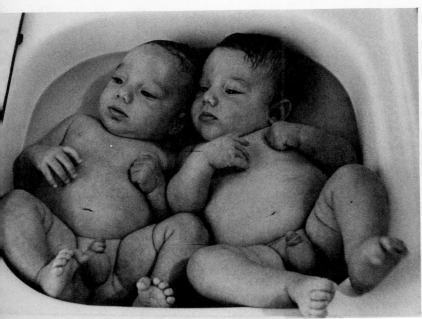

Identical twins have identical genetic characteristics because they develop from a single ovum and a single sperm. Fraternal twins are no more genetically alike than ordinary siblings.(Left: Marion Bernstein; right: Nancy Hays/Monkmeyer)

sperm. Dizygotic twins derive from two maternal ova and usually two sperm cells and are ordinarily no more genetically similar than ordinary siblings; dizygotic twins are just as likely, for example, to be of different sexes as of the same sex. The determination of monozygocity is based not merely on physical similarities but also on a complicated and still not foolproof technology (see Vandenberg, 1966). Without examining these procedural details, we will now consider how MZ and DZ twins are studied in order to find out the relative contribution of genetics to behavior. Basically the technique involves administering tests of the designated traits to each of the MZ and DZ twins. Emphasis is now given to the *variation* in performance for each pair of twins of each type rather than to mean performance. Logically, if a particular behavioral trait is determined entirely by genetics then one would anticipate less variation between MZ twins than DZ twins because MZ twins are genetically virtually identical, whereas DZ twins are not. Thus the technique employed is to compare statistically the variability occurring for the two types of twins. Holzinger (1929), Cattell (1960), and others have developed heritability equations that increase in complexity as the number of environmental components contributing to variation increase.

An important assumption in using the heritability index is that the environments of both the MZ and the DZ twins are basically similar. In actual practice the environmental variability of MZ twins is usually reasonably small. A similar, but somewhat more subtle, case can be made for DZ twins. It is probably true that some parents of MZ twins in fact standardize the environments of their twins, but it is also probably true that many parents encourage the development of individuality (this is the currently recommended practice). It is even more difficult to defend the assumption of environmental constancy for DZ twins. Among other possible differences, DZ twins can be of different sexes. To the degree that differential environmental pressure exists, differences between twins may be amplified. If genetics and environment are correlated, their relative roles cannot be sorted out.

An important variation of the twin method involves separating both types of twins at birth or closely thereafter and rearing them in different home environments. This procedure involves testing each pair of twins, looking for differences in the degree of common variance within the MZ pair and the DZ pair. The procedure assumes that, given differences in environments for both sets of twins, if genetics determine variation, then the MZ twins will show less between-twin variation than the DZ twins. A case can be made here, however, that social workers attempt to place twins in environments that are at least roughly equivalent in the educational level and socioeconomic status of the adoptive or foster parents.

PARENT-CHILD RESEMBLANCE.   Another procedure for assessing the relative roles of nature and nurture involves children adopted early in life or reared by foster parents. The standard method in this situation is to obtain scores on the behavioral traits of interest for the child's true mother and father, his or her foster parents, and the child. In some instances (Honzig, 1957, 1963) the correlations between the child and the true mother and the child and the foster mother are examined over time. This technique is exciting because it permits an assessment of the magnitude of the relationship as a function of the child's developmental level or as a function of the length of time the child lived in the foster home. The more typical procedure, however, is to obtain correlations between the child and its true mother, and the child and the foster parent, at a single point in time. The investigators must assume that children are randomly placed in foster homes; this assumption allows the investigator to claim that any differences in the correlation between true parent and child and foster parent and child are attributable to differences in environment. Unfortunately, from a scientific point of view, social policy dictates that a foster child be placed with couples whose general socioeconomic and religious background is similar to that of the true parents. Thus the assumption of random assignment is usually violated and environmental similarities may attenuate hereditary differences.

This concern with methodology is important, since it can be demonstrated that when we compare heritability indices across methods, the different methodologies yield different results.

Heritability of Intelligence

Research on the influence of genetic variation on intellectual ability has generated a considerable degree of controversy. The question has always been somewhat controversial because of the philosophical differences among those who are called *nativists* (representing genetic determinism) and those who are called *empiricists* (representing environmental determinism). Debate between these two camps pervades much of psychology and has influenced research directions and methodology. Unfortunately, the debate seems to have left the arena of scientific scholarship and has become a topic for shrill polemics. This increase in polarization has come about because some investigators concerned with the relative contributions of genetics and environment to intellectual ability have used apparent racial differences as a measure. Some laymen react to all studies of genetic determinants *as if* the study was directly concerned with racial differences, when it concerns differences within a race. We believe that the use of racial differences as a basis for estimating heritability is most unfortunate because the results of such studies are ambiguous at best and hence should not be used to make policy decisions that affect either group. To argue, on the other hand, that research on heritability should not be conducted because of potential political dangers seems equally inappropriate. Many heritability studies are not concerned with either race or sex and still provide an *empirical base* for estimating the degree to which a behavioral attribute is amenable to environmental manipulation. Further, these studies provide some idea of how such behavioral changes may be enhanced.

Intelligence is a man-made abstraction that can be measured only through specific behaviors; it is not an entity that occupies some specific region of the head. Some authors have said that intelligence is what an intelligence test measures, but some of these measures are very abstract and removed from direct environmental events, whereas others are tied much more directly to specific environmental events and can be described as more concrete. The degree to which genetics or environment influences intellectual ability depends on the degree to which the test is a reflection of the environment. There is also considerable logic in the argument that as the environment becomes more homogeneous, the effects of genetic variations will emerge more clearly.

The major research findings are summarized in Figure 3-6 adapted from Erlenmeyer-Kimling and Jarvik (1963). Examine the different categories of pairings upon which the correlations are based. The categories are arranged so that, as you read down the left side of the figure, the degree of relatedness between the pairs increases. For the most part, the data in this figure are based on studies using the method of degree of familial relationship. As the degree of relatedness between the

FIGURE 3-6 *Summary of Major Research Findings on Correlations of Genetic-Based and Nongenetic-Based Pairings.* The degree of relatedness between the pairs increases from top (unrelated persons) to bottom (monozygotic twins reared together).

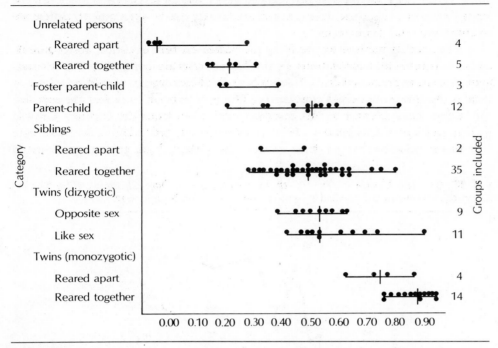

SOURCE: Erlenmeyer-Kimling, L., & Jarvik, L. F. Genetics and intelligence: a review. *Science*, 1963, *142*, 1477–1479.

pairs increases, the correlations also increase. The first category is called unrelated persons. When the IQ scores of randomly paired individuals are correlated, the median correlation is zero; rearing conditions yield only a slight difference. At the very bottom of the category listing are monozygotic twins, one group of twins reared apart and another group of twins reared together. The median IQ correlation for the twins reared apart is approximately +.78, whereas the median correlation for these twins reared together is approximately +.90. The difference in the magnitude of the two correlations is usually interpreted as showing the effects of environment. Since identical twins reared apart show higher correlations than fraternal twins reared together, we have strong evidence for the effects of genetics on intelligence.

The major criticism of these correlational studies is that among twins one would expect a greater commonality of environment than among siblings. Thus genetic and environmental similarities are confounded. Support for this conclusion comes from a study of identical twins reared apart reported by Newman, Freeman, and Holzinger (1937) (the correlations for their pairs of fraternal and identical twins are included in Figure 3-6). These investigators found that the identical twins reared apart in drastically different environments showed greater discrepancies in IQ than in the other cases; in one instance the difference was 24 IQ points. Thus, even the strong influence of genetic determinants apparently can be overcome by difference in environmental stimulation.

In another method for studying the nature-nurture question, foster parent- and true parent-child correlations on intelligence tests are compared. The environmental position predicts that the foster parent-child correlations should be at least as high as the true parent-child correlations. The genetic position makes the opposite prediction. Data relevant to this question were taken from the Berkeley Growth Studies and reported by Honzik (1957) and are summarized in Figure 3-7. First, note that the correlations for all three groups (true parent-child, true parent-adopted

FIGURE 3-7   *Intelligence of True Mothers in Relation to Their Children's IQ's.* The adopted children in the Skodak group had never lived with their true mothers.

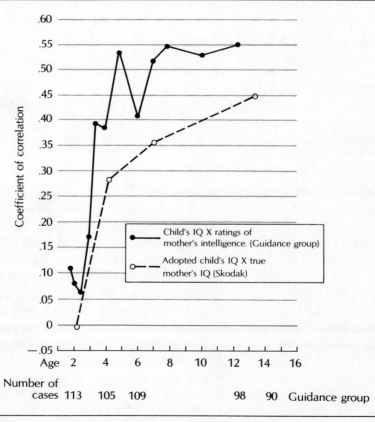

SOURCE: Honzik, M. P. Developmental studies of parent-child resemblance in intelligence. *Child Development*, 1957, 28, 215–228.

child, adopted parent-adopted child) are basically zero for approximately the first three or four years. These measures obtained in infancy are not predictive of performance at later ages. The reason for this lack of relationship is that the infancy tests measure sensorimotor abilities, which are unlike abstract cognitive demands (type of test problems) made by IQ tests for older children and adults. Secondly the IQ correlations between true parents and their children, whether or not the children lived apart, are high. These data strongly support a genetic interpretation, especially when the data show that the correlations between the IQs of foster parents and their adopted children are close to zero.

We must interpret these data with extreme caution. Skodak and Skeels (1949) and Skeels (1966) measured the intellectual ability of 100 adopted children over a period of approximately 16 years and found that their IQs averaged approximately 20 points higher than those of their true mothers. When they calculated the correlations using the same pairings as Honzik, they found that the correlations between true parent-child were higher than the correlations between foster parent-child, just as Honzik found. The explanation for this phenomenon requires understanding the concept of correlation. Even though the correlation between two sets of scores may be high, it does not follow that the actual scores, or the average scores, are similar. Correlation is an index of agreement between relative scores on two measures. In the Honzik study and the Skeels study, the relative values of the true parent-child scores were more similar than the relative values of the foster parent-child scores. In the case of the foster parent-child scores, however, the children made higher absolute scores—they were performing better than their true parents. These data suggest that normal children who are placed for adoption in stimulating environments will improve intellectually.

A study reported by Scarr and Weinberg (1976) represents a major methodological advance in research on the effects of taking children from home environments presumed to be detrimental to intellectual performance and placing them in home environments that seem to foster intellectual growth. Black children (defined as children with two black parents) and interracial children (defined as children with one black and one white parent) were adopted by upper middle-class white families. The data indicate that these families tend to raise children who perform well on IQ tests and also in school. This study is potentially important because the adoptees receive the same constant beneficial attention as the natural children of the adoptive parents as opposed to the piecemeal treatment available in compensatory programs. Also unlike similar studies done earlier, the change in environment is more dramatic, thus increasing the possibility that environment can have an impact.

One of the questions asked concerned the impact of the adoptive placement on IQ-test performance. If environment has no effect on performance, then the mean and variability of performance should remain equivalent to that of the black or interracial children. The results suggest that the impact of the upper middle-class environment was to raise test scores 10 to 20 points. Interracial children adopted early in life (8.9 months) scored higher than black children adopted later (32.3 months). The parents' biological children performed best of all groups on the IQ tests. Despite the impressive impact of the adoptive environments, the data also indicate that genetic variables contribute to the variation in IQ-test performance. According to Scarr & Weinberg (1976, p. 739) "The major findings of the study support the view that the social environment plays a dominant role in determining the average IQ level of black children and that both social and genetic variables contribute to individual variation among them."

A third strategy for studying the genetics of intellectual development, and possibly the least definitive, is the study of family histories. The history of the Kallikak family was presented as an earlier example of this approach. Other data, however, focus on children with unusually high IQs whose families and development were studied intensively by Terman (Terman, 1925; Terman & Oden, 1947, 1959). The approximately 1,000 children included in this work had IQ scores of at least 140. The parents of these children were themselves of superior intellectual ability; throughout their childhood and into adulthood, these children were taller and heavier than the average and experienced fewer health problems; these children had lower mortality rates; psychological and psychiatric assessments indicated that they had superior mental health, fewer were institutionalized or visited psychiatrists, and they were more popular and had more leadership roles in school. Their marriages resulted in both higher frequencies of happy marriages and higher divorce rates. Apparently, the gifted made their marriages work or got out of them—fewer gifted persons than controls reported unhappy but continuing marriages. They consumed more alcohol than the general population, but this finding may be a by-product of social class. As might be anticipated, these children did well in school, and most went on to complete four or more years of college. In turn, their children also were brighter than normal.

The children at all developmental levels exhibited a pattern of superiority on a number of different traits. Terman concluded that genetic endowment was mainly responsible for this pattern. His results are not isolated; Hollingworth and Galton reported similar findings in their separate studies of bright individuals. Let us note that unusually bright people are also above average in social competency according to these studies, which conflicted with the general belief that unusually bright individuals are mentally unbalanced, physically weak, and socially inept.

Clearly, genetic and environmental variables in these studies are completely confounded, making conclusions about either impossible. The data probably best fit an interaction model whereby parents with superior intellect and education not only provide an intellectually stimulating environment, but also provide their children with superior health and nutritional care. In part the children received superior health care because their parents could afford it; the parents, because they were brighter, were more likely to be aware of inoculation precautions, dietary needs, and other related matters. At the present time, for example, news broadcasts have been reporting outbreaks of smallpox and polio. Surveys have shown that large numbers of children, mostly lower class, are reporting to school without having received the mandatory inoculations. We agree with Terman and the others in their observations that positive traits tend to go together in populations, but in our judgment these correlations cannot be directly or exclusively attributed to genetic superiority.

What can we conclude about the heritability of human intelligence? There can be no doubt that intelligence is inherited and that environment influences its behavioral manifestations. We cannot estimate how much each factor contributes because presently genetic potential and environmental factors are hopelessly confounded. Although it is clear that environmental factors influence intelligence, unrestricted claims that environmental stimulation will substantially improve intelligence are, in our judgment, unwarranted.

Heritability of Personality (Temperament)

Within the last ten years, interest has focused on variations in children's and adults' emotional and general personality traits. The question has been asked whether these variations are produced exclusively by the environment (parents, teachers, peers) acting on the passive organism (Bell, 1968). Traditional correlational studies of parent-child interactions have made the implicit assumption that the parents are the cause of the children's behavior patterns. Bell raises the plausible hypothesis that constitutional differences among children may be the cause of behavioral variations among parents. (The term "constitutional differences" refers here not only to inherited differences but also to those arising from medical events during the prenatal period or birth trauma.) In effect, Bell is reminding us that social and emotional development, like intellectual development, is an interactive process; children act on their environment in various ways and the environment responds back in various ways, and so on. For example, Moss (1967) has shown that mothers are more responsive to their sons than to their daughters because male babies are more fussy and demanding than females. Thus it is probable that the same maternal and paternal behaviors may generate a wide range of responses among different infants. *If* we want to demonstrate genetic predispositions for certain personality traits, then we must give Bell's position greater weight in both our theoretical models and our research designs.

Research on the heritability of personality confronts many of the same methodological issues as intelligence—and a few more. First, the most common method of studying the heritability of personality is through the use of identical and fraternal twins. This method entails problems in separating genetic and environmental factors. In addition, however, the personality measures tend to lack the reliability of IQ tests. This lower reliability makes the problem of estimating heritability just that much more difficult. Secondly, there are many ways of measuring personality and there are many personality attributes that have been identified. Further, the developers of IQ tests agree more on what they mean by intelligence than the developers of personality tests concur on a definition of personality. Consequently two personality tests purporting to measure the same trait often fail to correlate as highly as they should. In addition, personality can be assessed by using paper-and-pencil inventories (objective tests); projective tests, such as the ink-blot test; or interviews. Different investigators use different procedures and specific techniques. Putting a cohesive picture together is difficult, therefore, and so we shall restrict our commentary to those relatively specific personality attributes that have received the greatest attention and for which some general consensus of findings emerges. In our discussion of the genetic predispositions to personality variations we shall use personality in a broad, loose fashion and include emotionality, timidity, introversion, extraversion, and activity level.

Everyday observation suggests that children vary their responses to emotion-producing situations. Some children merely whimper and turn toward a known adult for reassurance, whereas other children become uncontrollable and require considerable soothing before the emotional episode subsides. Although we could construct an environmental explanation (imitation and adult attention as a reward for emotional behavior), we have some evidence to suggest that differences in emotionality also have a genetic foundation. Jost and Sontag (1944) investigated the similarity of emotionality of identical twins, siblings, and random pairs of children. Reactivity of the autonomic nervous system was measured in several ways: skin resistance, systolic and diastolic blood pressure, heart rate, salivation, respiration, and vasomotor persistence time. A composite of these scores was developed and labeled an *index of autonomic balance*. The results of this study should be considered only an estimate of the genetic component, since only 17 identical twins took part and the measures themselves are not known to be highly reliable. The number of sibling pairs was 54, and the number of unrelated pairs 1,009.

Although the differences in the correlations between the emotionality scores of twins, siblings, and random pairs were not significantly different, in all cases the correlations for the identical twins were higher than for the other two groups. The sibling correlations were also consistently higher than the correlations for the unrelated pairs. Thus, in spite of the failure of the difference to reach statistical significance, the order of magnitude of the correlations corresponds to a genetic interpretation. When differences between mean scores are computed, it is clear that the identical twins differed significantly less than the siblings, and the siblings in turn produce fewer significant differences than the unrelated pairs. It seems reasonable to conclude that emotional reactivity has a genetic component, but probably not an overly powerful one; that is, it may be readily amenable to environmental manipulation.

Another behavioral attribute that may have genetic antecedents is activity level (Scarr, 1966). Scarr (1966 p. 664) indicates that there are "persistent individual differences in how much activity *per se* is initiated, how rapidly or slowly, how often, with how much vigor or apathy, with how much nervous activity or relaxation, and with how much patience or impatience." That great individual differences exist on this dimension is suggested in numerous studies of infants where investigators report varying percentages of babies who were uncontrollable. Kagan and Moss (1962) not only found individual difference among infants, but they also report that these differences persist into adolescence. The question then becomes whether the individuals' differences in activity have some genetic basis or whether they result entirely from environmental experiences.

Scarr compared 24 pairs of identical twins with 28 pairs of fraternal twins. All twins were females and ranged in age from 6 to 10 years. The indices of activity level were obtained from observations of the children on 2 games designed to measure curiosity, an interview with each child, and 3 sets of ratings (these ratings were based on scales measuring vigor, tension, and squirming).

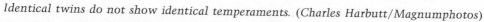

Identical twins do not show identical temperaments. (Charles Harbutt/Magnumphotos)

Analyses of the measures of activity level indicated 5 dimensions: reaction time, number of activities, percentage of active games, anxiety, and patience. The data are presented in Table 3-2 which shows 5 dimensions and the individual measures comprising each one. Among all of the measures, the ones that seem to have the highest heritability (see the column labeled H') are responses to quite different activities, anxiety and some of its correlates, and patience. Thus the data indicate that activity level and anxiety have moderate to high levels of heritability.

Scarr (1969) has also contributed to our knowledge about the heritability of the personality dimension of introversion-extraversion, an attribute fully described by Eysenck (1947) and Cattell (1960) and extensively developed as a personality concept. In this study by Scarr (1969, p. 824) the dimension is described as follows: "Social introversion-extraversion was defined in broad terms for this research to include sociability, social anxiety, friendliness to strangers, and social spontaneity. So conceived, the behavior dimension may be thought to extend from shy, introspective, anxious withdrawal to friendly, extraverted, self-confident engagement with the interpersonal environment."

Scarr used the same sample here and in studying activity levels. Numerous tests and interviews were administered to the twins and their mothers at home. The data show the degree to which members of a twin pair resemble each other on each measure. Scarr's data indicate that the heritability of introversion-extraversion is moderate to high. (Her heritability indices range from .55 to .83.)

In addition to her own findings, Scarr has also included data from several other studies of introversion-extraversion. All the studies also show moderate to high genetic contributions to social introversion-extraversion. Thus Scarr's data with children are consistent with general findings. Scarr also describes a number of additional studies in which she attempts to demonstrate longitudinal consistencies in sociability which she believes strengthens the case for a genetic component to this aspect of human behavior. Scarr (1969, p. 830) makes an interesting and, we believe, important point in discussing the results of her work and that of others.

> It seems probable that the reason introversion-extraversion shows remarkable longitudinal consistency is that much of the variance is found in the genotypes of the subjects. What MacFarlane calls "styles of behavior" can be thought of as ways of responding to the environment. Recently, Dobzhansky (1967) concluded that those aspects of behavior that are polygenically inherited are not specific traits, but patterns of growth and ways of *responding to the environment* . . . It is likely, therefore, that temperamental styles of behavior are produced by genotypes that predispose the individual to react in relatively outgoing or withdrawn ways to interaction with the cues and contingencies he meets in the environment.

Freedman (1967) and Kagan (1974) also report findings consistent with the notion of greater or lesser levels of predisposition to respond socially. These inves-

TABLE 3-2 Twin Studies of Social Introversion-Extraversion with Heritability Estimates

SOURCE, TESTS, AND SCALES	r_i MZ	r_i DZ	H'
Scarr:			
ACL nAff	.83***	.56**	.61
ACL counseling readiness	.56**	.03	.55
Fels friendliness	.86***	.36	.78
Fels social apprehension	.88***	.28	.83
Observer rating likeableness	.93***	.82***	.61
Eysenck (1956):			
Factor II intro.-extraversion	.50*	−.33	.62
Vandenberg (1962):			
Thurstone F sociable	—	—	.47
Gottesman (1963):			
MMPI O Si	.55***	.08	.71
HSPQ Q_2	.60***	.15	.56
HSPQ F	.47**	.12	.56
HSPQ H	.38*	.20	.38
Freedman and Keller (1963):			
Bayley IBP responsive to people; avoid examiner; avoid mother	All r_i MZs significantly greater than r_i DZs suggesting high heritability		
Gottesman (1966):			
CPI sociability		$F = 1.97$**	.49
CPI self-acceptance		$F = 1.85$**	.46
CPI social presence		$F = 1.55$*	.35
Partenan et al. (Loehlin 1969):			
Bruun soc.		—	.41
Vandenberg (1966):			
Myers-Briggs intro.-extraversion		$F = 1.84$*	.46
Vandenberg (1967):			
Comray shy		—	.48
Stern AI nAff		—	.35
Schoenfeldt (1967):			
TALENT SAI-SIB Soc.		—	.36

SOURCE: Scarr, S. Social introversion-extraversion as a heritable response. *Child Development*, 1969, Vol. 40, No. 3, 823–832.

*p < .05.
**p < .01.
***p < .001.

tigators were interested in the apparently spontaneous emergence of a smiling response among infants. Freedman, as noted earlier, views this response as adaptive, in the evolutionary sense, whereas Kagan's interest developed from his observation that some babies were more predisposed to smile than others. Both investigators agree that the behavior is determined to some degree by heredity. Schaffer (1966) has demonstrated that sociability and activity level play an important role in the development of children. Incidentally, this study adds some generality to Scarr's data, as the subjects here are Scottish. Basically, the study is concerned with individual differences among infants in reactions to relative stimulus deprivation occurring as a result of hospitalization. The infants were observed under standardized conditions within the last 3 days of their hospitalization and within 18 days of their return home. The basic data were taken on a seven-point scale of level of activity and on the Cattell Intelligence Scale (Cattell, 1940). The hypothesis was that because of the relatively deprived hospital situation, performance on the Cattell scale would decline. However, the more active infants might not show any decline at all. The hypothesis was supported by the data; people in the busy hospital environment largely ignored the passive and nondemanding infants, and their IQs declined. The more active and demanding infants received greater attention (if not admiration), and their IQs increased. Thus the dimension of introversion-extraversion and activity level have direct, long-term effects for the subsequent development of the child in a broad variety of areas, including cognition.

The material on the heritability of intelligence and personality suggest two reasonable conclusions: (1) the genetic antecedents of human behavior define a fairly broad range of reactivity; that is, many human behaviors are significantly influenced, positively or negatively, by environmental factors; and (2) our state of knowledge and methodological sophistication precludes dogmatic positions on either side of the issue. To reiterate our position, research on heritability is a legitimate scientific enterprise, and rather than reduce research support in this area for other than scientific reasons, more funds should be provided to improve the quality of the work and reduce the ambiguities that exist in the literature. Such efforts might just help us to improve the lives of children—an objective that is shared by everyone.

SUMMARY

This chapter has attempted to demonstrate that human development and behavior have substantial origins in biology and that these origins are important to understanding many facets of development. Although we are not yet prepared to go along with some sociobiologists in interpreting almost all aspects of human behavior as resulting from evolution and heredity (see *Time*, August 1977), we do find it reasonable that human behavior is influenced by its evolutionary history and current hereditary structures. Admittedly, it is sometimes difficult to understand how FAPs may operate in human behavior; yet their presence can be demonstrated in young infants. The material on genetic anomalies certainly provides further evidence that genetic structures operate to influence normal development. However, if one understands that environments can generate a range of reactions in children and adults, then the concept of the interaction of heredity and environment, which is crucial to understanding development and behavior, will become clearer.

CHAPTER 4

(Jean-Claude Lejeune)

THE DEVELOPMENT
OF PHYSICAL
AND MOTOR ABILITIES

CHILDREN EXHIBIT numerous behaviors, phenotypes, that appear to be independent but are in fact related. Our current knowledge does not allow us to give the following type of cause-and-effect statement: a change in one behavior causes a change in some other behavior. Although such inferences are occasionally very tempting we often can conclude only that two such changes are associated with each other, and not that they are causally related. From such patterns of associations between changes, child psychologists can develop hypotheses that integrate patterns of development. Data from the study of language development, for example, suggest that changes in physical and motor capacities are associated with changes in linguistic competency. Major advances in cognitive and perceptual competencies are associated with the onset of walking.

This chapter describes changes in physical and motor development from the prenatal period through 9 or 10 years of age. These data provide not only "normative" guidelines for motor and physical development, but also show how the organism interacts increasingly with the environment and thereby opens up more opportunities for learning. An underlying concept of this chapter is that the organism is active—it gains knowledge about the environment by being actively engaged with it. Not surprisingly, postnatal development is considerably easier to study than prenatal development, and consequently we know a great deal about the physical and motor components of growth. Measures of development—examples are height, weight, bone ossification, blood pressure, and heart rate—can be taken directly and with considerably greater accuracy.

Physical Development

Although we cannot describe fully all aspects of physical development, our aim is to provide enough information for the reader to grasp the complexities of the interrelations of the physical systems involved. We also intend to demonstrate that from the time of conception physical development is a continuing process of cell differentiation, with a concomitant process of differentiation and integration of systems. Finally, the material on physical development should be viewed as being specifically related to other aspects of the child's development. We describe these associated developmental changes in detail in the second section of this chapter which focuses on changes in motor development. Since the material on physical development is brief, the reader may want to consult other, more complete sources (Eichorn, 1970; Thompson, 1962).

Prenatal Period

Between the moment of conception and birth, all the biological mechanisms necessary for independent life become functional. When the sperm and egg unite in the fallopian tube (as the egg is descending to the uterus), mitosis begins immediately and the uterus is prepared with an extra blood supply to receive the fertilized egg. During its voyage to the uterus, the fertilized egg (zygote) receives nutrients from its yolk, but soon afterwards external structures—the umbilical cord, the placenta, and the amniotic sac—develop that provide protection and nutrients.

THE EMBRYONIC PERIOD.   The developing organism is called the **embryo.** If the zygote successfully attaches itself to the uterine wall, then development enters the embryonic stage which lasts for approximately 8 weeks. The cells of the embryo become so rapidly differentiated that by the end of the embryonic period, the organism's features have become distinctly human. These changes are shown in Figure 4-1, where the left-hand illustration indicates that by the end of the embryonic stage, the average organism is 41 millimeters long.

The process of cell differentiation responsible for the highly specialized functions of human structures is extremely complex (Fuller & Thompson, 1960). For example, let us consider neurological development. How do embryonic nerve fibers, each having some fairly specific function, find their way to their appropriate receptors, glands, muscles, and other parts of the central nervous system? At one time it was assumed that since each cell in the body contained the same number of genes, not all the genes in a particular cell were active. Successively smaller groups of genes were supposed to be active in each cell, that is, the process of cell differentiation

FIGURE 4-1 *Development of the Human Embryo from the Sixteenth Day to the Eighth Week.* Left, embryo aged about 16 days, enlarged × 23.5; middle, about fifth week, × 6.5; right, about eighth week, × 2.

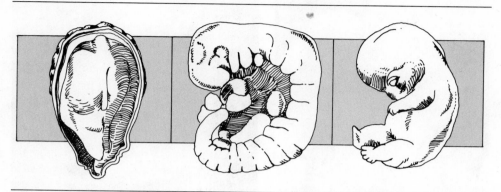

SOURCE: Adapted from Brooks, F. D. *Child psychology.* Boston: Houghton Mifflin, 1937, p. 32.

involved fewer and fewer active genes in each cell. However, it was not possible *empirically* to determine which genes were active and which were not. Anticipating future research, Sperry (1951) believed that the solution to this problem would be found in a complex biochemical "guidance system," a forerunner of the genetic coding system involving DNA and RNA. Sperry suggested that many nerve fibers are preprogrammed to serve specific functions (vision, audition, language). Nerve fibers become attached to only a few of the many dendrites (extensions of a nerve cell) emanating from nerve cells. The selection process determining which fibers attach to which cells depends on the physiochemical compatibility of the individual cells. Thus, brain cells develop specialized functions as well as specific nerve systems that control all bodily functions.

By the end of the second month, the termination of the embryo stage, the differentiation of body structures is 95 percent complete. The four limbs are clearly evident (see the right-hand illustration, Figure 4-1) and the beginning of eyes and ears, skeleton and muscles is detectable. In addition, a primitive nervous system is present.

THE FETAL PERIOD. The remaining 7 months of prenatal life are called the fetal period. Since 95 percent of the bodily structures are present at the end of the second month, the remainder of the prenatal period is taken up by general growth and the elaboration of these systems. An excellent example is the growth of the brain, which has developed all its principal structures by the end of the third fetal month. From that point on, nerve fibers become denser, which leads to the development of convolutions at approximately the seventh fetal month. However, the brain's speed of development is not matched by that of other structures. The more rapid

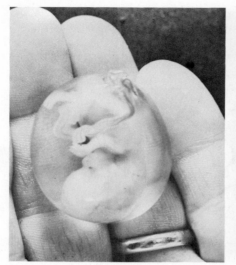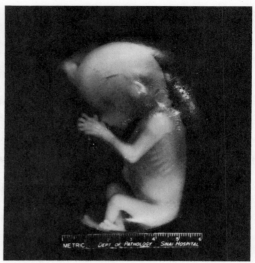

Human fetus at (left) 8 weeks and (right) 12 weeks (Donald Yeager/Camera M. D. Studios)

development of the head region is called the **cephalocaudal trend**. The pyramidal tract (nerve fibers that originate in the cortex and travel down the spinal cord) and the fiber of the spinal cord do not begin to develop rapidly until later, so that voluntary movement is not at first possible. While the systems that underlie voluntary motor behavior are becoming integrated, the other brain areas are also undergoing a similar integration.

Another process within the central nervous system that begins during the prenatal period is known as **myelinization.** Myelin is a white, fatty substance covering nerve fibers; it is thought to be responsible for the speed of nerve conduction, that is, making reaction time and sensory functioning more efficient.

Relatively little research has been published on the cardiovascular and endocrinological systems of fetuses. The fetal heartbeat, for example, begins approximately 3 weeks after *conception*, but the mechanisms triggering it are not understood. Further, there is evidence that within the cardiovascular system the blood flow from the placenta eventually opens systems so that the maternal blood flows through the fetal liver and returns to the heart, and accumulated wastes are drained through the placental membrane. The fetus has its own circulatory system but exchanges blood in both directions (fetus to mother, mother to fetus) by means of chemically permeable membranes, most notably present at the placenta. Thus, drugs, for example, thalidomide, taken by the mother will cross the placental membrane and may have deleterious effects on fetal development. Conversely, the infant transmits glandular secretions to the mother. Some fetal secretions, for example, bring about the remission of severe arthritic conditions, which, however, return after the baby is born.

Research on glandular development has focused mostly on newborns and older children. The major glands develop during the prenatal period but do not appear to have marked influence on behavior or development.

The fetus grows in length from 1.5 inches to approximately 20 inches at birth. Weight changes from approximately one-eighth of a pound to 7 pounds. By the time the fetus reaches 7 to 7.5 months, its physiological mechanisms are sufficiently well developed to permit extrauterine survival, albeit with some artificial-support systems. Fetuses also evidence primitive reflexes such as the palmar reflex (a grasping reflex in response to stroking the palm of the hand) and the plantar reflex (a curling of the toes in response to stroking the sole of the foot).

Development of Height and Weight

In describing prenatal development, we noted that the head region initially matures more rapidly than the structures below it. At birth, the head makes up some 22 percent of the infant's height, but the proportion (see Figure 4-2) changes dramatically with age. The average infant measures approximately 20 to 21 inches in length

FIGURE 4-2   The figures in the drawing have been adjusted to the same height in order to indicate more clearly the body proportion changes.

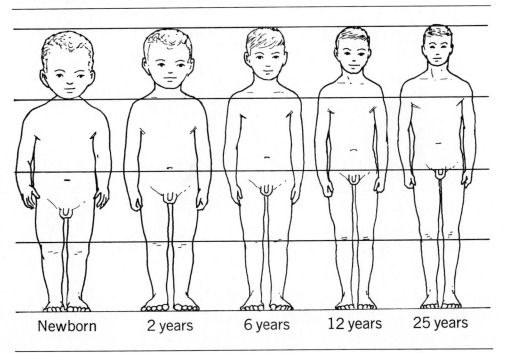

Newborn   2 years   6 years   12 years   25 years

FIGURE 4-3 *The Relation Between Individual and Mean Velocities During the Adolescent Spurt.* (a) The individual height velocity curves of five boys of the Harpenden Growth Study (solid lines) with the mean curve (dashed) constructed by averaging their values at each age. (b) The same curves all plotted according to their peak height velocity.

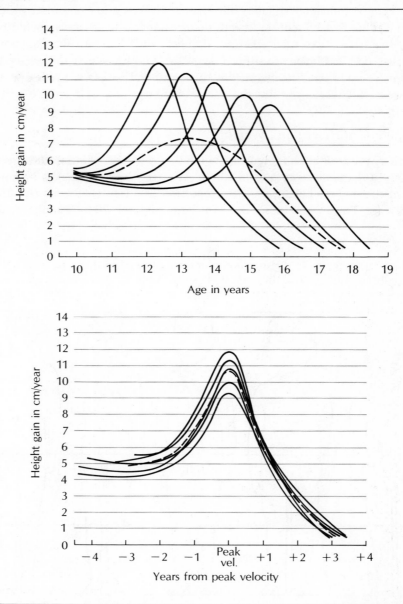

SOURCE: Tanner, J. M., Whitehouse, R. H., & Takaishi, M. Standards from birth to maturity for height, weight, height velocity and weight velocity: British children. *Archives Diseases of Childhood*, 1966, 41, 454–471; 613–635.

and weighs 7 pounds at birth. Slight sex differences are observed among newborns; boys tend to weigh somewhat more than girls and are also slightly taller. Trends in the development of height and weight involve some methodological issues, particularly that of the cross-sectional approach versus the longitudinal method (see Chapter 2). The curves shown in Figure 4-3, obtained by Tanner and colleagues (Tanner, Whitehouse, & Takaishi, 1966), show how the cross-sectional method distorts the actual growth pattern. The solid-line curves show the increments in height (the gains in height with age, called velocities); they indicate that each of 5 boys had a different point of most rapid acceleration. The dashed-line curve shows the average increment at each age point; the curve effectively smooths out the adolescent spurt in growth. This curve represents the growth pattern incorrectly— with the onset of pubescence, growth spurts up.

Figures 4-4 and 5 depict developmental trends in height and weight. Of special interest is Figure 4-4 which shows velocity curves for height that go back to 1 year of age. This curve indicates that height increases fastest between birth and approximately 4 years of age. The adolescent growth spurt does not approach the speed of growth during the earliest years. There is also a sex difference, with girls showing an earlier onset of rapid growth, but not achieving the same velocity as boys. At the end

FIGURE 4-4   *Average Increments Each Year in Height and Weight*

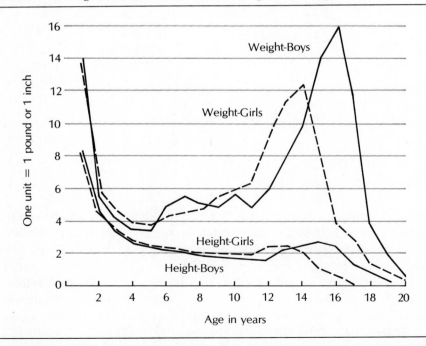

SOURCE: Pressey, S. L., Janney, J. E., & Kuhlen, R. G. *Life: A psychological survey.* New York: Harper, 1939, p. 127.

FIGURE 4-5   *Growth Trends as Related to Age at Maximum Growth (Girls)*

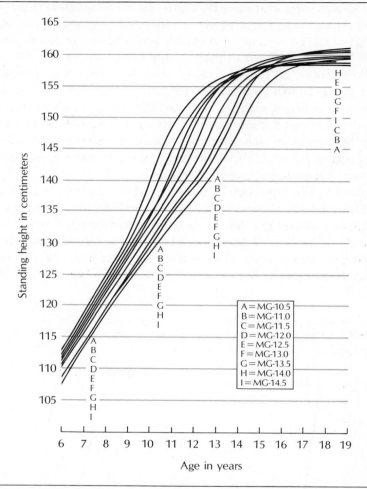

SOURCE: Greulich, W. W. *Physical changes in adolescence.* In 43rd Yearbook of the National Society for the Study of Education, Part I, 1944, p. 13.

of the growth period, males are taller and heavier than females. The curves presented in Figures 4-3 and 4 represent composite data on the average trends in the development of height and weight. Such curves are important in formulating mathematical functions for predicting terminal height or weight with data from an earlier age level. Figure 4-5 shows some individual differences in the rate of height development. Again, these curves take the same form as the composite curves but tend to accentuate the adolescent growth spurt. The composite curves shown in Figures 4-3 and 4-4 mask important individual differences that have implications for social and emotional development (Mussen & Jones, 1958). These investigators found that children who mature physically at a more rapid rate have superior self-concepts, are viewed as more socially and emotionally mature, and are more highly regarded by their peers.

REGULATION OF GROWTH.   Growth curves are affected by the physiological state of the organism. Severe illness or malnutrition, for example, slows down the velocity of development and can even alter the final level of growth. In most instances, however, if the debilitating cause does not last too long, the organism resumes growing at its original rate (trajectory). In fact, when the organism recovers, its velocity *exceeds* its normal rate until the normal height is attained. Once the projected height is reached, the velocity returns to normal. Waddington (1957) calls this phenomenon, which is not very well understood, **canalization** or **homeorhesis**. Tanner (1970) also presents data adapted from another of his studies (Prader, Tanner, & von Harnack, 1963) that show the effects of two periods of anorexia (the child severely reduced his food intake for psychological reasons). The relevant data are shown in Figures 4-6 (the distance curve) and 4-7 (the velocity curve). Tanner (1963, p. 823) interprets the data as follows: "The velocity during each period of catch-up reached more than twice the average velocity for the chronological age; it was nearly twice the average for the skeletal age, which was retarded in parallel with the retardation in length and caught up as the length caught up. The catch-up is apparently complete in that the child is quite normal in both length and velocity of length by age 5."

FIGURE 4-6   *Two Periods of Catch-Up Growth Following Episodes of Anorexia Nervosa in a Young Child*

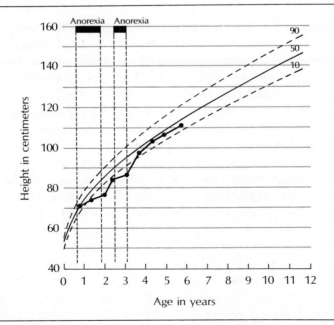

FIGURE 4-6   (cont.)

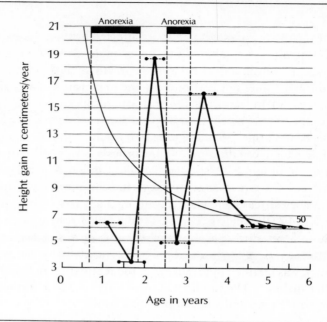

SOURCE: Prader, A., Tanner, J. M., & von Harnack, G. A. Catch-up growth following illness
or starvation: an example of developmental canalization in man. *Journal of Pediatrics*, 1963,
62, 646–659.

Seasonal effects.   The trajectory curves developed by Tanner and his associates have led to the discovery of other influences on development. The season of
the year appears to affect growth in height for many, but not all, children. Growth
velocity is greater between April and October than between October and April. The
cause of this seasonal alteration in velocity is not known.

Birth catch-up.   The phenomenon of catch-up is perhaps most dramatic at
birth. While most of the data are based on weight, there is enough information to
indicate that the phenomenon also occurs for height—indeed, the effect may be
even more marked for height. The data indicate that during the last phases of
prenatal development, velocity slows down, probably because of the limited space in
the womb; as the space available for growth shrinks, the rate of growth slows down.
This slowdown is particularly noteworthy when the mother is physically small and
the father is physically large. If the baby's weight and length reflected the mid-parent
level, the baby would be too large for the mother, requiring medical intervention,
probably before full term. Since velocity decreases, this does not happen. Postnatal
velocity again accelerates and continues for about 5 months, when catch-up is
completed. Evidence from cases of small mothers and large fathers suggests that the
velocity of these babies is greater than average. The correlations between adult
weight and weight at earlier ages, beginning with birth, yield certain inferences

FIGURE 4-7   *Catch-Up in a Hypothyroid Boy Following Treatment at Twelve Years Old*

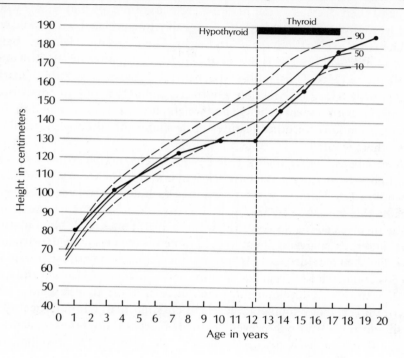

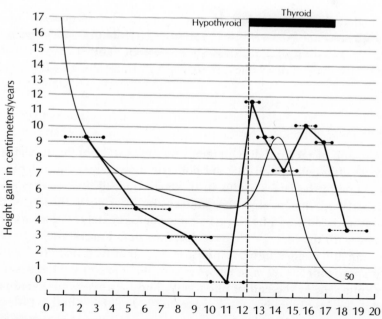

SOURCE: See Figure 4-6.

about this effect. The correlation between birth weight and weight gain at 6 months is −.15, and then decreases (the negative correlation means that babies who first weighed less gain more). Birth weight is probably uncorrelated with adult weight.

The same explanation applies to height. The correlation between height at birth and adult height is +.20. However, the correlation approaches +.70 at one year and +.80 at two years. Thus, built-in mechanisms apparently control prenatal and neonatal growth velocities, function adaptively, and help maintain population variability, at least with respect to height and weight. It remains to be seen if there exist comparable functions for other features of development, although logically it appears that there would be.

A number of other highly reliable and interesting measures also serve as indices of physical maturity. We have selected one of them because of its relevance to the work of Eric Lenneberg, who used it as an index of language development. Specifically, this measure indexes the density (ossification) of bone structure. The technique involves taking X-rays of the wrist (carpal) bones of children of different age levels and then analyzing them to determine the average bone density for each age level. The data obtained serve as "norms" for comparison with other individuals. Thus, a 5-year-old, whose **carpal age** is equivalent to that of a 7-year-old child, can be said to show advanced development. Such indices as these are often more accurate for determining the developmental levels of children than chronological age. The reader should not surmise, however, that carpal age, or any other measure of individual differences, is a perfect predictor. We have yet to develop errorless measures.

A final example of physical development after birth concerns muscles. At birth some 23 percent of the total body weight consists of muscle, but at 15 years of age this figure has risen to approximately 44 percent. This increase is substantial when one keeps in mind that bones are increasing in size, along with the amount of fatty tissue.

Cardiovascular System

In our discussion of prenatal development, we noted that the heart begins beating some 3 weeks after conception. We did not state, however, that during this period the heart is one of the larger organs in the body; indeed, it is at that time larger relative to body size than at any other time of life. After birth, the size of the heart increases rather rapidly and by the age of 6 is approximately 5 times its birth size. Concomitant with the increase in heart size, though not necessarily a consequence of it, is a dramatic change in blood pressure, which at birth is fairly low (systolic pressure is approximately 40 mm. Hg.). Systolic blood pressure increases to approximately 80 mm. Hg. at the end of one month and then rises more gradually. The normal adult level is generally considered to be 120 mm. Hg. There is little evidence of an age trend for diastolic blood pressure, but our picture may not be complete.

We can readily understand the reason for the dramatic increase in systolic blood pressure when we realize that the systolic measure indicates the amount of pressure the heart must exert in order to push the blood through the major arteries of the body. Since the arteries are large relative to heart size, and since the body is relatively small, we can see that the baby does not require nearly the same amount of pressure to pump the blood as a mature adult would. This interpretation is certainly confirmed by the fact that after the age of 50 the systolic blood pressure drifts upward as a consequence of structural changes both in the heart and also in the arteries and veins, largely through clogging as the result of accumulation of cholesterol.

Endocrinological Development

The glandular system consists of a large number of structures. We know relatively little about the functional significance of the pineal, the adrenal, and the thymus glands during childhood—or indeed, even in maturity and old age. The thyroid gland, which governs general metabolic activity and energy level, begins its development early in prenatal life, grows rapidly for the first four months, and appears to achieve its full adult status at about the age of 20. At that time, the size of the thyroid gland is twice as large as it was at birth.

The adrenal glands—the adrenal cortex, and the adrenal medulla—form part of the **sympathetic nervous system** and are generally thought to be related to emotional reactivity. Thus, when adrenalin is released into the blood stream, the organism may react by preparing for either flight or aggressive activity. Concomitantly, there is an increase in heart rate and blood pressure, the release of sugar, the admission of greater amounts of oxygen to the lungs, and the shunting of blood to the skeletal muscles. The adrenals are quite large at birth but decrease rapidly in size thereafter. It is largely unclear what these growth patterns indicate behaviorally. If, however, the adrenal cortex fails to secrete hormones, death will result. Unfortunately, no data have yet appeared on how the secretions of the adrenal cortex control the metabolism of salt, water, or carbohydrates.

The **pituitary gland** consists of the anterior and posterior lobes. Little is known about the posterior lobe, but the anterior lobe secretes hormones that influence physical growth, height, weight, and the metabolism of carbohydrates and proteins. In addition, the anterior pituitary also secretes a series of hormones (called *tropic* hormones) that influence the activity of most of the body's other glands. The pituitary gland is thus really one of the most important of the endocrine system. For example, among other things, the tropic hormones influence the gonadotropic hormones that affect the eventual development of male and female sex glands, which in turn will influence the development of secondary sexual characteristics. The pituitary gland can be observed by the end of the fourth fetal month; it exhibits a relatively slow rate of growth during the prepubertal years and attains maximum size and weight around the age of 35. One especially important secretion of the anterior pituitary is called **phyone,** which is essential to growth during childhood and puberty. Increased output of phyone during the growing years will lead to *gigantism,* whereas a decreased output during this period produces *dwarfism.*

The final area of endocrinological development we shall consider concerns the growth of the sex glands and their production of hormones. In males, the sex glands consist of the gonads; in females the sex glands are the ovaries. During the early prenatal period, even microscopic examination does not reveal the sex of the organism. Somewhere around the beginning of the eighth week, there is sufficient differentiation to make an accurate identification of the sex of the embryo. Chromosomal analyses of amniotic fluid are now possible which allow for a definitive sex identification. Perhaps one of the most interesting aspects of sex-gland development concerns the output of sex hormones during the prepubescent years. During this period both prepubescent males and females produce more **androgens,** the male sex hormone, than **estrogens,** the female sex hormone. Prepubescent males, however, show only a small difference in the output of androgens and estrogens. With the onset of pubescence, stimulated by the gonadotropic hormone of the anterior pituitary gland, the difference in androgens and estrogens for males and females becomes greater. However, the estrogen/androgen difference is greater for females than for males. Exactly what functional significance this difference has is not well understood. It is known, however, that the sex hormones gradually inhibit the production of phyone, thus bringing about the termination of physical growth. And, finally, the gonadotropic hormones generate secondary sexual characteristics typical of pubescence.

In this general overview of physical development, certainly one implicit finding should emerge, namely, that the newborn baby possesses all of the structures necessary for his functioning independently of the mother and, of greater psychological significance, to begin the long and arduous process of learning about his environment. Certainly, as the data from birth through maturity indicate, physical development is a continuing process so that, not surprisingly, the competencies of the organism also improve. However, this improvement now becomes an interactive function of developmental level and environmental stimulation.

Brain Development

Not a great deal is known. Much of the little that is known about the development of the brain has been reported by Conel and described by Tanner (1970) and, for the most part, this material consists of descriptions. Their primary significance, however, lies in their functional implications for behavior and development. For example, the newborn baby is capable of many motoric actions, somewhat less capable of sensory processing (relative to motor behavior), and capable of forming simple associations among stimuli. Examination of brain areas indicates a rough correspondence between area development and behavior. The motor area of the cortex, for example, is more highly developed than the other areas. Thus, functional capability corresponds roughly to the development of cortical structures. If this assumption is reasonably accurate, then we should be able to make certain inferences about brain development from behavior. Because of the knowledge of physiology required to understand brain development and because our interest is primarily in behavior, we shall not discuss the details of brain development. Recently, however, a considerable body of research has appeared that deals with the functional differences between the brain hemispheres. This work seems to have implications for such diverse aspects of human behavior and development as handedness, language, and the ability to make left-right discriminations, that is, to orient one's body in space.

The maturation of certain behaviors yields many inferences about cortical development. Most textbooks suggest that maturation ceases to have any important relation to motor development after the age of 6. It would be incorrect, however, to conclude that further maturational processes are no longer important, they are just harder to detect. According to Tanner (1970, p. 123),

> There is clearly no reason to suppose that the link between maturation of structure and occurrence of function suddenly ceases at age six or ten or thirteen. On the contrary there is every reason to believe that the higher intellectual abilities also appear only when maturation of certain structures or cell assemblies widespread in location throughout the cortex is complete. Dendrites, even millions of them, occupy little space, and very considerable increases in connectivity could occur within the limits of a total weight increase of a few percent. The stages of mental functioning described by Piaget and others have many of the characteristics of developing brain or body structures and the emergence of one stage after another is very likely dependent on (i.e., limited by) progressive maturation and organization of the cortex.

THE BRAIN HEMISPHERES.   The **corpus callosum** is a bundle of nerve fibers that connect the two large hemispheres of the brain. These hemispheres are commonly referred to as the left brain and the right brain. When the corpus callosum is severed, each brain seems to possess independent capacities (Sperry, 1975), which raises many questions about the functions of each brain and how these functions become integrated. The problem is complicated by the perhaps unique asymmetry of the human brain; that is, each hemisphere has primary control over certain aspects of behavior.

The primary control possessed by each brain over a specific function is called *dominance*. For motoric functions, such as handedness or footedness, the dominant cerebral hemisphere is usually contralateral (opposite) to the preferred hand or foot. A parallel concept is **laterality.** Laterality, according to Touwen (1972, p. 747), "is the name for the phenomenon by which, in an organism with paired faculties (hand, feet, eyes, ears), the performance of certain tasks, afferent or efferent, succeeds better on one side than on the other. Laterality describes an asymmetrical function."

Laterality does not refer to cerebral dominance but means merely asymmetrical performance characteristics. Performance capability depends on which side of the body is involved in the particular activity. The brain hemispheres themselves are also asymmetrical in structure.

Bilateral asymmetry.   Human beings are unique in possessing bilateral asymmetry (Corballis & Beal, 1970; Touwen, 1972; Zangwill, 1960; Benson & Geschwind, 1968). Corballis and Beale (1967) and Beale and Corballis (1967, 1968) trained pigeons to discriminate a mirror-image stimulus. In the experimental task, the pigeons were rewarded for pecking at the 135° line but not for pecking at a 45° line (the mirror image). After a considerable number of trials the pigeons could peck at the 135° line. But do these results mean that pigeons possess the ability to discriminate mirror images? The answer seems to be negative because further analysis of the pigeons' behavior indicated that the discrimination was brought about by what the investigators called "beak shift"; the pigeons tilted their heads so that one line became vertical and the other horizontal. In other words, rather than making a mirror-image discrimination, the pigeons had adaptively transformed the problem into one of discriminating between a vertical and a horizontal line.

The importance of this study is shown in two other studies summarized by Corballis and Beale (1971). The first study was conducted by Pavlov (1927), who reported that it was almost impossible to establish a conditioned salivation response in dogs by having them discriminate which side of the body was being touched. Specifically, animals were to salivate when touched on one side and not salivate when touched on the homologous point on the other side. However, when the corpus callosum was cut, thus severing connections between the left and right brains, the animals learned the mirror-image conditioned discrimination rather quickly. Pavlov's data have been interpreted as showing that each hemisphere (brain) is the mirror image of the other, with the fibers connecting the hemispheres also joining the mirror-image points. If this speculation is correct, communication between hemispheres may interfere with left-right discrimination.

Numerous studies support the conclusion that children, possibly below 8 years and certainly below 6 years, have difficulty telling left from right or in coping with certain problems involving mirror images. Gazzaniga (1968), cited by Corballis and Beale (1970), reported that the corpus callosum attains full development relatively late (7–8 years). Speech becomes localized in the left hemisphere at about 5 years, so that hemisphere specialization exists and, presumably, between-hemisphere connections are available before 7 years. However, the incomplete development of the callosum may explain why young children so often exhibit mirror-image writing and mirror-image discriminations.

Two interesting questions remain: Why does asymmetry occur; that is, why are structures and functions of the two hemispheres different? Further, what processes are involved in communication between the hemispheres?

Two alternative hypotheses have been suggested to account for the origins of asymmetry: genetic and environmental. According to Sperry (1975), hemispheric dominance and handedness are determined by two genes, each of which has two alleles. The genes and their associated alleles form 9 possible combinations of hemisphere dominance and handedness. Accordingly, some people will be strongly left-hemisphere dominant and right-handed; others will be more subject to environmental demands, whereas still others will be right-hemisphere dominant and left-handed.

The environmental view is actually more of an evolutionary theory. Basically, the theory holds that the human being's use of tools may have occasioned the beginning of cerebral asymmetry. When someone uses a tool, one hand holds and operates the tool while the other hand steadies what is being manipulated. But why the preponderance of right-handed people? No one really knows; it has been proposed that at one time genetic lateral dominance was equally distributed—there were as many left- as right-dominant individuals. Selection occurred as a result of hunting and fighting with the use of shields. People tended to incur wounds on the leading or more active side of the body. Those who were right-brained (left-handed) were more likely to receive wounds on the left side, where the heart is; that is, they were more likely to receive mortal wounds. Thus these people were killed earlier, reproduced less, and therefore a larger population of right-handed (left-brained) individuals remained. Clearly, this interpretation is speculative but not implausible.

How do the hemispheres communicate and what effect does this have on behavior? We have already indicated that interhemisphere communication occurs via the corpus callosum. We also indicated that each hemisphere appears to be a duplicate of the other, although that duplication is incomplete. Thus, the connections appear to produce mirror images and in fact make subsequent learning more difficult (the child cannot determine which information is correct). Before the corpus callosum develops, both hemispheres contain **engrams** (structures) for language and all sorts of perceptions. Thus, each hemisphere has the capability of performing acts before one hemisphere becomes dominant. As dominance has emerged, inhibitory processes suppress the cognitive and decision-making capability of the nondominant hemisphere (Gazzaniga, 1970). With such suppression, input from the **homologous points** in the nondominant hemisphere (the apparent cause of mirror images) can no longer interfere with the input to the dominant hemisphere; there are no longer competing systems of information. In this case, learning should be rapid.

Handedness.   One of the presumed indicators of cerebral dominance is handedness. Hemispheric dominance, as we noted, is usually contralateral to the preferred hand or foot (actually, we speak of handedness, but there is also footedness, eyedness, and other preferential functions). A majority (93 percent) of people are right-handed or show mixed dominance (right-eyed, left-handed, left-footed), whereas only 7 percent are left-handed (Benson & Geschwind, 1968; Zangwill, 1968). Since handedness is related to cerebral dominance, we should not be surprised to find both environmental and genetic interpretations. Although we do not disagree with the strict genetic interpretation, Sperry's view that some people are genetically more capable of adapting their handedness to external pressure is attractive. His theory is consistent with the findings of Zangwill (1960) and Benson and Geschwind (1968), who conclude that handedness is not an either-or-condition but is represented to varying degrees within a population. Thus, a strong dominance either way will not be influenced readily, if at all, by external pressure. A less-defined degree of genetic dominance will be more influenced by enviornment.

A series of studies reported by Hildreth (1949, a, b, c) suggest how the environment can be influential. She showed that parents use a variety of rewards and some frightening punishment techniques to promote right-handedness. Hildreth also found that more females than males were right-handed, which she attributed to the greater acquiescence of females to environmental pressures (although females may be more genetically predisposed to left-hemisphere dominance). Benson, Geschwind, and Subirana (1969) have offered another environmental interpretation. These investigators found that left-handedness is more prevalent among children when the mother, but not the father, is left-handed than when the father, but not the mother, is left-handed. According to the authors, these results are a consequence of mothers' greater influence on the development of children. To the degree that environment influences handedness, it becomes a less accurate predictor of cerebral dominance. This is consistent with Hildreth's findings that between 20 and 40 percent of the population exhibit mixed dominance. Eyedness or footedness may provide a better indication of dominance because these functions are less sensitive to social pressures.

When does handedness become established? Gesell and Ames (1947) collected the normative data shown in Table 4-1. According to their norms, it takes about 2 years before a consistent unilateral response appears. However, their data suggest that this early exhibition of handedness is transitory and that permanent handedness is not established until approximately 8 years. Coincidentally, it is at the age of 8 that Gazzaniga believes that the corpus callosum achieves full maturity and that hemisphere dominance becomes permanently established.

Neuropsychologists and developmental psychologists are also interested in handedness because it provides information about cerebral dominance. As noted, we have reason to suspect the accuracy of these data, but intensive testing ordinarily provides reasonably valid information. This information is used to identify people who are left- or right-hemisphere dominant, and researchers use that information to describe the major functions of each hemisphere.

The left hemisphere.   We have already seen that motoric activities that involve handedness (eyedness, footedness) are controlled by the **contralateral hemispheres.** This means that fibers cross from one hemisphere to the other. Both

TABLE 4-1   Schematic Sequence of Major Forms of Handedness

AGE	HANDEDNESS
16–20 weeks	Contact unilateral and, in general, tends to be *with left hand.*
24 weeks	A definite shift to *bilaterality.*
28 weeks	Shift to unilateral and oftenest *right hand is used.*
32 weeks	Shift again to *bilateral.*
36 weeks	Bilaterality dropping out and unilaterality coming in. Behavior usually characterized "right or left." *Left predominates in the majority.*
40–44 weeks	Same type of behavior, unilateral, "right or left," but now right *predominates in the majority.*
48 weeks:	In some *a temporary, and in many a last shift, to use of left hand*—as well as use of right—either used unilaterally.
52–56 weeks	Shift to clear unilateral dominance of *right hand.*
80 weeks	Shift from rather clearcut unilateral behavior to *marked, interchangeable confusion. Much bilateral, and use of nondominant hand.*
2 years	Relatively clearcut unilateral use of *right hand.*
2½–3½ years	Marked shift to *bilaterality.*
4–6 years	Unilateral, *right-handed* behavior predominates.
7 years	Last period when *left hand, or even both hands bilaterally,* are used.
8 years ff	*Unilateral right* once more.

SOURCE: Gesell, A., & Ames, L. B. The development of handedness. *Journal of Genetic Psychology,* 1947, 70, 155–175.

hemispheres control motor activities, but they apparently regulate different functions. Ingram (1975), for example, found that 3-, 4-, and 5-year-old children predominantly gesture with their right hands while speaking. The right hand also performed better in tests of strength and finger tapping. The left hand was superior on tasks of finger-spacing and hand posture. The preferred hand does not possess uniformly superior skills as compared with the nonpreferred hand. The superior performance of the left hand on the two tasks may be due to the visual-spatial components—a capability thought to be more of a right-hemisphere function.

Perhaps the most interesting and intensively studied function of the left hemisphere is its control over language. The complex features of language (syntax, abstract words, and concepts) are represented in the left hemisphere—for all right-handed people and for most left-handed people. But we should not assume that all language functions are located in the left hemisphere; some simple linguistic functions are apparently governed by the right hemisphere, for example, learning the names of objects. The illustration in Figure 4-8 shows the contrasting functions of the hemispheres (Calder, 1970).

Much of the research on the cerebral localization of language has employed subjects suffering from brain injury. In general, these studies suggest that injuries to the left hemisphere affect some aspect of language, whereas damage to the right

FIGURE 4-8   *The Two Sides of the Brain*—when split, they act like separate persons.

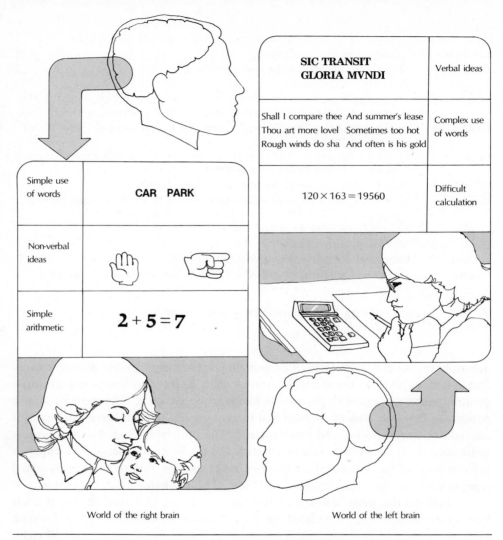

Simple use of words	**CAR PARK**
Non-verbal ideas	
Simple arithmetic	**2 + 5 = 7**

World of the right brain

SIC TRANSIT GLORIA MVNDI	Verbal ideas
Shall I compare thee And summer's lease Thou art more lovel Sometimes too hot Rough winds do sha And often is his gold	Complex use of words
$120 \times 163 = 19560$	Difficult calculation

World of the left brain

SOURCE: Calder, N. *The mind of man*. New York: The Viking Press, 1970.

hemisphere seems to have less dramatic effects. This research, however, is rather suspect because of the difficulty of determining with certainty what structures or nerve systems in the brain were damaged. Consequently, we shall base our generalizations on studies using normal subjects.

Kimura (1967, 1969, 1973) has made substantial contributions to our knowl-

TABLE 4-2   Mean Number of Digits Correctly Identified for Each Ear

GROUPS (N = 10 in each age-sex group)	LEFT EAR	RIGHT EAR	TOTAL
Age 5			
Male	19.2	23.4	42.6
Female	17.9	24.0	41.9
Age 6			
Male	18.7	29.1	47.8
Female	20.5	25.2	45.7
Age 7			
Male	22.9	29.6	52.5
Female	24.3	29.9	54.2
Age 8			
Male	24.7	29.9	54.6
Female	27.4	30.4	57.8

SOURCE: Knox, C., & Kimura, D. Cerebral processing of nonverbal sounds in boys and girls. *Neuropsychologia,* 1970, 8, 227–237.

Summary of analysis of variance:
Ear: F = 24.387, df = 1/72, $p < 0.001$.
Age: F = 15.449, df = 3/72, $p < 0.001$.
Sex: F = 0.107, df = 1/72. No significant interactions.

edge about both the left and right hemispheres. Her principal research technique is a **dichotic listening** task in which two different stimuli are presented, one to each ear simultaneously. The stimuli can be different kinds of words (nouns, verbs, and so forth), digits, or sounds. When digits are used, one digit is presented to the left ear and another digit to the right ear. Three such pairs are presented in rapid succession and after the 6 digits have been heard, the subject is asked to recall as many digits as possible. In a variety of studies using adult subjects, she reports greater recall of digits presented to the right ear.

Kimura adapted the dichotic listening task for use with children, reasoning that before cerebral dominance develops, presentations to each ear are equivalent; then, at the age when right-ear superiority appears, cerebral dominance should occur. The children in these studies had above-average IQs and were at least 5 years old. Surprisingly, in view of other studies, Kimura found right-ear superiority among the 5-year-olds and, subsequently, among 4-year-olds. Kimura replicated these results with other subjects. Among a group of lower middle-class children, right-ear superiority appeared somewhat later, and there was also a sex difference; girls exhibited right-ear superiority earlier than boys (see Table 4-2 for relevant data). The sex difference is consistent with the girls' earlier language development; the age dif-

FIGURE 4-9   Functional asymmetries of the cerebral hemispheres in normal, right-handed people are found in the auditory, visual and manual modalities. Test scores for the left and right sides were converted to ratios for comparison. The ratio for left-hemisphere dominance for perception of spoken words is 1.88:1, whereas the ratio for right-hemisphere dominance for melodies is 1.19:1. These ratios are not fixed values since they vary with the type of stimulus, the kind of response required and the difficulty of the task.

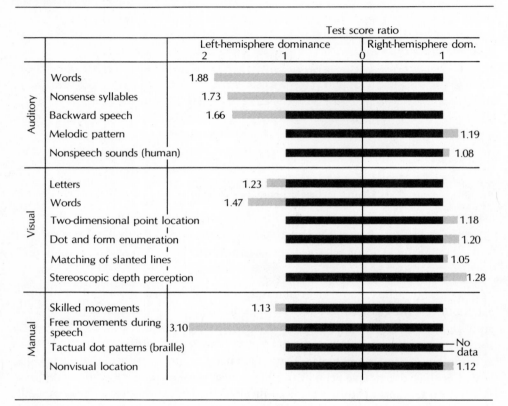

SOURCE: Kimura, D. The asymmetry of the human brain. *Scientific American*, 1973, *228*, p. 78.

ferences between socioeconomic groups is consistent with known differences in other developmental patterns.

The superiority of the right ear for auditory stimuli is not unrestricted. The graph in Figure 4-9 shows that melodic patterns and human nonspeech sounds are recalled better with the left ear (right-hemisphere function). The graph also includes data on visual and manual tasks. Note that language and language-related stimuli (printed letters) are left-hemisphere dominant. Tasks requiring visual-spatial ability appear to be more right-hemisphere dominant.

Knox and Kimura conducted a study on the cerebral processing of nonverbal sounds. The dichotic listening task was used with boys and girls aged 5 to 8, who listened to simultaneous pairings of various environmental sounds (dog barking—dishwashing; phone dialing—clock ticking; children playing—car starting, and so forth). The two members of the dichotic pairs were adjusted to be comparable in ease of recognition, pitch, and rhythm. The experimenters found that subjects correctly identified more nonverbal environmental sounds from the left ear than from the right ear. A replication of the digit task with this sample again showed the right-ear superiority for the speech sounds.

The dichotic listening task has been related to other laterality functions. Bryden (1970) studied laterality in dichotic listening and its relation to handedness and reading ability in children. His subjects—second-, fourth-, and sixth-grade children—were given the standard dichotic listening task with digits; handedness was assessed by several tests and a teacher interview. Reading ability and intelligence were also measured. The results show that right-ear superiority increases with age in right-handed children and decreases with age in left-handed children (40 percent of the subjects were apparently mixed dominant). Boys who were poor readers were more likely to show crossed ear-hand dominance than were boys who were good readers. This effect appeared in girls only at the second-grade level.

In an examination of other cerebral mechanisms underlying linguistic skills, Buffery (1971 a, b) compared easy-to-verbalize stimuli in two modalities—sight and hearing. He combined a technique of **tachistoscopic** presentation to a binocular visual hemifield with that of dichotic listening, and presented a visual stimulus initially to one cerebral hemisphere for comparison with an auditory stimulus presented initially to either the same or opposite cerebral hemisphere. The system, according to Kimura (1973, p. 72), works as follows:

> Although the visual system is crossed, its connections are different from those of the auditory system. The connections are not from each eye to the opposite half of the brain but from each half of the visual field to the visual cortex on the opposite side. Vision to the left of the point of fixation is received by the right half of each retina and the neural pathways from the right side of both retinas go to the visual cortex of the right hemisphere. Obviously the fibers from the right half of the retina of the left eye must cross the midline of the brain to get to the right hemisphere but the fibers from the right half of the retina of the right eye do not cross.

The subjects were 5-, 6-, and 7-year-old right-handed children. Buffery found that they compared a printed word with a spoken word, and vice versa, more accurately when the stimuli were presented consecutively to the left cerebral hemisphere. Simultaneous comparison was more difficult but was easiest when the printed word was presented to the right hemisphere and the spoken word to the left hemisphere.

In a second study, Buffery compared right-handed children, ages 3 to 4, 5 to 6, 7 to 8, and 9 to 10 on a conflict drawing test. This test required the children to draw simultaneously a square with one hand and a circle with the other. The majority of girls in all age groups showed left-hand superiority for drawing the square; boys did not show this superiority until 7 years of age. Girls exhibited greater right-hand preference than boys from 3 to 6 years 11 months, and for both girls and boys the degree of left-hand superiority on a conflict drawing test increased with age and with degree of right-hand preference. These results are consistent with the general finding that girls mature more rapidly than boys. Although the mechanisms are imperfectly understood, the data may also explain why girls read earlier than boys and why some children, regardless of their sex, encounter reading problems.

In summary, it seems clear that the left hemisphere is primarily concerned with abstractions, especially in language. Further, cerebral dominance, as reflected in language behavior, is established by 4 years and develops more rapidly in females than males.

The right hemisphere.   The right hemisphere may be considered something of an "orphan" because researchers have paid so little attention to it. Actually, as we have shown, the right hemisphere plays an important role in human behavior, particularly in visual-spatial ability. Sperry (1975) further suggests that the right hemisphere is involved in information processing of a mechanical nature. It handles verbal materials that are concrete or automatic but does not process more abstract verbal material.

At the outset of the discussion of brain hemispheres, we noted that the right hemisphere plays a more important role in the early part of life but diminishes in importance as the left hemisphere begins to dominate. Kinsbourne (1970), among others, is working on how the two hemispheres interact and how they function in maturity. One hypothesis he is exploring is that the auditory processing in the left hemisphere, which influences language, is facilitated by the superior ability of the left hemisphere in temporal integration, a process required for understanding language. Visual material may or may not require temporal integration and sequential ordering. Vision often does necessitate spatial integration, a right-hemisphere function. The availability of highly sophisticated instrumentation will surely provide further answers to many of the questions related to brain development and function.

Motor Development

The development of motor skills is one of the most important accomplishments of human beings. Motor skills are necessary for locomotion, extensive interaction with the environment, various forms of communication, voluntary recreational

The ability to construct a block tower involves complex perceptual motor skills which require several years to develop. (Michael Serino/The Picture Cube)

behaviors—indeed, survival. This section focuses primarily on early motor development, including walking, thumb-forefinger apposition, and the infantile reflexes, although we devote some attention to skills that normally emerge during the preschool years but only as they help us interpret the data on maturation, laterality, and dominance.

Our primary source for interpretive material is the work of Arnold Gesell (1954), a pioneer in the study of early motor development, who developed a photographic filming technique for obtaining extensive behavioral observations on many children. A frame-by-frame analysis provided a very suitable empirical basis for Gesell's theoretical formulations.

A second technique used by Gesell to study maturation is the **co-twin control method.** We have already seen how identical twins are used to study heritability; Gesell's method is an adaptation of that procedure. Because identical twins are genetically the same, differences in their development can be attributed to differences in environmental experiences. In the heritability studies, we noted that the separation of identical twins did not guarantee that their environments were functionally different. Gesell introduced systematic differences into the lives of identical twins by providing one of them, the training twin (Twin T), with special instruction designed to hasten the development of various motor behaviors. The control twin (Twin C) was only routinely tested to determine if the behavior was present or not. If Twin T exhibited a trained behavior, say walking, earlier than Twin C, then it could be concluded that the training had positive effects. If the twins showed no differences, then it could be concluded that training had no effects and that the behaviors resulted primarily from maturational processes. Gesell leaves little doubt that he believed that these maturational processes were genetically determined, evolutionary and adaptive in character, and not very susceptible to environmental influences.

The grasp reflex (palmar reflex) gradually gives way to a voluntary response involving thumb-forefinger prehension. (George N. Peet/The Picture Cube)

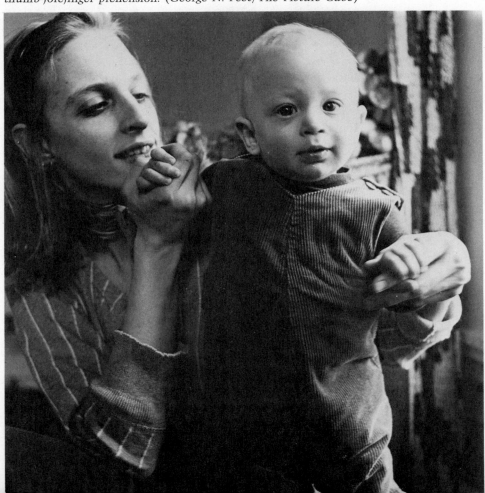

FIGURE 4-10   *Stages in the Development of Reaching and Grasping with Approximate Ages (in weeks) at Which They Appear*

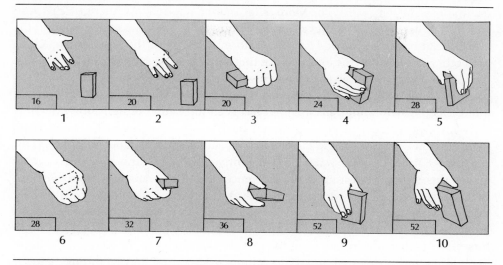

SOURCE: Halverson, H. M. An experimental study of prehension in infants by means of systematic cinema records. *Genetic Psychology Monographs*, 1931, *10*, 107–286.

Walking, or more precisely, erect bipedal locomotion, is a major human achievement. Children usually begin to walk, though not very well, somewhere between 13 and 15 months, a feat which signifies the acquisition of significant physical structures. The accomplishment of walking is preceded by a number of phases, all of which are necessary for the walking to occur.

The neonate's motor behavior consists of numerous movements that, for the most part, are uncoordinated and seemingly reflexive. Some reflexive movements in neonates are unique in that they are apparently completely innate and after a fairly short time disappear. For example, the **palmar reflex** can be elicited by lightly stimulating the palmar surface of the neonate's hand, whereupon the fingers close over the palmar surface. The hand stays closed until fatigue sets in and the grip is released. Grasping does not involve the thumb, as it does in adult primates. After about 4 to 6 months, stimulation of the palmar surface no longer generates a reflexive response and by 9 months thumb-forefinger grasping appears (see Figure 4-10) (Halverson, 1931). A second reflex exhibiting the same general history is called the **plantar reflex,** which is activated by stimulating the plantar surface of the foot (the sole of the foot) with a stiff hair. The neonate reacts by fanning out his toes. In the mature plantar response, the toes curl under. This response also disappears and a fully mature response emerges at around 2 years. The immature plantar reflex, known as the *Babinski reflex*, was named after a neurologist who observed, during World War I, that soldiers with certain head wounds had a higher incidence of the immature reflex. It is still used to diagnose brain injury, although some perfectly normal adults also exhibit the immature curling response so that this diagnostic technique is not very valid. The **Moro reflex** is often referred to as the *startle pattern* and it, too, has two distinct levels of development. In the immature response, the arms spread out from the body and then form a bow with the hands approaching each other. In addition, the lower part of the body becomes extended and somewhat rigid. In the mature phase, the response sequence is much more rapid; it becomes more a "bodily jerk" than any systematic sequence of responses. Another reflex of interest is the **swimming reflex,** which has been most fully described by McGraw (1934). If you place a newborn baby on its stomach, it will make characteristic swimming movements. These movements are sufficiently vigorous that the infant can propel itself through water. Subsequently, this reflex also disappears. What makes this reflex interesting is the existence of a clear transition from reflexive swimming to voluntary swimming, so that during the transition the baby may or may not demonstrate the reflex. Newborns also exhibit a **stepping reflex,** when, with proper support, they will walk. This reflex disappears at about 8 weeks. This transitory phase is characteristic of all of the reflexes that we have discussed and, indeed, as children move from involuntary to voluntary responses, they go through periods of acceleration and regression.

One reflex used by Gesell as a basis for much of his theorizing and to which he attributes considerable importance is the **tonic-neck-reflex (tnr).** The *tnr* is an asymmetric pattern of behavior that is virtually universal in the neonatal period. The major characteristic of the reflex is that while the face-arm and face-leg are in extension, the contralateral extremities are in flexion. During this stage, the infant might follow a stimulus but does so only until the stimulus reaches midline. When the stimulus passes the midline, the neonate is unable to continue the following response. In other words, the asymmetry appears to inhibit symmetrical behavior. According to Gesell's data, the *tnr* usually abates by 20 weeks of age. Gesell (1954, p. 353) discusses the reflex as follows:

> The process of transformation from *t.n.r.* to symmetric postures is extremely complex. It is not a process of simple substitution but one of progressive interlocking so that neither symmetry nor asymmetry gains permanent or complete ascendancy. The addition of the young infant to *t.n.r.* postures is both a symptom and a condition of his behavior growth. The infantile *t.n.r.* represents a morphogenetic stage in which fundamental neurological coordinations are laid down to form the framework for later postual, manual, locomotor, and psychomotor reactions. Indeed, the *t.n.r.* is part of the ground plan of the organism pervasively identified with its unitary, total action system.

This quotation echos some of the concepts attributed to the ethologists in Chapter 2. Actually, in his discussion of the *tnr*, Gesell suggests that it has adaptive significance during prenatal and neonatal development. Prenatally, the *tnr* helps the fetus adjust to the conformation of the uterus, and, neonatally, conforms to the postural requirements for breast feeding. Moreover, Gesell suggests that the *tnr* is even more important in the development of eye-hand coordination, prehension, and eventually, handedness. As we shall see later, many preschool and primary-grade children seem to have problems in handling tasks that require these competencies; the precursors to these difficulties may have been apparent during the neonatal period, or, more likely, the loss of the *tnr* may have been delayed.

As mentioned, each neonatal reflex disappears in a fairly short time. What implications does this phenomenon have for physiological development? It may be that the primitive reflexes occur because the cortex has no involvement in the behavior. The pathways of the central nervous system and the brain may be inadequately myelinated to provide the integration of actions required by the more mature responses. McGraw (1943) has postulated that the primitive reflexes are governed by structures lower in the central nervous system than the brain. She called these structures **"subcortical nuclei"** which she viewed as comprising a more primitive part of the brain and thus ready to control behavior at an earlier age than the cortex. As the central nervous system matures, myelinated fibers develop and the cortex assumes control over behavior by inhibiting the actions of the subcortical structures. The behavioral consequences of these changes are shown in Figure 4-11. This interpretation is similar to the explanation of how the dominant hemisphere

FIGURE 4-11 Suspension time for a group of children plotted on a logarithmic scale against chronological age, showing the trend of suspension behavior for all ages to eight years.

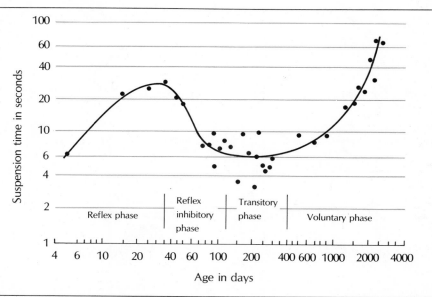

SOURCE: McGraw, M. B. *The neuromuscular maturation of the infant.* New York: Columbia University Press, 1943.
Note the probable phases of cortical control as indicated along the abscissa.

assumes control from the nondominant hemisphere. Direct evidence to support these assumptions is based largely on analyses of cortical structures and on the behavior patterns of abnormal children. There are also studies of animals in which the cortex has been cut away. The animal studies provide fairly strong support for McGraw's and Gesell's interpretation; the studies of abnormal children also support their interpretation but, because the nature of the abnormal condition is not always clear, the data are not as conclusive.

Walking

The stages in acquiring the ability to walk have been carefully described by Ames (1937), Gesell and Ames (1940), Shirley (1931), and McGraw (1935, 1940, 1941). It is remarkable that these investigators are in general agreement about the develop-

FIGURE 4-12   *The Fourteen Stages of Prone Progression Described by Ames*

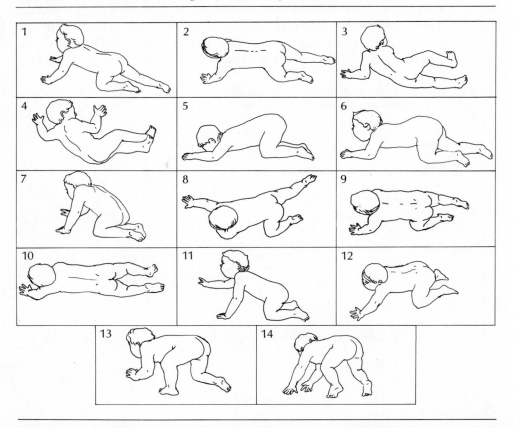

SOURCE: Ames, L. B. The sequential patterning of prone progression in the human infant. *Genetic Psychology Monographs*, 1937, *19*, 409–460.

mental stages involved in walking because they used different subjects, observational procedures, and analysis schemes. Ames' 14 stages are shown schematically in Figure 4-12. One identifiable stage is **crawling.** Crawling involves propulsion by use of the arms, while the legs drag along. **Creeping,** a more advanced stage than crawling, involves locomotion on all fours, thus involving coordination of the arms and legs. This sequence in which the legs are used later than the arms is also consistent with the cephalocaudal trend. Examination of the details of Ames' stages reveals the increasing individuation of bodily parts (arms, trunk, legs, and so forth). These developmental processes also involve apparent regressions; that is, as the child moves from one level of performance to another, behavior appears to be at a less mature level. This reversion to more primitive behavior also occurs in the development of cognitive processes. Figure 4-13 graphically demonstrates the principle as applied to the achievement of walking. As the child advances toward mature walking, certain cycles occur. Even with constant general advancement, the cycles show periodic regressions, but each cycle always terminates at a higher level. This principle is very similar to Werner's concepts of hierarchic organization and the genetic principle of spirality. Thus, it seems that regressions are a normal part of growth and probably represent a period in which new functions and forms are integrated into prevailing action patterns.

FIGURE 4-13   *Growth Cycles in the Patterning of Prone Behavior*

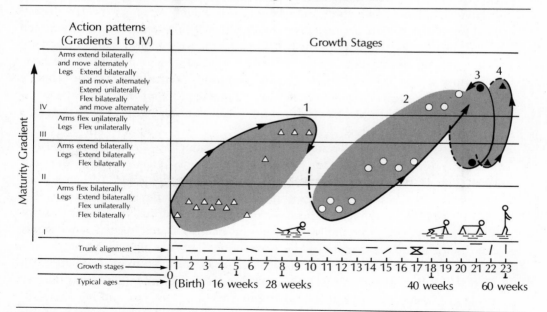

SOURCE: Gesell, A. The ontogenesis of infant behavior. In L. Carmichael (Ed.), *Manual of child psychology.* New York: John Wiley and Sons, 1954.

THE PROCESS OF MATURATION.   **Maturation** refers to a process in which morphological changes and consequent behavioral changes occur primarily because of genetically determined growth rather than learning or practice. The transitions from primitive reflexes to mature action patterns do not result from learning but from maturation, as do the developmental stages observed in the acquisition of walking. **Learning,** on the other hand, refers to behavioral changes that result from specifically taught associations or practice.

To demonstrate the validity of the concept of maturation, Gesell again used the co-twin control method using Twins T and C. These twins were seen 5 days a week. Twin T was given daily practice in crawling, creeping, walking, climbing, and thumb-forefinger prehension. All of these behaviors are exhibited by normal children, are parts of sequences of specific skill acquisitions, and appear to be strongly determined by genetic factors. Despite the daily practice received by Twin T, the twins showed no significant differences in the ages at which these behaviors appeared. Gesell concluded, therefore, that environmental variations do not influence these behaviors, which are thus innately determined action patterns that emerge with maturation.

Gesell's study was replicated and expanded by Myrtle McGraw, who also used the co-twin control method. The techniques for identifying identical twins had not yet been perfected and the twins used by McGraw, unlike those used by Gesell, turned out to be fraternal rather than identical. In McGraw's study Johnny was the experimental twin and Jimmy was the control. McGraw distinguished two kinds of behaviors: **phylogenetic** and **ontogenetic.** All members of a species display phylogenetic behaviors because they are members of that species. Furthermore, no special learning is required, for the behaviors are innately determined. Ontogenetic behaviors may or may not be acquired within a species. McGraw studied the same behaviors as Gesell, as well as jumping and swimming (actually swimming is both a phylogenetic and an ontogenetic behavior). One example of an ontogenetic behavior is roller skating which McGraw studied intensively. She also worked with the twins on ontogenetic swimming.

As regards the phylogenetic behaviors, McGraw duplicated Gesell's results; Johnny and Jimmy exhibited the phylogenetic behaviors at approximately the same time. The ontogenetic behaviors yielded a very different picture. When a child "showed signs of readiness" for a specific ontogenetic activity, she began training in that activity. For example, readiness for roller skating requires the ability to walk. When Johnny began to walk, McGraw put on training skates (regular roller skates, but the wheels do not contain ball bearings so that there is a high degree of friction) and placed Johnny on a thick gymnastic mat. She permitted him to acclimate to the skates and then started to make the mat thinner and thinner. Thinning the mat made the wheels easier to turn. Johnny often fell, but McGraw and her associates were always there to encourage him to continue. Eventually, she was successful in getting Johnny to skate on regular skates at the age of 18 months. A similar procedure

Learning a new skill (P. Simon)

was used to teach swimming. When McGraw noted that Johnny was going through the transition stage between involuntary and voluntary swimming, she developed a clever technique for teaching the baby voluntary swimming. She used a pulley system and harness with which she could lower him into the water. If he made swimming movements, he would propel himself through the water. Again by successive approximations, taking considerable care never to permit Johnny to become upset, McGraw was successful in getting him to swim the length of an Olympic-size pool by the age of 16 months. She also succeeded in introducing Johnny to other ontogenetic activities. Jimmy, who was given opportunities on these ontogenetic tasks only once a week, never approached Johnny's achievements. These data indicate that extra practice does not influence phylogenetic behavior but succeeds very well with ontogenetic behaviors.

McGraw's work gave rise to the concept of **readiness.** She believed that when a child showed signs of readiness, training procedures could be introduced with a reasonably high probability of success. Training before the appearance of such readiness signals, she argued, would be futile because the neuromuscular maturation would be insufficient to permit the child to profit from the learning experience. Thompson (1946, 115–116), in his review of McGraw's work, identified 6 educational principles that derive from her work:

Training in any particular activity before the neural mechanisms have reached a certain state of readiness is futile.

Exercise of newly developing functions is inherent in the process of growth, and if ample opportunity is afforded at the proper time, specific achievements can be advanced beyond the stage normally expected. (This generalization has significant implications for infant care.)

Periods of transition from one type of neuromuscular organization to another are an inherent part of development and are often characterized by disorganization and confusion [Gesell, 1943, describes this process of growth as spiral-like development].

Spurts, regressions, frustrations, and inhibitions are an integral part of organic growth, and there is reason to believe that they also function in the development of complete behavior activities.

Maturation and learning are not different processes, merely different facets of the fundamental process of growth.

Evidence that a child is ready for a particular educational subject is to be found in certain behavior "signals" or behavior syndromes which reflect the maturity of neural mechanisms.

These studies provided the prototype for at least 200 other studies performed with both children and animals. One of the better-known studies with children was conducted by Wayne Dennis (1940) with Hopi Indians. Dennis found a group of Hopi Indians who reared their infants on swaddling boards during the period when they would normally be creeping and crawling. In contrast, another group of Hopi Indians permitted their children complete motoric freedom similar to that of middle-class Americans. He found that the onset of walking for the Indian babies that were swaddled and those given motoric freedom was much the same. Both groups, however, walked later than the typical middle-class child. Dennis concluded that early environmental stimulation has only minimal effects on the onset of behavior. As you shall see in Chapter 8, Dennis later found an extremely impoverished environment for infants and changed his conclusions; specifically, he felt that improving extremely bad environments does improve performance.

EVALUATING THE MATURATION INTERPRETATION.   However impressive the quantity and quality of the research testing the maturation hypothesis, these studies rely on the incorrect assumption that the control subjects were not receiving any stimulation but that development occurred in spite of the lack of environmental stimulation. It would be more accurate to conclude that the extra stimulation provided to the experimental twin had no effects above and beyond the stimulation received by the control twin. Whatever stimulation the twins received in the studies by McGraw and Gesell was sufficient to stimulate normal development. These studies simply fail to make clear the characteristics of the stimulation received by the control subjects that contributed to their normal development. Flavell (1977) makes the further observation that in so-called "enrichment studies," even when they are successful, we cannot specify what attribute of the program contributed to growth;

in other words, we cannot specify the variables without which the treatment would *not* have worked.

The issues involved here have been recognized by other developmental psychologists. Wohlwill (1973, p. 319), for example, takes the following position:

> Once we grant the existence of "normal developmental processes," that is, acting independently of particular specifiable external agents or conditions, there follows a much more far-reaching consequence. That is that we can only hope to isolate necessary, those without which we can assert development does not take place, rather than those *thanks to which* it does take place. This would suggest, in other words, that the basic tool in the experimental study of development is the deprivation study, rather than the enrichment or special experience study.

A more productive procedure for investigating the crucial stimulus components in development is called the **deprivation strategy.** In this approach, the organism is denied an entire sensory system for an extended period of time. Perhaps the classic study in this area was performed by Austin Riesen (1947), who reared a chimpanzee in darkness from birth until just before it reached full maturity. If the environment does not play a role in the development of species-specific competencies, then the chimpanzee reared in darkness would not be expected to show differences from chimpanzees reared normally. Even after making corrections for nerve atrophy, the chimpanzee was found to be functionally blind even though the visual nervous system was intact. In the Nissen et al. study, a chimpanzee named Rob was reared in such a way that he was denied tactual-kinesthetic sensations (see Figure 4-14). Bandages were applied at the age of 5 weeks and effectively denied Rob of

FIGURE 4-14 *Rob's Sitting Position, Cylinders in Place*

SOURCE: Nissen, H., Chow, K., & Semmes, J. Effects of restricted opportunity for tactual, kinesthetic, and manipulative experience on the behavior of a chimpanzee. *American Journal of Psychology*, 1951, *64*, 485–507.

stimulation to the hands and feet. He was tested periodically and the bandages were finally removed at the age of 31 months. Compared with other chimps, he was found to walk normally but could not make use of tactual-kinesthetic stimulation. For example, when his trunk or head region was stimulated, he did not bring his fingers to that region as did the other animals. He did not show characteristic grooming behavior, grasp or cling to the attendent who carried him, or display the usual lip movements and sounds made by chimps; and his rough-and-ready poking with the finger showed none of the precision and perseverance typical of the behavior. Although Rob eventually learned to bring his finger to a given place with speed and accuracy, other innate behaviors did not appear. These data are not meant to suggest that the animals were totally deprived of an environment; such a condition is impossible. The data do, however, suggest that the genetically preprogrammed systems require appropriate stimulation in order to develop normally.

The hypothesis that genetically programmed neural structures require external stimulation to achieve maximal growth was fully explored by Hebb (1949). He proposed that through a complex biochemical process, the firing of nerve fibers actually triggered their growth. Recent research on the biochemistry of synaptic transmission, though only partially relevant to Hebb's hypotheses, nevertheless, suggests that he may be correct (Rosenzweig, Bennett & Diamond, 1972). In one of those experiments, for example, it was found that among rats a high level of extra stimulation was associated with heavier brains. The greatest growth took place in the visual areas of the brain, apparently because the major stimulation was visual. It should be noted that the stimulated and control animals were genetically identical, thus the differences can be attributed to environmental events.

These studies suggest that the effects of the environment are important for normal development, at least in sensory capacity. It is probably true that severe deprivation would also affect motoric activities. Thus, normal development clearly requires an intact active organism and a responsive stimulating environment.

Clinical Implications

This chapter has emphasized the relationship between structural development and behavior. The point was made that development involves a complex interweaving of action patterns, and it was explicitly assumed that the coordination of action patterns is a consequence of physical maturation, especially neurological and neuromuscular development. The material was presented as a basis for understanding developmental changes in more complex areas of behavior, including cognition, perception, language, and social behavior. As Tanner and Gesell indicated, the basic principles of neurophysiological development and their implications for behavior do not terminate with the onset of walking, or at age 6 or 9 or 13.

We also indicated that the material in this chapter, expecially the work on cerebral dominance and motor development, has implications for clinical assessments of children. For example, many of the conceptual views prevalent in the diagnosis of learning disabilities derive from various aspects of the material presented here. The reader interested in learning more about the relationships among cerebral dominance, laterality, Gesell's principles of development, and so forth, should consult any of the following major references: Cruickshank and Hallahan (1975 a, b), Ayres (1972), Kephart (1963), Myklebust (1971), and Reitan and Boll (1973).

Atypical Development

Our knowledge about the normal patterns of physical and motor development has provided a basis for identifying cases of atypical development. This is not simply a matter of diagnosing children who are grossly physically or mentally handicapped. Our concern is with children who show a lack of normal physical coordination, experience difficulties in copying geometric figures or in more grossly defined eye-hand coordination, or have difficulty in learning to read or in coping with complex mathematical problems. Frequently called learning disabled children, such youngsters display general intellectual ability and gross physical development that are well within normal limits. By all standard indicators they should develop normally.

Numerous hypotheses have been advanced about the causes of learning disabilities (Cruickshank & Hallahan, 1975), ranging from strictly environmental to strictly genetic. Gesell and his colleagues, Ilg and Ames, developed biological explanations based on the integration of neuromotor mechanisms, that is, the coordination of motor and perceptual functions. According to Gesell and his colleagues, these functions are genetically programmed and require an opportunity for expression through environmental stimulation. The environmental feedback from actions performed and consequent stimulation of the organism lead to increasingly integrated systems. As noted earlier, walking is a complex achievement requiring the integration and coordination of antagonistic muscles and neurological control. We might have added that children must also learn to locate themselves in space and to develop spatial-distance perceptions (which helps avoid spilled milk or knocking over a treasured vase).

Why do some children develop atypically? In general, the evidence suggests that these children have experienced a prenatal or neonatal trauma that places them "at risk." At risk refers to the *relative* biological integrity of a newborn baby. Risk is measured in numerous ways, including **Apgar** (1953) **ratings** (named after Virginia Apgar, a pediatrician) and more recent procedures developed by Brazelton (1973).

These techniques are administered within hours after birth or, when drugs were ingested during delivery, after the drugs have left the child's system. These techniques assess reflex strength, birth weight, degree of prematurity, the baby's alert-

Acquiring new motor skills may not always be pleasant. (Jamie Cope/The Picture Cube)

ness, as well as the adequacy of the life-supporting systems. The long-term validity of these techniques provides adequate differentiation between low-risk and high-risk babies, but their overall predictive power is not overwhelmingly strong. Even so, children born at high risk are more likely to encounter learning problems than children born at low risk (Pasamanick & Knoblock, 1966).

Risk involves two identifiable factors: maternal diet during pregnancy and the child's birth weight (low birth weight, though a correlate of prematurity, can also occur in full-term babies). Maternal diet is especially important because it provides the fetus with the nutrients required for physical growth. Diets severely deficient in protein and vitamins can cause a general slowdown in development or can actually cause irreparable damage to the nervous system. Some investigators (Birch & Gussow, 1970) suspect that neurological impairment resulting from dietary deficiencies is largely responsible for the incidence of high-risk babies. Not surprisingly, the dietary deficiencies, and the higher rates of infant mortality, prematurity, low birth weight, and so forth, occur among the poor.

Another variable that influences development is called neonatal **anoxia**. Anoxia is a state in which the baby fails to obtain sufficient oxygen to maintain life (neonatal **apnea** is a state where the baby fails to breathe). The best medical opinion is that babies can go without oxygen for 3 minutes without neurological damage, but thereafter grave consequences can occur. Stechler (1964) obtained permission to record the elapsed time between clamping the **placenta** (this severs the flow of oxygenated blood to the baby) and the beginning of the baby's breathing (the birth cry). A sample of 26 white middle-class mothers agreed to participate in the study. From this sample 9 (34 percent) of the babies (herein called experimental babies) failed to breath within the allotted 3 minutes. Stechler studied these babies for a period of 3 years, gathering test data and conducting interviews with the mothers. The mothers were not informed about the status of their babies. Several features of the data are interesting: as soon as 2 weeks after returning from the hospital, the mothers of the experimental babies made more negative statements and described more problems than did the control mothers (the mothers of the 17 normal babies); the test-score patterns of the anoxia babies varied more from testing session to testing session; the mean IQs of the 2 groups at 3 years were virtually identical and *above average*. Unfortunately, we do not know what happened to these children after entering school, but evidence on other anoxia babies suggest they may have encountered learning problems.

These are some of the causes of atypical or slower development. Dietary deficiencies and anoxia have obvious effects on neurological development. Gender is also related to development; boys are more likely to show slower maturation rates and atypical developmental patterns. Not surprisingly, boys are also more likely to experience learning problems in school. Recall that in Chapter 3 we noted that sex-linked deficiencies were more likely to occur among males than females. Although an environmental explanation of sex differences in maturation is appealing,

Many activities provide opportunities for strengthening eye-hand coordination. (Ed Buryn)

we believe that these differences are genetically determined. It is conceivable, of course, that a modified (school) environment might help boys to adjust and learn more readily—some clinicians have urged that boys begin school a year later than girls.

What behaviors do psychologists look at to determine if physical, motor, and neurological development is occurring within a normal range? Obviously, this depends on the child's age. While the child is still an infant, the psychologist may determine if the primitive reflexes (palmar, plantar, tonic-neck-reflex) are dropping out roughly on schedule. Motor integration can sometimes be assessed by examining sleeping postures. Somewhat later, one can examine creeping or crawling patterns and note the age of onset of walking.

As the child approaches the 4-to-7-year age period, the behaviors available for clues about development are more diverse and more complex. Skilled psychologists typically sample many aspects of behavior before making diagnoses. Performance on only one of these tasks is inadequate for diagnosing a dysfunction.

Kephart (1963) developed the "walk-a-beam" task consisting of a 2-inch by 4-inch board extending perhaps as long as 12 to 16 feet. Either the 4-inch or 2-inch side of the board is used, depending upon the level of difficulty desired. The child is asked to walk across the board, and while doing so, must fixate on a point in space located straight ahead; the child is not allowed to look down for foot placement. The successful accomplishment of this task requires the integration of spatial and motoric functioning. In a more advanced variation, the child has to walk the beam backwards while looking straight ahead—even adults find this task difficult, though most can do it. An interesting component of this task is the action pattern involved when the child falls off the beam. Some children go down in what can best be described as a "heap." Other children fall in a more controlled and systematic manner; for example, careful photographic analysis of their falling indicates an integrated coordination of the arms and legs. Thus, even the pattern of falling can provide relevant information.

Another task used by Kephart is "draw-a-circle." Illustrated in Figure 4-15 is a picture of a 4.5-year-old child performing the task. Given a piece of chalk in each hand, the child is told to stand with his nose touching the blackboard and to look straight ahead. The child is then asked to draw circles with both hands. Notice that the child is making a reasonably good circle with the right hand but seems to be having considerable difficulty with the left hand. In addition the child is placing the left-hand circle considerably below the right-hand circle, suggesting an inability to perform the task symmetrically. Further analysis of this task indicates another important feature of these early sensorimotor behaviors: the right-handed circle is being made in a counterclockwise direction. This behavior is somewhat advanced for a child this age (in fact this child has superior intellectual ability and was an early reader). Why children initially make circles in a clockwise direction and then shift

FIGURE 4-15

FIGURE 4-16

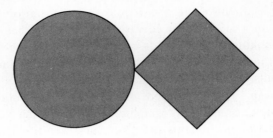

SOURCE: Bender, L. A visual motor Gestalt test and its clinical use. *American Orthopsychiatry Association Research Monograph*, 1938, No. 3 (A. of Plate I, p. 4).

is not understood. The task again provides an indication of the child's ability to coordinate a sensorimotoric pattern with visual-spatial competency.

A more formalized and better-known task was developed by Loretta Bender (1938). It consists of 10 geometric designs (see Figure 4-16 for example of one stimulus), which the child is asked to reproduce. Immature children will have considerable difficulty with this task: though they are usually able to draw a circle, an achievement well within the capabilities of most 5-year-olds, they will have considerable difficulty reproducing the square (actually shaped like a diamond). A frequent error is to draw the diamond in a vertical position; the child rotates the diamond. Sometimes the child accomplishes this by actually turning the stimulus card or turning the paper; this behavior is reminiscent of Corballis and Beale's pigeons who rotated the oblique angles that they were being trained to discriminate (see page 100). Koppitz (1964) has developed a scoring procedure that takes into account such matters as rotations, the inability to form angles, and the inability to perform other behaviors specific to each of the stimulus materials.

Ayres (1972) developed an interesting hypothesis that emphasizes the vestibular processes, that is, processes concerned with the ability to detect motion and to employ associations between sensory input and bodily movements. Ayres' hypothesis is extensively developed and well documented. Some of the implications that flow from her work, and other similar neurological hypotheses, involve the motoric skills of children during the age period from 5 through 8 years. Specifically, the child shows distinct developmental patterns in handwriting, the ability to learn to ride a bike, and in general the coordination of complex bodily movements into smooth action patterns. Let us take one more example in this area. When you ask a 4- or 5-year-old to hop on one foot, they often have considerable difficulty in achieving what is essentially a very simple feat. Sometimes they cannot perform the task at all, although many children can perform the task equally well on both the left and the right leg. In older children the task is, of course, much easier, but we also now see bilateral asymmetry; most children are able to hop with great agility on the right leg but perform rather poorly with the left leg. It takes more time before they are able to cope with this new asymmetry, but eventually they do so.

It should be noted that the few tasks we have described are related to neurological and neuromuscular development. Their diagnostic validity depends, in part, on the age of the children tested. For example, the Bender Gestalt has almost no diagnostic value with 10-year-olds because they can all perform the task; there is no variability. In general, these tasks have maximal value when the behavior is normally expected to first become manifest. For the Kephart tasks and the drawing and reproduction tasks, this age is between 5 and 9 years. Many of these tasks are part of so-called reading-readiness tests which are frequently used in school. Again, we reiterate, no one test or technique is foolproof; many tests should be administered.

SUMMARY

The phenomenon of developmental patterns is apparent almost from conception. Structures are formed and become integrated into complex functional systems. Each system has its own time table, but by 7 months these systems are sufficiently developed to sustain extrauterine life, at least with some artificial support. A major feature of the prenatal period is the rapidity with which growth occurs.

Growth continues to be very rapid after birth, especially in terms of height and weight. Phylogenetic behavior patterns, such as the palmar and plantar reflexes, thumb-forefinger prehension, and the developmental sequences leading to walking, are apparent. Research studies using the co-twin control method indicate that practice does not accelerate changes in phylogenetic behaviors. These studies do not imply that environment has little or no effect on development. Other studies, using a stimulus deprivation approach, have shown that normal growth requires environmental stimulation.

One of the major features of development described in this chapter is the lawful patterning of human development. This was demonstrated in terms of the "catch-up" phenomenon observed in physical growth and in terms of the interweaving of motor patterns. The catch-up phenomenon involves an acceleration in growth following a period of slow growth caused by illness. As soon as the child achieves normal height (weight), the rate of development returns to normal.

The interweaving of motor patterns is illustrated by the apparent loss of a physical skill while more elaborate skills are being acquired. This pattern of greater awkwardness followed by greater skill results from the integration of new skills with established skills. The interweaving of new and old behavior patterns is a feature of many aspects of development. It may well be the case that the physical, motor, perceptual, and cognitive components of development are totally interdependent.

CHAPTER 5

(Jean-Claude Lejeune)

PERCEPTUAL DEVELOPMENT

THIS CHAPTER and the two following it—Cognitive Development and Language Development—describe the development of the complex processes that eventually permit the normal adult to cope with the increasingly complex demands of the environment. We will examine such diverse aspects of behaviors as how human beings receive stimulation through the senses (vision, audition, touch, and so on); how they interpret this sensory stimulation; how they begin to define and categorize their perceptions; and how they communicate them. Finally, we will examine various mental operations, including memory and strategies for problem solving. Textbooks on child psychology and development have traditionally separated these related components of development—perception, cognition, and language—into separate chapters, but it will become clear that the materials are related in complex ways and thus cannot be considered as separate entities. The division of the chapters into perception, cognition, and language is somewhat arbitrary, a state recognized by Neisser (1966, p. 4), who dealt with it in his definition of the term "cognition."

> As used here, the term "cognition" refers to all the processes by which the sensory input is transformed, reduced, elaborated, stored, recovered, and fused. It is concerned with these processes even when they operate in the absence of relevant stimulation, as images and hallucinations. Such terms as *sensation, perception, imagery, retention, recall, problem solving,* and *thinking,* among many others, refer to hypothetical stages or aspects of cognition.

Thus, the reader should neither think of memory as independent of sensation or perception or view problem solving as independent of any of the other elements discussed. Our decision to place material in this chapter rather than the chapter on cognition was largely, but not exclusively, based on chronological age. That is, the material included herein tends to focus on infant behavior, whereas Chapter 6 emphasizes the more abstract and symbolic operations of the later years, according to Piaget's model of development.

It will be helpful to examine first one broad conceptual issue that pervades much of the discussion of perception and perceptual development. Specifically, the question arises whether or not perception is learned, according to the principles of S-R behaviorism, or whether perceptual processes and organization are in fact innately predetermined. The former position, in favor of learning, is generally referred to as **empiricism**, and usually assumes that the infant passively receives external stimulation and is controlled by environmental events. The latter view, that of innate predisposition, is called **nativism** and holds that the child is an active processor of the environment.

It is our position that the general principles of development tend to be consistent with the nativist viewpoint, for development is unidirectional and tends to occur in relatively fixed sequences. We do not, on the other hand, deny that environmental events are crucial, and we agree with the claim that many aspects of human behavior are the consequence of learning. Actually, this position restates McGraw's distinction between phylogenetic and ontogenetic activities where she very ably demonstrated that external events are relatively unimportant in phylogenetic activities but quite important in ontogenetic activities. Our general view holds that the organism is an active processor of environmental events and displays developmental patterns in the processing of these events. Horowitz (1975, p. 2) has stated the issue clearly in a very important monograph concerned with infant perception, culminating in a plea for a more adequate pool of data from which we may draw inferences concerning these theoretical issues:

> There have been almost no crucial tests of one position against the other. It is entirely plausible to think of the infant as an active environmental processor with a species-specific developmental sequence inherent in the appearance of processing strategies, while at the same time, conceiving of the infant as being under the kind of control of environmental stimuli that is represented in the traditional models of conditioning. The role of conditioning probably becomes increasingly complex as development proceeds. Indeed, the data bank of infant development may soon be sufficient for a serious integration of the two approaches to take place that might, almost ironically, bring us back to a "common sense" view of infant development.

Some investigators might disagree with Horowitz's conclusion that the two positions can be integrated. Nonetheless, the methods typical of each approach have provided us with basic knowledge about infant sensory capacities and perceptual processes. An understanding of the work done on the sensory capabilities of infants requires some acquaintance with the basic processes of classical and instrumental condition. We assume that most readers were exposed to these basic principles in their introductory psychology course and, therefore, the following description will be very brief and may serve as a reminder of basic theory. If this is not the case, then the reader should examine an introductory book for the relevant material.

Basic Principles
of Conditioning

An oversimplified statement of the behaviorist position is that behavioral change, learning, results from the association of a stimulus (S) and a response (R). A stimulus is a change in an internal or external feature of the organism which activates a receptor and serves as a signal for a response. A response is a change in behavior as a consequence of stimulation. Stimulation that occurs before a response serves not only an activating role but also has attentional, selective, and informational properties. Responses also generate stimuli, and these stimuli have rewarding or punishing functions; they will either strengthen or weaken the previous response.

Stimuli that follow a response and that increase its frequency are called **reinforcers.** The precise properties of reinforcing stimuli are subject to some debate. For example, Thorndike (1933) viewed this stimulus as a *reward*, which he defined as a satisfying state of affairs and which then had the effect of "stamping in" the S-R association or connection. According to the conceptual model of Hull and Spence, the crucial aspect of the reinforcing stimulus was its drive-reducing properties; that is, the terminal stimulus in the sequence, which they called a reinforcer, had to be capable of reducing a particular drive (food for hunger, water for thirst). The most general definition of a reinforcer is employed by Skinner, who states that a reinforcing stimulus is one whose occurrence is contingent on a response and strengthens that response. The difficulties with all of these definitions are of little concern in the present discussion. Suffice it to say that in other conceptions of behavioral change, especially those of a developmental nature, it is not entirely clear that reinforcement is a necessary condition, although some kind of reinforcing stimulus seems to be necessary for conditioning.

Classical Conditioning

The essential principles of **classical conditioning** are illustrated in Figure 5-1, which represents the now very famous experiment conducted by Pavlov with a dog. The stimulus that elicits the salivating response upon presentation and without any previous attempts to establish an S-R association, is the food powder. The food powder is called the **unconditioned stimulus,** or **UCS.** The response elicited by the UCS—the salivation—is called the *unconditioned response,* or UCR. The crucial component of classical conditioning involves presenting a stimulus such as a tone, which is called the **conditioned stimulus,** or **CS.** The UCS and the CS are presented in **contiguity** (very close in time); the interval for maximum rate of conditioning is approximately 1 or 2 seconds. Continual pairing of the UCS and CS eventually leads to the salivation response in the *absence* of the UCS; that is, the salivation now

FIGURE 5-1

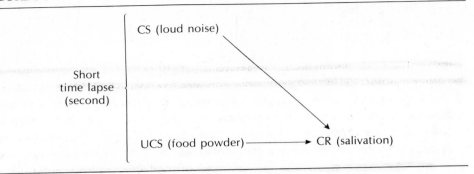

occurs upon presentation of the tone by itself. Now the salivation is called a *conditioned response*, or CR. You may ask where the reinforcing stimulus is to be found in this type of conditioning. Actually, in the learning phase of classical conditioning the reinforcing stimulus is the UCS, the food powder. In classical conditioning the reinforcing stimulus is always present during learning and the learner does not have to perform any act in order for it to occur.

A critical feature of classical conditioning is that the UCS elicits a *reflex response*. For Pavlov's dog, the reflex response was salivation; no one had to teach the dog to salivate to the food powder. Without a reflex response, classical conditioning is not possible. A number of reflex responses in human infants make it possible to demonstrate classical conditioning and thus some of the infant's sensory capabilities. It should be noted that the establishment of classically conditioned responses is very difficult, even with animals. A number of environmental variables (for example, extraneous noise) and varying states of the organism (fatigue or a general state of satiation) act as distractors that interfere with the process.

Instrumental Conditioning

In **instrumental conditioning**, the subject must make an appropriate response in order to receive the reinforcing stimulus. In other words, reward or reinforcement is contingent upon some *voluntary* behavioral act. Thus, when an experimenter wants a rat to make a right turn at a T-maze, the experimenter rewards it for right turns but not for left turns. With children, a large number of instrumental conditioning situations have been used. For example, to take a simple case, we may wish to have a child learn to press a triangular button instead of a square button. All the child's presses on the triangular-shaped button lead to reinforcing stimuli (M & M candies are widely used for this), but he or she receives no reinforcement for pressing the square button. Hence, the child learns the association between the stimulus, the triangular button, and the response of pressing that button. Of course, the principles of instrumental conditioning are not as simple as we have described them here.

Several theories have elaborated upon the basic principles and now include a number of variables that effect the *rate* of learning.

Instrumental conditioning is also often equated with *operant conditioning*, a term most closely associated with the work of B. F. Skinner. One way to apply instrumental conditioning to the study of the sensory capability of human infants is through discrimination experiments. Chapter 6 will elaborate on the instrumental conditioning model to include higher-order concept learning and explore how this basic learning model relates to language development.

Perceptual Attending

We will call another general approach that has been used extensively to study the sensory capacities of young infants "the method of perceptual attending." This method derives from the nativistic position that the organism has an innate tendency to examine, or attend to, unique stimuli in the environment. Sensory capacity is measured by determining if the baby can detect changes in the stimulus properties by attending to a slightly modified stimulus. The technique has been used to study sensory acuity and also has been the method of choice to study the characteristics of stimuli to which children respond. Thus, the implications of the method go beyond providing information about sensory acuity. Because of its importance, we shall examine the major attributes of perceptual attending and some of the essential features of methods that employ it.

The Orienting Reflex

The **orienting reflex** is an unlearned response in which the infant concentrates its full attention on the stimulus (Pavlov, 1927). If the organism is able to discriminate a stimulus (visual, auditory, gustatory, or whatever), if it is in a state that permits stimulus input to occur, and finally if the properties of the stimulus are compelling, then the infant will exhibit behaviors comprising the orienting reflex.

Not surprisingly, many of the behavioral indicators of the reflex are defined by involuntary physiological responses. One of the more thoroughly studied of these is heart rate. For example when a person is orienting, he undergoes cardiac deceleration, a slowing of the heartbeat (Steinschneider, 1967). Conversely, the presentation of some stimuli, notably those that are very intense, generates heart rate *acceleration*. Other physiological manifestations of the orienting reflex include a general decrease in motor activity, dilation of the pupils, and changes in galvanic skin response (electrical conduction of the skin). Yet another indicator of the orienting reflex is a marked, involuntary diminution in sucking behavior in the

Attentional behavior is critical in the formation of new concepts. (Paul Fusco/ Magnumphotos).

presence of a stimulus. Although it has been debated whether sucking is a true reflex or is learned, nevertheless, the majority of babies display what appears to be reflexive sucking behavior. After establishing a base rate of sucking (individual rates of sucking using a special pacifier described later), we can determine if rate of sucking diminishes upon presentation of a stimulus. If sucking is reduced, attending behavior is presumably occurring. To determine that the stimulus caused the decrease in sucking, we remove the stimulus and see whether the sucking rate returns to normal. Another technique is to present the stimulus for an extended period of time and see if the sucking response returns to normal.

The orienting reflex resembles what is also referred to as **attentional behavior,** in which the duration of examination of stimuli is measured. Perhaps the simplest distinction between the two terms is that the orienting reflex represents primarily the physiological aspects of attention, whereas attending behavior represents primarily the psychological aspects.

Habituation

If babies constantly attended to all novel or relatively novel stimuli in their environment, they would be unable to function because their behavior would constantly be expended in orienting toward any stimulus present in the environment. This does not occur; with repeated exposures to a particular stimulus object children exhibit less and less attention or orienting to it. This process is called **habituation.** As used in this context, we should not view habituation as merely a matter of stimulus adaptation in which the infant ceases to attend to the stimulus because of boredom or fatigue. Rather habituation means that the infant has formed a concept or representation of the particular stimulus object—it has become familiar (Soklov, 1963; Cohen, 1969).

The habituation of the orienting reflex has developmental features. During early infancy, orienting responses occur more frequently and last longer before habituation sets in because so much of the environment is new to the infant. As the child matures, the structures of the more common stimuli in the child's world become well established. With maturity, orienting responses occur less often and habituation to broader classes of stimuli becomes more rapid. Through orienting behavior, then, the child learns about the environment by examining it and forming representations. The process of determining the important dimensions of the world is apparently a matter of learning because children are reinforced differentially when they respond to appropriate rather than inappropriate stimuli and stimulus dimensions.

Wendell Jeffrey (1968) has developed a more detailed concept of habituation as it occurs in perceptual and cognitive development, which he calls the **serial habituation hypothesis.** Jeffrey contends that habituation is crucial for continued structural development and subsequent problem solving. When a baby has habituated to the most captivating cues, it then shows orienting reflexes toward less salient cues. With stimulus repetition, the infant develops a continuous, orderly sequence of attending responses to the stimulus. Eventually, this behavioral sequence ceases and the infant attends only to the most salient features. "It is both the integration of a pattern of attending responses and the discontinuity of that pattern with other attending responses or patterns that define an object percept or what we shall call more generally a **schema**" (Jeffrey, 1968, p. 325). Thus, the acquisition of knowledge about the world involves a sequence of attending, habituation, and the development of probabilities about what stimulus features are more likely to help identify an object.

Methods of Studying the Orienting Reflex and Habituation

There are two basic methods of studying the orienting reflex and habituation: (1) a single stimulus is presented, and fixation time is recorded over successive trials; and, (2) two stimuli are presented, and fixation time for each stimulus is recorded and subsequent comparisons are made. A variation of these two methods involves the presentation of a single stimulus (such as a tone) which is sustained or repeated until habituation occurs (the subject no longer exhibits an orienting response). At this point, a second stimulus differing in intensity, pitch, or some other feature, is introduced; if the child can detect the change, he or she will once again show the attending response.

Early Sensory Capacity

The techniques we have just described are useful in the study of sensory capacity because, obviously, infants are not able to give meaningful verbal responses about their sensory experiences. Thus our conclusions about sensory capability are based on inferences drawn from carefully designed experiments of the type already described.

Visual Capability

A number of studies, published some years ago and using relatively primitive observational techniques, indicate that the newborn infant is sensitive to some types of visual stimulation (Pratt, Nelson, & Sun, 1930). In these studies a flashlight was used to present light stimuli to newborn infants. The 24 infants responded to this stimulation—a pupillary or blinking response to the light—approximately 95 percent of the time. As might be expected, the newborn's response to light is more certain to occur, and with greater strength, when the light is strong. We have, unfortunately, no verified evidence that precisely defines the visual acuity of infants beyond their pupillary reflexes in response to light stimulation. Some research, however, enables us to make reasonably valid estimates of the visual acuity of very young children; it is approximately 10/30 at 21 months and shows distinct improvement by 40 to 45 months when the Snellen ratings were reported as 10/10.

Most of the research on the visual capacity of infants under 12 months has involved the discrimination of form and color. Visual discrimination in infants is possible but difficult to establish in comparison with older children. The physical arrangements for a color discrimination experiment conducted by Lipsitt (1963) are shown in Figure 5-2. The infants were 8 months old, and the reinforcing stimulus for pushing the correct panel was the sound of a buzzer. Half the subjects were reinforced for choosing the red stimulus, the other half for choosing the green stimulus. Notice in the figure that the infant had 3 panels to choose from even though the discrimination involved only 2 colors. Research with babies requires such special arrangements to prevent them from performing actions that confound experimental results. For example, when only two panels are used, the babies frequently pressed both panels at one time thus insuring a reinforcer. With the 3-panel arrangement, a press on the middle panel never led to a reinforcer. In addition, if two panels were pressed simultaneously, no reinforcers were delivered. The results of the study are shown in Figure 5-3; they indicate that the infants can discriminate between red and green and can also learn to associate the stimulus with a specific response. The results of the color experiment, and similar experiments with form, indicate that the

FIGURE 5-2 *Three-Panel Apparatus for Study of Operant Discrimination in Young Children*. Colors appear in windows of panels. Depression of "correct" panel produces buzzer sound.

FIGURE 5-3 Data for two subjects in 3-panel apparatus, one receiving buzzer reinforcement for response to the green panel, the other receiving reinforcement for response to either red or green depending on its being the odd color present.

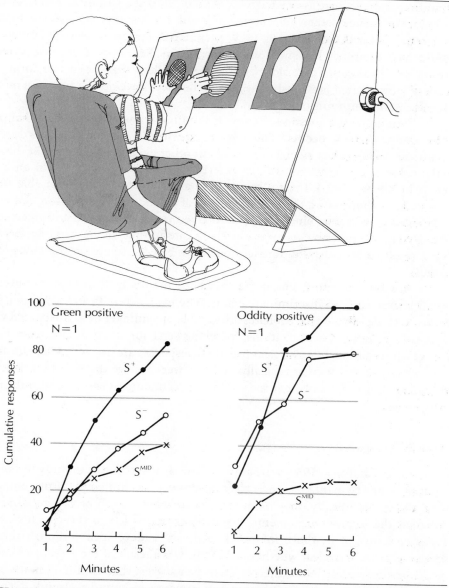

SOURCE: Lipsitt, L. Learning in the first year of life. In L. P. Lipsitt & C. C. Spiker (Eds.), *Advances in child development and behavior, Vol. 1*. New York: Academic Press, 1963, p. 181.

visual apparatus of infants below 12 months of age is sufficiently well-developed to permit adequate color and form discriminations. These data, incidentally, also indicate that infants below the age of 12 months are capable of rudimentary associative learning. It is interesting to note that the dimensions of color and form are learned more readily than other dimensions such as size or number; children's stimulus preferences are associated with chronological age. Children shift from form to color preference somewhere between 3 and 4 years and then return to form preference (Brian & Goodenough, 1929; Suchman & Trabasso, 1966). Relatively few studies have examined size and number preferences. Recent evidence discovered by Smiley (1972) suggests that older children and college students prefer form. The work of Jeffrey, cited previously, suggests preferences develop as a function of their usefulness in identifying objects.

Turning to the question of color discrimination, we might ask at what point color discrimination occurs. The Lipsitt experiment indicates infants can discriminate among colors by eight months, but other evidence suggests that they can make color discriminations even earlier (Haith and Campos, 1977). In an experiment by Chase (1937), infants between 15 and 70 days of age were able to discriminate, without error, the following pairs of colors: red versus green, red versus yellow-green, red versus blue-green, yellow-green versus blue-green, and green versus blue-green. The experimenter was especially careful that the discriminations were not a result of brightness differences but were based entirely on the color of the stimuli.

It would therefore appear that newborn infants have at least rudimentary visual acuity and can discriminate colors. The evidence indicates that acuity improves very rapidly, so that neonates are capable of a number of sophisticated visual activities including visual fixations, following behavior, color discrimination, and form discrimination. It is also clear that these responses are not very adequate at first but improve so rapidly that typically by 2 to 4 weeks of age the visual mechanisms, including acuity, are sufficient for the infant accurately to perceive stimuli in the environment.

Auditory Capability

Pratt, Nelson, and Sun (1930) were among the early investigators to study the hearing capacity of newborn infants. Their research strategy was similar to the one employed with vision. Specifically, they administered auditory stimuli of varying kinds and recorded the infants' movements. Their observations led to the conclusion that auditory acuity in newborn infants is relatively undeveloped, although their description leaves it unclear whether or not this was a result of the presence of mucus in the auditory canal. Nevertheless, their data suggest that within 48 hours babies performed distinct movement patterns in response to auditory stimuli. Other in-

FIGURE 5-4 Newborn with headpiece attached for recording head-turning responses.

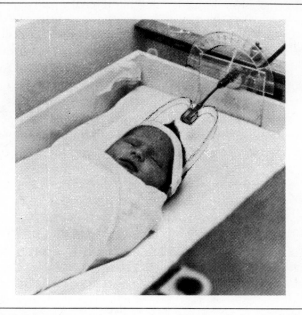

SOURCE: Siqueland, E. R., & Lipsitt, L. P. Conditioned head turning in human newborns. *Journal of Experimental Psychology*, 1966, 3, 356–378.

vestigators have noted that the stimuli used in these studies were not calibrated for intensity, frequency, or quality, so that it is difficult to arrive at specific conclusions about what attributes of sound were responsible for the bodily movements.

Siqueland and Lipsitt (1966) used conditioning techniques to demonstrate auditory discrimination in infants. They employed 2 groups of 8 infants each, ranging in age from 48 to 116 hours. In Group 1 the positive stimulus was a tone, whereas the positive stimulus for Group 2 was a buzzer. These stimuli were paired with tactile stimulation that produced a reflexive head turn in the direction of the stimulus. The apparatus that permitted precise measurements of the amount of head movement is illustrated in Figure 5-4. The results, illustrated in Figure 5-5, indicate rather clearly that auditory discrimination, and thus auditory acuity, can be demonstrated during the first few days of life.

Conditioned head turning as an indication of auditory discrimination has also been demonstrated in a series of studies of Papoušek (1967 a, b). The conditioned stimulus was a bell presented for 10 seconds. Each turn of the head to the left of at least 30 degrees occurring within 10 seconds after presentation of the bell was reinforced. After the left head turn in response to the bell was acquired, the buzzer stimulus was introduced. The infants were now required to make a right head turn

FIGURE 5-5   Comparison of percentage of responses to auditory stimulus (positive) and tactile stimulus (negative) during training and reversal trials.

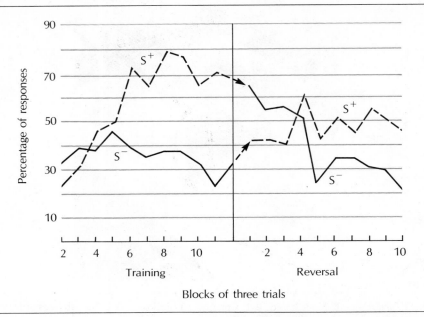

SOURCE: Siqueland, E. R. & Lipsitt, L. P. Conditioned head turning in human newborns. *Journal of Experimental Psychology*, 1966, 3, 356–378.

to the buzzer. The data in Figure 5-6 indicate that babies are capable of an auditory discrimination shortly after birth. Older infants, however, learned the discrimination more rapidly; that is, neonates required many more trials than infants who were 2 or more months of age. This difference suggests an ambiguity in the results of the work on auditory acuity; specifically, it is unclear whether the more rapid learning of the older babies resulted from a more refined acuity or improved conditionability. In view of the many attempts to condition neonates, it seems likely that newborn babies' capability for auditory discrimination is probably underestimated because of the complex methodological problems in conditioning studies. As an example, one of the real difficulties in conditioning the newborn baby is its propensity for falling asleep in the middle of the experiment or, conversely, becoming irascible and uncontrollable. The kinds of discriminations that Papousek has demonstrated probably do occur in newborn infants. It should be further noted that, as with earlier studies, the stimulus properties to which the infants are responding have not been carefully determined.

The auditory capability of young infants has also been observed in a study using the orienting reflex. Bronshtein and Petrova (1952) used a sample of infants ranging in age from approximately 2 hours to 8 days and a second sample of children ranging in age from 1 to 5 months. A pacifier with a rubber tube attached to one end,

FIGURE 5-6   Comparison of three age groups on mean number of trials to criterion on original discrimination problem and subsequent reversal problems.

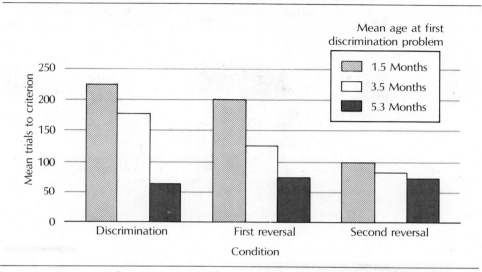

SOURCE: Adapted from Papousek, H. Experimental studies of appetitional behavior in human newborns. In H. W. Stevenson, E. H. Hess, & H. L. Rheingold (Eds.), *Early behavior: Comparative and developmental approaches.* New York: Wiley, 1967.

which in turn was attached to a recorder, provided the technique for recording the patterns of the infant's sucking behavior. Recall that in this procedure if the infant attends to a particular sound, sucking will be interrupted by an orienting reflex. With this apparatus one can record the onset and termination of an auditory stimulus and simultaneously record associated changes in sucking rates. A variety of stimuli were used including organ pipes in the range of 60–70 decibels (dB), a harmonica, and a whistle. In effect, the stimuli were musical tones, all of which were in the 60 to 70 decibel range.

Illustrated in Figure 5-7 is the sucking pattern of one of the very young children (4 hours and 25 minutes of age). The wiggly line indicates sucking by the infant and the straight lines indicate its cessation. During the period when the line is straight, the orienting reflex is assumed to occur. Notice in Figure 5-7 the sections labeled *a* and *b*. In Section *a* a distinct phase appears which involves an orienting reflex, but by the end of 9 trials, with the ninth trial illustrated in Part *b* of the figure, the orienting reflex no longer occurs. This is interpreted as evidence for habituation (recall now that habituation does not mean fatigue or boredom but is assumed to indicate familiarization or an assimilation of the stimulus by the baby). The rather rapid rate of habituation, especially for infants of this age, is probably not typical of newborn babies in general. In Part *c* of the figure the orienting reflex recurs upon presentation of a different tone. The reconstitution of the orienting reflex upon

FIGURE 5-7 *Differentiation of Musical Tones by a Child 4 Hours and 25 Minutes after Birth.* (a) The child is attending to the tones as they are first presented. (b) Nine tone presentations later, the child has habituated to the tones, as evidenced by the continued sucking. (c) The orienting reflex recurs when a different tone is presented.

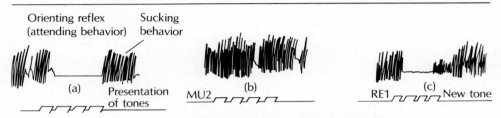

SOURCE: Bronshtein, A. J., & Petrova, E. P. (An investigation of the auditory analysis in neonates and young infants). Translated and reprinted in Y. Brackbill & G. G. Thompson (Eds.), *Behavior in infancy and early childhood: a book of readings.* New York: Free Press, 1967, p. 166.

presentation of a different auditory stimulus indicates that very young infants are probably capable of auditory discrimination. The results of this and other studies (Eisenberg, Coursin, & Rupp, 1966) support the conclusion that auditory discrimination occurs among young infants. There are, however, certain methodological difficulties that permit plausible alternative explanations. Spears and Hohle (1967) point out that the technique used by Bronshtein and Petrova (1952) included a long intertrial delay which frequently added to the recurrence of an orienting reaction to the same stimulus. Following up on their criticism, Spears and Hohle (1967, p. 63) observed:

> Second, following the disappearance of the responses to one stimulus, if a different stimulus was introduced, the orginal reaction, i.e., orienting, an interruption of sucking, could be revived. Both these phenomena could be interpreted in terms of sensory adaptation, of course: recovery of the response following an extended intertrial delay could have been due to recovery from adaptation effects, and the renewed response to a tone containing different frequencies could have resulted from stimulation of fresh unadapted receptors.

The long intertrial interval in the Bronshtein and Petrova study provides the basis for a serious criticism of their work and one which also applies to a study by Bridger (1961). The extended intertrial interval seems to be required in order to accommodate young infants because of their inability to remain attentive for extended periods of time. Interestingly, in the older sample employed by Bronshtein and Petrova, far fewer trials were required to bring about habituation, suggesting a pronounced maturational effect. But the maturational effect appears to influence the degree of the orienting reaction and rate of habituation rather than the capability to discriminate sounds. Thus, we conclude that young infants are capable of auditory discriminations, although, as noted, what features of auditory stimuli generate the discrimination capability is unclear.

Gustatory and Olfactory Sensation

Because the infant is equipped with a large number of taste buds, a baby is probably capable of distinguishing taste, but unequivocal evidence in support of that conclusion is simply unavailable. An infant cannot tell us whether one substance tastes different from another, and current experimental techniques are not sufficiently sensitive to detect these differences. The basic problem is that certain bitter-tasting substances may in fact cause the infant pain, which is different from having the infant distinguish between taste properties. The development of better instrumentation will probably provide the means for discovering taste preferences among infants (Reese & Lipsitt, 1970).

Similar problems have limited the study of olfaction among infants. Engen, Lipsitt, and Kaye (1963), using Engen's habituation procedure, were able to detect differences in responses of infants who were 2 days of age. The procedure involved placing an infant on a **stabilimeter,** a device that is sensitive to the child's movements. In addition, a *pneumograph* was placed around the infant's abdomen to record changes in breathing rate. Each infant was then given one of the odors, and changes in activity and breathing were automatically recorded. The stimuli—acetic acid, phenylethyl alcohol, asafetida, and anise oil—were delivered by placing a cotton swab saturated with the odorant 5 millimeters beneath the nostrils of the infant for 10 seconds. A control stimulus, a simple diluent, was delivered in exactly the same way and followed the presentation of each of the experimental stimuli. Although the results generally indicated that olfactory discrimination took place, the responses of the subjects to each of the 4 odors were different. Acetic acid, for example, was particularly effective, generating approximately 80 to 100 percent reaction. In contrast, phenylethyl alcohol initially only induced responses in the range of 10 to 25 percent of the trials. Consistent with habituation theory, it was found that repeated presentations of the same stimulus caused the responses of the infants to decrease rather dramatically. The investigators attributed these results to a decrease in novelty rather than to sensory adaptation, an interpretation entirely consistent with that offered by Bronshtein and Petrova. It suggests that the response declined because after several presentations the stimulus was no longer unique; if it were simply sensory adaptation, the infants would have been unable to distinguish the odorant from the diluent.

In summarizing the research on the sensory capacities of newborn infants and on the development of sensory capacity, we can plausibly conclude that the newborn infant does in fact have more than rudimentary sensory capabilities. Our technology is probably at a level where we *underestimate* the full range of the neonate's capabilities. It would, however, seem impudent to conclude that the neonate's sensory capacities approximate those of infants 2 or 3 months of age and older. Sensory development appears to be extremely rapid and so deserves some explanation. Sensory development is somewhat more rapid than motor development, but it is also probably true that the development within each area starts from a different base rate, with the motor area initially higher. For that reason we can interpret the rapid development of sensory capacities as a result of external stimulation after birth. Thus, the physiological structures required for sensory capacity are present at birth but require stimulation in order to activate development. When such external stimulation occurs, the rate of development appears to be dramatically accelerated. The reader should understand that this inference is speculative but plausible.

We have seen that from early on in life the sensory capacity for subsequent perceptual and cognitive development is present. It is these sensory capabilities that provide the raw material from which more complex perceptual competencies are derived.

A mobile easily captures the attention of infants and aids in the formation of sensorimotor schemas. (Karyl Gatteño/Taurus Photos)

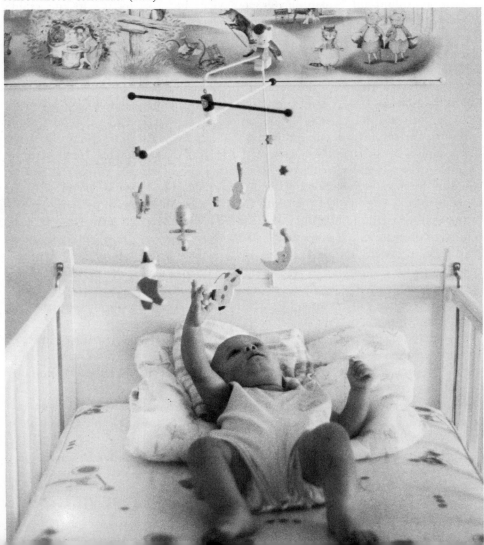

Perceptual Behavior
and Development

We have seen that the sensory input systems of the infant are functional. The material in the remainder of this chapter will focus on how perceptual processes are involved in early cognitive development and on age changes in several perceptual behaviors.

In our previous discussion of sensory capability in newborn infants, we referred briefly to the concept of the orienting reflex and habituation. We would now like to show the relationship between the perceptual properties involved in that system and the cognitive properties. We noted that the child's response to a particular stimulus is shown in the orienting reflex, a behavioral manifestation of a physiological system that responds to any novel stimulus (Sokolov, 1963). As children orient toward the stimulus on successive occasions, it has been postulated that they construct a neurological model of the stimulus. In citing Jeffrey on this issue, we noted that successive representations generate a "schema." The terms "neurological model" and "schema" tend to be used interchangeably although they do not overlap completely in meaning. Nevertheless, both terms are used to designate a mental representation of a stimulus object or event. Once children develop this representation, they no longer exhibit the orienting reflex unless some component of the stimulus complex is modified, thus generating a discrepancy between the original schema and the now altered or novel stimulus. From these primitive schemas emerges the substance of subsequent cognitive development. Thus, the orienting reflex and habituation form a basis for understanding cognitive and intellectual development not only during infancy but possibly over the lifetime of an individual.

Form Perception

Among the better known studies of form perception in young children are those conducted by Fantz (1961, 1963), who used the paired-stimulus method. A looking chamber, illustrated in Figure 5-8, contains space for the infant and the stimulus objects. The infant, depending upon age, is placed in a supine position or in an infant seat from which the pair of stimulus objects can be seen. Through a peephole the experimenter observes the infant's eye fixations and movements and determines the frequency with which each of the stimuli is examined and the duration of each fixation on the stimuli. These basic data yield inferences about the infant's stimulus preferences.

The nature of the stimuli used in one experiment are shown in Figure 5-9, which also shows the preferences of two samples of infants of different age levels; the children in the upper bar are between 2 and 3 months of age, and the sample in the

FIGURE 5-8 *Fantz' Looking Chamber*

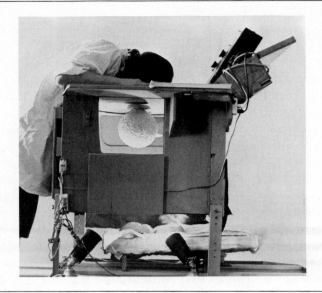

SOURCE: David Linton

lower bar are over 3 months of age. Regardless of age level, fixation time was greatest for the picture of the face and lowest for the plain colored circles. Among the numerous hypotheses suggested to explain this stimulus preference, the complexity explanation (at least in this experiment) seems to be the most tenable.

The attractiveness of complexity for young infants was demonstrated in an experiment by Horowitz, Paden, Bhana, Aitchison, and Self (1972). These investigators used black-and-white checkered boards which ranged from as few as 4 squares to as many as 1,024 (32 x 32). They included intermediate values of 16, 64, 256, and 576. In addition to these stimuli, they also used a gray square. The stimulus materials were shown to 5 infants once a week when the infants were between 3 and 14 weeks of age. A second sample of 5 infants was tested with materials when they were 3, 8, and 14 weeks of age. Finally, 6 infants at the ages of 3, 8, and 14 weeks saw the stimuli once. Although the results demonstrated that the checkerboard square was more interesting than the plain square and also indicated that the 2 × 2 checkered board was of less interest than the other checkerboards, the infants were not primarily captivated by the checkerboard with 1,024 squares. In actuality, the first presentation of the 8 × 8 checkerboard square elicited the longest fixation. The authors concluded that though complexity is a compelling dimension of infants' visual attending behavior, the relationship between visual scanning and stimulus characteristics is not as straightforward as other investigators had suggested. One possible interpretation of the Horwitz et al. data is that infants have optimal levels of

FIGURE 5-9   Importance of pattern rather than color or brightness was illustrated by the response of infants to a face, a piece of printed matter, a bull's-eye, and plain red, white, and yellow disks. Even the youngest infants preferred patterns. Upper bars show the results for infants from two to three months old; lower bars, for infants more than three months old.

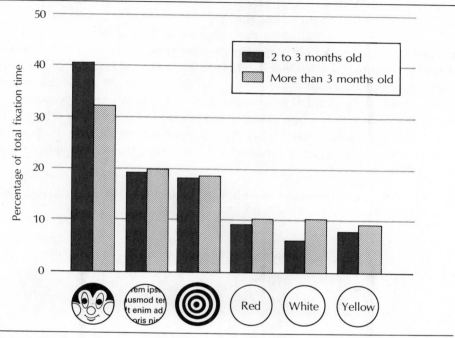

SOURCE: Fantz, R. L. The origin of form perception. *Scientific American*, 1961, *204*, 66–72.

Some research suggests that when infants encounter objects haptically they also form cognitive representations of them. (Sam Sweezy/Stock, Boston)

complexity, and that above or below these levels fixation time will be relatively short. This finding suggests the possibility that a very complex stimulus somewhat overwhelms young infants; they have no available schemas into which they can incorporate the complex stimulus pattern. In general, however, the research evidence lends itself to the conclusion that stimulus complexity is one of the variables influencing fixation time among infants (Jeffrey & Cohen, 1971).

Another stimulus attribute that appears to influence fixation time in infants is *novelty*. The typical study of novelty involves presenting the same stimulus until the subject habituates to it. Once habituation has been established, a variation of the stimulus is presented and it is expected that the subject will once again show the orienting reflex. This work is particularly interesting and important because it seems to indicate more directly how schemas can be elaborated; that is, a schema can be broadened to include variations on the original representation. In an experiment with pictures of human faces, Haff and Bell (1967) used the stimuli shown in Figure

FIGURE 5-10   *The Experimental Stimuli, Rank Orderings of Stimulus Characteristics, and Mean Percentage Fixation Time Scores for 36 Ss*

Stimulus	Degree of faceness	Amount of detail	% Fixation time
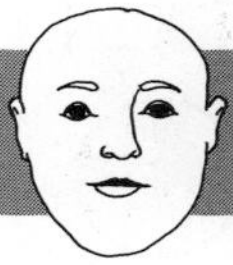	1	3	.33
	2	1	.28
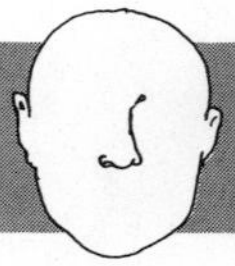	3	4	.19
	4	2	.20

SOURCE: Haaf, R. A., & Bell, R. Q. A facial dimension in visual discrimination by human infants. *Child Development*, 1967, 38, 893–899 (Fig. 1, p. 895).

FIGURE 5-11   *The Four Facial Patterns Displayed to the Infant*

SOURCE: Kagan, J., Henker, B. A., Hen-Tov, A., Levine, J., & Lewis, M. Infants' differential reactions to familiar and distorted faces. *Child Development*, 1966, 37, 519–532 (Fig. 1., pp. 522–523).

5-10. The infants fixated longest on the most realistic face and shortest on the figure with the least amount of detail. These data suggest that with infants below the age of 4 months, familiarity of stimuli is important. This finding is particularly interesting when we notice in Figure 5-10 that the second figure included more detail than the picture of the face. The authors believe their findings indicate that at this age level, faceness is more compelling than complexity. It should also be noted that the facelike stimulus with the least amount of detail had the lowest percentage of fixation time.

A relation between age and novelty is also suggested by the results of a study by Kagan, Hanker, Hen-Tov, Levine, and Lewis (1966), who found that infants over the age of 6 months were increasingly attracted to stimuli moderately discrepant from a more familiar stimulus. Their subjects were 4-month-olds and 8-month-olds. The stimuli used are illustrated in Figure 5-11. The index of the orienting reflex was cardiac deceleration, and habituation was defined as failure to obtain deceleration. Their results indicate that at 4 months the greatest degree of cardiac deceleration was exhibited for the regular face, a result consistent with the findings of Haff and Bell. The 8-month-old subjects, however, exhibited the greatest degree of deceleration in response to the scrambled face. Kagan et al. (1966, p. 532) interpret their results as follows:

> This is intuitively reasonable, for cognitive development is characterized by the continual creation of schema for new patterns. A stimulus that violates an existing schema at one time will be a familiar and easily assimilated pattern days, weeks, or months later. It appears that a wise combination of fixation patterns, cardiac deceleration, and smiling may allow one to explore the degree of articulation of varied schema in the infant and facilitate differentiation among stimuli that represent familiar, emergent, and novel schema.

This interpretation is consistent with that of Horowitz et al.; the infants failed to fixate on the most complex checkerboard but picked an intermediate level of complexity somewhere between the most and least complex. Both the interpretations of Horowitz and her colleages and that of Kagan and his associates are entirely consistent with the patterns of behavior observed in a number of behavioral domains. As children become familiar with a stimulus, they spend considerable time examining and learning about it. Only after children have completely incorporated the stimulus into existing schemas do they begin to ignore it or examine variations on it. Thus, the two features of form perception examined are so far entirely consistent with the general features of cognitive development. These results also conform to Hunt's (1961) hypothesis of the "match," according to which an optimal degree of discrepancy exists between the organism's schema—or familiarity with the stimulus object—and the organism's ability to cope with that discrepancy. Hunt argues further that too great a discrepancy overwhelms or frightens the child, who then avoids that stimulus. If, however, the stimulus matches some already existing schema, then the organism displays few, if any, fixations or other indications of interest. Hunt suggests that only when the optimal discrepancy occurs, does the organism get any pleasure from its *self-generated* attempts to incorporate the discrepancy into an already existing schema. Therefore, we can maintain curiosity in children by providing many opportunities for incorporating discrepancies into already existing schemas.

Despite methodological differences and difficulties, the results of the preceding experiments and a host of others are in general agreement that infants are attracted to novel stimuli. But why do children find the complexity or novelty of the stimuli compelling? The interpretation tends to rely on concepts like faceness, that is, concepts employed by adults. Some other, less apparent feature (less apparent at least to adults) may form the actual basis for the stimulus preference. For example, Salapatek and Kessen (1966) found that young infants were attracted to a triangle and seemed to be forming a triangle schema. The investigators measured the infants' visual fixations with a sophisticated device for recording eye movements. This sample of infants did not examine the entire triangle but fixated primarily on the angles, paying less attention to the perimeter and interior.

Additional research indicates that, with maturity, eye movements shift away from fixation on a single feature of a stimulus to a more integrated pattern of scanning. In a more elaborate study, Hershenson, Kessen, and Mussinger (1967) manipulated the following properties of stimuli: relative brightness, relative complexity, relative degree of organization, and patterning to show preference data for 20 newborn infants. Along the brightness dimension, the stimulus with medium intensity was more often fixated than those at the other two levels of brightness. As regards the degree of faceness, the data indicated no differences in preference among the stimuli for the three levels of faceness. The data on the dimension of relative complexity indicate that the least complex stimulus was preferred most,

Looking in the mirror helps an infant form a concept of self. (George Zimbel/ Monkmeyer).

the medium next, and the most complex the least. This finding is generally consistent with previous data for children under 4 months of age, like those in this study, but not older children. Finally, the infants preferred the medium level of complexity, but the only significant difference was between the middle value and the lowest value. The authors argue that a better understanding of the form perception of infants will require more sophisticated studies using a multidimensional approach. Certainly the results of the latter two experiments suggest that, although the orienting reflex and habituation to stimuli are verified events, the stimulus attributes responsible for these fixations have yet to be identified with certainty.

Depth Perception

Earlier in this chapter we briefly described the nativist and empiricist approaches to perception. The work on **depth perception** received much of its orginal impetus from this controversy, with research dating back to the late 1800s. Walk (1966) reviews much of this early work, which was conducted with animals, and concludes that, in general, the preponderance of evidence indicates that animals have an innate capacity to discriminate depth. Walk's conclusion is guarded; he does not assert that all animals can perceive depth immediately after birth. Furthermore he indicates animals reared too long in the dark will lose their capacity to discriminate depth visually. Finally, in some species (kittens and rabbits) the animal must interact with the environment before it can perceive depth.

Eleanor J. Gibson of Cornell University conducted a series of experiments on depth perception using human infants. The problem in conducting such research, of course, is that infants cannot verbalize their perceptions. Gibson and Walk (1960) developed an apparatus called the **visual cliff,** which is illustrated in Figure 5-12. The apparatus consists basically of a large glass-topped table, 6 feet by 8 feet and 40 inches high. An 8-inch-high border surrounds the edges of the top of the table to prevent the child from falling off. The glass extends across the length of the table top, but the apparatus is designed to give the impression of a shallow side and a deep side. The glass prevents the child from falling if it elects to go over the deep part, but it also allows him to see the deep side and the shallow side. The baby is placed on the table and its mother coaxes her child to cross over to the deep side. Some 43 percent of the babies under 10 months of age cross to the deep side. Of those babies 300 days of age or more, only 22 percent cross over to the mother at the deep side. Walk (1966, p. 101) draws the following conclusion from his extensive work conducted with Gibson:

> The human infant discriminates depth well. From a theoretical "innate-learned" point of view, he discriminates depth as soon as he can be tested. But his visual mechanisms are still maturing. He discriminates depth better when there is a definite pattern under both the deep and shallow sides than when either one is in any way indefinite, and as long as the depth or distance is far enough. This lack of discrimination is reflected in the fact that he can be coaxed across the deep side under certain conditions, but not under others. While all Ss respond by crawling more often across the deep side in the presence of the inadequate patterns of stimulation, it is the infants less than 300 days of age that are particularly affected.

Walk goes on to argue that the "insouciant" (nonchalant) behavior of the young infant is due to a lack of development in its depth discrimination. When depth is

FIGURE 5-12   *The Visual Cliff*

SOURCE: Gibson, E. J., & Walk, R. R. The "visual cliff." *Scientific American*, 1960, *202*, 65.

clearly perceptible, however, even the young infants cannot be coaxed to the deep side. As infants mature and develop more discriminations, they are able to differentiate the depth cues more readily and thus exhibit greater reluctance to cross to the deep side.

One of the difficulties with the conclusions drawn by Gibson and Walk is that the visual cliff requires that infants are capable of horizontal locomotion. By the time they can locomote, children must have interacted extensively with the environment so that the depth perception they exhibit on the visual cliff could have been learned. Campos, Langer, and Krowitz (1970) report a technique for assessing an awareness of depth which avoids this problem. It involves heart-rate response and was used with two samples of subjects; the median age of one group was 106 days and that of the second group 55 days. After obtaining base rates of heartbeat, the experimenters placed the infants on their stomachs with their eyes aimed down toward either the deep or the shallow surface of a visual cliff. The infants had comparatively slow cardiac responses on the shallow side of the cliff but a large deceleration on the deep side (recall that deceleration is usually taken as an index of the orienting reflex). This result is in fact somewhat surprising; from a common sense point of view, we would expect the infants to show not cardiac deceleration but acceleration, since the latter is ordinarily associated with fear and certainly the children should have feared falling on the deep side of the cliff. The authors recognize this apparent inconsistency and conclude that their results are in fact ambiguous. It is clear that depth perception does exist rather early, although it is less clear precisely what stimulus parameters govern this perception. Campos, Langer, and Krowitz (1970, p. 197) make the further interesting and sensible observation:

> The human infant does not appear to give evidence of much distress at loss of optical support on the deep side at the ages tested. This is in marked contrast to written and filmed observations of animals and studies of older infants in our laboratory. This suggests that the human infant can discriminate a stimulus and then undergoes a developmental process which allows that stimulus to elicit aversive responses.

Size and Shape Constancy

The most basic question about **size constancy** is, How are we able to judge accurately the size of an object despite changes in its distance from us? No matter what the distance of a familiar object, we perceive that object as having the same size. As is true of each of the behaviors we have discussed earlier, the basic question is whether or not size constancy requires extensive training, as the empiricist view would suggest, or whether size constancy is innate. One of the definitive studies on this question was conducted by T. G. R. Bower (1965, 1966) (see Figure 5-13). Bower reinforced a group of babies, ranging in age from 6 to 8 weeks, to turn their heads toward a 30-centimeter cube. This cube was approximately 1 meter from the eyes of the infants who had had no previous experience with the cube. To reinforce the infant's head-turning response, the experimenter popped up and said "Peek-a-boo"—a particularly effective reinforcer with infants this age. To determine if the infants gave evidence of size constancy, Bower systematically varied the size and distance of the cube. The manipulation involved the original 30-centimeter cube and another cube 3 times larger. The two cubes were positioned at 1 and 3 meters, respectively, from the infants so that the retinal image projects by the larger cube had the same size as that produced by the original stimulus. If the infants did not have size constancy, their head-turning response should have occurred as frequently to the one stimulus as to the other. In fact the infants responded rather infrequently to the large stimulus at the 3-meter distance, indicating that the infants were able to distinguish size and distance.

Shape constancy requires that an object is perceived as keeping the same form regardless of its orientation in space. Bower (1966) conducted an experiment using much the same method as in the study of size constancy. Specifically, 8 infants between 50 and 60 days old were trained to make a head-turning response of 45 degrees to a rectangular stimulus which stood on its long edge, turned 45 degrees back away from the infant. Once again, the experimenter came up in front of the infant and said "Peek-a-boo" as a reinforcer. After the response was conditioned

FIGURE 5-13   Size constancy was investigated with cubes of different sizes placed at different distances from the infants. The conditioned stimulus was 30 centimeters on a side and 1 meter away, test stimuli 30 or 90 centimeters on a side and 1 or 3 meters away. The chart shows how test stimuli were related to the conditioned stimulus in various respects.

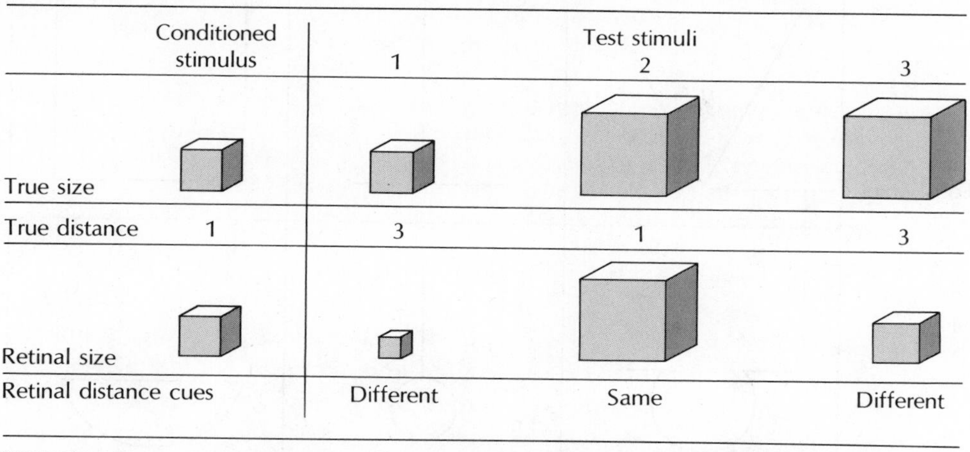

	Conditioned stimulus	Test stimuli 1	2	3
True size				
True distance	1	3	1	3
Retinal size				
Retinal distance cues		Different	Same	Different

SOURCE: Bower, T. G. R. The visual world of infants. *Scientific American*, 1966, 215, 80–92.

there were 4 test trials: the rectangle in its original 45-degree orientation, the rectangle in the frontal-parallel plane, a trapezoid in the frontal plane arranged so that its retinal projection equaled that of the slanted rectangle, and a trapezoid slanted at an angle of 45 degrees. The number of conditioned responses to the four test stimuli were ordered in the same way as described, with a very large difference occurring between the number of responses to the original stimulus (condition 1) and the trapezoid at the 45-degree angle (the fourth condition). The author viewed these results as indicating: "It is obvious that these infants have not learned to respond to a projective or retinal shape but to an objective shape, which could be recognized in a new orientation; to this extent they showed shape constancy" (Bower, 1966, p. 833).

Stimulus Orientation

Stimulus orientation concerns the degree to which an object can be rotated on its horizontal and vertical axis and still be recognized as the same object. Techniques for testing stimulus orientation are very similar to those in Bower's study of shape constancy. Whereas Bower was interested in the ability of infants to identify the same object, our interest is on the effects of rotations of stimulus objects on children's recognition of a standard object in an array of other objects.

It may be useful to describe an experiment in which Ghent-Braine (1965) examined the effects of stimulus orientation. Using a sample of 3-year-olds and

FIGURE 5-14 Figures commonly seen upside down by young children. Note that in each case the focal point is at the bottom of the figure.

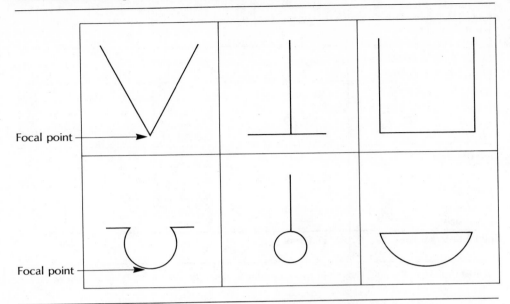

Focal point

Focal point

SOURCE: Ghent-Braine, L. Age changes in the mode of perceiving geometric forms. *Psychonomic Science*, 1965, 2 (Fig. 1, p. 155).

5-year-olds, she placed the stimuli shown in Figure 5-14 in different orientations; actually they were reversed. The keyholelike stimulus served as the standard, and the children were instructed to examine it carefully because they would later have to match it with one among other stimuli. In one display, the stimulus was presented with the round portion at the top, and in the other version with the round portion at the bottom. The triangle was also presented with the apex at the top in one condition, and the apex at the bottom in a second condition. The investigator reasoned that the round portion of the keyhole and the apex of the triangle were the focal stimuli for the preschool children and thus highly compelling. This hypothesis had an empirical basis in the matching-to-sample experiment of Salapatek and Kessen, which showed that young children tended to fixate most on the corners of the triangle. As you will note from the figure, each stimulus also has certain distinctive features that children actually use to pick out the standard from the other stimuli. Thus the investigator presented the stimuli in the upright position with the distinctive features at the bottom, and in an inverted position so that the distinctive features were on top. When the focal point was at the top, the experimenter hypothesized that the children would begin scanning at the focal point (at the top) and work their way down, finally examining the distinctive features. Conversely, with the focal point at the bottom (the inverted position), they would start at the focal point and *also* scan downward, thus missing the distinctive features. Ghent-Braine (1965) hypothesized that the natural trend of scanning is from top to bottom; thus, the orientation of the stimulus and the scanning strategy of the young children should lead to a deficient performance on the matching-to-sample task. Regardless of the orientation of the stimuli, the older children were expected to start at the top and systematically examine the stimuli in a downward direction. In this way they would always be certain to observe the distinctive stimuli. As it turned out, the success of the younger children varied with the orientation of the standard stimulus. When the focal point of the standard stimulus was at the top, the young children performed quite well, but when the focal point was at the bottom they performed poorly. The orientation of the stimulus did not influence the older children.

Other studies by Ghent-Braine gave similar results but raised certain questions about the method. These experiments used a tachistoscope, which presents stimuli at very brief exposures. Thus, the subjects had to identify the distinctive features very rapidly. It has been suggested that the speed of the tachistoscopic presentation was too great to allow for any eye movements (Pick & Pick, 1970). An experiment by Meyer and Dwyer (1974) supports this criticism. These investigators produced Ghent-Braine's stimuli and projected them on an opaque screen. The subjects were permitted to examine the stimuli for 8 seconds; they were told to examine the standard stimulus with care because they would have to pick it out later on. Each subject examined each stimulus 4 times; twice in the upright position and twice in the inverted position, for a total of 8 presentations. The aim of this study was to determine the degree to which children, when given more than sufficient time to examine a stimulus, employed different scanning strategies; eye movements were recorded. The subjects were a group of young children with mean age 3 years 7 months and a group of older children with mean age 4 years 10 months.

The primary finding of the study was that, no matter where the focal point was located, subjects, regardless of age, scanned both up and down in roughly the same proportion. It should be noted, however, that had these investigators employed the matching-to-sample task, their results would have been similar to those reported by Ghent-Braine. Specifically, it was found that the older children attended to—fixated more on—the distinctive features than the younger children. Thus, in the transfer task they would have probably performed better because they were more aware of these distinctive features.

One of the most influential studies on shape and orientation discrimination, Gibson, Gibson, Pick, and Osser (1962), developed a number of prototype letterlike forms along with a set of transformations of these forms that they believed to be either critical or not critical for the discrimination of English letters. The resulting array of stimuli are presented in Figure 5-15. The brief statements at the top of each column are expanded in order to make the transformation clearer.

These stimulus materials were used in a matching-to-sample procedure with

FIGURE 5-15 *The Standard Forms and Their Transformations*

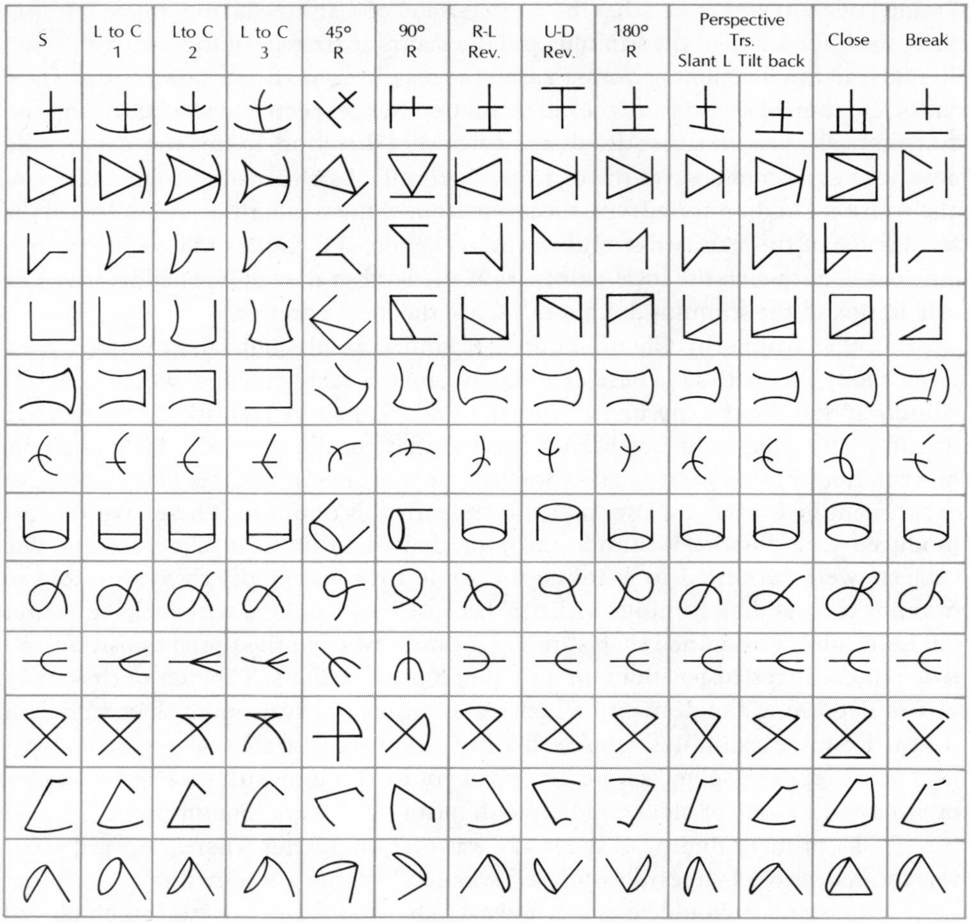

SOURCE: Gibson, E. J., Gibson, J. J., Pick, A. D., & Osser, H. A. A developmental study of the discrimination of letter-like forms. *Journal of Comparative and Physiological Psychology*, 1962, 55, 897–906 (Fig. 1, p. 898).

4- to 8-year-old children. Each prototype was placed at the top of a display rack containing 4 rows of 13 forms, of which 1 included the prototype. The child's task was to search the stimuli and find the form that was identical to the standard. The results of the experiment are summarized by the data shown in Figure 5-16. The data revealed a trend toward a decreasing number of errors, as might be expected, and that some of the transformations proved more difficult than others. The investigators interpreted the results as indicating that when children begin to read, at approximately age 6, they learn to detect the critical features of stimuli. This general interpretation is consistent with Gibson's (1969) view that improved performance on perceptual-discrimination tasks results from children's activities in which they encounter and learn to identify distinctive features of the environment. One of the findings in this study that has not been generally substantiated is that the level of errors for up-down mirror images was similar to the frequency of errors for left-right mirror images. In general, other investigators have found the right-left mirror-image transformation more difficult. Students familiar with the reading difficulties encountered by first-grade children will recognize that the left-right discrimination is often one that children find quite difficult for the letters *d* and *b* or *q* and *p*. This was reported some time ago by Davidson (1935), who found that children were able to make vertical discrimination of letters (*d* versus *q*; *b* versus *p*) approximately 2 years

FIGURE 5-16 *Developmental Error Curves for Four Types of Transformation*

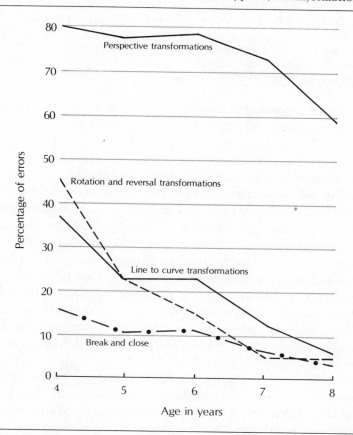

SOURCE: See Figure 5-15.

earlier than they were able to make horizontal discriminations. Jeffrey (1958) demonstrated that the difficulty with the left-right discrimination could be overcome by making the discriminative stimuli more distinctive. Several studies since Jeffrey's have supported the general finding that children can develop a left-right discrimination earlier than 7 years of age, but only through special procedures.

It may be quite instructive to understand why children have difficulty with the right-left discrimination as opposed to the up-down discrimination. Pick and Pick (1970, p. 81) have described the issue unusually well:

> Both transformations (right-left, up-down) are usually presented in horizontal alignment and this may make comparison of the left-right mirror images more difficult. Sekuler and Rosenblith (1964) and Huttenlocher (1967) have tested such a hypothesis. Sekuler and Rosenblith found a marked interaction, as predicted, in the situation involving same-different judgments. There were very few confusions of up-down mirror images when they were horizontally aligned, but a large number when they were vertically aligned. On the other hand there were very few diffusions of right-left mirror images when they were vertically aligned and a large number when they were horizontally aligned. Huttenlocher found similar results in a discrimination learning situation. Learning to discriminate between right-left mirror images was relatively more difficult when they were horizontally aligned than when they were vertically aligned. The converse was true with the up-down mirror images although the magnitude of the difference was rather small.

This interpretation suggests that the difficulties encountered are a consequence of the opposing representational demands that occur when the mirror image and its alignment are different rather than when they are the same. This interpretation seems to make considerable sense and indicates an aspect of perceptual experience that is quite difficult and yet quite necessary in reading.

The material we have presented in this section has been extensive and in some respects fairly difficult. Placing this material in some general developmental perspective, we think that two major themes emerge. First, the data indicate that very early in life children have formed or already possess certain essential perceptual abilities, including size constancy and depth perception. In addition, the evidence seems clear that certain built-in mechanisms are functioning effectively within days after birth, and with these mechanisms the baby can begin to learn the critical features that form its environment. Thus, from this perspective, as was the case for sensory capacity, the infant is capable of an extensive number of basic perceptual competencies which it makes use of to form a broader, comprehensive, and mature knowledge of the world.

The second theme that emerges is that neither the empiricist nor the nativist view of perception alone is entirely satisfactory in explaining the perceptual abilities of the infant. Some behaviors are very much a part of the behavioral repertoire of the neonate, whereas other behaviors would appear to require some extensive experience with the environment. It seems clear to us that, in conjunction with the data

Before being able to discriminate between stimuli, children must identify which features are distinctive. (Jean-Claude Lejeune)

described in Chapter 3 on stimulus deprivation, the normal development of *any* perceptual process requires interaction with the environment. Thus, even if it could be demonstrated that size constancy, for example, were present from the moment of birth, it would still be true that mature size constancy would require experience with the environment and that visual sensory deprivation would deprive the child of any normal functioning in this area.

The conclusions above are consistent with the theoretical views of Eleanor J. Gibson (1969, 1970), who has extensively studied perceptual development. According to Gibson, information about the environment comes directly from the senses, so that the identification of objects and events involves the perceptual detection of distinctive features. Perceptual acquaintance with objects and events does not require cognitive interpretation; the necessary stimuli and distinctive features required to construct mental models are present in the stimuli themselves. Development involves learning to detect stimulus features that are initially less immediately apparent. Unlike habituation theory, **detection theory** views development as leading to an ever-increasing ability to discriminate objects and events and to learn what features are invariant.

One interesting feature of Gibson's theory is that she views perception as an adaptive process in the same way as walking. Thus, both nativism and empiricism are essential to development. Some perceptual abilities (depth perception, for example) are available to the baby at or shortly after birth and serve to protect the baby from potential physical harm. Learning is required in order for the organism to detect more critical features and establish complexes of features. Learning for Gibson, however, is not of the S-R type, but rather results from the child's developing ability to detect more features. "But fine-grain differentiation of multi-dimensional complex sets of objects is high in the evolutionary scheme and in development, a process where adaptation is achieved only through education" (Gibson, 1970, p. 106). Her reference to education means that children must learn which features of a stimulus or event are relevant and which are not.

It should be noted that Bower's (1966) work has led him to a view of perception somewhat like Gibson's. His data, as we have seen, show that babies are perceptually competent—perhaps as competent in obtaining information from the environment as adults. Bower believed that babies do not have the information-processing capacity to handle the stimulus input. Thus, relationships among stimuli and events become manifest as the cognitive capacity of the child increases.

Perceptual Integration

We have already noted that as motoric competency increases, concomitant changes are occurring in the neurological structure of the organism. Naturally these neurological changes have no simple relation to motoric behavior but must encompass other aspects of development as well. The establishment of neurological networks tends to lead to the integration of behavior within domains (motor action patterns, for example) but also among domains (motoric action patterns, perceptual action patterns, and cognitive action patterns). In this section we will examine one system of integration within a domain (perceptual) and a set of behavioral patterns that would seem to emerge as a consequence of increased motoric competency, and finally, we shall describe the integration of motor and perceptual action patterns.

Intersensory Development

Human beings receive information about the environment through many sensory systems. Thus, an adult uses vision, audition, or touch to distinguish features in the environment. The question arises as to the degree to which sensory input to one system is translated into usable information in any one or all of the other systems. This topic is sometimes referred to as **cross-modal transfer** or **intersensory development.**

The major contributions in this area have come from the work of Birch and

Awareness of the stimulus properties of forms involves many senses. Practice with form boards helps develop form concepts. (Michael Serino/The Picture Cube)

various associates (Birch & Bitterman, 1951; Birch & Lefford, 1963; Birch & Lefford, 1967). To give the reader some sense of the general method in this area, we will describe one of these experiments in more detail than usual. In a study reported by Birch and Lefford (1963), visual, haptic, and kinesthetic modalities were examined for equivalency in the recognition of geometric forms. The term "haptic" refers to an active manual exploration of a stimulus object. Kinesthesia refers to the sensory inputs that occur in movement, in this case, arm movements. The procedure involved a series of paired comparisons: a form in one sensory system (the standard) is compared with forms presented in another sensory system. Thus, for example, the experimenter presents a visual stimulus to subjects and then asks them to match the

FIGURE 5-17   *Geometric Forms Used in All Phases of the Study*

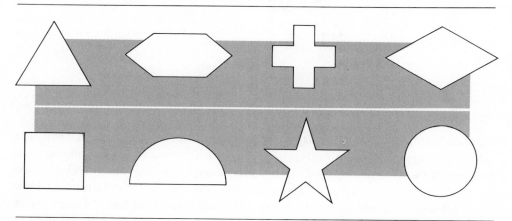

SOURCE: Birch, H. G., & Lefford, A. Intersensory development. *Monographs of the Society for Research in Child Development*, 1963, 28 (5, Serial No. 89), Figure 1, p. 6.

FIGURE 5-18   *The Relation of Empirical to Theoretical Developmental Curves for Intersensory Equivalence*

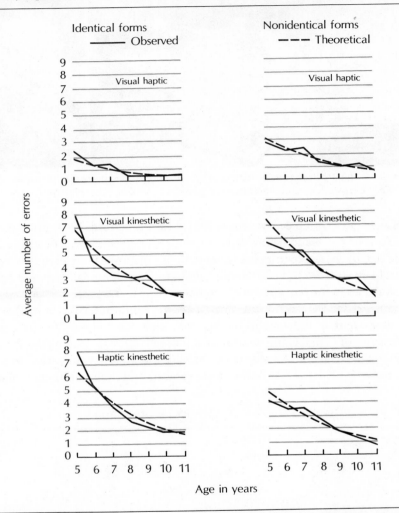

SOURCE: Birch, H. G., & Lefford, A. Intersensory development. *Monographs of the Society for Research in Child Development*, 1963, 28 (5, Serial No. 89), Figure 1, p. 6.

standard stimulus through the haptic sensory system or the kinesthetic systems. The geometric forms shown in Figure 5-17 were usually familiar to the subjects. The subjects in the study were 73 boys and 72 girls ranging in age from 5 through 11 years.

The results of the 3 pairings of sensory systems are shown in Figure 5-18. Note that the subjects made the fewest errors when the visual and haptic systems were paired, regardless of whether the comparison was between indentical forms or nonidentical forms. The poorest performance occurred with the sensory comparisons that involved kinesthesia. The data also indicate that girls performed better on this task than boys. Also noteworthy is the dramatic improvement in performance with age. The data also suggest that the most rapid development of visual-haptic equivalence occurs before 5 years of age.

In considering the results of this experiment, Birch and Lefford (1963, p. 40) observe:

> The slopes for the curves reflecting the development of visual-haptic and visual-kinesthetic equivalence indicate that the sixth through the eight years of life represent a period of rapid change in functional organization and capacity. During this period information derived from the external environment by a teloreceptor such as vision and a proximo-receptor complex represented by haptic stimulation achieve integration with and equivalence for inter-receptive information deriving from limb movement. The establishment of such interrelations contributes to behavioral organization the possibility of increased control of action by visual perception.

This interpretation is particularly interesting in view of the data on cognitive development presented in Chapter 6 showing dramatic changes in the cognitive organization of children in the same age period—6 to 8 years.

The concept of haptic input and its relation to other behaviors will become clearer if we examine some materials developed by Zaporozhets (1965), a Russian psychologist who, along with his colleagues, has made substantial contributions to our understanding of perceptual and motor development. The particular theoretical view that generated these materials is called the **motor copy theory,** which is primarily concerned with the relationship between visual, haptic, and kinesthetic sensory systems. According to this view, when children manually explore objects, they are also forming a visual image of that object. Thus, one can see a possible explanation for the Birch and Lefford data. The first pair of figures to examine are in Figure 5-19, which shows a picture of a child between 3 and 4.5 years of age, and in the lower half of the picture a child between 6 and 7.5 years of age. The area of the pictures to examine carefully is the child's hand on the stimulus object. Zaporozhets describes the younger child's performance as primitive because the exploratory behavior can not differentiate the object from any other object. Notice that the child's hand is grasped around the whole object, whereas in the second picture the child seems to be tracing the outline of the object and also examining it for other features, such as its solidity. The younger child, according to Zaporozhets, plays with the object and becomes incidentally acquainted with its characteristics. When the children are later asked to identify the object, the younger children make significantly more errors. Gibson would argue that the child does not yet know how to detect the critical features.

The second set of figures (Figure 5-20) shows children manipulating an irregularly shaped object. The youngster in the upper figure seems to have his palms on the edge of the figure and appears to be pushing it with his fingers. The author

FIGURE 5-19

SOURCE: Peter Vandermark, after Zaporozhets, A. V. The development of perception in the preschool child. In P. Mussen (Ed.), European research in cognitive development. *Monographs of the Society for Research in Child Development*, 1965, 30 (2, Serial No. 100).

FIGURE 5-20

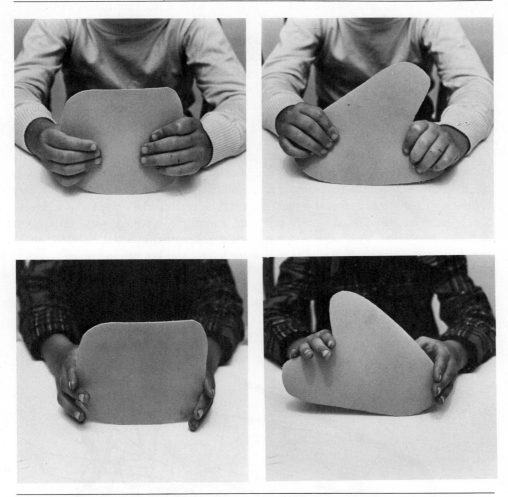

SOURCE: See Figure 5-19.

reports that throughout the entire period of filming the palm of the hand never moved. This finding seems to indicate that if it is important, which it is, to explore the perimeter of the object, this 3-year-old simply did not do it. The child in the lower figure is 6 years old and has placed his fingers along the perimeter of the object and throughout the filming systematically traced the whole outline of the figure with the fingertips. Figure 5-20 showed how an older and a younger child haptically manipulate a stimulus object. Birch and Lefford suggested the possibility of a relationship between haptic behavior and visual behavior, an observation supported by

Zaporozhets's evidence. In Figures 5-21 and 5-22 we see the eye-movement patterns, scanning strategies of children 6- to 7-years old. Notice the fascinating correspondence between the visual and the haptic movements of the children. The younger children tend to fixate mostly on the inside of the form, whereas the older children systematically fixate around the perimeter. When these children were later asked to pick out the figure from a set of other irregular figures, it should come as no surprise that the younger children could not. Thus it appears that the visual-haptic correspondence reported by Birch and Lefford is supported; furthermore, Zaporozhets's research indicates that the perceptual strategies (processes) of younger and older children are sharply different.

A final observation on this research. For some reason Birch inferred that the tactual manipulation of objects forms the basis for subjects' visual discrimination. In other words, he assumed that tactual manipulations are responsible for the primary formation of schemas and that visual input is then used to elaborate these schemas. Since, however, the visual system contains a motor component—eye-movement patterns associated with stimulus training—a perceptually based motor copy is possible for visually based forms as well as for haptic and kinesthetic ones.

FIGURE 5-21

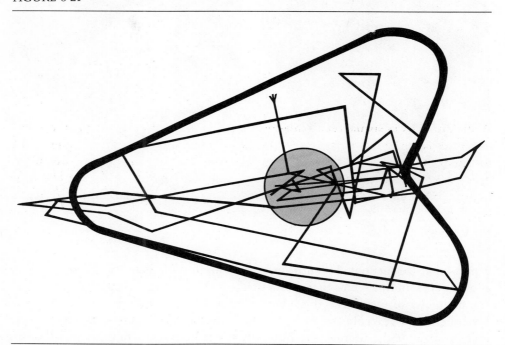

SOURCE: Zaporozhets, A. V. The development of perception in the preschool child. In P. Mussen (Ed.), European research in cognitive development. *Monographs of the Society for Research in Child Development*, 1965, *30* (2, Serial No. 100).

FIGURE 5-22

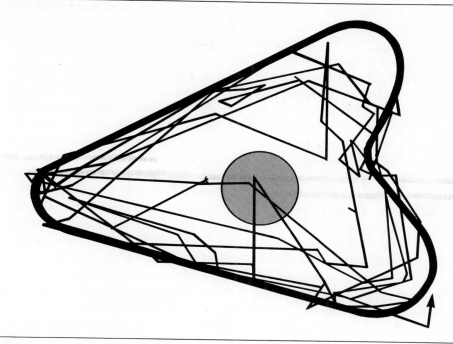

SOURCE: See Figure 5-21.

Spatial Representation

While the study of **spatial representation** has received less attention than other areas of perceptual development, this aspect of perception is important because it provides the ability to locomote from one area to another and to plan those moves intelligently. Spatial representation includes the child's ability to understand the relationship between his own body and that of other objects in space, particularly as the body changes position in that space. Although this particular material is interesting, we will concentrate on the development of children's ability to represent spatial relationships in the form of mapping behaviors.

By way of introducing the general topic, one of the authors observed his daughter, along with a number of other fourth-grade children, drawing a map of her school. The children were located in their classroom, had an enormous piece of paper, and were attempting desperately to make a reasonable schematic representation of the layout of the school—the school has the form of the letter H. To the chagrin of the teachers and parents, the final product was poor: the location of the gymnasium was approximately half in the principal's office and half in a courtyard. The cafeteria was located roughly in her classroom and the entrance to the school had been rotated 180 degrees. After leaving the school the somewhat chagrined father went to his office, shut the door, and sat down with a sheet of paper to see if in fact this was such a difficult task—he had only been in the school on three previous occasions. Not noted for his artistic ability, the father was able to make a reasonable and usable map of the school. Why the difference?

The material for this discussion is largely adapted from a recent paper by Siegel and White (1975), who have provided an historical overview of the concepts explaining spatial representations, as well as a very complete review of the research literature. One of the major features that emerges from their review is that the development and utilization of spatial representation is closely related to the degree of locomotion of the individual in the environment. As children become more mobile and freer to explore their environments, their exploration helps them to form spatial representations of their world. One might surmise, however, that the fourth-grade girl and her peers either do not locomote very much (quite the contrary) or that this explanation is simply not appropriate. Actually, Siegel and White make clear that the kinds of information that children obtain from exploring their environments will differ from those obtained with adults. Adults notice and remember landmarks. Furthermore, different landmarks are noticed. Siegel and White make the point that in their maps of their neighborhood young children tend to draw actual objects, whereas older children represent the same objects much more symbolically. In other words, the maps of older children are more *cognitively organized*. The evidence further seems to suggest that older children employ a cognitive transformation of visual input which helps their visual recognition; that is, the older child makes use of a sophisticated coding system that he employs spontaneously and that activates available schemas with fewer stimulus cues than young children require. Research tending to support that generalization was reported by Smothergill (1973) and in a series of studies by Keogh (1969, 1971; Keogh & Keogh, 1968).

A second basic assumption about the development of spatial representation, as viewed by Siegel and White (1975, p. 39) is, "Once landmarks are established, the child's acts are registered and assessed with reference to them." These landmarks, as we have hinted, serve as guides and organizers for the development of maps. It is from these cognitive cues that the child can either perform a series of actions or can do them mentally. The third assumption is that, given that the child becomes aware of landmarks, has associated them with a series of action sequences, and has cognitively developed a route system, he can then develop "minimaps." Eventually, through increased commerce with the environment and through continued development of representational competency, the child becomes capable of locating elements in space and can develop highly interconnected and hierarchically organized route maps. Siegel and White (1975, p. 36) state the major features of the developmental pattern as follows:

The development of the sequence of spatial representations in children conforms to the "Main Sequence" identified in the construction of spatial representation in adults. Landmarks are first noticed and remembered. The child acts in the context of these landmarks, and given landmarks and action sequences, route formation is accomplished. Landmarks and routes are formed into clusters, but until an objective frame of reference is developed, these clusters remain uncoordinated with each other. Survey representations appear as a system of routes arriving from and embedded in an objective frame of reference.

Perceptual-Motor Behavior

One of the most interesting features of children's perceptual development is their difficulty in copying forms. The typical experimental problem involves copying geometric forms, such as a circle, triangle, square, or diamond—the kind of problem discussed in Chapter 3. The order in which those forms are listed roughly approx-

The Draw-A-Man test measures children's ability to represent the human body. Scores on this test and IQ tests correlate. (Peter Vandermark)

imates.the order of difficulty children encounter in copying these forms. As we have already seen, children 2 years of age or even younger are able to discriminate among these forms and can even label these forms with fair accuracy. Despite these abilities, young children cannot copy the forms. A popular explanation for this inability is that they possess poor muscular development or little artistic ability. Depending upon what one means by artistic ability, this may be a partially correct explanation, but certainly the inability to copy the forms does not result from a lack of motor control. It is often argued, for example, when a child is asked to draw a man (a still widely used form of an intelligence test) that inadequate drawings are the result of poor artistic ability. Actually, a poorly constructed picture of a person indicates something much more important: it reveals the child's level of cognitive representation of the human form. An explanation as to why the sequence of events described occurs cannot be stated with any certainty, but we shall explore the concepts we suspect underlie the issue.

Maccoby and Bee (1965) have suggested that to copy a figure a child must attend to and incorporate more attributes of the model figure than is required to distinguish the model figure from other figures. Thus, for example, children can draw circles considerably earlier than they can draw diamonds. The Maccoby and Bee position is consistent with this developmental difference: drawing a circle requires the ability to reproduce the general form and connect the 2 points. Copying of a diamond, on the other hand, requires attending to 4 corners, which one does with a square, but in a diamond the corners are located at 45-degree angles in space. Thus, in addition to the 4 angles in a diamond, there is also the problem of representing the diamond in space. These are all cues that must be attended to and assimilated before the copying process can be successful.

This interpretation is certainly consistent with the data but probably does not account for certain other data that were not available at the time this explanation was given. In a book by Olson (1970), concerned with children's acquisition of the ability to copy or construct a diagonal, or what he called the acquisition of diagonality, the author agreed that while most adults have little difficulty in drawing a diagonal, for children the task requires considerable time and seems inherently difficult. In analyzing the Maccoby and Bee position, Olson makes a distinction between "perceptual space" and "representational space." Perceptual space involves the child's ability to recognize a square as distinct from a triangle, whereas **representational space** involves the question of whether the child knows what a square consists of. In making his case, Olson (1970, p. 74) cites Piaget and Inhelder (1956): "The fact that at least two year's work is required in order to pass from copying the square to copying the rhombus . . . shows pretty clearly that to construct a Euclidean shape, something more than a correct visual impression is required." Thus, a drawing is really an index of how a child represents space, and this attribute, as suggested in the discussion by Siegel and White, probably is responsible for the difficulty that children experience in handling many of the geometric forms they were asked to copy. It should be noted that Olson's diagonal and the drawing of a diamond are quite difficult, and, in fact, a diamond can be viewed as a series of 4 diagonals. Thus, diagonality must have some feature that makes it so difficult to draw.

In concluding this chapter, we might return to the mechanistic versus organismic views to assess how they relate to perceptual development. The evidence presented supports the contention that the organism is preprogrammed to be an active seeker of environmental stimulation. Many perceptual abilities are apparent at or shortly after birth, while others require more time and experience to attain maturation. Unlike older theories, the organismic view has substantially changed how developmental psychologists conceptualize and study perception. As Bower (1966) has noted, the early empiricist theories suggested that the perceptual world of infants is a frightening place where nothing remains constant and objects are never quite what they appear to be. Bower, through the clever use of conditioning techniques, provided a quite different picture—a world characterized by perceptual consistency. Though no theorist denies that experience enhances perceptual competency, the effects of experience are not viewed as mechanistic but rather as organismic.

SUMMARY

Newborn infants enter the world with a functional perceptual system. Studies using associative learning techniques (classical or instrumental conditioning) indicate that young infants are capable of making many sensory discriminations including those that are visual, auditory, and olfactory. Novel and complex stimuli capture their attention more than those that are familiar. Using conditioning procedures, it has been shown that infants can even classify stimuli. Other research studies using habituation procedures reveal that infants have preferences for visual and auditory stimuli. The habituation process is thought to represent a reasonable explanation of how children learn about the world. Although no complete theoretical explanation of early perceptual responding is available, it is clear that in the past scientists seriously underestimated the sensory capacity of infants.

As development proceeds past infancy, the child becomes more adept at determining those features of stimuli that make them distinctive from each other. Research studies of visual search behaviors show older children to be more efficient in isolating distinctive features and thus identifying objects. Concurrent with improving search skills, children evidence better sensory integration. Visual and tactual sensory systems, for example, become interchangeable—objects can be readily identified using either system. As representations of the perceptual world become more firmly established, children become capable of characterizing their representations in drawings and other abstract behaviors. Eventually, the distinctions between perception and cognition become blurred, each becoming an integral feature of the other.

CHAPTER 6

(Owen Franken/Stock, Boston)

COGNITIVE DEVELOPMENT: PROCESSES IN THE ACQUISITION OF KNOWLEDGE

IN CHAPTER 5 we described the perceptual capabilities of children from infancy to 5 years. The evidence indicates that infants possess both the sensory acuities and perceptual processes required to gain knowledge about their environment. Thus, the visual, auditory, tactual, olfactory, and somesthetic senses seem to be operative in varying degrees at infancy and become more acute with increasing age and experience. In some of these perceptual processes, we suggested that stimulus input provides the raw material that the child organizes into knowledge about the environment. In this chapter we shall discuss how the child elaborates on these structures, how these developmental changes in knowledge and cognitive processes influence performance on a number of different tasks.

Among the many cognitive theorists, we shall focus primarily on the work of Heinz Werner, Jerome Bruner, and Jean Piaget. Theorists of this persuasion share the following basic assumptions about the acquisition of knowledge or cognitive development:

1. Knowledge acquisition involves an *active learner* functioning in a responsive environment. Knowledge results from the interaction of environmental demands with the capabilities of the learner.
2. Development proceeds from primitive, reflexive responses, largely stimulus-bound, to ever-increasing levels of representation and abstraction.
3. Development takes place in a stage-hierarchical fashion where the next highest stage subordinates the preceding stages but at the same time depends on the earlier stages.
4. Behavior has certain biological antecedents that would never be realized without appropriate environmental stimulation.

Heinz Werner

We have already described some aspects of Werner's general theoretical position in the discussion of motor development. His theory, however, also has implications for cognition. **Orthogenesis,** Werner's major principle, includes two fundamental characteristics of development, **differentiation** and **hierarchic integration.** According to the principle of **differentiation,** primitive and generalized action systems become progressively differentiated but at the same time fuse with other systems to form a more integrated means of action. "Differentiation leads to progressive individuation into definite and well articulated part systems that are coherently related to each other" (Langer, 1970, p. 735). According to a cognitive interpretation of the principle of differentiation, the initial, primitive responses of the organism to the environment are overly generalized, undifferentiated systems. Thus the young learner responds in the same way to similar whole stimuli when certain distinctive aspects of the stimuli should control differential responses. One example might be the young child calling all men "daddy" because they wear pants.

According to the principle of **hierarchic integration,** as more advanced integrated systems emerge, they take over less developmentally sophisticated systems. Although each level of development depends on the previous level, it is nevertheless qualitatively distinct and takes over the governing of its behaviors. This concept is one of the most intriguing that organismic theorists have formulated and also distinguishes between theoretical orientations. The mechanistic position does not concern itself with qualitative distinctions but rather assumes that development represents the acquisition of more of a particular attribute rather than a change in the quality of the attribute.

Parallel to the concept of hierarchic integration is the **genetic principle of spirality.** As a child advances toward some ultimate state of maturity he will at times exhibit temporary regressions to an earlier level before resuming his inexorable growth. Werner categorized growth into three levels: sensorimotor development, perceptual development, and contemplative development. The interesting aspect of Werner's position is that while higher integrative levels subordinate lower levels, development within the lower levels continues parallel with the advanced stage. The integration of lower-order systems modifies the lower system; thus, though still subordinate, it is nevertheless at a more mature level of functioning. This assumption is important because Werner also believes that when a person faces a novel situation, the solution to the problem comes from the lowest to the highest developmental system. In other words, Werner postulates three levels of development, hierarchical in order, each of which follows its own developmental pattern. A schematization of the model is shown in Figure 6–1.

FIGURE 6-1   *Spiral Development: The Constructivist Assumption of Spiral Development*

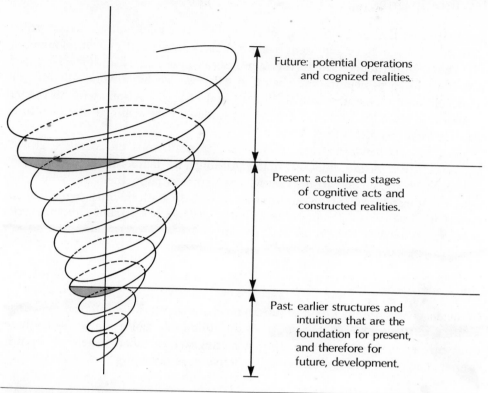

Future: potential operations and cognized realities.

Present: actualized stages of cognitive acts and constructed realities.

Past: earlier structures and intuitions that are the foundation for present, and therefore for future, development.

SOURCE: Langer, J. *Theories of development.* New York: Holt, Rinehart & Winston, 1969, p. 96.

Our description of Werner's substantial contributions to understanding general human development and specifically cognitive development is admittedly sketchy. Rather than attempt a definitive evaluation of it, we will quote Langer (1970, p. 768) whose evaluation of Werner's theory seems to fairly represent its current status:

Also, it is obviously too soon to pass any definitive judgment upon the theory as a whole. Yet it seems clear that the approach has already born fruit in a number of domains. It has been most successful in the study of cognitive phenomena, particularly phenomena of concept and symbol formation. It also has rich potential for the investigation of personality and social development from a genetic epistemological stance; but, to date, this potential remains relatively dormant except for some rudimentary stirrings.

Jerome Bruner

Jerome Bruner is one of those rare scientists who have made substantial contributions to both our basic knowledge of psychology in general and developmental psychology in particular and, furthermore, has also formulated an important theoretical model of perception and cognition. His research has covered infants, preschool children, elementary school children, and adults. Consistent with his general theoretical views, his work and that of his students have spanned many cultures (Bruner, Olver, & Greenfield, 1966).

Contrasts between Bruner's theoretical formulations on cognitive growth and Piaget's position are almost inevitable. Although we do not intend to make value judgments in these comparisons, we will nevertheless point them out when they serve to indicate vagueness in our knowledge. Clearly, both theorists agree that the course of human development can be characterized by a progression through a series of stages, each marked by *qualitative* differences. Bruner postulates three stages: the **enactive stage,** the **ikonic stage,** and the **symbolic stage.**

The Enactive Stage

In the enactive stage the infant acquires knowledge about the world from repetitive motor activities with familiar objects. As the child gains motor competencies, however, further opportunities arise for interacting with a broad variety of stimuli. Bruner et al. (1966, p. 16) describes the enactive stage as follows:

> The initial form of action is "looking at," as in eye movements or orientation of the head. It is obviously innate. Later, the actions of grasping, mouthing, holding, and the like further "objectify" and "correlate" the environment. Action, in this view, is the necessary condition for the infant's achievement of the ecologically valid "correlations" that constitute the segmented and segregated objects of experience. Action and some input from the distance receptors provide the necessary and sufficient conditions for such progress—assuming an intact nervous system.

Thus, according to Bruner, the early formation of knowledge probably depends most on the visual perception of stimuli in the baby's immediate environment. As Bruner sees it, babies go through a series of eye movements and fixations during which they are acquiring rudimentary knowledge about the world. As infants gain in motoric capacity, they continue to gain knowledge about the world through perceptual processes but now coordinate various perceptual input systems. For example, the infant can now look at a stimulus (form discrimination) and at the same time grasp it (distance discrimination). The visual input and the haptic input become coordinated and thus advance the knowledge that the child has about that and related objects. The enactive stage involves behavior that to the uninformed may seem

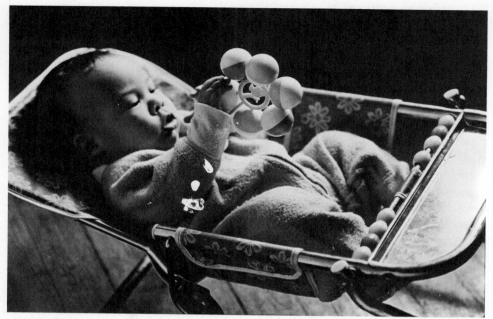

The development of an early schema is formed by the coordination of visual and tactual sensory input. (Joel Gordon)

extremely simplistic and of little or no functional consequence. This is hardly the case, however, and Bruner makes a persuasive argument that the enactive stage forms the very basis for the subsequent elaboration of knowledge and cognitive functioning.

The Ikonic Stage

In the ikonic stage, the child becomes less and less dependent on direct actions on objects and more and more capable of forming objective representations of the world; that is, the child becomes less reliant on direct physical contact with the environment and begins to rely more and more on *imagery*. For Bruner, this second stage represents an advance in the child's mode of representation, since it is during this period that the child begins to categorize objects on the basis of certain concrete features. This capability, which is of extraordinary importance for efficiently understanding the world, is acquired gradually and perhaps involves a series of qualitatively different substages before achieving maturity.

The Symbolic Stage

Bruner views the symbolic stage as the highest level of representation of which human beings are capable. The reader can think of the qualitative distinction between the symbolic level and the two previous levels as the distance of the symbol from either a descriptive gesture or a picture representing an object or event. The symbolic stage involves various changes in language that we discuss in Chapter 7. Suffice it to say here that for Bruner, language is a symbolic system that functions independently of the earlier systems and yet depends on events which occurred during the enactive and ikonic stages. It should be noted that the symbolic stage proposed by Bruner, and more specifically his emphasis on language as a symbolic system, is a point of difference between Bruner and Piaget. Although both theorists view development as moving from simple reflexive and associative actions to ever-increasing symbolic representations of the world, Piaget views symbolic representation as a prerequisite to language and language development. In other words, for Piaget, language becomes a vehicle for expressing knowledge and abstractions, whereas for Bruner, language *is* the abstraction. Clearly, Bruner believes that how one thinks is influenced by early enactive and ikonic experiences that are probably transcultural. However, the most important determinant of how one thinks is language. Language is clearly a function of culture. Piaget, conversely, stresses the equivalence of all languages as alternate means of communicating knowledge that has developed since the child's preverbal interactions with the world. This position is consistent with Piaget's insistence on translinguistic and cross-cultural universals in cognitive development.

Jean Piaget

There is a general consensus that the work of Jean Piaget has had a greater impact on developmental psychology than that of any other single theorist. His work is probably at least somewhat familiar to both psychologists and informed laymen. It is a curious fact that had we written this book 15 or 20 years ago, we might not have mentioned Piaget at all, or at most we would have described him as something of a curiosity. Piaget suffered this neglect in part because he writes in French and it is probably something of an understatement to describe the work, and Piaget's prose, even in translation, as less than clear. More importantly, the general philosophical atmosphere pervading American psychology was mechanistic, as opposed to organismic, and good research dictated the operationalizing of the philosophy of logical positivism. Thus, theories that employed terms like "stage," "schemas," or "structure" and referred to physiological structures were simply not accepted as science. What happened is described rather cogently by Sperry (1975, p. 33):

> After more than 50 years of strict behaviorist avoidance of such terms as "mental imagery" and visual, verbal, auditory, "images," in the past five years, these terms have come into wide usage as explanatory constructs in the literature on cognition, perception, and other higher functions.
> The revised interpretation brings the conscious mind into the causal sequence in

human decision making—and therefore into behavior generally—and thus back into the realm of experimental science from which it has long been excluded. This swing in psychology and neuroscience away from hardcore materialism and reductions toward a new, more acceptable brand of mentalism tends now to restore to the scientific image of human nature some of the dignity, freedom, and other humanistic attributes of which it had been deprived by the behavioristic approach.

Thus, as a consequence of a change in the prevailing philosophy and of the publication of a thorough description of his research and theory (Flavell, 1963), Piaget's work has become widely disseminated. It is now regarded as an imaginative and fairly complete description of the development of cognitive abilities from birth through maturity. One result of this wide recognition has been an outpouring of research on many of his assumptions and conclusions about development, research which has generated an expansion and modification of the theory.

Fundamental Assumptions, and Some Criticisms

Piaget's assumptions are probably not testable by experiments but become more or less tenable as the more testable aspects of his theory are found to be consistent with these broad assumptions. Piaget was originally trained as a biologist before his interests turned toward psychology, particularly child psychology. He also trained himself in the fundamentals of logic and physics, both of which are manifest in the details of his theoretical model. Piaget does not call himself a psychologist or a biologist, but rather a **genetic epistemologist,** an investigator of the *origins of human knowledge.*

In constructing his overall model, Piaget took two approaches, one conceptual and one methodological, that have led some psychologists to reject his work. His theory represents a blend of his early interest in biology and later interest in psychology. Biologically, his theory is based on innate behavioral mechanisms and action patterns. These action patterns emerge in an invariant sequence; each level incorporates the earlier levels but qualitatively modifies them (this concept is similar to Bruner's view of language as a symbolic system and to Werner's concept of hierarchic organization). His formulations tend to emphasize biological assumptions and, as one reads his original work, it is easy to understand how he was captivated by the orderliness of the developing behaviors he observed. But Piaget does not view the environment as playing an insignificant role. Unlike Bruner, he believed that the emerging cognitive processes do not vary among different cultures (transcultural), but he clearly recognizes that an organism must have an environment that acts on it and that it can act on if development is to occur. Some critics have argued that the seeming overemphasis on biology to the exclusion of manipulable psychological variables makes the theory ascientific, or at best, descriptive, and not capable of experimental test.

BEHAVIORISTS' CRITICISMS.   Not only philosophically incompatible with behaviorism (Reese & Overton, 1970; Overton & Reese, 1973), Piaget's model also includes broadly conceived concepts like **stages.** Kessen (1962) has contended that the use of "stage" as a synonym for age is not a useful addition to psychological terminology. Thus behaviorists have argued, persuasively, that psychology has no need for a concept of stage because it was theoretically empty. Furthermore, Kessen showed that to use this term in a descriptive way is also vacuous. "Stage" can be used to produce a tautology: "a child is in the walking stage because the child is walking" is merely a circular way of saying that a child is walking. Psychologists have often used the notion of stage either to refer to some descriptive aspect of the child's behavior or as a synonym for "age." The difficulty is that the term "stage" in these contexts seems to imply something more than is actually meant. Behaviorists rightfully objected to this usage. To be useful and productive, stages must be taken as "parametric variations of a fundamental set of theoretical statements" (Kessen, 1962, p. 69). In other words, given the broad fundamental aspects of Piaget's theory, a productive use of this concept is to demonstrate how changes in stages affect the fundamental theoretical statements. The construct of stage must help to predict how behavior changes from one stage to another and must lay out the rules of transition from one stage to another. So far, these transition rules are not very clearly defined.

CRITICISMS OF METHODOLOGY.   Piaget's methodology has been criticized most importantly on two basic issues: the limited number of subjects employed in his research, and the use of the **clinical method.** As regards the first criticism, there certainly is no argument that the empirical base from which Piaget derived his model of early development was three children, and worse yet, they were his own children. We can question the adequacy of a theoretical model based on three children who are probably not typical of children in general. This criticism would seem to have even greater weight when we recall that Piaget is steadfast in his belief that cognitive stages are invariant across cultures. His subjects represented only one culture and, furthermore, were not even typical of that culture. If Piaget were to reply to this criticism (it is likely he would not respond), he would probably argue that action patterns emerge in an invariant order and thus no need exists to expand on the population of subjects.

Curiously, one of the important modern behavioristic approaches, namely Skinner's position, agrees with Piaget's position. Skinnerians conduct their research on small numbers of subjects on whom they manipulate specifiable parameters. They justify their method of experimentation in much the same way as Piaget had; namely, that their principles of behavior are universal and will work with all organisms, although the parameters that define the properties of the stimulus and the stimulus situation may have to be modified depending on the characteristics of the organism studied or, with human subjects, age. Skinner's approach has met with much the same negative reaction, often from the same people who complained about Piaget! But since the initial formulation of his theory, Piaget, his colleagues, and his followers in many countries, have verified many of his deductions with countless numbers of children.

The second criticism of Piaget's work—the use of the clinical method—is perhaps more serious, and certainly more difficult to defend. The clinical method is compatible with Piaget's overall conceptual and philosophical orientation but is utilized in a unique fashion. An illustration may be useful here. For example, many psychologists interested in education want to know if 6-year-old children know the names of the primary colors. When they find children who are ignorant of color names, they try to find the best methods of teaching them colors. Their interest in this particular phenomenon comes from the relation between knowing the names of colors and reading performance, a relation that is not easily understood. Piaget, on the other hand, is not at all interested in whether children know their colors; instead, he would ask how children order colors, say, along the dimensions of intensity or brightness. The basic data for answering this more complex question must come from careful observation of the children on a variety of related tasks and from the children's own explanations of their behaviors. Piaget is usually unconcerned about whether a child's response to some cognitive demand is correct or incorrect. When the response is incorrect, Piaget uses interviews and manipulations of the stimulus materials to determine the kinds of mental assumptions the child is making and then to infer the mental processes that the child is using to arrive at the incorrect response. When a child gives a correct response, we cannot always assume that it results from the same rules or processes that adults use. According to Flavell (1963, p. 28),

> The approach does have much in common with diagnostic and therapeutic interviews, with projective testing, and with the kind of informal exploration often used in pilot research throughout the behavioral sciences. The crux of it is to explore a diversity of child behaviors in a stimulus-response-stimulus-response sequence; in the course of this rapid sequence the experimenter uses all the insight and ability at his command to understand what the child says or does and to adapt his own behavior in terms of this understanding.

Piagetian Theory

Piaget has certainly demonstrated that children are not simply miniature adults. His proposal of qualitatively different stages underscores his belief that children's ways of thinking are very different from those of the mature adult. But how can we determine what these differences are unless we have techniques for teasing them out? Very often, we must ask the children specific questions. One possibly unfortunate consequence of this approach is that the resulting manipulations and questions used are highly specific or situational. Consequently, we cannot tell if the children's responses are unique to the stimuli, the situation, or both. Few psychologists are as clever as Piaget in manipulating materials and asking children the appropriate questions. Although we cannot refute the criticism that his work is very hard to replicate, many of the major propositions of his system have been validated by others in better designed, standardized, and controlled situations than he ever used.

The Child as Active Investigator

We will begin our discussion of Piaget's theory with the general organismic assumption that the child is an active investigator. In observations similar to Bruner and to Werner, Piaget noted that children act upon their environments with reflexive responses during infancy and then with more complex responses that emerge from these early interactions. Piaget views the interaction of the organism and the environment as a two-way process, one of which is **accommodation** and the other **assimilation.** In accommodation, the child's knowledge of the environment is modified to incorporate new objects or experiences. Accommodation is the feature

Through play, children test hypotheses about the world. (Erika Stone)

of cognitive processing that is adaptive to the broad variety of cognitive demands imposed by the environment. In assimilation, the child incorporates a new object or experience into an existing structure; that is, the child fits it in with already acquired knowledge. The process of fitting new experiences or objects into already existing structures is almost never completely faithful to the actual attributes of the objects. In other words, the assimilatory process involves modification of the object so that it will be consistent with existing cognitive organization. It is impossible to separate accommodation from assimilation, and the reader should not assume that they are sequential or that either is more dominant or important than the other. They are truly reciprocal, and their interaction generates cognitive growth. The following explanatory statement by Flavell (1963, pp. 49–50) reveals both the complexity of the issue and its importance:

> Cognitive progress, in Piaget's system, is possible for several reasons. First of all, accommodatory acts are continually being extended to new and different features of the surroundings. To the extent that a newly accommodated-to feature can fit somewhere in the existing meaning structure, it will be assimilated to that structure. Once assimilated, however, it tends to change the structure in some degree and, through this change, make possible further accommodatory extensions. Also, as discussion of schemas will show, assimilatory structures are not static or unchanging, even in the absence of environmental stimulation. Systems of meaning are constantly being reorganized internally and integrated with other systems . . . thus, both kinds of changes—reorganizations of purely endogenous origins and reorganizations induced more or less directly by new accommodatory attempts—make possible a progressive intellectual penetration into the nature of things. Once again the twin invariance innervate each other in reciprocal fashion: changes in assimilatory structure direct new accommodations, and new accommodatory attempts stimulate structural organizations.

When Piaget talks about an active learner, he is referring to the accommodatory and assimilatory processes intrinsic to the organism. Thus Piaget need not invoke such concepts as incentives or reinforcers in order to provide an energy source for cognitive change. (Piaget would probably not deny that incentives or reinforcing stimuli are important for manipulating the performance of children, but he does not view such concepts as in any way crucial to cognitive development).

Cognitive Acquisitions

Given that assimilation and accommodation serve as the basic reciprocal processes through which cognitive development takes place, the question then arises how Piaget conceives of cognitive acquisitions. As we hinted earlier in our example of the child's knowing the names of colors as opposed to being able to order colors on some dimension, Piaget is not interested in any significant way in content. What he is interested in, and what the reciprocal processes arrive at, is the organization of knowledge which he calls **structure.** More specifically, Piaget is interested in how behavioral processes change in response to various cognitive demands. In determining the qualitative properties of these changes, he studies the structural properties of behavior under different conditions and with children at different developmental levels. He is thus able to draw up a "mapping" of the structural properties of tasks performed by children of different ages. This is a formidable undertaking, for it requires extremely careful analyses of the various properties in a cognitive domain (or the stimuli involved). Then one must examine how these properties are modified as the child matures. In any event, the reader should understand that structures are the product of the formation of new knowledge and represent, at any one point in time, the way in which a child organizes and represents his understanding of the world.

The Concept of Schema

Flavell notes that the concept of *schema* plays an important role in Piaget's theory. It is admittedly an oversimplification to define a schema as an action pattern that occurs on some particular occasion. However, in our earlier discussion of action patterns (see Chapter 4), we were careful to emphasize that they consist of a large number of related behaviors that seem to occur in a fixed sequence but which at least are closely associated with each other. As we can talk about a number of action patterns, in the Piagetian system we can speak of a large number of schemas. Thus, in effect, a schema represents a pattern of behavior. But if this is all it represents, that is, if it is only a descriptive term, then it is unnecessary in the same way that the concept of stage is unnecessary. A schema in fact implies not only a behavioral sequence but also a concomitant change in structures, that is, that a new or modified cognitive organization is now available to the child. For example, a child may have a schema of sight or a schema of grasping or a schema of reaching. Although at some point in infancy, these schemas are independent, eventually they become integrated, so that it is possible, for example, to speak of a schema of object-grasping. This term obviously is descriptive but it also reflects the infant's acquisition of a new form of cognitive organization or structure, namely, the integration of three schemas into one coordinated schema.

Piagetian Stages

Based on his extensive observations of his own children and on his intuitions, Piaget proposed that children progress through a series of four stages, beginning with rudimentary reflex responses and achieving full maturity with the attainment of formal deductive reasoning. The four stages are: **sensorimotor intelligence, precon-**

crete operations, concrete operations, and **formal operations.** The stages and sub-stages, along with brief behavioral descriptions and approximate age levels, are summarized in Table 6-1. The transitions from one stage to another are gradual and do not necessarily affect all features of the child's functioning. Within each stage there occur both a vertical development (what Piaget called a **décalage verti-cal**) that brings the child closer to a new stage, and a horizontal development (**dé-calage horizontale**) in which the child incorporates a broader range of behaviors into the same structural level. The age levels associated with each of the stages are approximations; that is, Piaget does not assert that all children reach each new stage at the same time.

TABLE 6-1   Characteristics and Achievements in Stages of Intellectual Development According to Piaget

STAGE	APPROXIMATE AGE RANGE, YEARS	MAJOR CHARACTERISTICS AND ACHIEVEMENTS
Sensorimotor period	0–2	Infant differentiates himself from other objects; seeks stimulation and makes interesting spectacles last; attainment of object permanence; primitive understanding of causality, time, and space; means-end relationships; beginnings of imitation of absent, complex nonhuman stimuli; imaginative play and symbolic thought
Preoperational period	2–6	Development of the symbolic function; symbolic use of language; intuitive problem solving; thinking characterized by irreversibility, centration, and egocentricity; beginnings of attainment of conservation of number and ability to think in classes and see relationships
Period of concrete operations	6/7–11/12	Conservation of mass, length, weight, and volume; reversibility, decentration, ability to take role of others; logical thinking involving concrete operations of the immediate world, classification (organizing objects into hierarchies of classes), and seriation (organizing objects into ordered series, such as increasing height)
Period of formal operations	11/12 on	Flexibility, abstraction, mental hypotheses testing, and consideration of possible alternatives in complex reasoning and problem solving

SOURCE: Hetherington, E. M., & Parke, R. D. Child psychology: a contemporary viewpoint. New York: McGraw-Hill, 1975, p. 255.

The Sensorimotor Period

The stage of sensorimotor development extends from birth to approximately two years of age. Initially, behavior consists almost exclusively of the reflexive movements characteristic of the newborn baby. These are not the reflexes discussed earlier—the reflexes that disappear in due course—but rather the reflexive behaviors of eye movements, arm movements, and sucking, to name just a few. In other words, Piaget's interest is in those reflexes that form the basis for later stages in cognitive growth. In characterizing this early stage of development, he lays stress on motor actions as opposed to any kind of representational or symbolic representations. This stage terminates when **symbolic operations** replaces it. The stage of sensorimotor intelligence consists of six substages and represents the area of some of Piaget's most detailed descriptive work.

SUBSTAGE 1.   The **reflexive stage** (0–2 months) is characterized largely by the reflexes just mentioned. The infant engages in a considerable amount of exercise of these reflexes, which appear to undergo slight alterations in structure. For example, the infant may begin sucking in the presence of a bottle or nipple, even without having the bottle or nipple touch the infant's lips.

SUBSTAGE 2.   **Primary circular reactions** (2–4 months) occur when the infant intensively practices the schemas developed in the reflexive stage as well as the new schemas that emerge during this period, including looking at stimuli, listening, and prehension. Piaget uses the concept *circular* to designate the repetition of these schemas. Perhaps the most important event, however, during this stage is the coordination of schemas. On hearing a sound, for example, the infant turns its head and eyes in the direction of the sound source. There also emerges the coordination of the sucking schema with the prehension schemas as well as a vision-and-prehension schema. Thus, the infant develops the ability to grasp an object and once having done so, brings it to the mouth for sucking. With the coordination of the vision and prehension schemas, the infant is able to view an object, locate it in space, grasp it, and then inspect it visually. It should be noted, however, that it appears as if a visual-prehension schema can occur only when both the eye and the hand are viewed simultaneously. If the object disappears from the infant's field of vision, the behavioral evidence seems to suggest the object no longer exists for the infant. In other words, during this stage the infant has no concept of **object permanence.**

SUBSTAGE 3.   **Secondary circular reactions** (4–8 months) indicate that the child becomes aware of the consequences of his own motoric actions, but unlike the earlier stages, the infant repeats these actions. One example of this behavior is the shaking of a rattle, an action the baby seems to make repeatedly in anticipation of the resulting sound. Some authors have suggested that the continual repetition results from positive reinforcement (the outcome of the motoric action on the object) and is thus similar to a conditioned response. Our description may seem to imply that Piaget is inferring some knowledge of cause and effect; that is, the infant is displaying intentional behavior. Actually Piaget argues that in this stage the infant is really not capable of understanding that its action generates the environmental result. During the latter part of this stage rudimentary object permanence appears; hidden objects do exist.

SUBSTAGE 4.   This stage is categorized as the *coordination of secondary reactions* (8–12 months). The major achievement is the appearance of intentionality, or **means-end behavior.** In addition, the infant further elaborates existing schemas and incorporates new objects into old schemas. What distinguishes this stage from the third stage (substage 3) is the capability of performing a number of subactions (multiple means) in order to obtain a desired goal (ends). Thus, whereas Piaget was unable to determine clearly that means were differentiated from ends in Stage 3, such separation is very clear in Stage 4.

Another major feature of the fourth substage is that **play** becomes clearly important. Flavell (1977, p. 32) describes an example:

> Play becomes much more clearly playful at this age. For instance, after "seriously" practicing a new means-end integration for a while (an instance of adapted intelligence), he may ignore the end and pleasurefully exercise the means (play). As a case

Endless repetition of a behavior is typical when a child first understands means-ends relationships. (Judith Sedwick)

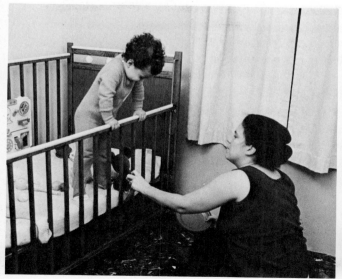

in point, one of Piaget's children began by practicing the feat of pushing an obstacle aside to obtain a toy and ended up ignoring the toy in favor of pushing the obstacle aside again and again for fun. Play, like imitation, is beginning to become differentiated from adapted intelligence to become a distinctive instrument of cognitive growth. For whatever other functions play might serve in the child's life (and there are probably quite a few), no one has ever doubted that it is a major vehicle for learning and mental development.

SUBSTAGE 5.　**Tertiary circular reactions** (12–18 months) are reflected by the infant exploring new possibilities in manipulating objects, in other words, he actively experiments with objects in the environment. The child also exhibits a more mature level of object permanence. Before this stage, infants tend to assume that an object hidden from their view must always be there, not understanding that it can be removed. In Stage 5, the child overcomes this incorrect notion and takes the actions of others into account in determining whether the object is still present or not.

The key difference between the circular reactions in Stages 4 and 5 is that in the earlier stages the circular reactions continue only if they achieve the same outcome. In Stage 5, circular reactions continue only if their outcomes vary, depending on how the actions are performed. Thus, in this stage the baby actually begins to experiment with objects by varying behavior with the object and examining how the variations affect the object.

SUBSTAGE 6.　The **internalization of schemas** (18–24 months) means that infants achieve some **representational ability;** that is, they are now capable of functioning with a symbolic reality as well as a concrete sensorimotor world. The child also begins to speak and understand words and to indulge in a primitive classification of objects. During this stage, and extending through much of the next stage, the child uses objects in a symbolic or representational way. For example, children can take a block and make it into an automobile with all of its characteristic motions and sounds. Ten seconds later, they may take the same block and make it represent an airplane. This ability to take objects as representations of other objects is an extraordinarily important cognitive acquisition. It assumes a major role in the play of children and has important implications for assimilatory processes.

Another aspect of the sixth stage that deserves comment is the role of **imitation.** We have not so far mentioned imitation because its precise function was unclear. Imitation is important, however, because of its role in accommodation. Imitative behavior has been occurring since approximately Stage 3, but during that stage it was difficult to distinguish between its assimilatory and its accommodatory aspects. Thus, in the third stage the imitated action patterns were already available to the infant, but not until Stage 4 is the child able to imitate new patterns of behavior. Furthermore, before Stage 4 imitative patterns can not be distinguished as separate from the infant's own body. It is not until the sixth stage that the child exhibits deferred imitation, the ability to imitate models that are not physically immediately present. In addition, the child is able to imitate nonhuman objects—how does a tree look? Thus, in effect, the full-blown mechanisms of imitation and play are apparent in the sixth and final stage of sensorimotor intelligence and continue to serve as important sources for assimilation, accommodation, and the extended elaboration of cognitive functioning.

The Preoperational Period (2–7 years)

Piaget (1951) views the shift to more representational processes as a critical transition in cognitive development and has marked off the change as the preoperational stage. However, the sixth substage of sensorimotor intelligence and the early phases of the preoperational stage actually represent a smooth gradation and not a sharp delineation.

The preoperational stage is subdived into the **conceptual phase** (2–4 years) and the **intuitive phase** (4–7 years). The most dramatic occurrence during the conceptual phase is the elaboration of symbolic processes and the use of representational skills. Much of this change is represented in the onset of language. For Piaget infant speech begins with the onset of the preoperational period, probably as the result of neurophysiological maturation. Unlike J. B. Watson who said that thought processes are actually small muscle movements in the larnyx, Piaget believes that language is a symbolic system that communicates concepts but does not embody the concept itself. As we noted in our comments about substage 6, the child exhibits an increase in fantasy play in addition to motor play with real objects. During the preoperational phase, these schemas are expanded so that stimuli come to have highly idiosyncratic meaning for children, a fact which often leads to difficulties in communication between children and adults. The cognitive behaviors, that is, the structures and schemas, of children in the conceptual phase of this stage reflect a substantial qualitative difference from the structures and schemas available to the child during the sensorimotor stage.

Unfortunately, extensive systematic research on various aspects of toddlers' behavior does not exist, largely, we suspect, because youngsters of this age are somewhat difficult to obtain as research subjects and also because they can be difficult to work with (in part because of the idiosyncrasy or egocentricity of their thought processes). What research has been done suggests that the conceptual child differs from older children in significant ways. For example, the thinking of children between 2 and 4 years is characterized by the absence of genuine concepts. Thus, though they may solve certain problems, they cannot produce accurate explanations and are unable to coordinate along more than one dimension; that is, they focus on a single attribute (called **centration**) rather than on the multiple attributes of objects and problems. Centration is one of the reasons children frequently cannot comprehend problems in **conservation.** Conceptual-level children are also unable to generalize one example of a concept to other objects and events. Actually, at this

Children experience great pleasure in creating, but adults sometimes fail to understand the product. (Erika Stone)

developmental level the child's thinking lies somewhere between deductive and inductive reasoning; the child does not go from the general to the particular (deduction) or the particular to the general (induction) but goes from one particular instance to another particular instance. Piaget calls this process **transductive reasoning.**

REVERSIBILITY.   The preoperational child cannot grasp the concept of **reversibility.** Piaget conceives of reversibility as a mental operation in which the person understands that objects can be transformed from one form to another and back again, or, in terms of simple equations, the operations within them can be reversed as in the following example: $6 + 3 = 9$ and $9 - 3 = 6$. The numerous conservation problems developed by Piaget and his associates exemplify this cognitive concept. Figure 6-2 illustrates the problem of the **conservation of liquids.** The children are asked: "Which beaker has more water in it, the tall one or the short one?" or "Do they have the same amount of water?" During the preoperational phase, children typically select either the tall beaker or the short beaker because it is wider (they actually choose the taller beaker more often because they associate tallness with quantity). If

FIGURE 6-2   *Conservation of Liquids*

(a) Two glass jars are filled to the same level with water. The child sees that they are equal.

(b) The liquid of one container is poured into a tall tube (or a flat dish). The child is asked whether each contains the same amount.

the child makes an incorrect response or gives an incorrect explanation for the selection of one or the other beakers, the experimenter then takes the water from the taller beaker and pours it into the shorter beaker. Then the child may be permitted to pour the water from the short beaker back into the taller beaker and to observe that the tall beaker is now filled to capacity. The child often comments that the tall beaker is filled or the short beaker is filled. After this operation is performed, the child is again asked to indicate which beaker has more water in it and to explain the reasons for the choice. Despite the fact they have performed the motoric operations, preoperational children persist in indicating that the taller (shorter) beaker has more water in it. In explaining their actions, they focus on the height or the width of he beaker as the reason why one contains more water than the other. Clearly, to give the correct response, the child must recognize that no water was added or taken away during the operation of pouring the liquid from one container into the other. Secondly, the child must comprehend that the greater width of one beaker compensates for the greater height of the other. We have here then two very important features of mental operations: the concept of reversibility illustrated by the fact that pouring the water from one beaker to the other is equivalent to pouring in the opposite direction. Secondly, the child must observe two dimensions simultaneously, both height and width, and must understand that they vary together in some constant relationship. In failing to solve this problem, the child is "captured" by a single perceptual feature of the stimulus material: either the height or the width of the beaker. The phenomenon of attending to only a single dimension or attribute was mentioned previously and is called centration.

Another conservation task concerns substance. A balance scale holding two balls of clay of equal weight is used to show that the child understands the word "same." Working in full view of the child, the experimenter rolls one of the balls of clay into another form, as shown in Figure 6-3. If the experimenter tells the child that the ball of clay has turned into a rocket, the preoperational child now states that the long ball of clay weighs more because rockets weigh more. If the experimenter does not comment on what the elongated clay shape represents, the child

FIGURE 6-3 *Conservation of Substance*

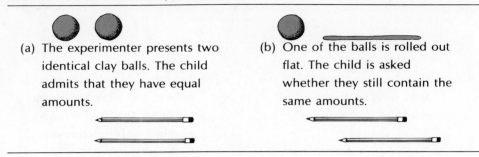

(a) The experimenter presents two identical clay balls. The child admits that they have equal amounts.

(b) One of the balls is rolled out flat. The child is asked whether they still contain the same amounts.

will say that the two clay figures are not the same because the transformed clay is now longer and therefore bigger, or the round ball of clay is taller and therefore bigger. After the transformed clay has been rolled back into a ball, however, the child says the two balls contain the same amount of clay.

CENTRATION.   In both examples of conservation, the children were captured by some perceptual attribute of the stimuli, a phenomenon we have labeled centration. Centration has been demonstrated in an imaginative study by O'Bryan and Boersma (1971), who recorded the eye movements and fixations of children performing the conservation-of-liquids task. Their subjects included younger and older children; the younger children were more likely to be captured by one or another perceptual feature of the task and thus were unable to solve the problem appropriately. The probability was reasonably high that the older group of children would be able to solve this conservation task. The investigators found that children who indicated that the tall beaker had more water tended to organize their successive eye fixations on the vertical axis (tallness dimension), whereas children who understood the reversibility of the task distributed their eye fixations over both dimensions.

By developing tasks for assessing children's ability to integrate identifiable parts into wholes, Elkind (1969) extensively examined centration and decentration as examples of perceptual and cognitive integration. The items used in the Picture Integration Test (PIT) are shown in Figure 6-4. Note that a child can either name the individual parts or integrate them into a whole figure, or both. Important features of integrative behavior are the making of multiple classifications and the coordination of parts into meaningful wholes. Elkind's data suggest that preoperational children are less likely to demonstrate integrative behaviors than older children. The younger children are more likely to name the individual objects rather than to see the perceptual pattern as a whole unit.

EGOCENTRICITY.   One behavior of the preoperational period that has received considerable attention is that of the **egocentric** nature of children's perceptions of the

FIGURE 6-4   *Items Used in the Picture Integration Test.* In describing each picture, the child can either name the individual parts or integrate them into a whole figure, or both.

SOURCE: Elkind, D. Developmental studies of figurative perception. In L. P. Lipsitt, & H. W. Reese (Eds.), *Advances in child development and behavior.* New York: Academic Press, 1969 (Fig. 2, p. 12).

world. Specifically, children at this stage of development are unable to take another person's point of view. This aspect of the child's mental operations is similar to the child's conversion of a block into a tank or an airplane, and then not understanding why no one comprehends his behavior and verbalizations.

Other examples can be given of the egocentric nature of children's thinking Piaget (1955) describes the preoperational children's asking of questions as reflecting their basic egocentricity. Thus, when children this age ask, "Why is it raining?" they are more likely to be asking, "Why is it raining when I want to go outside and play?" than a question about the physical cause of rain. Typical questions children ask in this stage begin with the interrogative, "why" and are mostly requests for explanations of physical events, for example, wind or rain (Meyer & Shane, 1973). Most of these same questions, when asked of the children, elicit illogical responses that suppose for example, that wind and rain are alive. Attributing life to inanimate objects, called **animism,** is a characteristic of the preconceptual child's questions and, also, answers. "Where does wind come from?", "Are clouds alive?", "Where does the wind go when it's calm?" are examples of the kind of thinking involved at this stage. Piaget postulates 4 stages of animism: (1) children between 4 and 6 years think everything is alive; (2) children between 6 and 7 years consider moving things alive; (3) children between 8 and 10 years consider anything that moves by itself as alive; and (4) children 11 years and older attribute life only to animals and plants.

The conceptual behavior of the preoperational child often gives the appearance of mature sophistication. However, when children are questioned carefully or are presented with problems creating conflict between perceptual and conceptual responses, their immature level of responding becomes evident. Such conflict is responsible for further cognitive growth.

Recently, Borke (1971, 1973) has raised the question whether children at this age are really incapable of understanding the feelings of others. Her data suggest that 4-year-olds are able to identify happy responses in other children and, between 4 and 7 years of age, become increasingly more competent in identifying fear, sadness, and anger. There is some difference of opinion about Borke's results. Chandler and Greenspan (1972), for example, suggest that rather than indicating empathic ability, the data show the psychological processes involved to be more similar to identification, where one accurately attributes one's own feelings to someone else's response. If Chandler and Greenspan are correct, their interpretation would be more consistent with the egocentricity found by Piaget. This issue remains unclear and requires more definitive research.

We have touched on only three aspects of mental operations during the early preoperational period. There are others, and we urge the reader to read Ginsburg and Opper (1969) for other features of this phase of cognitive development.

TRANSITION.   The second part of the preoperational phase is called the intuitive phase during which the child's behavior begins to show signs of adaptive intelligence. According to Flavell (1963, pp. 162–163):

> First, the child becomes noticeably more *testable* in formal experiments from age 4 or 5 on. He is much more able to address himself to a specified task and to apply adapted intelligence to it rather than simply assimilate it to some egocentric play schema. It is no accident that the lower age limit in most Piaget experiments is about 4 years. And not only does the child become testable *per se* in the late preoperational phase, he also becomes capable of reasoning about progressively more complex and extended experimental problems of displays in the testing situation.

The intuitive child is going through a transitional stage leading toward concrete operations. As with most transition stages, the children sometimes display immature behaviors in certain areas.

Although children in the intuitive phase show substantial growth in the quality of their mental operations, these operations are still limited. Children remain unable to deal with more than a single dimension and are thus unable to cope with multiple classification tasks. In addition, they do not yet possess a concept of reversibility.

Concrete Operations (7–11 years)

During the stage of concrete operations, the child achieves an understanding of the conservation of mass, weight, and volume and commands a highly flexible set of responses for coping with environmental demands. The child's mental operations now include reversibility, the ability to attend to more than a single dimension (height and width, for example), and the concept of equality; they also acquire the ability to arrange stimuli according to length and can thus perform **seriation** tasks. In addition, the child's ability to incorporate increasingly more abstract symbols shows decided improvement. Toward the end of the stage of concrete operations, the child becomes capable of handling **transitivity** problems (see p. 200). The period of concrete operations can be characterized as one in which children begin to demonstrate a mature understanding of the world and begin to recognize that they can resolve many problems through the use of logical reasoning and through measurement. The child relies less on perceptual attributes and more on symbolic concepts.

MULTIPLE CLASSIFICATION.   **Multiple classification** is one of the major new behaviors that the child acquires during the stages of concrete operations. An exemplary task might involve stimuli which vary in size (large, medium, and small), color (red, blue, and green, or black, gray, and white), and form (prism, sphere, and cube). The children are asked to group the objects according to how they go together. They may group the stimuli according to any of three stimulus dimensions or attributes: color, form, or size. After the stimuli have been sorted the first time, they are rearranged and the children are asked to sort them in another way. Ordinarily, children in the late part of the preoperational phase will sort the stimuli by form, fewer children will sort them by color, and fewer still will sort them by size. It is interesting that form tends to be the most salient dimension for children. If, however, one asks the children to classify the stimuli along more than one stimulus dimension, they are typically unable to do so. Concrete operational children have little or no difficulty making classifications on the basis of a single dimension, and most children will spontaneously classify on two dimensions; for example, all large green stimuli, medium-sized red stimuli, and small blue stimuli. Without a great deal of difficulty children are also able to classify using all three dimensions simultaneously.

DISTANCING.   Figure 6-5 illustrates another kind of classification problem. The stimuli were developed by Irving Sigel (1968). He was interested in how children

FIGURE 6-5 *Categorization Test Objects*

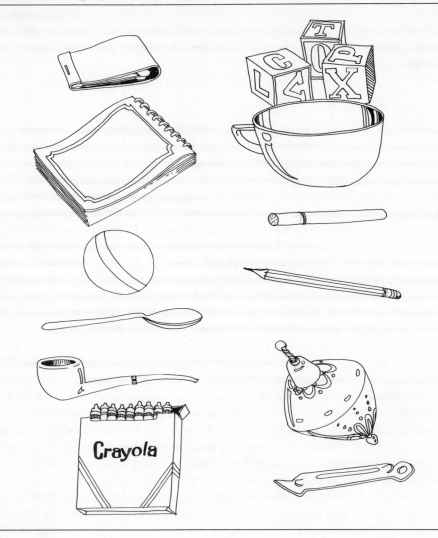

categorized stimuli and also in testing his concept of the **distancing hypothesis** according to which reality can be represented at some distance from its referent. Distancing is a manifestation of the ability to respond correctly to external representation and to respond in terms of schemas. Notice that all of the objects in this array are familiar, and indeed in the Sigel study and in a study by Meyer (1972) it was found that the children were able to name all of the objects. The task consists of taking one of the objects from the array, presenting it to the child, and asking the child to find other objects in the array that are the same. After the child makes his choices, he is asked to explain how the objects selected are alike. Scoring the behavior involves several categories: perceptual properties (form, color, or structure), a functional category (write with the pencil on the pad), thematic properties (you light the cigarette with the matches and while smoking, drink a cup of coffee), class labels (they are all toys), and a contextual category (the items were located in the same place). A nonscorable category included explanations not fitting any of the other categories.

The results of the studies illustrate several differences between the preoperational stage and the concrete operational stage. The subjects in Meyer's study were 108 middle-class preschool children and were tested on two occasions: when they were 4 years 2 months, and 4 years 11 months. The children were of high-average intellectual ability. Examination of the nonscorable category shows that approximately 51 percent of the children's responses on the pretest, but only 20 percent of their responses on the posttest, were nonscorable. In other words, the children had changed substantially in the very brief 9-month period. The main reason for the high frequency of nonscorable responses on the pretest was that the children's responses simply made no sense; that is, they often seemed to be unable to attend to any of the attributes of the stimuli. This is a characteristic of preoperational children. The low number of nonscorable responses before the age of 5 simply reflects the fact that these children were accelerated intellectually; their ability to handle the task at the age of 4 years 11 months does not in any way challenge the theoretical concepts. Indeed, when we analyze the basis on which these children made their classifications, we see that it fits the Piagetian position rather neatly. For example, almost all of the scorable responses on the pretest were in the *perceptual category*. Almost all of the categorizations were made on the basis of either form or color rather than a more abstract property of the stimulus objects. For example, the next most difficult category would be the functional basis of classification. Only 4 percent of the responses on the pretest fell into that category, as opposed to 16 percent of the responses on the posttest. This sample of subjects never used any of the other categories.

In a follow-up study of approximately 80 percent of this sample 2 years later, the children were able to handle this task with considerable ease and by the age of 8 they were giving class labels, an abstract classification, in their selection of stimulus objects. These results are entirely consistent with another task devised by Sigel, suggesting that the basis for classification moves from a single perceptual attribute to multiple perceptual attributes to increasingly more abstract conceptualizations.

One other interesting aspect of this study is the method Sigel suggested for assessing representational competence. The array of stimuli in Figure 6-5 is presented to the children, using either actual objects or life-size color photographs of the objects. In the study by Meyer, half the children were shown the actual objects first and the pictorial respresentations second, while the remaining half of the children saw the same stimuli in the reverse order. According to Sigel's distancing hypothesis, the young children should have had greater difficulty categorizing the pictures (representations) of the objects than the objects themselves. This is in fact exactly what happened, providing support not only for the distancing hypothesis but for the prediction that children would be able to cope with increasingly more abstract representational features of the stimulus.

CLASS INCLUSION.   A third kind of classification problem is called the *class-inclusion task*. In this task the experimenter presents pictures of 3 men and 2 women. The children are asked to tell how many men there are, then how many people there are, then if there are more men than people. Any number of variations of this task are possible, but the basic idea is to present a task with a superordinate category and two or more subordinate categories, and then determine if the children can distinguish between the two. The preoperational child is likely to say that there are 3 men and 5 people, but that there are more men than people. (Admittedly, if a woman were writing this book, the example would undoubtedly be reversed, but then we all do possess reversibility.) The child in concrete operations can understand the contributions of the attributes, men and women, that form the superordinate category of people. Thus, children in the period of concrete operations can solve class-inclusion problems, which are unusually important in defining the structure of the world.

SERIATION AND TRANSITIVITY.   In the seriation task the child is presented with sticks in random order and asked to make them into steps. The preoperational child is fairly likely to concentrate on only one of the relationships within the general ordering of sizes and ignore other aspects of the task, thus creating a fairly haphazard order. It is not until the child reaches the stage of concrete operations that he can understand the notion of the gradations of the sticks in a continuous series. This task, incidentally, involves another problem that the child in concrete operations can solve, a task of some difficulty known as transitivity. A verbal problem in transitivity is: "If John is taller than Bill and Bill is taller than Dan, who is taller, John or Dan?" The difference between this problem and the seriation problem is that the former also requires a mental transformation of "greater than" and "less than" as the basis for ordering the stimuli.

Formal Operations (11 +)

In the period of formal operations, the child can easily use abstract thinking and conceptualization and develops the capacity for systematic hypothesis testing. Piaget's postulation of this stage seems natural in view of his use of mathematics and logic as the basis underlying cognitive development, with deductive reasoning as the ultimate level of logical reasoning. The question has been raised whether all people achieve formal operations, and even whether these processes are in fact necessary for all people. There is also some question whether formal operations represent a ceiling beyond which human beings do not develop. Piaget (1972) has suggested that this stage may be limited to people whose mental activities *require* logical thought, such as mathematicians and physicists. Riegel (1973) examined this suggestion in light of the interaction of the indivdual and his environment (society in the broadest sense) and concluded that the attainment of formal operations is *not* a necessary terminal point. He suggests, however, that if an individual faces demands requiring deductive logical reasoning, he or she can develop the capability to cope with them.

Evaluation of Piaget's Theory

Without undertaking a complete and systematic evaluation of the whole of Piaget's theory, we will comment on some of the major questions that have been raised about the theory and that are currently providing an important impetus to research and refinements. We shall treat these issues in a rather general fashion, but the key references will provide the reader with the basic sources for obtaining more detailed descriptions of the issues.

In general, the major criticisms fall into 2 categories: (1) conceptual issues that are internal to the model and that frequently occur in broadly conceived theoretical models, and (2) conceptual issues that are derived from a basic disagreement or conflict with the structural or organismic orientation of the theory.

Issues Internal to the Theory

Piaget has made a numer of assertions about his theory that have either failed to gain consistent empirical support or that may be logically inconsistent. One such assertion concerns the invariant sequence of the acquisition of mental operations. The questions do not focus on whether or not the sequence—sensorimotor operations, preconcrete operations, concrete operations, and formal operations—is invariant; no one seriously disputes that sequence. The problem concerns sequences that are assumed to occur within a more narrowly limited range and that are more difficult to test empirically. A major issue at stake here is the difficulty of adequately assessing the child's developmental level. We may, for example, make an error in assessing one level of cognitive development, such as mental operation A, but we may make an accurate assessment of mental operation B. If we postulate that B depends on A, and if a child has B but lacks A, then the conceptual sequence would appear to be inaccurate when in fact it could be the result of measurement error. The research literature (Flavell, 1977) cites numerous instances of just such errors of evaluation.

Recently Flavell (1972, 1977) has published a detailed analysis of the concept of stages and has identified the concepts of structure, qualitative change, abruptness, and concurrence as crucial features required if we are to accept the Piagetian stage

The stage concept has obvious implications for methods of teaching. (Eric Roth/The Picture Cube)

theory. For example, Flavell concludes that the theory of stages would be far more convincing if the transition from one cognitive stage to another was abrupt. Arguing from previous research, he convincingly shows that the transition from one stage to another is in fact rather gradual. For example, when a child achieves conservation of weight, this accomplishment is not absolute. The first exhibition of conservation of weight does not mean that the child goes through no further development of that set of mental operations. A number of simultaneous growth patterns suggest that abruptness is indeed not a characteristic of stages. It is also extremely difficult to demonstrate that cognitive growth involves a network of interlocking competencies. If we are unable to make such a demonstration, then it may well be that the concept of stage is really rather empty. Flavell (1977, p. 249) summarizes his conclusions in the following way:

> My own hunch is that the concept of stage will not, in fact, figure importantly in future scientific work on cognitive growth. This does not imply a disbelief in the existence of undirectional and bidirectional developmental dependencies, wherein one development assists another and perhaps conversely. Nor does it imply that there is no unity or consistency in cognitive functioning across situations. But it does imply that there may be less unity, consistency, and developmental interdependence than theories like Piaget's would have us believe.

Certain other developmental psychologists, including Wohlwill (1973) and Kohlberg (1969), would certainly not agree with this statement. Nor should the reader imply from our quotation from Flavell that we particularly agree with it, either. It does seem to us, however, that his analysis is penetrating and will certainly provide an impetus for more research on the nature and usefulness of the stage concept as Piaget describes it.

A second internal feature of Piaget's theory that is now being seriously questioned concerns his assertions about the role of language in cognition. You will recall that he and Bruner appear to differ on this issue, with Bruner viewing language as an internally consistent symbolic system and Piaget viewing it as a social means of communicating the mental operations appropriate to a particular stage. Piaget's position has been challenged on the grounds that if the child does not understand the verbal instructions, then the child will not be able to solve the problem. For example, in the problem of conservation of volume, the subject is asked to determine whether one vessel contains the same, or more, or less than another vessel. This question assumes that the child understands the meanings of the abstract terms (same, more, less), and the child may not. Thus, one can ask the question: does language impede performance but not hinder competence?

Piaget's view has received strong support from the work of Hans Furth (1970). Furth and his colleagues have worked with deaf children in an effort to determine whether their hearing handicap changes the course of mental development or in any way modifies the sequence of cognitive development. The evidence supports the conclusion that the hearing deficit, which does affect language, does not substantially affect the rate of intellectual development and clearly does not influence the sequence of cognitive development, except when communications with the child are interfered with.

A second implication of Piaget's position is that providing the symbolic structure (giving the child the necessary vocabulary) is not sufficient to accelerate or influence cognitive development. Recently, Beilen (1976) has reviewed the entire area of the linguistic aspects of cognitive operations. His careful analysis of the available research lends some support to Piaget's position; specifically, providing children with the meaning of words does not seem to have a critical influence on the performance of those cognitive tasks associated with the theory. However, a number of experiments indicate that verbal-rule instruction does influence performance and thus may affect the development of mental operations. In view of the evidence on verbal-rule instruction, Piaget has in fact modified his position about the role of language. We shall present a summary quote by Beilin (1976, p. 100) that seems to indicate more simply and directly the nature of the changes that Piaget and his associates have suggested.

> This statement suggests the following: (1) Cognitive operations and preoperations do not direct language or language acquisition as a one-way relation (as in fact the Genevans had previously asserted). (2) What directs language acquisition is a reg-

ulating and organizing mechanism that has a counterpart in the regulating mechanisms in other (nonlinguistic) domains of behavior. These partially independent and at the same time coordinate mechanisms are the manifestations of a more abstract system. (3) Logico-mathematical operations and preoperations manifest these more abstract structures when there is a need for them. These abstract structures are evident in classification, seriation, and other behaviors that embody the logico-mathematical operations of inclusion, order relations, etc. (4) Cognitive structures do not derive then from linguistic structure, nor apparently do linguistic structures derive from cognitive systems. They both derive from a more abstract system of regulations and organizations common to all domains.

This important set of modifications suggests a higher order of mental operations that coordinate earlier mental operations and language. Thus, the linguistic system and the cognitive system originate in abstract logical structures and complement each other. If this theoretical modification in fact is correct, it would allow for the manipulation of mental operations by verbal means.

Issues Derived from the Mechanistic Position

The behaviorists are especially critical of his assertions about the relatively inactive role of cultural variations and Piaget's apparent dismissal of the basic behavioral principles of learning.

As regards the invariance of sequences and mental operations and its relation to cultural variations, we have already indicated that Bruner and his colleagues (Bruner et al., 1966) and Goodnow (1969) present the major evidence about the effects of cultural variations on mental operations. A summary of the literature based primarily on the contributions of Greenfield (Bruner et al., 1966) indicates some cultural effects on the performance characteristics and, presumably, the mental operations of children. Schooling appears to be a more important influence, rather than whether a particular culture is more primitive than Western society. Even here, the data seem to indicate, according to Goodnow's analysis, that many of Piaget's tasks are actually not influenced by school or nonschool factors, or more generally, cultural factors. Goodnow cites a number of examples of tasks in which the non-Western children seem to be most affected, and these influences seem to be in the nature of the representational or symbolic value of drawings and words. Cultural differences, on the other hand, seem to have comparatively little influence on the conservation tasks.

The viewpoint that mental operations required to handle the tasks the Piagetians use to demonstrate their model proceeds on the premise that the behavioral requirements of the tasks have to be clearly specified. After identifying the necessary tasks, the trainer then sets out to teach the child the necessary skills as identified by the task analyses. Clearly, this approach does not make any assumptions about how to order mental competencies or integrative mechanisms, but

The effect of training on cognitive competence, such as conservation, is unclear. (Eric Roth/The Picture Cube)

merely states that if the child's repertoire of responses contains the specific behaviors required, then the task will be solved. The research ensuing from this approach, summarized in detail by Beilin (1976), has generated a considerable amount of controversy about methodology. One issue is that the children inadvertently come to sense what response is expected of them, so that their performance suggests that important modifications have taken place in their mental operations. In other words, the techniques have modified performance rather than competence. The Piagetians argue that such studies never go far enough in proving that the mental operations have undergone significant modification. Specifically, they complain that the training techniques will also influence a number of different but conceptually related behaviors *if* competency has indeed been modified. In those instances where the appropriate tests have been attempted, the results have generally not been very satisfactory. Indeed, we might venture that task analysis has led to a sufficiently mixed set of successes and failures that suggests that this approach has not seriously threatened the Piagetian position. Gelman (1969) trained children to attend to two stimulus dimensions and succeeded in obtaining significant modification in their behavior. Her work has been criticized, however, on the grounds that her subjects may well have been going through a transitional phase and were therefore readily susceptible to the training procedures. Studies such as Gelman's have also been criticized on the grounds that the pretest designed to identify the children's level of functioning may in itself be sufficient to modify cognitive functioning. Thus, we must conclude that the effects ot training programs of the task-analysis type have probably not produced conclusive results, being plagued by a number of complicated methodological flaws. It does, however, seem safe to conclude that the studies of verbal-rule conditions do affect competency.

In examining the fundamental features of Piaget's model of cognitive development, our intention was to provide the reader with the major substantive aspects of the theory, and, equally important, a feel for his general approach. However, this theory, like almost every other one, is not without its problems. We have seen that Piagetian scholars and others are now questioning some of the internal assumptions of the theory, which could lead to major modifications. No doubt these challenges will continue and the model will see further modification. Despite all these inevitable problems, the theory seems to be sufficiently robust to withstand these challenges and will probably continue to have an important impact on how scientists, teachers, and child workers think about children for some time to come.

Concept Formation

Consider the Piagetian stages of development from the perspective of how the maturing child's behavior becomes increasingly more efficient. During the sensori-motor period, the child's knowledge of objects requires direct motoric action that is noticeable in both actions and outcomes. The child demands a maximum amount of direct contact and relies almost exclusively on perceptual cues. During the early part of this stage, the child requires that an object be present before he is capable of performing any behavior with that object. By the time the child can handle trans-formation problems and formal operations, he is in a position to cope with very high-level abstractions that he can communicate verbally. This means that the amount of information that the mature individual can absorb in a given amount of time is greatly increased, and by the same token the mature person can more rapidly understand components of the environment. The full capabilities of the mature human brain have never been duplicated, even by high-speed computers.

The material in this section comes from several different traditions in psychology, including behaviorism and what is now often referred to as information processing. We make no effort to integrate theoretical positions, except where they are obviously compatible, rather, our intention is to provide you with a broader view of the capabilities of children at different age levels and with a fuller description of the cognitive and perceptual processes involved. Some of the discussion here derives directly from materials mentioned in Chapter 5 on perceptual development, and, indeed, the work on behavior theory will require that the reader recall the principles of operant and classical conditioning. In this section we expand upon the operant-conditioning model in an effort to demonstrate how behavior theory has attempted to cope with complex information processing. We shall also examine how changes in the child's competencies modify the meanings of problems.

Hypothesis Testing

In Chapter 5, Perceptual Development, we examined a number of studies assessing the sensory capabilities of newborn babies. Many of those studies used either classical or instrumental conditioning, both of these techniques being based on the behavioristic concepts of S-R learning. In reviewing studies of infant conditioning we noted that the process is very difficult; indeed, some investigators are not persuaded that it is actually possible to condition infants. One possible obstacle to such conditioning is the incomplete development of basic neurological structures and myelin (see Chapter 4). We also noted that it is hard to bring the behavior of infants under stimulus control because their behavior patterns are very sensitive to such physiological states as hunger, fatigue, or general excitability. Although conditionability increases with neurological maturation, it does not continue to improve with age despite the great advances in the neurological development of older individuals. In fact, conditionability improves only up until approximately the age of 6 years. Razran (1933) observed that after this age, children become more resistant to conditioning. Although there are alternative explanations of this phenomena, White (1965) has proposed a plausible developmental explanation that in our judgment is consistent with, but more inclusive than, the observations of Bruner and Piaget and the research of behavioristic psychologists. Specifically, he contends that after the age of 6, children process information through the use of hypotheses. These hypotheses interfere with conditioning, which is primarily a low-level or automatic association of a response with a stimulus. There may be interfering effects, such as: "What does the experimenter *really* want?", or a statement that a very bright 6-year-old made to one of the authors, who was conducting a simple discrimination learning task which this child simply could not solve, "I would never have believed it was always the left one because that just seemed so simple that I thought you were trying to trick me." Thus, what seems to happen is that when children begin to approach concrete operations and become capable of forming hypotheses, the hypotheses are often completely irrelevant to the demands of the task.

A major feature of White's position is that information processing goes through a transition between the ages of 5 and 9. The transition period involves a change from an *associative* level of learning to a *cognitive* one. **Associative learning** is characterized by a rapid rate of response and can be likened to the behavior of an automaton. White suggests, and some research by the Russian psychologists supports this position, that at this level of cognitive functioning, **inhibitory mechanisms** necessary for careful analysis of the stimulus situation are too immature to permit

Picture stories help children learn that objects and actions can be represented by pictures and words. (Jean-Claude Lejeune)

abstract cognitive functioning. As the child matures neurologically and forms new S-R associations, information processing becomes more deliberate and abstract. Under certain conditions, adults will respond automatically and rapidly, but when presented with abstract problems, mature people tend to indulge in delayed, reflective thought. This capability is not readily apparent in the behavior of children under 5. White (1965, pp. 215–216) summarizes his position as follows:

> In summary, it is suggested that the data on temporal contingencies in learning, and the material on the various shifts in the 5–7 age period, may define something about the structure of adult mental processes. Adults may have available an "associative level" layed early in development, relatively fast acting, following conventional associative principles, and in the normal adult relatively often existing as a potential, but an inhibited, determinant of behavior. The "cognitive layer" layed down after the associative mode of response is taken to be relatively slower in action and to process information in ways which are only beginning to be understood.

White describes some 18 kinds of studies, mostly conducted within the behavioristic framework, that he believes lend support to this position. Two of these studies have been selected as examples of the kind of shifts that White describes. Incidentally, Whites's postulated shift from associative to cognitive learning approximates rather closely the major shift from preconcrete operational thought to concrete operational thought as viewed by Piaget. It appears to us that the evidence that White has marshalled in support of his hypotheses and the kinds of transitional events that Piaget describes are not coincidental. Both suggest that the period beginning about 5 years of age and lasting for the next 2 to 4 years in fact represents a series of major changes in the cognitive competency and organization of human beings.

TRANSPOSITION LEARNING.   Experiments reported by Margaret Kuenne-Harlow (1946) and by Alberts and Ehrunfreund (1951) used a **transposition** problem. The physical arrangement of the task is shown in Figure 6-6. The training stimuli consisted of a large and a small cylinder, and the initial training procedure involved a straightforward discrimination learning—the subject is rewarded for responding to the correct stimulus. In the Kuenne-Harlow experiment, the subject was trained to respond to the smaller of the two stimuli; the stimuli were randomly alternated from left to right to avoid any position bias. Further examination of the stimuli in Figure 6-6 shows a set of fairly large cylinders that represent a "near" transposition test, and a set of smaller stimuli that represent a "far" transposition. Examine the stimuli in the near transposition test. The smaller stimulus now is the same size as the stimulus that was incorrect in the training series. Transposition, or relational, rather than absolute, learning is a task in which pairs of stimuli are made progressively smaller in

FIGURE 6-6   *Stimuli and General Experimental Set-up Used by Alberts and Ehrenfreund in Their Study of Transposition Responses of Preschool Children.*

SOURCE: Alberts, E., & Ehrenfreund, D. Transposition in children as a function of age. *Journal of Experimental Psychology*, 1951, 41, 30–38. (Figure 2, p. 32).

FIGURE 6-7 *Percentage of Transposition Obtained by Younger and Older Preschool Children with Various Combinations of Test Stimuli*

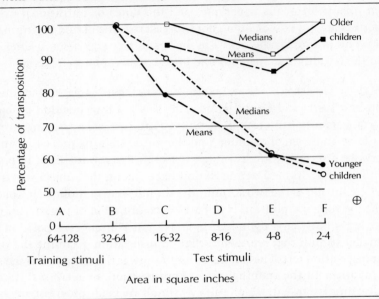

SOURCE: Alberts, E., & Ehrenfreund, D. Transposition in children as a function of age. *Journal of Experimental Psychology*, 1951, *41*, 30–38.

approximately equal units either down or up the scale (in the same way that one can transpose on a musical scale). After learning to select the correct stimulus (usually learning is defined as 10 out of 10 correct choices), the subject is given the near transposition test. Since the original correct stimulus is now the larger of the pair, it becomes the incorrect choice and the new smaller stimulus the correct choice. Following the near test, the far transposition test is given: the same height relationships are maintained (larger and smaller), but the stimuli are substantially smaller than those used previously. We assume that chance responding is approximately 50 percent; that is, children can guess the correct response 50 percent of the time without having identified the correct stimulus. The data in Figure 6-7 indicate that children between 3 and 5 years of age tend to choose the correct stimulus at a level better than chance on the near transposition test, but on the far transposition test they perform at chance level. With the older children, in this case children with *mental ages* of 7 years and above, selection of the correct stimulus on both the near and far transposition test is almost identical to their performance on the latter part of the training series. Thus, they are said to display transposition.

REVERSAL-NONREVERSAL SHIFT. In a series of experiments, Tracy and Howard Kendler (1962) devised a task known as the **reversal-nonreversal shift.** One way to use this task is illustrated in Figure 6-8. Note that the stimulus materials consist of a geometric form that is either black or white or large or small. The brightness and the size of the stimuli represent stimulus dimensions. An additional dimension, position, is necessarily included here, but position does not enter the task, for the position of the correct stimulus during initial training and for test trials is randomly alternated. The overall design in this experiment is fairly complex, requiring a diverse number of counterbalanced groups. One group of subjects learns (again, the criterion is 10 correct choices in 10 trials) to select the larger of the two stimuli. After reaching criterion, the group is shown the same pair of stimuli. However, half the subjects are now rewarded for choosing the smaller of the two stimuli (that is, the *reversal shift*). The remaining children are reinforced for selecting either the black or the white stimulus (subjects are randomly assigned to either the black or the white stimulus), and this is known as the *nonreversal shift*. In the reversal shift, the child selects the previously incorrect stimulus, but the stimulus is on the *same dimension* as the originally correct stimulus. In other words, in the reversal shift the dimension remains the same, but the cue value of the stimulus (large versus small or black versus white) is reversed. In the nonreversal shift, both the relevant stimulus dimension and the cue value are changed. Thus, instead of responding to the size

FIGURE 6-8   *Reversal-Nonreversal Shift*

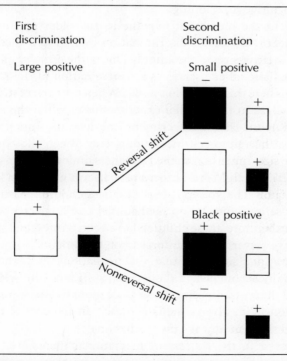

SOURCE: Kendler, H. H., & Kendler, T. S. Vertical and horizontal processes in problem solving. *Psychological Review*, 1962, *69*, 1–16 (Figure 2, p. 5).

dimension, the subjects now must shift to the brightness dimension. Again, half of the children are trained to select the black stimulus and half the white stimulus. The results of the numerous studies conducted using this experimental approach indicate that younger children learn the nonreversal shift more rapidly than the reversal shift. Conversely, children beyond the age of 6 and adults learn the reversal shift more rapidly than the nonreversal shift.

MEDIATION HYPOTHESIS.   The results of the experiments on the reversal and nonreversal shift and the transposition problems are interpreted as evidence for a **mediation hypothesis.** In more specific terms, mediational theory asserts that stimuli do bring about not only overt behavior but also internal responses, including muscle reactions and implicit verbal reactions. It was further assumed in the transposition task that the child who verbalized "larger than" was responding to the *size relationship* rather than to the *absolute value* of the stimuli. The notion of absolute values of the stimuli refers to the physical properties that impinge on sensory receptors. In straightforward instrumental or classical conditioning, the physical properties of the stimuli become associated with the response. Thus, mediation theory moves away from this reliance on the physical values of the stimuli and instead deals with the relationships between stimuli and responses in chains—a higher level of cognitive functioning.

According to the mediation hypothesis, the older and presumably more verbal children learn the initial discrimination and then a mediational cue associated with the relative sizes of the stimuli. One of the primary mediational cues is language. The mediational cue serves as a representation of the *reinforced dimension;* in the studies here this dimension is size. When the correct stimulus is changed from large to small, as in the Kendler experiments, or when the stimuli are transposed as in the Kuenne-Harlow experiment, the relevant dimension remains the same and so does the reinforced mediational cue. When the correct stimulus is changed from the size dimension to the brightness dimension (this only happens in a nonreversal shift), the child must learn a new discrimination and then associate it with a new mediator. The younger, less articulate children learn the nonreversal shift faster because, presumably, no mediational cue interferes with learning the new response. Furthermore, these children have been reinforced for the new correct response and have never been reinforced for the originally incorrect response. Incidental observations suggested that the mediational hypothesis was correct; children who readily accomplished the reversal shift and who were able to handle both the near and the far transposition task more often spontaneously verbalized the relevant dimension. ("It's always the larger one," in the case of the transposition study, or "It's still size, but now it's the smaller one".)

When viewed in the context of mediational theory, the results of these studies suggest that if children receive verbal training, or in some way are provided with the mediational cue, they can perform better on the reversal-shift problem than children with no such training. This did not occur! The children could be taught to verbalize the mediator, but they did not use it during the actual experiment. Reese (1962) suggested that a child's inability to apply a verbal statement is evidence for **control deficiency.** This means that though children can verbalize a concept, their verbalizations do not yet control their behavior. Other studies have suggested that mediation controls behavior only if the younger child could produce the mediator. This problem is called **production deficiency** (Flavell, Beach & Chinsky, 1966).

The mediational hypothesis excited great interest among child psychologists and served as the conceptual basis for a large number of research studies. Although mediation theory is used to explain memory strategies, its use in explaining reversal and nonreversal shift behavior has been somewhat modified. Psychologists still agree that some kind of mediation occurs, but it is not specifically verbal. The attentional hypothesis, discussed in Chapter 5, is viewed as an alternative to verbal mediation. Thus, a specific stimulus (S) becomes associated with an implicit response (r), which could be verbal but might also be a cue to search for relevant stimulus dimensions. The subject then selects from the available stimuli (s) and makes an overt response (R). The mediator in this analysis is stimulus selection that can be aided by a verbal response but does not depend on it.

ATTENTIONAL HYPOTHESIS.   An attentional theory was developed by Zeaman and House (1963) which grew out of their interest in the learning processes of mentally retarded children. Their data suggest that mentally retarded children learn more slowly because of their inability to attend to, or appropriately identify, relevant stimulus dimensions. This behavior resembles that of younger children who often are completely unaware of the possible relevant dimensions in the task.

Further support for an attentional interpretation comes from Meyer and Offenbach (1962), who examined the effects of positive and negative verbal feedback on the performance of 2 age groups of children (5 years and 7 years). The children were presented with a simple discrimination task in which the number of possible relevant dimensions was systematically manipulated. For one group of children, there was 1 relevant dimension and 1 irrelevant dimension (the relevant dimension was either size, color, or volume; the irrelevant dimension was position, which was counterbalanced). For the second group, the stimuli consisting of 2 irrelevant dimensions, and for a third group, the stimuli consisted of 3 irrelevant dimensions. It was hypothesized that the simplest task would be the one with 1 relevant and 1 irrelevant dimension and that the most difficult task would be the one with 1 relevant and 3 irrelevant dimensions. In addition to this manipulation, half of the subjects were told when their response was correct and the other half of the subjects were given verbal feedback only when their responses were incorrect. A series of other studies using this feedback procedure found it proved more effective to inform the subjects of errors than to inform them of correct responses. Regardless of feedback condition, the task with 1 relevant and 1 irrelevant dimension was significantly easier than tasks with 2 irrelevant or 3 irrelevant dimensions (which were not significantly different from each other). Furthermore, the experimenters did not find an age effect, which they took to mean that the children in the 2 age groups were equally aware of the available stimulus dimensions. This finding is in fact probably not surprising, for the youngest group, according to more recent data, was already familiar with all of the stimulus dimensions employed in the task. Of relevance to the concept of hypothesis testing, however, Meyer and Offenbach found no differences between the feedback conditions for the task with 1 relevant and 1 irrelevant task. There was, however, a significant difference in feedback conditions between the 1 relevant and the 2 or 3 irrelevant dimensions.

To interpret this study, remember that in the task with 1 relevant and 3 irrelevant dimensions, the pair of stimuli presented to the subjects for selection incorporated all of the available dimensions, both the relevant and irrelevant dimensions. For example, one of the pair of stimuli was a large green prism and the other was a small red sphere. The relevant dimensions may have been size, with the correct cue being the size of the larger stimulus. Notice that the larger stimulus also contains the color and form dimensions and is on either the left or the right side. Any one of these dimensions could be relevant. As Meyer and Offenbach analyze the ineffectiveness of the feedback for correct responses, they note that the subject might have chosen the correct response but was in fact using the wrong hypothesis. In the example given above, it could happen that the subject chose the large green prism because it was green, whereas the experimenter viewed that stimulus as correct because it was large. In that event the subject would be told he was correct and this positive feedback would therefore reinforce the dimension of color—in effect the child would have been given positive information for the wrong reason. On the next trial the subject may not be so lucky; the green stimulus was also smaller. Here the subject would not be told anything. Unfortunately, these investigators did not design their tasks to determine what happened after a failure to receive positive feedback. The group that received information for incorrect responses only learned faster because the moment the youngster gave an incorrect response, he or she could eliminate the entire dimension or at least that value of the dimension. The feedback for incorrect responses forced the children to use an elimination process, whereas the feedback for correct responses could not generate a useful research strategy.

Meyer and Offenbach (1962) also found that when the experimenter failed to respond in the condition where he gave only positive feedback, the subjects eventually understood that no response in fact meant that they were incorrect. Conversely, when feedback was given only for errors, the subjects learned that no response meant that they were correct. Thus, after a substantial number of trials, that is, when the subjects learned the meaning of the experimenter's failure to respond, the feedback conditions were then equivalent, and performance of the groups was similar. For this reason, Meyer and Offenbach speculated that the children in the group receiving feedback for correct responses eventually adopted a strategy known as win-stay or lose-shift. When compared with the elimination strategy generated by the feedback for incorrect responses, this strategy turned out to be less efficient.

This series of studies, among innumerable others, indicates that children do employ hypotheses and that older children are more likely to employ appropriate hypotheses than younger children. The major transition in the probability of employing hypotheses appears to begin at approximately the age of 5 and seems to reach almost complete adult status by approximately 8 or 9 years of age.

Attending Behavior

Although the mediation hypothesis is of interest because of its attempt to reveal the use of language in the formation of concepts, an attentional model along the lines suggested by Zeaman and House (1963) seems to have more explanatory power. Another kind of experimental arrangement, the **incidental learning task,** has been developed to examine developmental changes in attentional behavior.

THE INCIDENTAL LEARNING TASK.   In the incidental learning task, children are presented with a set of pictures. Each stimulus card is located on a panel and the children are told that some cards with drawings of animals and household objects on them will be shown to them and that they are to remember the position of the animals on the panel, that is, which animal will be found in each of the 8 panels. A single stimulus card at a time is placed on the panel for 2 seconds for the child to examine. After all 8 stimulus cards are exposed, the procedure is repeated for a total of 5 trials. The children are never instructed to remember anything other than the position of the animals on the panel. Using this design, Wheeler and Dusek (1973) tested the subjects for recall of the positions of the central stimuli (the animals) and the incidental stimuli (the other forms). The subjects in this experiment included children from kindergarten, third grade, and fifth grade. It was found that recall of the central stimuli increased with advances in grade level. There was also a general trend in the direction of lower recall of the incidental stimuli. Results similar to these have been reported by Hagen (1967), Drucker and Hagen (1969), and Hagen and Sabo (1967).

These data are usually interpreted as indicating that as children mature they pay more attention to the task-relevant stimuli than to the task-irrelevant stimuli. Actually, what appears to occur is that both older and younger children are almost equally aware of the task-irrelevant material, but the older children reject it in their cognitive processing and emphasize the task-relevant mechanism that we have previously seen operating among older children in other areas of cognitive and motor development.

One interesting variation in the incidental learning procedure is training one group to label the relevant stimulus. When shown a stimulus card, the labeling group is required to name the relevant stimulus. Verbal encoding helps the subjects to recall better the locations of the relevant stimulus. The results of these studies indicate that verbal labeling is more effective with the younger children; this finding confirms the observation of several investigators that the older children are not helped because they spontaneously label the relevant stimuli. These studies do not make clear whether the verbal labeling is effective because it provides children with a linguistic coding system, because it forces them to focus on the relevant stimuli, or because, in terms of mediation theory, it enables them to rehearse what they know verbally. It seems likely that the attention interpretation is more accurate, since labeling would not necessarily lead one to focus on the relevant stimuli. It should be noted that the effects of verbal labeling on the reversal and the nonreversal shift task as well as the transposition task have been equally equivocal. Thus it is not yet clear just exactly how labeling functions.

VISUAL SEARCH TASKS.   Another way in which experimenters examine attending behavior in older children resembles the procedures we have already explored with infants. With older children, however, it seems clear that the examination of stimuli for relevant perceptual features may well be guided by a set of cognitively determined hypotheses. The basic method employed in these studies involves measuring eye movements and eye fixations. We can now determine the sequence of movements used by children and adults in examining a stimulus which must later be identified either by naming the object or through finding it when embedded among other similar stimuli. A number of such experiments are reported in the literature (Mackworth & Bruner, 1970; Vurpillot, 1968; Zinchenko, Chzhi-tsin, & Tarakanov, 1963; and Zaporozhets & Zinchenko, 1966). We will examine the study by Mackworth and Bruner because the stimuli employed were closer to real-life situations than those used in other studies. The results of the other studies, however, indicate clear developmental differences in patterns of eye movements and fixations (herein referred to as **scanning strategies**); they also support the concept that the assessment of scanning strategies is a useful way of developing inferences about mental operations.

The stimulus employed by Mackworth and Bruner is an ordinary fire hydrant, but the clarity of the picture varies from clear to somewhat blurred to very blurred. Six-year-old children and adults served as subjects. Using a technique for measuring eye movements, the experimenters asked the groups of subjects to determine what the object was called. Several innovative measures of scanning strategies were taken, but the one of particular interest here is called a rated search score. This index was developed by asking samples of college students to indicate the parts of the fire hydrant that would be most useful in identifying it. The hydrant was superimposed on a grid composed of $1\frac{1}{2} \times 1\frac{1}{2}$ inch squares. The subjects were instructed to examine the stimulus until they were certain they could identify it. Illustrated in Figure 6-9 are the scanning strategies of a 6-year-old child and an adult. You will

FIGURE 6-9   Eye-movement patterns over a flat surface for an adult (a), a six-year-old (b), and another six-year-old (c). Compared to the adult, the children tend to cover less of the object and to fixate on a detail—not necessarily one that would provide information necessary for identifying the object, since they have not scanned the entire object for important features.

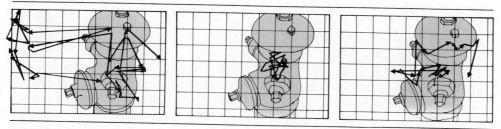

SOURCE: Mackworth, N. H., & Bruner, J. S. How adults and children search and recognize pictures. *Human Development*, 1970, *13*, 149–177 (Fig. 2, p. 157).

immediately notice that the adult has fewer fixation points, but each fixation lasted longer than that of the children. You will also notice that adults tended to concentrate their eye fixations within a relatively limited area and were not distracted by stimuli outside of the central features of the stimulus. When the fixation points for the children and the adults were compared, it turned out that under all conditions of clarity, the adults concentrated their fixations more frequently in the area of high information. The children were affected by the degree of blur but tended to fixate more frequently in the areas of high information as the picture became more clearly focused. Mackworth and Bruner (1970, pp. 172–173) concluded:

> The cognitive aspects of this visual selection were clear throughout the experiments. For instance, the highest Rated Search Scores per fixation were recorded while *Ss* were grasping the meaning of the picture. Furthermore, the averaged Rated Search Score per fixation fell off whenever a trial was repeated, as if *Ss* began with the important regions and then worked further afield the second time around. Children could not place their gaze so skillfully. These results were most clearly demonstrated whenever they were trying to identify out-of-focus pictures. The children were, however, able to find the important details in the sharp pictures. But in these sharp pictures, they became so hooked by the details that their eye tracks now averaged only two-thirds of the length of those made by the adults. Apparently some of the 6-year-old children lacked an effective program for visual search, which would have enabled them to achieve the parallel processing seen in healthy adults.

The research using eye movement, as exemplified in the Mackworth and Bruner study, seems to indicate that the attentional behavior of human beings is age related. As one becomes older, cognitive structures become more elaborate, more hypotheses become available; these in turn generate selective attention to relevant stimulus attributes. Thus, cognitively more sophisticated individuals will exhibit more efficient and more accurate identification and categorization.

MEMORY TASKS.   There are at least two broad classifications **memory** tasks: *episodic* and *semantic* (Brown, 1975). **Episodic memory** refers to a specific event. **Semantic memory** also refers to a specific event, but the memory has broader cognitive implication. Our discussion emphasizes the semantic memory system because it is more sensitive to developmental changes in cognitive functioning than the episodic system and therefore more germane to our discussion of concept formation. The semantic type of memory system requires a mnemonic strategy for satisfactory solution (Flavell, 1970).

Several kinds of experiments have been employed to demonstrate the conceptual character of semantic memory systems. In one type of task called free recall, subjects are presented with a list of words in which there are embedded two or more concepts that can serve as a basis for organizing the rest of the list. The presentation of the words is random. Subjects can attempt to recall the list of words in two ways: in serial order, in which they attempt to reproduce the words in the exact order in which they are presented; through the use of concepts, in which words belonging to a similar concept (for example, food, transportation, and so forth) are grouped together. In other words, the cognitively more mature subject will organize the stimulus words and in effect cluster the original list into meaningful categories. It is assumed that performance of this operation on the words requires meaningful concepts. This point has been emphasized by Flavell and Wellman (1976, p. 4): "Older individuals will presumably store, retain, and retrieve a great many inputs better or differently than younger ones, for example, simply because developmental advances in the content and structure of their semantic or conceptual systems render these inputs more familiar, meaningful, conceptually interrelated, subject to gap-filling, or otherwise more memorable for them."

Another reason why memory improves with age is related to the adequacy with which information is put into memory, or what is often called storage activity. The point is that with the increasing ability to distinguish between relevant and irrelevant dimensions and to improve one's attentional behavior, there is an increase in the amount and quality of information that can be reproduced.

Another developmental shift that makes more efficient retrieval is demonstrated in an experiment by Flavell, Beach, and Chinsky (1966). The children were required to reproduce the experimenter's behavior; in our categorization system this would be a serial memory task. The crucial aspect of the study is subsumed in two conditions: immediate recall of the experimenter's behavior and delayed recall of the experimenter's behavior. It was anticipated that the two older groups of children, in contrast with the kindergarten children, would produce more verbalization and rehearsal in both the immediate recall and delayed recall conditions. The youngsters in the delayed-recall condition were given an additional 15 seconds to rehearse or verbalize the task. In addition, a second treatment was added in which half of each group was induced to label the stimuli. The study clearly demonstrated that the older subjects spontaneously used verbal rehearsal as a mnemonic strategy and that

Psychologists have devised a number of ways to learn about the developmental aspects of memory. (Jean-Claude Lejeune)

the kindergarten children did not. The authors reject the view that the kindergarten children failed to exhibit verbal rehearsal because of their lower level of linguistic development. Rather, they take the view that older children engage in more active kinds of intellectual activities in order to meet what they perceive to be the demands of the task, in this case, verbal encoding and rehearsal. In this respect the behavior is identical to verbal mediation discussed earlier. Thus, this study, like all the others discussed in this section, indicates that the qualitative aspects of the mental operations influence how a task is seen, which is a kind of hypothesis testing in the broadest sense, and this in turn generates mental activities designed to maximize the likelihood of success in solving the particular cognitive task.

Individual Differences

The performance on any one of the several cognitive tasks discussed in this chapter as well as tasks that occur in the natural setting of the school (reading, arithmetic) vary among children. Obviously, one factor responsible for the variability is that some children develop at faster rates than others and thus at any one time will exhibit more competency on the task than other children. Children vary in their performance on tasks in another interesting way. Kagan and his colleagues (Kagan, Rosman, Day, Albert & Phillips, 1964) developed a task known as the Matching

FIGURE 6-10   *Sample Items for MFF*

SOURCE: Kagan, J., Rosman, B. L., Day, D., Albert, J., & Phillips, W. Information processing in the child: significance of analytic and reflective attitudes. *Psychological Monographs*, 1964 (Whole #678) (Fig. 8, p. 22).

Familiar Figures Test (MFFT), an example of which is illustrated in Figure 6-10. The subject is shown a standard picture and asked to examine the 6 pictures accompanying the standard and to identify the one that matches the standard figure. As the reader will notice from our example, the identification of the matching figure is not a particularly easy task, so that in fact a considerable degree of response uncertainty is involved. The basic question answered by this test is the degree to which a child is capable of responding carefully (slowly) and also the degree to which such careful analyses generate a correct response. Thus in scoring the MFFT, a measure is taken of the amount of time elapsed between presentation of the 6 alternative responses and the child's first choice. This is called the latency measure. A second recorded response is the number of errors the child makes before identifying the correct stimulus. In order to obtain the error score, the subject is permitted to continue responding until either the correct stimulus is found or 6 errors occur, whichever comes first. Thus, for each child, both a latency score and an error score are obtained, and it is possible within a sample of children to make a distribution of latency scores and a distribution of error scores. The distribution of scores is then divided in half (this is called a median split) at the fiftieth percentile for each distribution, and all the children above the median are put in one category and those below the median are put in another category. This technique produces 4 groups: fast responders-high errors, fast responders-low errors, slow responders-low errors, and slow responders-high errors. The children in the category fast responders-high errors have been labeled impulsives and children in the category of slow responders-low errors have been called reflectives. The children in the other 2 categories have typically been excluded from further research analysis. It might be noted in passing that children who are slow responders with high errors seem likely to exhibit intellectual dullness, whereas children who exhibit fast responding and low errors are likely to be fairly intelligent. However, reflectives and impulsives do not differ in basic intelligence; they differ in their problem-solving strategies. These observations are based on the authors' work with a variety of learning-disabled children.

Considerable research has been done on the implications of impulsiveness and reflectiveness for cognitive performance on a variety of different tasks. Impulsive children typically respond so rapidly on the MFFT that they may never examine all if any of the figures. Siegelman (1969), who examined the eye movements of children while they performed on the MFFT, reported impulsives indeed do not look at all the pictures. Hence, errors are likely to occur. When they are told that their first choice is incorrect, they simply jump to another stimulus but never really analyze with any care the basic components of the task. These children might be described as inattentive to relevant stimulus dimensions, as showing some inability to form hypotheses because time is required, or as displaying a random pattern of responding to task demands. Conversely, reflective children examine the standard stimulus with considerable care and then examine each of the possible alternatives with equal care. When they think they have found the correct stimulus, they often return first to the standard to make certain that all features are common. Their behavior is deliberate and careful and reflects a fairly systematic approach to the task. It might be noted that the impulsive child is somewhat similar to the highly active child described by Scarr (see Chapter 3).

Given that most cognitive tasks require at least some attention to the salient dimensions or stimulus characteristics and also involve the use of higher order abstractions, it should not be surprising that the impulsive child tends to perform less satisfactorily on reading tasks and on more complex problem-solving tasks. It would appear that impulsiveness tends to take its greatest toll on tasks requiring the greatest degree of systematic detailed analysis. However, Zelnicker and Jeffrey (1976) have shown that impulsives may be superior on tasks requiring speed but not precision. It should be somewhat encouraging to note that several efforts to modify the behavior of impulsive children have met with success, particularly those approaches in which the adult serves as a model demonstrating reflective behavior. Thus, despite the apparently genetic causation of the behavior, impulsiveness would appear to be modifiable through environmental intervention.

SUMMARY

Cognitive theorists such as Bruner, Piaget, and Werner agree that the formation of knowledge about the world involves active organisms acting on, and reacting to, environmental stimulation. These theorists also agree that there are identifiable stages experienced by all children as they progress toward cognitive maturity. Each stage is dependent upon the previous stage, but their qualitative properties are distinctive.

Piaget views cognitive development as resulting from the processes of accommodation and assimilation. Accommodation is the process whereby the child's knowledge of the environment is modified to incorporate new objects or experiences. Assimilation is the process whereby a new object or experience is incorporated into an existing structure. These reciprocal processes are responsible for changes in cognitive schemas. Schemas are cognitive organizations which are manifested in behavioral sequences; object-grasping, for example. Normal children progress through 4 stages: (1) sensorimotor intelligence, (2) preconcrete operations, (3) concrete operations, and (4) formal operations. The major features of each stage are fully described in Piaget's research and have been intensively researched. These research studies have produced important new information about cognitive development and the features of cognitive performance at different age levels. Many of these research studies have caused some scientists to question the usefulness of the stage concept in understanding cognitive development. An alternative view is that the stage transitions are not abrupt but are more continuous than Piaget thought.

Several scientists have studied concept development using a variety of associative learning techniques. The relevance of this work has been to further illustrate the qualitative changes that occur in children's cognitive development. The insights derived about these qualitative changes are now being applied to the study of memory.

(Jean-Claude Lejeune)

CHAPTER 7

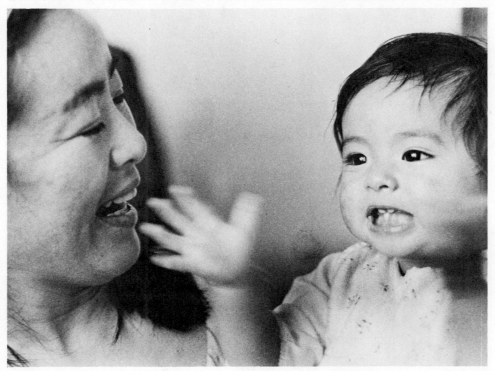

(Ed Buryn)

LANGUAGE DEVELOPMENT

CHAPTERS 5 AND 6 described the very rapid changes in perceptual and cognitive processes from birth to five years. However, the speed with which language develops may be even more impressive. For example, consider the fact that vocabulary expands to approximately 270 words at 2 years, from the first word spoken at about 1 year. At this early stage, single-word utterances such as "Mommy" or "ball" apparently communicate ideas (i.e., single words require other information in order to be correctly interpreted in different contexts). By 4 or 5, children use sentences that contain most of the grammatical constructions used by adults. As children rapidly advance from single words to complex sentences, they seem to have a notion of which rules to apply in particular linguistic situations. Thus, young children rarely use the incorrect progressive form of certain verbs: "I am wanting dinner" or "I am knowing my name." They do correctly use the progressive form for appropriate verbs: a first approximation is "I running," then "I am running," and finally "I'm running."

When we examine in detail the various aspects of sentence formation we have to ask how can such a complex behavior or set of skills be acquired in the relatively short span of two or three years? In this chapter some explanations of language acquisition will be explored and then evaluated with this question in mind. After the various theories have been described and the relevant data have been presented, it will become clear that no single theory satisfactorily accounts for the phenomena of language development.

Theories of Language Acquisition

How *is* language learned? Common sense suggests that imitation plays a key role; children acquire the language they continually hear. But can imitation processes account for all that is known about language acquisition? The principles of classical and instrumental conditioning, discussed in Chapter 6, may also seem like an obvious explanation. However, it should come as no surprise that many students of language acquisition accept a set of assumptions that are biological (nativistic) and do not believe that imitation explains any more than children's learning of speech sounds. In order to give a basis for interpreting the research literature, we shall first examine several theoretical explanations of language learning.

Imitation and Conditioning

An imitation theory of language development seems intuitively correct because, on the surface, it is so simple. How could a sensible person not agree that children learn the sounds and grammatical structures from others (parents in particular)? Let us examine first the learning of sounds. Data exist that show the range of sounds emitted from birth to 12 months becomes progressively more similar to the native language. Parents not only serve as models for these sounds but are also likely to reinforce appropriate sounds—especially when they approximate real words ("ma ma," "da da"). Eventually the baby learns to differentiate those sounds that are likely to produce reinforcement from those which will not. Through this process the sounds themselves become reinforcing and thus self-sustaining.

Imitation theory has also been used to explain how children learn correct word sequences or grammer. Again the model relies on the child's imitating mature speech and being reinforced for the appropriate responses. Thus, after a sufficient number of repetitions involving a broad variety of word classes (nouns, verbs, prepositions, etc.), children discriminate among the word classes and learn what classes of words can follow (or precede) other word classes. Staats (1971), a principal theorist for the learning view, refers to acceptable word sequences as the **privileges of occurrence** learned by conditioning. According to his analysis, children learn to say, "See the horse" but not "Horse the see" because such an utterance is not likely to be heard by a child nor is it likely to be reinforced.

Privileges of occurrence actually represent grammar for Staats, who further assumes that this grammar is learned by means of complex stimulus-response (S-R) mechanisms. He has enumerated numerous such mechanisms, and we shall explore one of these for illustrative purposes. Recall (Chapter 5) that in both classical and instrumental conditioning a stimulus and a response become associated. Thus, when a particular discriminative stimulus (S^D) elicits a response and this response is quickly followed by a reinforcement, the S^D is likely to elicit the same response upon its subsequent presentation. The more often the pairing of the S^D and R with reinforcement, the stronger the association between S^D and R. But what constitutes an S^D and R in a sentence (a sentence is defined as two or more words occurring together)? Staats solves this problem by assuming that the words used in a sentence are simultaneous reponses and stimuli. To understand how this works, we shall take a simple two-word utterance which can be represented as

Word 1   Word 2

Staats uses the word "please" as Word 2 which might be paired with "bread": the child says "bread," meaning "I want a piece of bread," and the mother says, "bread, please." The child repeats the entire phrase and receives the bread. The bread is a reinforcer. Repetition of the entire sequence eventuates in the child automatically using the two words in the learned sequence. Staats views the word "please" as the S^D which controls the response "bread, please." As used here, "bread" is a response and is also the stimulus for the word "please." If several different words ("milk, bread, apple") are consistently paired with "please," they form a class that is associated with a single response. Elaborations of this basic conditioning model generate various functional classes of words and their acceptable positions in sentences. Sentences not previously heard by children ("All gone mommy") are explained in terms of the principle of generalization.

Braine (1963) reports a series of experiments demonstrating how classes of word stimuli can be conditioned to appear in specific positions within sentences. Nonsense words were used which possessed common identifying features permitting the subjects (college students) to form functional classes. Braine was able to demonstrate that words can be conditioned to appear in certain positions. More importantly, however, his experiments demonstrated that new nonsense words (words not previously seen or heard, but functionally related to the familiar words) were correctly placed by the subjects. "The learning of locations is a case of perceptual learning—a process of becoming familiar with sounds of units in the temporal positions in which they recur" (Braine, 1963, p. 348).

Learning theory explains the acquisition of word meaning in a relatively direct way. Specifically, various objects and actions that occur in the child's environment become associated with distinctive speech responses. This form of conditioning is frequently called labeling, i.e., associating names with objects. Meaning occurs as the verbal label becomes associated with the various properties of stimulus objects. Thus, balls bounce, can be caught and thrown, or may involve a game to be played with someone. Actions (running, talking) and variable stimulus properties (red ball, large man) are also learned by association. Although we have not provided much detail on this aspect of theory there are many studies showing that learning

Imitation accounts for some of language learning. Biological correlates are increasingly important for contemporary linguists, however. (Anna Kaufman Moon/Stock, Boston)

labels can be easily produced by instrumental conditioning. These techniques in fact have been widely used in the vocabulary development of preschool children.

Learning theory was widely accepted in the late 1950s and early 1960s as an explanatory model of language acquisition (Skinner, 1957). There were, of course, disagreements on some details of the theory, but there was general agreement about basic principles. Two of these principles deserve consideration: language acquisition can be understood by applying the behavioristic principles of conditioning without recourse to mentalistic concepts (cognitive process or structure); and the only way to understand (predict and control) language acquisition is through the systematic manipulation of independent variables as they influence dependent variables (presumably some aspect of language). Staats (1971, p. 142) summarizes the case this way:

In summary it may be stated that it is important to indicate the nature of theory in the context of language. There are antecedent-consequent (S-R, or causal) theories. These could conceivably be of two types—learning or biological. In either case it is necessary to observe the antecedent conditions and their relationship to language. An even more convincing act is to manipulate the antecedents and thus produce the language behavior. When this has been done in detail the result is a theory by which the behavior can be manipulated, and thus explained, as well as predicted.

Modern Linguistics

Interest in explaining—as distinguished from describing—language development was increased by the appearance of Noam Chomsky's *Syntactic Structures* (1957) and B. F. Skinner's *Verbal Behavior* (1957). Skinner, as previously noted, applied the principles of instrumental conditioning to the study of language, whereas Chomsky's explanation is closely tied to a biological-structural interpretation, more generally referred to as the "nativist" position. It was Chomsky's book that fundamentally changed the study of language and stimulated the interest of developmental psychologists in language development. As might be expected from earlier discussions of the behavioral and organismic views, Chomsky's views challenged the very essence of the learning view. The resulting controversy has stimulated a considerable amount of fresh research and has generated new insights about the early language behavior of children.

CHOMSKY'S VIEWS.   There can be little quarrel with the conclusion that Chomsky's conceptualizations of language acquisition are, at the very least, provocative. He proposed that language acquisition is *instantaneous* and not gradual (Chomsky, 1965). This nativistic theory assumes that human beings have an innately determined (prewired) knowledge of language which alone can explain both the rapidity of language acquisition and the compexity of the system acquired. Chomsky and other modern linguists have been impressed by the near-universality in the sequences with which language is acquired. They appropriately contend that the principles of associative learning simply cannot handle these data and other new information which has emerged since the publication of *Syntactic Structures*.

For Chomsky, the goal of **linguistics** is to try to discover a finite set of rules that explain the infinite number of grammatically correct sentences of a language, but none of the grammatically incorrect sentences (actually nonsentences). **Linguistic rules** represent the knowledge of the language that Chomsky refers to as **competence**: "the set of rules which allow the user to speak and understand the language by relating the sound system to the meaning system, the phonetic representation to the semantic representation" (Palermo, 1970, p. 140). Competence is an abstraction referring to a native speaker's knowledge of grammatical rules; actual speech is called performance. Competence is not always reflected in performance, as when the speaker becomes distracted or forgets and utters an ungrammatical phrase or sentence. That competence is really present is shown by the fact that the speaker can recognize the errors and correct them. The rule systems are not necessarily apparent to the user, since linguistic rules occur without conscious effort. Chomsky believes that general rule systems can adequately describe all particular languages, regardless of how different their grammars may be. Thus, diverse grammars are viewed as variants of a universal grammar whose origins are in the structure of our brains and are known intuitively and innately to the young child. According to McNeil (1970, p. 1088):

> In the case of syntax, some universals describe characteristics of the deep structure of sentences (Chomsky, 1965). Every language utilizes the same basic syntactic categories, arranged in the same way—such categories as sentences, noun phrases, verb phrases. Every language utilizes the same basic grammatical relations among these categories—such relations as subject and predicate of a sentence, verb and object of a verb phrase and modification within a noun phrase. Every language can recursively include sentences within sentences. And every language distinguishes deep and surface structures, and so is transformational.

The important implication of a universal **grammar** is that children naturally "look for" the regularities in adult language that conform to the kinds of rules contained in the universal grammar. This built-in language detection system enormously simplifies the problem of acquisition, since children need not proceed inductively, trying out all the rules that seem consistent with the limited samples of native language actually heard. Rather, children explore a very limited set of grammatical possibilities that are consistent with their experience and with the universal grammar.

Perhaps the key argument supporting Chomsky's innateness principle is based on the fact that children develop full competence within their native language based on fragments of the language. Chomsky labels this phenomenon "poverty of the stimulus," meaning that the rules of a language are learned by hearing a very small sample of the language. Without a special language detection system there is no way that the fragments of language to which a child is exposed could generate adequate rule systems to explain the complexity and subtlety of the language children actually use.

The concepts of **surface** and **deep** structure are another unique feature of Chomsky's analysis of language. Surface structure refers to the characterization of sentences in terms of grammatical units, their interrelationships, and their representation in phonetic form. Thus, surface structure consists of groups of words that go together and which can be broken down into constituent components. In the sentence, *John hit the ball*, for example, *hit the ball* is a constituent component which can be further broken down into *hit* and *the ball*. Deep structure is a more abstract aspect of syntactic description and is concerned with meaning. At this level a message cast in diverse syntactical forms will be perceived as possessing similar meaning.

Consider the following sentences:

The meat was sold by the butcher.
The meat was sold by the pound.

In these sentences, the constituent elements are the same, thus the sentences have identical surface structures. Their deep structures, or meanings, are different.

Next, consider these sentences:

David made a touchdown.
The touchdown was made by David.

These sentences have different surface structures; the first sentence is stated in an active mood, the second in the passive. Despite the differences in the surface structures, the meanings are common; the deep structures are similar.

The modification of the active sentence to the passive is one example of how a sentence can be changed without violating meaning. There are other examples:

David did make the touchdown.
Was it David who made the touchdown?
David did not make the touchdown.

The set of rules that permit these changes in the surface structure are called **transformational rules.** These rules also provide the means for understanding that the sentences are related in meaning and serve as a basis for translating deep structure into surface structure. It is possible from this analysis to understand a sentence almost without regard to how the words are ordered. Thus transformational rules play an integral part in Chomsky's systems and explain why it is known as transformational grammar.

Chomsky's strongly biological position was shared to a greater or lesser degree by psychologists interested in language (psycholinguists). McNeil (1970), for example, has postulated a **language acquisition device (LAD).** He uses this expression metaphorically to designate a biological but uniquely human system which detects linguistic features in speech sounds and uses this information to generate the rules of language. Although the actual LAD processes are not specified, the concept of feature detection is entirely consistent with Chomsky's formulations.

Lenneberg (1967) developed a more detailed account of the innate mechanisms involved in language learning. He believed that language development is a function of a highly specialized logical system, also unique to human beings. He further hypothesized specific brain areas for language, an articulatory apparatus, and an auditory system for distinguishing speech from other sounds. This last hypothesis has been experimentally confirmed. Lenneberg believed that children need some minimal level of language stimulation (such as a voice on a radio) so that all the components of the system would develop. In his opinion the whole system is governed by maturation, in much the same way as motor development depends on maturation rather than learning. The data in Table 7-1 illustrate the parallels between motor and language development that support Lenneberg's maturational hypothesis.

Although Chomsky chose to emphasize **syntactics,** his generative grammar also includes a **phonological** component and a **semantic** component. The phonological component is discussed more fully later in the chapter. In the present context, this component involves the detection and discrimination of speech sounds (phonemes), intonation patterns, and the relations among sounds. A fundamental assumption is that there exist innate structures designed to discriminate and categorize speech sounds.

The semantic component is a system for interpreting the meaning of a sentence. Specifically, semantics is concerned with the meanings of words, phrases, and sentences. Children must learn that words (phrases, sentences) represent objects and actions in the world. At a more advanced developmental level, subtleties in meaning and double meanings may also be learned.

Until the late sixties and early seventies, research emphasis was on the syntactic component and the assumption that syntactics could explain meaning. Bloom (1970, 1973), among others, showed that there are both syntactic and semantic regularities in language. From this work came the current interest in the relation between language and cognition. Lois Bloom (1975, p. 3) describes a basic assumption as follows: "Children learn language as a means of representing or coding information that they have already acquired about objects, events, and relations in the world. Language development, in this view, follows from and depends upon conceptual development in a logical way." Her basic idea is that we can understand language development better if we examine children's language with semantic concepts like *agent, action, object,* and *location,* rather than with syntactic concepts like *subject* and *predicate.* Semantic analysis is still in its infancy, and is represented by more theoretical conceptualizations that we can consider here. These conceptualizations are extraordinarily complex and, in certain areas, conflicting, so that any brief synthesis of this work would be unfair to the theorists discussed. Since, however, this work is extremely important for understanding language development, we do make an effort to present the main concepts, with examples of the data on which these concepts rest.

Semantic theories of language, relying heavily on Piaget's notion of levels of cognitive development, generally accept the proposition that language reception and production reflect knowledge. Linguistic complexity is also viewed as a product of cognitive formulations, namely, elaborations of syntactic relations and the use of grammatical rules. This last assumption is reminiscent of Chomsky's views about the innateness of language ability. The relationships between cognition and language have been carefully examined by McNamara (1972, p. 1). Summarizing on the basis of studies of vocabulary, and of syntactical and phonological development,

McNamara concludes that cognitive awareness (knowledge) is the basis of language development: "The thesis of this paper is that infants learn their language by first determining, independent of language, the meaning which a speaker intends to

TABLE 7-1 Developmental Milestones in Motor and Language Development

AT THE COM-PLETION OF	MOTOR DEVELOPMENT	VOCALIZATION AND LANGUAGE
12 weeks	Supports head when in prone position; weight is on elbows; hands mostly open; no grasp reflex	Markedly less crying than at 8 weeks; when talked to and nodded at, smiles, followed by squealing-gurgling sounds usually called *cooing*, which is vowel-like and pitch-modulated; sustains cooing for 15 to 20 seconds.
16 weeks	Plays with a rattle placed in his hands (by shaking it and staring at it), head self-supported; tonic neck reflex subsiding	Responds to human sounds more definitely; turns head; eyes seem to search for speaker; occasionally some chuckling sounds
20 weeks	Sits with props	The vowel-like cooing sounds begin to be interspersed with more consonantal sounds; acoustically, all vocalizations are different from the sounds of the mature language of the environment
6 months	While sitting, bends forward and uses hands for support; can bear weight when put into standing position, but cannot yet stand with holding on; reaching is unilateral; no thumb apposition yet; releases cube when given another	Cooing changes into babbling resembling one-syllable utterances, neither vowels nor consonants have very fixed recurrences; most common utterances sound somewhat like *ma, mu, da,* or *di*
8 months	Stands holding on; grasps with thumb apposition; picks up pellet with thumb and fingertips	Reduplication (or more continuous repetitions) becomes frequent; intonation patterns become distinct; utterances can signal emphasis and emotions
10 months	Creeps efficiently; takes side steps, holding on; pulls to standing position	Vocalizations are mixed with sound play such as gurgling or bubble-blowing; appears to wish to imitate sounds, but the imitations are never quite successful; beginning to differentiate between words heard by making differential adjustment

SOURCE: Lenneberg, E. Biological foundations of language. New York: John Wiley & Sons, 1967, pp. 128–130.

"Why is it raining?"
Piaget believes that the preoperational child's questions
indicate a lack of ability to separate intentions from
causes. (Mike Mazzaschi/Stock, Boston)

convey to them, and by working out the relationship between the meaning and the language. To put it another way, the infant uses meaning as a clue to language, rather than language as a clue to meaning."

Lenneberg (1971) suggested that Piagetian cognitive development takes place in parallel to linguistic cognitive development and that these processes eventually combine to form an integrated system. This convergence of different processes may be seen in children's ability to grasp the meaning of sentences whose deep structure is not obvious.

Children use certain words and word orders more than others because these words and their order have meaning for them. Recall that the development of sensorimotor intelligence (Chapter 6) involved the child (subject) acting (predicate) on a variety of things (object). It seems reasonable to suppose that children's language would focus on actions, requests for information (learning the names of objects), and more complex relations, reflecting children's acting on objects. Several investigators' analyses of speech samples have brought to light a remarkable uniformity in the semantic content and in the sequence with which words are used (Brown, 1973; Bloom, 1970, 1975; Bowerman, 1973; Greenfield & Smith, 1976).

Nelson (1973) proposes that semantic components may be acquired on a more individualistic basis rather than in terms of sensorimotor relations. She reports data showing initial vocabularies may be either referential or expressive in content. Referential content refers to objects and their properties (round). Expressive content is more social, referring to people and relations. It is Nelson's view that early semantic development reflects children's language experiences, most likely with their mothers.

What is the current state of theory, and what hypotheses seem useful in furthering understanding of language development? Although we cannot conclude with certainty that the semantic relations among words correctly explain language development it does seem that children initially learn the semantic relations between words. Subsequently they learn syntactic relations, such as subject and predicate. When we consider how children manage to produce complete adultlike sentences, however, a strict semantic account is also inadequate. It can be shown, for example, that young children can communicate meaning without using adultlike complete sentences. How do they come to adopt the adult sentence forms?

There seem to be two possible explanations of linguistic development. First, after the child becomes aware of linguistic rules (a cognitive event), the detection and elaboration of these rules run parallel to cognitive elaborations. At some point these interdependent systems intersect, at which time the comprehension of how syntactic structures relate to meaning can generate new cognitive structures. The second explanation would place the fusion of cognitive and linguistic elaborations as occurring at the same time as the first awareness of grammatical structures. According to this view, syntactic and cognitive elaborations are interdependent. Both these positions require extensive work with older children before any conclusions may be made; neither may be tenable.

Bloom (1975, p. 291), a major contributor to the field, gives an excellent summary of the changes in theories of language development since Chomsky introduced transformational grammar.

1. Attempts to explain how children learn to talk have had two main thrusts. On the one hand, it was proposed that the course of language development depends directly on the nature of the linguistic system, and more specifically, on those aspects of language that may be universal and represented in an innate, predetermined program for language learning.

2. On the other hand, evidence began to accrue to support a different hypothesis that emphasized the interaction of the child's perceptual and cognitive development with linguistic and nonlinguistic events in his environment.

3. The issue remains to be resolved, and neither linguistic determinism nor cognitive determinism has yet received unequivocal empirical or theoretical support. Research in semantic development, however, has led to an increasing awareness of the correlates of language acquisition in the development of perception and cognition.

Prelinguistic Development

A number of accomplishments precede the emergence of language. The sounds associated with the native language must be discriminated, categorized, and reproduced. Combinations of sounds to form words are learned, and also, eventually, their meaning. As the research indicates, these complex accomplishments are acquired very rapidly; the first recognizable word occurs at approximately 12 months. The rapidity of these events lends further support to the general concept of an innate system sensitive to language. One component of this system involves language reception; the ability to detect language signals simplifies the acquisition process.

Receptive Language

In our earlier discussion of Chomsky's theory, it was assumed that human beings possess a special language detection system. Support for this interpretation requires a demonstration that infants can discriminate basic sound units (phonemes) and **morphemes** (the smallest units of meaning). Given that babies have the acuity to discriminate sounds (see Chapter 5 for evidence), the nativist position would be supported by evidence showing that: (1) babies discriminate between language and nonlanguage stimuli; (2) they have a preference for linguistic stimuli; (3) they categorize, at least primitively, phonological features of speech; and (4) they understand words that do not appear in their own oral vocabularies.

That babies do discriminate between the human voice and other sounds was demonstrated by Wolf (1966). This investigator also found the human voice was more effective in soothing a baby than other noises. This latter result does not directly show infants' preference for linguistic sounds, but it does suggest that such stimuli are more effective in gaining their attention.

Infants' discrimination and categorization of phonological elements has been demonstrated in two studies. Moffitt (1971), using the method of habituation of the orienting reflex (see Chapter 5), showed that 24-week-old infants could reliably discriminate between the "ga" and "ba" sounds. Eimas, Siqueland, Jusczyk, and Vigonito (1971), used the same method to show that 1- to 4-month-old infants can distinguish the /p/ and /b/ sounds. Eimas' work suggests that familiarity with these sounds influenced discriminability of other sounds. The increased discriminability occurs because the infants may have formulated classes of speech sounds and fit new sounds into these categories. If Eimas is correct, then it appears that infants can discriminate and categorize phonetic elements nearly as well as adults. This research permits the conclusion that the reception of speech begins at birth and serves as a basis for elaborated detection, comprehension, and production.

If infants process linguistic stimuli, can they comprehend words? That is, is their **receptive vocabulary** larger than their productive vocabulary? Vincent-Smith, Bricker, and Bricker (1974) studied this question using two age groups: 22-month-old and 29-month-old infants. The experimenters paired familiar and unfamiliar objects and asked the babies to pick up the object named. Some of the pairs consisted of a known and an unknown object (drum/megaphone), and some consisted of 2 unknown objects (gas pump/camel). In the known-unknown pairs, children in both age groups performed better than with the unknown-unknown pairs. When asked what a certain unknown object was, the children used the known object as a referent: "It can't be the drum, the experimenter asked for a megaphone." In the condition with two unknown objects, no referent was available, and performance was at chance level. This study suggests that infants confronted with new words use cues other than the words themselves. It should be noted that when again presented with the unknown pairs just after having been corrected the first time, the children's performance improved. Thus, it appears that by using many cues, children develop a receptive vocabulary.

The research evidence provides support for each of the four propositions derived from the nativist position. While the evidence is sparse and limited in other ways, the possibility that special detectors of linguistic features exist continues to be a plausible hypothesis.

FRIEDLANDER'S RESEARCH.   A discussion of receptive language would not be complete without describing Friedlander's (1970) research. He examined preferences in the receptive language of babies between 11 and 15 months; his studies reveal the ingenuity research with infants often calls for. Figure 7-1 shows the stimulus complex named PLAYTEST: its critical feature is two switches that the baby can operate. Each switch activates one of two audiotapes, each producing stimuli with different features. One experiment examined the effect of redundancy on stimulus preference. One tape contained a short (20-second) story segment. This tape is highly redundant because the story is repeated after 20 seconds of listening. The second tape contained a 140-second segment; the low redundant tape. The infants in this study were tested at home and were free to press either tape whenever they so desired. The range of listening is from approximately 1,200 to 1,500 seconds per day to 65,000 seconds of responding (the equipment was available for 20 days, averaging more than 3,000 seconds of listening per day). The results of the redundancy experiment, shown in Figure 7-2, indicate that the two infants clearly preferred the less redundant story.

Friedlander also studied babies' reactions to the voice intonation and vocabulary of different speakers (mother versus stranger). The babies preferred the sound of the mother's voice, but they were sensitive to changes in the intonations of both mother and stranger. When the mother spoke in a flat, monotonous tone of voice and used unfamiliar words, and the stranger spoke in a dynamically varied

FIGURE 7-1 *Twelve-Month Boy with PLAYTEST Mounted on Crib at Home.* Control units are normally placed below crib, out of reach.

SOURCE: Friedlander, B. Z. Receptive language development in infancy. *Merrill-Palmer Quarterly,* 1970, *16,* 7–51 (Fig. 1, p. 14).

tone using familiar words, some babies preferred the stranger. Friedlander (1970, p. 19) observes " . . . listening to sounds and voices seems to have hitherto unsuspected potency as a desirable form of activity to babies whose own speech is barely advanced to the stage of one and two word sentences." We can reasonably conclude that babies are specifically aware of language during infancy.

Productive Language

The first sound emitted by the newborn infant is typically the **birth cry.** Although the psychoanalytic (Freudian) interpretations of behavior have attached considerable psychological significance to the birth cry, Thompson (1961), in his survey of the research, concludes that it most likely results from a sudden influx of air across the vocal cords. No empirical evidence supports the contention that the birth cry represents a protest against leaving the womb; in fact, for the fully developed infant, the womb is not an ideal environment.

It is unclear just what physiological capability the vocal cords have for producing different sounds. McCarthy (1954) concluded that during the first months of life, speech sounds are emitted at random and that it has proved difficult to identify speech sounds reliably. These data contradict the popular belief that mothers can reliably distinguish between the basic sounds made by their infants. It would probably be fruitless for us to challenge this belief, because we lack solid proof one way or the other. If mothers can tell the difference between these sounds, they are probably relying on contextual cues (such as time of day or hours since eating) rather than on specific features of the sounds themselves.

Vocalizations during the **prelinguistic period** consist of babbling—a variety of sounds whose origin seems to be innate. It is plausible to assume that all the sounds contained in adult speech in all languages can be heard in the baby's early babbling. Any changes in the phonemic properties of babbling are the result of learning. Shown in Figures 7-3 and 7-4 are data collected by Orvis Irwin (1947, 1948) which show how consonant sounds change over a period of 2.5 years; the data also show how the production of these sounds (their formation in the oral cavity) changes during this period. These data indicate that during this age span infants' speech sounds come to resemble the speech sounds of others. Although infants have the biological capability for many speech sounds, the sounds the infant does not hear rapidly disappear, and only the sounds he does hear remain.

FIGURE 7-2 *Two Children Showing Cross-Over Effect of Self-Selected Listening Preference in Preverbal Infants.* These curves show initial listening preferences for short, highly redundant story segments, followed by a shift to greater preference for larger, less redundant segments of the same story. The data were collected with automated Playtest toys attached to the infants' cribs in the normal environment of their own homes. The infant in A (left) was a bright boy 12 months old. The infant in B was a bright girl 16 months old.

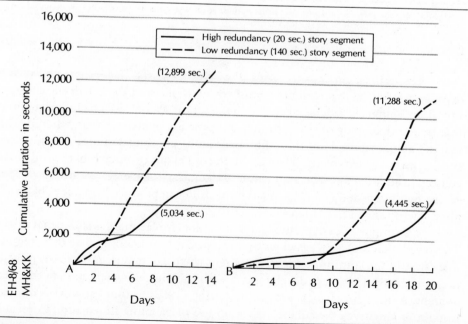

FIGURE 7-3   *Percentages of Consonant Sounds Produced in Various Oral Positions at Fifteen Different Age Levels*

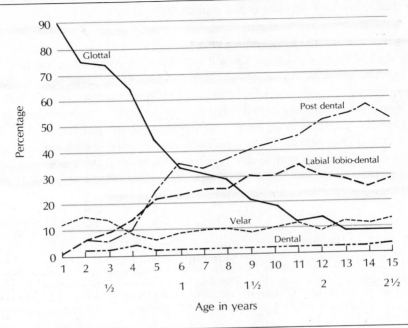

SOURCE: Irwin, O. C. Infant speech: Consonantal sounds according to manner of articulation. *Journal of Speech Disorders*, 1947, *12*, 402–404.

The earliest linguistic sounds identifiable in infant speech are vowels, not consonants. For the first 6 months, most vowel sounds and about half the consonant sounds of a language can be identified in the infant's babbling. The infant maintains this greater frequency of vowel sounds until the age of about 1 year, when he utters his first actual word. After that, the infant emits consonants more and more often until at least 2.5 years of age. Then children emit about two-thirds of the full range of consonant sounds. The development of phonemes is most rapid during the first year of life. By the age of 30 months, the typical child can produce 77 percent of all adult phonemes in the native language.

The importance of prelinguistic utterances for language is somewhat unclear. The developmental view, as expressed by McCarthy (1959), is that they represent one phase in the continuous development of language; that is, emphasis is placed on the continuity of language development, with babbling being one stage of that development. A different view, expressed by Carroll (1960), is that babbling is unrelated to mature language; the infant makes no use of babbling in learning to form the

FIGURE 7-4   *Age Trends in the Relative Proportions of Consonant Categories According to Manner of Articulation*

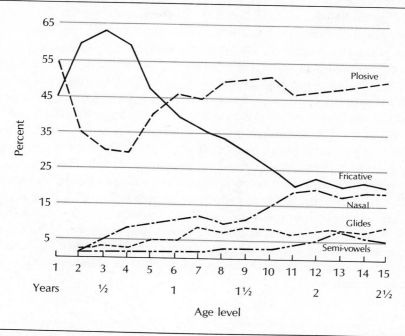

SOURCE: Irwin, O. C. Infant speech: consonantal sounds according to manner of articulation. *Journal of Speech Disorders*, 1947, *12,* 397–401.

phonetic elements of the language. Carroll (1960, p. 746) describes the discontinuity as follows: "Despite the fact that the phonetic diversity (frequency) noted during the period of babbling increases considerably these phenomena have little specific relevance for the development of true language. It is as if the child starts learning afresh when he begins to utter meaningful language." An assessment of these two opposing views suggests that McCarthy and Carroll are discussing two different issues. McCarthy would appear to be correct in holding that the child who rapidly acquires the phonetic elements of his language begins speaking that language earlier than other children (McCarthy, 1959). A child must have the speech sounds before uttering words. Carroll's position is that mere sounds do not constitute true language—sounds must have meaning in order to qualify as true language. The evidence suggests that the first emergence of meaningful sounds, "Ma Ma," "Da Da" for example, lack any representational meaning to the infant. Thus, if true language requires understanding, then it would appear that Carroll is also correct.

We noted earlier that, typically, the child utters his first meaningful sound at the age of 1 year. A more demanding definition of "meaningful sound," however, requires that the sounds refer to something external in order to be considered examples of true language. One frequent early utterance is "Da Da," which is ordinarily taken to show that the child is referring to Daddy, and which thus has meaning. But it is probably not until some time later that the child actually applies a particular combination of phonemes to its appropriate referent. Thus, it is probably accurate to conclude that language occurs only at this later stage. Evidence from research indicates that meaningful words first appear at 12 months, or toward the end of the sensorimotor period of development. Studies by Smith (1926) and Lenneberg (1967) show that vocabulary grows very rapidly from 12 months through 6 years. Smith's findings (summarized in Table 7-2) show that vocabulary grows from some 270 words at 2 years to well over 2,500 words at 6 years. But the estimate of the number of words used is well below the child's functional (receptive) vocabulary. Children's receptive vocabulary is undoubtedly much higher than their productive vocabulary—both children and adults understand more words than they themselves actually speak or write. The rapid growth of vocabulary is consistent with the rapid cognitive development also taking place during the child's early years. Whether these two courses of development are interdependent or merely parallel is a question of great interest.

TABLE 7-2 The Average Size of Oral Vocabularies of Children from Eight Months to Six Years of Age.

YEARS MONTHS		NUMBER OF WORDS	GAIN
	8	0	
	10	1	1
1 —	0	3	2
1 —	3	19	16
1 —	6	22	3
1 —	9	118	96
2 —	0	272	154
2 —	6	446	174
3 —	0	896	450
3 —	6	1222	326
4 —	0	1540	318
4 —	6	1870	330
5 —	0	2072	202
5 —	6	2289	219
6 —	0	2562	273

SOURCE: Smith, M. E. An investigation of the development of the sentence and the extent of vocabulary in young children. *University of Iowa Studies, Child Welfare*, 1926, 3, No. 5.

Development of Grammar

Contemporary language theories are concerned with children's developing abilities to make up sentences and to make them longer and longer. As noted earlier, the study of sentence structure is called *syntax*. This section concerns the development of sentence length, the emergence of the various parts of speech, and the variables associated with individual differences in development in these aspects of language, as well as changes in question-asking.

The first word the child speaks, at around 12 months, is regarded by many investigators as a sentence (Greenfield & Smith, 1976). If the word has meaning for the child, this claim makes sense. One-word sentences are called **holophrastic,** because it is assumed the child means the word to communicate ideas, feelings, or actions. Sometimes after 24 months, children produce 2-word sentences. Two-word sentences communicate more than single words, but the listener relies on the utterance's context in order to understand them. Two-word sentences are sometimes called **telegraphic** because key parts of speech are missing. "Eric ski," for example, may mean "See Eric ski," "Those are Eric's skis," or "Eric can ski." These 1-word and 2-word sentences have been studied to discover any regularities in early speech that provide clues for later learning of syntactic rules.

Studies of syntax have relied heavily on large samples of children's speech, most of them from infants (Braine, 1963, 1976; Bloom, 1970; Bloom, Lightbown, & Hood, 1975; Brown, 1973; Bowerman, 1973; Greenfield & Smith, 1976). Brown's study exemplifies the general method very well. He used average sentence length as an index of language competence; he called the index **mean length of utterance,** or **MLU.** The collection and analysis of samples of speech is time-consuming and expensive because the productive output is usually large, especially among older children. Thus, such studies use very few subjects. Brown's study included Adam, Eve, and Sara. Like Piaget, these investigators assume the existence of universal sequences of language acquisition and universal syntactic structures. Thus, all that is really needed is a reasonably sized sample of a child's language in order to make generalizations about all children. Not everyone accepts all, or even any, of these assumptions.

Eve was the daughter of a graduate student; Adam, the son of a minister; and Sara, the daughter of a clerk. Sara's parents had graduated from high school but had not attended college. The data were transcriptions of each child's spontaneous speech. Observations were made in the home with the mother present. A minimum of 2 hours' speech for each month of the child's participation in the study was obtained. Eve, the youngest child, was studied beginning at the age of 18 months. Adam and Sara entered the study at 27 months of age. Eve remained in the study for

FIGURE 7-5   *Mean Utterance Length and Chronological Age for Three Children*

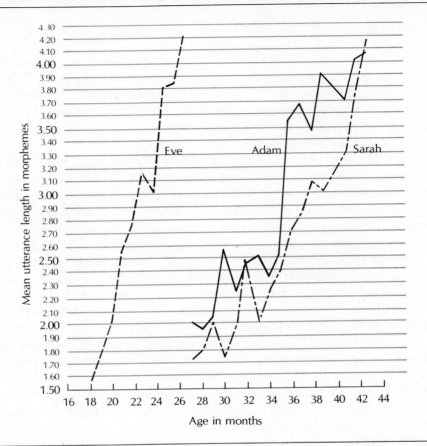

SOURCE: Brown, R. *A first language: the early stages.* Cambridge, Mass.: Harvard University Press, 1973 (Fig. 1, p. 55).

8 months; Adam, for 15 months; and Sara for 21 months. Figure 7-5 shows the changes in MLU for each child. As Figure 7-5 shows, Eve exhibited the most rapid increase in MLU, and Sara lagged somewhat behind Adam. Eve's MLU at 28 months, when she left the study, was 4.25 words. Adam attained a comparable output at 42 months. Individual differences of this magnitude are rather common among children at this age level.

The data in Figure 7-5 have certain implications for syntactic development. Note the numerals I through V, on the right-hand side of the figure, and the associated horizontal lines. These lines represent developmental stages when the children's language behavior changed in identifiable ways. The stages were not based on a conceptual analysis but were derived empirically.

The best characterization of Stage I is that early on, children produce a few 2-word utterances which are intermingled with a number of single-word utterances (holophrases). Later in the same stage, the MLU is expanded to include 2- and 3-word utterances, and as children approach the end of Stage II, they utter some 4-word sentences.

To characterize the sentences produced at Stage I, Brown uses the term telegraphic. As this expression implies, children use only the words critical for communicating the meaning. At this level, prepositions, conjunctions, articles (these words are sometimes called **functors**), and auxiliary verbs are typically omitted. Thus, sentences consist mainly of nouns and verbs. Further, **inflections** are consistently omitted; the -*ed* marker signifying the past tense is dropped, as is the -*s* to form plurals. One interesting feature of telegraphic speech was shown in a study by Brown and Fraser (1963) using the imitation method we described earlier. Level I children omit inflections when they are imitating an adult. Despite the omissions, however, they maintain the same sequence of words. Thus it appears that at Level I, children have a grammar but omit words that are not crucial for comprehension.

PIVOT-OPEN CONSTRUCTIONS.   Two-word utterances have received considerable attention from a number of investigators. Braine (1963, 1976) is foremost among those interested in 2-word sentences. Braine believed, on the basis of the 1963 study, that 2-word utterances were not random combinations of words, but rather reflected an underlying order. He later substantially modified this claim, but the data for his original concepts are still interesting.

Table 7-3 shows data from one of Braine's subjects. The language behavior of 3 young children—Gregory, Andrew, and Steven—was observed directly. Braine developed the concept of **pivot** and **open** words to explain the consistencies in 2-word sentences. Pivot words categorize a few words that occur very frequently. In a 2-word utterance, a pivot word can come either first or second, but it also serves as the focal point of the sentence. Open words are any other expressions attached to the pivot word, regardless of position. For example, Andrew used the word "more" in the sentences, "more car" and "more juice." Here, "more" is the pivot word, and "car" and "juice" are open words. In the second example, the word "off" is a pivot word in the second position with "boot" and "light" as open words. Two-word constructions can also mention 2-object class words: "Mommy sleep," "Milk cup." Brown contended that the pivot-plus-open construction implies that children have some knowledge of "what words are permitted to go where." If he is correct, it would appear that children at this stage have some conceptual knowledge of language rules. It also suggests that we have underestimated the information children are capable of communicating at the 2-word level.

The pivot-open construction has attracted the interest of many scholars because it has appeared to be a fairly simple example of early linguistic behavior governed by rules. One critical assumption is that pivot words never occur alone, or

---

TABLE 7-3 Andrew's Word Combinations

---

more car[a]	no bed	other bib	boot off	see baby
more cereal	no down[c]	other bread	light off	see pretty
more cookie	no fix	other milk	pants off	see train
more fish	no home	other pants	shirt off	
more high[b]	no mama[d]	other part	shoe off	hi Calico
more hot	no more	other piece	water off	hi mama
more juice	no pee	other pocket	off bib	hi papa
more read	no plug	other shirt		
more sing	no water	other shoe	airplane all gone	airplane by[h]
more toast	no wet[e]	other side	Calico all gone[f]	siren by
more walk			Calico all done[f]	mail come
outside more	down there		all done milk	mama come
	clock on there		all done now	what's that
all broke	up on there		all gone juice	what's this
all buttoned	hot in there		all gone outside[g]	mail man
all clean	milk in there		all gone pacifier	mail car
all done	light up there		salt all shut	our car
all dressed	fall down there			our door
all dry	kitty down there		byebye back	papa away
all fix	more down there		byebye Calico	look at this
all gone	sit down there		byebye car	pants change
all messy	cover down there		byebye papa	dry pants
all shut	other cover down there		Calico byebye	
all through	up on there some more		papa byebye	
all wet				

SOURCE: Braine, M. D. S. The ontogeny of English phrase structure: the first phrase. *Language*, 1963, 39, 1–13 (Table 2, p. 5).

[a]"Drive around some more."   [e]"I'm not wet!"
[b]"There's more up there."   [f]Said after the death of Calico the cat.
[c]"Don't put me down."   [g]Said when the door is shut: "The outside
[d]"I don't want to go to mama."   all gone."
                                                 [h]"A plane is flying past."

---

together with other pivot words. Several studies have failed to substantiate this assumption, and it is now believed that pivot grammar is inadequate to account for constructions at Stage I. In a more recent study (1976), Braine acknowledges this conclusion and suggests that children's linguistic categories are probably semantic (based on word meanings) as well as grammatical.

WH-QUESTIONS.   During Levels I and II, children's questions take the grammatical form of a declarative sentence, but the tone (inflection) of a question. Thus "Sit?" or "Daddy sit?" can be a question or not, depending on the inflection. Either of these expressions could be a command, since nothing in their syntactical forms makes them necessarily questions. During the latter part of Level II, children begin to form Wh-questions by placing the Wh-form (*why, who, when, what, or where*) before a declarative sentence, as in "Where daddy sit?" This construction may be explained by examining the use of auxiliary verbs in children's language.

The proper use of auxiliary verbs (*can, did, have, should*) in forming questions appears no earlier than 4 or 5 years of age. The initial use of auxiliary verbs is quite interesting. Rather than use any transformation, the usual subject-predicate order is maintained. For example: "Why the boy can't play?" "Where mommy should have gone?" Finally, the Wh-question is properly formulated by a seemingly simple transformation: "Why can't the boy play?" "Where should mommy have gone?" Apparently the actual transformation of the subject-predicate relationship occurs later than the use of auxiliary verbs.

NEGATION. There is a developmental progression in the formation of sentences intended to negate ("I don't want to study tonight"). The sequence is somewhat similar to the Wh-sequence. At the 2-word level, the child simply places the negation before the object: "No milk," "No go." The second phase involves placing the negation early in a positive statement: "I no like milk." With the emergence of auxiliary verbs, children begin to master the adult form of negation: "I don't want the milk," "Mommy, don't go."

Complex Rules of Grammar

From the single- and double-word sentences, children make steady progress to adult sentence lengths of 7 to 8 words (McCarthy, 1954; Templin, 1957). At about 8 or 9 years, children's spoken sentences closely resemble those of adults. Templin's study revealed that the average length of sentences increased from that found in her study 20 years earlier. She attributed this finding to television and the increased permissiveness in the rearing of children. Sentence length varies with sex and socioeconomic status: girls are more loquacious than boys, and children from higher socioeconomic classes use longer sentences than less privileged children.

With the increase in sentence length a concomitant increase occurs in the use of clauses within sentences. Until the age of 6, adverb clauses predominate; after that noun clauses predominate slightly. By the age of 5, children have begun to speak using correct grammar, i.e., their speech comes under the rules of grammar. For example, the modification of a verb to denote time (*-ed* marks the past tense of regular verbs) takes place without deliberate training, a phenomenon reported as early as the age of 4. Sometimes the *-ed* rule leads to errors, for example, "goed" rather than "went." But this error signals the application of a rule. Thus, as children gain experience with language, they learn its distinctive features and rules. Consequently they learn the ordering of words, the use of markers (including word endings—*s, -ed*, for example) and possessives, function words (*the, her*), and the typical patterns of intonation and stress called prosody.

There are innumerable rules of grammar that children may learn. In the process of learning they often generate incorrect sentences based on those rules. Several instances of rule learning and their incorrect application have been studied.

TABLE 7-4 Age Differences on Inflexional Items

ITEM (PLURAL)	PERCENTAGE OF CORRECT PRE-SCHOOL ANSWERS	PERCENTAGE OF CORRECT FIRST-GRADE ANSWERS	SIGNIFICANCE LEVEL OF DIFFERENCE
glasses	75	99	.01
wugs	76	97	.02
luns	68	92	.05
tors	73	90	—
heafs	79	80	—
cras	58	86	.05
tasses	28	39	—
gutches	28	38	—
kazhes	25	36	—
nizzes	14	33	—

SOURCE: Berko, J. The child's learning of English morphology. *Word*, 1958, *14*, 150–177.

In one test of the use of rules, Berko (1958) designed a study to determine the ability of preschoolers and first graders to form plurals. She used 1 real word ("glass") and 9 nonsense words (see Table 7-4). Pictures were used to represent the nonsense words. Figure 7-6 shows one of the stimuli and its associated verbal task. Each sentence was read aloud, and the children were asked to complete the unfinished sentence. In spite of some age differences, most young children could provide the correct ending *-s* but were much less proficient with *-es*. The errors, however, tended to be consistent. Everyday observation of children forming the plural of a word like "mouse" also supports the ideal of rule-governed behavior. Instead of saying "mice," young children often say "mouses."

Another example of language rules is the use of the past tense. Most regular verbs' past tense is marked by *-ed*. Problems occur with irregular verbs such as "come." Ervin (1964) found that children who had not learned the *-ed* marker used "went" correctly. After learning *-ed*, however, they said "comed." The incor-

FIGURE 7-6 *"This is a wug"*   *"There are two wugs"*

rect use of -s and -ed is called overregularization of rules, a common occurrence in early speech.

Overregularization was found in a study by Porter (1955), described by Ervin and Miller (1963). Porter asked children between the ages of 7 and 13, and a sample of adults, to find a word most similar to "jumped" in the nonsense-word sentence: "Dosib heggof gufed rupan tesor." (Intonation was not an influential variable because the words were written.) Children more often than adults chose "heggof," while the adults chose "gufed." Thus, the children, especially the younger ones, made their choices on the basis of position, because in the simple sentences used by young children, the verb is often the second word (subject-predicate). Adults responded to the marker, -ed.

In their report of a more complex study, Fraser, Bellugi, and Brown (1963) reported similar results. They set out to discover whether 3-year-olds could understand active and passive sentences. The children were presented with pairs of sentences and pictures corresponding to the meaning of the sentences. One of the 2 sentences was repeated, and the children were asked to point to the corresponding picture. For the sentences "The boy pushes the girl" and "The girl pushes the boy" (active voice), the children had little difficulty choosing the correct picture. They encountered difficulties, however, with passive constructions: "They boy is pushed by the girl" and "The girl is pushed by the boy." For the first sentence, they chose the picture of the boy pushing the girl (and for the second, the reverse). Here the children seemed to be following the rule of placing the subject before the verb. We described other examples of rule-governed utterances earlier in this chapter in the section on receptive language. Altogether, the data support the claim that language performance of young children is governed by rules.

The Influence of Imitation

Does the research evidence support the view that the acquisition of linguistic rules is better understood in nativistic terms rather than in terms of learning theory? The issue concerns the importance of imitation in the early phases of language acquisition; specifically, do interactions between parents and child influence later linguistic performance? The research indicates that imitation does have some *slight* effect on early language performance. Cazden (1965) compared the effects of having adults systematically elaborate children's utterances (age range: 28 to 38 months) rather than giving the children examples of well-formed sentences. Each group received 30 to 40 minutes of the treatments each day for 3 months. The group exposed to well-formed sentences showed the most progress. Cazden concluded that expansion merely repeats the children's ideas, whereas full responses broaden ideas and provide children with the words needed to express their ideas.

Brown, Cazden, and Bellugi (1969) studied parental reactions to their children's ungrammatical utterances. The learning position requires that parents reward correct sentences and ignore (extinguish) incorrect sentences. It was found that parents respond differently to the substance of their children's utterances, rather than to their form. Thus, parents reward a sentence that is grammatically incorrect but substantively accurate. If we can generalize from this evidence, we suggest that reinforcement of good grammar does not explain children's learning of simple or complex sentence structures.

The study of receptive language has also been used to investigate the development of grammar. Closely related to this research are studies of the relations between change in language structures and comprehension. Our review of this work covers children over 5, and shows, as Palermo and Molfese (1972) contend, that language competence is probably incomplete until early adolescence. The method of these studies is to present sentences with different grammatical structures, and then to ask the child to repeat the sentence or to act out what it means.

Although parents try to use language appropriate for their child's age (see Phillips, 1973), children probably still hear grammatical constructions that are too complex for them to grasp. Even so, they can apparently get the information they need to understand these sentences. Wetstone and Friedlander (1973) hypothesized that children simply ignore the syntactic structure of sentences that are too complex for them. Children obtain meaning, these investigators contend, by attending to the familiar words or semantic elements in the sentence. Twenty children, ranging in age from 2 years to 3 years 1 month, were shown sentences in normal word order ("Put the marble in the truck."), misplaced order ("Put marble the truck in the."), and scrambled order ("Truck the marble in the put.") Each child's spontaneous speech was sampled to determine his average sentence length. The sentence stimuli were commands (as in our example) and questions. Appropriate materials were made available to carry out the commands. The percentage of relevant responses for the normal, misplaced, and scrambled orders were, respectively, 90, 81.5, and 79.5. The most fluent children (those who used the longest sentences, and who were, incidentally, the oldest) did least well with the scrambled sentences. Wetstone and Friedlander interpret these data as support for their hypothesis. The performance of the more fluent children suggests that they are more sensitive than the other children to syntactic constraints.

The toddlers' freedom from syntactic constraints may not be surprising, but some evidence suggests that 5- and 6-year-old children are similarly unresponsive. Bohannon (1976) studied kindergarten and first- and second-grade children. He used three tasks: a discrimination task in which the children determined whether or not a sentence was syntactically correct; an imitation task requiring children to repeat normal and scrambled sentences; and a comprehension task in which children matched both normal and scrambled sentences with corresponding pictures. They imitated normal sentences more easily and obtained higher comprehension scores with them than with scrambled sentences. The older children imitated better than the younger ones, and also had higher comprehension scores. Children who learned to discriminate normal from scrambled sentences performed better than the non-discriminators, but only with the normal sentences. This study suggests that children can produce grammatically correct sentences even though their mastery of grammar is still imperfect. In other words, they use the rules but are unaware of doing so. Bohannon (1976, p. 679) proposes a twofold system of rules for receptive and productive language: "a child's ability to discriminate syntax may not be a determining factor in language acquisition but may be a *result* of attaining a certain level of grammatical skill." The postulation of such a dual system has also been suggested as an explanation of cognitive development and linguistic competence.

Bohannon unfortunately fails to describe the errors of imitation. However, Menyuk (1969) has described fairly completely how children change improper sentences. She shows convincingly that changes in syntactically proper sentences are independent of their length, so that the data may not be considered a reflection of memory ability. Accurate repetition depends rather on the sentence's structural adequacy. Three categories of responses were used: a repetition (the transformation or nongrammatical structure was repeated), a modification (a change in the syntactic structure of a good sentence), and a correction (a nongrammatical form was appropriately changed). A correction might be to reproduce "He wash his dirty face" and "He washes (or washed) his dirty face." The data by age groups are presented in Figure 7-7. The most frequent deviations were modifications of transformational

FIGURE 7-7   Mean percentage of children modifying transformational structures, spontaneously correcting nongrammatical structures, and correcting nongrammatical structures in sentences when asked to do so at various age levels.

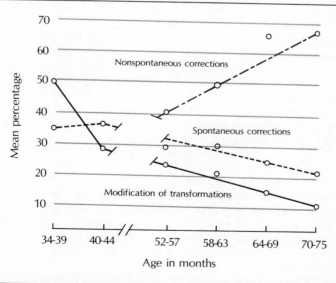

SOURCE: Menyuk, P. *Sentences children use.* Cambridge, Mass.: MIT Press, 1969, p. 114.

structures and spontaneous corrections of nongrammatical forms. Menyuk (1969, p. 118) observes:

> the results of these studies indicate that the child does not listen passively to the language in his linguistic environment, attempting merely to reproduce only what he can remember of what he has heard, but, rather, actively goes through a process of matching what he hears to structures that he has internalized in order to regenerate or generate sentences.

This observation provides a clear summary statement of the essential processes in language acquisition.

Language and Cognition

The later development of linguistic structures (MLUs of three or more words) presumably continues to reflect cognitive growth. Unfortunately, we lack data directly relating cognitive events and linguistic structures. Brown (1973) has described some aspects of the development of the formation of words (morphology)—for example, the formations of the past tense, plurals, or possessives—and has related them to meaning. His data are based on the language samples of Adam, Eve, and Sara in which he found 14 grammatical morphemes. The morphemes' order of appearance is remarkably similar among the three children and is consistent with data from other studies as well. The order is: present progressive, in, on, plural, irregular past, possessive, uncontracted copula, articles, regular past, regular third person, irregular third person, uncontracted auxiliary, contracted copula, and contracted auxiliary.

1. *Present Progressive.* This involves using the inflection *-ing* and in adult speech is accompanied by the auxiliary *be*. At Level II, this takes the form "I talking," "I walking." The auxiliary is omitted. Brown believes this morpheme is meant to express temporary duration (a state or action that will not last.)

2, 3. *In* and *On.* These prepositions are assumed to communicate containment and support, respectively: "in box," "on floor."

4. *Plural.* The formation of plurals requires the inflection *-s* and communicates a singular-plural distinction or number: "two hats."

5. *Irregular Past.* These forms involve verbs whose past tense is something other than *-ed*. Brown interprets their intended meaning as *earlierness*, i.e., occurring before the utterance: "it gone."

6. *Possessive.* The possessive is formed by using the *'s* inflection: "Eric's boots."

7. *Uncontracted Copula.* A copula involves a form of the verb *to be* without contraction. It is used with the third person singular and the present tense and communicates number and presentness: "There it is."

8. *Articles.* This means the nonspecific article *a* and the specific article *the*: "Here a toy"; "Here the book."

9. *Regular Past.* These morphemes include regular past tense verbs (taking *-ed*) and communicate *earlierness*: "Beth jumped."

10. *Regular Third Person.* These forms communicate number and presentness: "He talks."
11. *Irregular Third Person.* These forms communicate number and presentness: "He goes."
12. *Uncontracted Auxiliary.* This form combines previous forms (1, 7) and communicates temporary duration, number, and presentness: "That is walking."
13. *Contracted Copula.* This form involves the verb *to be* in contracted form: "That's hat." Its meaning involves number and presentness.
14. *Contracted Auxiliary.* This morpheme is formed by contracting the verb *to be* and using the *-ing* inflection. Its meaning includes temporary duration, number, and presentness: "I'm talking."

The grammatical morphemes form the basis for subsequent language development. Is there evidence to support the assumption that changes in linguistic structures (complexity, length) are associated with changes in cognitive development? If the question is posed in terms of associations or relationships, the answer is clearly affirmative. But this question is not particularly important because the association is mediated by maturational processes (see Lenneberg, this chapter). The more critical question is whether a possible cause-and-effect relationship exists—is the onset of the preconcrete operational stage marked by changes in linguistic features? Are there distinctive features within stages that are reflected in children's language? Answers to these questions have been derived by examining children's speech samples in terms of word meanings rather than inferred syntactical relations. Again the major emphasis is on early speech, Levels I and II.

BROWN'S RESEARCH. Brown has proposed that there are at least 11 forms of sensorimotor concepts in Level I and Level II of children's language. The first 3 are forms of reference: naming, recurrence, and nonexistence. Naming and questions about the names of objects occur in speech because 18-month-old children know (are cognitively aware) that objects have names. Typically, utterances meant to communicate a name, or information about a name, contain the words "this," "that," "see," "there," and "here": "Here Mommy, here Mommy?" "See Daddy." Reference to recurrence reflects the children's awareness that events can be repeated. The words "more," "another," and "other" often show up in this context: "More cookie." "Another milk." Some understanding of nonexistence (the knowledge that objects can disappear) is associated with words such as "no more," "all gone," "no," "gone" "Milk gone." "No more cookie."

In addition to reference meanings there are semantic relations that require at least words. According to Brown, the action relations are (1) agent and action, (2) action and object, (3) agent and object, and (4) action and location. Object attributes prevalent in 2-word utterances that seem related to sensorimotor knowledge are: (1) object and location, (2) possessor and possession, (3) object attributes, and (4) demonstrative entity. Recently, Gardner (1977) developed a useful summary of

TABLE 7-5

TYPE	UNDERSTANDING IMPLIED BY DUO	EXAMPLES
Naming	There exists a world of objects, whose members bear names.	It ball. There doggie.
Recurrence	A substance or activity can be prolonged, made to reappear, added to, or otherwise enriched or lengthened.	More ball.
Nonexistence	An object can disappear from a situation.	Allgone ball. No doggie.
Agent-action	People do things.	Johnny fall.
Action-object	Objects are acted upon.	Put truck. Change diaper.
Agent-object	A person can perform actions on an object.	Johnny stone. Me milk.
Action-location	An action can occur in a specific place.	Sit chair. Fall floor.
Object-location	An object occupies a specific place.	Book table.
Possessor and possession	People possess objects.	My ball. Adam ball.
Attribution	Objects have characteristics.	Big ball. Little story.
Demonstrative entity	One of a set of objects can be specified.	That ball.

SOURCE: Brown, R. *A first language: The early stages.* Cambridge, Mass.: Harvard University Press, 1973.

Brown's 11 categories, which is reproduced in Table 7-5. The meanings of the semantic relations and the examples of these seem consistent with Piaget's descriptions of the types of behavior associated with sensorimotor knowledge. Clearly, however, precise interpretation of the meanings of 2-word sentences requires additional cues—particularly stimulus context and the child's tone of voice. Brown notes that the order of the words is not crucial (agent-action or action-agent), does not restrict the semantic analysis, and therefore is consistent with the observation that word order is variable.

SINCLAIR-DE-ZWART'S RESEARCH. Sinclair-de-Zwart (1969) reports a somewhat more direct test of the relation between cognitive awareness and language. She compared the linguistic patterns of children who had achieved conservation of liquids and seriation (the ability to order objects or numbers in stepwise progressions) with those of children who had not mastered these concepts. Conservers were more likely to use comparatives (more, less) and also described attributes simultaneously along two dimensions (big/little, fat/thin). The nonconservers used sentences expressing absolute values (a little, a lot) and did not distinguish between dimensions.

One important feature of the study was Sinclair-de-Zwart's success in persuading the nonconserving children to use the language of the conservers. Despite her success, however, the nonconservers were still unable to produce conservation responses. She interpreted these findings as showing that language reflects and depends on cognitive structures. Bloom (1976) concludes that the evidence from studies of early language development supports Piaget's position.

RESEARCH ON WH-QUESTIONS.   Earlier in this chapter, the formation of the *wh*-question was discussed. The question-asking behavior of children may also reflect cognitive functioning. Piaget (1955) proposed that children's questions reflect their thought processes. Although he has devoted a major part of his theory to questions beginning with "why," his model also applies to a number of other interrogative forms. He has observed that children at the preoperational stage ask a great many questions about physical causality. These questions seem to reflect a desire to understand physical events: "What (who) makes the wind?", "Why does a plane fly?" Piaget believes that these questions reflect undifferentiated cognitive structures in which the child does not distinguish motives and intentions from causal explanations. For example, on the day planned for a picnic, a child may ask, "Why is it raining?" This question could be a request for a physical explanation. It could also mean that the rain is spoiling the picnic. Preoperational children often mean the latter because they cannot separate themselves from their environment. When the child progresses to the stage of concrete operations, his questions reflect a distinction between physical and psychological causality. Questions about physical causes become requests for causal explanations. Instead of "Why is it raining?" the question may take the form "What causes rain?" The child eventually asks fewer questions about physical causes as he learns more physical laws that explain them.

Although Piaget has been most interested in causal questions, he has also studied other types of questions, including those about reality, human actions, justification, and classification. Questions about reality concern facts and events, time, and place; questions about human actions concern an understanding of the motivations behind people's behavior. Examples of questions about human actions might be, "Why did he hit the boy?" and "Why do teachers yell so much?" Questions calling for justifications might include "Why must we do homework?" and "Why can't we talk in class?" Classification typically involves questions about the names of objects, their value, the classes they belong to, and comparisons among them. Overall, it appears that as children pass from the preoperational to the concrete stage, their concern with understanding physical causes becomes of primary importance. As the child assimilates these concepts, he or she asks fewer questions about physical causes, and the subjects of the questions asked shift to other categories.

Two studies, conducted some 33 years apart, examined Piaget's analyses of children's questions (Davis, 1932; Meyer & Shane, 1973). Figures 7-8 and 7-9 show the frequency of questions asked at each of 4 age levels for each of Piaget's categories. These tables include a sixth category called social relations, added by Davis, and also by Meyer and Shane, even though it was not one of Piaget's original concepts. Despite the 33 years between the studies, as well as different methods used in each, the developmental trends they reveal are strikingly similar. The data on physical causality are entirely consistent with Piaget's postulations.

The form of the interrogative was also analyzed. Specifically, the frequency of the words *how, when, why, who, what, where,* and the use of auxiliary verbs (*could, does,* and the like) were examined. Examination of the data in Table 7-6 shows that "how" used as an interrogative form predominates in the youngest group, and that children in grades 10 through 12 use it less often. The use of the auxiliary verb form, however, increases over time and becomes the predominant interrogative form by the seventh grade.

FIGURE 7-8 *Percentage Distribution Among the Functional Categories of Questions Asked by Three Age Groups*

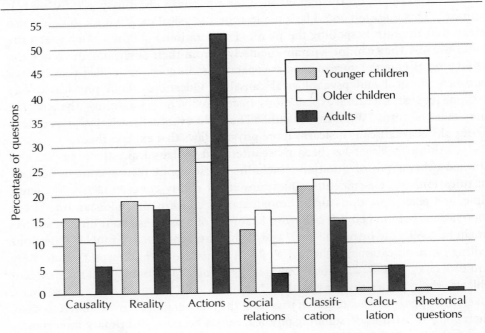

SOURCE: Davis, E. A. The form and function of children's questions. *Child Development,* 1932, 3, 57–74 (Fig. 3, p. 66).

FIGURE 7-9   *Percentage of Questions in Functional Categories*

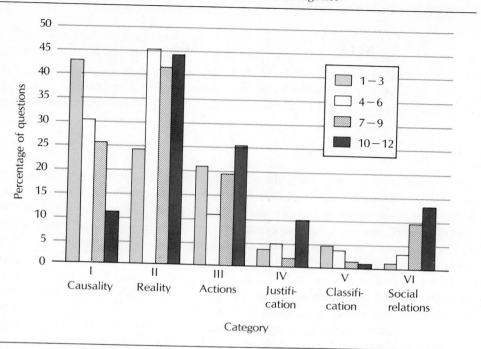

SOURCE: Meyer, W. J., & Shane, J. The form and function of children's questions. *Journal of Genetic Psychology*, 1973, *123*, 286–296 (Fig. 2, p. 293).

TABLE 7-6   Percentage of Types of Interrogatives

| | GRADE LEVEL × SEX | | | | | | | | | | | |
| | 1–3 | | | 4–6 | | | 7–9 | | | 10–12 | | |
INTERROGATIVE	M	F	T	M	F	T	M	F	T	M	F	T
How	43.6	38.0	40.7	40.2	24.2	32.0	22.2	18.0	20.2	12.7	12.8	12.8
Why	21.3	28.9	25.2	14.8	26.8	21.0	25.3	35.3	30.1	22.1	41.9	32.3
When	2.1	3.1	2.6	1.9	1.4	2.7	1.4	1.3	1.2	4.1	1.8	2.9
Who	3.3	2.6	2.9	3.6	1.7	3.4	1.7	2.9	2.3	1.4	1.3	1.3
What	13.4	9.4	11.3	13.4	15.3	15.8	15.3	14.3	14.8	19.6	10.5	14.9
Where	1.8	3.1	2.5	0.5	1.0	0.8	1.0	0.4	0.7	1.9	0.5	1.2
Auxiliary verbs (pooled)	14.4	14.9	14.6	18.6	29.5	24.2	33.0	27.9	30.5	38.1	31.1	34.5

SOURCE: Meyer, W. J., & Shane, J. The form and function of children's questions. *Journal of Genetic Psychology*, 1973, *123*, 285–296 (Table 2, p. 290).

Communications Skills

In the most general sense the acquisition of language provides the user with a remarkably efficient system of communication. Thus, through language one can express emotion and desires and can communicate and receive information. The aim of this section is to examine children's ability to develop messages that effectively provide a listener with definitive information. This form of message is called *referential communication*.

Referential Communication

Until recently, the referential skills of children were largely ignored by scientists (Glucksberg, Krauss, & Higgins, 1975). In part, this can be attributed to the prevailing belief that communicative competence simply required linguistic competence. This assumption is now no longer accepted. Lack of interest can also be attributed to Piaget's influence. He concluded that children under the age of 7 years do not have the cognitive skills necessary for communication. Piaget's position is that the young child is an *egocentric* organism. The term "egocentric" refers to an inability to be sensitive to, and unconcerned about, the needs, intentions, or opinions of other people. Egocentric children are aware only of their own perspectives and are not able to view situations from the perspectives of others. This view incorporates both cognitive and social variables, especially social learning in the form of role taking, role playing, or empathy.

Possession of role-taking skills makes it possible for the speaker to accommodate messages in terms of the characteristics or reactions of the listener. We noted earlier, for example, that parents usually modify their messages to children in accordance with the age level of the children. Thus, when communicating with a 2-year-old, parents typically use very short sentences involving simple syntactical constructions. It is conceivable that in communications between adults, the speaker might modify a message if there is reason to believe that the listener is unfamiliar with the content of the message or, for other reasons, may have difficulty in understanding the speaker's intent. Everyday adult conversation reveals that speakers are sensitive to the reactions of the listener: the listener's furrowed brow, indicating a failure to understand the message, will generate changes in the message. Piaget believed that young children were incapable of making these modifications.

Flavell and his colleagues (1968, p. 208) conducted an extensive set of experiments concerning role taking and communication development. They formulated a set of 5 major skills that appear to be necessary for adequate communication. They are as follows:

1. *Existence*—that there *is* such a thing as "perspective," that is, that what you perceive, think, or feel in any given situation need not coincide with what I perceive, think, or feel.

2. *Need*—that an analysis of the other's perspective is called for in this particular situation, that is, that such an analysis would be a useful means to achieving whatever one's goal is here.
3. *Prediction*—how actually to carry this analysis, that is, possession of the abilities needed to discriminate with accuracy whatever the relevant role attributes are.
4. *Maintenance*—how to maintain in awareness the cognitions yielded by this analysis, assuming them to be in active competition with those which define one's own point of view, during the time in which they are to be applied to the goal behavior.
5. *Application*—how actually to apply these cognitions to the end at hand, for example, how to translate what one knows about the other's listener role attributes into an effective verbal message.

These skills clearly involve social-cognitive functions and may be thought of as a as a consequence of the interaction of cognitive development and social interactions.

In addition, Glucksberg et al. (1975) suggest that there are linguistic skills involved in the development of communication skills. Specifically, they differentiate between the **referential** and **denotative** meanings of words. Referential meanings of words are highly specific and context-bound, referring to particular events, objects, or relationships. The authors use as an example the word "table," which refers to a particular piece of furniture or a particular class of furniture. Denotative meanings refer to "that class of items which are exemplars of the generic idea or concept represented by a word." For example, the referential meanings of *Mars* and *planet* are identical, but their denotative meanings are different. According to Glucksberg et al., the major developmental task for children is the acquisition of the denotative meanings of words. In other words, children must learn to use those words, from a set of alternative words, that most precisely define the referent object referred to in a message.

Roger Brown (1958), in his fascinating book *How Shall a Thing Be Called?*, makes the point that a single word can refer to a number of different things, and conversely any given thing can be referred to by a large number of words. For example, children often refer to *all* dogs by using the name of their *particular* dog (Rover). Thus, for that child all dogs are called Rovers. Unfortunately, in communicating about dogs to another individual, this particular use of the word would not contribute substantially to referential communication. What children need to acquire is a knowledge of the *most frequently used* name for a thing. That this often influences the referential communication skills of young children will become clearer as we examine some of the relevant research literature.

Research Models

There are two basic general research designs that have been employed over the years in the study of children's communicative abilities. In the first design, direct observations of the interactions of children are made and examined for specific instances of attempts to describe a particular object. The assumption made in these studies, but not directly tested, is that role taking is necessary for effective communication. The older studies using direct observations involved frequency counts of the use of the personal pronoun *I*.

The second research approach is more structured. In these situations one child is asked to provide another child with sufficient information to determine which one of a set of possible objects is being described. With this approach it is possible to vary the stimuli in terms of such variables as familiarity and interest value. The data consist of the frequency with which the communicator employs denotative language and the frequency with which the listener is able to make appropriate use of the communicator's messages. In addition, the data are examined for variations in the communicator's behavior as a function of the stimulus materials and the characteristics of the listener (age, sex).

PIAGETIAN RESEARCH.   Among the earliest studies of direct observations of spontaneous verbalizations were those conducted by Piaget (1926). The children in these studies ranged in age between 4 and 7 years. He reports that approximately 38 percent of the utterances of the children involved the pronoun *I*, which he interpreted as evidence of egocentricity. In addition, there were numerous instances of utterances which seemed to lack a genuine communicative aim—the child was alone or was not directing the utterance to any particular individual—or where the utterances apparently were not intended to have any effect on the listener. The greatest proportion of these observed egocentric utterances were seen among the younger children, but evidenced a substantial decline with age. In considering the percentage of *I* utterances reported, it should be noted that other investigators failed to find this high a percentage. For example, in studies by McCarthy (1930), less than 4 percent of the children's speech contained egocentric remarks. It is unclear what features of the two samples may have been responsible for these differences, but it is generally conceded that Piaget's estimates of egocentric speech are probably high.

An example from a second experiment reported by Piaget is particularly informative with respect to the issue of role taking and communication. The study simply involved telling a story to an 8-year-old child named Gio, who in turn repeated the story to a listener. The material is taken from Piaget (1955, p. 99), and the story told to Gio was the following:

> Once upon a time, there was a lady who was called Niobe, who had 12 sons and 12 daughters. She met a fairy who had only one son and no daughter. Then the lady laughed at the fairy because the fairy only had one boy. Then the fairy was very angry and fastened the lady to a rock. The lady cried for ten years. In the end she turned into a rock, and her tears made a stream which still runs to-day.

The following is Gio's account of the story:

Gio (8-years-old) tells the story of Niobe in the role of explainer: *Once upon a time there was a lady who had 12 boys and 12 girls, and then a fairy, a boy and a girl. And then Niobe wanted to have some more sons* (than the fairy. Gio means by this that Niobe competed with the fairy, as was told in the text. But it will be seen how elliptical is his way of expressing it). *Then she* (who?) *was angry. She* (who?) *fastened her* (whom?) *to a stone. He* (who?) *turned into a rock, and then his tears* (whose?) *made a stream which is still running to-day.*

Although the results of this experiment are not without ambiguities (for example, one cannot be certain whether Gio's rendition is a function of inadequate memory), nevertheless it provides a good example of how the lack of role-playing ability can interfere with communication.

Perhaps the most extensive study of role taking as related to the development of communication skills was conducted by Flavell and his collaborators (Flavell, Botkin, Fry, Wright & Jarvis, 1968). These investigators used numerous tasks to assess both role taking and communication in the context of role taking. These tasks are quite complicated, consequently no effort will be made to describe them here. The subjects involved in the various experiments ranged from preschool age through adolescence. The general sense of the findings was that role-taking performance increased with age, as did communicative performance. The finding of developmental changes is generally consistent with Piaget's view, suggesting that perspective differences are not very much in evidence before 7 years of age. The authors do suggest, however, that preschool children develop a number of role-taking skills that seem to go beyond the capabilities described by Piaget.

EVIDENCE AGAINST PIAGET.   While the research evidence we have cited lends support to Piaget's position, recent studies have led to a reappraisal of the communicative ability of young children. Shatz and Gelman (1973), for example, demonstrated that 4-year-olds will modify their speech according to the characteristics of the listener. The speech modifications include length of sentence, complexity, and style. The direction of the adjustments was entirely sensible; utterances directed toward 2-year-olds were shorter and simpler than those directed toward adults. It was also found that in conversations of 4-year-olds with their peers, as opposed to conversations with their mothers, peers were treated like adults in terms of message properties. It was concluded that 4-year-olds adjust their speech to the changing capacities of different-aged listeners. In terms of our general conceptual framework, these results are consistent with the notion that 4-year-olds can role-play.

In another study by Maratsos (1973) it was demonstrated that 3½-year-olds modified their messages when the listener was blindfolded; that is, when the listener's need for clear communication was very obvious. Wellman and Lempers (1977) examined the interactions of 5 boys and 5 girls aged 2 years 2 months, to 3 years. Video tapes were taken and examined for instances where the speaker's intent

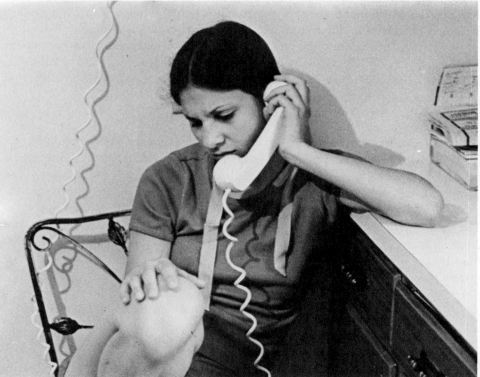

Some psycholinquists believe that the development of language skills parallels the development of cognitive skills as described by Piaget. (Top: Clif Garboden/Stock, Boston; bottom: Michael Serino/The Picture Cube)

was to point out, show, or display a particular object. The results of the study indicate that children *as young as 2 years* were differentially responsive to the feedback provided by other children. These investigators also indicate that these very young children actively engaged other listeners about 80 percent of the time. This finding is clearly in contradiction to the egocentrism suggested in Piaget's findings.

SOME CONCLUSIONS.   The apparent contradictions in the research literature clearly require more rigorous theory and experimentation. However, certain tentative explanations for the contrasting findings seem apparent. One of the more obvious differences among the studies is in terms of the difficulty of the tasks from which the children's communications were derived. In the earlier studies, the tasks were developed by the experimenters and were relatively structured and admittedly difficult. In those instances results tended to support the concept of poor role-taking ability and poor communication ability. Communication ability was probably affected by a lack of an adequate vocabulary. In the more recent studies, the research designs have involved natural settings, settings in which the children naturally interacted with their peers and with adults. In those settings the findings are in distinct contrast with the earlier work and indicate that even children as young as 2 years have communicative ability and are sensitive to the responses of the listener. These situations are familiar to the children so that their communicative skills are not adversely influenced by inadequate knowledge or inadequate vocablulary.

In concluding this section on communication skills, we would like to express our concurrence with the views of Glucksberg, Krauss, and Higgins (1975) based on their examination of the studies. In essence, their argument is that the demands of interpersonal communication seems to be a more likely candidate for motivating language acquisition than the acquisition of syntax. "It is not unreasonable to suppose that one source of pressure upon a child to differentiate his surface utterances in order to differentiate explicitly his propositions (meanings) is the need to be understood" (Glucksberg et al., 1975, p. 339). With Rommelveit (1968) these authors suggest that there is real potential in examining how children become effective communicators with others. The crucial issue in language is really messages, not words, sentences, or paragraphs.

SUMMARY

This chapter began with the seemingly simple idea that language acquisition is a function of imitation. This concept was elaborated to include the principles of conditioning and reinforcement, or in the more general sense, the principles of associative learning. The point was made, however, that these principles seemed inadequate to explain the very rapid language learning that occurs in human beings

and the enormous complexities involved in language development. An alternative view, the nativist position, proposes that human beings possess innate mechanisms peculiarly adapted to foster language development. The precise mechanisms or structures are not well understood at this time. However, the fact that young children can generate most of the grammatical constructions of their native language on the basis of relatively small samples of the language provides rational support for the nativist position.

Acceptance of the nativist view did not lead to a uniform set of theories. Some scientists believed that language learning was instantaneous and were primarily concerned with its syntactical components. Other scientists believe that the semantic component of language is crucial because it is concerned with meaning. Interest in semantics is more closely linked to the relationship between cognitive and language development. Thus, the former view represents a linguistic determinism of language development, whereas the semantic emphasis represents a cognitive determinism. Neither position has yet to receive unequivocal empirical support.

Research studies have shown that there are some universal syntactical structures; structures that appear in many languages. Evidence also shows that children are remarkably similar in their patterns of language acquisition, but sufficient variation exists to seriously question the concept of a prewired program of language acquisition. Semantic analyses of children's 1-word and 2-word sentences show an unanticipated capability of expressing meaning. In most instances, however, intended meaning is clearer when it is known in what context the utterance was made.

Studies of children's receptive language were also examined. These studies show that young infants enjoy listening to human speech, a finding that is consistent with the nativist view. Other studies show that young children do not imitate the syntactical structures they hear but rather use their own, usually incorrect, constructions. These constructions are not random but are based on previously learned syntactical rules.

Recent research studies have examined the development of communication skills. These studies show that 2-year-olds evidence communication skills that are limited primarily by their inadequate vocabulary. A majority of the studies fail to confirm Piaget's assertion that young children's thought processes are too egocentric to permit communication.

The study of language development is increasingly capturing the interest of many scientists and the knowledge gained in the past 20 years is clearly very exciting. With the possibility of new theories about language development 20 years from now, research interest will continue to be intense.

CHAPTER 8

(Erika Stone)

THE MEANING
AND ASSESSMENT
OF INTELLECTUAL
DEVELOPMENT

ALTHOUGH INTELLIGENCE tests have generated considerable controversy, they are among the better known products of psychologists. Before examining the issues underlying the quarrel about IQ tests, we shall first examine what is meant by intelligence and by the IQ, the different kinds of measures of intellectual ability, and the variables that influence performance on intelligence tests. Finally, we will attempt to evaluate the usefulness of these tests.

Concepts of Intelligence

Intelligence is what an intelligence test measures (Spiker & McCandless, 1954). Philosophically, this position is an example of **operationalism**—the philosophy of science that defines an abstract concept, such as intelligence, by *observable behaviors* (responses to test items). This definition of intelligence is difficult to dispute, and furthermore in its very simplicity avoids controversy involving "mentalistic" concepts that may not be directly observable. This definition could generate a number of different intelligence tests, but they might not correlate with performance of value to a particular culture. In other words, those behaviors that best predict the criterion would comprise the best measure of intelligence for that particular criterion, whatever it might be (reading in the primary grades, ability to operate a lathe, or the ability to learn to drive an automobile). You may already suspect that the operational definition of intelligence, despite its several advantages, has not deterred psychologists from attempting to develop more abstract and less circular conceptions of intelligence. The operational approach did not gain wide acceptance largely because psychologists are interested in *why* performance on some test items is predictive of a broader range of behaviors than is performance on other test items. In other words, most psychologists assume that intelligence is something more than the aggregate of performance on individual behavioral indices or test items.

Intelligence as a General Ability

One concept of intelligence that has had a great impact on how we measure it is that intelligence is a **unitary trait.** This feature means that behaviors (phenotypes) that seem diverse are correlated. These correlations vary in magnitude; for example, we would expect that a measure of vocabulary would correlate more highly with a measure of verbal reasoning than it would with a measure of spatial abilities. However, verbal abilities will still be related to spatial ability. Thus, according to the concept of general ability, "bright" people differ from "dull" people on the basis of a unitary trait of general ability. The concept of a unitary trait was most completely explored by Charles Spearman (1927), who viewed intelligence as "psychical energy" which he labeled g (**general intellectual ability**). According to Spearman, all individuals possess mental energy in varying degrees and that energy functions in all mental activities to a degree commensurate with the demands of the task.

Lewis Terman, who was a professor at Stanford University, accepted the concept of intelligence as a unitary trait. Terman developed the Stanford-Binet Intelligence Test, which was originally published in the United States in 1916 and which has undergone several revisions, most recently in 1960. Terman expanded the original Binet test (a test originally developed in 1908 in France by Alfred Binet and Theofile Simon to screen mentally retarded children) by adding items measuring the ability to reason abstractly and to manipulate abstract symbols. The original test devised by Binet and Simon stressed psychomotor (sensorimotor) tasks such as copying forms and stringing beads. This emphasis is not surprising, since the test was designed for preschool children. Under Terman's guidance the test was expanded and presently encompasses items from year 2 through approximately year 16. The kinds of items that Terman added to the test included vocabulary, general reasoning, analogies, and arithmetical problems. Estimates of g values associated with items on the Stanford-Binet were reported by McNemar (1942), who performed extensive statistical analyses on the standardization data of the 1937 revision. His data indicate that the verbal-abstract reasoning tests are more related to g than the psychomotor tests. McNemar's evidence indicates that the Stanford-Binet Scales largely measure one general factor of intelligence, a unitary trait.

We should not conclude that g is a measure solely of verbal abstract reasoning ability. These measures capture the essence of the concept of a unitary trait better than other kinds of measures (spatial abilities). Raven (1960) developed a nonverbal test that requires the use of such intellectual abilities as matching analogies, and a kind of "mental imagery" in problem solving. Somewhat like the Stanford-Binet, the items tend to vary in the degree to which they measure g. The research evidence indicates that Raven's Test, known as Raven's Coloured Progressive Matrices (RCPM), correlates with performance in reading, arithmetic, and general achievement. It is regarded as one of the purer measures of g now available.

Intelligence as Multiple Abilities

The view that intelligence is a unitary trait was predominant in the United States until David Wechsler published the Wechsler Adult Intelligence Scale (WAIS) (1937, 1958). Wechsler contended that intellectual ability consists of two large **group factors** that are relatively **orthogonal** (independent) of each other. He labeled these factors verbal (V) and performance (P). In actuality, Wechsler's conception is not too dissimilar from Spearman's. Although Spearman emphasized the general intellective factor, he also postulated a number of group factors and even identified a number of **specific factors** (factors associated with tasks and with people). Wechsler believed these group factors were largely uncorrelated. He also developed an instrument designed for children called the Wechsler Intelligence Scale for Children (WISC) and the Wechsler Preschool Intelligence (WPSI) Test.

The verbal scale items from the WAIS and the WISC include the following subscales: general information, comprehension, arithmetic, similarities, digit span, and vocabulary. With the exception of the digit span task, which seems to measure short-term immediate memory, and perhaps the general information task, the remaining items all seem to require abstract reasoning ability similar to that

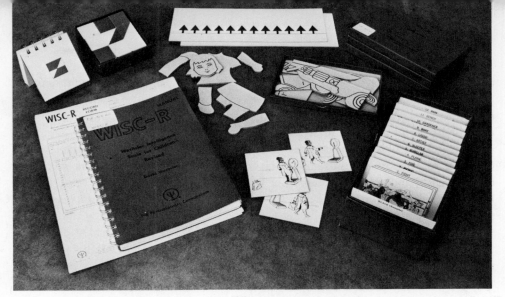

Intelligence tests measure a number of correlated abilities through standardized procedures. (Peter Vandermark)

demanded on the Stanford-Binet. The performance scale consists of the following subtests: digit symbol substitution, picture completion, block design, picture arrangement, and object assembly. The digit symbol substitution task requires the child to learn a code and substitute the code for numbers. The block design task, which incidentally correlates substantially with the verbal scale, consists of 9 colored blocks that the subject must use to reproduce a set of designs. The picture completion task requires the subject to examine a picture and determine what is either missing or incorrect. For example, a picture might show a tree with a shadow located incorrectly with respect to the sun. The picture arrangement task consists of a series of pictures presented in random order. The subject must rearrange the pictures so that they make a coherent story. Finally, the object assembly test, which resembles a jigsaw puzzle, requires the subject to put together a set of pieces into a meaningful figure. All of the subtests are timed, suggesting that one important component of intelligence is *speed of response*. In fact, speed is a reasonable index of intellectual ability; a person who can solve a problem both correctly and rapidly is probably "brighter" than a person who requires a prolonged period of time.

A logical extension of a group-factor model is to postulate a number of factors as orthogonal. L. L. Thurstone (1946), who viewed intelligence as made up of a number of relatively independent traits or abilities, did just this by using a mathematical procedure known as **factor analysis.** Factor analysis takes a set of inter-correlations (that is, the correlations among a battery of subtests) and identifies the subtests that cluster together. Imagine a **correlation matrix** consisting of say, 60 different subtests (called a 60×60 correlation matrix). Factor-analytic procedures make it possible to reduce this matrix to a smaller set of independent factors. The independence of the factors, however, is a *function of the mathematical procedure* imposed on the data and not a function of the subtests comprising the factors themselves. In other words, the researcher imposes a conceptual model on the mathematical procedure; according to the conceptual model here, the factors are independent. Psychologically, the factors may in fact be correlated. The result of Thurstone's work is a series of tests known as the Primary Mental Abilities (PMA) (Thurstone, 1946). Some versions of this test contain 5 factors; other versions consist of 7 factors. The difference is attributable to the chronological age of the subjects, with more factors for the older subjects. The following are some examples of Thurstone's primary mental abilities:

1. Verbal Comprehension (V): this subtest is similar to the vocabulary subtest on the Binet and the WISC.
2. Reasoning Ability (R): this factor measures abstract and symbolic reasoning ability and is again similar to items on the Binet and Wechsler.
3. Numerical Ability (N): this factor measures the ability to perform numerical calculations rapidly and accurately but does not require arithmetical reasoning as does the WISC.

Intelligence tests measure aspects of problem-solving ability that are related to school performance. (Cary Wolinsky/Stock, Boston)

4. Space Relations (S): this factor assesses the ability to visualize spatial relations. You may be familiar with the task in which you have to count the number of blocks in a figure, many of the blocks not being visible.

5. Word Fluency (W): The subject is required to think as rapidly as possible of words that begin with a particular letter. For example, think of all the words that you can with 3 or more letters beginning with the letter C. You would then have one minute to produce these words.

Despite Thurstone and his co-workers' strenuous efforts to develop independent facts, the evidence indicates that the factors are correlated; in some cases, the correlations are rather high. Meyer and Bendig (1961) administered the PMA to 100 eighth-grade children and factor analyzed the intercorrelations resulting from the 5 × 5 matrix (each variable in the matrix consisting of one of Thurstone's primary factors). Theoretically, this analysis should have resulted in 5 independent factors; that is, the correlations among the factor scores should have been close to zero. The results of their analyses indicated, however, 2 factors: Factor I was comprised of vocabulary, reasoning, and numerical ability, and Factor II was comprised of spatial ability. The word fluency factor seemed independent of the other factors, but the investigators had reason to believe that this test was unreliable and they omitted it from further analyses. The investigators then correlated the 2 factors and found that the correlation was extremely high, suggesting the presence of a single unitary factor, or g. The first factor includes the subtests recommended for predicting school performance. This factor requires verbal abstract reasoning ability—a factor predominant in the Stanford-Binet, the verbal subtests of the Wechsler, and usually identified with general intellective ability.

Some Conclusions about Concepts

A considerable body of evidence can be brought to support either the unitary or multiple factor viewpoint. The evidence in support of the multiple trait model is probably greater, but the reader is reminded that the multiple trait reflects a mathematical concept more than a psychological one. At a more speculative level, the functions of the brain hemispheres may correspond with the major Thurstone factors, verbal (left hemisphere) and spatial (right hemisphere). The g factor may describe integrated brain function which depends more on the left hemisphere. We take the view that intelligence is a unitary trait that approximates the functions Spearman attributed to it. We are not suggesting that intelligence is made up entirely of verbal abstract reasoning abilities or even that such abilities are superior to some outstanding competence in another area, such as spatial ability. (It is, nevertheless, true that abstract verbal-reasoning ability is important for success in the traditional scholastic subjects). We do believe, however, that as a general rule individuals scoring high on the g type tests tend to perform better on all kinds of tests.

FIGURE 8-1 *Hierarchical Theory of Human Abilities*

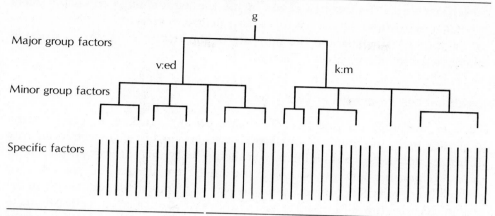

SOURCE: Vernon, P. E. *The structure of human abilities.* London: Methuen, 1960.

Vernon (1960) has proposed a plausible model of intelligence that incorporates the basic features of both the unitary and multiple-trait concepts. This model postulates a hierarchical ordering of traits or abilities. At the apex of this hierarchy is g. Vernon suggests a number of group factors derived from g, and because of the common origin of these factors, they would be more or less correlated with each other. As we have already noted, the correlations between vocabulary and verbal reasoning tend to be fairly high, whereas the correlations between vocabulary and spatial relations tend to be more modest. In this model, group factors give rise to a number of specific factors, again more or less correlated because of their association with g. Finally, Vernon postulates that each specific factor is associated with factors particular to individuals. Vernon's model is presented in Figure 8-1 and, in our judgment, seems most consistent with a psychological conception of the structure of the intellect.

Measuring
Intellectual Ability

The form and content of an intelligence test will be consistent with the conceptual model of the person developing the instrument. For example, the Stanford-Binet test provides a single score or index of intellectual ability (the **IQ**), the WISC provides 3 scores (a Verbal IQ, a Performance IQ, and a Total IQ) and the PMA provides scores for each of the 5 factors in addition to an overall score. This means, however, that in developing each of these tests, expecially a factor test, items specific to each factor must be included. In constructing a test such as the Stanford-Binet, this requirement becomes less stringent. The actual content of intelligence tests will also vary with the age of the target population, the purposes of the test, and whether the test is administered to individuals or to groups.

Psychometric Properties of Tests

All tests, including psychological ones, have certain statistical or psychometric properties. Since the results of intelligence tests are used to make extraordinarily important decisions about children, you should be familiar at least with some of these psychometric concepts, which are also crucial to understanding the criticisms of intelligence tests. Since intelligence tests play an extremely important role in the lives of children, it will be useful to those readers who are or expect to be parents to be familiar with not only their conceptual properties but with some of the more technical properties as well. Hence, we will briefly examine the concepts of reliability and validity and some of the techniques for selecting items to be included on an intelligence test. The reader should be aware that psychologists take the considerations in this section quite seriously: the American Psychological Association has published a manual defining the minimal psychometric standards required for decision making about human beings. This manual is available for a minimal fee by writing to the American Psychological Association.

RELIABILITY.   **Reliability** refers to the degree of consistency in obtained scores, that is, the degree to which an individual's performance on a test is stable, replicable, and internally coherent. Reliability is frequently defined, operationally, as consistency of performance on two separate occasions. We can also obtain excellent reliability estimates from a single test administration. Most simply, however, we can think of reliability as the stability of performance.

Reliability coefficients can range from 0 to +1.00. According to the standards prescribed by the American Psychological Association, decisions (placement in special education programs or institutionalization) about *individuals* must be made with those tests that are administered individually, such as the Stanford-Binet or the WISC. The reliability of these instruments approximates .90, which is extremely high and indicative of a very stable estimate of an individual's ability. Decisions affecting groups of individuals, such as a classroom, permit the use of group-administered intelligence tests with a slightly lower reliability of .85. Regardless of their reliability, however, group tests cannot be used to make decisions about individuals.

TEST VALIDITY.   Indices of **validity** answer the question: does the test measure what it purports to measure? A test may have a high degree of reliability but it may in fact be impossible to demonstrate its validity. Thus the essential question is whether or not a test predicts anything of functional significance. Considerable controversy has developed in this area over the past several years. Most research on the validity of intelligence tests has been done using these tests to predict academic achievement of schoolchildren. Although the magnitude of the correlations between intelligence test and measures of achievement vary, intelligence tests predict academic achievement at a level *substantially better than chance* (they surpass phrenology every time). You may well ask what this means for the actual accuracy of predictions about scholastic achievement. Predictions about groups, especially when they are large, are substantially more accurate than inaccurate. Predictions for *individuals* are generally less accurate or valid.

Since intelligence tests have been constructed with great technological sophistication, why should there be a validity problem? Several answers to this question are possible, and the one that we emphasize simply reflects our bias in that no one of the causes is preemptory. In capsule form the problems of validity are as follows:

1. Not all scholastic behavior requires the same intellectual skills; academic materials can be learned in many ways, including rote memory.
2. Neither the intelligence test nor the achievement test assesses all of the intellectual processes that children possess; how much the two types of tests differ in their assessment of these processes is the degree to which the validity is lowered.
3. A measure may be inappropriate to the particular group of children being examined; that is, the test may be too easy or too hard. For example, one of the authors found data showing that the correlation between performance on an intelligence test and performance on a reading achievement test was $-.10$. (Actually this correlation is not significantly different from 0, but the negative sign serves to make the point.) Further examination of the IQ test scores revealed that almost all of the third graders received a perfect score; in other words they varied very little. Clearly, this intelligence test was inappropriate for the age group; they had simply outgrown it.
4. Since we will have occasion to touch on the motivational and personality variables affecting test performance, we will only mention them here: poor motivation, fear of examinations, and built-in cultural biases in both the intelligence test and the achievement test.

Deriving the IQ Score

All of the preceding discussion has assumed that scores are derived from tests. The kind of score obtained with an intelligence test is related to the chronological age for which the test was developed. For example, with scales for infants, we commonly speak of **developmental quotients** (DQs). As the child progresses through the toddler, preschool, and elementary school years, we most often use the term **intelligence quotient** (IQ). Finally, for high school and college students, we used the term **aptitude.** These differences in terminology have no special significance.

Of the three labels denoting intellectual ability, the IQ score is of course the best known. How is an IQ score derived, and what does it mean? IQ scores are derived in two ways. One of the earliest methods, and still one of the best known, involves the concept of **mental age** (MA). Mental age refers to the chronological age at which an average group of children show the same performance as the individual tested. For example, a 6-year-old child may correctly answer as many questions as the *average* 9-year-old child. We would then conclude that this child has a mental age of 9 years. Ordinarily, mental-age scores are established by administering a test to large samples of children at different age levels. The test may be regarded as suitable for children say, between the ages of 6 and 10. The investigator may obtain samples of 5,000 children at each age level from 6 through 10. The next step is to compute the average number of correct responses made by the children at each age level. Obviously, this process assumes that the items in the test are age related; that is, a large enough sample of items are appropriate for each of the several age levels. The average number of correct responses at each age level then becomes the score necessary for the equivalent mental age. (A very similar procedure is used in establishing **grade equivalent scores** on achievement tests.) If we assume that the growth of mental ability is linear, in the same sense that chronological age changes are linear, then the *ratio* between MA and CA (IQ = MA/CA × 100) indicates whether an individual's mental ability is growing at a faster rate than the chronological age, at the same rate, or at a slower rate. The index of rate of growth is known as the IQ. Thus, for example, a child who has an IQ of 120 is developing intellectually at a considerably more rapid rate than the chronological age. Conversely, a child with an IQ of 80 has a slower rate of mental growth than change in chronological age. The use of this ratio in estimating the IQ makes an additional assumption: the variability in performance at each age level is equivalent. This assumption must be met so that the derived IQ score at one age level has the same meaning for all other age levels. Since this is a difficult concept, let us give a facetious example of what happens: if we tell you that an infant of 3 months of age is 20 pounds underweight, you would undoubtedly express considerable concern for the health of the infant. Why? Because you know intuitively that the range of healthy weights for 3-month-old infants is not very great and certainly does not encompass 20 pounds. On the other hand, if we tell you that among a sample of college sophomores some students are 20 pounds underweight, you would be less concerned because you realize that weight among college sophomores varies considerably. Thus, the effects on **relative position** of being 20 pounds underweight at 3 months of age and at 20 years of age are substantial. The same logic holds for the IQ measure; the IQ is an index of relative position, and in order for the meaning of that relative position to be equal across age levels, the variability in performance on the test must be equivalent across age levels. Until the 1960 revision of the Stanford-Binet, the MA/CA equation found in the Stanford-Binet was used. However, this method was dropped because the variability in performance was not equivalent across age levels, therefore invalidating the equivalence of meaning of the IQ scores thus derived.

The 1960 revision of the Stanford-Binet uses standard scores for determing IQ. This is the most widely used technique. A **standard score** is a derived score that takes into account the variability in the distribution of scores. Thus, when a test is administered to each of several different age levels, it is possible to derive a standard score IQ for each age level; the standard scores are equivalent over age levels because they have been corrected for differences in variability. This technique permits the psychologist to compare the relative positions of children regardless of their age. The concept of relative position plays a prominent role in our subsequent discussion of the effects of cultural variation on IQ test performance.

Psychological Properties of IQ Tests

In the discussion opening this chapter, we presented an operational definition of intelligence and suggested that this approach seemed destined to prohibit our learning very much about the nature of intellectual ability. In this section we examine the developmental changes that occur in intellectual functioning as currently measured on tests (as opposed to a theory such as Piaget's).

Interpreting IQ Scores

In its simplest and most precise form, an IQ score is an index of relative position in a definable group. At a psychological level, the interpretation of IQ scores depends very much on the age of the children tested. Interpretations vary with age because the content of IQ tests varies considerably with age. For example, the content of IQ tests for infants consists mainly of psychomotor/sensorimotor items and does not include items that require language. Conversely, IQ tests designed for the age group of 6 to 7 years are comprised of items that mostly require verbal abstract reasoning ability. In fact the interpretation of an IQ score varies with both the chronological age of the children and the conceptual orientation of the instrument.

PREDICTIVE ABILITY.   One way in which we can assess the implications of an IQ score is to examine the research on the **predictive ability** of test scores at different ages. Admittedly, using subsequent intellectual status or academic achievement as validity indicators is too narrow; nevertheless, that is the state of the current literature. Recalling that tests of infants assess psychomotor behaviors, we can then ask the question about the predictive ability of the IQ scores obtained by children at age 6 years or older. In effect, the predictive ability is just about zero; that is, the average correlation between performance on an infant IQ test and performance on a test such as the Stanford-Binet at age 6 is zero. This implies that either one or the other IQ test is not reliable or that the psychological processes that are being assessed at the two times are different. The reliability interpretation is not persuasive; it is true that the reliability of infant scales tends to be somewhat lower than the reliability of the WISC or the Stanford-Binet at 6 years, but not of sufficient magnitude to warrant the expectation of a zero correlation.

Thus, the explanation appears to be that the psychological processes being assessed are different or nonoverlapping. Before pursuing that interpretation, we should recognize that the infant IQ tests are not completely devoid of predictive power. Infant IQ tests usually do provide a reasonable long-term predictive validity for children who are severely retarded. The likely reason that the predictive validity is so low is that average and above-average performance of infants involves a set of mental processes that are largely independent of those involved in the later acquisition of more abstract intellectual abilities. Some investigators, however, claim great success in predicting subsequent intellectual development when using clinical methods, that is, individualized diagnostic procedures. Unfortunately, these investigators have not been able to provide a description of the key discriminative cues they employ in their diagnostic work.

Returning then to the question of the differences in psychological processes, it would seem that the psychomotor tasks require relatively little of Spearman's g factor, whereas the kinds of behaviors that are expected of children at age 6 and beyond require more g. Hofstaetter (1954) performed a factor analysis of the IQ test data in the Berkeley Longitudinal study. These data were based on the same children from infancy through 18 years of age. The results of his extensive analyses indicate that the intellectual factors being measured change significantly between infancy and approximately the age of 4. Specifically, Hofstaetter reports an initial factor which he called "sensory-motor alertness." This factor reflects the infant's awareness of the stimuli, and his or her reaction to them. Between the ages of 2 and 3, there appears a factor which Hofstaetter labeled "persistence." This factor is self-explanatory; that is, performance at this stage is very much a function of keeping at the task until the appropriate response is made. Some time after the age of 4, a third factor emerges which Hofstaetter interpreted as being similar to Spearman's g, the general intellective factor. This third factor increases in magnitude as children grow older, and he concludes that performance variation thereafter results from differences in g. It should be noted that Hofstaetter's findings are based exclusively on the Stanford-Binet and may not generalize to other intelligence tests. It is interesting that he finds this decided shift to a general intellective factor at approximately 4 or 5 years of age. This is consistent with our earlier discussion of Sheldon White's interpretation that human beings become capable of functioning at an abstract level some time during the age level from 5 to 7 years (White, 1965).

Cronbach (1965) criticized the statistical methods employed by Hofstaetter and concluded that his results should not be taken seriously. Nevertheless, the problem of describing early mental development remains. Using more sophisticated statistical methods, McCall, Eichorn, and Hogarty (1977) examined the nature of developmental changes during the first five years. A portion of their data was also used by Hofstaetter. It is important to note that these investigators, unlike so many others in this area of study, *expected* to find age differences, which may mean the end of the futile efforts to explain the low correlations. We believe this approach will generate more knowledge about early mental development.

The results of this extensive study suggest that there are 5 stages of intellectual functioning during the first 36 months of life. McCall et al. conclude that their 5 stages are very similar to those proposed by Piaget. They further show that their data is largely consistent with the data reported by Uzgiris (1976) using a test specifically designed to measure Piaget's stages. Consistent with Hofstaetter's findings, McCall and his associates found that symbolic relationships emerged some time after 21 months. Thus, it seems likely that there is a general trend toward more abstract ability with increasing age.

ITEM CONTENT.   Changes in the interpretations of IQ scores can also be examined in terms of the items that comprise the mental-age score. How does item content change? Before age 6, the Stanford-Binet assesses vocabulary by asking children to label a number of familiar objects (airplane, ball, knife, cane, leaf). The ability to identify these objects is reasonably predictive of subsequent mental development, but it represents a more concrete behavior than a subject's giving a definition of word without a physical stimulus present. Vocabulary items first appear at the 6-year level. At that level, the average child is expected to define correctly the following words: orange, envelope, straw, puddle, tap, and gown. Very often children cannot define the words without the help of a picture corresponding to the word. Thus when asked to define an orange, the child may not be able to do so, but when an orange is placed in front of the child, an adequate definition is forthcoming. The transition from the picture vocabulary test to the vocabulary test seems to require a different ability, perhaps the ability to employ mental abstractions. It is also of interest that the vocabulary subtest of the Stanford-Binet is the best predictor of overall performance. This finding, incidentally, is not unique to the Stanford-Binet but typical of most intelligence tests that include a vocabulary item of this kind. To put this distinction in some perspective, it is analogous to the difference between a multiple-choice examination and an essay examination; the multiple-choice exam is basically a test of recognition, whereas the essay examination tests recall and the integration of related concepts.

The mental processes involved in IQ measures have not been extensively examined. Clearly, on an instrument such as the WISC, each cluster of items making up the various subtests becomes increasingly more difficult and is correlated with chronological age. Thus, the expectation that older children can handle more difficult items is the essential ingredient entering into the item selection. The vocabulary items on the Stanford-Binet, for example, become progressively more difficult because they become increasingly more abstract and subtle and also because the words are used more rarely. A good example of how rarity operates is shown from the Stanford-Binet where the word "Mars" is rated at the 8-year level, but since 1960 "Mars" is a more frequently used word. Undoubtedly, if we were to restandardize the vocabulary items of the Binet, we would view the word "Mars" as considerably easier. But to make the point concerning how the vocabulary items change, consider that on the Binet the fourteenth word on the list is "brunette" and the forty-fifth and last word is "parterre" (that part of the theater beneath the balcony and behind the parquet). Indeed "parterre" is a good example, for although it is not a particularly abstract word, it certainly is not used with great frequency. Thus the strategy is to make items harder, by whatever means, without any particular concern about the mental processes being measured. Of course, the ultimate objective in item selection for intelligence tests is to maximize the predictive power of the test and not necessarily to increase our understanding of the mental capabilities required to be successful with these items. This strategy, as we have noted earlier, has proven to be only moderately successful.

CONSTANCY OF IQ. One of the important questions that has been raised about IQ scores is the degree to which they remain constant within individuals. Obviously, for psychometric reasons (lack of reliability) we cannot expect perfect constancy; that is, scores will vary as a result of error. The basic issue, however, is whether developmental rates among children vary beyond expected error. This issue is at least tangentially related to the question of whether IQ-test performance is genetically or environmentally determined. According to a strictly genetic position, the IQ is fixed and not influenced by environmental events. Two major studies have investigated this question (Honzig, McFarlane & Allen, 1948; Kagan, Sontag, Baker & Nelson, 1958). Both studies involve longitudinal data extending over a period from infancy to 18 years. The Honzig et al. study, which was conducted at the University of California at Berkeley, found clear evidence that IQ is not constant. Using a sample of 222 children, they found that 59 percent of them changed 15 or more IQ points. A total of 37 percent of the sample varied 20 or more IQ points. The matrix of correlations showing the age levels, the tests employed at each level, and the intercorrelations of test performance indicate that as the subjects grow older, or as the interval between testing decreases, the magnitude of the intercorrelations improves. Thus the correlation of a test administered just before 2 years of age and IQ at the age of 18 is essentially zero. Conversely, when the IQ test is administered at age 14, its correlation at age 18 is .73. As an example of the kinds of variables that influence test scores, we will examine two individual children with very different levels of intellectual functioning, each of whom shows how personality considerations relate to

Environments can influence intellectual growth. (Joel Gordon)

the changing scores. Case 423 shows a youngster of relatively high intellectual ability. The following case report is quoted from Honzig et al. (1948, p. 313):

> *Relatively consistent high scores.* Case 423 presents a high-scoring girl whose mother is a normal-school graduate and whose father obtained a postgraduate university degree. Her highest test score was obtained at age six. Her scores continued high, but sagged during late adolescence. She is attractive, artistically talented, and socially successful. She got very high grades in the elementary and junior high school years. Her lowest test scores are at age nine and ten, a period of fatigue and poor posture, and a period during which she strained to excel, and at year eighteen where her Sigma score [a derived score] showed a drop. Her high school years were characterized by much less interest in intellectual success, which she regarded as unfeminine and interfering with getting good dates; and her motivation in all test situations was markedly below that of her early years. Scholastic mediocrity was consciously sought and obtained, serving not only her date objective, but her emancipatory revolt against her parents who placed a high value on grades and a very low value on her boyfriends.

In the following description, involving steadily decreasing mental test scores, Honzig et al. (1948, pp. 313–314) state that Case No. 764

> is an example of a gradual lowering of IQ from 133 to 77, and Sigma scores from +1 to −3. She is an only child, born when her mother was forty four, the father thirty seven. The estimated IQ of the mother is sixty five to seventy. The father is a skilled

mechanic. The parents went to school until age fourteen. Obesity began in late preschool years and increased steadily until medical advice was finally followed at age fourteen (height 5'2", weight 160 lbs. at thirteen). Weight was normal at seventeen. There were, however, no IQ variations in relation to these physical changes. She was always over-indulged by the mother who lived to feed her and keep her young, and who was always complaining that her daughter never gave her enough affection.

The first case is interesting because it conforms very closely to the currently popular idea that women have been taught to avoid outstanding academic achievement because it is unfeminine. We might even describe the behavior of this young woman as consistent with the position that females are taught to fear success.

The second case is more difficult to interpret along environmental lines because of the low IQ estimated for the mother. This low estimate suggests that the child's poor performance results from a lack of genetic potential, an interpretation that is strengthened somewhat by the fact that when she overcame her obesity, her IQ score showed no shift. On the other hand, the change in her weight did not occur until the age of 17, which may have been too late for her to demonstrate any gains. What is interesting about the second case, however, is the indication that the mother was creating an emotionally dependent child. This interpretation is entirely consistent with data reported by Kagan et al.

In the Kagan et al. study, a sample of children who had been examined every year for 18 years served as the basis for selecting children who showed constant fluctuations in IQ scores over that time period. The investigators examined the IQ scores of the subjects between the ages of 6 and 10 and selected those children who showed consistent gains or losses in IQ. The gainers showed an average increase of 17 points, while losers' scores went down 5 IQ points. The investigators then administered a series of projective tests including the **Rorschach Test** (the ink-blot test) and the **Thematic Apperception Test.** In addition, the investigators made use of detailed data on the parent-child relationships based on direct observations made in the homes over a period of time. It should be noted that the general sample is predominantly middle-class with a very large majority of parents having attended college. One of the major findings of the studies was that the children with decreasing IQs tended to be more emotionally dependent on their parents. Children with increasing IQs tended to be more achievement-oriented and display more aggressive responses on the projective tests. The results suggest that children who interact more with their environment tend to increase in intellectual ability over time. In addition the authors observed "achievement-oriented children from homes in which intellectual activity was praised would probably be more likely to master intellectual skills than achievement-oriented children from homes in which such accomplishment was not rewarded. In a cultural environment where athletic ability, fighting prowess, or success with the opposite sex is highly valued, one might expect the child to choose these behavioral channels to gratify his achievement and competitive needs" (Kagan et al., 1958, p. 265). This interpretation by the Kagan group is in fact quite consistent with the cases cited from Honzig et al. and also consistent with prevailing notions that environmental factors play a significant role in motivating children toward intellectual achievement. We must remember, of course, that such an interpretation is based on the premise that the child has the intellectual potential to take advantage of a stimulating environment and is able to respond to parents' demands for achievement. It seems likely that where the intellectual competence of the child does not meet the demands and expectations of the parents, important adverse psychological consequences are likely to follow.

Psychologists have known for a long time that the IQ is not constant but is sensitive to environmental variations. Sherman and Key (1932), for example, showed that children growing up in a rural mountain village of Appalachia show IQ scores that are approximately average when they are between 6 and 8, but by the time they reach the age of between 14 and 16, their IQ scores drop, on the average, to the low 70s. This finding has been replicated on numerous occasions. In understanding why the IQ declines as an apparent function of environmental impoverishment, we must understand that the content of almost all IQ tests is based on the assumption that as children mature chronologically, society's demands and expectations on them make commensurate increases. This is clearly reflected in the curriculum of schools for middle-class children. The theory then assumes that the normal child will take advantage of all new environmental stimulation and thus will show commensurate improvement in intellectual competence. If, however, the environment is not stimulating, or not consistent with the kinds of intellectual competencies assessed by IQ tests, then we would expect decreases in IQ scores. This intepretation is somewhat tentative at this point in our discussion and will be examined in greater detail when we discuss the literature on programs for combating the debilitating effects of impoverished environments on children by providing more stimulating environments.

The Course of Mental Growth

Earlier in this chapter we discussed one of the first operational definitions of IQ, namely, the ratio of MA to CA. One assumption was left implicit. In order for the ratio of MA to CA to make sense, we must assume a linear (straight line) relationship between mental age and chronological age. The material discussed in this section will show different forms of mental growth that depend in part on the method employed and in part on the kind of mental ability being examined. We also include in this section a brief discussion of what happens after the age of 18 because of the considerable interest in the development of mental abilities during adulthood and particularly during the older years.

A typical curve of mental growth is depicted in Figure 8-2. The form of the curve indicates a period of very rapid acceleration that tapers off at approximately 20 to 25 years of age; the curve then seems to decline gradually but steadily thereafter.

FIGURE 8-2   *Curve of Mental Growth and Decline as Measured by the Wechsler-Bellevue Full Scale.* Note the deceleration in mental growth during the early teens, and the peak of mental growth near age twenty.

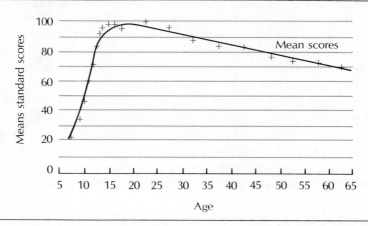

SOURCE: Wechsler, D. W. *The measurement and appraisal of adult intelligence.* Baltimore, Md.: Williams & Wilkins, 1957.

The form of the growth curve is **negatively accelerated;** that is, growth is extremely rapid in early development and then tapers off. Curves like the one shown in Figure 8-2 are based on the assumption that the units of mental measurement employed in intelligence tests are equal over all points in time. For example, the curve assumes that the increment of growth between 2 and 3 years of age is exactly equivalent to the increment in growth that occurs between 7 and 8 years. To make this assumption, the psychological scale must have an absolute zero point or at least an inferred zero point. Such a scale can be found on a Fahrenheit or a centigrade thermometer, that is, an **interval scale** that has a derived zero point. (The zero point on the Fahrenheit scale is 32 degrees below the point where water freezes, and the zero point on the centigrade scale is that point at which water freezes.) Although the interval does not have an *absolute* zero point, it does have equal intervals and thus allows us to assume that the increment in mental ability units between 2 and 3 and between 7 and 8 are equal. The curve in Figure 8-2 does not have a zero point; thus, the intervals are unequal.

Figure 8-3 gives a set of growth curves for the Primary Mental Abilities Test that were derived by L. L. Thurstone (1955); he used an equal-interval scale, defining zero as that point where the variation in performance was zero. In Figure 8-4 Thurstone and Ackerson (1929) converted the Stanford-Binet data into an inferred ratio-scale with equal units and an arbitrarily defined absolute zero. Notice that this curve takes a quite different form from that of the curve in Figure 8-2. In fact, the curve derived by Thurstone and Ackerson is called an S-shaped or **ogive curve;**

FIGURE 8-3   *Mental Growth Curves for Seven Primary Mental Abilities:* perceptual speed (P), space relations (S), reasoning ability (R), numerical ability (N), immediate memory (M), verbal comprehension (V), and word fluency (W). In this scale Thurstone arbitrarily defined zero as that point where there is no longer any variation among subjects.

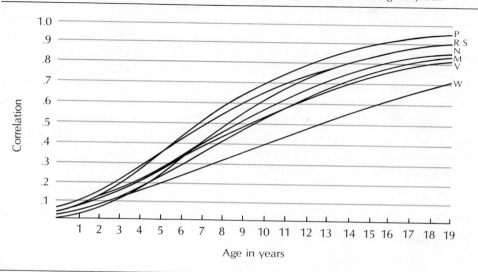

SOURCE: Thurstone, L. L. *The differential growth of mental ability.* Chapel Hill, N. C.: University of North Carolina, The Psychometric Laboratory, 1955.

FIGURE 8-4   *The Intellectual Growth Function Obtained by Thurstone and Ackerson by Statistical Analysis.* Note that this curve is based on an inferred ratio-scale with equal units and an absolute zero.

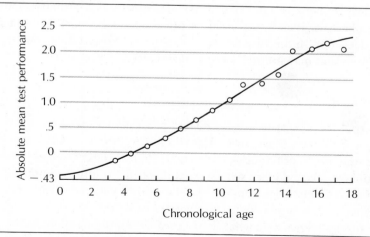

SOURCE: Thurstone, L. L., & Ackerson, L. The mental growth curve for the Binet tests. *Journal of Educational Psychology,* 1929, *20,* 569–583.

growth is relatively slow in the initial or early years and then accelerates during the middle portion of the scale and then begins to taper off toward the upper end. A contribution of major importance is shown in the set of curves in Figure 8-3, which employed the same procedure and which generates a set of curves that also are consistently ogival in form. This particular study involved a form of the Primary Mental Abilities containing 7 scales from which we can roughly compare the rates of maturation of these abilities. In descending order of maturation rate we find perceptual speed, space and reasoning, number and memory, verbal comprehension, and finally, word fluency, which appears to be fully developed at about 20 years of age. This hierarchy of maturational rates corresponds roughly to the kinds of behavior described by Piaget, and the kinds of behavior assessed on various kinds of intelligence tests. It also seems to indicate that verbal abstract reasoning ability, which is perhaps the most complex of all the factors, takes the longest to achieve maturity. (It is difficult to interpret the word fluency factor because of its fairly low reliability.)

Variables Influencing Test Performance

Our discussion of the variables affecting test performance now becomes more specific as we consider the problems in establishing the reliability of intelligence tests. We indicated that motivation, age, characteristics of the examiner, and features of the test could serve to enhance or hinder the child's performance. We have already made the point that these variables might function differently on two occasions, thus lowering reliability. In the everyday use of intelligence tests, consistency of measurement is not the primary concern (it is a primary assumption); instead, emphasis is given to the child's score as a basis for making extraordinarily important decisions. In this discussion we examine in greater detail the characteristics of children that may influence test performance.

Sex Differences

In considering the effects of sex on IQ-test performance, we look for differences among types of abilities. Maccoby and Jacklin (1974) have written an excellent analysis of research on sex differences. Girls are generally thought to have greater verbal ability than boys; the evidence suggests that this belief is quite accurate. The verbal abilities of male and females from preschool to early adolescence are very similar, although females show some slight superiority. After the age of approximately 11 years, the sexes diverge somewhat, with females improving more rapidly, at least through the end of high school. This generalization holds for both receptive and productive language, fluency, and on abstract mental activity including verbal analogies. In contrast, boys apparently excel on visual-spatial tasks, and this superiority becomes more pronounced during adolescence and adulthood. At about the age of 12 to 13, boys tend to increase their mathematical skills more rapidly than girls. A possible explanation for this finding is provided by Maccoby and Jacklin (1974, p. 352):

> The greater rate of improvement appears to be not entirely a function of the number of math courses taken, although the question has not been extensively studied. The magnitude of the sex differences varies greatly from one population to another, and is probably not so great as the differences in spatial ability. Both visual-spatial and verbal processes are sometimes in the solution of mathematical problems; some math problems can probably be solved in either way, while others cannot, a fact that may help to explain the variation in degree of sex differences from one measure to another.

The difference in favor of males is very carefully specified as having to do with mathematical ability. Meyer and Bendig (1961) found that on the numerical abilities subtest of Thurstone's Primary Mental Abilities Test, there was a significant difference in favor of females. This seeming discrepancy is readily resolved; the numerical abilities test on the PMA consists of arithmetical operations (addition, subtraction, multiplication, and division) and depends heavily on the acquisition of number facts, accuracy, and speed. These skills differ from mathematical ability which apparently requires visual-spatial ability. There do not seem to be any other significant sex differences in intellectual ability.

Ethnic and Socioeconomic Background

There is a very extensive literature on the ethnic and socioeconomic variables that influence performance on IQ tests. One of the difficulties in investigating this complex issue involves separating socioeconomic status from racial factors; in reviewing the relevant research, it is often unclear whether the socioeconomic status of the children is the major feature of the sample or the race. Our discussion here will be somewhat elaborate, for we include a number of different issues, for example, **cognitive style,** motivation, and the cultural fairness of IQ tests for certain ethnic and other minority groups. Finally, we give an overview of efforts to remediate the effects of impoverished environments through such practices as Head Start and Follow-Through.

Before examining the relations between socioeconomic status and IQ-test performance, we should note a few facts about the ambiguities inherent in a socioeconomic classification. Significant relations exist between socioeconomic status and rate of mental growth in children. An estimated 21-point difference exists in the average IQ, as measured on the Stanford-Binet, between children whose parents are classed as professionals, and children whose parents are classed as day laborers.

The socioeconomic classification does not really explain the performance differences. The distributions of IQs for each of the socioeconomic classifications overlap, so that placement in any one category does not provide complete assurance that the child will perform better or worse than children in the adjacent categories. Furthermore, when we speak of lower-class homes, the term tends to carry an excess of meaning; for example, we tend to think of the parents as being possibly indolent, possessing a different set of moral standards, disinterested in the educational progress of their children and the educational process itself, and a kind of general family disorganization that may involve a disproportionate frequency of one-parent families. In point of fact we are not at all certain how the social structure of the lower-class culture influences intellectual development. All we can say at present is that it does apparently have an influence. Perhaps Scarr (1976) stated it best by noting that upper middle-class families know how to prepare children for IQ tests and school achievement. The ensuing discussion is an effort to operationalize the meaning of socioeconomic status as it affects performance on IQ tests.

MOTHER-CHILD INTERACTIONS.   Hess and Shipman (1968) examined mother-child interactions to find possible explanations of how they might influence performance on intelligence tests as well as performance in school. The research focused on 3 characteristics of the mother-child interaction. The first cluster of variables were concerned with the properties of the mother-child interaction where the mother's intent was to control or regulate the child's behavior. The second characteristic involved the degree to which the communication employed by the mother is either elaborated or restricted. The third set of variables concerns what the authors refer to as the "development of educability in the child," which refers to motivation to perform well in school, teacher-child relationships, and the authority system of the school.

The sample consisted of 40 mother-and-child pairs from the upper-middle and upper-lower class, 36 mother-and-child pairs each from the lower-lower class, and a group receiving aid for dependent children (ADC). The verbal IQs of the mothers as measured on the Wechsler Adult Intelligence Scale ranged from 109.4 for the highest status mothers to 82.4 for the ADC mothers. The Stanford-Binet IQ scores did not show as great a range: 109.4 to 94.5. The children were all of preschool age.

This study employed a number of cognitive tasks in which the mother and child worked together in solving different problems. In characterizing the results of their study Hess and Shipman (1967, pp. 57–81) make the following observation:

> The cognitive environment of the culturally disadvantaged child is one in which behavior is controlled by imperatives rather than attention to the individual characteristics of the specific situation, and one in which behavior is neither mediated by verbal cues which offer opportunities for using language as a tool for labeling, ordering, and manipulating stimuli in the environment, nor mediated by teaching that

relates events to one another and the present to the future. The meaning of deprivation would thus seem to be a deprivation in the early cognitive relationships between mother and child. This environment produces a child who relates to authority rather than to rationale, who may often be compliant, but is not reflective in his behavior, and for whom the consequences of an act are largely considered in terms of immediate punishment or reward rather than future effects and long-range goals. If this general picture is valid, it would seem that the goal of early education is to promote the development of strategies or structures for dealing with information, rather than merely transmitting a supply of concepts, information, and mental skills.

The lower-class mothers tend to use imperatives in controlling the child. The typical control mechanism is an appeal to power and authority, which appears to have the effect of restricting the child's ability to consider alternative behaviors or strategies. This treatment may also restrict the language of the children (Bernstein, 1960). Hess and Shipman suggest that such appeals may produce an impulsive youngster because, in fact, the child has not had any opportunities to consider alternatives, which means that they will move to a solution very quickly rather than test out a range of possibilities.

RESPONSES TO TEST TAKING.   Another set of related data were collected by Hertzig, Birch, Thomas, and Mendez (1968), who were interested in the behavioral characteristics of lower-class and middle-class Puerto Rican children *during* test taking. All 116 middle-class Puerto Rican and 60 lower-class Puerto Rican children were between 3 and 4 years of age, and all of them took the Stanford-Binet, Form L. Two broad classifications of behaviors were observed. The first general category is called "work responses," which meant that the child attempted to do what was asked of him. The child did not have to obtain the correct response nor did a verbal response have to be evoked. It was simply a matter of the observer's judgment that the child was making an effort to respond to the examiner's cognitive demands. The second category of responses were called "nonwork responses." Again the responses could be either verbal or nonverbal but included negative responses ("I won't do it"), substitutive responses ("I want a drink of water"), and requests for aid ("You do it for me"). One other category of nonwork response was a refusal on the basis of incompetence ("I don't know how to do that").

The middle-class children responded to the examiner's demands by making a significantly greater proportion of work responses than the lower-class children. The middle-class children not only showed a greater tendency to be task-oriented on an initial demand but also altered their initial nonwork responses more rapidly upon re-presentation of the question. A second and quite pervasive difference was the tendency for the middle-class children to respond through the use of verbalization as opposed to action or gestures. The most typical nonwork behavior for the lower-class children was silent unresponsiveness. Of the several interpretations of the findings in the Hertzig et al. (1968, p. 46) study, the one that seems most relevant to our concern states:

> It may be that the Puerto Rican children come from a person-oriented rather than a problem-oriented culture and that they lack sufficient opportunity for the exercise of independence in advance of task mastery, which would permit the development of successful problem-solving behavior under conventional educational conditions. The style of the culture may be one in which verbalizations are heavily weighted to communicate affective and social contents rather than task-directed ones, with the result that the ability to engage in verbal behavior in response to a cognitive demand fails to develop in the same way that it does in the middle class children.

The pervasive effects of home environments has been demonstrated in a series of studies using a more experimental methodology (Zigler & Butterfield, 1968; Zigler, Abelson & Seitz, 1973; Goldstein, Meyer & Egeland, 1978). Each of these studies tested the hypothesis that standardized tests may underestimate the ability of lower-class children. It was reasoned that lower-class children have had less experience with testing, are more suspicious of the examiner, and are more likely to avoid errors by not responding.

The basic strategy of Zigler et al. was to develop a procedure for administering tests that they felt would optimize the child's performance. In effect this meant giving the children a fairly simple task designed to assure at least some degree of initial success. Then, during the course of the formal examination, the procedures were designed so that whenever a failure occurred, a child was given an item with a high probability of success. Gentle encouragement was continually employed. The control condition used the standard individual testing procedures. The results of the manipulation are rather striking: the children in the optimal condition performed significantly better than those in the standard condition. The studies permit the conclusion that when a child is unfamiliar with an examiner, he or she will take longer to respond. The result is a lower estimate of the child's true intellectual ability. Similar results are reported by Goldstein et al. These investigators manipulated both familiarity with the examiner and with the setting of the test. The children in the familiar-examiner condition met and engaged in activities with the tester for 5 days before taking the Stanford-Binet tests. For a familiar setting, the test was administered in the homes of the children. This condition was based on the premise that the strangeness of the examiner contributed to poor performance. In a third condition, the children were given 2 pretests: the Stanford-Binet was administered on the first day of a 6-week Head Start program and then was readministered one week later. This procedure was designed to familiarize the child with the examiner and with the kinds of cognitive demands required. All children took a posttest during the last 3 days of the Head Start program. A fourth group was a control group; these children were administered the Stanford-Binet without any previous experience with the examiner and without any time to become accustomed to the new environment. The results indicate that the children who were familiar with the examiner scored higher on the pretest than the other groups. The effects of testing the children at home were adverse; it turned out that the testing conditions in the homes of these children were very poor. Further confirmation of the general hypotheses came when the groups were tested at the end of 6 weeks; the initial differences resulting from familiarity with the examiner had disappeared. In a similar study using middle-class children, there were no effects attributable to familiarity or nonfamiliarity with the examiner. Thus the evidence so far accumulated clearly seems to indicate that lower-class children perform more poorly because they develop expectations about examiners and cognitive demands that are simply not like those of middle-class children, who serve as the standard for developing testing procedures and for defining appropriateness of responses.

CULTURAL DEPRIVATION.   A number of other studies demonstrate what appear to be quite negative environmental effects. The research focuses on the effects of stimulus deprivation on infant development. The reader is already familiar with the concepts underlying the research; namely, that in order for neuromuscular development to occur, the organism requires extensive environmental stimulation. For example, recall the grave consequences for the perceptual development of chimpanzees who were completely deprived of visual and tactual stimulation. Naturally, experiments of this kind have not and cannot be conducted with children. There do exist, however, two naturalistic studies in which the infants were reared under conditions of apparent stimulus deprivation (Dennis & Najarian, 1957; Dennis, 1960). These studies examined the development of infants reared in orphanages located in Lebanon and Iran under extremely impoverished conditions. For example, the ratio of the number of children to caretakers was approximately 15 to 1, which meant that infants were left unattended for long periods of time. In addition, in an effort to keep the infants quiet, their cribs were covered with white sheets. Riesen's study suggests that such visual deprivation could have very serious effects on development. The infants were not handled very often, nor were they given very many opportunities, except within the confines of their cribs, for motor activity. In the first study (Dennis & Najarian, 1957) it was found that the infants' motor development was markedly retarded, as was their general responsiveness. In the Iranian orphanages, the results were even more dramatic. Two of the three institutions investigated were almost completely devoid of stimulation—they were demonstrably poorer than those found in Lebanon. The third institution provided at least minimal care and stimulation.

Dennis reported that not only was the motor development of these children retarded by 2 to 3 years relative to American children, but that the *sequence of development* among the children was atypical in comparison with other Iranian children. When placed on the floor, these children propelled themselves by **scooting**—a form of locomotion in which the child remains in a sitting position and is propelled forward by pushing with the arms and legs. Normal children, when placed in the sitting position and urged to locomote, will turn and get on their hands and knees and propel themselves by creeping. Thus not only was development retarded, but the pattern of development was also different. Dennis argued that these findings are not the result of malnutrition or **marasmus** (a disease in which the body slowly wastes away), but rather a consequence of the lack of opportunities to learn. The results of his data are even more impressive because the infants in the third institution did not show the same degree of retardation, nor did they show the atypical developmental pattern (scooting as opposed to creeping). The inclusion of this third group is particularly important because it demonstrates that the behaviors observed in the other institutions were not a result of sampling peculiarities.

That the institutions described by Dennis have effects on the cognitive, social, and emotional development of children has been well documented (Casler, 1967; Yarrow, 1964). Socially, these children typically show marked disturbances in interpersonal relations. Many of these children were unable to distinguish between their primary caretakers and other adults, a discrimination that normal infants acquire readily, and they displayed a marked degree of apathy. Goldfarb (1949) has suggested that these disturbances continue through adolescence. It is clear that performance on IQ tests declines steadily with the length of time spent living in the institution, a finding similar to findings reported by Sherman and Key with respect to the Hollow's Mountain children.

The institutional experiences of these infants were extremely deprived, with little or no effort put forth to help the children. The concept of sensory deprivation is often used to describe the environments of lower-class children; hence the term "environmental impoverishment." In actuality, no one could describe a lower-class neighborhood as devoid of stimulation; sometimes it almost seems as if the level of stimulation is too great. The implications of these studies of institutionalized children for lower-class youngsters therefore seem somewhat limited. A reasonable conclusion is that the type of deprivation experienced by lower-class children is more consistent with the kinds of experiences described by Hess and Shipman and Hertzig et al.

Dennis's work contains one compelling feature that makes it extremely important. He compared the infants we have already described with children who had lived in the institution anywhere from 6 to 15 years. Dennis (1960, p. 56) made the following observation:

> So far as the permanency of motor deficiencies is concerned it should be noted that Institution 2 had many children between ages 6 and 15 who presumably were as retarded at ages 2 and 3 as were the children whose behavior was described above. Yet these children were attending school, playing games, doing chores, and being trained in difficult skills, such as the weaving of Persian rugs. There was nothing in their general behavior to suggest that any permanent consequences issued from the extreme retardation in motor development during the early years.

In addition to these studies, Kagan and Klein (1973) report work on groups of Guatemalan Indians growing up in isolated and primitive settings. The Indian children's developmental patterns were compared with those of American children and Guatemalan children reared in a city. The results may appear somewhat surprising. Among one group of Guatemalan Indians, adults rarely allowed the infants to crawl on the dirt floor, and believed the sun, fresh air, and dust are harmful. Interactions between the infant and adults were infrequent. "A few with pale cheeks and vacant stares had the quality of tiny ghosts and resembled the description of the institutionalized infants that Spitz called marasmic" (Kagan & Klein, 1973, p. 950). These comparisons were made throughout infancy and then through the age of 11 years. Their results indicate that although the Indian children reared in rural settings never achieved the same average performance as the American children or the city-reared children, their improvement over what might be expected was quite dramatic. Specifically, in late infancy these infants showed a surge in cognitive performance. Kagan and Klein (1973, p. 958) make the following observation:

> These data have implications for America's educational problems. There is a tendency to regard the poor test performances of economically impoverished minority group 6-year olds in the United States as indicative of a permanent and perhaps, irreversible defect in intellectual ability—as a difference in quality of function rather than slower maturational rate. Guatemalan data . . . suggest that children differ in the age at which basic cognitive competencies emerge and that experiential factors influence time of emergence. Economically disadvantaged American children and isolated rural Guatemalan children appear to be one to three years behind middle-class children in demonstrating some of the problem-solving skills characteristic of Piaget's stage of concrete operations. But these competencies eventually appear in sturdy form by age 10 or 11. A common practice of arbitrarily setting seven years—the usual time of school entrance—as the age when children are to be classified as competent or incompetent confuses differences in maturational rate with permanent, qualitative differences in intellectual ability.

These authors further argue that retardation in academic achievement is relative and does not mean that these children show no intellectual growth. The evidence suggests that the rate of growth is similar to that of middle-class children and that these lower-class children will achieve competencies that are sufficient for conducting complex tasks in adulthood. Unfortunately, the attainment of these competencies is delayed, relative to middle-class children, and thus early opportunities to make use of these abilities become severely restricted.

CULTURAL BIAS OF INTELLIGENCE TESTS.   Hess and Shipman, and more recently Scarr, have suggested that the lower- and middle-class children acquire different cognitive styles; the middle-class style is consistent with the cognitive demands of intelligence tests, whereas lower-class style is less compatible. We can interpret the effects of cultural bias in another way that involves the actual content of the items that are being measured. Among the intelligence tests that stress abstract verbal reasoning ability, assessment requires the use of words. The test constructor, in determining what words will be used or what areas of knowledge will be tested, will use stimulus materials that reflect the individual's culture. Thompson (1962, p. 428) makes the point rather directly:

> Intelligence tests have a cultural reference. They are constructed by psychologists who have accepted the broad social values of a much smaller subgroup within which they have the greatest number of social contacts. Their value judgments of what constitutes intelligent behavior is likely to be most favorable to the particular stratum of society from which they come. It has been facetiously said that if a lion were to construct an intelligence test he would most certainly turn out to be the most intelligent of all beasts, surpassing even Man in mentality.

Almost no one disputes the idea that cultural variables influence the content of intelligence tests and therefore children's performance. Efforts to resolve the problem have not proved to be very successful. Logically, it seems impossible to imagine a "culture-free" test. How would you choose items? Some tests are less biased culturally than others; a totally nonverbal test such as Raven's Coloured Progressive Matrices exemplifies such a test. The core problem, it seems to us, is the failure to recognize that intelligence tests were not designed to compare performances of different cultural groups. Their purpose was to screen children who are likely to have academic difficulties because of slow or otherwise inappropriate intellectual development. Our instruments do that with something less than complete accuracy, and this in part reflects some of the cultural biases we are now discussing. But it would seem that we need primarily to determine the cognitive processes, or intellectual skills, required for success in school and to isolate these attributes as they may occur on intelligence tests. Modifications in the education program should then be made commensurate with the cognitive styles, culture, and intellectual skills of the child.

A study by Lesser, Fifer, and Clark (1965) provides some information on socioeconomic status and ethnic patterns of intellectual abilities. This study involved 320 first-grade children aged 6 years 2 months and 7 years 5 months. The sample was divided into 4 cultural groups (Chinese, Jewish, Negro, and Puerto Rican) and within each cultural group 2 social-class levels (lower and middle). Twenty children in each of 16 categories (4 cultures × 2 class levels × 2 sexes) participated. All the children were from public schools in the New York City area.

The main results of this study are summarized in Figures 8-5 through 8-9. Not shown are the data comparing the groups strictly on the basis of social class. The middle-class children, combined over all groups, performed significantly better than the lower-class children. Figure 8-5 indicates that each of the ethnic groups summed over social class and sex have unique patterns of performance on the 4 areas ex-

FIGURE 8-5   *Pattern of Normalized Mental Ability Scores for Each Ethnic Group*

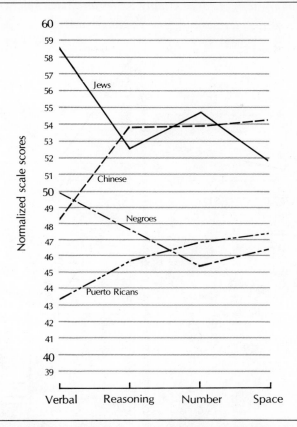

SOURCE: Lesser, G. S., Fifer, G., & Clark, D. H. Mental abilities of children from different social-class and cultural groups. *Monographs of the Society for Research in Child Development*, 1965, *30* (4, Serial No. 102).

amined. More interesting are the next 4 curves (pp. 296–297) showing that these cultural patterns are consistent over social-class levels. The differences in the environmental encounters of lower- and middle-class children *within* each cultural group do not influence significantly the *pattern* of performance on specific abilities. Sex differences were relatively few: boys were significantly better than girls on the picture vocabulary test but not on the total verbal scale. There were no overall differences on the reasoning scale, but boys performed better on the total space scale.

This very carefully conducted study does not permit unequivocal conclusions about what caused the pattern differences, that is, what specific cultural components contributed to the results. The authors appropriately find the patterns of mental abilities to be one of the more important results of their study because of

FIGURE 8-6 *Patterns of Normalized Mental Ability Scores for Middle- and Lower-Class Chinese Children*

FIGURE 8-7 *Patterns of Normalized Mental Ability Scores for Middle- and Lower-Class Jewish Children*

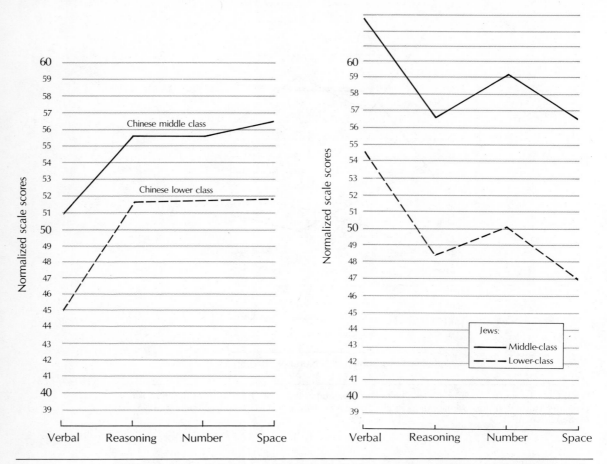

SOURCE: Lesser, G. S., Fifer, G., & Clark, D. H. Mental abilities of children from different social-class and cultural groups. *Monographs of the Society for Research in Child Development,* 1965, *30* (4, Serial No. 102).

their implications for possible variations in educational programs. Lesser et al. (1965, p. 83) state:

> Ethnic group affiliation also affects strongly the pattern or organization of mental abilities, but once the pattern specific to the ethnic group emerges, social-class variations within the ethnic group do not alter this basic organization. Apparently, different mediators are associated with social-class and ethnic-group conditions. The mediating variables associated with ethnic-group conditions do affect strongly the organizations of abilities, while social-class status does not appear to modify further the basic pattern associated with ethnicity.

FIGURE 8-8 *Patterns of Normalized Mental Ability Scores for Middle- and Lower-Class Negro Children*

FIGURE 8-9 *Patterns of Normalized Mental Ability Scores for Middle- and Lower-Class Puerto Rican Children*

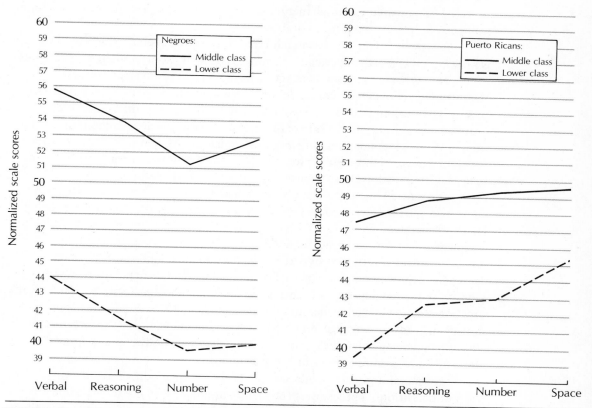

SOURCE: Lesser, G. S., Fifer, G., & Clark, D. H. Mental abilities of children from different social-class and cultural groups. *Monographs of the Society for Research in Child Development*, 1965, *30* (4, Serial No. 102).

INTERVENTION PROGRAMS.   In recognition of the disadvantage faced by lower-class children entering the public elementary school with its predominantly middle-class values, massive federal programs were developed in the 1960s to help these children develop the skills and attitudes necessary for success. The two programs examined here are known as Project Head Start and Project Follow-Through. These programs undertook teaching children the intellectual skills, both cognitive and social, that would help them perform satisfactorily in school. In other words, if success in school requires middle-class intellectual skills and values, then those values and skills would be taught to lower-class children—a position not received with universal acclaim. Despite some objections, the programs seemed acceptable to the general electorate and were viewed as an enormously valuable opportunity and challenge by preschool educators, child development specialists, and other interested professionals. A massive amount of money was appropriated, and these projects were launched with considerable promise and optimism. As will be seen, the problems confronted by those responsible for implementation were very complex indeed, and simple solutions simply were not forthcoming.

Project Head Start.   Although **Head Start** is the label by which the program is known, it was less than perfectly uniform. Indeed, it is only a slight overstatement to say that there are as many Head Start programs as there are Head Start classrooms. For this reason, we cannot conclude that Head Start was either successful or unsuccessful; the varieties of Head Start programs indicate that different kinds of approaches to teaching children affect the course of cognitive development in different ways. This result is not trivial; before the availability of data showing the effects of different kinds of educational programs for young children, it was largely assumed that programs uniformly influence the course of development.

We can characterize the philosophical approaches of Head Start programs along two related dimensions. One dimension involves the degree to which the child is an active learner or a passive recipient of environmental input. The latter dimension involves a considerable degree of program structure (drill), while the former involves undirected opportunities for learning. The second dimension involves the degree of emphasis placed on social behavior as opposed to cognitive behavior. These dimensions are correlated, although not perfectly so. One of the programs was developed by Bereiter and Englemann (1966) and made extensive use of drill in reading, language, and arithmetic. The atmosphere of the classroom for this program was academically oriented and very businesslike. Evaluation of the social and emotional outcomes of the program proved to be very difficult.

A second approach made use of the behavior modification techniques, or operant conditioning procedures (Bushell & Brigham, 1971). Again the objective of this program was skill development with some interest in socialization, especially in attempting to reduce aggression.

Other programs used less formal structure in the classroom and viewed the child as being intermediate between an active and a passive learner. Klaus and Gray (1968), Weikart (1972), and the Montessori Schools (1964) are some of the examples of this general approach. These programs provided the children with relatively structured experiences. In addition, however, they used a variety of other stimulus materials and paid particular attention to using techniques for fostering language and social development. These programs were more child-oriented and more concerned with helping children to gain skill in using abstractions.

A third kind of program is typically referred to as the **open environment.** This program has very little structure; the children are viewed as active learners who can profit from their interaction with the environment. The adults serve as a mediator between the child's active explorations with the environment and the development of concepts from these interactions.

Finally, we return to the traditional program of preschool education, one that evolved from the needs of middle-class children. The basic focus in these programs according to Kagan (1958) is on the development of values and attitudes, as opposed to the learning of skills. We cannot give a detailed description of the operational features of each of these kinds of programs, nor does our description include all kinds of programs. Anyone interested in learning more about the operational features of preschool programs with different philosophical views should read Miller and Dyer (1975), Hess and Bear (1968), and Stanley (1972).

The Miller and Dyer report is one of the most careful and skilled comparisons of different preschool programs. Four programs were examined: the Bereiter and Engelmann program, the Klaus and Gray program, a Montessori program, and a traditional program. In addition, there was a control group of children with no preschool experience. It was possible to follow these children from prekindergarten through kindergarten, grade 1 and grade 2.

The prekindergarten data indicate that the program philosophy, as operationalized in this study, had different effects on different aspects of cognitive development. If the distinction between competence and performance is translated into the various measures employed by Miller and Dyer, the highly structured programs emphasizing skill learning produced the greatest progress in performance. Programs less concerned with specific skills and more concerned with children's acquiring abstractions of various kinds show somewhat poorer performance at prekindergarten than the other groups. The control group in all instances performed least satisfactorily, but this may well be a result of their relative inexperience with strange adults (see Zigler & Butterfield, 1968; Goldstein et al., 1978). Thus, the impact of highly structured, skill-oriented programs in prekindergarten and kindergarten is reflected in the performance of the children on those skills. It should be noted that it is those skills that are also important in determining IQ estimates at this age level, thus it is not surprising that these children maintain relatively high IQs.

This study is extremely important, for the children were studied through the second grade for a total period of 4 years. At the end of 4 years, differences among the groups on the various indices of cognitive performance were negligible and seemingly random. The authors suggest that there were some differences in the social and emotional measures, but these were very small. The authors (Miller & Dyer, 1975, p. 131) make the following carefully considered conclusion:

> To some extent our data also indicate that immediate academic success is not adequate criterion for the value of prekindergarten programs. Montessori appeared to be the best program for males with respect to second-grade IQ and achievement, and yet on immediate impact there was no evidence of MONT. (Montessori) superiority in tests such as the Preschool Inventory, arithmetic, etc. The BE (Bereiter-Englemann) Program, as implemented in the study, produced the best results on achievement as

well as IQ in prekindergarten, but there followed a steady decline in IQ resulting in a loss of approximately 11 points in the mean over a 3-year period and disappointing reading achievement test results at Grade 2.

An earlier study reported by Karnes (1973), using some of the same programs as reported by Miller and Dyer, found much the same results. Specifically, in the Karnes study, which extended through the third grade, early variations that appeared to result from the preschool program had disappeared at the end of the third grade. It is interesting to note that one of the programs in the Karnes study was designed and implemented by parents from the local neighborhood. Although these children intially looked rather unpromising in comparison to the other groups, by third grade their performance was quite as good.

Returning to the question of whether or not Head Start works, it would seem that on the basis of the studies discussed here, and other unpublished reports as well, that if success is measured by a sustained gain in IQ points and scores on achievement tests, then Head Start has been less than a stunning success. Proponents of Head Start have admitted that the current state of knowledge concerning early childhood curriculum is not nearly as well developed as thought but that we would be foolish to think that the gains obtained in preschool can be sustained when the child returns to a deprived home environment or when the child moves from a highly stimulating preschool program to a more ordinary elementary school program. Thus, they contend that Head Start without strong parent education programs, as well as programs that maintain high levels of stimulation in the elementary grades, will fail.

The Follow-Through Program.   The **Follow-Through Program,** as the name suggests, was developed to extend the extra stimulation of the Head Start Programs through kindergarten and the primary grades. These programs are substantially similar in the variation of underlying philosophies; indeed, many of them are direct outgrowths of programs originally developed for the preschool projects. Since Follow-Through is a more recent program and because it requires approximately 3 to 4 years for completion (kindergarten through third grade), only limited, preliminary research findings are available.

In the Miller and Dyer study, part of the sample that went from prekindergarten through second grade were enrolled in Follow-Through Programs similar in philosophy to those they had gone through in preschool. A separate analysis of the performances of these children at the end of second grade does not suggest that maintaining an intervention program has any particular beneficial effect. Miller and Dyer found that the structured, skill-oriented program tended to produce accelerated cognitive growth during the kindergarten or the first grade (depending upon when the program was introduced), followed by a leveling off in performance over the ensuing grades. The less structured, more cognitively oriented program showed substantially slower beginnings but very rapid improvement after the first grade. The net consequence is that at the completion of the third grade, differences among the various groups in terms of reading, arithmetic, and other measures of achievement are essentially equivalent. Indices of social and emotional development fail to suggest any strong effects as a consequence of program content.

The Future of Intelligence Testing

The future of intelligence testing in the United States involves two fundamental issues. The first issue seems to be relatively straightforward, concerning the use of current or future intelligence tests as instruments for furthering our understanding of cognitive development. We believe that the work of McCall, Applebaum, and Hogarty (1973) and McCall, Eichorn, and Hogarty (1977) are examples of research which will advance our understanding of intellectual development and mental operations. Unfortunately, not many studies of intelligence testing have had a developmental orientation. The prevailing view, and one that we think has led to some of the current difficulties in the applications of these tests, is that people acquire more of any number of different traits as they get older but that the qualitative properties of these mental traits remain constant (a quantitative as opposed to a qualitative conceptualization of intellectual ability). This view has simply not been productive. We also believe that comparing the IQ scores of children from different social and ethnic backgrounds is unproductive. Research needs to focus more intensively on the mental operations demanded by test items and on how these operations change with age.

Recommendations for the application of intelligence tests are a little more difficult to determine. On the negative side, the evidence we have examined here indicates that intelligence tests have a built-in cultural bias in favor of middle-class white children. The nature of this bias is inherent in both the content of the tests and the kinds of noncognitive responses required—for example, achievement-motivation, relative ease with strangers, and a willingness to work at a task in the face of apparent difficulties. Further, the evidence has shown that though the tests have moderate predictive capability for groups, their predictive capability for the individual is less satisfactory. In this connection, it should be noted that the predictive ability of intelligence tests is no worse with disadvantaged populations than with advantaged populations (Cleary, Humphreys, Kendrick & Wesman, 1975). On the positive side, IQ tests do provide a reasonable estimate of the relative position of individuals with respect to intellectual development. Such information could be of importance whenever we need to form groupings of children for some educational purpose. This use of intelligence tests would, of course, be enhanced greatly if we had more information about the mental operations required for performance on the

Many psychologists believe that intelligence is a general trait that pervades diverse areas of abilities. (Eric Roth/The Picture Cube)

test and for performance on the tasks for which the children are being grouped (reading, for example). But without such information, intelligence tests are superior to *subjective* bases of appraisal. It is our general conclusion that the use of intelligence tests on a mass basis is probably overly time-consuming and expensive, considering the knowledge gained, and that they can too easily be misinterpreted, especially with disadvantaged children. Our position, which has been documented by Dusek and O'Connell (1976), is that an alert teacher can very quickly determine the intellectual capabilities of children based on their *actual performance* on the *criterion tasks*. Since the purpose of intelligence tests is prediction, the information they provide duplicates that provided by perceptive teachers. Perhaps some of the problems can be resolved by allocating our fiscal resources toward supporting better teachers rather than expensive tests.

SUMMARY

There are a large number of published intelligence tests. Although these tests overlap considerably in terms of the intellectual processes measured, many of them reflect different conceptual views. Some tests, for example, primarily measure abstract reasoning ability. These tests reflect the concept of a single general intellectual ability, Spearman's g factor. Another group of intelligence tests consists of two major factors that are assumed to be independent. The Wechsler Intelligence Scale for Children (WISC), for example, consists of a set of verbal subtests and a set of performance subtests. Still other tests are called multiple-factor tests and consist of a variable number of independent subtests. These tests are based on the assumption that intelligence consists of a number of relatively independent abilities. Individuals, according to this view, can be strong in some abilities, average in others, and weak in still others. This view is in opposition to the concept of a general ability which holds that ability is relatively uniform.

Intelligence tests also vary according to the age level for which they are intended. Considerable effort has been put forth in developing intelligence tests for infants. These tests generally measure sensorimotor abilities and provide reasonable estimates of early intellectual development. Infant tests, however, do not predict long-term intellectual ability. Unlike infant tests, tests designed for older children reflect more verbal-reasoning (abstract) items and fewer sensorimotor items. The long-term predictive power of tests improves markedly after the age of 5 years, probably because the nature of the intellective processes measured change less. It should be remembered, however, that despite the general stability of test performance for groups, individuals frequently vary as much as 15 or more points over a period of 16 years.

Much of the debate about intelligence tests is focused on relevance of the test for different ethnic and socioeconomic groups. Specifically, the charge is made that minority groups, especially among the lower classes, are penalized because the tests demand behavior that is incompatible with their cultural experiences. There is a certain validity to the charge: IQ tests are developed by highly educated, usually white, upper middle-class males. Typically the tests measure verbal reasoning, a skill crucial for success in school. But the tests were originally designed for predicting school performance; this function is performed moderately well. The tests were not designed to compare groups. Analyses of the situation indicate that good teachers are sensitive to the abilities of their pupils and do not need IQ scores. It might be better to spend money, not on remedial programs, but on training teachers to be more effective with minority lower-class children.

CHAPTER 9

(Peter Simon)

EMOTIONAL DEVELOPMENT

SCIENTISTS AND LAYMEN alike have long been fascinated by how the newborn baby changes from an organism that exhibits only generalized emotional reactions into a mature adult capable of subtle emotional responses. Interest in emotional development has been further stimulated by the practical concerns of the cause and treatment of the emotionally disturbed child. This chapter concentrates on the mechanisms of normal emotional development and developmental patterns of various emotions and emotional behaviors.

Despite our assertion that emotional development and the psychology of emotions have generated considerable interest over the years, our understanding of emotions is relatively primitive; at least, comparatively little agreement exists about how best to conceive of emotions and their development. The inadequacy of our knowledge and the disagreements in this area are reflected in a series of papers presented at a symposium several years ago (see Arnold, 1970). Some 20 well-known scientists were able to agree on only a broad outline of what an adequate conception of the emotions should include. In order to grasp the problems, we will have to examine the history of the study of emotions, particularly the basic concepts that may have inhibited conceptual and research progress.

First, the question arises whether emotions are innate or learned, an issue that appears in almost every aspect of developmental psychology. Associated with the question of innateness is the view that emotion can be regarded only as a set of more or less *specific physiological responses*. The emotion of fear, for example, has been assumed to be measurable only by assessing activity in the **autonomic nervous system.** Anger, another important emotion, was also assumed to be assessable only by measuring autonomic reactions, and it was further assumed (correctly, as it turns out) that one could differentiate **anger** and **fear** by the different physiological response patterns. **Jealousy** is an emotional response that makes trouble for a strictly physiological position because the physiological reactions involved are not specific. Most adults who have experienced jealousy report introspectively that they felt either fear or anger. But since the physiological position does not admit feelings as scientific evidence, jealousy could not be accepted as an emotion. Similarly, it was physiologically impossible to differentiate emotions such as **love, joy,** and **delight,** the so-called positive integrative emotions. The logical alternative, and one which was seriously postulated, was to restrict the range of human emotionality to those few physiologically specifiable emotional reactions. Many psychologists eventually rejected this view because it was so contrary to everyday experience and observation.

Another theory of emotions attempted to integrate physiological processes with learning. This position adopted conditioning as a basic explanation. But a conditioning (or S-R learning) view also could not account for the full range of emotions, nor for the numerous occasions when children showed an observable emotional response although no conditioning could have occurred. For example, it is not uncommon for children between 4 and 7 years of age to exhibit fear of numerous imaginary creatures, such as dragons. The problem is that children have these fears without any *apparent* aversive conditioning. An alternative explanation is that as a result of increased cognitive development the child acquires an incomplete understanding about dragons. Learning that dragons are dangerous, children have not yet discovered that dragons do not exist. If their concept of dragons is aversive, we can use conditioning to explain an aversive response, but inclusion of a cognitive component in the model means we are no longer dealing with a simple S-R association. The situation now involves a mediational mechanism or cognitive process.

The incorporation of cognition into our general conception of emotions represented a major breakthrough, since models of emotion were no longer restricted to physiological reactions or S-R learning but could integrate physiological processes with development. Also, context (external stimulation) came to be recognized as critical to the identification of specific emotions. Thus, as Leeper (1970) has suggested, emotion can be conceived as involving the interaction of cognition, perception, and affect (physiological state). This broadening of the concept leaves psychology free to deal with the richness of human feeling and emotion.

Concepts of Emotion

Biological Concepts

According to the earliest views, the emotions consisted of physiological reactions that were instinctive and thus evolutionarily adaptive. The consequent approach to the study of emotion was to assess physiological reactivity, usually by measurement of the **sympathetic** or **parasympathetic** (autonomic) **nervous system** and by the observation of behavior. A sharp distinction was made between the emotional and the rational behavior of human beings. The emotional component was understood as more primitive behavior governed by lower-level neurological mechanisms. Recent evidence (Brady, 1970) suggests that the important neurological structures activated in emotion are the **reticular formation,** the **hypothalmus,** and the **limbic system.** Brady's work has shed light on the neurological and endrocrinological components of emotion, showing that emotional arousal is sustained at a level commensurate with the maintenance of physiological involvement.

The biological approach to the study of emotions also focused on emotional *behaviors* and hence, helped direct psychology away from **introspectionism.** Because the method of introspection relies on subjective reports on the state of the self, it makes the replication of experiments difficult. Thus, the biological approach, however useful, faces certain problems. Although we can differentiate the physiological states belonging to certain specific emotions, this work has made limited progress and probably cannot cope with the full range of human emotions. Arnold (1970, p. 184) summarizes this view:

> [I]t is possible to account for the physiological changes in various emotions, and even to work out the neural circuits that trigger them. But only on the basis of a phenomenological analysis of the psychological activities from perception to emotion and action will it be possible to work out a theory of brain function that provides a neural correlate for psychological experience. Without such a theory, the scores of detailed findings resulting from the massive research effort of the last few decades are bound to remain isolated and disconnected nuggets instead of clues to the rich mains of future knowledge.

Thus, according to Arnold physiological arousal does not exhaust the concept of emotion. Rather, the emotion—and the behavior it leads to—depend on how the individual "appraises" the contextual situation associated with the emotional arousal.

Buss (1961) and Schacter (1970) have noted yet another problem with a strictly biological view of emotion. In a behavioral analysis of **aggression,** Buss persuasively argues that not all aggression results from anger. A person's anger might sometimes lead to aggression, but it does not follow that aggression is always a result of anger. He distinguishes between an involuntary response (anger) and an instrumental response (aggression). According to this view, it cannot always be determined if aggressive behavior involves an emotional response or not. Thus, behavior is not an entirely adequate index of someone's emotional state.

A series of experiments carried out by Schacter has demonstrated that emotional behavior cannot be fully explained by arousal alone; indeed, Schacter contends, an emotional state includes a cognitive component that gives meaning to the physiological state. In one of these experiments (Schacter & Singer, 1962) the subjects (college students) were told that they would receive (if they agreed) an injection of Suproxin—a vitamin compound influencing vision. Actually, the subjects took either a **placebo** or epenephrine (adrenalin), which brings about numerous symptoms associated with emotional arousal. Subjects receiving the **adrenalin** were given one of the following sets of instructions: that the Suproxin would cause side effects—which were specified to the subjects—that last about 15 to 20 minutes, or that the Suproxin would have no side effects at all. Thus, one group expected arousal; the second group did not. The final manipulation was to place subjects from both groups (one at a time) in a room with a confederate of the experimenters (a stooge). In one case the stooge behaved in a euphoric-manic fashion; the second stooge became outrageously angry. The purpose of these conditions was to provide settings from which the subjects might derive explanatory cognitions (it provides the contextual stimuli to explain the physiological arousal).

Neither the manic stooge nor the angry stooge had any special effect on the informed subjects. The second group, the uninformed subjects, however, behaved similarly to the stooges and reported feeling either manic or angry. The control (placebo) subjects behaved similarly to the informed group. Schacter (1970, p. 116) makes the following observations.

> In other contexts, I have suggested that precisely this condition would lead to the arousal of evaluative needs; that is, pressures would operate on such an individual to understand and evaluate his bodily feelings. His bodily state roughly resembles the condition in which it has been at times of emotional excitement. How would he label his present feelings? I would suggest that such an individual would label his bodily feelings in terms of the situation in which he finds himself. Should he at the time be watching a horror film, he would probably decide that he was badly frightened. Should he be with a beautiful woman, he might decide that he was wildly in love or sexually excited. Should he be in an argument, he might explode in fury and hatred. Or, should the situation be completely inappropriate, he would decide that he was excited or upset by something that had recently happened. In any case it is my basic assumption that the labels one attaches to a bodily state, how one describes his feelings, are a joint function of such cognitive factors and of a state of physiological arousal.

This conception of emotion resembles Cannon's (1929) position. Cannon argues that emotional arousal occurs physiologically, but the identity of the emotion does not lie in the physiological reaction but in the person's perception of the meaning of the arousal, or the general stimulus context in which the arousal occurred.

Cultural Concepts

Schacter's data provide a point of departure for examining the role of culture in identifying emotion. Stating the results of Schacter's study in a slightly different form, we can conclude that the subjects perceived the effects of the arousing drugs as a result of cultural definitions of emotional stimuli. Lazarus, Averill, and Opton

Is this child expressing love for her grandmother or living up to parental expectations?
(Michael Serino/The Picture Cube)

(1970) agree that cultural values and expectations are important in identifying emotions and that certain stimuli sensitize some emotions more than others. They argue, however, that cultural expectations developed through association can acquire some emotion-producing stimulus value of their own. They use, among many examples, mourning rites. Anyone who has lost a close relative or friend has probably gone through mourning rituals that seem intentionally designed to generate intense emotional expression. Lazarus et al. make the point that the distinction between social expectations and genuine emotion is a very fine line; in the example of mourning, the line probably becomes blurred. A more germane example is the admonition that children should love certain people such as their parents and grandparents. The emotion of love between a child and an adult takes certain culturally defined forms, such as hugging or kissing. We can raise the question as to whether children exhibit such behaviors as a genuine expression of love or because cultural expectation dictates the behavior. Yet another example is how males express the emotion of love to other males, if they dare to do so. In European societies it is commonplace that a father and son, regardless of the son's age, will kiss. This behavior is rare in the United States and indeed tends to be associated with a quite different, and unfortunately negative, connotation about its emotional meaning. It should be clear that cultural expectations play a mediating role, and a decisive one, in the form of emotional behavior and, furthermore, in the definition of stimuli that produce emotion. Thus, we see here an interaction between the biological mechanisms and cultural demands. The mediation of these two circumstances is handled by cognitive processes.

Cognitive Processes

Of the three concepts of emotion, psychologists have paid most attention to the cognitive theory. In this view a person's cognitive processes provide stimuli with meaning. Some stimuli acquire meaning through conditioning—the child who touches a hot stove becomes less likely to repeat the behavior. But cognitive processes include more than associative learning (see Chapter 6); they make up a system of representations of objects and events in the environment. These systems change developmentally, and such changes are reflected in behaviors (problem solving, concept formation, memory) that increasingly resemble the features of adult knowledge.

Emotional development in children is reflected in their changing cognitive competence. That is, children exhibit increasingly subtle emotional behavior as they mature, eventually displaying the full range of adult emotional responses. They also respond differently to specific stimuli, depending on their age; children under 2 have no fear of snakes but later come to fear snakes even without direct contact. Explanations of these events do not require associative learning, but rather an understanding of children's changing cognitions. Cognition translates the interaction of the individual and his environment into specific action systems and interpretations of stimuli.

General Characteristics of Emotional Development

The study of emotional development has been largely atheoretical, that is, purely descriptive and nonexperimental. Consequently, we have only rudimentary knowledge about emotional behavior and its development. The conceptual and methodological advances that have been made have almost exclusively concerned the emotion of fear, especially among infants. Despite these limitations, we can provide a fairly accurate description of emotional development, especially of fear, anger, and jealousy, and a somewhat less adequate description of the development of positive emotions (joy, love).

Neonatal Emotions

Predictably, the issue of innate versus acquired emotions is not completely resolvable. We agree that the physiological mechanisms necessary for experiencing emotions are innate. We make this claim on the basis of Schacter's and Brady's work, among others, as well as the apparent universality of certain characteristic behavioral responses. You will recall Freedman's study (mentioned in Chapter 3) which showed the nearly normal emotional reactions (behaviors) of a child born deaf and blind. We interpret this study as showing that the arousal mechanisms and behavior patterns associated with emotions are innate. We also described a study by Jost and Sontag (1944) showing higher correlations among identical twins on a measure of emotionality. Other studies in Chapter 3 provide support for a genetic basis of **temperament.** Furthermore, at least one study indicates that the facial expressions of emotions across different cultures are highly similar. Thus it would seem that emotionality—the degree to which stimuli can arouse a person—and many responses to arousal are innate.

Which stimuli elicit emotions is probably a matter of learning, though not necessarily associative learning. Among the supposedly innate elicitors of fears are snakes. If that assumption were true, then we would expect that newborns, or very young babies, with no experience of snakes, would be afraid of them—this is not so. Since a remarkably high proportion of people express a fear of snakes, it has been suggested that some latent developmental mechanisms is operating to produce an eventual fear of snakes. This argument fails on two counts: (1) not all people report any fear of snakes, and (2) many people either directly or indirectly have had bad experiences with snakes and, thus, clearly learned to fear them.

In summary, the arousal and response components of emotion are largely innate, with such emotions as fear and anger more closely associated with biological mechanisms than the emotions of joy and surprise. What stimuli actually elicit emotions are more a consequence of learning, although not purely S-R association.

WATSON'S THEORY.   In 1919, John B. Watson, the renowned behaviorist whose work we have already discussed, proposed three innately determined emotional responses: fear, rage, and love. He also argued that the behavioral patterns characteristic of these emotions were also innate and universal. Finally, he claimed that the eliciting stimuli for these primary emotions were also innately determined and present at birth. Fear, for example, could be elicited by a sudden noise or the loss of physical support. Babies would respond to such stimulation with a stereotyped pattern of movements described in Chapter 4 as the Moro reflex. Rage or anger results from some form of unwanted restraint, such as holding the baby's arms and legs down and pinching the nose. The behavior characteristic of anger is rapid and intense movements of the head and trunk—behavior that seems designed to free the child from the restraint. Finally, Watson stated that love could be elicited by gentle rocking; he described the love response as a state of quiescence or homeostasis. Unsurprisingly, Watson saw all other manifestations of emotion (elaborations on the primary emotions and emergent new emotions, as well as the character and quality of eliciting stimuli) as the result of associative learning.

While Watson's theory seems naive to us today, it was, unlike other theories of the time, amenable to empirical confirmation or disconfirmation; and the theory was extensively tested (Dennis, 1940; Taylor, 1934; Irwin & Weiss, 1934). Sherman

TABLE 9-1 Judgments made by 23 observers as to the emotional characteristics, if any, of the crying of infants between three and seven days of age. The only cues available to the observers were the cries of the infants in response to the stimuli indicated in the following table.

JUDGMENTS	STIMULI CAUSING THE CRYING			
	HUNGER	DROPPING	RESTRAINT	STICKING WITH NEEDLE
Hunger	6*	2	2	5
Pain or hunger	1	—	—	—
Pain	—	3	5	5
Colic	4	7	3	2
Fear	3	1	4	—
Anger	2	5	2	—
Rage	—	1	—	1
Irritation	—	—	3	1
Discomfort	—	1	—	1
Sleepy	2	2	—	—
Awakened from sleep	1	—	3	4
Grief	1	—	1	—

SOURCE: Sherman, M. The differentiation of emotional responses in infants: II. The ability of observers to judge the emotional characteristics of the crying of infants, and the voice of an adult. *Journal of Comparative Psychology,* 1928, 8, 385–394.

*Number of observers making the response.

(1927), in a most damaging study of the theory, asked a group of medical students to identify the emotions displayed by each of several infants after they had been dropped, restrained, or stuck with a needle. The infants' responses were recorded on film, but the students could not see the stimuli being applied. The data in Table 9-1 reveal that the observers were unable to determine at better than chance level the emotion displayed under each of the conditions of stimulation.

The other studies cited examined the effects of the stimuli Watson proposed as innate elicitors of emotion. These studies also failed to support his hypothesis. In some of the studies, many of the children seemed to enjoy the fear-eliciting stimuli, whereas the love-producing stimuli sometimes elicited either fear or rage. In other words, responses to the eliciting stimuli varied too much to support Watson's claims.

THE EMERGENCE OF SPECIFIC EMOTIONAL RESPONSES. Studies of neonatal emotion indicate that their emotional responses are generalized undifferentiated behaviors. Indeed, we have reason to doubt that the behavior of the newborn is emotional if we include cultural and cognitive variables. It does appear, however, that the newborn infant is capable of autonomic responding (Jones, 1930, 1935).

Building on the research that Watson's theory generated, Katherine Bridges-Banham (1930, 1932) hypothesized that the newborn's emotional responses are undifferentiated and that this undifferentiated reactivity later gives rise to specific identifiable emotional responses. Figure 9-1 gives a schematic diagram of her theory for the first 2 years of life. Approximately 3 months after birth, a state of **distress,** characterized by crying and generalized muscular tension, can be distinguished from delight, which she describes as a state of relaxation and smiling. These responses involve skeletal and visceral reactions to intense stimulation, either internal or external. Some of the **visceral reactions** become differentiated from the rest, conditioned to certain stimuli, and combine with particular skeletal responses as a result of experience to form the various well-known emotions. The continued differentiation (illustrated in Figure 9-1) results from combining the patterns with new stimuli. Out of this differentiation come the emotions of fear, disgust, anger, and—at 18 months of age—jealousy. The positive emotions of **elation** and **affection,** first toward adults and later toward other children, emerge at 12 months from the general emotion of delight. The emotion of joy becomes distinguishable at 24 months. In an extension of her work, Bridges-Banham postulates that by 5 years of age, the child

FIGURE 9-1   *The Approximate Ages of Differentiation of the Various Emotions During the First Two Years of Life*

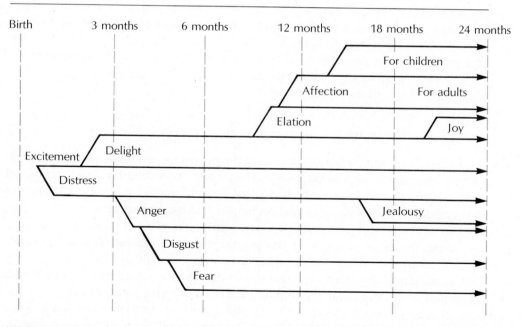

SOURCE: Bridges-Banham, K. Emotional development in early infancy. *Child Development,* 1932, 3, 324–341.

differentiates the emotions of anxiety, shame, disappointment, and envy from the general emotion of distress, while hope and parental affection spring from delight.

Bridges-Banham's position that emotional responses result from the differentiation of visceral responses is consistent with the general developmental principle of differentiation. Her model relies rather heavily on the interaction of maturation and learning; physiological maturation makes the organism more sensitive to environmental stimulation, and it is simultaneously gaining increased differentiation in the functioning of the central nervous system. Bridges-Banham seems to have been aware that not all emotional reactions result from associative learning, insisting that the differentiation of emotions is partially controlled by maturation. This interaction hypothesis may be a rudimentary form of the cognitive interpretation of behavior.

We should make one point explicit about Bridges-Banham's data: they are based on children living in an orphanage during the 1920s and 1930s, where the level of social stimulation may have been less than ideal. Perhaps the safest conclusion we can draw from her data is that the sequence of the differentiation of emotions may be approximately correct, but she may have underestimated the age levels.

The work of Bridges-Banham has not generated very much research, although the few studies that have been done lend support to her general position. It may be that her conjectures did not stimulate more research because her descriptors of emotion are sometimes difficult to distinguish. For example, elation and delight, or joy and delight, have different meanings if we attempt to define them on the basis of "feeling tone." Psychologists, however, are concerned with behavior, so the problem becomes one of distinguishing the behavior of joy from the behavior of delight. But this problem seems trivial in comparison with the general lack of theoretical concepts needed to frame research questions about the development of more subtle and sophisticated emotional responses.

Emotions after Infancy

At the beginning of this chapter, we made the point that psychologists tend to focus almost exclusively on the physiological antecedents of emotion and emotional behavior and have only recently recognized the importance of contextual variables and cognition. Although John Watson helped remove introspection from the psychology of emotion, the current interest in cognition may mean that introspection is returning. Indeed, Singer (1975) has suggested that introspection is a legitimate scientific method. While not denying that Singer and others have persuasively argued the case for introspection for the study of certain problems, we think that introspection may be a less appropriate method to use with young children because of problems in communication. In the final analysis, however, the most direct way of understanding a child's feelings and emotions will be to ask for a self-description of them!

The development of some fears seems to parallel cognitive development. Further cognitive development usually ends the fear. (Eric Roth/The Picture Cube)

THE COGNITIVE-AFFECTIVE RELATIONSHIP.   With the exception of some research published in the past few years, most material on emotional development is purely descriptive. Investigators have devised many sophisticated techniques for observing the behaviors of fear, anger, joy, laughter, and jealousy, which enables us to talk about the waxing and waning of fears, changes in anger and stimuli that produce it, and variables associated with jealousy. This information describes what happens but may not help us understand why these changes occur. We are not presumptuous enough to think that we can enlarge that understanding, but we do think that the work of people like Donald Hebb, Richard Lazarus, Magda Arnold, and Robert Leeper have given us at least the outline of how psychologists ought to proceed in studying emotional development. Now we will examine the work of Donald Hebb on the relationship between cognitive development and emotional arousal.

Relying heavily on neurophysiology, Hebb takes a structural view of the human being. His approach to neurophysiology, however, is closer to Piaget's than to, say, Brady's. According to his view, the development of emotions is the product of learning and neurological maturation; thus, it is neither strictly innate nor learned. Hebb's use of the term "learning" refers to the formation of structures similar to Piaget's. These structures determine which stimuli produce an emotional response and also which pattern of responses will be elicited. Hebb's position is entirely consistent with the conceptions of Arnold and Lazarus but is unique in that he has addressed the question of cognitive structure to developmental problems. This position is similar to the material on infant perception discussed in Chapter 5, which holds that developing infants grow in their awareness of the world around them and the concepts of familiarity and novelty emerge.

For example, in the case of the fear of snakes, Hebb contends that this is not innate but is not acquired by associative learning. The developing organism becomes *aware* that the slithering object can in fact be harmful and thus is an appropriate object to fear. Before this point in cognitive development, the child does not exhibit fear in the presence of a snake. Eventually, the child will advance toward a snake, an action that reveals a great deal of cognitive growth. The child may have also learned a good deal of discrimination. In some parts of the world, people can instantaneously discriminate between poisonous and harmless snakes. People living in climates where snakes are rare tend to be less sensitive to these discriminations, and their response is likely to be indiscriminate fear. Hebb (1949, p. 243) describes the developmental changes in behavior as follows:

> I discovered accidentally that some of the chimpanzees of the Yerkes colony might have a paroxysm of terror at being shown a model of a human or chimpanzee head detached from the body; young infants showed no fear, increasing excitement was evident in the older (half-grown) animals, and those animals that were not frankly terrified were still considerably excited. These individual differences among adults and the difference of response at different ages, are quite like the human differences in attitudes towards snakes, the frequency and strength of fear increasing up to the age of 17 or so in persons who had never been injured by a snake.

It might be helpful to relate an anecdote about a perfectly normal youngster, the daughter of a friend of one of the authors. The parents reported that their 6-year-old girl was convinced that a whale was going to come to the house and take her away. Since she lived in a large industrial city several hundred miles from the ocean, her fear was wholly imaginary and irrational, yet nonetheless genuine. The parents, both intelligent, bought the youngster books about whales, explained to her that no self-respecting whale would go to such trouble, and in numerous other ways tried to allay her fear through intellectual means. All to no avail. Four or five months later, the fear vanished. When asked about the whales in the area, the girl glibly explained that they simply did not exist. We are pleased to report that this story, unlike most psychologists' stories, has a happy ending—she is now a highly educated, mature, and delightful woman, and unafraid of whales.

This anecdote points out once again that during the age period from 5 to approximately 8 or 9 years—the transition from **preoperations** to **concrete operations**—major changes take place in the thinking and understanding of children. When stimuli produce fear, the consequences are neither amusing nor pleasant, *but they are normal.*

Development of Fear

Of all the emotions discussed in this chapter, fear has received the most attention in both empirical research and conceptual analysis. Thus, we can with a reasonable degree of certainty discuss early fears from a conceptual viewpoint and place in a conceptual context the older research on the different fears that children exhibit.

Fears During Infancy

We have already seen that Bridges-Banham reports the first onset of fear at about 4 months of age and noted that this may be an underestimate. A full review of the literature by Scarr and Salapetek (1970) suggests that the 4-month estimate may in fact be quite accurate. The research literature does indicate that noise and the agents of noise may be among the first class of stimuli to elicit fear in infants. Previous discussions, however, should remind the reader that Gibson and Walk (1960) found that infants 6 months or older showed signs of fear while on the visual cliff, with older infants showing more fear than the younger ones. Thus, the evidence suggests that at 4 months, at least, infants display some fear, however ill defined or unstable.

Developmental psychologists have long been interested in the fear that babies exhibit toward strangers. Consequently, research on this fear has developed sound methods, a reasonable conceptual basis, and implications for the development of attachment (described in Chapter 11). Efforts to identify the exact age at which infants exhibit stranger anxiety have encountered difficulties. Different studies indicate that children first develop stranger anxiety anywhere between 7 and 8 months (Sroufe, 1977) and that there is a consistent increase in the frequency and intensity of stranger anxiety through the first year. Findings differ depending on where the study takes place, at home in familiar surroundings, or in the laboratory. Other variables also affect the age at which stranger anxiety first appears.

A systematic, careful experimental analysis of the onset of stranger fear was conducted by Morgan and Ricciuti (1969). The investigators used 80 infants equally distributed among 5 age levels: $4\frac{1}{2}$, $6\frac{1}{2}$, $8\frac{1}{2}$, $10\frac{1}{2}$, and $12\frac{1}{2}$ months. In the experiment, a stranger approached the infant in successive stages. In one condition, the infants were seated on their mother's lap; in the second condition, they were seated at a feeding table (a baby tenda) about 4 feet from the mother. Figure 9-2 summarizes the results of the study. The $12\frac{1}{2}$-month-old infants showed a distinct negative reaction to the stranger. This negative reaction increased with age, although the stranger's presence had the least effect when the infants were sitting on their mothers' laps. Morgan and Ricciuti conclude that their results call into question Spitz's (1965) claim that stranger anxiety occurs at 8 months, the age when attachment had been assumed to show itself. Another condition in this experiment, not

FIGURE 9-2   *Infants' Response to Strangers as a Function of Age and Distance from Mother*

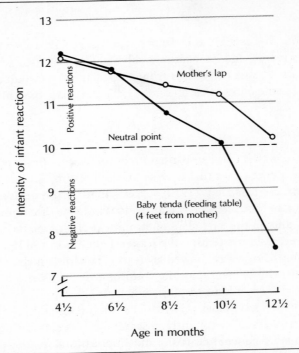

SOURCE: Morgan, G. A., & Ricciuti, H. Infants' responses to strangers during the first year. In B. M. Foss (Ed.), *Determinants of infant behavior*, Vol. 4. London: Methuen, 1969, pp. 253–272.

shown in the table, concerned the presence of male and female strangers. The male stranger evoked more fear responses than the female. It is unclear whether the greater fear of the male resulted from "maleness" or the greater physical size of the male. The sex of the infants seemed to have no significance.

In an extension of the Morgan and Ricciuti study, Lewis and Brooks (1974) used 24 children ranging in age from 7 to 19 months. These investigators exposed the infants to a male and a female stranger of roughly the same physical stature and to a 4-year-old girl. Emotionality was assessed with the strangers at 4 distances—the farthest when the stranger first entered the room and closest when the stranger tried to touch the infant. Table 9-2 shows the scales used to assess emotionality; their content is similar to those used by Morgan and Ricciuti. The results of the study are rather clear: as the adult strangers approached, the infants showed increasing agitation. With the size of the male and female strangers controlled, sex of stranger made no difference in the infants' reactions. They tended not to respond to the unfamiliar 4-year-old. Proximity also affected reaction—as the stranger approached, the infants

TABLE 9-2   Behavioral Scales

FACIAL EXPRESSION		VOCALIZATION	
+2	Smile broad	+2	Laugh or giggle
+1	Slight smile	+1	Coo, babble
0	Neutral expression	0	Neutral vocalization
0	Sobering	0	No vocalization
−1	Slight frown	−1	Fuss, whimper
−2	Marked and pronounced puckering	−2	Cry, scream

MOTOR ACTIVITY TO *M* AND TO *E*	
+2	Reaches out to *E*, tries to approach, cling
+2	Touches *E*'s hand or body when nearby
+1	Makes gross body movement—hand waving toward *E*
0	Looks at *E*
0	Inattention—sleeping, squirming
0	Explores surroundings (to room)
0	Attention directed away from stranger (to *M*)
−1	Waves arms and legs while looking at *E* with negative expression
−1	Avoids *E*'s glance
−1	Pulls hand away from *E*
−2	Attempts to escape from *E* (withdraw)
−2	Reaches for mother, tries to approach, touches

SOURCE: Lewis, M. M., & Brooks, J. Self, other, and fear: infants' reactions to people. In M. M. Lewis & L. A. Rosenblum (Eds.), The origins of fear. New York: John Wiley & Sons, 1974.

became more agitated. The effect of age is shown in Figure 9-3. The older children reacted more negatively to the adult stranger than did the younger children.

Reaction to strangers is also influenced by the context of the encounter. Sroufe, Waters, and Matas (1974) have suggested that the laboratory setting may raise the infants' level of emotionality even higher than the approach of strangers. These investigators conducted a series of experiments in which they saw children both at home, a presumably familiar environment, and in the laboratory. The ''approaching stranger'' technique was used, but instead of behavioral measures of emotionality, they recorded heart rate, heart-rate *acceleration* defining emotionality. The data indicate greater heart-rate acceleration in the laboratory than at home, substantiating the hypothesis of the importance of context in the reactivity of infants to strangers. The position that unfamiliar persons do not constitute an innate stimulus for fear has also been suggested by Rheingold and Eckerman (1973). These investigators report a study that in fact obtained quite the opposite effect from the fear caused in other studies—the infants actually began playing with the stranger.

FIGURE 9-3 *Mean Data by Age*

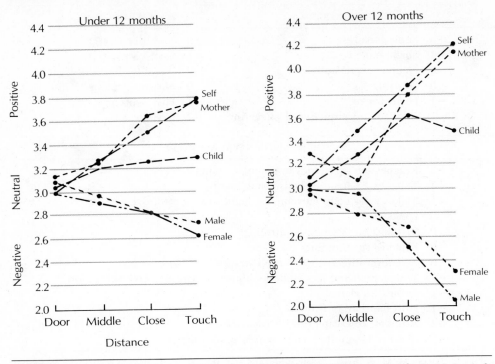

SOURCE: Lewis, M., & Brooks, J. Self, other, and fear: Infants' reactions to people. In M. Lewis & L. A. Rosenblum (Eds.), *The origins of fear*. New York: Wiley, 1974, p. 203.

However, these observations were made in the home. Skarin (1977) reported more fear in the laboratory and more rapid reaction when the mother was not present.

We clearly have here conflicting research findings. In the experimental situation, emotional reactivity tends to rise with increasing age. The stimulus of a "stranger" does not generate intense reactivity, which is more highly correlated with the stranger's proximity and the unfamiliarity of the setting. The infants in these studies varied quite a bit in their reactions to the stranger. Some showed awareness of the stranger but continued playing; others became disturbed and required calming; still others actually approached the stranger. The picture that emerges is that the infant's age, the situational context, and possibly the infants' general temperament are the key variables causing both the intensity and the quality of the emotional response. Sroufe and his colleagues have suggested that "focusing on either the infant's fear behavior *or* its affiliative behavior alone yields a distorted view of the infant's development" (Sroufe, Waters & Matas, 1974, pp. 69–70). They further observed: "Rather than inducing negative or positive affect, it is clear that novel situations and strange persons activate *both* strong approach and strong avoidance tendencies, with the affective outcome being determined by factors such as setting, sequence of events, and familiarization" (Sroufe, Waters & Matas, 1974, p. 69).

The interpretation given to these key studies is that emotional behavior undergoes important developmental changes during the latter half of the first year. We are still left with the question whether infants before the age of 8 months react emotionally to unfamiliar objects or people. Data collected by G. W. Bronson (1972) indicate that, indeed, babies show distress during their first 6 months, with particularly reliable signs of *wariness* toward strangers appearing in the fourth month and becoming more frequent during the second half of the first year. It may be coincidental that it was also the fourth month that Bridges-Banham postulated that fear emerges from the distress side of general excitability—and what she may have observed may have been a wariness of strangers. It is also important to note that Bronson's conclusions about infants from 3 months to 9 months are almost identical with those of Sroufe and Rheingold and Eckerman; namely, the older infants' reactions to unfamiliar events depend upon a number of variables that we have already mentioned, and can be either wariness or fear or, on the positive side, affiliation and exploration.

Fears in Older Children

Arthur Jersild has conducted more extensive and detailed studies of children's fears at different age levels than any other single investigator (Jersild & Holmes, 1935 a, b; Jersild, Markey & Jersild, 1933; Jersild, 1954). His work concerns not only the kinds of fears that children exhibit at different ages but also correlates of these fears. He has used several methods, ranging from diaries in which parents recorded their children's fear to experiments in which children's behavior was observed in various standard situations. In one experiment, Jersild had the parents record the fears of their children, who ranged in age from 2 to 6 years, categorized these fears according to 3 age groupings, and then selected 8 sources of fear to be used in the experiment. Figures 9-4 and 9-5 summarize the categories and age trends of the fears gleaned from the diaries and interviews.

The 8 situations to which the subjects were exposed were as follows:

1. *Being left alone.* The child and the experimenter are seated at a table. The experimenter then leaves the room and remains absent for two minutes. The child has never seen the room. You will recognize this situation as an example of stimulus novelty.
2. *Sudden displacement or loss of support.* A bridge-like apparatus was used, with two boards connected in such a way that when the child stepped on the second board, it gave way. The boards were 2 inches above the floor. The investigators note that this loss of support was not complete and therefore did not strictly meet the criterion.

FIGURE 9-4 *Relative Frequency of Various Fear Situations as Described by Parents and Teachers*   This includes 146 records of observation of children for periods of 21 days (31, 91, and 24 at the respective age levels), combined with occasional records of 117 additional children (27, 67, and 23 at the respective age levels).

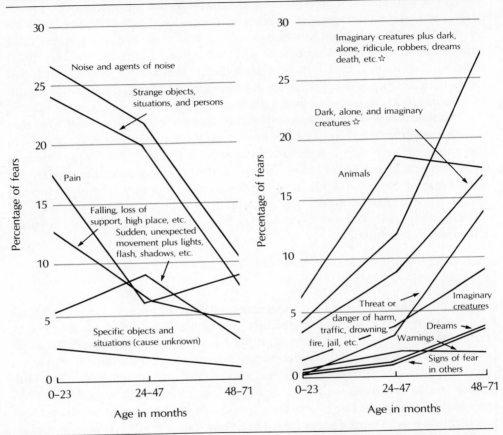

SOURCE: After Jersild, A., & Holmes, F. B. Childrens' fears. *Child Development Monographs*, 1935, No. 20. From L. Carmichael (Ed.) *Manual of child psychology*. New York: Wiley, 1946, p. 763.

NOTE: Starred items represent the cumulative tally of two or more categories that also are depicted separately.

3.   *Dark room.* The experimenter throws a ball down an 18-foot dark passageway and asks the child to retrieve it.

4.   *Strange person.* While the child is out of the experimental room, a female assistant dressed in a long gray coat, a large black hat, and a veil that obscured her features, entered the room and sat near the entrance. Both the stranger and the odd costume served to provoke fear.

5.   *High place.* The experimenters placed a board (12-inches wide, 8-feet long and 2-inches thick) on 2 ladders to that they could vary its height. They first placed it

at 4 feet and then raised or lowered it, depending upon the child's reaction (lower when the child was afraid, and higher when the child did not hesitate at the 4-foot level).

6. *Noise.* An iron pipe suspended from the ceiling and out of the child's sight was hit by a hammer while the child was working with the experimenter at a table located elsewhere in the room. You will recognize this situation as one having a lot of potentiality for producing fear.

7. *Snake.* A harmless garter snake, some 22½-inches long was placed in a box deep enough so that it could not get out. The child saw the snake being placed in the box but when later occupied with other matters did not see that the snake was removed and replaced with a length of ribbon. The box also contained an attractive toy which the child was asked to retrieve.

8. *Large dog.* The child and the experimenter sat working at a table when a familiar adult entered the room with a large collie on a leash. The adult moved to a certain part of the room, at a constant distance from the child, and the child was permitted to examine the dog and then urged to go and pet the dog.

The data (summarized in Figure 9-5) indicate a decided trend toward fewer manifestations of fear with age and also tentatively suggest an interaction between type of fear and age. The fears of the dark room, being left alone, and the snake

FIGURE 9-5   The percentage of children at various age levels who showed fear in response to several experimental situations designed to induce a fearful response. Note especially the rise and fall of the fear response to "snakes" and "being alone."

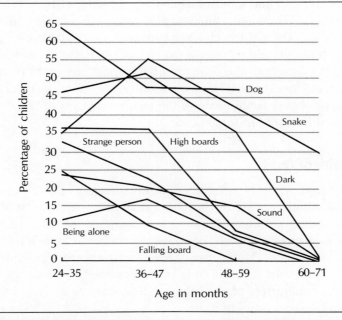

SOURCE: After Jersild, A., & Holmes, F. B. Children's fears. *Child Development Monographs*, 1935, No. 20. New York: Teachers College Press, 1935.

appeared to increase slightly with age. Provisionally, we suggest that these fears require more imagination about potential harm and thus may reflect more sophisticated cognitive functioning.

A high percentage of the children showed some fear of the large dog. Interviews revealed, however, that few of the children had been directly attacked by a dog. Parental admonitions to be wary of strange dogs may have been in effect here. Many of the fears of young children, however realistic, do not result from any painful experiences. Data such as these, we suspect, will eventually lead to conceptions of fear that are consistent with a cognitive view.

SEX DIFFERENCES.   On the average, girls manifested more fear than boys. Since we know of no biological reasons for such results, it seems likely that the data reflect sex typing. Keep in mind that these studies were conducted some 40 years ago, when girls in American society were more protected and also expected to be more fearful than boys. It would be interesting to find out how their parents accepted or did not accept fear in their sons and daughters, and also what kinds of experiences they permitted their sons and daughters to have. We would guess that the boys in this study had been encouraged to perform some of the more fear-producing acts and also to inhibit their fears.

FEARS AND INTELLECTUAL ABILITY.   A statistical examination of the relation between number of fears and intellectual ability revealed a slight but significant correlation of $+.30$. When the children were separated by age, different results emerged: the IQs of the younger children correlated $+.53$ with the number of fears, but the older group showed no correlation. We can interpret these data as meaning that the bright children perceived the potential harmfulness of the situations earlier than their less intelligent peers. However, even the dullest of the older children (all were average or above) could perceive the possible dangers of the situation, thus canceling out differences in intelligence.

Age and Kinds of Fears

The work we have reported so far does not even begin to tap the vast number of studies of fear at different age levels. Rather than review all these studies, we have elected to reproduce an interesting summary compiled by Wake (summarized in Table 9-3) who adapted the results of numerous studies of human fears with age as the independent variable. Notice that the age groupings overlap—different studies used different age groups. Also, different samples and methods were used, along with slightly different definitions of fear behavior. Despite these limitations, the data are interesting and deserve close attention.

Of the various fears reported in the studies, Wake developed three categories: concrete, personal inadequacy, and imaginative. The *concrete* category includes

TABLE 9-3   Age Changes in Types of Fears Between Infancy and Adulthood

TYPES OF FEARS	JERSILD'S BOYS AND GIRLS, AGES 0-8	JERSILD'S SUBJECTS, AGES 5-12		WAKE'S SUBJECTS, AGES 11-16		WAKE'S SUBJECTS, AGES 18-24	
		BOYS	GIRLS	BOYS	GIRLS	MEN	WOMEN
Concrete, percentage	83.8	45.1	40.0	56.2	59.4	50.8	56.4
Personal inadequacies, percentage	4.7	4.6	5.5	28.8	21.6	43.1	28.2
Imaginative, percentage	11.4	50.2	54.5	13.6	16.2	6.1	15.0

SOURCE: After Wake, F. R. Changes in fear with age. Doctor's dissertation, McGill University, 1950, p. 44. From Zubek, J. P., & Solberg, P. A. Human development. New York: McGraw-Hill, 1954, p. 322.

fears of things that can actually happen to a person: being hit by an automobile, falling out of a tree, breaking an arm. These are fears that most normal human beings acquire in order to avoid the dangers of modern living. The category, *personal inadequacy*, includes such fears as the loss of friends, personal failure, and performing in public. The *imaginary* fears include the fear of being alone, the fear of imaginary creatures (dinasaurs, witches, and the like), and other events that are extremely unlikely to occur (the end of the world).

Concrete fears are clearly highest in the youngest age group, and made up 84 percent of the total number of fears reported. At this age level, concrete fear can be realistic; parents continually admonish children to avoid many objects, animals, and situations that their immature motoric capacities make them not quite capable of handling. In the next age category, the percentage of concrete fears drops to 45 percent and remains largely unchanged for the remaining age groups. This appears to mean that after the first contacts with the world, the child identifies those things that are apt to be dangerous and hence require caution.

The first 2 age groups show virtually no fear of personal inadequacy, but with the beginning of adolescence (the 11-to-16-year age group) this fear increases dramatically. This fear is quite prevalent in adulthood, especially among males. The reasons for this sex difference are unclear, although they may be related to the anxieties of seeking employment and achieving professional success. Again, we hasten to remind the reader that most of these studies were conducted at a time when few women aspired to careers outside the home. It could be argued, of course, that an equally high percentage of females would have fears about marriage. It is possible, however, that most of the females studied were in fact already married.

The category of imaginary fears best illustrates Hebb's cognitive-development hypothesis. These fears increased from 11 percent in the first age group to 52 percent in the next higher age group and then dropped dramatically to a steady level of 14 to

15 percent. According to Wake, these data indicate that some time between the age of 5 and 9, children exhibit fears that reflect both their increasing cognitive maturity and their lack of fully mature cognitive schemas. Recall Hebb's description of the chimpanzees and our example of the youngster who was afraid of whales. Children younger than 5 probably do not suffer from many imaginary fears; indeed, we suspect from the analyses presented by Sroufe et al. that the strangeness or novelty of stimuli such as dragons and witches is pleasantly arousing. It appears that children younger than 5 are in fact captivated by dragons and witches, but after that age such stimuli upset them because they think these creatures can do them harm. Eventually, the majority of people realize that these creatures are purely imaginary and so cannot be harmful. Many seemingly irrational fears displayed between the ages of 5 and 9 result from cognitive immaturity rather than emotional difficulties.

THE LEARNING OF FEAR.   Although cognitive-developmental variables play an important role in the development of fear, we have substantial evidence that children also acquire specific fears through associative learning, or conditioning. With laboratory animals as subjects, for example, it has been shown that when an initially neutral stimulus (CS) is paired a number of times with the noxious stimulus (UCS—such as electric shock), the CS will elicit an avoidance or fear response. This response has all the characteristics of other conditioned responses, including stimulus generalization and extinction. Stimulus generalization, as employed in conditioned fear, means that the subject tends to avoid stimuli that are similar to the conditioned stimulus. Watson and Raynor (1920), for example, conditioned a 9-month-old to make a withdrawal response to a white rat. After fear conditioning, the child also avoided other furry objects, such as a rabbit and a Santa Claus beard. **Stimulus generalization** often makes it difficult to determine the original source of specific fears in children and adults.

In another well-known study, Jones and Jones (1924) conditioned a 15-month-old child to fear a rabbit. Before conditioning, the child approached the rabbit with no apparent anxiety or wariness. In conditioning, the child heard a very loud sound when the child touched the rabbit. The conditioning was very rapid, and, as in the Watson and Raynor study, the child showed a generalized fear of other furry objects. The child continued to exhibit this fear for a month. In a follow-up study of this child, the experimenters employed the technique of **counterconditioning** to help the youngster overcome his fear of rabbits and other furry objects. Jones brought the rabbit into a room where the child was eating. He first presented the rabbit at a distance of 20 feet from the child, then gradually brought it closer and closer, each increment being small enough not to evoke an emotional response (physiological arousal). After a fairly short time, the youngster approached the cage and released the rabbit. With the rabbit free, the child eventually touched it with no apparent emotional reaction. The child later showed no residual fear of the rabbit, and the fears of other furry objects also disappeared. Jones and Jones concluded that counterconditioning is more effective than such other techniques as verbal appeal, disuse, and distraction.

The reduction of fears is not always as readily achieved as it was by Jones and Jones. Mowrer (1960) proposed that fears are difficult to overcome because the physiological arousal caused by the feared stimulus is *involuntary*; it is very difficult to control intellectually the visceral responses. Because the response is involuntary, it is difficult to prevent the cycle of: feared-stimulus → physiological reaction → behavioral response (avoidance) → reduction of fear (a reinforcement).

We now have techniques for "curing" many fears. These **desensitization** procedures resemble the approach used by Jones and Jones. The person is encouraged to relax, that is, to reduce muscle tension. The second step in the procedure is to work on the fear hierarchy, the objects or events related to the original fear. The degree of relationship is defined by the intensity of the stimulus's emotion-arousing properties, which are usually a function of its physical similarity to the feared object. For example, a person who is afraid of snakes will experience a strong emotional reaction in a room with a snake. A less intense reaction might occur if the snake were caged; an even weaker response might occur to a picture of a snake; or perhaps little or no response to a picture of a jungle. The desensitization procedure involves having the person look at the stimuli (or imagine them), beginning with those lowest in the fear hierarchy. If fear occurs, the picture is removed and the person is asked to relax again. This procedure is repeated until the stimulus no longer evokes fear. The same procedure is used for each stimulus in the hierarchy (Lang, 1960; Wolpe, 1969). Desensitization has been very successful in treating a great variety of fears. Its crucial feature, as in the counterconditioning used by Jones and Jones, is to prevent the person from becoming strongly aroused; in other words, the physiological response to the stimulus is extinguished.

Another successful technique for reducing fears is **modeling.** Bandura, Grusec, and Menlove (1967) designed 4 treatments for overcoming preschool children's fear of dogs: (1) the 4-year-old model exhibited increasingly brave behaviors toward the dog in a jovial, partylike atmosphere; (2) the same "brave" behavior was shown but in a neutral context; (3) the fearful children watched the dog in a partylike context; and (4) only the jovial party context was experienced but no dog. The curves in Figure 9-6 (p. 328) show that the modeling conditions were most successful in overcoming the children's fear.

Anxiety Effects

Although professionals and laymen alike often use the term **anxiety,** its exact meaning is not entirely clear. Few people reach maturity without having experienced anxiety and without the anticipation of future anxiety. But just exactly what is anxiety? Mowrer, suggests that anxiety involves visceral autonomic responding. The question then becomes how we distinguish between anxiety and fear. One common

FIGURE 9-6   *Mean Approach Scores Achieved by Children in Each of the Treatment Conditions on the Three different Periods of Assessment*

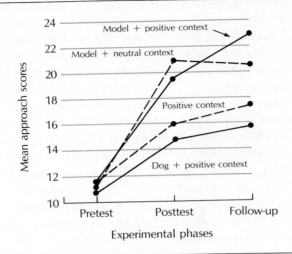

SOURCE: Bandura, A., Grusec, J. E., & Menlove, F. L. Vicarious extinction of avoidance behavior. *Journal of Personality and Social Psychology*, 1967, 5, 16–23.

distinction is that the physiological manifestations of both anxiety and fear are similar (some people argue that fear has more *intense* physiological concomitants, but there seems to be no evidence for this) but that fears are attached to specific referents or objects, while anxiety is more diffuse—anxious people cannot specify what precisely is causing their physiological state. Unfortunately for psychologists, this distinction does not clarify matters very much—closer examination usually reveals the arousing stimulus. Even so, people experience a diffuse state of heightened anticipation or arousal in varying degrees, sometimes over long periods of time. Furthermore, anxiety serves as an important source of motivation for the acquisition of both cognitive and social behaviors.

ANXIETY AS A TRAIT VARIABLE.   We encountered the concept of **trait** in our discussion of temperament (Chapter 3) in which we said that individuals vary in the degree to which they become aroused by stimuli. Some individuals are more prone to anxiety than others; that is, they experience anxiety over a broader range of stimuli. Research studies are not particularly helpful in explaining how some people come to be generally more responsive, or anxious, than others. Some psychologists interpret anxiety as a genetically determined characteristic of temperament, while others contend that some environments are more conducive to high sustained anxiety.

Psychologists have studied the effects of high levels of anxiety in numerous ways. One popular technique is the Children's Manifest Anxiety Scale (CMAS), an adaptation of a scale for adults by Castaneda, McCandless, and Palermo (1956). This 42-item paper-and-pencil scale indicates whether or not an item does or does not apply to an individual. For example, to the items, "I blush easily," "I worry most of the time," "I wonder why some children are afraid of the dark," children can indicate that the items describe them, do not describe them, or, in effect, respond "I don't know." These items generally do not identify the source of the worry, but rather induce individuals to describe themselves as fretful or not. The scale also includes a large number of items directly related to the visceral component of anxiety: "I blush easily." Items describing physiological arousal are probably the best operational definition of the *trait* concept of anxiety.

The CMAS was not designed to study emotional disturbance, sources of anxiety, or other clinical phenomena. Instead its purpose is to assess levels of motivation. The rationale is that highly anxious children will show heightened states of arousal and thus perform more intensively. Extensive studies comparing the performance of high- and low-anxious children on different learning tasks indicate that high-anxious children perform better on comparatively simple tasks (2-choice discrimination tasks) than low-anxious children. These findings are consistent with the learning principle that the more highly motivated an organism, the more rapidly it will learn a particular task. However, in a series of similar studies using *complex* learning tasks involving multiple responses, the low-anxious children performed better than the high-anxious children. If we interpret the evidence in terms of *anxiety*, then these results appear to make sense; we usually expect very anxious people to perform less well on achievement tests and other complex materials. If we look at the results in the context of learning theory, the results appear to be contradictory. Actually, they are not. In complex tasks, heightened motivation generates competing responses. Thus, very anxious people often cannot make crucial discriminations among stimuli or among possible solutions to a problem. One consequence is that they make errors or cannot respond at all.

Although the CMAS was not designed for clinical purposes, the items were taken from a clinical instrument known as the Minnesota Multiphasic Personality Inventory (MMPI). Thus, it is not surprising to find that highly anxious children tend to be less liked by their peers, to be more self-deprecating, and to perform less well on intelligence and achievement tests.

ANXIETY AS A STATE. The conception of anxiety as a state means that stimuli—or, more broadly, external and internal conditions—generate a temporary arousal with all of the feelings of physiological stress. Thus, anxiety as a trait refers to a more-or-less constant level or predisposition, while anxiety as a state is transitory. This view of anxiety has been explored most fully by Seymour Sarason and his colleagues

Test-anxious children perform less well on tests than other children. (Charles Gatewood/Magnum Photos)

(Sarason, Davidson, Lighthall, Waite & Ruebush, 1960; Mandler & Sarason, 1952; Wine, 1971). Their major research instrument is the Test Anxiety Questionnaire (TASC), which was developed on the premise that individuals become anxious as a consequence of having to perform tasks under stressful conditions. Wine (1970, p. 92) describes the general conception as follows:

> The low-test-anxious person is focused on task-relevant variables while performing tasks. The highly-task-anxious subject is internally focused on self-evaluative, self-deprecatory thinking and perception of his autonomic responses. Since the difficult tasks on which the test-anxious person does poorly require full attention for adequate performance, he cannot perform adequately by dividing his attention between internal cues and task cues.

Extensive studies indicate significant negative correlations between test anxiety and performance on achievement and intelligence tests. These studies also show that test anxiety increases during the elementary grades and therefore accounts for increasing amounts of variability in test performance as children progress through the elementary grades. One of the most interesting observations of Sarason and his colleagues was the near impossibility of reducing the test anxiety of school-age children, even first graders. In one anecdotal account, the children were told that what they were going to do later that week was not a test nor was it something that they should be concerned about. When the experimenters walked in with their questionnaire booklets, all the children said, "Oh, here comes the test!" This is probably not surprising to any reader of this text who has spent much of his life taking examinations in school and worrying about his performance.

The consequences of anxiety, whether a state or trait, are generally negative. This is not entirely true, for anxiety does alert the individual to the necessity for a response, and it is probably a good thing that all human beings possess some degree of anxiety. The problem becomes serious when the level of anxiety is so high that it interferes with effective performance. Again, we face the question of how individuals learn to cope with their anxieties; without going into the issue in any detail, we should nevertheless point out that many people come to rely on anxiety-reducing agents such as drugs and alcohol. It would seem crucial that as parents and child workers we become sensitive to children's anxiety and help them to develop adaptive responses to it. The procedures for alleviating fears are also applicable to anxiety and provide several possible approaches to helping anxious children.

Development of Anger

We generally consider anger a negative—not to say destructive—emotional reaction, but it too can be adaptive. The physiology (visceral reactions) associated with anger or rage prepares the organism for combat. While in certain circumstances in modern society physical combat is adaptive, in general it is no longer so. Hence, the socialization of anger (see Chapter 11) becomes extremely important. Here, we examine the causes of anger, its frequency and form, changes over time, and the effects of context and cognitive variables. As we have already noted, however, anger has not received nearly as much attention as fear. We will make every effort, however, to get as clear as we can about the cognitive and contextual aspects of this emotion.

Age and the Expression of Anger

Recall that in Bridge-Banham's model of emotional development, we can first discern anger at 6 months of age. Data from studies by Florence Goodenough (1931), Jersild and Markey (1935), and Muste and Sharp (1947) indicate that before 6 months of age clearly defined anger is rather infrequent. However, after 6 months, the frequency of outburts of anger increases sharply, reaching a maximum at approximately 18 months. This conclusion was based on systematic observations of children by their *mothers* at home (Goodenough, 1931). The results of the other studies cited do not make clear whether anger increases after 18 months. Some investigators have suggested that anger becomes more and more frequent until approximately 4 years of age, while other investigators are more in agreement with Goodenough's conclusions. Buss (1961) has attributed these conflicting results to age changes in the expression of anger. The evidence lends some support to his interpretation because children between 6- and 24-months of age express anger in a direct physical way, whereas older children express it verbally. Of perhaps greater significance is the reason why anger occurs after 6 or 7 months. The answer seems most likely to be a function of context demands. After 6 or 7 months of age, parents expect and demand more mature behavior from their children. They expect them to be quieter, more responsive to requests, and to deviate less from daily routines. At the same time, children are also becoming more mobile, more capable of satisfying their curiosity; they thus encounter more and more forbidden, potentially dangerous objects. In support of the context interpretation, Ricketts (1934) found that more than a third of the immediate antecedents to anger in children occur over basic routines—dressing, washing, doing homework.

Understanding Anger

The preceding discussion provided a very general description of the typical antecedents of anger in children from infancy through approximately 7 years of age. We can summarize these data in the claim that anger in young children results from the interaction of biological and context variables. Furthermore, as children mature, they gain considerable control of their anger. However, anger comprises more than merely the maturation of physiological systems and the management of daily routines. Since we examine material on this subject in later chapters, particularly the socialization of aggression, we shall comment here only briefly on some of the more directly relevant analyses of aggressive responses resulting from anger.

THE FRUSTRATION-AGGRESSION HYPOTHESIS.   The **frustration-aggression hypothesis,** originally introduced by Dollard, Doob, Miller, Mowrer, and Sears (1939), stated that all frustration leads to aggression and that all aggression results from frustration. The theory grew out of studies of associative learning and dealt with a variety of behavior resulting from frustration. We do not propose to examine postfrustration behavior but rather to examine the basic claim that frustration always causes aggression. According to this hypothesis, frustration works like an automatic triggering mechanism, not unlike Watson's stimuli for eliciting fear, rage, and love. This position encounters much the same problems that Watson's theory did—frustrated children do not always become angry or aggressive. Davitz (1952) suggests that responses to frustration may vary depending on how frustration-induced behavior has been rewarded. The learning process is consistent with behaviorism—frustration may be an arousing stimulus that can be followed by any number of responses,

Parents should match toys to the child's abilities, to reduce frustration/anger. (Judith Sedwick)

including aggression. Davitz, who conducted an experiment demonstrating that the postfrustration behavior of children between the ages of 7 and 9 can be manipulated, concluded that understanding postfrustration behavior requires a knowledge of what responses have previously been rewarded, ignored, or punished. This interpretation is consistent with Buss's (1961) view that when aggression "pays off," which in our society it frequently does, then it is likely to become a highly frequent response. Socioeconomic differences in the incidence of aggression, for example, have been widely documented; lower-class children tend to behave aggressively more frequently than middle-class children.

DEVELOPMENTAL INTERPRETATIONS. The cognitive and physiological factors associated with aggression and violence have been reviewed by Singer (1971). Little work has been done on the development of this behavior. In Moyer's thorough examination of the physiology of aggression, he indicates that different kinds of aggression have different physiological correlates. In a statement that suggests a cognitive interpretation, Moyer (1971, p. 61) claims, "each kind of aggression can be defined by the stimulus situation which elicits it and the particular topography of the response." This position is very similar to Singer's summary of the predominant theorists: "They stress the way in which the *interpretation* of situations (a cognitive function) interacts with a limited but differentiated affect system in producing an ultimate reaction" (Singer, 1971, p. 4). Unfortunately, we have neither experimental nor descriptive evidence to show how the interpretation, or cognitive appraisal, of stimulus situations undergoes developmental change with experience; hence, we cannot as yet grasp the relation between the level of cognitive functioning and aggression. To oversimplify, the stimulus contexts that generate emotional arousal are more likely to produce aggression when aggression is the predominant response of a particular culture. For example, one of the authors tried to construct a physiological explanation of the higher incidence of anger and aggression among boys as compared to girls. The argument was based on animal studies showing that male sex hormones (testosterone) are associated with greater aggressiveness. In the case of female rats regular injections of testosterone induced unusually high aggressive behavior. Thus, it seemed plausible to suppose that boys are more aggressive than girls because of differences in male and female hormones. An examination of the literature reveals, however, that prepubescent human males and females have the same ratios of male and female hormones. This ratio remains constant until adolescence. Thus, the physiological explanation, at least by endocrinological differences, simply does not work.

The interpretation remained, therefore, that males make different cognitive appraisals of stimulus situations than do females, reflecting differences in cultural rules about appropriate sex roles. It should be noted that the *failure* of prepubescent males to act aggressively in certain situations can often lead to counteraggression by their peers. Thus, as Buss suggests, in many circumstances, aggression pays.

Although we are somewhat dissatisfied with the current state of knowledge about the development of anger and aggression, we do believe that the developmental-analytic model given for fear also holds promise for anger. Perhaps the ever-increasing level of violence in the United States and throughout the world will stimulate psychologists and others to try to comprehend better the dynamics of aggression. Although we do not reject the notion that television may contribute to violence, we are no more convinced that it does so any more than seeing horror movies causes persistent fears in children. It seems to us that a more productive question, both scientifically and socially, is, How the vast majority of children, adolescents, and adults are so nonaggressive, or aggressive only after extreme provocation? An answer to this question might help us to understand better how physiology, contextual stimuli, and cognitive systems interact in the development of this important emotion.

Jealousy

Like anger, the emotion of jealousy has received considerable attention, but almost all of the work has been purely descriptive. Curiously, we understand fairly well the contextual and cognitive influences on jealousy, but our knowledge of the physiological reactions is spotty. Some investigators have suggested that jealousy is not in fact a "true" emotion because it lacks any specific physiological reaction. This supposition reflects a strict and narrow behavioral definition of emotion. However, any reader who has either experienced jealousy or observed it in others knows the absence of clearly specifiable physiological reactions does not make jealousy disappear.

Antecedents of Jealousy

Jealousy among children has probably received more attention from laymen than from professional psychologists. Indeed, many current assumptions about jealousy in children are based on only one study (Seawall, 1930), involving 40 boys and 30 girls ranging in age from 12 months to 5 years 10 months at the time that a new sibling was born. One difficulty in the study of jealousy is how to define it. The Seawall study exemplifies this problem by giving no true definition of the term; the following behaviors, however, were included as typifying the emotion: (1) bodily attack on the younger sibling, (2) ignoring the presence of the sibling, (3) denial of the existence of the younger sibling, and (4) "definite" personality changes in the older sibling at birth. These indicators of jealousy appear to be consistent with Lazarus's definition of an appraisal indicating future damage or hurt. The children studied came from families ranging from low to high middle class, and the data were collected through the study of clinical case records, personal observations, and other family contacts.

Thirty-nine out of 70 children (or slightly more than 50 percent) showed at least one of the 4 behaviors indicating jealousy. The great majority of instances of jealousy took the form of bodily attacks on the younger sibling (67 percent of the reported behaviors were in that category). The other categories did not contribute significantly to the overall incidence of jealousy. Perhaps of greater interest are the variables that seem to distinguish between the children who showed jealousy and those who did not. Whether or not the child had been told that a baby would arrive seemed to have no effect one way or the other on the child's jealousy. Jealousy occurred slightly less often when the baby was wanted by the parents. One variable that had some influence on jealousy was the number of siblings already in the family. When the family already had 2 siblings, there were more instances of jealousy; but with 3 or more siblings, no differences in jealousy were found. Perhaps the most notable factor was the age of the child when the new sibling was born. Jealousy occurred most frequently between 18 and 42 months. Coincidentally, the child is more apt to display negativistic and resistent behavior within this age range (Levy, 1936) and thus may be more easily provoked by the presence of a new sibling. Another, equally plausible interpretation of this age effect is that children between 18 and 42 months still depend very much on their parents for their physical and emotional well-being, and so feel the effects of a new sibling more acutely. Before the baby is 18 months, the parents are in no position to relinquish their attentiveness to

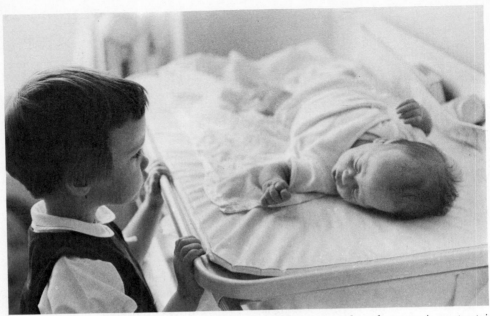

How a new sibling will be received depends on many factors, but the most important is the child's previous emotional status. (Elizabeth Wilcox/Photo Researchers)

the child; after 42 months, the child probably depends less on the parents for meeting his or her physical and emotional needs. Another extremely crucial variable—and the one that seems to make the greatest psychological sense—was the consistency of discipline. Those parents who were judged by clinicians to use consistent discipline encountered significantly fewer instances of jealousy, whereas parents whose discipline was inconsistent (today's acceptable behavior causes punishment tomorrow) encountered significantly more jealousy. If consistency of discipline is taken as an indicator of family adjustment, then the best predictor of jealousy—or the most important *antecedent* of jealousy—may be the level of adjustment of the family, including the child, before the birth of the sibling. This interpretation makes particularly good sense when we recall that the highest incidence of jealousy was physical attack on the new sibling.

Seawall's study, as well as others (Smalley, 1930, 1931; Baldwin, 1947; Levy, 1936), do not reveal any patent techniques for preventing jealousy. Consistent with Lazarus's view, the emotion involves a significant cognitive element, and we are rarely certain precisely what cues a child is responding to. These studies do demonstrate a significant cognitive component—more intelligent siblings show more jealousy than less intelligent siblings. Thus, the more intelligent sibling may appraise the situation as more damaging to the self than less intelligent children. At any rate, families living in an atmosphere of harmony and trust may foster less jealousy in the older sibling. Further, where such harmony and trust prevail and where there are a large number of children, jealousy becomes much less probable. Finally, Seawall's data suggest that parents should plan the births of their children so that the older sibling is *not* between 18 and 42 months older than the newborn child.

A great deal of research needs to be conducted on how jealousy develops. Adults who have experienced jealousy report that they felt either anger or fear at the time, but they are relying on long-term memory and may not be recalling their feelings accurately. So research is needed to find out the *feelings* of children displaying jealousy.

Positive Emotions

The research on the positive emotions is sparse. Perhaps this is understandable since our information about fear, anger, and jealousy can be used to improve the lives of children. Children who are happy, well-adjusted, and generally in tune with the world demand less of our services and attention. On the other hand, if we ask the general question how emotional development takes place, then the paucity of research is indeed unfortunate. However, it should be noted that many of the concepts used to describe positive emotions (joy, elation, delight, and the like) are difficult to differentiate behaviorally and do not fit in with the approach to the study of emotions that we discussed earlier. Thus, we shall restrict our discussion to the positive emotions that have clear behavioral indicators.

Development of Laughter

The serious study of laughter dates back to at least 1929 when Washburn (1929) described the kinds of stimuli that elicit smiling and laughing in infants during the first year of life. He reported that one highly successful and uniform elicitor of laughter among infants was the "threatening head" stimulus—a looming of the head toward the child's abdomen. Any parent will readily recognize this as a familiar phenomenon. Other early studies indicate that children rarely laugh when alone, apparently requiring company as a catalytic agent (Brackett, 1934). In another study Justin (1932) found that incongruity and contrast consistently evoked laughter; his observations anticipated more current interpretations of the development of children's humor.

ROLE OF COGNITION.   The basic interpretation of cognition in the development of humor has been extremely well stated by McGhee (1974, p. 722). It is:

> proposed that once a conceptual level of cognitive mastery has been achieved, the child can assimilate or interpret incongruities in a pretend or fantasy sense, again a necessary condition for perceiving humor and discrepancies in the physical environment. Finally [it is] suggested that logic plays no part in preschool children's

incongruity humor. Upon acquiring concrete operational thinking at the age of 6 or 7, children acquire the capacity to perceive humor in the violation of logical relationships between stimulus elements. While the perceptual orientation of the preoperational child restricts him to humor based upon violation of perceptual expectancies, the logical thought capacity of the concrete operational child enables him to see humor in more abstract relationships.

The features of McGhee's interpretation should be reasonably familiar to the reader by now: he has applied the principles of cognitive development to children's humor. His interpretation is entirely consistent with Sroufe et al. (1974), in their discussion of the development of fear, in which they explained the responses of smiling, laughter, and fear by the principle of cognitive incongruity, with the contextual situation determining the eventual emotion or behavioral reaction. In one experiment by Sroufe and Wunsch (1972), the mother wears a mask. This stimulus produced laughter in between 50 and 80 percent of 10-month-old infants when they were tested at home, but in only 33 percent when they were tested in the laboratory. Thus, we might conclude that infants' humor requires both arousal and a familiar context. For older children, contextual cues are probably less important, for they may depend more on the incongruity of the stimuli.

The principle of cognitive congruity developed by Zigler, Levine, and Gould (1966) is based on a study of children in grades two through five. They selected a series of 25 nonverbal cartoons from the Children's Mirth Response Test (CMRT). These items were individually administered to 64 children in four grade levels. The cartoons were first presented face down; after each was turned up, the following behaviors were recorded: spontaneous laughter, the child's verbal judgment of whether it was funny or not, and other spontaneous responses. After these judgments had been made, the series was then repeated and the children were asked to explain each joke. Figure 9-7 shows the results of the study and includes an index of mirth (whether the child thought the picture was funny or not) as well as an index of comprehension. The curves from grade two through four clearly indicate that as the children's ability to understand the humor increased, so did their "That is funny" responses. Fifth-grade children, however, often got the point of the joke but did not find it very funny. This discrepancy between comprehension and funniness generated the cognitive congruency hypothesis. The authors (Zigler, Levine & Gould, 1966, p. 514) interpret their findings as follows:

A possible explanation for this generally lower level of mirth response in the fifth grade as compared to the fourth grade can be subsumed under a principle of cognitive congruency. This principle would generate the prediction that cartoons which made few cognitive demands elicit a lower mirth response than those that are in keeping with the complexity of the child's cognitive apparatus. That is, it is possible that for the fifth grade many of the cartoons are too easily comprehended, and this very ease of comprehension reduces their funniness.

FIGURE 9-7   *Mean Mirth and Comprehension Scores in Percentages for Second, Third, Fourth, and Fifth Grades*

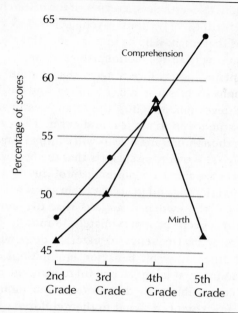

SOURCE: Zigler, E., Levine, J., & Gould, L. Cognitive processes in the development of children's appreciation of humor. *Child Development*, 1966, 37, 507–518.

McGhee has argued that a conceptually more sophisticated experiment would test specific aspects of cognitive congruency as exemplified in the various Piagetian tasks described in Chapter 6. He has reported a number of such experiments that provide support for Zigler's position but that also suggest additional dimensions of humor, especially among older children. In one experiment, for example, McGhee and Johnson (1975) found when the contextual setting permits the child to use fantasy and minimizes the demands of reality, the cognitive incongruencies are more likely to produce humor. According to McGhee, the cognitive interpretation that seems to explain the first onset and development of humor becomes less satisfactory as children get older. He suggests, in agreement with Goldstein, Suls, and Anthony (1972), that with increasing age, comprehension becomes less important, while emotional factors and the personal salience of the humorous material assume greater importance.

Enhancing Emotional Development

It is not our intent here to provide prescriptions that guarantee that a child will grow up with a mature and stable control of his or her emotional reactions. Even if that were our purpose, we do not know enough about the development of positive emotions—or, for that matter, the development of the less positive emotions—to permit such prescriptions. Nevertheless, a review of the research, conceptual models, and the clinical observations of various psychologists and psychiatrists suggests certain generalizations that might help us in understanding the emotional behavior of children and in fostering healthy emotional development.

First, developmental psychologists agree that certain patterns of behavior associated with emotions such as fear, anger, smiling, and laughter, always occur in the course of normal development. Thus, the infant's early smiling is biologically adaptive, but by the same token so are fear and anger. The evidence also indicates that children between the ages of 5 and 8 years will exhibit fears that are very difficult to cope with rationally. This evidence suggests that the best way to understand the origin of these fears is to see them as a normal part of the transition from immature to mature cognitive functioning and to accept them as such.

As regards anger, the evidence suggests that the most intense outbursts, usually temper tantrums, occur at approximately 18 months of age. Extreme anger most likely results from the frequency of external demands and restraints that inhibit curiosity and other enjoyable behavior. Prohibitions are still necessary for the child's safety. In addition, it might be helpful to manipulate the environment in ways that are more compatible with the curiosity and motoric capability of the 18-month-old child. How parents respond to their children's anger may well determine how children later respond to their own anger. Suffice it to say parents provide important models for the expression of anger.

Finally, we return to the concept of innate temperamental traits (see Chapter 3). The evidence suggests that the general level of emotional arousal is inherited, and that fact has important implications for the interaction of child and parents. Parents report that the easily aroused child exhibits a high number of irritating behaviors, including temper tantrums and fear. The importance of these apparently innate behavioral tendencies has been dramatically demonstrated by Thomas, Chess, Birch, Hertzik, and Korn (1963). These investigators systematically followed the emotional adjustment of 135 children from birth to at least 6 years of age and to a maximum of 12 years. These children differed in temperamental characteristics during infancy, and these differences were found to be fairly constant over the entire time in which the children were studied. One important finding was that although the parents did not treat their children differently as infants, after infancy the parents behaved differently toward their more difficult children. Thus, these clear interactive effects may well have antecedents in the child's genetic endowment. Remember that parent and child begin to interact at birth, and the quality of these early interactions may very well be indicative of future patterns of behavior. *Constructive* parental behavior is important for all children, but even more so for emotionally labile children. The one characteristic of parental behavior that emerges in many studies, including clinical cases, as being of paramount importance is *consistency*—always handling similar problems in similar ways. Our reading of the literature suggests that this recommendation is especially critical for children whose emotional arousal is readily triggered and intense.

SUMMARY

The study of emotional development has been largely ignored by psychologists. Essentially the problem has been of conceptualizing emotions. Are emotions purely innate physiological responses? Are emotional behaviors learned? Are cognitive processes involved? The answer appears to be "yes" on all counts. A state of physiological arousal has no "affective" meaning by itself; the individual defines the arousal state in terms of context. How arousal is defined and expressed behaviorally appears to be largely learned. There are research studies, however, showing that predispositions to emotional arousal and certain behavioral responses are genetically determined.

There are developmental changes in the stimuli associated with fear arousal. An interesting feature of these changes is the increase in fears of the supernatural that emerge at about 6 years and diminish after age 9 years. These data indicate that fears are influenced by cognitive functioning; dragons may be perceived as real and frightening by normal 6-year-olds but not by normal 12-year-olds.

Not all unusual or debilitating fears weaken with age. Fear of heights, snakes, or enclosed spaces may be very powerful and interfere with normal living. Although there are many treatment procedures available, the most successful appears to be behavior therapy. This approach makes no assumptions about the cause of the fear but concentrates on changing the behavior.

Research studies on the development of anger are largely descriptive. The same situation prevails for the study of jealousy. These important areas of human emotion clearly require more research studies and better theories.

Our understanding of emotional development has not progressed sufficiently to warrant guaranteed prescriptions for preventing problems. The data suggest that all normal children evidence fears and temper tantrums. They also smile, laugh, and experience joy. Parents should understand that "peculiar" fears at a specific age level are normal and that certain environmental conditions, such as cramped space, may cause anger. However, temperament also makes some children more emotionally volatile than others. Our best guess is that parents can markedly influence the behavioral expression of emotion but will be less successful in controlling emotional reactions. The mark of emotional maturity, however, is expressing feelings in socially acceptable ways.

CHAPTER 10

(Burk Uzzle/Magnum Photos)

IDENTIFICATION AND THE DEVELOPMENT OF SEX ROLES

IN THIS CHAPTER we discuss two important aspects of socialization: identification and sex-typing. Each is a complex pattern of behavior that is idiosyncratic because each child's environment is different. Both are learned in part without direct training, although such training may affect their development. Thus, while children may not consciously intend to learn the behavior that indicates identification or sex-typing, they do learn to behave like their parents and other important people (identification) and to behave in ways considered appropriate for their sex (sex role).

Defining Socialization

Human beings live in social systems with rules and norms that specify appropriate modes of behavior. As infants, children, adolescents, and adults we learn to behave in a manner deemed appropriate by society. The term **socialization,** although difficult to define precisely, refers to what, why, and how we learn social behavior, including that indicative of identification and sex-typing. The systematic study of socialization phenomena has its roots in anthropology, sociology, and psychology.

Brim's (1966, p. 3) definition seems well suited to the needs of the psychologist: "the process by which individuals acquire the knowledge, skills, and dispositions that enable them to participate as more or less effective members of groups and the society." This definition indicates that the individual must *learn* certain behaviors. As noted in Chapter 2, there are two theories about the nature of learning: cognitive-developmental theory and learning theory. Their most important implication for socialization is the distinction between learning and performance. That is, *how* children learn appropriate social behavior versus *why* they learn it. The "how" question concerns the psychological processes underlying socialization. The "why" question concerns specifying the processes determining peoples' behavior. How, or in what ways, do children behave like their parents, and why do they do so? In what ways do boys and girls behave differently, and why do they come to do so?

According to Brim's definition socialization is a process in which the individual's behavior changes in accordance with societal standards. Behavior that is acceptable at one point in the life cycle may be unacceptable at some later time. We expect children to behave differently from adolescents or adults. As children grow up, we expect their behavior to change in ways commensurate with their new level of maturity. Socialization involves interaction with others—such as parents or teachers—who interpret societal standards for children. As social standards change, children are socialized differently. For example, we expect 10-year-olds to behave more maturely than 5-year-olds, to take more responsibility for their personal hygiene, to act appropriately in social situations, and the like. The specific behavior we expect depends on the culture. As the culture changes, so do our expectations about the behavior of children of different ages.

Socialization is a two-way street (Bell, 1968; Rheingold, 1969), in that it demands changes by both the parent and the child. For example, as children grow up, they are expected to show more independence; at the same time parents must learn to act differently toward their child's strivings for independence. Just as parents bring up children, children bring up parents. Goslin (1969, p. 6) emphasizes the importance of studying the interactional components of interpersonal relations by noting that each participant influences the behavior of the other and that social role learning and role teaching go hand in hand.

Consider some of the many ways in which you have been socialized and the many factors affecting the way you behave: You are, for example, either a male or a female, a son or a daughter, of a certain age, religion, and social class. Add to these descriptors the various patterns of acceptable behavior that go with these roles and changing social standards, and the attempt to describe how socialization occurs becomes mind-boggling. All these factors are relevant to socialization, how the individual learns to behave in our society. Psychologists studying socialization have tried to sort out the most important influences for large segments of a society, or for societies in general, and have constructed theories to explain socialization in terms of these variables.

Identification

Sigmund Freud first used the concept of **identification** to describe how children come to think, behave, and feel like some other person (a model) (Bronfenbrenner, 1960). The most important models for young children are their parents. Older children may identify not only with parents but also with peers, such as members of the same school club or athletic team, or with some other adults, such as teachers. They also identify with broad classes of people who fit within a common grouping, such as male or female, adolescents, or schoolmates. All the models with which the child may identify share the common element of similarity to the child (Lynn, 1969). If the child perceives some similarity between himself or herself and some model, then he or she is more likely to identify with that person. Thus, the child's perception of similarity forms the basis for identification. Research demonstrates

Dressing up is one way to show identification with a role model. (Elizabeth Hamlin/Stock, Boston)

that similarity between an observer and a model increases the probability that the observer will imitate the model (Bandura, 1969a, 1969b; Gewirtz, 1969). By imitating a model, the child can learn new behavior. Hence, identification is often regarded as one of the most basic ways in which children become socialized.

Examples of children's identification with their parents illustrate both the strength of identification and its function in socialization. The 2-year-old playing house is imitating the parents' behavior by exercising control over the doll children. These children may call themselves "mommy" or "daddy," indicating a sex-based similarity to the parent. Other examples are a young boy imitating his father's shaving and a young girl helping her mother in the kitchen. These behaviors, too, illustrate children's awareness of differences in sex roles and the children's identification with the parent of the same sex. The similarity between the child's and the adult's behavior provides evidence that identification has taken place. The differential imitation of mother and father by the girl and the boy illustrate the power of identification in learning sex-typed behavior.

We might well ask why children imitate their parents at all. It is generally accepted that children imitate their parents' behavior—and probably their attitudes and feelings as well—in order to be more like their parents, to feel more secure and adequate and more able to please them. This is especially true when parents actually teach their children to behave like adults. Children also imitate their parents in order to acquire some of the things that their parents have, such as power over rewards and punishments, and competence in dealing with the environment. Through imitation, children come to believe that they possess these competencies. Parents and other adults reinforce this imitation when they announce that the child behaves "just like daddy" or "just like mommy."

The child comes to perceive his similarity to the parent, especially one of the same sex, in a number of ways—by dressing like the parent, being told that he looks and behaves like the parent, having the parent's skills ascribed to him, and in countless other ways. This perception of similarity increases the likelihood the child will model the parent.

Identification Versus Imitation

Identification is not simply imitation. To be sure, "identification" and **imitation** both refer to behavioral similarity between the child and a model. The child can imitate any one of a wide range of models but selects only certain ones. It is the imitation of *selected* models, such as the parents, out of the wide range of adults that indicates identification and distinguishes it from simple imitation.

Selective attention to specific models has two important consequences that help to distinguish between identification and imitation. First, the child attends to a wider range of behavior of the models selected than to models not selected. As a result, the child acquires a more detailed set of behaviors from the model selected

Child-rearing techniques used early in development may help children develop androgynous role behaviors and break away from traditional role behavior. (Left: Ruth Silverman/Stock, Boston; right: Bobbi Carrey/The Picture Cube)

than of the behavior of other potential models. This detail may include both gross motor patterns as well as more subtle gestures, word phrasing, voice inflection, and mannerisms peculiar to the model.

Second, the child is more likely to attach significance to the behaviors of the model in specific situations. If the model is competent, the child is likely to learn adaptive behavior for that situation. If the model is incompetent, the child may not learn how to deal appropriately with the situation.

Selective attention to specific models has its basis in the child's first contact with adults—specifically the parents. The parents' power over rewards and over the environment no doubt teaches the child to give parents special attention. In addition, parents directly teach their children to attend selectively to others by pointing out other's appropriate or inappropriate behavior. In this way, the child learns to pick models to imitate and with whom to identify.

Consequence of Identification

The socialization resulting from identification seems to be automatic (Bandura, 1969a, 1969b; Bronfenbrenner, 1960) and to result from processes other than deliberate training of the child. This function of identification manifests itself in two ways. First, the child develops a **sex role,** a set of behavior patterns consistent with the masculine or feminine roles in the child's culture. Second, the child develops a **superego,** or conscience, that internalizes the society's standards of moral conduct. We shall discuss sex-typing in this chapter and reserve our discussion of moral development for Chapter 12.

Sex-Typing

Sex-typing refers to the child's acquisition of the motives, attitudes, values, and behavior regarded by the culture as masculine or feminine. This learning begins in infancy when the parents label the child a boy or a girl and then respond differently to the child according to his or her sex. Through these different responses and expectations of different behavior from boys and girls, the parents shape the child's behavior along lines considered appropriate to his or her sex. Although some evidence indicates that biological predispositions also affect sex-typing, most psychological research has been aimed at explaining the role of environmental contingencies in the acquisition of sex-appropriate behavior.

Most cultures view the male role as controlling, independent, assertive, competitive, aggressive, and manipulative of the environment. The female role is seen as passive, dependent, nurturant, nonaggressive, and warm. In some cultures, however, these roles are reversed, indicating that humans are not strictly biologically predestined to certain sex roles by their gender alone. The cross-cultural study of sex-typing and sex-role development (Barry, Bacon & Child, 1957; Block, 1973) proves to a large extent that the most important determinant in the acquisition of sex roles is the historical context of the culture, and the resultant training undergone by the child. Either males or females may assume the aggressive or the passive role in the society. Indeed, the current women's movement is based on the notion that many if not all of the differences in the behavior of men and women are due to the socializing influences that have made the female role a restricted, subservient one. One of the aims of the movement is to establish a cultural atmosphere in which women are free to choose alternate roles. If culture is as strong a determinant of sex roles as many believe, several interesting questions arise. For example, how do preferences for alternate sex roles relate to child-rearing practices, to traditional sex roles, and to societal expectations about the patterns of behavior that differentiate the sexes? Does having a working mother help the female child acquire the desire to have a career?

Opposed to the cultural argument is the thesis that at least some sex differences in behavior have a biological basis. Data on stress in infants and life expectancy, for example, show that males are much more susceptible to prenatal and postnatal difficulties and illnesses than are females. In general, females can withstand pain and stress better than males. Girls are "ready" for school earlier than boys, at least in terms of their psychomotor and perceptual-motor abilities. Females also mature earlier than do males, achieving full adult height and reproductive capacity earlier than males the same age. Might there not be other biological differences between the sexes that relate more directly to behavior? And in what ways do the biological differences that we know exist between the sexes relate to differences in sex-typing and in its result, the sex-typed roles that we have?

Two fairly complete surveys of the development of sex differences and sex-typing (Maccoby, 1966; Maccoby & Jacklin, 1974), and a critique of the most recent of these (Block, 1976), will be of interest to those who want to read a thorough survey of the literature.

Sex-Role Stereotypes

We are all familiar with the traditional stereotype ascribed to a person on the basis of his or her sex. There is considerable historical evidence (Hartly, 1960; Parsons, 1955; Bennett & Cohen, 1959) that both children and adults expect men to be independent, competitive, assertive, and the like, while they expect women to be nurturant, dependent, passive, and so on. These traditional sex roles, however, have been challenged by women concerned with the detrimental effects of sex-typing. It is an interesting question whether sex-role stereotypes have changed as a result of the feminist movement.

PRESENT ATTITUDES.   Several recent surveys by Broverman and her colleagues (Broverman, Broverman, Clarkson, Rosenkrantz & Vogel, 1970; Rosenkrantz, Vogel, Bee, Broverman & Broverman, 1968; Broverman, Vogel, Broverman, Clarkson & Rosenkrantz, 1972) have concerned changes in sex-role stereotypes. They first asked approximately 100 male and 100 female undergraduates to list the characteristics on which men and women differ. A checklist was devised of the traits mentioned and this list was administered to 74 male and 80 female college students. Of the 60 items on the list 41 were identified as indicating sex-typed behavior, as assessed by 75 percent agreement among subjects of both sexes. Table 10-1 shows the items discriminating beween the sexes, divided into those in which the masculine trait is viewed as more desirable and those in which the feminine trait is viewed as more desirable. More of the masculine traits were thought to be desirable than the feminine traits. It is of some interest that when asked to indicate the degree to which an item was characteristic of an adult man, both males and females showed a high degree of agreement. The same was true of items characterizing the adult woman. In other words, both males and females agreed about the traits they thought masculine and those they thought feminine. On the basis of these and other findings, Broverman et al. (1972) conclude that general agreement exists across sex, age, religion, marital status, and educational level about the characteristics of the sex roles that differentiate between men and women. In addition, the male traits were more highly valued than the female traits. This and other research (Bem, 1974, 1975, 1977; Urberg & LaBouvie-Vief, 1976; Heilbrun, 1976) strongly suggest that the traditional sex roles are still with us.

TABLE 10-1 Sex-Role Stereotypes

| COMPETENCY CLUSTER: MASCULINE POLE IS MORE DESIRABLE | |
FEMININE	MASCULINE
Not at all aggressive	Very aggressive
Not at all independent	Very independent
Very emotional	Not at all emotional
Does not hide emotions at all	Almost always hides emotions
Very subjective	Very objective
Very easily influenced	Not at all easily influenced
Very submissive	Very dominant
Dislikes math and science very much	Likes math and science very much
Very excitable in a minor crisis	Not at all excitable in a minor crisis
Very passive	Very active
Not at all competitive	Very competitive
Very illogical	Very logical
Very home-oriented	Very worldly
Not at all skilled in business	Very skilled in business
Very sneaky	Very direct
Does not know the way of the world	Knows the way of the world
Feelings easily hurt	Feelings not easily hurt
Not at all adventurous	Very adventurous
Has difficulty making decisions	Can make decisions easily
Cries very easily	Never cries
Almost never acts as a leader	Almost always acts as a leader
Not at all self-confident	Very self-confident
Very uncomfortable about being aggressive	Not at all uncomfortable about being aggressive
Not at all ambitious	Very ambitious
Unable to separate feelings from ideas	Easily able to separate feelings from ideas
Very dependent	Not at all dependent
Very conceited about appearance	Never conceited about appearance
Thinks women are always superior to men	Thinks men are always superior to women
Does not talk freely about sex, with men	Talks freely about sex, with men

| WARMTH-EXPRESSIVENESS CLUSTER: FEMININE POLE IS MORE DESIRABLE | |
FEMININE	MASCULINE
Doesen't use harsh language at all	Uses very harsh language
Very talkative	Not at all talkative
Very tactful	Very blunt
Very gentle	Very rough
Very aware of feelings of others	Not at all aware of feelings of others
Very religious	Not at all religious
Very interested in own appearance	Not at all interested in own appearance
Very neat in habits	Very sloppy in habits
Very quiet	Very loud
Very strong need for security	Very little need for security
Enjoys art and literature	Does not enjoy art and literature at all
Easily expresses tender feelings	Does not express tender feelings at all easily

SOURCE: Broverman, I. K., Vogel, S. R. Broverman, D. K. Clarkson, F. E., and Rosenkrantz, P. S. Sex-role stereotypes: a current appraisal. *Journal of Social Issues,* 1972, 28, p. 63.

Sex-typed behaviors may result in large part from imitation of and identification with same-sex parents. (Left: Burk Uzzle/Magnum Photos; right: Owen Franken/Stock, Boston)

GENDER IDENTIFICATION.   One important aspect of the child's increasing acquaintance with sex-role stereotypes is the learning of **gender** identification (Mussen, 1969). In a study of children aged 2, 2½, and 3, Thompson (1975) found that 2-year-olds could clearly identify pictures of people or dolls as belonging to one or the other sex. The 2-year-olds, however, were inconsistent in applying gender labels to themselves. The 2½-year-olds could not only identify gender but could also correctly categorize themselves as male or female. They also indicated that they felt they were more similar to a same-sexed doll than to an opposite-sexed doll. These children were clearly aware of their own sex. They also showed an awareness of cultural sex-typing of clothes and household articles. The 3-year-olds easily identified another person's sex, as well as their own sex and sex-typing. They preferred "good" and "same-sex" objects and appeared to have accepted their own gender label and incorporated it into their own sex-role behavior. Gender identification, then, precedes sex-typing and the learning of sex-typed behavior. Since gender identification is a task requiring cognitive evaluation by the child, these findings suggest that cognitive development may be an important component to the learning of sex roles.

Williams et al. also investigated the awareness and expression of sex stereotypes (Williams, Bennett & Best, 1975). They used a picture-story technique to assess sex stereotyping in kindergarten, second-, and fourth-grade boys and girls. The kindergartners were highly aware of traditional sex stereotypes, and the second-graders even more so. The fourth-graders, however, showed no further increase in this awareness. Furthermore, the fourth-graders' knowledge of sex stereotypes was incomplete; they did not achieve the maximum possible scores on the assessment questionnaire. The investigators suggest that many traits do not become sex-typed until adolescence, particularly those that are hard to define, such as frivolous, shy, and boastful. In both this study and others (Mussen, 1969), children of both sexes learn the male stereotype earlier than the female stereotype. Williams and his co-workers suggest as an explanation that descriptors of the male stereotype (e.g., aggressive, loud, adventurous) have more obvious behavioral referents than do descriptors (e.g., gentle, dreamy, sophisticated) of the female stereotype.

The child's concept of gender follows a sequence of stages (Slaby & Frey, 1975). First, the child recognizes that he or she is a male or female—*gender identity*. Next, the child comes to realize that girls grow up to be women and boys grow up to be men—*gender stability*. Finally, the child develops *gender consistency*, the belief that one's gender does not change with time or situation. This sequence of development is linked to the child's developing cognitive competence and to the child's selection of models to emulate (Slaby & Frey, 1975).

These developmental trends are consistent with those reported in other research (Flerx, Fidler & Rogers, 1976; Slaby & Frey, 1975; Mussen, 1969; Kohlberg, 1966). Further evidence (Flerx et al., 1976) suggests that boys exhibit more stereotyped responses than girls, perhaps because boys receive stronger disapproval for engaging in opposite-sex behavior (Hartley & Hardesty, 1964). As Flerx and her colleagues note, society may value the male sex-typed behaviors more than the female ones, and boys may more readily accept sex-typing than girls.

In summary, by about age 3 both boys and girls are aware of sex-typed behavior and, with development, show increasing knowledge of sex stereotypes. Adolescents and adults show no lessening of sex stereotypes (Urberg & LaBouvie-Vief, 1976). Finally, boys seem to be more aware of sex-appropriate behavior, interests, and vocations (Garrett, Ein, & Tremaine, 1977) than girls, whose sex-typed preferences are more variable (Mussen, 1969; Hartup & Zook, 1960).

ADAPTABILITY OF SEX ROLES.   Recent investigations (Bem, 1974, 1975, 1977; Hefner, Rebecca & Oleshansky, 1975; Heilbrun, 1976) have focused on the concept of **androgyny** and the transcendence of sex roles. "Androgyny" refers to the adaptability of sex roles. According to Bem (1977, p. 196):

> It is possible for an individual to be both assertive and compassionate, both instrumental and expressive, both masculine and feminine, depending upon the situational appropriateness of these various modalities; and it further implies that an individual may even blend these complementary modalities in a single act, being able, for example, to fire an employee if the circumstances warrant it but with sensitivity for the human emotion that such an act inevitably produces.

The concept of androgyny suggests that an individual can express both masculine and feminine traits, depending on the situation.

TRANSCENDENCE OF SEX ROLES.   The concept of **sex-role transcendence** is quite similar to that of androgyny. It assumes that assigned gender is irrelevant to one's orientation to life, which ideally should be flexible and dynamic. The person should be able to engage in the fullest possible range of life-styles and behavior, limited only by the individual and his or her needs. Hefner and his colleagues have presented a stage theory representing the development of sex-role transcendence. In stage 1, the child has an undifferentiated conception of sex roles and sex-typed behavior; he or she is unaware of the differential ascription of behavior to people on the basis of sex. The child then learns to attend to dichotomies in the society and gradually comes to realize the existence of a male-female dichotomy and that appropriate behaviors are related to the sex of a person. In stage 2, which Hefner and his colleagues call polarized, the child identifies with the societally determined sex role and learns the behaviors appropriate to his or her sex. The child accepts the conventional sex roles and rejects the opposite sex role. More importantly, the child learns that he or she has no choice, because the society places him or her on one side or the other of the

Learning gender identity (Jean-Claude Lejeune/Stock, Boston)

gender dichotomy. The third stage is called sex-role transcendence. Here, the individual learns to move freely between the characteristics and behavior associated with either sex, depending on the situation. Rigid adherence to sex-typed behavior drops out as the individual transcends sexual stereotypes. Hefner and his colleagues conclude that there is little support for an ongoing transition between stage 2 and stage 3 in our society at the present time.

Although Hefner and his colleagues have not done extensive research on this sequences of stages, the research we have discussed here is in line with stages 1 and 2. The stage analysis of gender identity (Slaby & Frey, 1975), discussed above, suggests a basis on which the first stage of sex-role transcendence may be founded, viz., the child learns gender identity.

The Study of Sex Differences in Behavior

To investigate the impact of sex-typing, psychologists have tried to assess the ways in which the sexes differ in intellectual and other achievement areas, social behavior, emotional development, and personality. Most of the research is aimed at determining the impact of socialization on the development of sex differences in behavior. Only a little research has been aimed at assessing the biological basis for sex differences in behavior.

THE BIOLOGICAL BASIS OF SEX DIFFERENCES.   Research on biological factors in the development of sex roles is fairly new, and only recently have certain trends begun to appear. Interest in these biological influences stems in part from our knowledge of prenatal and postnatal differences between the sexes. For example, males are miscarried more often and are more susceptible to diseases throughout their lives than are females. Female infants tend to be physically more mature at birth than male infants. For example, they are more sensitive to touch, pain, and sound. Girls also begin to walk and talk earlier than boys. Puberty begins about 2 years earlier in girls than in boys. These early sex differences have stimulated considerable research on possible biological components determining sex differences in behavior.

Biological research on sex differences has focused on the effects of **hormones** on sex-typing (Beach, 1958; Money, 1961; Money & Ehrhardt, 1972). The hormones of primary interest here are **progesterone** and **testosterone.** The hypothesis is that hormones absorbed prenatally may contribute to differences in behavior between the sexes. Injecting pregnant monkeys with testosterone (a male hormone), for example, results in **hermaphroditic** female offspring who exhibit not only physiological alterations but also show behavior patterns more similar to those of males than to those of females (Quadagno, Briscoe & Quadagno, 1977). Injecting male hormones into an infant monkey after birth does not alter its physical attributes but can result in changed behavioral patterns. Clearly, with lower animals, hormones affect prenatal development and also behavior after birth (cf. Quadagno et al., 1977).

Research with humans is much less conclusive, partly because of the ethical issues involved in research on hormonal reactions. Much of the research that has been done has concerned the relation between hormones and aggressive behavior. Males seem to be universally more aggressive than females. This sex difference appears early in life, before social pressures might cause differential behavior through shaping or other learning. It is of major interest whether aggressiveness has a biological basis, particularly a hormonal one.

Research with humans shows that male hormones masculinize the prenatal development of girls—both their physical attributes and postnatal behavior. Ehrhardt and Baker (1973) studied 17 fetally androgynized girls and their sisters, who served as a control group. The androgynized girls, who were exposed to excessive prenatal **androgens** because of genetic anomalies or because the mother took hormone therapy, exhibited masculinized behavior: a preference for playing with boys, little interest in doll play and other girlish pastimes, and a preference for outdoor sports. In general, they were described as tomboys. Clearly, these androgynized girls exhibited behavior that was more "masculine" than "feminine." This finding suggests a hormonal basis for sex-typed behavior. These and other data suggest that the presence of sex hormones before or just at birth predisposes the individual to behave in ways—in this case, aggressively—that are sex-typed. Although it is plausible to conclude that hormones may determine some sex-typed behaviors, Quadagno et al. (1977) have recently suggested an alternate explanation based on socialization practices and parental expectations. The parents may have expected their daughters to act like tomboys and thus may have interpreted their behavior that way. The girls were also undergoing **cortisone** replacement therapy, which may have been the real cause of their more aggressive, rough-and-tumble behavior.

SOCIAL FACTORS AND BIOLOGY.   Criticisms made by Quadagno and colleagues and the research of Money, Hampson, and Hampson (1955) and Money and Ehrhardt (1972) demonstrate that hereditary influences on the development of sex roles may be modified by social factors. Many of the androgynized females studied by Money had normal internal reproductive systems but abnormal external genitalia. Although these girls showed an interest in marriage and having children and although they dated like other girls, they also behaved in ways typically considered unfeminine. Our point here is that these girls *learned*—were socialized—to play the feminine role in spite of their biological abnormalities; that is, cultural and social influences overcame the biological anomalies.

Money and his co-workers also studied children who were assigned the incorrect sex at birth because of deceptive external genital anomalies (Money & Ehrhardt, 1972). Babies with male chromosomal patterns were raised as girls, and babies with female chromosomal patterns were raised as boys. In all 19 cases, the child learned to behave in a manner consistent with the assigned sex, which was opposite to the chromosomal sex. Thus, socialization triumphed over biological attributes. No matter what the biological predispositions toward different behavior between the sexes, social factors still have an influence. Biological factors may predispose an individual to behave in ways that society labels masculine or feminine—for example, aggressively or nurturantly—but the individual's social situation and learning temper these predispositions. Hence, socialization plays a critical part in the development of sex roles; it can even have an effect opposite to that of the biological sex.

Socialization of Sex Roles

The study of the learning of sex roles has emphasized socialization factors. As Bandura (1969a) has pointed out, the reasons for taking this perspective are obvious when one considers that immediately after birth the child is given a name indicative of sex, is dressed in sex-typed clothes, and is given sex-typed toys. Later, haircuts, playmates, and reinforced behaviors all reflect sex-role learning.

Psychoanalytic theorists assume that the child learns a sex role through identification with the parent of the same sex. Social-learning theorists have translated the concept of identification into the notion of imitating the parents (Mischel, 1970; Bandura, 1969a; Gewirtz, 1969) and emphasize the parental training of sex-typed behavior. Biological predispositions are assumed not to be critical in determining the sex role learned by the child. Rather, it is the child's socialization—both through deliberate training and modeling—that constitutes the major influence on the child's acquisition of a sex role.

In the remainder of this section, we discuss 3 aspects of parent-child interaction that seem to be necessary for identification and the development of sex roles. The first is children's imitation of models of the same sex. The second is the influence of absence of a father on the development of sex roles. The third is the effect of the mother's employment on sex-role development.

SELECTIVE MODELING.   Several investigators have suggested that children will more readily imitate a model of the same sex than one of the opposite sex (Bandura, 1969a; Mischel, 1970). In support of this hypothesis, Grusec and Brinker (1972) found that for 5- and 7-year-olds, the sex of the model was significantly related to the amount of material remembered. Boys remembered the male model's behavior better than the female's; girls showed a less clear, but nevertheless present, tendency to remember a female model's behavior better than a male model's. Grusec and Brinker (1972, p. 155) conclude that children are socialized to attend more closely to the behavior of people of their own sex.

> While boys at an early age may even be equally familiar with the behaviors displayed by both their mothers and their fathers, as they grow older and are exposed to more and more direct training for masculine behavior, they may come to be less familiar with the behaviors that females in our culture display. When they grow up they may

Intergenerational modeling can serve to maintain the consistency of sex roles. (Left: Suzanne Szasz/Photo Researchers; right: Peter Vandermark)

be unskilled at sweeping, dusting, and making beds not just because they have not had practice in doing these things, but because they have never really concentrated too closely on how they are done.

Slaby and Frey (1975) tested the notion that the child's concept of gender is related to selective attention to models of the same or opposite sex. They report that children's preference for attending to a model of the same sex increased as the children became more aware of their own gender constancy. In fact, gender constancy was a better predictor of attending to the model's behavior than was age. These results point up the importance of cognitive components in socialization (Kohlberg, 1966). As children mature cognitively, they acquire a clearer idea of gender, and, accordingly, attend more closely to the behavior of others of the same gender. Both the boys and the girls in this study showed similar amounts of gender constancy and a similar increase in attention to the same-sex model. Identification with the parent of the same sex may simply reflect the child's cognitive development about notions of gender.

Not all research, however, supports the hypothesis that children imitate models of the same sex more than those of the opposite sex. Maccoby and Jacklin

(1974) reviewed 20 experiments on children's imitation as a result of exposure to male and female models. Sixteen of these studies provided no evidence that children imitated the same-sex model more than the opposite-sex model. Similarly, Barkley, Ullman, Otto, and Brecht (1977) reported that in only 18 out of 81 studies did children imitate the same-sex model more than the opposite sex model. They suggest that this inconsistency in the research results may be due to either of 2 variables: the sex-typed behavior (e.g., aggressiveness) of the model or the sex-appropriateness of the behavior for the child. If a child observes a model who is behaving inappropriately for the sex of the child, the child is less likely to imitate that behavior. If the model's behavior is sex-typed appropriately for the sex of the child, the child should be more likely to imitate that behavior.

Barkley et al. tested the hypothesis that the sex-typed nature of the model's behavior was critical for the children's imitation. Boys and girls from 4- to 11-years old observed either a male or female model exhibiting masculine or feminine behavior. The children's imitative behavior during free play with the same materials was recorded. The results indicated that, regardless of the sex of the model, the girls imitated feminine behavior much more than masculine behavior, and boys imitated masculine behavior more than feminine behavior. The effect was much stronger for girls than for boys.

Early sex-role learning is not simply a matter of the child's selectively observing the behavior of a model of the same sex. Maccoby and Jacklin (1974) suggest a twofold model of the social learning of sex-typed behavior. First, the child acquires a certain amount of nonsex-typed behavior. Second, the child selects the behavior that is relevant to a particular situation. Thus, the acquisition of behavior through the observation of models is not sex-typed, but the performance of behavior may well be sex-typed. For example, if a girl "knows" that she is a "good" girl, she is more likely to behave in a feminine way than in a masculine way. This does not mean that the girl does not know masculine sex-typed behaviors. Rather, the girl will do "girl things" because she has been reinforced for sex-appropriate behavior. The same holds true for boys and masculine behavior.

Gender constancy is also related to sex-typing (Thompson, 1975). Since gender constancy reflects the child's developing cognitive competence, we are suggesting that cognition has a significant impact on the child's learning of social behavior (Kohlberg, 1966). It seems that learning, whether through the imitation of a model or through direct training, interacts with the child's cognitive competence to determine behavior. As a result of the interplay of these influences, we observe children engaging in highly sex-typed behavior.

Maccoby and Jacklin (1974) have recently published a summary of the extensive literature on the development of sex differences in behavior. The areas discussed include perception, illusions, learning, memory, intellectual abilities, verbal ability, quantitative ability, analytic ability, moral judgment, self-esteem, anxiety, prosocial behavior such as empathy and helping, aggression, and parent-child interactions. Their conclusions are listed in Table 10-2. The well-established sex differences include the female's greater verbal ability and the male's greater visual-spatial and mathematical ability and greater aggressiveness. There are a number of areas in which no sex differences were found or in which the evidence was too scanty or ambiguous to allow definite conclusions.

Although several reviewers (Block, 1976; M. Hoffman, 1977) have pointed out defects in Maccoby and Jacklin's categorizations of experiments and have argued that some of their conclusions may be premature (M. Hoffman, for example, has demonstrated that girls are more empathic than boys), it is clear that sex differences in behavior are not as pervasive as many have believed.

PATERNAL ABSENCE AND SEX TYPING.   The ever-increasing divorce rate in the United States prompts the question how appropriate sex roles develop in homes without fathers (Herzog & Sudia, 1973). Does the boy with no father at home still develop appropriate social behavior and a sex role? Related issues include the reason for the father's absence, death or divorce, and the role of the stepfather.

TABLE 10-2   Summary of Research on Sex Differences

BELIEFS NOT SUPPORTED	WELL-ESTABLISHED SEX DIFFERENCES	AREAS WITH AMBIGUOUS OR TOO LITTLE EVIDENCE
1. Girls are more "social" than boys.	1. Girls have greater verbal ability than boys.	1. Tactile sensitivity
2. Girls are more "suggestible" than boys.	2. Boys excel in visual-spatial ability.	2. Activity level
3. Girls have lower self-esteem.	3. Boys excel in mathematical ability.	3. Fear, timidity, and anxiety
4. Girls are better at role learning and simple repetitive tasks that require higher-level cognitive processing and the inhibition of previously learned responses.	4. Males are more aggressive.	4. Competitiveness
5. Boys are more "analytic."		5. Dominance
6. Girls are more affected by heredity, boys by environment.		6. Compliance
7. Girls lack achievement motivation.		7. Nurturance and "maternal" behavior
8. Girls are auditory, boys visual.		

SOURCE: Compiled from Maccoby, E. E., and Jacklin, C. N. The psychology of sex differences. Stanford: Stanford University Press, 1974.

The effects of the father's absence on sex-typing depend on the child's age at the time of separation (Biller, 1971; Herzog & Sudia, 1973; Hetherington, 1966; Santrock, 1975). Boys who were over 6 when the father left home behaved similarly to boys from intact families (Hetherington, 1966). However, boys who were under 6 when the father left the family had less masculine sex-role preferences, were more dependent and less assertive than other boys, and tended to have more feminine self-concepts. These effects of the absence of the father seem to hold true of children from various subcultures, including black (Santrock, 1970) and Mexican-American children (LeCorgne & Laosa, 1976).

We have much less information on the effects of absent fathers on the personality development of girls. In a study by Hetherington (1972), girls from homes without a father—whether because of death or divorce—did not differ in interests, preferences, or behavior from girls who had fathers present in the home. They did, however, show different patterns of sexual development; they tended to be either very shy and uncomfortable with boys or to be promiscuous and inappropriately assertive with boys. If the father had died, anxiety and shyness were most prevalent. If the father had left the family because of divorce, promiscuity and assertiveness were more manifest.

The effects of the absence of a father have also been investigated in the development of moral thought and behavior (Santrock, 1975). When moral behavior is assessed by resistance to temptation (the ability to hold off doing something forbidden) boys from father-absent and father-present homes do not differ as long as IQ, socioeconomic status, and age are controlled (that is, if the 2 groups are equivalent in these respects). This result suggests that some of the earlier research on the effects of father-absence may be contaminated because inequivalence on these measures may cause the differences reported. However, even with equivalent intelligence, age, and social class, teachers found boys without fathers to be less advanced in moral development than boys with fathers (Santrock, 1975; LeCorgne & Laosa, 1976). Santrock suggests that the teachers' ratings of the boys' moral development differed from those in the laboratory because the teachers observed the boys for longer periods of time and in a greater variety of situations. Perhaps more research in naturalistic settings is necessary.

Only a few studies have examined the effects of a stepfather on children's moral development. In principle, the presence of a stepfather should provide boys with an adequate male model for identification and for the development of an appropriate sex role. Some research suggests that an older brother or other father-substitute provides an important model for the boy's development (Brim, 1958; Oshman & Manosevitz, 1976). A stepfather living in the home should have an even greater effect in promoting appropriate social growth. Oshman and Manosevitz (1976) found that boys with fathers or stepfathers scored higher on measures of ego development than did boys without fathers. The cause of father's absence, death or divorce, appeared to have no effect on the stepfather's favorable influence.

MATERNAL EMPLOYMENT AND SEX-ROLE DEVELOPMENT.   Considerable evidence (cf. L. Hoffman, 1977) demonstrates that in the United States more women are now employed than ever before. Taking into consideration smaller family size and a longer life expectancy, motherhood may now be seen to occupy less of a woman's adult life. How much is sex-role stereotyping weakened in a family where the mother works? In such families, the mother has taken on a role usually considered masculine. Do the children—particularly daughters—of working mothers have less stereotyped sex roles, or do they perceive sex roles as less stereotyped than the daughters of nonworking mothers? Moreover, since some of the husbands of women who hold jobs share some of the housework and child care, we might expect that this difference would influence the development of sex roles in boys (L. Hoffman, 1974).

Several recent reviews (L. Hoffman, 1974, 1977; L. Hoffman & Nye, 1974) generally support the notion that maternal employment alters children's conception of sex roles. Elementary school girls with working mothers indicated that both their mothers and fathers engaged in behaviors traditionally ascribed to the opposite sex (Hartley, 1961). The daughters of nonworking women did not make statements of this sort as frequently. Children whose mothers work are more likely to approve of their employment than children whose mothers do not work, especially if the father takes a significant role in household management (L. Hoffman, 1974). Moreover, both elementary school and adolescent girls with working mothers expressed a greater interest in going to work when they are mothers than girls whose mothers did not work (L. Hoffman, 1974). The literature suggests that having a working mother promotes a less restricted view of the female sex role.

Studies of the views of children and adolescents toward the male sex role when the mother works are much less clear. Lower-class adolescent boys with working mothers are less likely to name their fathers as the person they most admire than are lower-class boys with nonworking mothers. Some data indicate that these children even disapprove of their fathers (McCord, McCord, & Thurber, 1963; Douvan, 1963). In a study of Canadian children from 9- to 16-years old (Kappel & Lambert, 1972, reported by L. Hoffman, 1974) lower-class sons of working mothers rated their fathers lower than did the lower-class sons of mothers who did not work. Among the middle classes, there is some evidence to suggest that the father whose wife works is viewed as more nurturant and kind (cf. L. Hoffman, 1974). Hoffman suggests that these fathers are more involved in child care and thus play a more nurturant role.

The daughters of working mothers develop more positive views of the female role, views that include a wider range of activities, autonomy, and independence (Douvan, 1963). Female college students with working mothers are more career-oriented and have a higher achievement level than the daughters of nonworking mothers (L. Hoffman, 1974). When the mother's employment produces conflict in the home these positive benefits are diminished (Kappel & Lambert, 1972). As L. Hoffman (1961) has pointed out, mothers who work but are unhappy with their jobs tend to have poorer relations with their children than mothers who are happily employed. Hence, it appears that the mother's reasons for going to work as well as her satisfaction with her job affect her child's development.

One interesting consequence of maternal employment concerns the child's conception of traditional sex roles. If both parents work, the child may develop a view of sex roles that combines both working and doing things around the house. Since the husbands of working mothers tend to participate in house care to a greater extent than the husbands of nonworking mothers, the child may come to see both sexes as working and doing house care (L. Hoffman, 1974, 1977). This may be especially true of middle-class children (Stein, 1973). Indeed, some evidence (Broverman et al., 1972) suggests that daughters of working mothers have a less negative view of femininity than daughters of nonworking mothers.

Marantz and Mansfield (1977) investigated the impact of maternal working on girls aged 5 to 11. The daughters of working mothers had more flexible perceptions of both male and female sex roles. The daughters of working mothers viewed women as more competitive, less dependent, and emotionally more secure than did the daughters of nonworking mothers. No relation was found, however, between maternal work status and the girls' aspirations for a career. Career choices seemed to reflect the sex appropriateness of the mother's occupation. Daughters of mothers who had feminine occupations chose that kind of career more often than did the daughters of mothers who had less feminine occupations. Older girls, however, tended to be less constrained by sex-role stereotypes about occupations than did younger girls. With increasing age, girls aspired to more masculine occupations.

Because husbands of working women often engage in role behaviors traditionally considered feminine, they present a less stereotyped male model for their children. (Charles Gatewood)

Finally, at all ages, girls whose mothers worked were more egalitarian in their ascription of traits to both the male and female roles than were the daughters of nonworking mothers. The authors explain these age trends according to Kohlberg's theory about the importance of cognitive development in sex-role acquisition and stereotyping, discussed below, noting that the child must be cognitively ready and sophisticated to attend to and integrate the behavior of other people before it can affect the stereotypes the child develops.

The Consequences of Sex-Role Stereotyping

We are all now quite familiar with the negative consequences of sex-typing, particularly as they affect women. Because of extreme sex-typing and its concomitant discrimination, women tend to be underemployed, to be less well paid for doing the same job that a man does, and to enjoy fewer career opportunities just because they are women. Rigid stereotyping makes career women out to be less feminine and more aggressive than women ought to be (Horner, 1972; L. Hoffman, 1974; M. Hoffman, 1977). It is well documented that children are aware of the sex-typing of occupations and that this stereotyping increases with age (Garrett, Ein & Tremaine, 1977).

Parents play a significant role in developing sex stereotypes in their children. Boys are raised to prefer male toys and activities, and girls are raised to prefer feminine toys and activities (L. Hoffman, 1977; Fein, Johnson, Kosson, Stork & Wasserman, 1975; Masters & Wilkinson, 1976). Such stereotyping even affects children's preferences for stories with heroes of their own sex (Jennings, 1975). Although parents may not consciously force their children to play with same-sex toys or read same-sex stories, reinforcing children for doing so also reinforces their behaving in sex-typed ways. As a result, parents teach sex-typed roles in these areas. Similar parental impact on sex-typing has been noted in parental encouragement for achievement strivings, independence training, and expectations for doing household chores (cf. L. Hoffman, 1977). In her summary of the literature on sex differences, Lois Hoffman (1977, pp. 655–656) points out the historical nature of the parents' role and suggests that currently changing parental roles may lead to a diminution of sex differences in future generations:

> [T]he traditional family roles reflect the fact that women are the childbearers. Technological-medical advances, however, have altered the significance of this fact. At present, a woman spends more of her life working than mothering. The father's traditional breadwinner role is shared with his wife, and he in turn may participate in more of the child-rearing functions than previously. Although socialization patterns still reflect traditional role expectations, shifts more in keeping with the new adult role requirements are already beginning. At present there are differences between males and females, and these, at least to some extent, reflect the traditional, sex-differentiated socialization patterns. Thus, these sex differences may be expected to

diminish—some even to disappear—as socialization practices accommodate to the reality of the new adult roles. Fewer children, longer life, and working mothers—none of which are new, but all of which are now pervasive, normative, and I think here to stay—add up to new family roles, new socialization patterns, and a decrease in the differences between the sexes.

The prediction of a reduction in sex-role stereotyping should largely reduce the negative impact of rigid sex roles. As noted above, psychologists have only recently become interested in the consequences of rigid sex stereotyping (M. Hoffman, 1977; Hefner et al., 1975; Block, 1973; Bem, 1974, 1975, 1977; Heilbrun, 1976). Evidence from these investigators indicates that people with a rigid sex-role orientation tend to have lower self-concepts and to be less flexible in social interaction than those who have less rigid sex-role orientations. For example, a strong masculine orientation leads to lowered tenderness in college men, while a strong feminine orientation leads to low resistance to social pressure in college women. Androgynous college students of either sex are high on both these traits. Since adult roles demand that men sometimes show tenderness, as when rearing children, and that women do not feel compelled to conform to a sex sterotype, as when on the job, it may be maladaptive to rear children with rigid expectations about sex roles. Evidence from the Berkeley Growth Study (Pleck, 1975) indicates that boys rated high on masculinity during adolescence lost ground on measures of adjustment in later life, perhaps because they never acquired other than highly masculine attributes. During later life, interpersonal relations require traits other than those associated with extreme masculinity.

Psychologists' interest in androgynous child-rearing practices is likely to have its greatest effect in achieving better social adjustment for all people. The androgynous individual can take either the traditionally masculine or feminine role, depending upon the particular situation. He or she has a flexible sex role that allows behavior to be dictated by the situation, creating a wider range of possible reactions, and leading perhaps to a more satisfying life.

Theories of Identification and Sex-Typing

Both identification and sex-typing are pervasive tendencies shown in the child's imitation of a model. We have already mentioned some of the factors that lead the child to imitate the parents or other models, for example, children's perception of similarity between themselves and a model. Parents also teach imitation through games like peek-a-boo and through rewards for imitation. Since the parents are the adults with whom the child has the most contact during the first several years, their importance in socializing the child would be hard to overemphasize. And although peers, siblings, teachers, and others become important socializing influences as the child grows up, the parents' influence on identification and sex-typing remains very strong.

Psychoanalytic Theory of Identification

Sigmund Freud was the first to formulate a comprehensive theory of identification. He believed there were two types: *anaclitic identification,* based on the fear of the loss of the parents' love, is especially important in girls' development, and *identification with the aggressor,* sometimes called *defensive identification,* based on fear of the powerful parent and aimed at avoiding punishment. This form of identification is particularly important in boys' development. Freud believed that identification was critical to the development of the superego (the conscience or ego ideal) and to sex-role development. The superego represents the internalization of the society's standards for acceptable behavior.

Freud's theory of the mechanisms of identification evolved gradually over several decades (Bronfenbrenner, 1960). To appreciate the importance he attributed to identification and how it develops, it will be helpful to explain Freud's theory of personality development. The reader interested in a more detailed treatment of Freud's theory is referred to the excellent summaries by Langer (1969) and Baldwin (1967).

ANACLITIC IDENTIFICATION.   Freud (e.g., 1930, 1935, 1950) believed that the neonate is basically an asocial creature. The infant is an *id* (an it), with all its sexual energy (libido) invested in seeking pleasure through tension reduction, for example, release from hunger or physical discomfort. Freud called this hedonistic behavior *primary process functioning.* When the id cannot reduce tension, that is, cannot produce pleasure, part of the id is transformed into the *ego.* The **ego** is rational and copes with reality, for example, by initiating behavior to get food. Functioning within the framework of reality, which Freud termed *secondary process functioning,* is substituted for pure hedonism, and, with development, becomes the child's preferred mode of interacting with the environment. The ego, which begins to form sometime during the first year of life, dominates the **id** in normal development, and the child behaves in accordance with the reality of the social environment. The ego's main coping mechanism is conforming to adult attitudes, values, and demands. In this mode of adaption to the environment, part of the ego is transformed into the *superego,* the third and final structure governing the child's personality. The **superego** represents the ideals and moral standards of the larger society, learned through parental training and the mechanism of identification.

Psychoanalytic theory holds that the bases of personality development lie in the maturation of the body's erogenous zones. Hence, the Freudian theory of development includes what are called the psychosexual stages. The individual passes through 5 stages, each based on a different erogenous zone from which primary pleasure is derived. (Table 10-3 summaries the 5 stages.)

Boys and girls come to identify with the parent in somewhat different ways. Because of the child's initial dependence, both boys and girls form a strong attachment to the primary caretaker, usually the mother. **Anaclitic identification** begins when the mother leaves the child and does not respond to his or her needs. Since no mother can attend to her child constantly, there will be times when it is hungry, lonesome, or otherwise in a state of tension. According to Freud, these occasions create anxiety about the loss of the mother's care. By learning to do some of the things the mother does, the child can reduce this anxiety and regain a sense of security. Hence, both boys and girls identify with the mother.

Freud believed that anaclitic identification was especially important to the development of girls. Contemporary psychoanalytic theory (see Baldwin, 1967; Langer, 1969) explains this identification in the following way. At about the age of 3 or 4, the girl develops a strong affection for the father, rivaling the mother for the father's affection. Because she feels that this will make her mother jealous, and perhaps reject her, the girl gives up her strong desire for the father and identifies with the mother. This identification is due to a fear of the loss of the mother's love. In identifying with the mother, the girl learns social standards (morality) from the mother as well as the female sex role.

IDENTIFICATION WITH THE AGGRESSOR.   Identification in boys results from the resolution of the **Oedipal complex.** At about age 3 to 4, the boy develops the desire to possess the mother and becomes the father's rival for the mother's love. Because the boy realizes his father is bigger, stronger, and more powerful, he fears his father's retaliation for his incestuous wishes. Freud believed, in fact, that the boy feared the father would castrate him. To avoid this punishment, the boy identifies with the father (**identification with the aggressor**), which in turn reduces his anxiety about castration and provides the mechanism for him to develop an understanding of the male sex role and the culture's moral norms.

FIXATIONS.   The final result of a successful passage through these psychosexual stages is a healthy, normal adult personality, especially with respect to heterosexual relationships. For Freud, then, infantile sexuality is the precursor of mature adult sexuality. Under adverse conditions—excessive frustration or excessive satisfaction, for example—the child may become *fixated* in a given stage rather than progressing to the next. As the child grows to adulthood, his or her personality is characterized by the behavior patterns typical of the stage fixated on. For example, the adult behavior resulting from fixation at the anal stage—perhaps because of overly strict toilet training—is characterized as excessive hoarding, neatness, and an extreme reluctance to throw things out. A child may also *regress* to behaviors characteristic of an earlier stage of development.

TABLE 10-3   Freud's Psychosexual Stages

STAGE	DEVELOPMENT	AGE
1. Oral	The main source of pleasure is sucking, swallowing, and biting. The ego begins to develop during this stage.	From birth to about 1 year
2. Anal	The major pleasure comes from expelling or retaining feces. The ego is strengthened and, as a result of parental pressures in toilet training, the superego begins to develop.	From approximately 1 to 3 years
3. Phallic	The major source of pleasure is the genital region. It is during this stage that the Oedipal complex develops. The child becomes sexually attached to the opposite-sex parent. When the parent rejects the sexual attachment, the child identifies with the same-sexed parent. A successful resolution of the Oedipal situation results in normal personality development through identification, as a result of anaclitic or defensive identification. Identification results in the child taking on the values of the same-sex parent and, therefore, learning socially appropriate behavior.	From about 3 to 6 years
4. Latency	As a result of the resolution of the Oedipal situation, the child experiences a reduction of libidinal energy in the genital zone and enters a latency period.	From about age 6 to the onset of puberty at about age 11.
5. Genital	The major source of pleasure is again derived from the genital zone. Interest in the opposite sex reappears, and the adolescent seeks out heterosexual relationships, but with peers, not the same-sex parent.	Through adulthood.

The identification concepts noted in the third psychosexual stage (the phallic stage) are the most important for childhood socialization. It should now be clear that the psychoanalytic explanation for socialization phenomena rests on identification. The processes of identification are internal and not directly observable. Like the id, ego, and superego, these identification concepts are hypothetical constructs that help explain development. By identifying with the parent of the same sex, the child learns how to be a male or female, learns the rules of society, and learns that they should be obeyed. This identification, based on the child's fear of the loss of parental love or of punishment, is responsible for the development of a sense of guilt and therefore for the willingness to follow social standards. These processes are due to maturation and the psychological forces of the id, ego, superego, and the psychological defense against guilt. Freud's theory minimizes the role of external societal influences, which are represented primarily through the parent's interpretation

Social learning theorists claim that children learn sex roles by positive reinforcement and imitation. (Jean-Claude Lejeune)

of social norms, because of the child's very close contact with the parents, and concomitantly limited contact with others, during the first 5 years of life.

Social Learning Theory of Identification

The social learning theorists explain identification using the principles of instrumental or operant conditioning together with imitation. These theorists redefined psychoanalytic concepts in S-R terms to test hypotheses derived from psychoanalytic theory.

SEARS' RESEARCH.   One of the first psychologists to use learning theory to investigate psychoanalytic concepts of socialization was Robert Sears (e.g., 1950). For the most part, his research focused on the relation between mother and child (Sears, Maccoby, & Levin, 1957; Sears, Rau, & Alpert, 1965). His basic thesis was that the child's personality development is determined by the parents' child-rearing practices (Sears, 1950). One corollary of this hypothesis is that individual differences in personality are due to differences in the way parents raise their children. By investigating these practices, Sears hoped to gain insights into the development of identification.

Sears' research strategy was interesting in that it included: observing parent-child interactions; extensive interviews with parents about their child-rearing techniques and how they perceived their child's behavior; and observing children in peer interactions, play, nursery school, and experimental tasks. Sears and his co-workers (Sears et al., 1957; Sears et al., 1965) attempted to relate parent types, such as restrictive or permissive, to the child's identification and sex-role development. The basic thesis underlying these investigations was that parents shape (teach) dependency, aggressiveness, conscience, and the like by the types of child-rearing practices they employ. Generally speaking, the results of Sears' investigations provided little support for this thesis, largely because of the difficulties involved in relating global child-rearing variables to global measures of child behavior. More recently, researchers have shown that relating specific child behaviors to specific antecedents is a more fruitful way to investigate child development.

GEWIRTZ' RESEARCH.   The research and theory of Jacob Gewirtz (1969) epitomizes the learning-theory approach to socialization. According to Gewirtz, social learning, that is, learning involving stimuli and responses of people living and interacting within a culture, follows the same general principles as nonsocial learning. To describe socialization Gewirtz thus emphasizes the development of S-R relations within the context of operant conditioning.

The paradigm for operant conditioning is as follows:

$$S^D \ldots R\_\_\_\_\_\text{Reinforcement}$$
$$(S^R)$$

A discriminative stimulus (S^D) triggers a response (R) which leads to reinforcement (S^R). This type of learning may involve a number of stimuli and responses, the length of the S-R chain depending upon the complexity of the behaviors to be learned. All the principles of stimulus-response learning are applied to explain social development through reference to observable stimuli and responses. As noted in Chapter 2, learning theorists do not feel that unobservable concepts, such as id or ego, are useful in explaining development because they cannot be accurately observed or measured. The principles of conditioning deal with observable stimuli and responses.

Using these principles, Gewirtz (1969) has attempted to explain certain phenomena in socialization such as identification, dependence, and attachment —all without recourse to mentalistic, unobservable processes. Accordingly, the child is said to acquire social behaviors in two ways. The first is through direct instrumental conditioning. The socializing agent—the parent, for example—uses differential reinforcement techniques to teach the child to emit a specific response. That is, the socializer positively reinforces responses he or she wants the child to learn and ignores or punishes other responses. For example, the parent may respond positively to a child's request if it is preceded by "please" and may ignore the request if the child does not say "please." The same methods may be used to teach the child more complex social skills, such as behavior characteristic of sex roles. Little girls may be taught to do stereotypically girlish things and not to do boyish things. Boys, too, may be taught sex-typed behaviors through parental use of rewards and punishments. The child's use of the word "please" or conformity to expected role behaviors, in turn, reinforces the parent and the parent's use of these training techniques. In this simple way the child acts as a socializer of parental behavior. As the parents shape their children the techniques used are reinforced by the child's learning.

Socialization also takes place through *imitation*, the term used by learning theorists to describe what Freud called identification. Imitative learning occurs when the child matches his or her behavior to that of some other person or "model." Picture a little boy's face covered with shaving cream or a little girl putting on lipstick and makeup. Both children are imitating the behavior of a parent. Gewirtz believes that imitative learning is extremely important in socialization, because it becomes generalized to a wide range of behavior. **Generalized imitation refers to the processes by which the different responses of a model are emitted by the child in a variety of situations.** Although few if any of these imitative responses are directly reinforced, they are acquired in the same way as instrumental conditioning. In other words, imitative learning is assumed to be a special case of instrumental learning.

The child's imitative responses may first occur by chance, or they may be deliberately taught, as in playing games with the parents. Once learned, they are maintained by reinforcement. The child continues to emit imitative responses because they are intermittently reinforced. With occasional reinforcement, the child does not know which responses will be reinforced, and which will not. Hence, many imitative responses enter the child's repertoire without being reinforced. In other words, the reinforcement given by socialization agents for specific imitative behavior tends to strengthen a whole class of imitative responses. As a result, the child acquires a number of patterns of imitation of adults and emits these behaviors even though they may never have been directly reinforced.

Imitative learning, then, is the result of intermittent reinforcement of "matching" responses and serves as the basis for generalized imitation. Gewirtz (1969) believes that generalized imitation is the basis for such socialization phenomena as identification and dependence-attachment. Rather than explaining similarities in the behavior of the parent and the child on the basis of unconscious, unobservable psychoanalytic processes such as Freud's anaclitic identification or identification with the aggressor, Gewirtz has proposed that such similarity is best explained by generalized imitation describable in terms of observable stimuli and responses.

BANDURA'S THEORY.   The most extensive studies of the role of imitation in social learning are found in the work of Albert Bandura (1969a, 1969b; Bandura & Walters, 1963). Bandura's research and theory have been focused on the acquisition of responses through **observational learning,** learning which accounts for the manner in which the child patterns his thoughts, feelings, and actions after another person and which thus explains identification.

According to Bandura, the observation of a model may have several effects on the observer. First, the observer may learn an entirely new response (a **modeling effect**). This is a true acquisition effect which Bandura calls observational learning. Observation of a model may have two effects on the performance of responses already in the observer's repertoire. The first is an **inhibition-disinhibition** effect. After the model emits a given response, the reinforcement experienced either inhibits (if negative) or disinhibits (if positive) the observer in repeating the response. A second way in which observation of a model influences the observer's performance of an already-learned response is through **response facilitation.** In this case, the model's behavior acts like a discriminative stimulus to facilitate the recurrence of a response already in the observer's repertoire.

To clarify these effects, consider again the little boy imitating his father's shaving or the little girl putting on makeup. In both cases, the child has *learned* an imitative behavior by observing a model. Since it is unlikely that the child's repertoire already contained this behavior, this result is termed a modeling effect. A number of other modeling effects, for example, aggressive behavior and concept learning, have been demonstrated in experimental settings. Inhibition-disinhibition effects owing to observation of a model have also been experimentally demonstrated. A series of experiments by Walters and his students (Parke & Walters, 1967; Walters, Leat & Mezei, 1963; Walters, Parke & Cane, 1965) showed that children who observed peers being punished for playing with some toys that belonged to someone else later played less with these toys than children who had not been exposed to the punished models. In another study, Bandura (1965) showed that children who had observed a model who was either rewarded, or experienced no consequences, for behaving aggressively later showed more aggression than children who had observed a punished model. This finding represents a response-disinhibition effect. Response facilitation is exemplified by "social contagion" such as increased volunteering or helping that results from observing models engage in such behavior. As with inhibition-disinhibition effects, the individual's behavioral repertoire already contains relevant responses. As a result, the observer learns no new behavior. Rather, the observation of the model acts as a "releaser" for the behavior of the observer.

Bandura contends that the mechanisms of observational learning and imitation are largely responsible for the child's acquisition of social behavior, including identification and sex-typing. Like Gewirtz, he believes that these mechanisms (illustrated in Table 10-4) can account for identification better than psychoanalytic principles. The behavior observed is coded into a representational mediator that can be retrieved and reproduced in the presence of appropriate environmental cues. In other words, observational learning and imitation are the result of a number of psychological processes, including attention, retention, motoric reproduction, and motivation.

TABLE 10-4   *Bandura's Observational Learning Paradigm.*   Modeling Stimuli (coded into→) Representational Mediators (mediate→) Response Retrieval and Reproduction

| | PROCESSES | | | |
	1. ATTENTIONAL	2. RETENTION	3. MOTORIC REPRODUCTION	4. INCENTIVE OR MOTIVATIONAL
Subprocesses (Influence the content and degree of observational learning)	a. Observer characteristics	a. Overt practice	a. Availability of component responses	a. A number of performance-related variables
	b. Prior training in discriminative observation	b. Covert rehearsal	b. Physical limitations	
	c. Presence of incentive-oriented sets	c. Coding	c. Availability of model's responses	

SOURCE: Dusek, J. B. Adolescent development and behavior. Palo Alto, Calif.: Science Research Associates, 1977.

An organism will not acquire a model's response if it does not attend to, recognize, or discriminate the distinctive features of the response. A number of factors influence attention to a model, including such characteristics of the model as sex and competence, such characteristics of the observer as self-esteem and dependency, and the presence of incentives. For example, the observer will pay closer attention to models perceived as more competent or powerful.

The modeled response must be stored in a cognitive, representational form, especially if the observer does not overtly perform the response. Bandura has termed this *"no trial learning,"* since the observer learns the response and stores it in memory without actually making the response. Two representational mechanisms aid retrieval and reproduction: one imaginal and one verbal. Imagery formation occurs through conditioning. During exposure to a model, modeled behavior acts as a stimulus that causes the observer to emit perceptual responses that become associated with the stimulus because they occur contiguously with the stimuli. These stored representations of the modeled behavior are either imaginal (pictorial) or verbal. Overt or covert rehearsal of the model's responses will aid retention by stabilizing and strengthening the acquired responses.

Response retrieval and reproduction are influenced by both motoric reproduction processes and incentive/motivational processes. Motoric reproduction processes that are critical to response retrieval and reproduction include the physical capabilities and limitations of the observer and the extent to which the model's performance is a function of subtle, internal cues which are difficult for the model to communicate to the observer. The observer cannot reproduce a response if it is composed of several parts which are missing from the observer's behavioral repertoire, if the response is beyond the physical capabilities of the observer, or if the model's response depends on subtle internal physiological or psychological cues which are difficult to communicate to the observer. Reproduction of observed behavior is also affected by incentive-motivational processes. For example, if the observer is not sufficiently positively reinforced for imitating, the observed response may cease to be performed. In addition, if a model is positively reinforced for some behavior, the observer is more likely to imitate the behavior than if the model is punished, although an equal amount of behavior may be learned in either case.

BANDURA'S EXPERIMENTS.   The distinction between imitation and observational learning and the influence of incentives are illustrated in Figure 10-1, which shows the imitation of aggressive responses by children who had observed an adult model's aggressive behavior toward a bobo doll (Bandura, 1965). One group of children observed the model receiving positive reinforcement after attacking the doll; one

FIGURE 10-1   Mean number of different matching responses reproduced by children as a function of response consequences to the model and positive incentives.

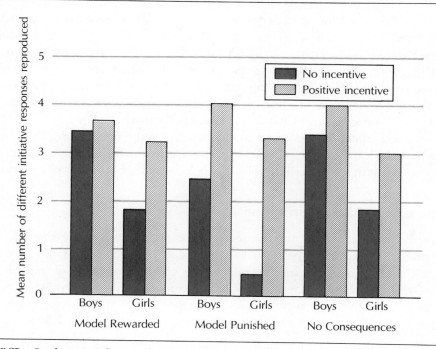

SOURCE: Bandura, A. Influence of model's reinforcement contingencies on the acquisition of initiative responses. *Journal of Personality and Social Psychology*, 1965, 1, 589–595.

group saw the model being punished; and the third group saw the model receive no reinforcement. All the children were then placed in a room with a bobo doll and the same toys as the model had had available. For the first 10 minutes, the behavior of the children was observed, and their spontaneous imitation recorded (the no-incentive condition). Then the children were offered positive reinforcement (cookies and 7-Up) and asked to do what the model did (a measure of observational learning). During the first 10 minutes, children who had observed a model who was rewarded or who received no reinforcement for aggressing toward the bobo doll spontaneously imitated more of the model's aggressive behavior than children who observed a punished model. All 3 groups, however, showed equal amounts of observational learning (see Figure 10-1) as assessed during the last 10 minutes of the experiment. Imitation, as assessed in the first 10 minutes the children played with the toys, may not accurately reflect all that the children learned while observing a model. The results of this experiment highlight the importance of the model's reinforcement contingencies on the observer's imitation.

Up to this point, we have been discussing modeling as though the only models relevant to the child's socialization were live human adults. A number of experiments have explored the possibility that symbolic models—films or cartoon characters, for example—exert equally strong influences on the child's social learning. Seeing films of aggressive adults or cartoon characters has been shown to have as strong an influence on the child's aggressive behavior as observation of live human models (Bandura, Ross & Ross, 1963 a, b; Stein & Friedrich, 1975). These findings are important for 2 reasons. First, there is no theoretical reason why symbolic models should affect children's behavior less than live models. In fact, any such difference would be hard to explain by any current learning theory. Second, the effects of symbolic models indicate the importance of studying the content of children's movies and TV programs (see Chapter 11) (Stein & Friedrich, 1975).

Bandura contends that observational learning is the basis of identification, and, indeed, the learning of most social behavior. His research has therefore focused on the conditions that govern the imitation of behavior learned through observation.

Cognitive Theories of Identification and Sex-Typing

Neither the psychoanalytic nor the social-learning theories include the role of cognition in their explanations of social development. This is an important omission because the child is a thinking organism. The child's evaluation of a model's behavior and the child's understanding of someone else's point of view are two examples of ways in which cognitive skills influence social interactions. To ignore the role of cognition is to neglect an important factor in the child's social development.

Interest in the role of cognition in social development, which has become known as social cognition, has only recently become widespread (Flavell, 1977;

Shantz, 1975). **Social cognition** refers to how the child characterizes others and infers their inner experiences (Shantz, 1975). Thus, the study of social cognition is the study of how children come to understand others' thoughts, emotions, and viewpoints. Shantz (1975, p. 1) points out two reasons why the relation between cognition and social behavior is important for understanding socialization: "First, it provides a more complete picture of the child's cognitive development indicating what types of concepts and processes are evident in both the nonsocial and social domains at particular age periods. Second, the way in which children conceptualize others presumably has an important effect on their social behaviors with others." Research on social cognition has concentrated on the child's understanding of other people's thoughts, intentions, feelings, and perceptions. One basic assumption in this study is that as the child's cognitive competence increases, the child's conception of the social world and other people also changes (e.g., Aronfreed, 1969; Flavell, 1977; Shantz, 1975).

A cognitive theory of socialization assumes the existence of an internal cognitive representation of the world that acts as an "effective environment" by guiding the child's behavior. It is the child's perception and understanding of the environment, not the objective environment, to which the child responds. Thus, two children who have different perceptions and understandings of the same objective environment will probably respond differently to it. This representation of the environment changes as the child matures and reaches higher stages of cognitive development. With learning and maturity, this representation becomes a broad, complex coding of the environment (Aronfreed, 1968). For example, the preoperational and the concrete-operational child viewing the same model will code the information differently because their cognitive structures are different. More importantly, the two children will show different kinds of *evaluative control* over their own behavior because their cognitive competencies will produce different evaluations of the behavior they observe. By "evaluative control," Aronfreed means *internal control* over behavior. For example, by considering how others might react to their behavior, or whether their behavior is right or wrong as regards the welfare of others, children exhibit control over their behavior. This cognitive evaluation is carried out with reference to similarity to models and the child's understanding of the rules of the social order.

KOHLBERG'S THEORY.   Kohlberg (1963, 1969a, b) has proposed a cognitive theory of socialization which makes several assumptions about development. Since these are similar to those of Piaget's theory of cognitive development (see Chapter 6), we mention them briefly here. First, development involves basic changes in the structure of the organism. Second, cognitive structures develop through the interaction of the structure of the organism and the structure of the environment, rather than through maturation or learning. Third, cognitive structures represent organized actions on objects. Fourth, the development of cognitive structures is directed toward greater equilibrium in the interaction between the organism and the environment.

The further assumptions are specific to social development. Fifth, cognitive and affective development occur simultaneously and simply represent different perspectives on structural change. Sixth, social development involves structuring the relationship of the self to others who live in the same social world. Seventh, social development is directed toward an equilibrium between the actions of the self and those of others toward the self.

These assumptions together make up a stage theory of social development in which the organism's structure interacts with that of the environment within the constraints mentioned here. All the assumptions of the stage theory of cognitive development apply to this social theory, for example, qualitative differences in mode of functioning at different developmental levels (stages), the invariant sequence of stages, and so on.

Kohlberg has been primarily concerned with applying the principles of cognitive-developmental theory to moral development (see Chapter 12), and the end product is a stage theory of moral development. Presumably, the same sort of analysis can be applied to other social phenomena, and Kohlberg (1966) has attempted to do so in the development of sex roles. His notion is that children's cognitive representations of the social world determine their learning of sex roles. The theory is cognitive because of its emphasis on children's cognitive organization of roles and role learning in their identification with boys or girls. One result of this view is that concepts of sex roles change with age because of changes in cognitive organization as children mature.

Kohlberg suggests that gender identity (self-categorization as a boy or a girl) is the basic organizer of attitudes toward sex roles. Gender identity is a result of a cognitive judgment made by the child very early in development (Thompson, 1975; Slaby & Frey, 1975). According to this cognitive theory, the child says, in effect, "I am a boy, therefore I want to do boyish things and therefore the opportunity to do boyish things . . . " is rewarding. This view stands in direct contrast to that of social-learning theory, which states that the child wants rewards, is rewarded for doing boyish things, and as a result wants to be a boy.

For Kohlberg's theory to be tenable, gender identity must be established early in life. The evidence discussed above is that children learn gender identity by about 3 years of age (Flerx et al., 1976; Slaby & Frey, 1975). Gesell & Ilg (1946) reported that between two-thirds and three-fourths of 3-year-old children can correctly identify themselves as little boys or little girls. They soon learn to label other people in the same way. Therefore, the child's gender identity may become the basis for learning sex-typed behavior. Somewhat later, around the age of 5 or 6, the child develops notions of masculine and feminine stereotypes in behavior (Slaby & Frey, 1975; Thompson, 1975; Williams, Bennett & Best, 1975).

Figure 10-2 shows how Kohlberg's view differs from that of the psychoanalytic and social-learning theorists. As you can see, the cognitive-developmental view is very nearly the opposite of the social-learning view, and both differ considerably from the Freudian view. Kohlberg disagrees with the psychoanalytic view on several counts. First, he does not agree that identification is fixed and established early in the child's psychological structure. Rather, he believes that attitudes about identification change with development. Second, he notes the pathological nature of the evidence on which psychoanalytic theory is based and believes this may distort the picture of sex-role learning.

In accord with the social-learning theory, Kohlberg believes that reinforcement and imitation play an important role in the learning of sex roles. However, he reverses the sequence of the behavior (Figure 10-2). By knowing what boylike and girllike behaviors are, the child is capable of determining the behavior to be adopted for his or her own sex identity. Both reinforcement and imitation, however, depend on developmental changes in cognition as well as the child's evaluation of his or her own sex identity and the appropriateness of some behavior for that identity.

FIGURE 10-2 *Theoretical Sequences in Psychosexual Identification*

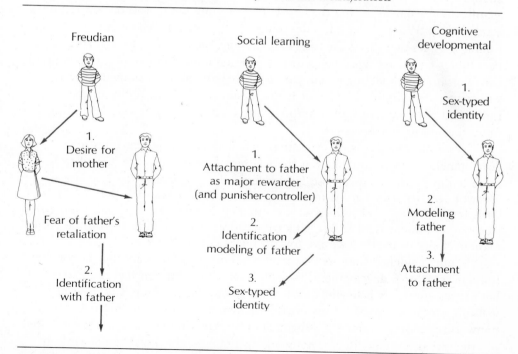

SOURCE: Kohlberg, L. A. Cognitive-developmental analysis of children's sex-role concepts and attitudes. In E. E. Maccoby (Ed.) The development of sex differences. Stanford: Stanford University Press, 1966.

SUMMARY

In this chapter we have discussed some of the basic concepts involved in socialization of the child. Socialization is the process that teaches the child the skills and knowledge that are needed for getting along in the society. The process is one of interaction between parent and child, each of whom influences the behavior of the other. One aspect of socialization is identification and another is sex-typing of behavior.

Indentification refers to the child coming to behave, think, and feel like the parents. Freud believed this was a result of resolution of the Oedipal conflict. Social-learning theorists believe identification simply refers to the tendency of the child to behave like someone else, a result of imitating those who are powerful or who are similar to the child. Cognitive theorists insist that the child's developing intellect is the basis for identification. Some support exists for each of these theoretical views, which may together provide a relatively inclusive basis for considering the many factors that influence identification.

Sex-typing refers to the learning of the motives and behaviors consistent with the child's gender. The behaviors considered sex-typed appear not to have changed very much, if at all, during the past decade, even though there is a significant movement to alter the female role. An important aspect of sex-typing is gender identity. This concept is developed in the child by about 3 years of age. Kohlberg argues that this is the basis of sex-typing. Social-learning theorists believe the child is taught sex-typed behaviors by parental reinforcement of sex-appropriate behavior and by modeling of the parent's behavior. Some current theorizing suggests that the optimal behavior is one of androgyny, the ability of the individual to behave in ways traditionally masculine or feminine depending upon the situational demands.

Paternal absence is one situation that may adversely affect sex-role development. Boys separated from their fathers before about age 6 tend to be more feminine than boys whose fathers leave the home after the boys are 6. The younger boys tend to be more dependent and less assertive than other boys. Girls from father-absent homes do not differ in interests or activities from girls from father-present homes. But, girls from father-absent homes tend to be either extremely shy or overly assertive toward males.

Some evidence suggests that maternal employment is another factor that influences sex-role development. In such homes the children feel the parents of both sexes engage in behavior that is masculine and feminine. Children of working mothers approve of maternal employment more than children of nonworking mothers, and the daughters of working mothers are more interested in careers than the daughters of nonworking mothers. The daughters of working mothers also develop a more positive view of the female role and see it as including the traits of autonomy, independence, and competitiveness. In general, children of mothers who work outside the home have a more flexible view of both male and female sex roles than children of mothers who do not.

CHAPTER 11

(Bill Stanton/Magnum Photos)

PARENT-CHILD INTERACTIONS

WITHOUT ANY DOUBT, the single most important influence in the socialization of the child is the family, particularly the parents. During the preschool years, the typical child spends more time with the parents than with peers, and more time in the home than in any other social setting. Thus, the likes, dislikes, values, attitudes, and general home background provided by the parents have a tremendous effect on the child's development and adjustment during these early years. Even in later childhood and adolescence, current parental demands and past child-rearing practices exert considerable control on the developing individual's behavior.

The powerful, long-term influence of the parents on children's social and personality development formed the cornerstone of Freud's (1935) theory of personality development. In our discussion of his theory (Chapter 10), we noted several of its implications for early childhood development. Perhaps the most important is the notion that the child has to identify with the same-sex parent to develop normally. Through identification, the child learns some acceptable social behaviors and begins to acquire a sex role. Parents also use rewards and punishments to teach their children how to behave. Hence, the parents' personalities and behavior are important because they influence the way parents socialize children through modeling and other child-rearing techniques.

Although social-learning theory (Bandura, 1969a. 1969b; Gewirtz, 1969) has also focused on child-rearing practices to explain personality development (e.g., Mischel, 1970; Sears, Maccoby & Levin, 1957; Sears, Rau & Alpert, 1965), emphasizing the role of parents as models and as reinforcers of social behavior, approaches to socialization based on learning theory have led to a view of socialization as an interaction (Bell, 1968; Martin, 1975; Rheingold, 1969) in which not only do the parents socialize the child but the child socializes them as well. As a result of this emphasis on the interaction of parents and child, psychologists have gradually abandoned the parent-causation model according to which parents cause the child to behave in certain ways. For example, the child behaves aggressively because the parents behaved aggressively toward him or her, thereby modeling and teaching aggression. The interactive-causation model emphasizes the roles of both parent and child as they interact and attempts to pinpoint the circumstances that maintain the interaction. Martin (1975, p. 464) gives the following illustration of this approach.

> Tommy begins to tease his baby sister; mother says, "Don't do that"; Tommy continues to tease; mother, somewhat louder, "Tommy, stop that"; Tommy continues to tease; baby sister starts to cry; mother yells loudly and slaps Tommy; Tommy stops teasing baby sister. These kinds of data almost force one to think interactively. Tommy is "teaching" his mother to escalate her response to yelling and slapping; the mother is providing a model of aggressive behavior and perhaps, somewhat paradoxically, providing reinforcement for his teasing by her dramatic display of attention.

As this example shows, the parent and child interact, each influencing the other's behavior. The nature of this interaction must be explained in order to understand the importance of parent-child relations in the socialization process.

Early Research on Child-Rearing Techniques

Early research on child rearing and its importance for personality development received most of its impetus from Freud (1935), who emphasized the importance of parental discipline on the development of stable, long-term personality traits. Hence we are led to ask how parental discipline and the child's identification with the parent are related.

Dimensions of Child-Rearing

Early research on parent-child relationships aimed to discover the psychological **dimensions of child-rearing** practices. Grouping parents along these dimensions and then studying the behavior of their children made it possible to relate child-rearing practices to children's behavior. Another common strategy was to study the child-rearing practices of parents of children who shared some common characteristic, for example, delinquency, aggressiveness, or emotional disturbance (Martin, 1975). The purpose of these studies was to determine which patterns of child-rearing would be predictive of childhood difficulties.

Schaeffer (1959) analyzed the interactions of mothers with their 1-month-old to 3-year-old children and categorized maternal behavior on two dimensions—love versus hostility, and control versus autonomy. Using factor analysis—a statistical technique for determining the number of dimensions needed to describe the correlations among a number of variables—Becker (1964; Becker & Krug, 1964) has claimed that describing parental behavior involves 3 dimensions—restrictiveness versus permissiveness (control versus autonomy), warmth versus hostility (love versus hostility), and anxious-emotional involvement versus calm detachment. The end points of these dimensions are defined by various parental acts. Warmth, for example, is defined as encompassing acceptance, approval, positive responses to dependency, the lavish use of praise in discipline, little use of physical punishment, and the like. The hostility end of this dimension is defined by the opposite behaviors. The restrictive end of the restrictive-permissive dimension is defined by the enforcement of demands for modesty, table manners, obedience, aggressive behavior, and so forth. Anxious-emotional involvement refers to babying, overprotectiveness, and other similar behaviors.

A parent's behavior may be scored on these dimensions, and differences in child-rearing practices among parents exhibiting various behavior patterns may be discovered. For example, Becker (1964) has described both the democratic and the indulgent parent as having a high rating on the dimensions of warmth and permissiveness, with the difference that the indulgent parent scores high on emotional involvement and the democratic parent scores low on this dimension, that is, the democratic parent is calmly detached. Figure 11-1 shows other types of parental behaviors that may be classified along two of the dimensions.

Types of Parent Discipline

Hoffman (Hoffman 1970; Hoffman & Saltzstein 1967) has clarified the roles of various disciplinary practices by noting there are at least 3 forms of punishment parents use. **Power assertion** refers to the use of physical punishment, the deprivation of desired things or privileges, or the threat of these. In using this form of punishment, the parent controls the child through the child's weakness rather than through guilt arising from the child's identification with the parent.

Two forms of disciplinary techniques are "psychological" or **nonpower-assertive** in nature. Discipline through **love-withdrawal** involves nonphysical expression of parental anger or disapproval, such as ignoring, isolating, and expressing a dislike for the child. These techniques may be more punitive than physical punishment because of their implicit threat of abandonment. In turn, guilt may arise and begin to control the child's behavior. Unlike power assertion, love-withdrawal may last for a long period of time rather than ending relatively quickly as occurs with physical punishment.

The other nonpower-assertive technique is **induction.** When the parent explains why the child should not engage in some behavior—such as warning the child of the dangerous consequences of touching a hot stove or playing with matches—the parent is using inductive discipline. The parent tries to convince the child to alter this behavior through appeals to the child's ability to understand that certain situations require specific forms of behavior (Hoffman, 1970). An additional aspect of induction discipline involves pointing out the effects of the child's behavior on others. This fosters the child's understanding of other's perspectives and helps the children realize the impact of their actions on others. Examples of induction discipline might include pointing out the dangers of running in the house, carrying scissors incorrectly, pushing other children, and the like. As we shall see in our discussion of moral development, this form of discipline promotes aspects of moral development. Unlike the use of power-assertion and love-withdrawal, induction makes no attempt to punish the child. The parent tries to train the child to understand the consequences of his or her actions within the context of a punishment situation.

FIGURE 11-1   *Schaeffer's Hypothetical Model of Parental Behavior*

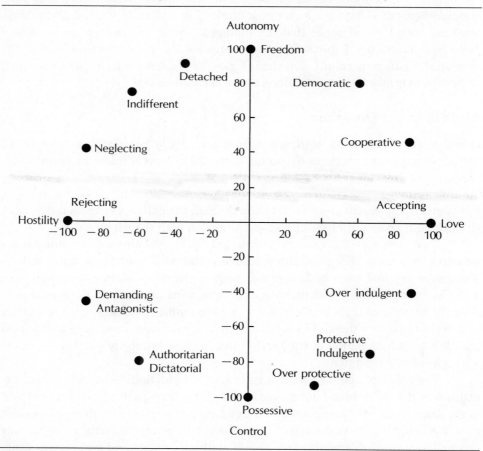

SOURCE: Schaeffer, E. S. A circumplex model for material behavior. *Journal of Abnormal and Social Psychology*, 1959, 59, 226–235.

Love induction and withdrawal exert different effects on the child's development. (Left: Elizabeth Hamlin/Stock, Boston; right: Jim Harrison)

We have some evidence that parents who score high on hostility tend to use power-assertive discipline. Parents high in warmth tend to use praise and induction (Becker, 1964). Since parents who use physical punishment have more aggressive children (Martin, 1975; Becker, 1974; Feshbach, 1970), we would expect that more hostile parents will rear more aggressive children. This is indeed the case.

Parent Discipline and Children's Behavior

Some research has related these child-rearing, discipline patterns to children's behavior. Becker (1964) has summarized this research in the framework of the dimensions of parental behavior discussed above. Generally speaking, there is considerable evidence to demonstrate that parents who use high amounts of physical punishment rear children who are aggressive on measures taken in the home, in school, and in doll play situations (Becker, 1964). This relationship between parent and child aggression is apparently due to 3 factors. First, parental use of physical punishment may be frustrating to the child. In turn, this may produce anger which is expressed through aggressive behavior. Second, parents who use physical punishment in attempting to control their children's behavior are models for the use of aggression. In effect, these parents may teach their children to behave aggressively.

Third, punitive-hostile parents may directly reinforce aggressive behavior in their children. No doubt there is some truth to each of these explanations. At the present time we cannot do more than state that each hypothesis has some support in research. At the practical, parenting level, however, the fact remains that physically punitive parents rear aggressive children.

The largest body of research on parental discipline effects on children's behavior deals with the restrictive-permissive dimension. In general, the research confirms the common-sense supposition that restrictive parents, those who force the child to adhere to their standards, raise children who are inhibited, passive, socially withdrawn, and noncompetitive. In comparison parents who are permissive, that is, those who do not demand high conformity to parental standards, rear children who act in a more uninhibited fashion and who tend to be somewhat more aggressive. Information from the Fels Research Institute longitudinal study (Kagan & Moss, 1962) indicates that the effects of maternal restrictiveness during the early childhood years (from birth to age 3) has long-lasting effects. The children of restrictive mothers tend to be more conforming and dependent on adults and less aggressive and competitive. Maternal restrictiveness during the years 3 to 6 exerted somewhat more complex influences. Boys who were restricted acted in fearful and dependent ways during the later childhood years but were more aggressive (competitive and assertive) as adolescents. The general pattern of peer interaction revolved around

TABLE 11-1 Interactions in the Consequences of Warmth vs. Hostility and Restrictiveness vs. Permissiveness

RESTRICTIVENESS	PERMISSIVENESS
Warmth	
Submissive, dependent, polite, obedient	Active, socially outgoing, creative, successfully aggressive
Minimal aggression, boys	Minimal rule enforcement, boys
Dependent, not friendly, not creative	Facilitates adult role taking
Maximal compliance	Minimal self-aggression, boys
	Independent, friendly, creative, low projective hostility.
Hostility	
"Neurotic" problems	Delinquency
More quarreling and shyness with peers	Noncompliance
Socially withdrawn	Maximal aggression
Low in adult role taking	
Maximal self-aggression, boys	

SOURCE: Adapted from Becker, W. C. Consequences of different kinds of parental discipline. In M. L. Hoffman, and L. W. Hoffman (Eds.) Review of child development research, vol. 1. New York: Russell Sage Foundation 1964.

NOTE: Where sex of child is noted, findings are limited to that sex.

attempts to gain peer acceptance. Similar trends were present for girls during late childhood and early adolescence but as adults the restricted girls remained passive and dependent. Hence, it seems that early restrictiveness results in a passive and dependent mode of social interaction and later permissiveness results in a person being more aggressive, albeit appropriate and acceptable aggression.

The influence of parental restrictiveness-permissiveness on the child's development is related to the general home atmosphere, hostile or warm, in which it occurs (Becker, 1964). Permissiveness coupled with a hostile home atmosphere has been related to aggressiveness in children and to juvenile delinquency. The combination of permissiveness and hostility produces maximal aggression and noncompliance with respect to restrictions on behavior. Restrictiveness in a hostile atmosphere leads to higher levels of self-aggression, anxiety and worry, or other neurotic symptoms. The combination of permissiveness and warmth results in children who are independent, friendly, creative, and relatively low on measures of hostility. Children reared in homes that are restrictive but warm tend to be dependent, unfriendly, less creative, and more hostile. Children from permissive but warm homes tend to be socially assertive and domineering, but within appropriate bounds that are acceptable to others.

In summary, it is important to note that, in general, restrictiveness and permissiveness each has positive and negative consequences. While restrictiveness results in highly socialized, controlled behavior it also fosters dependency and reduced intellectual striving. Permissiveness results in sociable and outgoing behavior but also leads to increased aggressiveness. The relationships between children's behavior and the combinations of warmth-hostility and restrictiveness-permissiveness are summarized in Table 11-1. Permissiveness in a hostile atmosphere maximizes aggression and poorly controlled behavior. Restrictiveness combined with hostility increases self-aggression (suicidal tendencies) and social withdrawal. Warmth and permissiveness maximize individuality and socially outgoing characteristics. Finally, restrictiveness in a warm atmosphere results in a highly conforming child.

These generalizations must be interpreted with some caution. In most research little if any evidence about fathers was obtained. In addition, the findings are largely limited to the middle classes. The descriptions given here, then, offer some clues about parenting but should not be taken as absolute truths. In the final analysis, there are many acceptable modes of parenting and child rearing and we cannot specify which might best suit the individual parent.

Child-Rearing and Child Abuse

No discussion of child-rearing can be complete without considering the difficult and complex problem of child abuse. Perhaps no single aspect of child-rearing has stirred the general public more in recent times. Since we can touch on only a few of the many issues involved, the interested reader may wish to consult the excellent reviews of Spinetta and Rigler (1972), Parke and Collmer (1975), and Fontana and Besharov (1977).

DEFINITION OF CHILD ABUSE.   Child abuse is most commonly the result of excessive use of power-assertive, physical punishment disciplinary techniques (Parke & Collmer, 1975). However, an adequate definition of child abuse must consider other factors in addition to the physical injuries suffered by the child. Since approximately 93% of parents use physical punishment to a greater or lesser degree (Stark & McEvoy, 1970) definitions limited to the use of physical punishment are likely to be nondiscriminatory and of little practical use.

One additional factor involves the concept of intent—did the parent intend to inflict serious physical injury on the child? Inclusion of intent in the definition of child abuse is necessary to rule out accidental occurrences of injury as being a form of child abuse. The difficulty of judging the intent of the parent, however, becomes an issue. Since inferences of intent are difficult to make in a reliable way, some errors of judgment about child abuse will be made.

A second additional factor that must be included in a definition of child abuse is community standards with respect to child-rearing, particularly with respect to parental use of physical punishment (Parke & Collmer, 1975). An injury may be labeled abuse in one social class but not another, for example. Child abuse is partially defined by community standards, which vary as a function of social class, area of the country, religious groups, and the like. Inclusion of community standards in the definition allows it to be more precise and useful.

Parke and Collmer (1975, p. 513) have suggested the following definition which takes all the above factors into account. Child abuse is evidenced by "any child who receives nonaccidental physical injury (or injuries) as a result of acts (or omissions) on the part of his parents or guardians that violate the community standards concerning the treatment of children."

INCIDENCE OF CHILD ABUSE.   It is extremely difficult to obtain reliable statistics on the incidence of child abuse in the United States. A number of factors contribute to the unreliability of the statistics (Parke & Collmer, 1975). Some of these are: failure of parents to take the injured child for medical treatment; failure of doctors to report possible cases of child abuse; shifting of doctors and hospitals by parents who repeatedly injure their child; inconsistencies in reporting abuse because of varying legal definitions of abuse. As a result of these and other difficulties the incidence of child abuse can be estimated only roughly, and even these estimates are suspect. Moreover, figures on increases in incidence are difficult to interpret because it is not possible to determine if the increases represent simply an increase in *reported* child abuse, due to improved reporting procedures and requirements, or a *real* increase in child abuse. For example, Parke and Collmer (1975) report a 549 percent increase in child abuse in New York between 1966 and 1975. However, it is unclear whether this represents a real increase in incidence or is a result of the newly instituted central registry procedures.

Despite these difficulties, it is possible to gain some estimates of incidence of child abuse. A conservative estimate is that in 1970 there were approximately 500,000 abused children in the United States (Light, 1973). Others have suggested that reported incidence is only about 50 percent of actual incidence. A yet more extreme estimate of incidence is given by the United States Department of Health, Education and Welfare (1976), which suggests that between 2.5 and 4 million children are abused. Whichever estimate one believes, it is clear that a significant number of children are abused and that the problem is serious.

CAUSES OF CHILD ABUSE.   Research on the causes of child abuse has tried to determine personal, sociological, and parent-child interaction characteristics that relate to child abuse. We shall confine our discussion to a consideration of information on the personality characteristics of abusing parents and the characteristics of parent-child interaction that relate to child abuse.

Child-abusing parents have been described as impulsive, self-centered, rigid, immature, and the like (Parke & Collmer, 1975). These descriptors indicate that abusing parents have a personality defect that allows them to express aggressive behavior rather freely and in extreme forms (Spinetta & Rigler, 1972). But, there is little consistent evidence pointing to specific traits or clusters of traits that reliably distinguish child-abusing from nonabusing parents (Parke & Collmer, 1975).

There is considerably more aggreement that child-abusing parents were themselves abused and neglected as children (Parke & Collmer, 1975; Spinetta & Rigler, 1972). Abusive parents also come from homes where they were criticized and lacked for care and for being cared about. It appears that abusive parents learn to rear children in an abusive manner in part because they model their own parents' child-rearing procedures. As a result, there is a degree of intergenerational consistency in child abuse.

We have stressed in this and other chapters the importance of studying parent-child interactions in describing the child's development. This is highlighted by the *selectivity* that occurs in child abuse; not all children in a family are abused. Parke and Collmer (1975) indicate two factors related to ways in which the child may contribute to his own abuse. First, the child may have some genetic, physical, or behavioral trait that makes him a likely target for abuse. Second, the parent-child interaction may teach the child behavior patterns that lead to further abuse. Of particular relevance is the child's reaction to punishment. For example, a child who reacts to punishment in a defiant manner is likely to cause the parent to intensify the punishment in the future. A vicious circle may develop, culminating in the parent using such intensified physical punishment that the child is injured.

There is much yet to be learned about the causes of child abuse, and how to treat it effectively. The interactional approach appears to be promising in this regard. It is clear at the present time, however, that parental use of extreme physical punishment is not only detrimental to the child but promotes intergenerational consistency in child-rearing techniques that are detrimental to the society. Later in this and other chapters we shall discuss the relations between power-assertive and other discipline techniques in the child's development.

Development of Attachment

Attachment in both humans and animals is a precursor of more general social development (Ainsworth, 1973; Martin, 1975; Schaffer & Emerson, 1964; Maccoby & Masters, 1970). Over the past decade, psychologists have become increasingly interested in the developmental course of attachment—its stability over time, the types of parental interactions that foster it, and its importance for cognitive, emotional, and personal development.

Attachment is difficult to define. Most developmental psychologists believe it is indicated by proximity-seeking responses by the young of a species. Schaffer and Emerson (1964, pp. 6–7) define attachment as "the tendency of the young to seek the proximity of certain other members of the species . . . Attachments are generally focused on certain specific individuals only, while to others fear responses may be shown." The key feature of attachment is the specificity of the responses to a particular member(s) of the species. This singling-out of specific objects of attachment distinguishes it from the more global patterns of behavior called dependency, which we attribute to older children.

Many species of animals exhibit attachment (Hess, 1959, 1964; Bowlby, 1969; Ainsworth, 1973; Maccoby & Masters, 1970). The young of a species seek visual, auditory, or physical contact or proximity to certain other members of the species. Another index of attachment is the young's protest or distress when separated from another member(s) of the species. For human infants, a number of behaviors have been used to index attachment (Ainsworth, 1963, 1964, 1973; Bowlby, 1969, Maccoby & Masters, 1970; Schaffer & Emerson, 1964). These include protest at separation from the parent, use of the parent as a secure base from which to explore the environment, approaching the parent, fear of strangers, smiling and vocalizing to the parent, and clinging to the parent. In most research these attachment behaviors have been measured toward the mother. However, as we shall discuss below, children also become attached to the father or to other people or objects.

Theories of Attachment

Concern with the human infant's attachment grew out of Freud's theory of psychosexual development (Chapter 10) and the concept of identification. According to

Attachment of the young to the parent occurs in many species of animals. (Irven De Vore/Anthro-Photo)

Freud, infants are biologically predisposed to relate to the humans around them (Maccoby & Masters, 1970). He saw attachment as a **cathected** object choice—the infant invests some libidinal energy in another person, the mother or her substitute (Freud, 1959). This was presumed to take place for both boys and girls during the first year of life.

LEARNING THEORY. The learning theorists translated Freudian theory into their terms, formulated testable hypotheses, and systematically collected data on the development of attachment in human infants (Gerwirtz, 1969). Much of their research dealt with the role of child-rearing practices and concluded that infants develop attachment primarily during feeding, usually with the mother. Sears, Whiting, Nowlis, and Sears (1953, p. 178) note that behaviors indicative of attachment

> ... appear to result from the pervasive presence of others' performance of the nurturant role. From birth the child is fed, warmed, dried, snuggled, has his thirst quenched and his pains and discomforts reduced, by others. In American society, this "other" is usually the mother. As a consequence, the child learns early to manipulate his mother, to secure her help whenever his primary drives require some change in his environment in order that they may be reduced.

Because of their association with the pleasurable experience of feeding, mothers were assumed to become secondary reinforcers. The infant learns that mother's approach signifies pleasure and contentment. In other words, the learning theorists assume that the mother comes to signify relief from discomfort or the onset of pleasurable stimulation. They also assumed that the upset, frightened, or otherwise uncomfortable child would seek out its mother as a source of release from fear, discomfort, or other unpleasantness. According to Bijou and Baer (1965, p. 123), "the mother herself will, as a stimulus object, become discriminated as a time and a place for either the addition of positive reinforcers to the baby's environment or the subtraction of negative reinforcers from it ... Thereby, she acquires positive reinforcing function, and lays the foundation for the further social development of her infant."

IMPRINTING.   A considerable body of research on **imprinting** or attachment in animals casts doubt on this view. The work of Eckard Hess (1959, 1964) and Konrad Lorenz (1943) on imprinting in chicks and ducks suggests that learning theory is an inadequate explanation. In imprinting, for example, the baby duck will follow (attach itself to) any moving object that it sees, particularly between 13 to 16 hours after hatching. Normally, the duckling will follow its mother and thus will become attached to an adult. When this happens, the duckling learns to behave like other members of its species, for example, to engage in normal procreative behavior. If the duckling does not imprint to an appropriate member of its species, but to, say, a block of wood or even a human being, then it does not learn the social responses appropriate to its species. Thus, for ducks at least, imprinting seems to be a precursor of normal social development. Imprinting does not result from secondary reinforcement but represents a fixed action sequence in which an environmental stimulus (a moving object) acts as a **releaser mechanism** for the duckling to make following responses (Hess, 1959, 1964). Moreover, imprinting seems to occur only during a critical period from birth to about 24 hours of age. After this period, animals do not usually imprint. This notion of critical periods is important in understanding the development of animal responding and also may be important for understanding human development (Caldwell, 1962).

HARLOW'S RESEARCH.   The most well-known research on attachment in animals was performed by Harry Harlow, who researched the development of attachment in infant monkeys raised with two types of surrogate (substitute) mothers. One surrogate mother was made of wire; the other had a terry cloth covering. Half the monkeys were fed from the wire mother and half were fed from the cloth covered mother. According to the learning theory of attachment, the infant monkey should learn to "love" (become attached to) the mother that fed them (Harlow & Zimmerman, 1959). But the data showed that this was not true. The monkeys fed from the wire mother spent only enough time with her to be fed. They preferred to sit on, play, and maintain contact with the cloth-covered mother. The monkeys fed on the cloth-covered mother spent virtually no time with the wire mother. Moreover, in a fear-provoking situation both types of monkeys ran and clung to the cloth-covered

One of Harlow's surrogate mothers (Dr. Harry Harlow)

mother, which provided what Harlow called contact comfort. Contact with the cloth-covered mother reduced the fear that the monkeys experienced, and they would often explore novel frightening objects, using the mother as a secure base from which to explore. These findings, which have been demonstrated a number of times, suggest that there is a great deal more to attachment than can be explained by secondary reinforcement principles. The ecological approach underlying much of the research on human infant attachment has been offered as an alternative explanation.

EVOLUTIONARY FACTORS. One of the earliest to investigate human infant attachment from an ecological perspective was John Bowlby (1958, 1960, 1969, 1973). He believes that human attachment has a biological basis that can be understood only within an evolutionary framework. Although he acknowledges the role of learning in human attachment, he believes that the human organism is endowed with some relatively stable behavioral patterns which reduce the risk of the infant dying prior to reaching maturity. These patterns, which are seen as necessary for survival of the species, have resulted from human evolutionary history and serve functions similar to those of attachment in lower animal forms, largely the protection of the young. In order to be effective these behaviors must be aimed at adult members of the species, primarily the mother. These behaviors, then, ensure appropriate care from adults and, hence, function as ways in which the infant can ensure that it will survive the relatively long human infancy period.

Attachment has the goal of bringing the young into close contact with some member of the species and is activated when the young are separated from the attached member or are threatened. Attachment behavior is terminated by visual, auditory, or tactile stimulation by the attached member of the species, usually the mother. The more intense the separation or threat, the greater the amount of contact required to end the attachment behavior. For example, extreme threat may produce attachment behaviors that terminate only when the young make contact with the attached member whereas a lesser threat may produce attachment behaviors that are terminated by simply seeing the attached member.

Bowlby (1969, 1973) believes that humans have evolved behavior patterns that reflect attachment. By aiming attachment behavior at adults, usually the primary caretaker, the infant ensures appropriate care and maximizes its chances of surviving a prolonged infancy. Bowlby argues that infants have 5 kinds of species-specific behavior which help them to bring about and sustain contact with adults. *Clinging, sucking,* and *following* maintain contact with the species. *Crying* and *smiling* bring an adult into social contact with the infant. As the infant matures, these behaviors become integrated and focused on the mother and form the basis of attachment to her. With increasing age, the behavior is assumed to shift from physical contact with the mother to more distant contact, including emotional support.

RESEARCH BY SCHAFFER AND EMERSON.   Schaffer and Emerson (1964) conducted one of the first longitudinal studies of attachment in humans with a group of 60 Scottish infants. These investigators defined attachment as the tendency of the young to seek out proximity of other members of the species as indexed by protest at separation from these others. In their research they wished to explore the age of onset, the intensity, and the objects of attachment. They observed and tested 31 males and 29 females. Attachment was measured in a number of conditions of separation from the mother: being left alone in a room, being left with other people, being left in a buggy outside the house or outside a store, being put to bed at night, being put down after being held, and being passed by while in bed. The data, which were collected through interviews with the mothers every 4 weeks for the first year of life and then again at 18 months of age, included: the infant's form of protest at separation, its frequency, intensity, and the person to whom the protest was directed, that is, whose departure elicited the response.

Attachment first appears during the third quarter of the first year. During the first 6 months, the infant typically protests when anyone leaves, a form of indiscriminate attachment. Schaffer and Emerson suggest that during the first 6 months the infant seeks contact and attention from strangers and familiar people alike, indicating a general attachment to people. Only during the second 6 months of life does the infant make any protest at separation from specific individuals and so demonstrate attachment to specific people, particularly the mother. These intense attachments reach a peak between 12 and 18 months of age.

Figure 11-2 shows the growth curves for specific attachments, attachments to the mother, and indiscriminate attachments. Note that the onset of specific attachment does not exclude protest to separation by people in general (indiscriminate attachment). The infants protested somewhat when anyone left them, but after about 7 months, they protested much more vigorously when specific people left them. Individual children form specific attachments suddenly rather than gradually, as Figure 11-2 suggests. These curves represent average scores for each age; infants at any one age level vary considerably in their protests. The age at which specific attachments begin also varies. One child showed specific attachments at age 22 weeks, but others not until they were a year or older.

If only one specific object was attached, 65 percent of the subjects chose the mother. The remaining infants most often chose the father. Other objects of specific attachment tended to be family members rather than members of the general

FIGURE 11-2   *Developmental Course of Attachments*

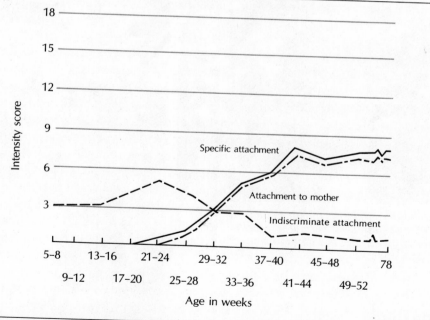

SOURCE: Schaffer, H. R., and Emerson, P. E. The development of social attachments in infancy. *Monographs of the Society for Research in Child Development,* 1964, 29.

community or friends of the parents. By the time the infant has formed specific attachments, the number of people attached slowly increases so that the average infant becomes attached to a number of different people by age 12, 13, or 14 months.

These results suggest that the attachment process consists of 3 stages (Schaffer & Emerson, 1964). In the first or *asocial stage,* the individual seeks arousal from all parts of its environment. This stage lasts until about 7 months of age. In the *prosocial stage,* the individual singles out human beings as particularly satisfying objects and actively seeks them out. In the final or *social stage,* which begins at about 8 months of age, the infant forms attachments to specific persons.

Protest at separation decreases at about 18 months of age, when the development of object permanence is complete. The infant now understands that the parent still exists even when no longer in view. This finding suggests that cognitive factors play a significant role in the development of attachment and separation protest.

ATTACHMENT AND EXPLORING.   Attachment can also be viewed as an adaptive mechanism for exploring the environment (Ainsworth, 1973), which is necessary for the child to learn about his surroundings. Young infants use the mother as a secure base from which to explore. Attachment keeps the infant in safe contact with

One consequence of attachment is that the infant uses the attached person as a secure base from which to explore the environment. (Peter Vandermark)

TABLE 11-2   Episodes and Time in the Strange Situation

EPISODE	TIME
1. The mother carried the baby into the strange room, accompanied by an observer who left.	3 minutes.
2. After placing the baby on the floor the mother sat in a chair.	3 minutes.
3. The stranger entered, sat quietly for one minute, talked to the mother for one minute, then slowly approached the baby. Three minutes later the mother left.	6 minutes.
4. Stranger and infant alone in room.	3 minutes.
5. Mother returned and stranger left, leaving mother and infant alone.	3 minutes.
6. The baby was left alone.	3 minutes.
7. Stranger returned and stayed with baby.	3 minutes.
8. Mother returned and stranger left.	Session terminated.

the mother, away from danger, and also acts to make the infant seek out the mother if peril should arise. This view of the relation between attachment and exploration is basically an ethological statement, such as that suggested by Bowlby. Caretaker-infant attachment ensures the protection and caretaking the young of the species require in order to mature and propagate the species. Ainsworth and her co-workers devised what has become known as the **strange situation** (see Table 11-2), which consists of a series of planned mother-child separations and reunions along with a planned sequence of encounters between the infant and a stranger. The coding of the infant's behavior in this situation reveals several different aspects of attachment.

Ainsworth and Wittig (1969) used the strange situation to study the development of attachment in 56 infants aged 49- to 56-weeks old. These investigators recorded exploration, proximity- and contact-seeking, and contact maintaining. Locomotor, manipulative, and visual exploration occurred most frequently when the mother was present and decreased sharply when a stranger entered the room. Contact-seeking and maintaining were weak during the early episodes but increased during separation. At the first reunion with the mother, contact maintaining was very high and increased even more during the second reunion. These findings indicate that the mother acts as a secure base for exploring a novel environment. When the mother is present, the infant goes exploring and suppresses its attachment. When the mother leaves, the infant stops its explorations and intensifies its attachment.

The Mother and Attachment

Much current research on attachment is aimed at identifying child-rearing patterns related to the child's ways of dealing with the strange environment. Ainsworth, Bell, and Stayton (1971) have devised a scheme for classifying children according to their reactions to the strange environment. The scoring for this system has even been objectified (Connell 1974, 1977) so that it can be done with computer programs. Three groups of infants—As, Bs, and Cs—have been identified on the basis of their behavior in the strange situation.

The As show little desire for contact or proximity to the mother; when picked up, they do not cling or resist being put down. They tend to avoid or ignore the mother when she returns, for example, by moving away from her and by not looking at her face. These infants are sometimes called "unattached." The Bs seek out and maintain contact with the mother after a brief separation; they also exhibit a high degree of contact maintenance. Moreover, they rarely avoid or resist the mother. These infants are sometimes called "securely attached." The Cs react quite violently to separation from the mother. They tend not to explore the environment even when the mother is present. Some of them actively seek proximity and contact, while at the same time pushing away from mother; other Cs show no sign of actively seeking the mother. These infants are sometimes called "insecurely attached."

SOME CONCLUSIONS FROM THE RESEARCH.   Ainsworth et al. (1971) have argued that mothers of A and C children are less sensitive than mothers of B infants to signals and communications in the home. The mothers of infants in Group B seem to have the best interpersonal relations with them. These mothers are more sensitive, accepting, and cooperative than mothers of A or C infants. The mothers of A infants appear to be more rejecting (Ainsworth et al., 1971). The mothers of C infants are not obviously rejecting, but their interaction with their children is not harmonious. Bowlby (1973) has suggested that these differing mother-child interactions may cause children in Groups A and C to develop less well-integrated personalities than Group B children, particularly in the traits of self-reliance and trust in others.

This basically one-dimensional interpretation of attachment does not take into account the interaction between parent and child. In noting this failing, Sander (1964) has suggested that harmony between parent and child may well affect attachment. Harmony depends on the adaptive abilities of both mother and child. The mother must be sensitive to the infant's signals as well as to the environmental conditions that affect the infant's well-being. The infant must be socially responsive and provide feedback to the mother. Harmonious interactions involve a lack of conflict and a mutually active, positive relationship. According to Ainsworth et al. (1971, pp. 46–47), such interpretations of mother-infant interaction are important for understanding the behavior of C infants in the strange situation: "A disharmonious or unsatisfactory relationship with the mother evokes insecurity in the infant ... which generally manifests itself in heightened proximity and contact seeking as well as a low threshold to separation distress."

There is additional evidence to link parent-child interaction to type of attachment (cf. Martin, 1975). The mother's responsiveness to her infant's crying is related to strength of attachment (Schaffer & Emerson, 1964) as is responsiveness to the infant's initiativeness (Clarke-Stewart, 1973). The mothers of B infants give more stimulation, exhibit a more positive attitude toward their infants, and respond more frequently to their infant's behavior. More recent evidence (Blehar, Lieberman & Ainsworth, 1977) indicates that the mothers of B infants maintain a higher quality of interaction than do the mothers of A and C infants. The mothers of B infants also encourage more interactions as well as warmer interactions, terminate fewer interactions, vocalize more to their infants, and touch them more (Connell, 1977).

Maternal stimulation of the infant is also related to attachment. Infants who exhibit strong attachment in the strange situation and who use the mother as a secure base from which to explore the environment have mothers who are highly sensitive to the infant's feeding demands and allow the infant to set the timing, pacing, and duration of feeding (Ainsworth & Bell, 1969; Caldwell, Wright, Honig & Tannenbaum, 1970). Mothers who are insensitive to their infant's initiatives in feeding rear infants who tend to reject the mother and who show less interest in maintaining contact with her (Martin, 1975). In general, it appears that when mothers ignore their infant, the infant in turn orients less to them (Beckwith, 1972).

Studying only the effects of the parent on the child's behavior ignores half of the parent-child dyad as well as the interactive nature of parent-child relationships (Bell, 1968; Rheingold, 1969; Martin, 1975). The parent-child relations we have discussed here are clearly interactive and it is appropriate that we discuss the child's contribution to this interaction.

TEMPERAMENT AND SEX OF THE CHILD.   One especially important characteristic in parent-child interaction is the child's **temperament.** Schaffer and Emerson (1964) divided their sample of infants into those who liked to be cuddled and those who objected to cuddling. Although mothers of noncuddlers tended to interact primarily in nonphysical ways with their children, the difference between them and the mothers of cuddlers was not statistically significant. Mothers of cuddlers seemed equally at ease with physical and nonphysical contact with their infants, with the mothers of noncuddlers preferring nonphysical contact. These findings suggest that differences in infants' temperaments are related to the types of parent-child interactions discussed above.

The most extensive and informative studies of the relation of infant temperament to parent-child interaction have been reported by Thomas and his co-workers (Thomas & Chess, 1977; Thomas, Chess & Birch, 1968). To distinguish temperament from ability and motivation, which also affect behavior, Thomas and Chess (1977) define it as a behavioral style; that is, the *way* the individual behaves. Temperament, then, refers to the stylistic characteristics of behavior. It is influenced by environmental conditions, is partly learned, and may also have a genetic basis (cf. Thomas & Chess, 1977). Analysis of temperament ratings gleaned from observations of children as well as parent and teacher questionnaires identified three temperamental styles. The *Easy child* readily adapts to change, develops regular eating and sleeping patterns, is flexible and adaptable. The *Difficult child* exhibits much the opposite behavioral patterns. These children are moody, have irregular eating and sleeping patterns, and do not adjust easily to changing or new stimuli. The *Slow-to-Warm-Up child* has a style between the two extremes. These children adapt, but slowly, exhibit mild negative responses to change, and are more regular than the difficult child in regard to eating and sleeping patterns.

The child's particular temperament disposition affects the parents' interactions with the child. For example, in infancy, the child's temperament affects how the parent performs daily care-taker functions. The Easy child can be very reinforcing to parents because the parents can readily feel they are doing a good job. The opposite may occur with a Difficult child, the parents perhaps coming to feel that they are inept and that the child is a burden. A danger is that they will react with negative feelings, thereby heightening the infant's negative responses. The vicious cycle may continually escalate throughout childhood until open hostility between parent and child results. As this example clearly shows, the combination of child-parent characteristics determines to a significant degree parent-child interactions related to attachment. Although there are no data, it is interesting to speculate that the pattern of interactions with the Difficult child result in the C-type of attachment behavior. The A-type children in terms of attachment may be composed of Easy children, and the B-type of children may come from the Slow-to-Warm-Up temperamental group. If this were to be demonstrated, it would highlight even more the importance of studying parent-child relations in an interactive framework.

Also related to parent-child interactions are the sex of the infant and temperamental differences associated with sex (Martin, 1975). Boys sleep less and are more fussy and more irritable than girls (Moss, 1967). As a result, mothers hold boys more than girls, provide boys with more stimulation, and respond more readily to terminate stress in boys (Corter & Bow, 1976). Mothers also spend less time in social, affectional, and caretaking activities with later-born children, especially girls (Jacobs & Moss, 1976). These findings show how individual difference characteristics of children promote individual differences in parent-child relations and attachment.

The Father and Attachment

Infant attachment to the father has been studied only recently (Lamb, 1975, 1976b). There is considerable evidence that infants are attached to both the mother and the father from the very beginning of attachment relations (Cohen & Campos, 1974; Feldman & Ingham, 1975; Kotelchuck, Zelazo, Kagan & Spelke, 1975; Willemsen, Flaherty, Heaton & Ritchey, 1974). Michael Lamb (1975, 1976a, 1976b, 1976c, 1977) has investigated the role of the father as an attachment figure. He assumes than the infant will exhibit differential attachment behaviors under stress but under non-stressful conditions will show no differences in attachment to the mother and the father. In order to test this hypothesis, Lamb devised a standardized situation with

Under stress infants show greater attachment to the mother than to the father. Lamb believes this develops partly because of differences in the mother's and father's typical interactions (caretaking and play, respectively) with the child. (Peter Vandermark)

the systematic presence or absence of mother, father, and stranger. During the first episode, the mother, father, and infant are together. During the second episode, only the mother (or father) is with the infant. The third episode involves the other parent with the child. The final episode involves the mother, the father, a stranger, and the infant (Lamb, 1976a). The infant behaviors recorded included smiling, vocalizing, looking, reaching, touching, approaching, and being near to another person. Lamb divided infant behaviors toward the parents into 2 sets. **Affiliative** behaviors are distal responses to the parent, for example, smiling, looking at, and laughing. **Attachment behaviors** are proximal responses that include touching, seeking to be picked up, approaching, and being in the immediate vicinity of a parent.

Both at home (Lamb, 1976b) and in the laboratory (Lamb, 1976c), infants did not show any differences in attachment to the parents in the relatively stress-free first episode. They did, however, display more affiliation toward their fathers than toward their mothers. During the more stressful fourth episode, the infants showed more attachment behaviors to their mothers than to their fathers. The infants also directed more affiliative behaviors to the mother during the stressful situation. When given a choice, in a stressing situation the infants preferred the mother.

These differences in attachment and affiliative behaviors are related to the types of day-to-day interactions the mother and father have with the infant (Lamb, 1977). Mothers make physical contact with the infant primarily during caretaking, while fathers make physical contact primarily during play. Lamb suggests that infants can discern a difference between these interactions and that differences in their attachment behaviors under stress reflect this perception. Given a choice the infant prefers to attach itself to the mother—the parent most strongly associated with nurturance. If, however, the mother is absent, the father can act as an acceptable substitute for attachment. If both parents are absent, the infant will display attachment behaviors to a stranger (Rosenthal, 1967).

Attachment in infants is also indicative of cognitive development, as shown in the different ways the infant interprets its environment. Infants must have achieved a certain level of cognitive development before they can even realize that they are in a novel environment or that some individual is a stranger. And they must make certain cognitive evaluations that reflect their different interpretations of their interactions with the mother and father.

Consequences of Attachment

We have seen above that one consequence of attachment is exploratory behavior. Attachment has two other consequences of historical interest. First, responses to the attached caretaker will generalize to other people. Attachment thus sets the stage for the child's learning of social behavior. Second, the infant develops a scheme for the caretaker's face, form, voice, and so forth. This result of attachment is important in the development of separation anxiety, exemplified by protest at being separated from the attached person.

In a now classic study, Rheingold (1956) showed the importance of attachment for social learning. Her investigation probed whether infants' general social responsiveness would be greater when they had only one caretaker instead of many. In order to investigate this question Rheingold mothered 8 institutionalized infants. Eight control infants received normal institutional care, with many caretakers and necessarily low responsiveness by the staff to the infants' needs. The 8 experimental infants were mothered, fed, played with, changed, and so on by Rheingold herself for 7.5 hours a day, 5 days a week. At the start of the experiment the infants were 6 months old. Tests of social responsiveness to the experimenter (Rheingold) and to an examiner, who saw the infants periodically for other tests, were given a week before the experiment began, biweekly during the experiment, and biweekly for a month after the experiment was concluded. At the end of the 8 weeks of the experiment, all the infants were tested for social responsiveness to Rheingold, to the examiner, and to a stranger. The results graphed in Figure 11-3 show the growth of social responsiveness to Rheingold and to the examiner. The social responsiveness of the infants mothered by Rheingold was higher both to Rheingold and to the examiner than was

FIGURE 11-3   *Means of Social Test for Experimental and Control Groups in Response to Experimenter and Examiner.*

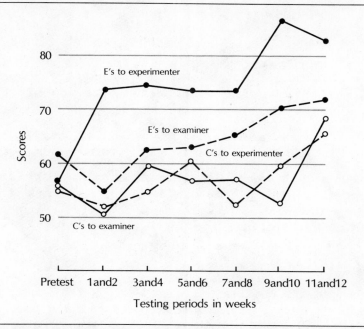

SOURCE: Rheingold, H. L. The modification of social responsiveness in institutional babies. *Monographs of the Society for Research in Child Development,* 1956, 21, (2), Serial no. 63, p. 23.

the social responsiveness of the control group, which was low both to Rheingold and to the examiner. The data collected at the eighth week of the experiment showed that the experimental infants were generally more responsive than the control infants and were also more responsive to the examiner and the stranger than were the control infants. Behavior learned in response to a nuturant socially stimulating caretaker generalized to other adults, whereas multiple caretaking, especially in an institutional setting, seemed to retard social responsiveness. However, since children raised by many caretakers in an Israeli kibbutz are as strongly attached to their mothers as children raised in American homes (Maccoby & Feldman, 1972), the lower responsiveness of the Rheingold control infants may have been caused by other aspects of institutionalization, such as a general lack of stimulation. Although Rheingold reports that the general institutional care was of a high quality, stimulating interactions of the staff with the infants were limited.

SEPARATION.   Infantile **separation anxiety** is an obvious phenomenon. Recall in Schaffer and Emerson's research (1964) that protest at separation served as the criterion for attachment. In American infants, separation anxiety begins at about 7

Separation anxiety (Judith Sedwick)

to 8 months of age (before sophisticated object permanence) and ends at about 18 months of age (with the development of object permanence), at least in its more extreme forms. All parents have witnessed such behavior when they leave their infant at home with a babysitter. On leaving, the parents often hear the child scream "bloody murder." On returning home, however, they are usually informed that the child only cried for a few moments.

Separation anxiety might be explained by the following sequence of events consistent with the ethological perspective. If the child is interacting with an individual who then leaves the child, there is a break in the response chain that the child is making; that is, the child's response chain is disrupted. The infant may then begin to cry in an attempt to reestablish contact with the individual to whom the responses were being made.

Separation anxiety has 3 components: one, the discrepancy produced by being separated from the attached person; two, the disruption of responses that follows from this separation; three, a response on the part of the infant to reestablish contact with the person. Separation anxiety should disappear when the absence of the attached person is no longer a discrepant event or when the child can successfully maintain contact. Both of these possibilities occur between 12 and 18 months of age. When object permanence is established (at about 18 months), the child views the person as another object and realizes that "out of sight is not absence forever." In other words, the child realizes that people continue to exist even though out of sight. Also, since the child can move around better, he can follow the attached person and thus maintain contact in many, albeit not all, situations. In these circumstances, the child will show less separation anxiety because the child can maintain contact by itself.

HOSPITALIZATION.   Other, less common separations, for example, the behavior of children going into or returning home from a hospital, may be of interest to the reader. Hospitalization makes it possible to study both the infant's separation from and reunion with the parents. The kinds and severity of reactions to hospitalization vary depending upon the age of the child, with developmental changes in reactions appearing at about 7 months of age. Children younger than 7 months at separation are normally responsive to strange adults and show little sign of disturbance at being separated from the parents. Older infants and young children show a variety of marked disturbances. Between 2 and 3 years of age, children react with extreme severity. Crying, anger, vomiting, loss of bowel and bladder control, and eating and sleeping problems are frequent among children this age. Four- to 6-year-olds show similar problems but not with the same severity.

The period from 7 to 12 years of age is another developmental marker. These children tend to show fairly low separation anxiety but fairly high free-floating anxiety. They tend to be concerned more about the extent of their illness and about what is going to happen to them in the hospital than about being separated. Since

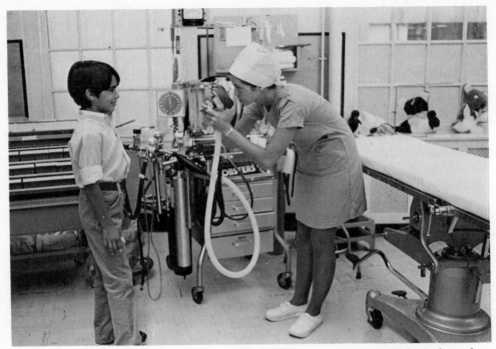

Showing the child the operating room and explaining the procedures helps reduce the child's fear about surgery. (Judith Sedwick)

hospitalization is usually a new experience for children and since they have reached fairly high levels of cognitive competence, this is not surprising. Younger children rarely know what a hospital is, while older children know that people go to the hospital when they are very ill. These older children may be concerned that they are extremely ill and therefore more anxious about what may happen to them in the hospital than they are about being separated from their parents.

We have very little data on the reunion of parents and child after hospitalization, but the literature seems to reveal the following trends. On returning home, children less than 7 months of age show few manifestations of hospitalization. The child may vocalize less than usual, spend more time staring at the environment, and have some problems in sleeping and eating. However, these changes are short-lived and unlikely to pose problems for the family. The return to the family may provoke much stronger reactions in older infants—extreme dependence on the mother, rejection of the parents, anxiety about separation from the mother, as well as troubles in sleeping and eating. Such problems may last several months.

These are normal reactions of children upon entering and returning home from the hospital. They are not necessarily abnormal or likely to cause aberrant development. Still, parents should understand that children who are hospitalized may behave in these ways.

Hospital personnel, who have long been aware of these problems, have recently introduced procedures to make it easier for the child to enter the hospital and to cope with the anxieties of hospitalization and the return home. Daily parental visits or parental stays with their children in the hospital; play programs such as those found in a nursery school; preparation of children for therapy; and familiarization of children with operating rooms, operational procedures, and apparatus are now routine strategies in larger hospitals.

In our opinion, attachment in infancy has warranted such lengthy discussion because it represents the beginning of children's interpersonal social development. The individual differences in strength or type of attachment and its developmental course demonstrate its importance for psychological development. Nevertheless, there is still much to learn about various influences, such as the effect of parents, on individual differences in attachment and its development over the life span of the individual.

It should now be obvious why we have discussed attachment as an effect of child-rearing practices. As Ainsworth (1973) and her colleagues have hypothesized, the parents, through the use of certain child-rearing techniques, shape not only the immediate behaviors of the child, but also, as mediated by attachment, indirectly influence the child's long-term socialization. But the data we have reviewed also suggest that children themselves play a significant role in their own socialization. Parental influences are undoubtedly mediated by the particular nature of the child, for example, the child's level of cognitive development, learning history, and predilections toward behavior of a certain sort, perhaps as biologically predetermined.

Dependency

We noted above that the greater the social stimulation the mother provides, the more strongly the child becomes attached to her. We also discussed evidence indicating that mothers who are more sensitive and responsive to their infants' needs rear infants who are more strongly attached to them. Developmental psychologists have extended the study of the effects of child-rearing techniques to **dependency** during the childhood years (Sears et al., 1957; Sears et al., 1965; Kagan & Moss, 1962).

Defining and Measuring Dependency

Hartup (1963, p. 333) has defined dependency behaviors in the following way: "Whenever the individual gives evidence that people, as people, are satisfying and rewarding, it may be said that the individual is behaving dependently." Indices of dependency include seeking physical contact or nearness to someone, seeking praise or approval from someone, attempting to obtain another's attention, and resisting being separated from another person (Maccoby & Masters, 1970). Many of these behaviors bring attachment to mind. Hence, we might expect a close relationship between measures of dependency and measures of attachment. And we might further expect that the infant's degree of attachment should be related to the degree of childhood dependency. The evidence, however, indicates that neither expectation is borne out (Maccoby & Masters, 1970).

There are several possible reasons for the lack of correspondence between measures of attachment in infancy and those of dependency in childhood. In some instances, we have no one measure that crosses the periods of infancy and childhood. Or if the same variable is relevant to different developmental levels, it has often not been investigated in both. One example of the latter is responsiveness to crying, which has typically been measured only in infancy (Maccoby & Masters, 1970). Another problem is that various indices of dependency are not closely related (Maccoby & Masters, 1970; Martin, 1975), suggesting that dependency is a fragmented concept, covering a diverse set of behaviors (Martin, 1975). Some conceptual order has been achieved by distinguishing between clusters of dependency behaviors, such as affectional dependency (seeking contact with another person because that contact is rewarding) versus instrumental dependency (seeking help from someone else in order to achieve some nonsocial goal, for example, having an adult set up an electric train set so it can be played with) and proximity-seeking versus attention-seeking. The two types of dependency in each pair seem to be independent (Maccoby & Masters, 1970; Martin, 1975) and are similar to Lamb's (1977) distinction between affiliative and attachment behaviors that are directed differently toward father and mother. Future research may show relationships between clusters of attachment measures and clusters of dependency behaviors.

Child-Rearing Techniques and Dependency

Parents affect their children's expressions of dependency partly through the use of rewards and punishments. Children whose dependency is rewarded become more dependent than children whose parents do not reward such behavior. Parents who punish dependency behavior rear children who are less dependent than children whose dependency overtures are not punished or are ignored (Hartup, 1963; Maccoby & Masters, 1970; Nelson, 1960). However, the relation between reward or punishment of dependency behavior and its occurrence are not always straightforward.

Some investigators (Sears, Rau & Alpert, 1965; Sears, Maccoby & Levin, 1957; Yarrow, Campbell & Burton, 1968) report that if the mother is involved in some task and ignores or punishes the dependency responses of her child, they are likely to increase. This apparently anomalous finding reflects the history of interaction between mother and child. The child has previously learned that dependency will eventually get its reward; that is, since the child has learned to expect reinforcement for dependency behaviors, it will continue to exhibit them even if the mother ignores or mildly punishes them. The child knows that sooner or later the parent will give in and attend to him. Therefore, it comes as no surprise that some investigators (Sears, Whiting, Nowlis & Sears, 1953; Martin, 1975) have found that the highest percentage of dependent children come from homes where the mother both rewards and punishes dependency.

Although maternal warmth is positively related to infant attachment and warmth (Stern, Caldwell, Hersher, Lipton & Richmond, 1969; Martin, 1975), parental warmth is not related to dependency directed toward the parents (Hatfield, Ferguson, Rau & Alpert, 1967; Sears et al., 1957; Becker, 1964). The degree of parental hostility and rejection is also unrelated to parent-directed dependency. Some evidence, however, suggests that, at least for boys, high dependency toward peers and other adults is related to being reared by rejecting mothers and fathers (Sears et al., 1953; Sears et al., 1965; Martin, 1975).

The evidence about the relations between maternal permissiveness-restrictiveness and dependency in preschool children is ambiguous (Martin, 1975). Some researchers report that maternal permissiveness correlates postively with negative dependency (attention-seeking) in preschool children, but others do not (Kagan & Moss, 1962).

Permissive parental behavior does seem to be related to high peer-dependency for older boys (McCord, McCord, & Verden, 1962). And boys who were highly dependent on adults had a high proportion of restrictive parents. Other researchers (e.g., Kagan & Moss, 1962) find that maternal restrictiveness during early childhood correlates with dependence during the midchildhood years (ages 6 to 10). Martin (1975) suggests that dependency directed toward adults is related to authoritarian and restrictive child-rearing that is absent in a warm, accepting home atmosphere. Dependency directed toward peers is likely to arise from parental permissiveness in an atmosphere that lacks warmth and acceptance.

Aggression

Psychologists have long been interested in the causes and development of **aggression** in children (Feshbach, 1970). Recent discussions about the effects of violence on television have fueled the fires of this concern. Feshbach (1970) has thoroughly reviewed many of the theoretical issues in aggression, Martin (1975) has related child-rearing practices to the learning and expression of aggression, and Stein and Friedrich (1975; see also Friedrich & Stein, 1973, 1975) have discussed the effects of TV violence on children's aggression.

Definition

One major problem encountered in studying aggression is its definition (Feshbach, 1970). Some define it as behavior that causes injury or destruction. By this definition, even some accidental acts are considered aggressive. But such unintentional aggression should be distinguished from intentional aggression. Hence, we adopt Martin's (1975, p. 509) definition: "Aggression is behavior whose *aim* is to hurt or injure a person or object. The injury may be accomplished physically or verbally, as with insults." (Italics ours). This definition has several advantages. First, it distinguishes between intentionally aggressive behavior and accidents. Second, this definition fits the data collected on aggression in childhood.

Age and Sex Differences

We can discern a few general developmental trends in children's aggressive behavior from observations of aggression in children's play with each other, in doll-play situations that allow the assessment of fantasy aggression, and through verbal reports. Some researchers (e.g., Jersild & Mackey, 1935; Green, 1933) report that between the ages of 2 and 5, physical aggression decreases while verbal aggression increases. In playing, older children tend to be more verbally demanding and aggressive, while younger children aggress more by taking toys (Muste & Sharpe, 1974). In playing with dolls, children show an increase in aggression up to age 4 (Sears, 1951; Walters, Pearce, & Dahms, 1957). Verbal aggression increases between the ages of 2 and 4. The best longitudinal study (Goodenough, 1931) showed that aggression peaked at about age 2 and gradually declined until about age 5. Undirected temper tantrums slowly decreased until about age 3, and then rapidly declined after age 4. Aggressive behavior aimed at injuring someone or damaging something generally increases with age throughout the childhood years.

Aggression in older children has received much less study. Some evidence indicates that children aged 7 to 8 and up engage in more fantasy aggression than younger children (Feshbach, 1956), but this trend ends at adolescence (Bender & Schilder, 1936). Finally, data from the Berkeley Growth Study (Tuddenham, 1959) and the Fels longitudinal study (Kagan & Moss, 1962) indicate that aggressive behavior remains highly stable during the adolescent years and into adulthood.

A large number of studies have assessed sex differences in aggression (Feshbach, 1970; Oetzel, 1966). From age 2 to adulthood, boys show a much greater amount of direct physical aggression than girls. According to measures of indirect aggression, however, girls are more aggressive than boys (Feshbach, 1970). Hence, girls quite probably are as aggressive as boys, but, in line with traditional sex roles, girls express their aggression quite differently. Since aggression is a sex-typed behavior, this seems to be a plausible hypothesis, although the evidence is not yet conclusive.

Child-Rearing Techniques

The harsh use of power-assertive discipline (especially physical punishment) is closely related to aggressiveness in children (Martin, 1975), regardless of age and, with minor differences, sex of the child. The explanation given for this relation is that highly punitive parents instigate aggression because they frustrate the child and act as models for aggressive behavior (Bandura, 1969a, 1969b; Martin, 1975; Feshbach, 1970). The view that children's observation of aggressive models makes them more aggressive has received considerable support from experimental research (e.g., Bandura 1969a, 1969b) and from investigations of the effects of TV violence (Stein & Friedrich, 1975).

Lack of parental warmth is also related to aggression. McCord, McCord, and Howard (1961) investigated this relation in a group of boys studied from ages 9 through 14. After classifying the boys as aggressive, normally assertive, or nonaggressive, McCord reported that 95 percent of the aggressive boys had rejecting, nonwarm parents. The boys in the other two groups had affectionate parents. Cold, rejecting child-rearing practices foster aggressive behavior in children. As Feshbach

Parents who spank their children or who use other forms of aggressive behavior are modeling and teaching aggressive behavior. (Bruce Roberts/Photo Researchers)

(1970, p. 217) points out: "The child's aggressiveness may elicit rejecting responses from the parent, which in turn fosters further aggression, thereby establishing an unhappy cycle of rejection-aggression."

The child's aggressive behavior has also been related to permissive-restrictive practices in child-rearing (Feshbach, 1970; Martin, 1975). And, research (Sears, Maccoby, & Levin, 1957) indicates that the highest percentage of aggressive children (41.7 percent for boys and 38.1 percent for girls) come from homes with highly permissive and highly punishing mothers and the lowest percentage of aggressive children (3.7 percent for boys and 13.3 percent for girls) come from homes with mothers who score low on these two dimensions. This finding does not hold, in general, for younger children. The findings for delinquents also indicate that permissiveness coupled with parental hostility and rejection maximizes the aggressive behavior of children (Feshbach, 1970; Martin, 1975). Finally, some evidence (Martin, 1975) indicates that we must consider the role played by both parents in order to best understand how child rearing relates to childhood aggression. McCord, McCord, and Zola (1959) reported that the greatest percentage of 5- to 13-year-old boys *subsequently* convicted of crimes came from homes in which both mothers and fathers were rejecting. The lowest percentage of boys—32 percent—convicted of crimes came from homes where both parents were loving. Thirty-six percent of the boys from homes with a loving mother and rejecting father, and 46 percent of the boys from homes with a rejecting mother and a loving father were subsequently convicted of crimes. This information clearly demonstrates the importance of assessing the behavior of both parents toward the child. One loving parent more than counteracts the influence of a rejecting parent. And, the data indicate that two rejecting parents have a more deleterious influence than one rejecting parent.

Modeling

Research on the modeling of aggression has dealt with the child's modeling of parental aggression or the modeling of aggression shown on TV or other media. The study of children's modeling of parental aggression stems from research demonstrating that aggressive parents have aggressive children (Bandura & Walters, 1959). This relation holds true particularly for delinquents, whose parents have been characterized as aggressive and prone to conflict (Glueck & Glueck, 1950). Parents are an excellent source of learning social behavior because their children see them as powerful. Unfortunately, children model not only their parents' prosocial but also their inappropriate behavior. In effect, aggressive parents teach their children to behave aggressively. The children learn aggressiveness as a dominant mode of dealing with daily frustrations.

The extensive research on the learning of social behaviors through modeling, especially the seminal work of Albert Bandura (1969a, 1969b) and his colleagues on the imitation of aggression, has led to a significant concern over the effects of the

Watching a violent cartoon
(Peter Vandermark)

amount of aggression children observe on TV. As a result of these concerns, a number of researchers have investigated the effects of TV violence on children's aggressive behavior. (See Friedrich & Stein, 1973, and Stein & Friedrich, 1975 for thorough and easily readable reviews.)

Without doubt, violence pervades television programming. The 3 major networks show an average of 8 violent incidents per prime-time hour (Stein & Friedrich, 1975). Violence here means the use of physical force that involves pain, injury, or killing. Cartoons, which are aimed at young children, are the most violent programs, with 30 violent incidents per hour in 1969. This was reduced to 17 incidents per hour in 1972. Although demonstrating that violence does not pay is said to reduce its potentially harmful effects, the research indicates that even the "good guys" are violent and violence does pay for them.

What then, are the effects of this violence on the child's propensity to engage in aggressive behavior? According to Stein and Friedrich (1975), seeing violent cartoons increases young children's expression of aggression. This holds true more for children who are already aggressive than for those who tend to be unaggressive. For older children, the influence of TV violence on aggression is less clear. Some research shows an increase in aggressiveness after watching violence on TV, but other studies show either no effect or an actual reduction in aggression (Stein & Friedrich, 1975). Older children seem to be more attuned to the situational context of TV violence and are more distressed by it than younger children. Finally, filmed violence is related to increases in adolescent aggressiveness.

We cannot doubt that TV violence *can* result in increased aggression and *does so* both in laboratory and in naturalistic settings. The effects of TV violence on prosocial behavior are still open to question because of the paucity of research. As regards lessening the impact of TV violence on the child, Stein and Friedrich (1975, p. 225) suggest: "The most effective action parents can take is to limit viewing in the early years. If they also convey a definite value system disapproving of aggression, violence may have slightly less impact. If disapproval is combined with child-rearing practices that lead the child to be relatively nonaggressive, the child will probably be less responsive to violence."

SUMMARY

The most important socialization influence on children is the parents, who shape behavior by providing models and by dispensing rewards and punishments. However, children also socialize their parents and influence their behavior.

Studies of the dimensions of restrictiveness versus permissiveness, anxious-emotional involvement versus calm detachment, and warmth versus hostility describe the wide range of parental behaviors and parent types. Parents described by differing combinations of these dimensions use different types of discipline. Hostile parents tend to use power-assertive discipline, i.e., physical punishment or deprivation of privileges. Other forms of discipline include love-withdrawal, expressions of parental anger or disapproval, and induction (explaining why what the child did is not a good thing to do).

The nature of attachment to parents has been extensively studied in both humans and animals. In general, attachment refers to a tendency of the young to seek the proximity of other members of the species. Some have argued that this tendency reflects the evolutionary history of humans. Others feel that attachment in humans is learned through caretaking activities. The infant's clinging, sucking, and following behaviors maintain contact with other members of the species, while crying and smiling act to bring others into contact with the infant. Attachment first appears at about 7 months of age and reaches a peak intensity between 12 and 18 months of age. One consequence of attachment is that the attached person acts as a secure base for exploring the environment. A second is that attachment to other people prepares the child for learning social behavior.

Attachment is related to parental interactions with children. Some infants are unattached and others are insecurely attached. These infants tend to have mothers who are less sensitive to them and who communicate little with them. Securely attached infants have mothers who are sensitive to their infant's signals and who communicate with them and are accepting of them.

Attachment to the father has only recently been extensively studied. The evidence indicates that infants are attached to their fathers as much as to their mothers. However, under stress the infant seems to prefer comforting from the mother, probably because she has provided this more frequently than the father in the past. In less stressful situations the father is sought out equally as much as the mother, which probably relates to the more frequent play activities in which the father engages with his children.

Dependency also develops during very early childhood. Dependency refers to the child behaving as though people as people are rewarding in and of themselves. Dependency is learned by parental rewards. Investigations of the relationship between parental types and dependency indicate no general correspondence.

Aggressiveness, too, is learned, especially by parental reward and modeling. As children get older they use more verbal aggression and less physical aggression. Fantasy aggression also increases until about adolescence. Boys tend to be more aggressive than girls, but this may be due to differences in socialization.

CHAPTER 12

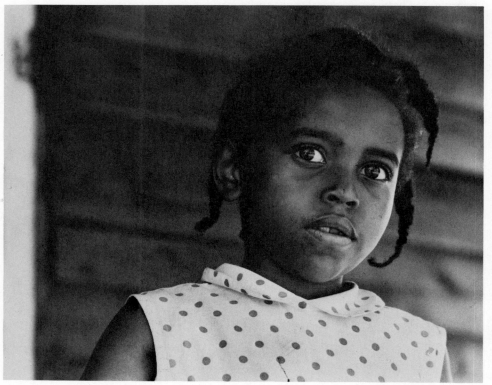

(Bob Combs/Photo Researchers)

THE DEVELOPMENT
OF MORAL THINKING
AND BEHAVIOR

PSYCHOLOGISTS' RECENT increased interest in studying moral development stems from several sources. One is a concern about better understanding how societies evolve social rules and codes (Kohlberg, 1969). All societies have systems of written and unwritten rules and values that govern the interpersonal behaviors of people.

A second impetus to studying moral development comes from advances in psychological theory that make the systematic study of morality more feasible now than it was previously (Aronfreed, 1976). Early writing on the issues was left to philosophers, who formulated 3 doctrines concerning moral development (Hoffman, 1970) and from whose work contemporary theory and research stem. The doctrine of *original sin* assumed that parents had to intervene to save the child's soul. This point of view is currently represented by Freud's psychoanalytic theory (1949) which is concerned with the development of conscience, which Freud called the superego. As we noted in Chapter 10, the superego represents the internalization of the parents' moral standards.

According to the doctrine of *innate purity*, the child is basically moral, or pure, and learns immorality from adult society. As a result, the corrupting influence of adult society on the child must be minimized. This philosophical view is represented in the theory of Piaget (1932), who argues that morality develops from the acquisition of autonomy emerging from the need to get along with peers. Piaget believes parents alone do not allow autonomy to develop, since the child's behavior is governed by the parents rather than the child.

The third philosophical doctrine is the notion of a *tabula rasa* (blank slate), which assumes the child is neither innately pure nor corrupt. Rather the child's moral behavior reflects only environmental influences. The contemporary representative of this position is the learning-theory approach to child development.

A third impetus to the study of moral development may be found in psychologists' attempts to extend their theories to the exploration of increasingly wide-ranging aspects of human behavior (Aronfreed, 1976). Social-learning theories about the role of models and reinforcement in controlling behavior have found fertile ground in the study of moral behavior (Aronfreed, 1976; Mischel &

Mischel, 1976). Similarly, cognitive developmental theorists, working from Piaget's (1932) seminal writing, have tried to extend cognitive theory to explain the development of morality.

A number of social psychologists, e.g., McDougall (1908) and Parsons (1960) have also written about moral development. After the early works of Freud (1949) and Piaget (1932), however, all writing on the subject was sparse until the late 1960s, when much research and theorizing were undertaken on the processes involved in moral development.

In this chapter we review theory and research on children's moral behavior and moral thinking as well as a number of factors that influence them.

Although definitions of **morality** vary with the theory being discussed (Lickona, 1976b), Hogan's (1973) definition is sufficiently broad to cover most instances. He defines morality as "a system of rules that are external to people, designed to guide social or interpersonal behavior, and which may to some degree be codified and spelled out" (Hogan, 1973, p. 219). Note that this definition includes all types of social interaction, including prosocial behavior (Chapter 13), and not just those we typically associate with morals; it includes behavior toward friends, teachers, and peers, as well as behavior falling under formally codified laws.

Psychoanalytic Theory

Since Freud's psychoanalytic theory of superego development was detailed in Chapter 10, we will explicate only those aspects of the theory that are relevant to moral development. According to Freud, the formation of the conscience, or super-ego, and thus the acquisition of moral behavior, is conceived as a result of the resolution of the Oedipal complex. The superego, which represents the internalization of adult standards, develops through identification with the parent of the same sex (Freud 1923, 1924). Society ensures its survival through identification by imposing its standards on the individual, who conveys these standards to the next generation.

Both boys and girls identify with the same-sex parent out of fear or anxiety about parental behavior (loss of love or aggression). As Bronfenbrenner (1960) notes, the child may identify with any or all of three aspects of the parent: overt behavior, motives, or aspirations for the child. Which of these are incorporated by the child is a question for research and may depend on the form of identification. "It may be that one process, such as anaclitic identification, is more likely to result in the emulation of standards, while another, such as identification with the aggressor, leads to the adoption of parental motives and acts" (Bronfenbrenner, 1960, p. 24).

Stopping a child from doing something wrong is more effective in promoting moral development than punishing after the fact. (Elizabeth Hamlin)

Although the exact basis of identification is unclear, and, indeed, is the subject of considerable controversy, Freud's theory has stimulated considerable research on the effects of parents' behavior on the child's development.

Hartshorne and May Research

One implication of Freudian theory is that because of identification with a single individual, the various aspects of moral behavior should be highly consistent with each other since they are all part of the same integrated personality structure. This implication was tested by Hartshorne and May (1927, 1928, 1929, 1930), who administered a series of tests to children and adolescents aged 8 to 16 in order to measure cheating, lying, and stealing. The most important findings of the Hartshorne and May research were that (1) cheating was normally distributed and (2) that cheating in one situation did not predict it very well in another situation. In other words, the children could not be classified as "cheaters" or "noncheaters." Almost all the children cheated, but they varied in the amount of risk they would take in being caught. Hartshorne and May concluded that cheating was largely determined by the situation and that there was no general trait of honesty or morality.

A reanalysis of Hartshorne and May's data by Burton (1963, 1976) tempers this last conclusion. Burton's analysis of these tests revealed a general "honesty" trait, indicating some stability in honesty across situations, specifically with regard to resistance to temptation to cheat, lie, or steal. Like Hartshorne and May, Burton concluded that similar situations tended to elicit similar cheating, but he did not argue that this implied people could be classified as either honest or dishonest. That this might be the case, however, was demonstrated in research by Peck and Havighurst (1960) who reported a trait of outward conformity to rules. At one end of this dimension is the person who follows rules; at the other end is the person who thinks social rules do not apply to him and who regularly violates them. The evidence on the consistency of moral behavior, then, indicates that people behave consistently in similar situations but that there is little consistency across situations (Burton, 1976).

Parental Discipline

As noted in Chapter 10, psychoanalytic theory relies heavily on the importance of parents' child-rearing practices. In identification, the child learns to experience guilt as a form of self-punishment based on parental discipline. Guilt arises whenever the child violates a prohibition or is tempted to do so (Hoffman 1975c, 1976). To avoid guilt, the child must behave in a manner consistent with the values and morals incorporated through identification with the parent. When this is done the person feels pride, which reinforces continuing to behave according to the rules. Early in childhood, the individual's behavior is controlled by parental dictates, not because of fear of punishment by the parents but rather because the child has identified with the parents' values and moral standards. These standards become part of the child's own value and moral system and guide his behavior to some extent.

Investigations of the relation between parental disciplinary practices and childrens' moral development have employed a number of indices of children's internalization of adult moral standards: **resistance to temptation,** the degree to which a child will resist violating a standard when the chances of getting caught are remote or nonexistent; **guilt,** the internal emotional response following transgression; *reactions to transgression*, the child's moral judgments about wrongdoing; and, *confession*, admitting a transgression.

HOFFMAN AND SALTZSTEIN RESEARCH.   In a well-designed study, Hoffman and Saltzstein (1967) assessed the relation between moral development and parental discipline and affection in a sample of 146 middle-class and 91 lower-class boys, and 124 middle-class and 83 lower-class girls. All were seventh-graders. Hoffman and Saltzstein hypothesized that induction techniques (explaining the basis for dissatisfaction with the child's behavior) would be most closely related to moral development. This hypothesis was based on the notion that, unlike punishment based on power assertion or love-withdrawal, induction techniques provide the child with knowledge that his behavior may be harmful to someone else, thereby capitalizing on the child's capacity for empathy. Hoffman and Saltzstein argued that this appeal to empathy motivates the child to develop moral controls. Since neither power assertion nor love-withdrawal appeal to the child's capacity to experience empathy, this cognitive component of discipline is lost.

Two measures of morality were obtained from each child. Guilt was assessed by asking the child to complete two stories about a child of the same sex and age who had broken a rule. The subjects were asked to tell what happens and how the child in the story thinks and feels. Responses giving evidence of self-critical reactions were scored as guilt responses. Moral judgment was assessed by having the child judge several hypothetical situations involving transgressions, for example, stealing and committing various other crimes. Children's overt reactions to transgression were assessed with teachers' reports of the child's behavior when "caught doing something wrong" and with measures of the child's confessions obtained from the mother. Consideration for other children was measured by **sociometric techniques,** that is, through nominations by peers of children who cared most about the feelings of others. Identification was assessed by measuring the child's perceived similarity to his or her parents, admiration for them, and desire to emulate them.

Parental disciplinary practices were determined by reports from the children and, for the middle-class subjects, through interviews with the parents. Both the child's and the parents' responses were coded to indicate the predominant type of parental discipline—power-assertive, love-withdrawal, or induction. Parental use of affection was determined by asking the children to rate their parents' use of 19 forms of behavior indicating affection. Parents were also asked to estimate their use of approval when the child behaved well. In sum, there were 6 indices of moral development and 4 measures of parental discipline. The data for each sex-social subgroup were analyzed separately. For each index of moral development children

Inductive discipline encourages the development of moral thinking. (Peter Vandermark)

scoring high and children scoring low were identified and then compared on the child-rearing scores and, for the middle-class children, the interviews with the parents.

The findings may be summarized as follows.

1. For middle-class children:
   a. Maternal use of power assertion was consistently related to weak moral development.
   b. Maternal use of induction was consistently associated with advanced moral development.
   c. Maternal use of love-withdrawal related negatively, but infrequently, to moral development.
   d. Paternal discipline techniques related infrequently and inconsistently to moral development.
   e. Parental affection related positively to moral development, much more so for the mother than the father.

2. For lower-class children:
   a. There were few relationships between children's moral development and children's reports of parental discipline techniques. The relationships which were significant were inconsistent and inconclusive.
   b. There were few (3) relationships between parental affection and moral development. The 3 significant relationships were positive.

SUPPORT FOR HOFFMAN AND SALTZSTEIN. Hoffman (1970, 1976) and Saltzstein (1976) have reviewed the findings of a number of investigations of the relation between disciplinary techniques and children's moral development. The findings support the results of the Hoffman and Saltzstein (1967) study. The mother's frequent use of power-assertive discipline was related to weak moral development, and maternal induction and affection were associated with moral growth. The literature also supports Hoffman and Saltzstein's finding that love-withdrawal does not relate to moral development. These findings are most clear-cut for the moral development measures of guilt and internal moral orientation, and they are less clear for resistance to temptation and confession. Hoffman (1970, 1976) has noted that the latter two measures may involve complex decisions that mask or alter the relationships. Measures of such states as guilt do not involve decisions based on consideration of consequences and alternate courses of action. Saltzstein (1976, p. 209) has summarized these findings and interprets them as follows:

> Frequent use of power assertion, especially physical punishment, retards the development of any kind of internal morality. Psychological techniques, especially pointing out the consequences of actions for others, facilitate the development of internal morality. Reasoning is conducive to the development of an altruistic or humanistic morality, that is, one based primarily on consideration for others. Love withdrawal is conducive to the development of a conformist or conventional morality, that is, one based on rigid conformity to rules for their own sake or in deference to authority.

Research also supports the findings of Hoffman and Saltzstein on the importance of the father's use of discipline to the moral development of children (Saltzstein, 1976). Few relationships between the father's disciplinary techniques and children's moral development have been reported, and the few that have appear to fit no pattern. For boys, however, the presence of the father seems to be important. Boys without fathers tend to score lower on indices of moral development than boys with fathers (Hoffman, 1970). This finding may have two explanations. First, fathers may provide instruction about moral standards in nondisciplinary situations. Second, the father's disciplinary role may be critical only in exceptional circumstances (delinquency, for example), since mothers handle discipline in ordinary circumstances.

The social-class differences reported by Hoffmann and Saltzstein have not been investigated in other research, most of which has been conducted with middle-class children. Hoffman (1970) conjectures that the basis of the social-class differences lies in the predominantly power-assertive disciplinary practices used in the lower classes. When power assertion is the primary mode of discipline, it may wash out the relationships between other disciplinary practices and moral development. In addition, the father tends to be the primary disciplinary agent in the lower classes, thus diluting the mother's influence on moral development. The effect of the mother's disciplinary techniques may also be weakened by the greater need for the mother to spend time away from her children, for example, if she works. This combination of factors apparently lessens the relation between maternal discipline techniques and moral development in lower-class children. As Hoffman (1970) suggests, one result of the mother's lack of influence may be that peers play a more important role in moral development among lower-class children than among middle-class children.

These naturalistic investigations support the hypothesis that discipline is an important factor in the child's development of morality. We should keep in mind, however, that data from self-reports and from naturalistic settings are often difficult to interpret in terms of cause and effect. Therefore, we review some of the laboratory research on the effects of discipline on moral development.

Discipline and Moral Development: Laboratory Research

Punishment administered when the child begins to perform the transgression should be more effective in preventing repetition of that behavior than punishment administered later, for example, after the undesired behavior is over. Mowrer (1960a, b) has argued this point of view by noting that punishment administered near the beginning of a behavioral sequence will produce a strong association between fear and these first responses in the sequence. This fear will arouse anxiety in subsequent attempts to initiate the deviant behavior. If the anxiety is strong enough, it will produce avoidance responses, which in turn will be reinforced by anxiety reduction. As a result, the deviant behavior will not be performed.

In contrast, punishment administered late in the sequence, or after it is over, will produce anxiety that is only weakly associated with the beginning of the deviant behavior. If the completion of the behavior is highly reinforcing, the anxiety may have no effect. As a result, the deviant behavior may be repeated. One testable hypothesis, then, is that the earlier punishment occurs in a response sequence, the more effective it should be in preventing subsequent occurrences of the punished behavior.

The research generally supports Mowrer's hypothesis. In two experiments (Aronfreed, 1966; Aronfreed & Reber, 1965) 8- to 10-year old children were presented with 10 pairs of attractive or unattractive toys and were instructed to pick up one toy from each pair and describe it. If the child chose an attractive toy, the experimenter said "no" and deprived the child of candy. The children were randomly assigned to 1 of 4 timing-of-punishment conditions. Children were punished either (1) when the child reached for the toy, (2) immediately after the child lifted the toy, (3) 6 seconds after the child lifted the toy, or (4) when the child had completed describing the toy (10 to 12 seconds after the toy had been lifted). After 10 trials, during which the children quickly learned to pick the unattractive toy, they were left alone with an attractive and an unattractive toy and the time until they began to play with the attractive toy was recorded. Time to play with the attractive toy was related to the timing of punishment in the direction predicted by Mowrer's theory. The sooner the punishment after the beginning of the disapproved act during the 10 training trials, the longer the time before handling the attractive toy in the test situation. This finding held for both boys and girls, and with both male and female experimenters. Others have reported similar findings (e.g., Leizer & Rogers, 1974; Parke & Walters, 1967; Walters, Parke & Cane, 1965). These studies lend support to the hypothesis that punishment administered early in a behavioral sequence aids the development of resistance to temptation.

It is unfortunate that there has been little laboratory research on the relation between discipline by induction and moral behavior. The naturalistic studies we have reviewed indicate that this form of discipline was closely related to moral development. Some research (e.g., Leizer & Rogers, 1974) supports the notion that induction techniques are superior to physical or verbal punishment—both immediately and two weeks later—but other research (e.g., LaVoie, 1974) does not. In both of these studies, resistance to deviation was used as the measure of morality. Until further research on the use of induction is conducted, the issue remains confused.

Some Conclusions About Psychoanalytic Theory

The findings of both the naturalistic and experimental research on the relation between disciplinary techniques and moral development provide only partial support for the psychoanalytic theory of moral development. Both types of research indicate that power-assertive discipline is related to moral development—negatively in the naturalistic studies and, with respect to timing of punishment, positively in the experimental studies. We can account for this discrepancy if we assume that parents use power-assertive techniques primarily at the end of an undesired act, thus producing the negative relations reported in the naturalistic studies. In contrast to this stable relationship, love-withdrawal showed only a weak, inconsistent relation to moral development in both types of research. This lack of relation is unfortunate for psychoanalytic theory, since it is at the heart of the concept of identification, particularly anaclitic identification.

The naturalistic evidence relating the use of induction to moral development indicated that it fostered moral development, probably by providing the child with a cognitive basis for making decisions about the morality of behavior. The paucity of experimental evidence, however, leaves the direction of causality unclear. In addition, the cognitive component in moral development may be explained in more productive ways than those employed by psychoanalytic theory.

Social-Learning Theory

According to learning theory, moral behavior is acquired through the same mechanisms as any other behavior, namely, teaching (Gewirtz, 1969) or modeling and generalized imitation (Bandura, 1969a; Gewirtz, 1969).

The bulk of research on imitation in moral development has dealt with the internalization of moral standards (Mischel & Mischel, 1976). As noted in Chapter 10, social-learning theorists (e.g., Bandura, 1969) believe the psychoanalytic concept of identification is identical to the social-learning theory concept of imitation. Identification is said to occur when an individual's behavior matches that of a model. According to social-learning theory, identification is a continuous process of response acquisition and modification resulting from teaching and vicarious experiences with parents and other models. This is in contrast to the psychoanalytic view which sees identification as a process ending by the age of 4 or 5.

Whereas psychoanalytic theory emphasizes unobservable processes, such as id, ego, or superego, social-learning theory stresses observable processes. For example, the psychoanalytic concept of conscience, or superego, is explained through the conditioning of anxiety to specific situations or behaviors. This is a result of the pairing of punishment with disapproved behaviors; the pain and anxiety that results is conditioned to the undesirable behavior and becomes a conditioned response to doing or even thinking about doing the forbidden act (Eysenck, 1976). Eysenck (1976, p. 109) further points out that "this conditioned anxiety is experienced by the child as conscience. The acquisition of this conscience is, of course, facilitated by labeling, as is its generalization over different types of actions. By calling a variety of actions bad, evil or naughty, we encourage the child to identify them all in one category, and to react in the future with anxiety to everything thus labeled." The conscience, then, is viewed as a result of learned responses to specific actions or classes of actions. As learning progresses the external control of others over the child's behavior becomes unnecessary; the child comes to administer its own rewards (pride) and punishments (guilt) for its behavior (Maccoby, 1968).

Like psychoanalytic theory, social-learning theory stresses the role of parents or other models in this learning. Parents both teach and model behavior for their offspring. Maccoby (1968, p. 242) has emphasized this point in her discussion of how children learn social behavior.

> . . . the parents serve as the most consistently available and salient models as well as the primary dispensers of reinforcement during the early part of the child's life. Furthermore, although a child may *acquire* elements of social behavior through observation of a model with whom he is not directly interacting, the *performance* of the behavior tends to be controlled by the immediate reinforcement contingencies; hence the people who are in a position to control these contingencies will have the greatest effect on what the child *does*, even if they have less exclusive control over what he learns how to do. The parents, then, are the central figures in early socialization, and this makes them central for the whole of moral development, for in social-learning theory, early learned behavior tends to persist. Behavior once learned will be maintained unless the reinforcement contingencies are changed.
> . . . Stability of behavior tends to be maintained by the tendency of the individual to seek or stay in environments which will not demand change of him.

The social-learning approach, then, has concentrated on behavioral manifestations of morality. Resistance to temptation, the ability to delay engaging in a forbidden act, has been a popular experimental paradigm in part because it reflects the child's willingness and ability to follow a moral rule.

Slaby and Parke Research

A study by Slaby and Parke (1971) is a good example of research on children's ability to resist commiting a transgression. The experiment examined two aspects of modeling on resistance to deviation: (1) the consequences experienced by an observed model and (2) the reaction of the model to these consequences. The subjects were 7-year-old boys and girls, 66 of each sex. Each child was seated at a table on which were several attractive toys. The experimenter told the child that they were going to play a game, but he could not remember where it was. The experimenter also said that the toys on the table were for someone else and that the child was not to play with them. The child then saw a film in which an adult told a boy to read a book and not play with some toy. The adult in the film then left, and the child played with the toys for 3 minutes, after which the adult returned. Half the subjects saw the adult reward the child for playing with the toys and half saw the child punished. The boy in the film showed either positive affect (smiling), negative affect (crying), or no affect following the adult's reward or punishment. At this point, the film ended, and the experimenter gave the child a dull book to read and left him or her alone in the room for 15 minutes while going to look for the game. The number of times the child played with the toys, the latency to the first touching of the toys, and the duration of playing with the toys were recorded by observers looking through one-way mirrors.

Slaby and Parke hypothesized that children observing a model who was rewarded would deviate more than children who had observed a model being punished, and, furthermore, that the frequency of deviation would increase if the model exhibited a positive affective response and decrease if the model exhibited a negative affective response, compared with the frequency of deviations shown by children observing a model showing no affective responses. The first hypothesis was supported—children observing a rewarded model deviated more frequently and longer than children who observed a punished model, although this effect was significant only for boys, perhaps because a boy model was used in the film. The second hypothesis was only partially supported. Children who observed a rewarded model deviated more and longer if the model displayed positive rather than negative affect, with deviation following no affect falling in between. Children observing a punished model deviated more if the model exhibited negative affect than if the model exhibited positive affect, with the no affect group again falling in the middle.

These findings about the effects of reward and punishment to a model replicate the findings of a number of other experiments (e.g., Walters, Leat & Mezei, 1963; Walters & Parke, 1964; Walters, Parke & Cane, 1965). These studies make it clear that exposure to a rewarded model has a **disinhibitory effect** and exposure to a punished model an **inhibitory effect** on the child's behavior.

The findings about the affect displayed by the model point up the complexity of this research. The results owing to the affect displayed by the model were as predicted for the children observing a rewarded model, but not for children observing a punished model. Slaby and Parke argued that the children observing a rewarded model cry and a punished model smile must have rejected them as models because of the inappropriateness of the affect, given the child's knowledge of his own behavior in similar circumstances. Similarity of the observer's affect to the model's appears to be important in eliciting imitation. Since the child finds it incongruous to be sad about a reward or happy about punishment, the model is seen as dissimilar to the child. Support for this conjecture comes from experiments (e.g., Fry, 1977) indicating that children who experience success and have positive affect resist temptation longer than those who experience failure and feel sad.

A number of experiments have been conducted to investigate how much the similarity of the model to the child influences the child's imitation (e.g., Rosekrans, 1967; Tannenbaum & Gear, 1965). Similarity appears to heighten the inhibition/disinhibition effects (Chapter 10) of observing a model. However the dimensions along which similarity may vary are many, and, unfortunately, many of those critical to imitative behavior have yet to be isolated.

Research within the tradition of social-learning theory has been conducted on a number of other aspects of moral development, for example, aggression (e.g.,

Bandura, Ross & Ross, 1963; Bandura, 1965), self-reward (e.g., Bandura & Kupers, 1964; Bandura & Whalen, 1966; Thelen & Fryreur, 1971), and delay of gratification (e.g., Mischel, 1965; Bandura & Mischel, 1965). In all these areas the behavior of a model influences the subsequent performance of the observing child.

Some Conclusions About Social-Learning Theory

Research on moral development from the social-learning theory tradition has dealt mainly with environmental effects on children's performance in situations quite similar to those in which a model was observed. In describing the processes of observational learning and imitation, researchers have identified several motivational factors in children's moral behavior. The model of morality in this research is basically a **hedonistic** one (Hoffman, 1970), in which the child relies on rewards and punishments for clues to appropriate behavior. In other words, the child's notions of morality are initially based on external sanctions. Before we can evaluate this research, however, we must consider the cognitive contributions to understanding morality.

Cognitive-Developmental Approach

The cognitive-developmental approach to moral development follows the principles detailed in our discussion of cognitive development (Chapter 6) and the cognitive-developmental approach to social development (Chapter 10). The cognitive-developmental approach tries to describe the thought processes involved in moral

Younger children play games with less complex rules than older children. This is partly because they have a less mature understanding of the nature of rules. (Michael Serino/The Picture Cube)

judgment. It thus has a focus somewhat different from the social-learning theories, which deal primarily with behavior and not judgment. The basic notion is that these thought processes develop in a sequence of stages in the same manner as the stages of intellectual development discussed in Chapter 6. First, each stage is an integrated whole, qualitatively different from any other stage. Second, as development progresses, the processes of thinking in each stage are integrated into those in the next higher stage, so that an emerging stage is an integration of the old and the new. Third, the stages of development make up an invariant sequence. Fourth, age is not equivalent to stage.

Piaget (1932) and Kohlberg (1963 a, b; 1969, 1976) are the chief advocates of the cognitive-developmental approach. Those interested in more detail are encouraged to read the reviews of Hoffman (1970), Flavell (1963), and Lickona (1976b).

Piaget's Theory

Piaget has studied the development of two aspects of childhood morality—the child's respect for social rules and the child's sense of justice (Flavell, 1963)—and has tried to explain the cognitive-developmental changes in these two areas.

To study children's respect for social rules, Piaget studied their conformity to the rules of a game. He gave children some marbles and asked them to explain how the game was played. He also asked them whether new rules could be made up and if they would be fair. This last question tested the child's understanding of the nature of rules (Flavell, 1963).

From these investigations, Piaget developed a stage theory of the child's understanding of and conformity to rules (Flavell, 1963). Up to about age 3 (Stage 1), the children play with marbles in an apparently ruleless fashion. In Stage 2, from about 3 to 5, children imitate the rule-governed behavior of older children, but their play is idiosyncratic and socially isolated until about 7 to 8 years of age (Stage 3). At about this time, children regard rules as unchangeable, as though they came from some divine source. New rules and changes in old rules are seen as unfair even if everyone agrees to them. After about age 11 to 12 (Stage 4), children alter rules to fit unusual situations and may invent new rules to cover special circumstances. Rules are then seen as changeable.

To investigate the child's developing sense of justice, Piaget told children stories about people engaged in wrongdoing. The child was then asked why the acts were wrong or which of two acts was more wrong and why. For example, in one story the children were asked to judge who was naughtier, a child who broke 15 cups through an unavoidable accident or a child who broke 1 cup while sneaking some jam. As a second example, children were asked which of two girls was guiltier, the one who stole a roll to give to a poor and hungry friend or the one who stole a (less costly) ribbon for herself. Each story juxtaposes differences in intent (good or bad) and differences in damage (large or small).

On the basis of these and other data, Piaget formulated certain ideas about children's understanding of rules and justice. **Retributive justice** concerns two ways in which children think punishment should be meted out for misdeeds. One form of punishment, used more by younger children, was **expiatory justice:** the punishment should be in direct proportion to the seriousness of the offense, but its form need not be logically related to the misdeed. Older children seemed to think that the punishment should fit the crime in some way so the wrongdoer will better appreciate the consequences of his act. The purpose of this form of punishment, which Piaget called **punishment by reciprocity,** is not to inflict punishment for its own sake but rather to show the consequences of an act through punishment that is logically related to the misdeed (Flavell, 1963). An example from Flavell (1963) illustrates this point. Suppose a child fails to bring home food after being requested to do so. A spanking would be an example of expiative punishment for there is no logical connection between the misdeed and the punishment. Reducing the size of the child's meal or refusing to do a favor for the child would be examples of retributive punishment, the former because less food is available and the latter because the child refused to do a favor.

From these findings, Piaget (1932) developed a theory of the emergence of moral judgment. He found two stages of moral development. In the first stage, called **morality of constraint** or **moral realism,** a person obeys rules because they are believed to be rigid and unalterable. Behavior is viewed as either right or wrong, depending on whether it follows established social rules. Younger children believe in what Piaget has termed **immanent justice,** the notion that God punishes people for their misdeeds.

The older child operates according to a **morality of cooperation** or **reciprocity.** At this second stage of development, rules are viewed as being determined by reciprocal agreements and depend on the social circumstances. The child realizes that there is no absolute right and wrong. Rather, notions of justice include considerations of intention. Breaking 15 cups accidentally is viewed as less bad than breaking 1 cup while trying to take some forbidden jam (Lickona, 1976c). Following moral rules is viewed as necessary to the functioning of society, and punishment is viewed as suited to the misdeed rather than simply meted out by authority.

Maturation affects moral development through its function in promoting general cognitive development (see Chapter 6). Experience affects moral development primarily through peers. The interactions between adults and children are mostly **heteronomous**—one-sided and authoritarian; that is, since adults tend to be dominant over children, children view adult rules as absolute (Lickona, 1976c). According to Piaget, moral development cannot take place under these conditions. Rather, mutual give-and-take, which occurs primarily with peers, is necessary. Interactions with peers can affect the child's conception of morality in two ways. First, by sharing decisions with peers, children gain confidence in their ability to apply rules to situations and to change rules. Rules thus come to be viewed as the result of

Isolation from peers may be detrimental because peer group interaction promotes moral thinking. (Leonard Freed/Magnum Photos)

agreement and cooperation among people. Rules also come to be viewed as flexible rather than unchanging. Second, through experiences in **role taking** (Selman, 1976) with peers, children become aware that they think and feel about things in ways similar to their peers. Psychologists use the term "role taking" to refer to how we learn to understand others by taking their point of view as well as the relation between their perspective and ours (Selman, 1973, 1976; Shantz, 1975). This realization helps the child view the utility of rules as benefiting the group. It also helps the child understand the motives behind the actions of others and thus provides a basis for moral judgments to be made on intention rather than overt behavior alone.

SOME CONCLUSIONS ABOUT PIAGET'S THEORY.   Piaget's writings make it clear that the importance of interaction with peers in promoting moral development is due to its **reciprocity.** The heteronomous nature of the interaction between adults and children precludes the child's testing alternatives in a neutral give-and-take manner. Interaction with peers, on the other hand, is mutual and many-sided. The child is allowed to participate in making up and changing rules and to take various roles that provide insight into alternative views of rules and situations. This mutual and reciprocal interaction, together with cognitive development, promotes the moral development of the child. Unless development is arrested, for example, by overstrict parents or cultural constraints that minimize mutual and reciprocal interactions with peers, the child will move from a state of moral realism to a state of autonomy, a new and higher level of moral orientation.

Research stimulated by Piaget's theory has aimed at assessing stages of moral development in 5 areas: (1) relativism of perspective versus absolutism, (2) objective view of punishment versus immanent justice, (3) intentions versus consequences,

(4) relative versus expiative justice, and (5) conformity to peer expectations versus obedience to adult authority (Hoffman, 1970; Lickona, 1976b). With few exceptions, the findings have supported Piaget's theoretical assertions about age trends for these traits. This impressive array of data is very compelling, for the age trends were not tempered by IQ, social class, or race. The only limiting factor of Piaget's theory is that it may be applicable only to Western cultures (Hoffman, 1970).

SOCIAL LEARNING ARGUMENTS.   The stages postulated by Piaget have stimulated some controversial research. Social-learning theorists have argued that morality does not develop in stages and is unrelated to age. They think it develops and is modifiable through environmental intervention. Exposing the child to differing environmental experiences should alter moral judgments through learning regardless of the child's cognitive level of development.

The influence of models on children's moral judgments was assessed in an experiment by Bandura and MacDonald (1963). The subjects, boys aged 5 to 11, were divided into 2 groups, one of which exhibited primarily an **objective moral orientation** and the other primarily a **subjective** one. The former made judgments on the basis of damage done and the latter on the basis of the transgressor's intentions. Each of these 2 groups were further divided into 3 experimental treatments. One group observed an adult model who expressed moral judgments counter to those of the child's orientation, and the child was verbally reinforced for imitating the model's responses. The second group observed the adult model but received no reinforcement for matching the model's responses. Children in the third group observed no models but were reinforced for expressing moral judgments opposite to their dominant orientations. The dependent variable was the number of objective judgments made by subjectively oriented children and the number of subjective judgments made by objectively oriented children during the base (initial assessment) period, the experimental treatment period, and the immediate posttest period, which was conducted in a different social setting with the model and reinforcement procedures absent.

The results are illustrated in Figure 12-1. Children who observed a model altered their moral judgments and matched those of the model regardless of the reinforcement contingencies. Children who did not observe a model but were reinforced for moral judgments opposite to their primary orientation tended not to change, especially if they were subjectively oriented. Bandura and MacDonald argued that these data supported the notion that children may learn moral behavior from observing models. Such a notion conflicts with the conceptions of Piaget (1932) and others who have argued that moral development unfolds in a series of stages as a result of a cognitive restructuring of interactions between the child and the environment.

The shifts in moral judgment reported by Bandura and MacDonald (1963) have also been reproduced in several other experiments (e.g., Crowley, 1968). These

FIGURE 12-1   *Mean Percentage of Moral Judgments Opposite to Child's Primary Orientation*

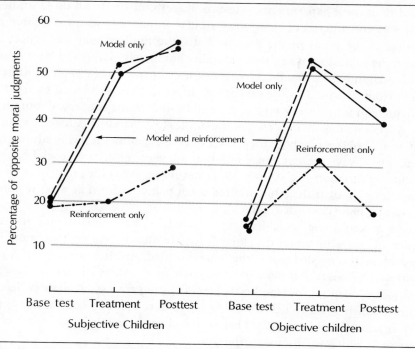

SOURCE: Bandura, A., and MacDonald, F. The influence of social reinforcement and the behavior models in shaping children's moral judgments. *Journal of Abnormal Social Psychology,* 1963, 67 (3), 274–281.

changes seem to persist for some time following exposure. Cowan, Langer, Heaven-rich, and Nathanson (1969), for example, reported shifts in moral judgments that lasted 2 weeks, and LeFurgy and Woloshin (1969) reported shifts in adolescents' moral judgment that lasted as long as 3 months. These experiments seem to show that moral judgments may be shaped through learning.

Although this evidence seems to call into question the theory that moral development takes place in stages in conjunction with intellectual development (e.g., Piaget, 1932; Kohlberg, 1963a, b; 1969) this may not be so (Cowan et al., 1969). Low-level moral judgments—for example, those concerning the consequences experienced by the central character of a story depicting a moral dilemma—predominate in young children. According to strict interpretation of social-learning theory, this should not be the case, since adults presumably do not exhibit these low-level judgments in their everyday interactions. If children do make moral judgments modeled on the adults they encounter, then it is difficult to explain this low-level behavior in young children and also the subsequent changes in moral judgments with age.

DEFECTS IN THE SOCIAL-LEARNING STUDIES.   Hoffman (1970) has noted two defects in the design of the social-learning studies of moral stages that he rightly argues limit the validity of these experiments as tests of Piaget's theory. In all three studies, the posttest was constructed of items very similar in nature and on the same moral dimension as the items of the pretest. Thus, the findings may not reflect a real change in the subject's notions about morality but merely changes in overt responses to a particular moral dimension. Were the posttests made up of items on a dimension different from that used in the pretesting, the results could be used to argue more convincingly in favor of a change in the child's underlying concept of morality.

A second problem in several of the studies (e.g., Bandura & MacDonald, 1963; Cowan et al., 1969) is that both the model and the experimenter were adults and one of them was always present. Since children are very sensitive to social cues in an experimental situation (e.g., Dusek, 1971; Stevenson, 1961) they may have given the response they thought the adult wanted them to give, a form of what is known as experimenter bias (Rosenthal, 1966).

As a result, the social-learning research is inconclusive as a test of the sequence of stages of moral development postulated by Piaget. One view is that further research is needed before the issue is settled. An alternative view, suggested by Kohlberg (1969), is that moral development does involve structural changes but that Piaget's conception and methods of investigation are less adequate in describing morality than they are in describing cognitive development. Following a very persuasive argument, Kohlberg (1969) has proposed an alternative stage theory of moral development which we discuss further on.

INTENTIONALITY AND PIAGET'S TECHNIQUES.   A third area of research on Piaget's theory has examined his techniques for assessing moral development. These studies specifically focus on the issue of the child's use of intentionality rather than the consequences of the act in judging moral acts. One line of research, concentrating on the stories developed by Piaget, is an attempt to clarify the nature of children's responses. An experiment conducted by Costanzo, Coie, Grument, and Farnill (1973) exemplifies this research.

Recall that Piaget's stories involve either good or bad intention, which is always paired with a bad consequence. One aspect of the study by Costanzo et al. examined the children's use of outcomes and intentions in making moral judgments. Both good and bad intentions were followed by either good or bad outcomes. The subjects were 20 children each from kindergarten and second and fourth grades. Each child heard 2 stories from 1 of the 4 combinations of intention and consequences and judged the goodness or badness of the main character and whether or not he was helpful or nice. The findings indicate that age differences in children's use of intentionality in evaluating another's actions depends upon the consequences. For stories with good consequences, all children used intention, which is presumably a higher level of moral thinking. For stories with bad consequences, the use of intention increased with age. These findings conflict with previous studies using Piaget-type stories and suggest that children may use intentionality considerably earlier than previously thought (Buchanan & Thompson, 1973).

Indeed, it now seems that the construction of Piaget's stories (Berg-Cross, 1975; Feldman, Klosson, Parsons, Rholes & Ruble, 1976; Keasey, 1977; Peterson, Peterson & Finley, 1974)—whether or not the child is asked to use intention to judge his own or somebody else's behavior (Keasey, 1977)—and the order of the statements concerning intention and consequences in the story (Austin, Ruble & Trabasso, 1977; Feldman et al., 1976) all influence the use of intention in moral judgments, especially by younger (ages 5–8) children. By age 5 or so, children are aware of the significance of considering somebody's intention when they judge that person's behavior (Imamoglu, 1975). Most kindergartners and first-graders also apply the criterion of intention to judgments about their own behavior more than they do to the behavior of another child (Keasey, 1977). Children's memory abilities are also related to their use of intention cues in judging someone's behavior. If the cue to intention (for example, to eat forbidden cookies or trying to help mother) is noted later in the story, it influences judgments more than if it occurs earlier (Feldman et al., 1976; Austin et al., 1977). If the stories are repeated until the child can say what it was about, intention becomes a more important determinant of the child's judgments than damage (Austin et al., 1977). Finally, it has also been shown that the use of cues to intention and damage in children's judgments of the behavior of others is influenced by whether or not the character's behavior was provoked by someone else (Hewitt, 1975). When the wrongdoer's misdeed was strongly provoked by the victim, the wrongdoer was seen as less naughty than when the misdeed was not provoked. Other research (Berndt & Berndt, 1975) demonstrates that children as young as 5 understand motives and intentions but may ignore them when making moral judgments.

The mode of presentation of the moral dilemma story also seems to influence children's responses (Chandler, Greenspan & Barenboim, 1973; Berndt & Berndt, 1975). Chandler and his co-workers investigated this issue with 7-year-olds. Each of the 40 boys and 40 girls heard one Piaget-type story and saw a film of another. The usual judgments about who was naughtiest and why were categorized as based on intention or consequences. The results were dramatic. For the film stories, 4 times as many (32) judgments were based on intention as were based on consequences (8). For the orally presented stories, judgments based on consequences (24) outnumbered judgments based on intentions (16). The mode of presenting the story may thus bias the moral judgments given by children and thereby creates the impression that young children are insensitive to the intent of an act in judging its morality.

These findings may seem to indicate that Piaget's theory is incorrect. We should keep in mind, however, that although the methodological artifacts discussed here may distort age trends in moral development, we have no evidence that Piaget's hypothesized sequence of developmental stages in moral thinking is incorrect. This sequence may simply occur earlier than expected. Clarification of this issue must await further research.

ROLE TAKING.   Several investigators have tested Piaget's notion that peer interaction and role taking promote moral development. Selman has described the stages of role taking and concluded that role-taking ability increased with age in a series of stages that roughly parallel Piaget's stages of cognitive development. Selman gauged role taking by reading a moral dilemma to the child and assessing his ability to understand the viewpoints of the characters in the story and how these viewpoints related to his own. The child's role-taking ability thus influences his understanding of the social world and of how conflicts should be resolved. Selman (1976, pp. 307–308) has described the relationships among role-taking skills, cognition, and moral judgment:

> . . . [T]he child's cognitive stage indicates his level of understanding of physical and logical problems, while his role-taking stage indicates his level of understanding of the nature of social relations, and his moral judgment stage indicates the manner in which he decides how to resolve social conflicts between people with different points of view. Moral judgment considers how people *should* think and act with regard to each other, while social role-taking considers how and why people do *in fact* think about and act toward each other. The stage at which the moral claims of self and others are considered builds on the structurally parallel role-taking stage of understanding the relationship between the perspective of self and others. If the subject has not reached a given stage of role taking, he cannot apply this stage of social cognition to the moral domain.

Moir (1974) administered moral development tests and tests of nonmoral role taking (understanding the motives and feelings of others) to 40 11-year-old girls. The scores on the two types of tests were positively correlated, indicating that higher levels of moral thinking were associated with higher levels of role-taking ability. This held true even when the correlations were corrected for IQ; intelligence, as assessed by IQ, was not the reason for the correlation between the two measures. Moir's results and those of others (e.g., Selman, 1971; Ambron & Irwin, 1975) strongly suggest that the child's developing ability to take the perspective of others is a necessary precursor to the development of mature levels of moral thinking (Selman, 1976; Shantz, 1975).

Role taking is important for moral judgment because it increases the child's understanding of someone else's point of view, which in turn reduces the child's egocentrism and thereby allows for moral judgments of increasing subtlety. Studies in which children are given opportunities for role playing demonstrate both immediate and delayed (1 week) changes in moral judgments (Arbuthnot, 1975). Moreover, this is a result of actually engaging in the role playing. Children exposed to the same arguments but who do not do role playing show little change in moral-judgment level. Cognitive development, especially as applied to the social world, is intimately related to the development of moral judgments.

Kohlberg's Theory

Lawrence Kohlberg, like Piaget, has argued that conceptions of morality develop in a manner consistent with cognitive-developmental theory (Kohlberg, 1963 a, b, 1964, 1969, 1976). His main interest is the thought structures revealed in moral judgments. In other words, his interest is in moral thought, not moral behavior. He assumes that humans are moral philosophers, be they children or adults, and that children have a morality of their own, different from adult morality. The problem is to determine the psychological processes underlying the child's transition from an immature morality to a more mature, adult form of moral thought.

Kohlberg has conducted interviews with a large number of boys and girls, ranging from 6 to 16 years of age (Kohlberg, 1963 a). During the interviews, the child heard 10 stories that posed a moral dilemma. Two examples are given in Table 12-1. Kohlberg was less interested in the alternative selected by the children than in the reasons they gave for their choices, which reflected their way of thinking about the moral situation. Their choices presumably reflected their moral values, which were not of interest to Kohlberg. The responses each child made during the interview were classified according to the stage of moral development they reflected and dimensions of that stage. Each child could thus be classified by the percentage of use of each stage.

Kohlberg has postulated 3 levels of moral development composed of a total of 6 stages. These stages are listed in Table 12-2 in addition to a description of what is considered right, the reasons for behaving in the right way, and the relationship of moral stage to social perspective.

TABLE 12-1   Examples of the Moral Dilemma Stories Used by Kohlberg

---

1. Joe's father promised he could go to camp if he earned the $50 for it, and then changed his mind and asked Joe to give him the money he had earned. Joe lied and said he had earned only $10 and went to camp using the other $40 he had made. Before he went, he told his younger brother Alex about the money and about lying to their father. Should Alex tell their father?

2. In Europe, a woman was near death from a special kind of cancer. There was one drug that the doctors thought might save her. It was a form of radium that a druggist in the same town had recently discovered. The drug was expensive to make, but the druggist was charging ten times what the drug cost him to make. He paid $200 for the radium and charged $2,000 for a small dose of the drug. The sick woman's husband, Heinz, went to everyone he knew to borrow money, but he could only get together about $1,000 which is half of what it cost. He told the druggist that his wife was dying and asked him to sell it cheaper or let him pay later. But the druggist said: "No, I discovered the drug and I'm going to make money from it." So Heinz got desperate and broke into the man's store to steal the drug for his wife. Should the husband have done that?

SOURCE: From Kohlberg, L. The development of children's orientations toward a moral order: I. Sequence in the development of moral thought. *Vita Humana*, 1963, 6, pp. 11–33.

TABLE 12-2 The Six Moral Stages Identified by Kohlberg

| | CONTENT OF STAGE | | |
LEVEL AND STAGE	WHAT IS RIGHT	REASONS FOR DOING RIGHT	SOCIAL PERSPECTIVE OF STAGE
Level I—Preconventional			
Stage 1—Heteronomous Morality	To avoid breaking rules backed by punishment, obedience for its own sake, and avoiding physical damage to persons and property.	Avoidance of punishment, and the superior power of authorities.	*Egocentric point of view.* Doesn't consider the interests of others or recognize that they differ from the actor's; doesn't relate two points of view. Actions are considered physically rather than in terms of psychological interests of others. Confusion of authority's perspective with one's own.
Stage 2—Individualism, Instrumental Purpose, and Exchange	Following rules only when it is to someone's immediate interest; acting to meet one's own interests and needs and letting others do the same. Right is also what's fair, what's an equal exchange, a deal, an agreement.	To serve one's own needs or interests in a world where you have to recognize that other people have their interests, too.	*Concrete individualistic perspective.* Aware that everybody has his own interest to pursue and these conflict, so that right is relative (in the concrete individualistic sense).
Level II—Conventional			
Stage 3—Mutual Inter-personal Expecta-tions, Relationships, and Interpersonal Conformity	Living up to what is expected by people close to you or what people generally expect of people in your role as son, brother, friend, etc. "Being good" is impor-tant and means having good motives, showing concern about others. It also means keeping mutual relationships, such as trust, loyalty, respect and gratitude.	The need to be a good person in your own eyes and those of others. Your caring for others. Belief in the Golden Rule. Desire to maintain rules and authority which support stereotypical good behavior.	*Perspective of the individual in relationships with other individuals.* Aware of shared feelings, agree-ments, and expectations which take primacy over individual interests. Re-lates points of view through the concrete Golden Rule, putting yourself in the other guy's shoes. Does not yet consider generalized system perspective.
Stage 4—Social System and Conscience	Fulfilling the actual duties to which you have agreed. Laws are to be upheld ex-cept in extreme cases where they conflict with other fixed social duties. Right is also contributing to society, the group, or institution.	To keep the institution going as a whole, to avoid the breakdown in the system "if everyone did it," or the imperative of conscience to meet one's defined obligations	*Differentiates societal point of view from interpersonal agreement or motives.* Takes the point of view of the system that defines roles and rules. Considers individual relations in terms of place in the system.

SOURCE: Adapted from Kohlberg, L. Moral stages and moralization: The cognitive developmental approach. In T. Lickona (Ed.) Moral development and behavior: Theory, research, and social issues. New York: Holt, Rinehart, & Winston, 1976.

TABLE 12-2   The Six Moral Stages Identified by Kohlberg (*continued*)

CONTENT OF STAGE

LEVEL AND STAGE	WHAT IS RIGHT	REASONS FOR DOING RIGHT	SOCIAL PERSPECTIVE OF STAGE
Level III—Post-Conventional, or Principled			
Stage 5—Social Contract or Utility and Individual Rights	Being aware that people hold a variety of values and opinions, that most values and rules are relative to your group. These relative rules should usually be upheld, however, in the interest of impartiality and because they are the social contract. Some nonrelative values and rights like *life* and *liberty*, however, must be upheld in any society and regardless of majority opinion.	A sense of obligation to law because of one's social contract to make and abide by laws for the welfare of all and for the protection of all people's rights. A feeling of contractual commitment, freely entered upon, to family, friendship, trust, and work obligations. Concern that laws and duties be based on rational calculation of overall utility, "the greatest good for the greatest number."	*Prior-to-society perspective.* Perspective of a rational individual aware of values and rights prior to social attachments and contracts. Integrates perspectives by formal mechanisms of agreement, contract, objective impartiality, and due process. Considers moral and legal points of view; recognizes that they sometimes conflict and finds it difficult to integrate them.
Stage 6—Universal Ethical Principles	Following self-chosen ethical principles. Particular laws or social agreements are usually valid because they rest on such principles. When laws violate these principles, one acts in accordance with the principle. Principles are universal principles of justice: the equality of human rights and respect for the dignity of human beings as individual persons.	The belief as a rational person in the validity of universal moral principles, and a sense of personal commitment to them.	*Perspective of a moral point of view* from which social arrangements derive. Perspective is that of any rational individual recognizing the nature of morality or the fact that persons are ends in themselves and must be treated as such.

PRECONVENTIONAL LEVEL.   At the *preconventional* level of development, the child's conception of good and bad, and right and wrong, are determined by the physical consequences of actions, that is, by rewards and punishments or by the power of those in authority. In *Stage 1*, the physical consequences of an act completely determine its goodness or badness. There is an unquestioning deference to authority motivated by desire to avoid punishment. In *Stage 2*, acts are considered right if they are satisfying to the self or perhaps to others. There is some indication of a concept of fairness and egalitarianism of a reciprocal nature, but it is the naive "you do for me and I'll do for you" sort. It is not reciprocity based on justice.

CONVENTIONAL LEVEL. At the *conventional* level, the immediate physical consequences of an act become subservient to the maintenance of the accepted social order and to living up to the expectations of others. The child not only behaves as others expect him to, that is, in terms of their anticipated praise and blame, but he also incorporates the rules of others and respects their judgment. *Stage 3* is a "good-boy" morality. Good and bad are defined by what pleases others. The child may well conform to the cultural stereotype of what is good and bad behavior and begins to judge others on the basis of their intentions. *Stage 4* may be characterized as a "law-and-order" orientation toward authority, rules, and maintenance of the social order. Right behavior is defined as doing one's duty, showing respect for authority, and maintaining the social order for its own sake. Stage 4 morality indicates respect for an underlying social order maintained by reward and punishment. At this stage, the individual also is able to take the perspective of others who have rights.

POSTCONVENTIONAL LEVEL. At the *postconventional* or *principled* level, moral values and principles are defined by sharable standards or rights, and the possibility of conflict between socially accepted standards is realized. An effort is made to define morality apart from authority and from the individual's identification with various groups. In *Stage 5*, morality is defined by mutually agreed-upon standards, that is, contracts. The legal point of view is emphasized, but with the knowledge that laws are formed on some rational basis and can be changed to fit changing social situations. This latter characteristic is an important distinction between Stages 4 and 5. There is also an awareness that personal opinions are relative and that conflict can be resolved through a set of agreed-upon procedures. *Stage 6* is characterized by defining "right" according to universal ethical principles such as the Golden Rule or the greatest good for the greatest number. The basic notion is that the individual adheres to universal principles of justice, equality, and human rights.

Invariability and Universality of the Theory

Kohlberg (1969, 1976) believes that this sequence of stages is invariant. Each stage represents a qualitatively different way of organizing the social world in which the child grows up. As the child attains a new stage, the preceding stage is displaced. All the characteristics of stage theory discussed in Chapters 2 and 6 apply to Kohlberg's theory. It is important to keep in mind that, for Kohlberg, transitions from one moral stage to the next are a result of cognitive development in an environment that supplies the information on which cognitive processes operate. Thus, Kohlberg believes his moral stages reflect the underlying cognitive components of moral development.

Kohlberg (1969) has suggested that these stages are universal. Because of their cognitive basis, they should be the same in all cultures. To date, Kohlberg (1969) has reported data collected from children and adolescents in the United States, Taiwan,

Mexico, Great Britain, Turkey, and Yucatan. For children at age 10 in each country, the order of the stages is the same as the order in which they mature. That is, judgments are based on Stage 1 most often, Stage 2 next most often, and so on. In the United States the trend is increasingly on judgments based on Stages 3, 4, and 5. Stage 6 is found rather rarely. Differences between cultures may be due to 2 factors. First, individuals may pass through the stages at different rates. This may also be true within a culture. Second, the demands imposed on individuals living in different cultures may cause them to proceed through the stages at different rates and even perhaps not to reach the upper levels (Rest, 1976). Although the structural aspect of the stages may be universal, the content (behavior) may reflect specific cultural teachings (Rest, 1976).

The claim that these 6 stages are culturally universal has met with several criticisms (Simpson, 1974; Rest, 1976). One is that the data come from a small number (12) of cultures. If further data were collected from other cultures, both Eastern and Western, they might support Kohlberg's claim. On the other hand, it may be that Kohlberg's conceptual framework, measurement techniques, or procedures for scoring and classifying are unsuitable as an index of moral development for cultures with widely differing requirements for thinking, role taking, and problem solving. In other words, the explanation of moral development in other cultures may require different theoretical conceptions, measurement techniques, or scoring procedures. That this may turn out to be the case is suggested by the notion that morality is culturally defined and, as Kohlberg (1969) notes, development of morality is a function of organism-environment (culture) interaction.

Some psychologists (e.g., Kurtines & Greif, 1974) have strongly criticized Kohlberg's theory and research because of problems concerning the reliability and validity of the scoring methods (Rest, 1976; Kohlberg, 1976). Indeed, the scoring system is rather subjective and leads to low test-retest correlations ($r = .44$) (Rubin & Trotter, 1977). New scoring systems are being devised (Kohlberg, 1976; Rest, 1976), as are new assessment techniques (Rest, 1976). These may solve the problems raised about Kohlberg's formulations.

Research on Kohlberg's Theory

TURIEL'S RESEARCH.   Turiel (1966, 1969) has conducted research on Kohlberg's claim that the stages are invariant and that the higher stages represent reorganizations of preceding stages. The experiment was both clever and well designed. The subjects were 44 middle-class boys ranging from 12 to $13\frac{1}{2}$ years of age. To assess each boy's dominant stage of moral development, he was asked to respond to 6 Kohlberg-type stories. The dominant stage was that used at least twice as often as the next most-used stage. Boys with no dominant stage were dropped from the analysis. The subjects were distributed among Stages 2, 3, and 4. The subjects in each stage were then randomly assigned to either a control group or 1 of 3 experimental groups.

Two weeks after the initial testing, the subjects in the experimental groups were exposed to a situation calling for moral reasoning. An adult experimenter read 3 Kohlberg-type stories. Each boy was asked to play the role of the main character in the story and to seek advice from the experimenter who advised once pro and once con to the dilemma in each story. For a third of the subjects, the reasoning behind the advice, whether pro or con, was one stage below the boy's dominant stage (the −1 group). For another third, the reasoning was 1 stage above their dominant stage (the +1 group) and for the remaining third, it was 2 stages above their dominant stage (the +2 group).

The posttest measure was the boy's response to each of the 9 stories. The posttest was given 1 week after the treatment for subjects in the experimental groups, and 3 weeks after the pretest for subjects in the control group. One of Turiel's hypotheses was that an individual would assimilate concepts 1 stage above his current level of thinking more readily than concepts 2 stages above. The rationale for this hypothesis was that existing reasoning ability limits the acceptability and assimilation of reasoning above that of the child's current stage. This hypothesis was supported for both the 3 stories used in the training (direct posttest scores) and the 6 stories used in the pretest (the indirect posttest scores). The subjects in the +1 group showed greater change than the subjects in the other 2 groups. These findings suggest that Kohlberg's stages do represent a succession of increasingly advanced cognitive stages, with a skipping of stages being unlikely.

Turiel's second hypothesis was that each of the subsequent stages represented a reorganization of the preceding stages rather than just an addition to them. One implication of this hypothesis is that children will reject thinking at a stage lower than their current level. Turiel therefore predicted that subjects in the +1 condition would shift in the +1 direction more often than subjects in the −1 treatment condition would shift in the −1 direction. The findings were exactly opposite to the predictions. For both the direct and indirect scores, the −1 group shifted slightly more in the −1 direction than the +1 group did in the +1 direction. Neither group, however, shifted more than the control group, which shifted more toward the −1 than the +1 direction.

In another experiment, Turiel and Rothman (1972) examined the relation between level of moral reasoning and behavior in 13-year-old boys. Two weeks after determining each boy's level of moral reasoning by his responses to 6 Kohlberg-type stories, each boy participated as a teacher along with 2 adults in a learning task. The task was to read a list of words to a third adult, who was then to spell them. Each time the adult made a spelling error, poker chips—representing money—were taken away from him. The speller, who was a confederate of the experimenter, made a predetermined number of spelling errors. One of the 2 adults was the first teacher. After presenting 6 words, this adult said the experiment should be stopped and presented an argument that was either 1 stage above (+1) or 1 stage below (−1) the boy's level of moral reasoning. The second adult presented a counterargument either 1 stage below or 1 stage above the boy's level of moral thinking. These two adults then left, presumably to resolve their conflict, and the boy was given the choice of taking his turn or not participating. The reasons for the boy's choice were then assessed. A week later, a posttest was given to redetermine the boy's level of moral reasoning.

Boys whose moral thinking level was at Stage 2 or 3 continued the task regardless of the arguments presented. Boys at Stage 4 behaved consistently with the +1 argument. That is, if the argument presented for stopping the experiment was 1 stage above the child's current level, the Stage-4 child would stop, and if the +1 argument was to continue the experiment the boy would continue. The behavioral choices of the Stage-4 boys were integrated with their understanding of moral reasoning. This was not so for the boys at Stage 2 or 3. The posttest scores, however, revealed no long-lasting changes in moral reasoning as a result of the experimental situation.

These findings relating stages of development to behavioral choice were replicated in a study (Rothman, 1976) with boys in grades 7–9. Boys whose moral reasoning was predominantly at Stage 4 were better able to integrate and coordinate moral thinking and moral behavior than were boys from lower stages.

CONCLUSIONS FROM TURIEL'S RESEARCH.   These experiments are important for several reasons. First, they are among the few studies investigating the relation between level of moral reasoning and behavior. The results show a relationship between moral reasoning and behavior for Stage 4 boys and suggest that these two domains may be integrated before the child reaches Stage 4 of moral thinking. The second important finding of the experiment was its failure to find lasting changes in the level of moral reasoning. This is especially interesting for the level-4 subjects, whose behavior was affected by the experimental situation. It suggests that research from the social-learning approach (e.g., Bandura & MacDonald, 1963) may not demonstrate a change in the child's level of moral reasoning. Rather, the experimental manipulations used in these studies may simply alter behavioral choices rather than the cognitive processes presumed by Kohlberg to underlie moral reasoning. The findings from the social-learning approach and those of Turiel and Rothman suggest that the modeling procedures employed in the former represent a more effective way to alter behavioral choices than the procedures used by Turiel and Rothman, at least for Stage 2 and 3 boys. There is no way at present to determine which procedure would be better, if either, for Stage 4 subjects. This view is consistent with theorizing by Kohlberg about processes related to progression through the stages of moral development.

RESEARCH ON ROLE TAKING.   Kohlberg (1969, 1976) has argued that progression through the stages may be facilitated by opportunities for role taking. That is, moral development may be enhanced through social interactions that allow the child to play various roles and to learn to take somebody else's point of view. For example, a young child would not be expected to give an advanced moral response to any of Kohlberg's stories since the child lacks the ability to take the role of the central character and has no conception of that character's position. Opportunities for role playing promote understanding of other's views, reduce egocentrism, and as a result lead to advances in moral thinking. Such opportunities may be the cause of cultural differences in the rate of progression through these stages and in the predominant level of moral judgment in the culture (Rest, 1976, Selman, 1976).

For example, complex cultures may provide more opportunities for the child to take other roles than less complex cultures. More primitive societies may show slower rates of moral development and the predominant use of a lower stage of moral thinking than more technologically advanced societies for this reason. It should also be true that children who engage in higher-quality or a larger number of social participations in groups should show more advanced moral reasoning than their less socially active peers.

The role of social participation in moral development was tested in an experiment (Keasey, 1971) with 75 boys and 69 girls from predominantly lower-middle-class homes. Their level of moral development, determined by their responses to Kohlberg's Moral Judgment Interview, ranged from level 1 to level 4. About 2 months later, measures of social participation were obtained for each subject. These were measures of quantity (for example, the number of clubs or social organizations the child belonged to during the past 2 years) and quality (for example, the number of leadership positions held by the child at the time of the testing) of the child's social participation. In total, there were 8 measures of social participation, 2 relating to quantity and 6 to quality, based upon self, peer, and teacher ratings of each child. These 8 measures formed a composite description of the child's social interactions.

Keasey then compared the social ratings to the indices of moral development. For all 3 sources of data (self-report, peer ratings, and teacher ratings), and for both boys and girls, higher levels of moral development were related to greater participation in clubs and social organizations and to being a leader. Participation in a relatively large number of social roles (quantity) as well as assuming leadership responsibilities (quality) is linked to having a relatively higher level of moral reasoning. The causal basis of this relation, however, is unclear—higher levels of moral reasoning may cause the child to interact more socially, or the reverse.

RESEARCH ON CORRELATION BETWEEN COGNITIVE AND MORAL STAGES.   Piaget's stages of morality have not been related to either cognitive stages or behavior, but Kohlberg's theory has. One recent experiment by Tomlinson-Keasey and Keasey (1974) examined the relation between cognitive and moral thinking in sixth-grade and college-level females. The investigators found high correlations between stages of cognitive development and stages of moral development, supporting the notion that cognition underlies moral thinking. Table 12-3 shows the relations between Kohlberg's stages of moral development and Piaget's stages of cognitive development. In addition, Kohlberg's stages of moral development have been shown to relate to

TABLE 12-3 The Relationship of Kohlberg's Moral Stages and
Piaget's Cognitive Stages

COGNITIVE STAGE	MORAL STAGE
Symbolic, intuitive thought	Stage 0: The good is what I want and like
Concrete operations, Substage 1 categorized classification	Stage 1: Punishment-obedience orientation
Concrete operations, Substage 2 reversible concrete thought	Stage 2: Instrumental hedonism and concrete reciprocity
Formal operations, Substage 1 relations involving the inverse of the reciprocal	Stage 3: Orientation to interpersonal relations of mutuality
Formal Operations, Substage 2	Stage 4: Maintenance of social order, fixed rules and authority
Formal Operations, Substage 3	Stage 5: Morality of contract, democratically accepted law
	Stage 6: Universal ethical principle orientation

SOURCE: Adapted from Kohlberg, L. Continuities in childhood and adult moral development revisited. In P. Baltes and K. Schaie (Eds.), Life-span developmental psychology: personality and socialization, pp. 179–204. New York: Academic Press, 1973.

behavioral dispositions, at least in experimental situations. Although the evidence is scanty and the measurement techniques not as precise as they might be, it appears that Piaget and Kohlberg have presented sufficient empirical evidence to warrant the conclusion that children's moral development has a cognitive basis.

Perhaps the clearest demonstration of a close relationship between cognition and moral development has been reported by Lee (1971). The subjects were 195 middle-class boys, 15 each from kindergarten through twelfth grade. Lee first determined the Piagetian stage of cognitive development by administering a series of conceptual tasks, for example, conservation of mass or conservation of liquids. Lee then administered Kohlberg's 9 moral judgment stories, which had been modified so that the younger children could understand them. The child's responses to each story were scored along lines similar to those used by Kohlberg to determine the child's level of moral reasoning.

The results showed that cognitive level, independent of age, correlated highly with the level of moral reasoning. For example, concrete-operational thinking predicted an increase in Level 4 (societal) moral reasoning. This relationship between cognitive and moral development is more clearly illustrated in Figure 12-2, which shows the relation between the cognitive level of the 6-year-olds and the moral reasoning in Levels 1, 2, 3, and 4.

For both Kohlberg and Piaget, a child's reasoning about morality reflects cognitive processes. They do differ, however. Kohlberg's Stage 1 is similar to Piaget's heteronomous stage and Kohlberg's Stage 2 is similar to Piaget's stage of autonomy.

FIGURE 12-2   *Mean Frequency of Moral Responses of Conservers and Nonconservers Among Six-Year-Olds*

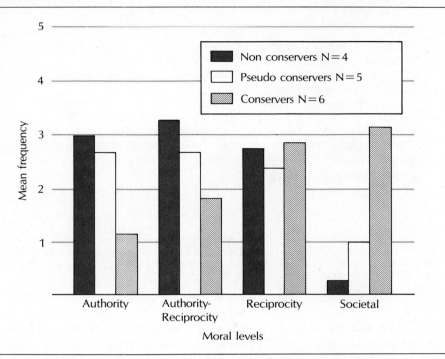

SOURCE: Lee, L. C. The concomitant development of cognitive and moral modes of thought: a test of selected deductions from Piaget's theory. *Genetic Psychology Monographs*, 1971, 83, pp. 93–146.

Hoffman (1970) has noted that Kohlberg believes Piaget has overemphasized the younger child's respect for authority. Kohlberg has also argued that Piaget attributes too much egalitarianism to children at the autonomous stage. We can clarify these issues if we assume that Kohlberg's levels of moral reasoning incorporate and add to the notions of Piaget. Kohlberg's scheme may produce more fine-grained levels of development because it takes into account a greater range of behavior.

SUMMARY

The old philosophical doctrines of original sin, innate purity, and tabula rasa are represented today in the schools of psychoanalytic theory, Piaget's cognitive theory, and learning theory, respectively. Psychoanalytically inspired research on the relation between child-rearing practices and moral behavior show that—for middle-class children—the maternal use of power assertion and love-withdrawal are associated with weak moral development, while maternal affection and the use of induction are associated with advanced moral development. For lower-class children, few significant relations have been found between children's moral development and their parents' disciplinary techniques.

Social-learning studies of moral behavior stress the importance of models, especially the parents, and reinforcement contingencies in the child's learning of moral behavior. Research based on this orientation indicates that children observing a rewarded model deviate more than children observing a punished model, with perceived similarity to the model having a significant effect on imitation.

The cognitive-developmental approach to moral development focuses on the thought processes underlying moral judgment and has tried to determine the sequence of stages of moral thought. Piaget has developed a stage theory of morality based on studies of children's understanding of rules of games and their reactions to wrongdoing by story characters. They seem to progress from a morality of constraint, in which they view rules as fixed, to one of cooperation or reciprocity in which they view rules as changeable according to circumstances. Moral development is seen as resulting primarily from interactions with peers, who provide the opportunity for more give-and-take than the heteronomous relations with parents do. While studies of the influence of models on children's moral judgments seem to show that modeling can produce lasting changes in moral thinking, various defects in these social-learning studies indicate that they are inconclusive as disproofs of Piaget's sequence of stages of moral development. The mode of presentation of Piaget's stories—whether oral or filmed—also affects children's judgments. Studies of role taking show that an understanding of interpersonal relations, and particularly the ability to take the perspective of others, is necessary for moral development.

Kohlberg's 6 stages of moral reasoning were developed from studies of reasoning about stories depicting moral dilemmas. Research has so far been inconclusive about the cultural invariance and universality of these stages, but it does suggest that the stages do represent increasingly advanced cognitive levels. Opportunities for role taking and for social participation seem to facilitate progression through the stages and may explain differences in moral development both within and among cultures. There is also some evidence that the development of moral thinking has a basis in cognition.

CHAPTER 13

(Shirley Zeiberg/Taurus Photos)

DEVELOPMENT OF PROSOCIAL BEHAVIOR

PARENTS, TEACHERS, AND RELIGIOUS institutions all try to promote behavior that is beneficial to society. Virtually all children are taught to share and cooperate with others and to help and comfort them. This behavior, which emerges during the preschool and elementary school years, is called "prosocial" (the opposite of "antisocial") because it promotes positive social interactions (Bryan, 1975; Rosenhan, 1972; Wispé, 1972).

Prosocial behavior reflects the child's use of behavior that is considered moral in his culture, for example, sharing. Similarly, cooperativeness, altruism, empathy, and helpfulness—all examples of prosocial behavior—are considered not only beneficial to the recipient but also to be ingrained in the "moral fiber" of our society.

Although we can trace investigations of this behavior back at least forty years (Murphy, 1937), intense interest in it has sprung up only in the last fifteen to twenty years (Mussen & Eisenberg-Berg, 1977). The burgeoning research literature on this topic now provides us with considerable knowledge about the emergence of prosocial behavior. Bar-Tal (1976) and Mussen and Eisenberg-Berg (1977) provide very readable and complete surveys of the area.

In this chapter we review developmental trends in the emergence of prosocial behavior in children as well as research and theory on cooperation, helping, altruism, empathy, and sharing. We also discuss factors that promote the child's learning of such behavior, for example, modeling and parental child-rearing techniques, reinforcement, and situational factors.

449

Definition

While examples of prosocial behavior are easy to provide, it is important to define the term in a way that makes it scientifically useful. **Prosocial behavior** refers to actions that result in aid to others and that may have some risk or self-sacrifice to the person acting prosocially. Psychologists also limit the term to behaviors for which the actor anticipates no external rewards (Mussen & Eisenberg-Berg, 1977), although some may be received. And, some internal rewards—feeling good about helping or sharing, reinforcing yourself by saying you are a good person for behaving prosocially—may also be obtained. Children are usually not rewarded for helping others, for being cooperative, or for sharing with others, for example, and some of these behaviors may even entail a cost to the child—sharing may mean less candy, and empathy may result in feeling sad and unhappy, for example. A final point in defining prosocial behavior is that it must be voluntary; the person must have the freedom to decide whether or not to act in this manner (Bar-Tal, 1976).

The above conceptualization suggests that the child must have some knowledge of societal norms regarding prosocial behavior (Mussen & Eisenberg-Berg, 1977) in order to act prosocially. As noted in the introduction, children are taught to behave in this manner. This teaching reflects and takes place within societal and subcultural norms describing acceptable behavior. As children internalize these norms they learn how they are expected to behave. However, knowledge of how one ought to act is no guarantee that one will act this way. A number of factors, situational as well as personal, influence the child's performance. Mussen and Eisenberg-Berg (1977, pp. 5–6) point out the complexities in describing the child's willingness to engage in prosocial behavior:

> To act in accordance with learned or internalized norms, the child must first perceive the other person's needs, interpret them accurately, and recognize that he or she can be helped. In addition, the child must feel competent in this situation, that is, capable of providing what is needed, and the cost or risk entailed in helping must not be prohibitive. Unless these preconditions are met, even the child who knows the norm of social responsibility is not likely to render aid. A self-concerned or egocentric youngster may not be aware of the needs of others or may be unable to interpret these needs accurately, and many failures to conform with the norm of assisting others are the results of ignorance of how to help in certain situations. In short, while societal norms bearing on prosocial behavior are undoubtedly widely accepted, even among children, they guide behavior only some of the time and under particular circumstances. Internalization of norms is not an adequate explanation or predictor of prosocial behavior; in fact, there is very little evidence that knowledge of norms exerts control of children's actions.

Psychologists, then, have studied a number of situational factors that influence children's performance of prosocial behavior, many of which we shall discuss below.

Sharing and helping are two forms of prosocial behavior that children learn. (Left: Heath Paley/ The Picture Cube; right: Guy Gillette/Photo Researchers)

Theories

Most theoretical explanations of prosocial behavior are based on the theories of moral development discussed in the previous chapter. Therefore, we highlight only those aspects that are directly pertinent to explaining prosocial behavior.

Psychoanalytic Theory

Psychoanalytic theory explains the child's learning of prosocial behavior through the identification mechanism. If the parent with whom the child identifies exhibits prosocial behavior and espouses rules of prosocial behavior—for example, the norm of social responsibility, which asserts that we should help those who need our help—these will be incorporated into the developing superego and become part of the child's understanding of the rules of society. Some research indicates that people who are highly altruistic, such as in helping others (London, 1970) or in being activists on behalf of others (Rosenhan, 1970), strongly identify with one or the other of their parents. These data not only show the importance of identification but also emphasize the need to examine child-rearing variables that may affect the learning of prosocial behavior.

Social-Learning Theory

Social-learning theory emphasizes the role of rewards, punishments, and modeling to explain how and why children learn to behave prosocially. Rewards strengthen childrens' sharing, helping, and other prosocial behaviors. As the child learns to act prosocially, the norms for doing so slowly become internalized and direct the child's behavior. The child then may behave in prosocial ways in the absence of external rewards, perhaps because the child rewards (praises) himself or herself for behaving prosocially. Children learn which behaviors bring adult praise and reinforce themselves for behaving in those ways. Prosocial behavior, then, comes under the control of self-reinforcements. Modeling, too, facilitates the child's learning of prosocial responses. As we pointed out in Chapter 12, parents and others act as effective models for moral development, which encompasses prosocial behavior. Observing appropriate models elevates children's helping, sharing, generosity, and other prosocial behaviors. All the factors (e.g., the model's power and nurturance) that influence the observational learning and modeling of moral behaviors affect the learning and performance of prosocial behaviors as well. We review research findings in support of social-learning theories later.

Cognitive-Developmental Theory

Cognitive-developmental theory assumes prosocial behavior emerges from cognitive changes and increasing role-taking abilities. These skills underlie increases in moral development, which in part is reflected in increases in prosocial behavior (Rubin & Schneider, 1973). Other research (Harris, Mussen & Rutherford, 1976) demonstrates relations between measures of moral maturity and prosocial behavior. Prosocial behavior, then, reflects changes in cognitive structures that relate to **social cognition**—that is, the child's changing understanding of social rules promotes prosocial behavior. Cognitive theorists focus their research efforts on understanding how the child comes to view and comprehend rules for prosocial behavior, rather than on the behavior itself, much as in our previous discussion of moral development.

As in other areas of child development, the three approaches stress different antecedents and mechanisms for explaining prosocial behavior. And, each makes a unique contribution to understanding this phenomenon. None of the theories alone can adequately or entirely explain all the emerging facts about prosocial development. Hence, following a brief discussion of possible biological bases for prosocial behavior, we shall discuss findings based on research from all three perspectives.

The Role of Biology

The systematic study of the biological basis of social behavior is a new field of study ushered in by Edward O. Wilson's (1975) book *Sociobiology: The New Synthesis*. In this work, Wilson points out that prosocial behavior occurs in many animals, not just humans. Insects, birds, dolphins, dogs, and chimpanzees engage in helping, sharing and other behaviors which, when observed in humans, are called prosocial. Sharing of food, protection of the young, and defense of the bee hive are a few of the examples Wilson gives of prosocial behavior by those species lower than humans on the phylogenetic scale.

Wilson explains these altruistic acts by lower animals through the concept of *kin selection*. By acting prosocially the animal increases the chances that its kin, those who share its genes, will survive. Of course, other members of the species may also benefit from the altruistic behavior of one or several members. A bird warning its family of approaching danger may well be warning other birds, too. And often this warning to the family is *intended* for other members of the species as well. The concept of **reciprocal altruism** is invoked to explain altruistic behavior to other than family members. The idea is that altruistic actions toward another member of the species may result in reciprocal altruistic actions in the future. Wilson (1975) contends that this altruistic behavior is promoted by, and contributes to, genetic predispostions toward altruism. The notion rests on the process of natural selection, through which traits become characteristics of a species. Wilson (1975, pp. 3–4) sees social behavior, including altruism, as reflecting natural selection processes.

According to Wilson's sociobiological theory, prosocial behaviors in humans and lower animals occur in part because of biological predispositions. (James Moore/Anthro-Photo)

As more complex social behavior by the organism is added to the genes' techniques for replicating themselves, altruism becomes increasingly prevalent and eventually appears in exaggerated forms. This brings us to the central theoretical problem of sociobiology: how can altruism, which by definition reduces personal fitness, possibly evolve by natural selection? The answer is kinship: if the genes causing the altruism are shared by two organisms because of common descent, and if the altruistic act by one organism increases the joint contribution of these genes to the next generation, the propensity to altruism will spread through the gene pool.

Wilson suggests that human social behavior, too, may be controlled by genes. However, this assertion has met with considerable resistance (e.g., Campbell, 1975; Gould, 1976; Washburn, 1976). The prevalent opinion seems to be that humans inherit the potential for exhibiting a variety of social behaviors, including altruistic ones, but, the behavior that is exhibited is a result of psychological and social determinants, not biological ones. Hence, psychologists have searched for the determinants of prosocial behavior in the mechanisms of learning, thinking, identification, modeling, and the like.

Research on Prosocial Behavior

Research on the development of **altruism**—any behavior that benefits others and that produces no gain, and perhaps a loss, for the actor (Bryan, 1975)—has been conducted in two types of situations: helping or rescue, and sharing or donating.

Helping

In studies of children's helping or rescuing, children are led to believe that another child needs help. The children's rescuing effort, including the type of behavior (intervening or telling an adult experimenter) and the speed of rescue, is assessed.

AGE DIFFERENCES. The most extensive studies of children's rescuing have been conducted by Staub (1970a, 1970b, 1971a, 1971b, 1972), who in one study (1970a) investigated age differences in helping in elementary-school children. The children were brought alone or with a same-sex classmate to a room where they were presumably going to draw and color some pictures. After entering the room, the experimenter recalled that she had forgotten the crayons. Before going to get them, she announced that she had better check on a child in the next room. After checking and coming back to the subjects, the experimenter commented that the child was all right and that she hoped the child would not stand on the chair again. She then left to get the crayons. About a minute later, the child, or pair of children, heard a noise, a scream, and then crying come from the next room. (The noise, scream, and crying were produced by a tape recording, not by a child actually hurt in the room. The subjects were unaware that the sounds were tape-recorded.) The child, or pair of children, could help by going into the next room or by telling the experimenter when she returned. Or the child, or children, could say nothing. The first two measures were considered attempts to help the child in the next room.

Helping, as measured by entering the room or by volunteering information to the experimenter, increased from kindergarten to second grade and then declined. Children in pairs helped more than those who were alone (see Figure 13-1). Staub speculated that the older children were afraid to help for fear that the experimenter would reprimand them for going into another room. Staub (1970a, p. 137) goes on to note:

[O]ne effect of the socialization process is that the child's behavior comes increasingly under the control of norms, either explicit or implicit, which determine what is

FIGURE 13-1   *Percentage of Help at Each Grade Level*

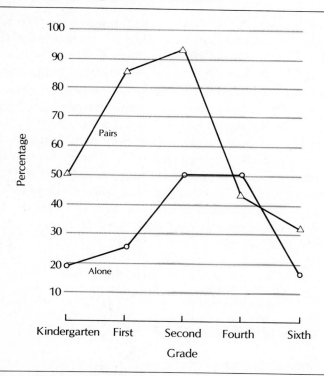

SOURCE: Adapted from Staub, E. A child in distress: the influence of age and number of witnesses on children's attempts to help. *Journal of Personality and Social Psychology*, 1970, 14, 130–140.

appropriate behavior in a particular situation. In an unfamiliar environment, when the norms are unclear, he may be unwilling to initiate action, fearing disapproval for possibly inappropriate behavior. If this explanation of the decline in helping with age is correct, it would suggest that the learning of standards of "appropriate" behavior for certain times and places, as part of the socialization process, may be a factor which negatively influences children's readiness to respond to another's need.

Staub also suggests that in an unfamiliar environment with no clear rules for behavior, the child may have thought it inappropriate to enter the other room. Children in pairs may have helped more because the presence of a peer may have reduced the fear and distress aroused by the apparent harm that was taking place.

These speculations were partially supported in a subsequent study (Staub, 1970b). Using the same situation, Staub told some children that they were in charge of things when the experimenter left the room. Others were told nothing. Those who were told they were in charge helped more than those who were told nothing. This finding suggests that the older children helped less than the younger children in the earlier study because they feared breaking a rule and felt they should not enter the other room.

EMPATHY TRAINING AND HELPING SKILLS.   Other research (e.g., Staub, 1971a, 1971b, 1972) has been aimed at determining how children learn to help and the factors that promote this behavior. Staub and others (e.g., Bryan, Wispé, 1972) believe that the ability to empathize with others and the possession of the skills required to help are two critical factors in determining whether or not one will extend aid to others. If this supposition is correct, Staub reasoned, training in **empathy** and provision of the skills needed for helping should increase helping. To test these notions, Staub (1971a) exposed pairs of kindergarten children to one of four experimental treatments: role playing, induction, role playing with induction, or control.

Role playing consisted of putting the pairs of children in situations in which one of them needed help and the other provided it. The children took turns at each of these roles. They were encouraged to help in every way they could think of and the experimenter then suggested other ways. Each of these was acted out. Five situations were used (Staub, 1971a):

1. A child had fallen out of a chair in an adjoining room.
2. A child was trying to carry a chair that was too heavy for him.
3. A child was distressed because another child had taken his building blocks.
4. A child was standing in the path of an oncoming bicycle.
5. A child had fallen and hurt himself.

The children either helped, gave verbal consolation, or called someone else to help.

In the induction training, the same five situations were described, and the children were asked to say how help could be provided. Following the children's suggestions the experimenter provided others. The experimenter pointed out the positive consequences of all the helping acts, including improving the physical and psychological well-being of the person in need of help. The intent of this training was to make the children aware of the consequences of their behavior for others.

Children in the role-playing with induction training group were exposed to both methods. These children acted out the various roles of helping, and the experimenter explained the positive consequences of helping. The control group participated in activities unrelated to helping and did not exchange roles.

Three measures of help were taken: active help, volunteering information, and no help. Since the distress situation closely resembled the training of children in the three treatment groups, it was of interest to see how the helping generalized to other situations. To test for the generality of helping, Staub used a situation quite different from those used in the role-playing and induction training. The child and the experimenter began to play a game, during which the experimenter "accidentally" dropped a box of paper clips. The experimenter then expressed mild alarm ("Oh, my dear") and began picking up the paper clips. The measure of helping was the number of clips the child picked up either voluntarily or with mild prompting (e.g., "Could you help me a little bit?").

Role playing proved to exert an influence on helping, but induction did not. The effect of role playing was especially pronounced for girls, who helped the distressed child more than did the boys. Following role playing of prosocial scenes, girls helped the child in distress more and boys shared more than did control subjects who role-played scenes unrelated to helping. Induction *reduced* helping (picking up paper clips) of the adult. This was an unexpected finding because other research (Green & Schneider, 1974) shows that, in general, there is an increase in this form of helping (from 48 percent of children aged 5 to 6 to virtually 100 percent of children aged 9 and over) as children get older. Staub speculates that the effects for the induction training may result from the children feeling pressured to be "good" because of the induction techniques used. As a result, the children may have felt their freedom to act had been taken away, and they resisted by refusing to help. These findings indicate that children may be trained to act prosocially, especially through role playing. It appears that when parents admonish their children to put themselves in the parents' place or in a friend's place (role playing), they foster prosocial behavior in their children.

ADULT MODELS.   Other researchers (e.g., Staub, 1971b; Yarrow, Scott & Waxler, 1973) have also been concerned with how children learn to behave altruistically. These researchers have examined the importance of adult models on children's learning of altruism, especially as indexed by helping others in distress. These studies give some insight into how children learn prosocial behavior in the home and specifically shed light on the importance of parental modeling of altruism for children's learning of prosocial behavior.

Observing models who engage in prosocial behavior, such as helping, promotes similar behavior in children. (Shirley Zeiberg/Taurus Photos)

Generally speaking, children who observe a model who helps, learn to help in similar circumstances (Staub, 1971b; Yarrow et al., 1973). In other words, adult modeling of altruism is an effective means of increasing children's willingness to help others, probably because it provides knowledge of how to help others and indicates the appropriate responses to others in distress (Aronfreed, 1968; Staub, 1971b; Yarrow et al., 1973). Research on the effectiveness of a model's influence on children's imitation indicates two important individual difference characteristics of models that must be considered: the **model's power** and the **model's nurturance.**

The power of a model relates to the model's control of resources, usually defined in terms of rewards and punishments the model can administer to the child. Research generally shows that children imitate powerful models to a greater degree than they imitate less powerful models (Bandura, 1969a, 1969b; Gewirtz, 1969). Some research (e.g, Bryan, 1975; Grusec, 1971) demonstrates that children imitate the sharing of a powerful model more than the sharing of a less powerful model, perhaps because children are more likely to feel a powerful model will reward them.

NURTURANT ADULT MODELS.   A number of researchers (e.g., Grusec, 1971; Rosenhan & White, 1967; Staub, 1971b; Yarrow et al., 1973) have examined the effect of
model nurturance on children's imitation of prosocial behavior. In these studies,
nurturance is usually defined by a warm, kind, friendly and interested model who
interacts with the child for a short time (10 to 15 minutes) prior to the start of the
experiment. In general, if the model in an experiment is nurturant prior to modeling,
for example, helping, children show more imitative helping than if the model is not
nurturant (Bryan, 1972, 1975). The model's nurturance apparently indicates to
children that they may do what they wish to do and that the adult is unlikely to
punish them.

The influence of long-term nurturance as related to children's imitation of
modeled sharing was investigated by Yarrow and her colleagues (Yarrow et al., 1973).
The specific procedures used in this experiment make it a very good analogue to the
family situation. As a result, it provides better clues about how parents influence
prosocial development than do other studies.

Prior to the start of the experiment the base-line levels of helping were
measured in a group of nursery school children aged $3\frac{1}{2}$ to $5\frac{1}{2}$. The experimenters
observed the children's reactions to pictures of people or animals in distress (e.g., a
child caught under a barbed-wire fence, birds in a nest being attacked by a cat), and
to four actual behavioral examples of distress (e.g., the contents of an adult's purse
fall on the floor). The child's verbal and behavioral responses were recorded, including recognition of a misfortune, action to alleviate the misfortune, expressions
of sympathy and concern, and the like. After these measures were obtained, the
children were divided into small groups of 6 to 8 people. These groups met in a
playroom for 5 sessions of 30 minutes each with an adult leader who behaved
nurturantly to some groups and nonnurturantly (somewhat aloof) to other groups.
After these sessions the adult leader acted as an altruistic model for some of the
children. This was done with dioramas (miniature reproductions) of distress situations—one diorama for the child and an identical one for the model. The nurturant
modeling included verbal statements showing awareness of the distress, sympathy
for the victim, and the like, and behavioral manipulation of the diorama to help the
victim. After the modeling the child was allowed to take a turn. For some children
the model not only worked with the dioramas but also helped another person in real
distress (for example, helping another adult who had banged her head on a table).
Two days after the modeling sessions were completed the children's altruistic tendencies were again tested with a new series of pictorial and behavioral incidents.
Two weeks later the children's altruism was again tested to check for durability of
the effects of modeling. This was done by taking the child to a house adjacent to the
school to visit a mother and her baby. The children could help the mother by picking
up some spools or by getting toys that the baby had dropped out of the crib.

The results for the two types of modeling were very different. Modeling with
the dioramas *and* "live" situations increased the altruistic responses of the children

more than modeling with the dioramas only. On the 2-day posttest the latter group showed increased altruism with the diorama situations but not with picture situations or "live" incidents. Modeling with dioramas, then, influenced symbolic altruism only. Exposure to a model who not only preached but also practiced altruism, especially if it was a nurturant model, increased symbolic and "live" altruism. On the 2-week posttest, 84 percent of the children who observed a nurturant model in the diorama *and* live situations helped the mother. This was more than in any other group and was a significant increase over the percent (24 percent) of these children who helped on the pretest. Altruistic behavior, then, was fostered most in those children exposed to extensive training with a nurturant model.

LEARNING GENERALIZED ALTRUISM. Yarrow and her co-workers made some practical suggestions for parents who want their children to be altruistic and sensitive to those in distress: model such behavior, don't just preach it. Verbalizing altruistic motives and behaving symbolically with dolls or toys has little impact on the child's altruistic behavior outside the symbolic situation (Yarrow et al., 1973, pp. 252–253): "Modeling in symbolic form was highly effective in developing similar symbolic altruism, including the generalization of helping and sympathy to new situations of distress . . . However, symbolic modeling has little impact on live altruism . . . Only when extensive training (symbolic plus behavioral) was conducted in the context of a developed, nurturant interaction was altruistic behavior significantly increased." Yarrow et al. (1973, p. 256) go on to suggest some socialization principles to parents:

> The parent who conveys his value to the child didactically as tidy principles, and no more, accomplishes only that learning in the child. Generalized altruism would appear to be best learned from parents who do not only try to inculcate the principles of altruism, but who also manifest altruism in everyday interactions. Moreover, their practices toward their children are consistent with their general altruism.
>
> Emphasis on the role of nurturance in the rearing environment does not suggest that it alone is sufficient. The data demonstrate its importance along with the specific modeling, accompanied by the model's verbal communications. The model communicated a good deal about her altruism by identifying the cues to which she was reacting, the inferences she was making about the victims, and her affect in aiding them. She also supplied a bridging label of "help" which was common to each of the events. The cognitive aspects of the training, the labels for her behavior, it is assumed, were probably significant aids to the child's acquiring and generalizing helping.

Sharing and Donating

Sharing is important in any moral system (Larsen & Kellogg, 1974). Hence, the child's learning of norms for sharing has been of interest to psychologists (Bryan, 1975; Bryan & London, 1970). Piaget (1932) has suggested that the child's understanding of these norms progresses from an attitude that the just distribution is whatever those in authority say it is, to a mechanical and strict orientation toward

One function of school during the early years is to teach cooperative behavior. (Elizabeth Hamlin)

equal distribution of resources, to a principle of equity in which sharing is based on situational and personal factors. This description implies an age gradient in children's sharing reflecting their understanding of rules (see Chapter 12).

AGE DIFFERENCES.   Recent findings (e.g., Bryan, 1975; Green & Larsen, 1974; Larsen & Kellogg, 1974; Rushton, 1975; White & Burnam, 1975) indicate that sharing increases during the childhood and early adolescent years. In these studies, children are given the opportunity to share candy, marbles, money, or tokens than can be traded for prizes with friends or "needy children" in the community. The amount shared with these others increases with the age of the children. Moreover, the percentage of children who share reaches nearly 100 by age 9 (Green & Schneider, 1974).

Systematic studies of sharing in infants are less common. Rheingold, Hay, and West (1976) reported several components of sharing in children about 1½ years of age. Sharing was defined as showing or giving an object to another or playing with an object with another person. All children shared toys with their mother and father. The number of children who shared toys with a stranger and the percent of children who showed all sharing behaviors increased with age. The children also shared new toys as well as old ones. Hence, it seems that sharing is a universal trait and that age differences in sharing are probably the result of learning.

ENVIRONMENTAL DIFFERENCES.   Most of the recent investigations of children's sharing have focused on environmental influences within the social-learning paradigm (Bryan, 1975; Bryan & London, 1970). The variable attracting the most interest is the effect of models. Modeled behavior is viewed as analogous to what the child observes in the home and elsewhere. The influence of models who share or do not share, and of models who preach sharing or not sharing, has been examined (e.g., Bryan & Walbek, 1970a, 1970b; Bryan, Redfield & Mader, 1971; Midlarsky, Bryan & Brickman, 1973; Presbie & Coiteux, 1971; Rushton, 1975; White & Burnam, 1975). Children who observe a generous model share more than children who observe a stingy model; those who observe no model usually share at a level between these two groups (Rushton, 1975).

The influence of the model's statements about the norm of sharing on children's subsequent sharing is somewhat more difficult to understand (Bryan et al., 1971; Rushton, 1975). Rushton had children aged 7 through 11 observe a model play a bowling game. The model either shared or did not share the tokens he won by putting some or none in a bowl marked "Save the Children Fund." The model also preached sharing, selfishness, or neither by making comments about the positive or negative aspects of sharing or by simply commenting about the game. Children's sharing was measured immediately afterward and again 2 months later. The results, which are presented in Table 13-1, indicate that modeling is a potent determiner of children's generosity. Models who shared or were neutral elicited more sharing from the children than did the selfish models. And this effect lasted 2 months after the completion of the experiment.

Preaching had no effect on the immediate posttest but was a significant determiner of sharing on the 2-month posttest. Models who preached generosity or who made neutral statements elicited more sharing than models who preached selfishness. It appears that at first the model's actions override the model's statements, perhaps because children attend more to actions than verbalizations. After

TABLE 13-1   Mean Number of Tokens Donated for Each Modeling and Preaching Group on the Immediate and Delayed Posttests

POSTTEST	MODEL	GENEROUS	PREACHING NEUTRAL	SELFISH
Immediate	Generous	7.6	7.6	6.1
	Selfish	1.8	.9	1.7
Two-month	Generous	5.2	6.8	3.3
	Selfish	3.2	2.8	2.4

SOURCE: Adapted from Rushton, J. P. Generosity in children: immediate and long-term effects of modeling, preaching, and moral judgment. *Journal of Personality and Social Psychology*, 1975, 31, pp. 459–466.

a time, however, the child may find it easier to recall what the model said than what the model did, and therefore preaching may have a greater influence on behavior.

Some Conclusions

It appears that the power of the experimental manipulations is strong enough to mask individual differences in sharing that might be attributable to cognitive growth. Not only does observation of a model increase sharing, but thinking happy (rather than sad) thoughts (Isen, Horn & Rosenhan, 1973; Moore, Underwood & Rosenhan, 1973), instructions to share (Bryan, 1975), and "overpayment" in the form of giving children more than they think they deserve (Olejnik, 1976) also increase sharing and donating. Since these manipulations often interact with the age of the child—having different effects on the sharing of children of different ages—they may be interpreted differently by children at different levels of cognitive development. At present, however, we cannot tease out the exact nature of this influence of cognitive functioning on children's sharing. Only weak relationships between sharing and conservation have been reported (e.g., Larsen & Kellogg, 1974). More promising relationships between level of moral judgment and sharing have been found (Rushton, 1975). Children high in moral judgment donated more on the immediate but not the 2-month posttest in the study by Rushton just described.

Cooperation and Competition

The recent increase in interest in how children learn to behave cooperatively stems partially from the tenor of the times (Bryan, 1975; Cook & Stingle, 1974) and partly from an interest in moral codes (Bryan, 1975). Concerns about violence and aggression, the limits of natural resources, and the peace movement of the early to mid-1970s have highlighted the importance of our gaining further knowledge about the factors that promote cooperative and other prosocial behavior.

Research Methodology

Most research on children's cooperative and competitive behavior has been done in the laboratory, although some has also been done in naturalistic settings (Friedrich & Stein, 1973; Hartup & Keller, 1960). Cooperation is usually defined as a coordination of actions among individuals to allow for the attainment of a desired goal. When the reward is for a group (such as a team) the child loses nothing if the group does not win; when the reward is for the child a loss may occur if the child does not win (Bryan, 1975; Cook & Stingle, 1974). In both cases, cooperation may result in gaining

FIGURE 13-2   *Games Used to Study Cooperation*

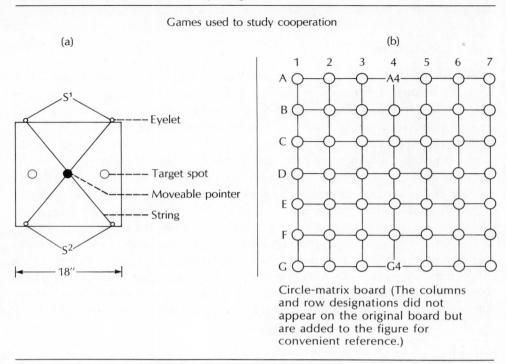

Games used to study cooperation

(a)

(b)

Circle-matrix board (The columns and row designations did not appear on the original board but are added to the figure for convenient reference.)

SOURCE: (a) Nelson, L., and Madsen, M. C. Cooperation and competition in four-year-olds as a function of reward contingency and subculture. *Developmental Psychology*, 1969, 1, 340–344. (b) Kagan, S., and Madsen, M. C. Cooperation and competition of Mexican, Mexican-American, and Anglo-American children of two ages under four instructional sets. *Developmental Psychology*, 1971, 5, 32–39.

something. In this respect, studies of cooperative and competitive behavior differ somewhat from our earlier definition of prosocial behavior: cooperation can result in a reward for the child. Interest has centered on age, sex, and cultural differences in the degree to which children cooperate or compete in games designed to assess this behavior.

Two examples of the games used in this research are shown in Figure 13-2. In the cooperation-board game, each child (S1 and S2) holds a string in each hand. Pulling on the strings makes the pointer move across the board. If it is pulled to one of the target spots, the child whose name is in that spot wins a prize. For one child to win a prize, the other player must cooperate; a player cannot move the pointer to his target spot by pulling his strings only. In the circle-matrix board, a token is placed in the center of the board (D4). The players (seated behind G4 and A4) alternately move the token one circle at a time, vertically or horizontally. If the token ends up in the circle belonging to one of the players (A4 or G4), that player gets a prize.

Cooperation is the rational strategy in these games because nothing can be gained by competitive behavior. In either of these games, children can cooperate in such a way that each gets equally rewarded by alternating who gets the prize on each trial.

Age Differences

Studies of age differences reveal that cooperation declines as children get older, and competitiveness and rivalry increase (Bryan, 1975; Cook & Shapira, 1974; Cook & Stingle, 1974; Kagan & Madsen, 1971, 1972b). Using the circle-matrix board, Kagan and Madsen (1971) found that 4- to 5-year-olds cooperated more than 7- to 9-year-olds. Over 70 percent of the moves made by the 4- to 5-year-olds, both Anglo-American and Mexican-American, were completely cooperative. In contrast, the Anglo-American 7- to 9-year-olds made over 70 percent conflicting (competitive) responses. The Mexican-American 7- to 9-year-olds made 50 percent conflict responses, indicating that they, too, were highly competitive. In a subsequent study (Kagan & Madsen, 1972b), the same authors reported that 5- to 6-year-olds were more rivalrous than 8- to 10-year-olds. The older children acted to lower the gains of other children to a greater degree than did the younger children, even though it limited their own personal gain. This increase in rivalry among older children was more apparent in the American than the Mexican children.

Cultural Differences

As the reader may have noted, these invesitgators not only found age effects, but also noted that children from different cultures differed in their cooperation with each other. This observation led Madsen and colleagues (e.g., Madsen & Shapira, 1970; Nelson & Madsen, 1973; Kagan & Madsen, 1972a; Nelson & Madsen, 1969; Shapira & Madsen, 1974), and others (e.g., Thomas, 1975) to conduct a series of investigations of cultural differences in children's cooperativeness and competitiveness. Children from urban areas are generally less cooperative and more competitive than children from rural areas. And American children from urban areas (Afro-American, Anglo-American, and Mexican-American) are more maladaptively competitive than rural Mexican children (Madsen & Shapira, 1970), while Mexican-American children are more cooperative than Anglo-American children. Finally, Israeli children from a Kibbutz are more cooperative than Israeli children from urban areas (Shapira & Madsen, 1969, 1974). These differences seem to reflect different cultural emphases in cooperation and competition. As Kagan and Madsen (1971, p. 37) put it: "The environmental milieu in which United States children develop during the early school years, given the high value placed on individual achievement through competition, may lead to a strong I orientation by age seven which masks any potential for behaving on the basis of an autonomous morality of cooperation."

Team activities promote a "we" orientation that increases cooperation and reduces competition. (Eugene Richards/The Picture Cube)

This highly competitive spirit can be overcome, however. By organizing the task to produce a "we" rather than "I" attitude, Kagan and Madsen (1971) increased cooperation on the circle-matrix board. The we versus I attitude was induced by an instructional set. "I" set instructions stressed individuality and possessiveness (e.g., by the experimenter speaking of circles that belonged to him). "We" set instructions stressed a group orientation and deemphasized possessiveness (e.g., by stating "*We* want to move the token . . . "). This instructional set had less impact on the 4- to 5-year-olds than on the 7- to 9-year-olds, but the younger children were already highly cooperative.

Reinforcing group rather than individual performance also increases cooperative responding (Madsen & Shapira, 1970; Nelson & Madson, 1968; Shapira & Madsen, 1969). In the case of reinforcement, "taking turns" was the most common response for group orientations, while a dominance-submissive orientation (one person dominated the other, who allowed the domination) emerged when rewards were given to individuals. Reinforcement for cooperation also promotes it both in play (Bryan, 1975; Cook & Stingle, 1974) and in verbal interactions (e.g., Slaby &

Crowley, 1977). Cooperative models also exert a positive influence on the expression of cooperation among children (Liebert, Sprafkin, & Poulos, 1975). Finally, changing the contingencies for rewards from competitive to cooperative results in an increase in cooperation (e.g., French, Brownell, Graziano, & Hartup, 1977).

These results seem most easily explained by assuming that when a child desires something, and the only way it can be obtained is if the group reaches a certain level of performance, cooperation will ensue. If reward is contingent on the performance of the individual, the result will be competition. Rewarding collective (group) performance, then, increases cooperation among children.

Sex Differences

One interesting question is the degree to which the sexes differ in cooperativeness and competitiveness. The sex-role stereotype prevalent even today is that females are, or should be, less competitive than males (Broverman, Broverman, Clarkson, Rosenkrantz & Vogel, 1970; Maccoby & Jacklin, 1974; Rosenkrantz, Vogel, Bee, Broverman & Broverman, 1968). Since such stereotypes may act as guides to behavior, we may expect sex differences in cooperation and competitiveness. The evidence from research, however, is unclear (Bryan, 1975; Cook & Stingle, 1974). Studies with children aged 4 to 9 (e.g., Kagan & Madsen, 1971) have shown no sex differences. When sex differences do appear, they indicate boys are more willing than girls to take a loss in order to keep their peers from winning (Kagan & Madsen, 1972b). The best estimate is that there are no significant sex differences in cooperative behavior (Bryan, 1975).

Relationships Among Prosocial Behaviors

The developmental trends reported above suggest that measures of the various kinds of prosocial behavior should be related. Children who cooperate should be likely to be more helpful and ready to share than less cooperative children. Similarly, we would expect that children who behave prosocially would not behave antisocially. Highly cooperative children, for example, should be less aggressive.

Several investigators have presented data that suggest these common-sense notions are incorrect. Although Rubin and Schneider (1973) reported a positive correlation between a measure of helping and a measure of sharing for 7-year-olds, Green and Schneider (1974) did not. In the latter study, helping, sharing, and volunteering (another measure of helping) were measured in children ranging in age from 5 to 14. The 3 measures of prosocial behavior were unrelated to each other. Yarrow, Waxler et al. (1976) studied sharing, helping, and comforting in 3- to

7½-year-olds. Scores on sharing were significantly correlated (r = .32) with scores on comforting, but neither sharing nor comforting was significantly related to helping. In naturalistic settings, none of the correlations among the 3 prosocial measures was significant. Finally, Levine and Hoffman (1975) reported that 2 measures of cooperation (using the cooperation board) taken 2- to 4-weeks apart were unrelated. Moreover, cooperation was unrelated to measures of empathy in this study.

Data such as these indicate that different forms of prosocial behavior do not form a unitary set (Yarrow, Waxler et al., 1976). The situational context children find themselves in, for example, danger, with someone in pain, or in a situation indicating inequity, strongly influences whether children will behave prosocially. In addition, the child's expectations for approval, knowledge of norms of behavior, and competence all determine whether the child will act prosocially. This suggests that we may not be able to speak of a global personality trait that disposes children to behave prosocially.

In a now classic study Lois Murphy (1937) investigated some precursors and correlates of children's sympathy. Her definition of "sympathy" included the behavior that now falls under the rubric "prosocial." Although the nursery school children she observed demonstrated sympathy, its frequency was quite low. Surprisingly, however, Murphy reported a positive correlation between sympathy and aggression.

More recent research on the relationship between prosocial behavior and aggression reveals that this relationship is not as simple or unidirectional as that reported by Murphy (1937). Harris and Siebel (1975) reported that aggression was unrelated to sharing. Feshback and Feshback (1969) assessed aggression in boys and girls aged 4 to 5 and 6 to 7 as a function of empathy. Empathy was assessed by reading the child a story and showing a series of slides depicting the story. At the end of the story, the child was asked how he or she felt about it. Empathic responses were those that indicated the child felt similar to the main character in the story. Aggression was measured by teachers' ratings of the children's behavior. Girls in both age groups showed no relation between empathy and aggression. For boys, age was a critical variable. At the younger age level, the high-empathy boys were more aggressive than the low-empathy boys. For the older group, those low in empathy were more aggressive than those who were highly empathic.

Finally, Yarrow and her colleagues (Barrett & Yarrow, 1977; Yarrow, Waxler, et al., 1976) have pointed out other complexities in the relation between prosocial and aggressive behavior. Helping is generally unrelated to aggression, as are sharing and comforting (Yarrow, Waxler, et al., 1976). However, low-aggressive boys tend to score higher on a combined measure of sharing-comforting, with no relation for boys who are high on measures of aggression. No relation among these measures was found for girls (Yarrow, Waxler, et al., 1976). But assertiveness (attempts to direct or stop another person's activity) was positively related to prosocial behavior.

The information provided by these studies indicates complex relations between prosocial and antisocial behavior. Situational and motivational factors seem to override the influence of stable personality predispositions that might incline the child to behave prosocially. The information also suggests that situational influences have a more important effect on the behavior than do cognitive factors.

Factors Influencing Prosocial Development

Cognition and Empathy

Martin Hoffman (1975a, 1975b, 1976, 1977) has suggested that children's prosocial behavior—especially helping—results from the development of **empathy** and cognition. He believes that empathy, which is a vicarious affective response to someone else's feelings (Hoffman, 1977), contributes to our altruistic motives to help others. Developmental changes in helping are due to the child's changing cognitive competence which allows the child to take someone else's point of view (role taking) and to understand better the difference between the self and others (see Chapter 5 for a discussion of object and person permanence). Since the child's role-taking ability and understanding of the environment develop along with advances in cognitive competence, the child's behavior in situations, for example, distress, will change. As Hoffman (1975a, pp. 610, 614–615) has put it:

> The central idea of the theory . . . is that since a fully developed empathic reaction is an internal response to cues about the affective states of someone else, the empathic reaction must depend heavily on the actor's cognitive sense of the other as distinct from himself, which undergoes dramatic changes developmentally.
>
> . . . [O]ne's cognitive sense of the other may be presumed to determine the meaning of his affective response to cues about the other's inner states. A major change may therefore be expected when the child begins to discriminate between the stimuli from his own body and those from without, acquiring a sense of the other as separate from himself.

The child first reacts to someone else's distress as though what is happening to that person is happening to him. At about 2 years of age, the child begins to realize that others have feelings and thoughts of their own and that they can differ from his. Because the child can make this discrimination, he can put himself in the other's place and find the source of distress. At about 6 to 9 years of age, the child gradually learns that each individual has his own distinct identity and personal history. As a result, the child can take into account not only the immediate state of the person but also that person's general condition. This results in what Hoffman calls *sympathetic distress,* a concern for the victim. The child then helps the person in distress out of sympathy for him or her (Hoffman, 1975a, 1976).

This formulation links the child's cognitive sense of the other person to prosocial behavior, specifically to empathy. We have some evidence to support this link. Children with a greater ability to decenter (to show less egocentrism) shared and helped more than children who were more egocentric (Rubin & Schneider, 1973). Training in role taking has also been found to increase sharing in 6- to 9-year-olds (Iannotti, 1975). Other researchers, however, report only very weak relations between prosocial behavior and skills in perspective taking (e.g., Zahn-Waxler, Radke-Yarrow & Brady-Smith, 1977) or report very complex relationships between these two abilities (e.g., Barrett & Yarrow, 1977). As better measures are devised, we shall probably find cognitive development to be an important contributor to the development of prosocial behavior.

Child-Rearing

Hoffman (1975a, 1975b, 1976, 1977) has also discussed the role of child-rearing practices for promoting prosocial behavior. In one study children's consideration for others, assessed by peer ratings of caring for other children's feelings and being willing to stick up for another child, were related to parents' discipline techniques, measured by parents' statements of how they would react if their child misbehaved in various ways. There was an interesting sex difference in the findings. For girls induction discipline was related to perceived high consideration for others; power assertion was related to peer ratings of low consideration for others. Girls' prosocial development was facilitated by parents' use of induction and diminished by parents' use of power assertion. For boys, induction had no relation to prosocial behavior, but power assertion promoted it. It may be that consideration for others is motivated by boys' need for peer approval and is a more deviant trait for boys. This would account for the sex difference.

Other research has related prosocial behavior to parents' use of induction (e.g., Hoffman, 1963), parents' affection (Rutherford & Mussen, 1968; Mussen, Harris, Rutherford & Keasey, 1970), the child's perception of the parent as warm and nurturant (Rutherford & Mussen, 1968), and the parents' altruistic values (Hoffman, 1975a, 1975b). Parents who espouse altruistic values and behave as altruistic models have children who are rated by their classmates as caring about other children and sticking up for them (Hoffman, 1975c). In addition, nurturant parents model prosocial behaviors such as sympathy and compassion and promote identification (Rutherford & Mussen, 1968). Prosocial behavior is clearly learned through identification and modeling, which are facilitated by the warm, nurturant use of induction discipline. Interestingly, the use of victim-centered discipline—suggesting reparation to a victim of the child's behavior—also relates to higher empathy, with the father being more important for girls and the mother for boys.

Television

Although considerable research has been done on the effects of television violence on childrens' aggressive behavior, it is only recently that the effects of television on childrens' prosocial behavior have been intensively researched (Friedrich & Stein, 1973, 1975; Mussen & Eisenberg-Berg, 1977; Stein & Friedrich, 1975). We have already discussed the role of parental modeling on prosocial learning. The research indicates that television models can positively influence children's prosocial behavior, although concomitant decreases in aggressive behavior are not very often observed (Stein & Friedrich, 1975; Friedrich & Stein, 1973, 1975).

Much of this research has been conducted with television programs designed to carry a prosocial message. The popular program for this purpose is "Mister Rogers," which is specifically designed to promote prosocial behavior through modeling and teaching. "Sesame Street" and "Fat Albert and the Cosby Kids" are examples of other programs designed to illustrate prosocial behavior. Scripts of these shows indicate they contain a variety of prosocial themes: cooperation, sharing, helping, persistence, understanding others' feelings, delaying gratification, and valuing individual uniqueness are some examples.

FRIEDRICH AND STEIN RESEARCH.   Friedrich and Stein's (1973) extensive study of the effects of aggressive and prosocial television programs on childrens' social behavior in preschool is an excellent example of this research. The 97 children were enrolled in a 9-week summer nursery school program. During the first 3 weeks childrens' behavior in the classroom was observed. The childrens' behavior was scored for aggression, task persistence, self-control, and regression in frustrating situations and in regard to requests or demands made of the child. Then the children were divided into 3 groups. During the next 4 weeks each group observed 12 television programs or films. One group observed aggressive programs—e.g., "Batman" and "Superman" cartoons. A second group observed prosocial programs—e.g., "Mister Rogers Neighborhood." A third group observed neutral films—childrens' films that had neither aggressive or prosocial themes. The childrens' behavior in the classroom was also recorded during this phase. During the last 2 weeks of the program, behavior was observed to check on any lasting effects due to observations of the various film contents.

Children exposed to aggressive television programs engaged in more interpersonal aggressive behavior than children who viewed the neutral program, especially if they were already prone to behave aggressively. The aggressive behavior of children initially low in aggression did not change as a result of viewing aggressive films. But these children also evidenced a decline in their ability to delay gratification and in their willingness to follow rules. Viewing prosocial films increased the prosocial behavior of lower-class but not middle-class children, whose prosocial behavior increased after viewing aggressive or neutral films. The researchers suggest

It has been found that television shows in which helping and sharing are stressed promote prosocial behavior in children. (Eric Roth/The Picture Cube)

this latter unexpected finding occurred because these children do not usually watch aggressive television programs (based on parent interviews) and watching them in the experiment heightened their number of interpersonal interactions, which were already highly prosocial. Those who observed prosocial programs also showed an increased ability to persist at tasks, were better able to delay gratification, and obeyed rules and followed commands better.

CONCLUSIONS FROM RESEARCH.   Observation of prosocial television films, then, increases prosocial behavior. And, these effects are discernable as long as 2 weeks after the viewing is stopped. Of some interest were the findings indicating that increases in aggression were not accompanied by decreases in prosocial behavior; and increases in prosocial actions were not paralleled by decreases in aggression. Since the measures of childrens' behavior were taken in settings very different from those shown in the films this experiment shows the strength of generalizability of the effects of viewing aggressive or prosocial films.

Other research (e.g., Friedrich & Stein, 1975) also demonstrates the generalizability of prosocial behaviors learned through television content. In their summary of this research Stein and Friedrich (1975) note some implications for educational programming on television. First, increased cooperation, altruism, sharing, and other prosocial behaviors occur after viewing prosocially oriented television programs. The researchers suggest that maximal effects are obtained when prosocial behavior is followed by positive consequences that are intrinsic to the behavior and that are real for children. Second, the use of warm, nurturant, and powerful models will enhance the benefits of prosocial programs. Finally, rehearsal of what is observed through play situations should be encouraged. Although the viewing time in this and other research is small compared to that typical of childrens' television viewing habits, Friedrich and Stein (1975, p. 37) point out:

> The clear effects of television . . . suggest that this type of prosocial television can have a strong impact on children who watch it in naturalistic contexts where viewing can occur over a much longer period of time than 1 week. These results appear to be readily applicable to naturalistic settings because the children generalized both learning and behavior to situations quite different from those to which they were exposed in the television and training, and because this generalization occurred in measures administered 2 to 3 days after the television viewing.

SUMMARY

Prosocial behavior, acts that help other people, includes helping, cooperativeness, altruism, and empathy. Experimental studies show that children help more with age but that situational factors, such as the presence of adults, can bring about a decline in helping. Practice in role playing and the observation of altruistic models, both live and televised, promotes helping. Sharing also increases with the age of the child, with modeling being a potent influence on the child's generosity. Cooperation seems to decline with age, while competitiveness and rivalry increase; cultural norms seem to have a strong influence on this behavior. Studies of the relations among various kinds of prosocial behavior indicate that they do not form a unified set. Situational and motivational factors seem to affect prosocial behavior more than any one enduring personality predisposition. Nonetheless, cognitive competence, empathy, and socialization seem to be related to the development of prosocial behavior.

CHAPTER 14

(Jerry Berndt/Stock, Boston)

PEER GROUP INTERACTIONS IN CHILDHOOD

OUR DISCUSSION of social development has been confined thus far to broad cultural influences and situational contexts. We have ignored for the most part the important role the child's peers play in social development. Much of the child's early socialization is controlled by adults because of the child's close contact with parents and other adults. But as the child enters a new world dominated by peers, they come to have an increasing impact on socialization. The theory and research discussed in this chapter focus on the roles played by the child's peers as he or she spends more and more waking hours away from the parents and under the influence of the peer group.

Interaction with the **peer group** has consequences that are sometimes obviously important and sometimes subtle. One unique feature of peer relations is the opportunity to practice adult roles. The child may, for example, practice being both a leader and a follower and thereby learn which role is more suitable. The child can also practice roles other than those encountered in child-adult relations. In this way, the child can learn how to behave in various situations and may develop behavior patterns or roles that will serve well in adulthood. Of course, if the behavior patterns are inappropriate, new ones will have to be developed. In childhood, this change is fairly easy. The child's mistakes usually do not have irreversible consequences, as they might have in adulthood.

The peer group also provides the child with the opportunity to interact with age-mates with similar conflicts, beliefs, likes, and dislikes. The child's peers may serve two functions, one therapeutic and the other bridging the generation gap. The peer group's influence on the child's adjustment becomes particularly important during adolescence (Chapters 15 and 16) but is significant even in childhood when strivings for independence and dominance arise (Cooley, 1909).

Investigators of childhood peer relations have attempted to find answers to such questions as: How do peer groups form and what changes do they undergo in formation, stabilization, and breaking apart? What is the course of friendship, both with same- and opposite-sex peers? How does the peer group influence the child's learning of social norms? How do peers influence the development of the child's self-esteem and self-concept?

This chapter describes group formation in childhood, the effects of the peer group on the individual child, the reinforcement of children's behavior by peers, and the role of peers as models for social development. It would, however, be beyond the scope of this chapter to review all the research in this area. We refer the interested reader to other recent surveys (for example, Campbell, 1964; Hartup, 1970a; Lewis & Rosenblum, 1975). Much of the material presented here is aimed at providing information needed for theoretical advancements in the explanation of the effects of peers. But this research also provides valuable descriptive information. In addition, research on such topics as peer reinforcement and modeling effects provides techniques for changing children's undesirable behavior through the use of peers.

Difficulties in Studying Peer Relations

To find answers to their questions, psychologists have used both experimental and observational techniques. As with much of the research on questions about socialization, there are problems that limit the research that can be done and that cloud the interpretation of the findings (Campbell, 1964). Much of the data obtained in research on peer relations comes from questionnaires or interviews that yield faulty (for example, people forget or unintentionally distort their recollections) or incomplete information and that are difficult to use with younger children, whose answers may be utterly unrelated to the question asked. The alternative is to use observation, which presents the problem of what is to be observed. For example, if we want to find out how peer groups are formed, we must choose a research setting—the playground, the classroom, the neighborhood gang, and so forth. To observe formation of groups in all these settings would require a great deal of both time and money. In addition, the samples of children studied are not usually representative of any large group but rather represent a narrow segment of the population, for example, middle-class 3- to 4-year-olds attending a private nursery school. Obviously, findings from this select sample may not reveal the same processes as those operating in the peer relations of middle-class children not enrolled in nursery school or of children from different social and economic backgrounds.

We note these difficulties for two reasons. First, the researcher must be aware of these problems and must learn how to deal with them. Second, we must reconcile apparently conflicting findings. We need to keep in mind that several investigators studying the same phenomenon in different situations or with different techniques or samples of subjects, may come to different conclusions about the processes underlying peer relations. Such diverse findings point the way for future research aimed at clarifying inconsistencies. Nonetheless, even at this early stage the research data do tell us something about peer relations and their effects on the growing child.

Age Differences

Most research on peer relations in childhood was conducted from the late 1920s through the early 1950s. The earlier developmental research was spurred on by the establishment of university nursery schools during the 1920s and 1930s. Since then, research on peer relations has focused on nondevelopmental hypotheses or on methodological advances. By far, most current research on the formation of groups and on group processes is done with adults.

Nursery School Children

Among the classic research of this kind is an investigation by Parten (e.g., 1932), who studied the patterns of play of 42 nursery school children between the ages of 2 and $4\frac{1}{2}$. Their behavior was coded into 6 categories: unoccupied behavior, **solitary play,** onlooker behavior (the child was an onlooker but not a participant in play activity), **parallel play** (playing alongside but not with other children), **associated play** (playing with other children and sharing toys), and **cooperative play** (playing games with rules). Sixty 1-minute observations of the children's play behavior were recorded. Parten reported that social participation increased with age—the older children spent more time in associated and cooperative play and less time in the other forms of play than did the younger children (see Figure 14-1). Parten and others (Herron & Sutton-Smith, 1971) have suggested that solitary play is a low-level activity indicating nonsociability or a preference for fantasy play.

More recent investigations of solitary play (Moore, Evertson & Brophy, 1974; Rubin, Maioni & Hornung, 1976) and fantasy (Sanders & Harper, 1976) have clarified the former's function. Moore and her colleagues (1974) had kindergarten teachers record instances of solitary play by their students during free-play sessions. She reported that, contrary to Parten's conclusion, nearly 50 percent of all solitary play consisted of goal-directed and educational activities. Large-muscle solitary play also accounted for 24.5 percent of all solitary play. The most mature forms of solitary play, then, occurred much more frequently than less mature forms indicative of social withdrawal. Sulking, pouting, daydreaming, and wandering were infrequent. The solitary play took place with blocks, arts and crafts, puzzles, workbooks, or reading—all of which are task-oriented and suggestive of maturity. In their review of their own and others' findings, Moore et al. (1974, p. 834) suggest "a continuum in solitary play, in which children move from passively watching to acting in more active and expressive activities to becoming independently involved in more challenging, problem-solving activities. Further, [the data] suggest that for most children

FIGURE 14-1   *Age Changes in Types of Play Patterns*

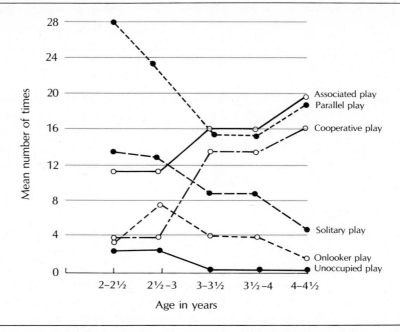

SOURCE: Parten, M. C. Social participation among pre-school children. *Journal of Abnormal and Social Psychology*, 1932, 27, pp 243–269.

at least, solitary play is a normal and probably functionally beneficial activity rather than an indicant of poor social adjustment."

Other research on children's play supports this view of the function of solitary play (Rubin et al., 1976). Rubin and his colleagues observed the play of lower- and middle-class boys and girls at a nursery school. These investigators coded 4 types of cognitive play based on Piaget's (1962; Smilansky, 1968) classification of the relation of play to cognition: *functional play,* involving repetitive muscle movements; *constructive play,* including the manipulation of objects to build something; *dramatic play,* involving substituting an imaginary situation that satisfied the child's needs; and *games with rules.* These 4 forms of cognitive play were coded within each of Parten's (1932) categories of social play. Rubin and his coworkers analyzed the data for social class and sex differences.

CLASS FACTORS.   Middle-class children engaged in more constructive, associative, and cooperative play than did the lower-class children. The latter group engaged in more parallel and functional play than did the middle-class group. Girls engaged in more constructive and less dramatic play than boys.

These investigators suggest that the lower-level play patterns of the lower-class children reflect the lack of relevant materials at home. The lower-class child may find the nursery school materials unfamiliar and may therefore spend time examining and manipulating them (functional play) but not yet using them for constructive or dramatic play. The middle-class child is likely to be more familiar with the materials and will consequently use them in more advanced activities, such as constructive or dramtic play (Feitelson & Ross, 1973; Feitelson, Weintraub & Michaeli, 1972; Rubin et al., 1976). Social-cognitive measures also reflect these differences, with lower-class children engaging in more solitary-functional and parallel-functional play and less associative-constructive and cooperative-dramatic play than middle-class children. The lower-class children, then, exhibited a lower level of social-cognitive play than the middle-class children.

The data for the middle-class children replicates Parten's (1932) findings of 40 years earlier, thus indicating the intergenerational stability in Parten's play hierarchy. But the descriptive value of the hierarchy may be limited to middle-class children. Lower-class children come from backgrounds that produce a different sequence in play behaviors.

IMPORTANCE OF SOLITARY PLAY.   The findings of Rubin et al. (1976) for solitary play are especially interesting because they confirm the results of Moore et al. (1974) that most solitary play is goal-directed. Rubin et al. suggest that solitary play has typically been misunderstood as a low level of play. They believe that parallel play occupies the lowest level on the social-cognitive hierarchy of play in preschool children. Rubin et al. (1976, pp. 418–419) interpret solitary play as an attempt by the child "to get away from it all, while those who play beside others may desire the

Younger children engage largely in parallel play (Hugh Rogers/Monkmeyer)

company of other children but may not be able to successfully take their points of view in order to play in an associative or cooperative manner. This notion is supported by a recent finding that ... preschooler's role-taking skills are ... positively related to associative play, and not related to solitary play."

SEX DIFFERENCES.   We have noted that boys engage in more **fantasy play** than girls (Moore et al., 1974) and that middle-class children engage in more fantasy play than lower-class children (Rubin et al., 1976). Psychologists are interested in the role of the situation and playthings in promoting fantasy play (Fein, 1975; Singer, 1973). Sanders and Harper (1976) investigated age and sex differences in the fantasy play of 3- to 5-year-old preschoolers. Boys engaged in more fantasy play than girls, as did older children more than younger ones.   For example, boys and older children more often pretended to be animals, pretended objects were other things, attributed human feelings and behavior to inanimate objects, played pretend games, and adopted pretend roles. Younger children's fantasy play increased over the course of the year, indicating a possible developmental trend, perhaps cognitive, in fantasy. Sanders and Harper suggest that the sex differences found in fantasy play may reflect situational circumstances, for example, open spaces and materials favoring large-muscle activities, that facilitate fantasy play for boys. This supposition is consistent with the finding that boys engage in more pretend assaults than girls, who play more passive and physically restrained games.

A FOLLOW-UP STUDY.   These measures of peer relations among preschoolers have important connections with peer relations during early childhood. Waldrop and Halverson (1975) investigated this relationship in children at age $2\frac{1}{2}$ and again at age $7\frac{1}{2}$. Both boys and girls who at $2\frac{1}{2}$ were friendly and involved with their peers were at ease with peers and spent considerable time with them at age $7\frac{1}{2}$. Hence, social interaction, of which play is an important part, at this early age was predictive of peer social relations 5 years later.

Pre-Nursery School Children

Studies of peer interactions among children younger than age $2\frac{1}{2}$ to 3 are rare (Mueller & Lucas, 1975). One study of a group of 19-month-olds with their mother and with a familiar peer revealed clear peer-oriented interactions (Rubenstein & Howes, 1976). When both the peer and the mother were present, the child spent over 50 percent of the time interacting with the peer—talking, offering or exchanging toys, imitating the peer, and indulging in very little aggressive behavior. These toddlers "preferred" peer interaction to interaction with their mother. This preference resulted in a more mature interaction with the inanimate environment. Peers enhanced the quality of the child's play, perhaps by serving as models. This finding is interesting in light of Piaget's claim that peer interactions have an important influence on the child's cognitive development. When the peer was present, the child talked less to the mother and imitated her less than when the peer was absent. Peers, then, exert a dual influence on children aged 1½: they encourage higher levels of play with toys and they act to lower the level of interactions with the mother.

We have some evidence about the developmental course of this type of peer interaction among infants and toddlers (Eckerman, Whatley, & Kutz, 1975). Eckerman and her colleagues recorded the play behavior of 60 middle-class boys and girls in 3 age groups: 10–12 months, 16-18 months, and 22–24 months. In over 60 percent of the observations made during the 20-minute play period, the children at all ages were interacting with the peer. Direct involvement with the peer's play—for example, imitating the peer or coordinating toy play with that of the peer—increased with age. Solitary play remained stable at all 3 age levels, but social play increased with age (see Figure 14-2A), making up some 60 percent of the oldest children's behavior. As Figure 14-2B shows, the increase in social play with age reflected an increase in play with peers. By 2 years of age, children's toy play typically involves another person who, in this study, was more likely to be the peer than the mother. These results suggest an orderly progression in the social interaction of children with their peers.

Young infants interact very little with their peers. By about 1½ years of age, peer interaction occurs but does not exceed interaction with the mother. At about 2 years of age, the child prefers toy play with peers and shows a decline in play with the mother when a peer, either a stranger (Eckerman et al., 1975) or a friend (Rubenstein & Howes, 1976) is present. Eckerman et al. suggest that this progression reflects the generalization of responses learned to familiar adults. In our discussion of the consequences of forming attachments (Chapter 11), we pointed out this response

FIGURE 14-2   In social play the child involves others—peer, mother, or new adult—in his activities with nonsocial objects.

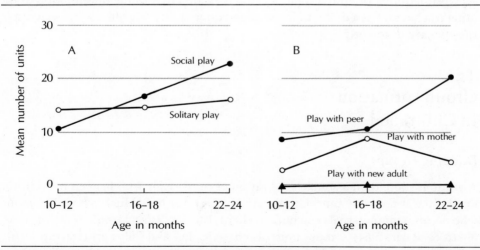

SOURCE: Eckerman, C. O., Whatley, J. L., and Kutz, Stuart L. Growth of social play with peers during the second year of life. *Developmental Psychology*, 1975, *11*, pp. 42–49.

generalization as an important result of attachment. Both the age progression and the behavior toward peers correspond closely to what we would expect on the basis of attachment theory.

SOME CONCLUSIONS. The developmental changes in play reflect the changing nature of children's peer interactions. Concomitant changes have been noted in other social behaviors of children in this age range. Attention seeking from adults, for example, decreases during this age span (Hattwick & Sanders, 1938; Heathers, 1955; Maccoby & Masters, 1970; Martin, 1964). Competition and rivalry increase between the ages of 2 and 5 (Leuba, 1933). In a peg-inserting task children performed both alone and with the help of another child. The performance of 2-year-olds was the same under both conditions, but the performance of 3- and 4-year-olds was lower in the peer condition than in the alone condition, apparently because of the distraction of the peer's presence. The 5-year-olds performed much better with a peer than they did alone. Leuba argues that by the age of 5, the children could channel their competitiveness into an adaptive outlet, in this case performance at the task.

These and other studies demonstrate dramatic changes with age in children's reactions to groups and in their responsiveness to peers. The causes of these age differences probably lie in changes in cognitive abilities (Flavell et al., 1968, 1977; Hartup, 1970; Piaget, 1932; Kohlberg, 1969). The important cognitive skill here is role-taking ability (Chapter 12; Selman, 1976).

Skills in role taking, defined as the ability to see things from another's point of view (Selman, 1976), depend on age (Flavell et al., 1968; Selman, 1976) and level of cognitive development. Children's cognitive skills enlarge their role-taking abilities and alter their perspective on social situations and on the points of view of others; preoperational and concrete operational children have different views of the same social situation or of other people because they are interpreting the situation or the other's behavior from different levels of cognitive ability (Flavell, 1977). As a result, they behave differently.

Group Formation in Childhood

Defining Groups

A group is more than a simple aggregation of individuals who happen to be in the same place at the same time. Groups are composed of individuals who interact and who possess common goals and norms (Sherif, Harvey, White, Hood, & Sherif, 1961; Sherif & Sherif, 1964). Groups must also have leaders and followers (Hartup, 1970), and probably a division of labor. These defining characteristics apply equally to long- and short-term groups and to spontaneous and ad hoc groups.

Types of Peer Groups

The child's first peer group is probably based on sex. From the preschool years until about sixth or seventh grade, children associate almost exclusively with others of their own sex. Before that, a child who associates with members of the opposite sex to any great degree is likely to be labeled a "sissy" or a "tomboy." Only after puberty is it acceptable for children to have close associations with members of the opposite sex. This grouping seems to reflect social stereotypes in children's games as well as intentional or unintentional attempts by the parents to encourage the development of "appropriate" sex roles.

Another important determinant of membership in peer groups is age. During childhood, members of a peer group are likely to be of roughly the same age. This phenomenon probably stems from age differences in interests and physical ability in games as well as competence in following the rules of the game. Age differences in cognitive abilities also affect the formation of groups and suggest that age groupings for peer associations reflect more than chance happenings.

Peer Group Formation

Sherif and his co-workers have carried out a number of excellent studies of the formation of children's groups. In one study, Sherif and Sherif (1953) investigated the formation of groups in white, middle-class boys in a camp setting. In the first phase of the experiment, 2 groups of boys were formed. They named themselves the "Red Devils" and the "Bull Dogs." The groups were kept apart and allowed to remain intact for 3 days to allow friendships to spring up. In the second phase, the 2 groups were split in half and 2 new groups were formed and observed for 5 days. These 2 groups were carefully matched in personalities and abilities based on the judgments of the camp staff. Again, the groups were kept apart while each engaged in its own activities. In the third phase, the 2 groups were put in competition with each other.

This experiment tested 3 hypotheses: (1) individuals brought together in a haphazard way will acquire the characteristics of a group—leaders and followers, friendships, division of labor, and the like; (2) shared norms, attitudes, and values will develop; (3) hostility between groups will arise if they are placed in competition. The data clearly supported each of these hypotheses.

Phase 1 saw the emergence of friendship and status patterns, but these changed and new friendship patterns formed in Phase 2 (although half the boys in each group knew each other from the first phase). In Phase 2, both groups developed a hierarchy of leaders and followers. Although the leaders tended to be the more popular members of the group, leadership and popularity were not perfectly correlated. Each group also formed its own norms during the 5 days of Phase 2. For example, attitudes about each other, the camp and the activities in it, and the other group—we versus they—developed in each group. Although the boys in each group expressed disparagement of the other group, there was no genuine hostility. Friendships were formed mostly with members of the current group. In Phase 3, 1 group happened to win consistently in the contests. The result was considerable frustration in the losing group, with consequent hostility between groups, and a loss of solidarity within the losing group.

Sherif et al. (1961) replicated and extended this experiment in a study of the formation of groups among 22 fifth-grade boys, also in a camp setting. The boys were separated into 2 equal aggregates, with neither being aware of the other's existence. Again, the aggregates quickly took on the characteristics of groups. In this study, however, the competition between groups was controlled in such a way that both groups had the same number of successes and failures. However, competition had the same result as in the previous experiment, namely, considerable hostility between groups, although the solidarity within the groups remained strong. During the competitive phases, the groups' structure did change, with new leaders coming to the fore, primarily as a result of excelling in the contests (leadership roles in groups may depend on the group's immediate goal). In the last stage, the groups had to cooperate to meet a common need, for example, to restore the water supply. This forced cooperation, reduced conflict beween the groups, and increased friendship choices across group lines.

These and other studies by Sherif and his colleagues (e.g., Sherif & Sherif, 1964) have important practical implications. Forming new groups out of two or more hostile groups and providing a common goal should reduce hostility. Providing the opportunity for two hostile groups to work together also should reduce intergroup hostility. These implications have been tested with racial groups in camp settings and have been partially verified (e.g., Mussen, 1950; Yarrow, Campbell, & Yarrow, 1958). These two studies showed that racial integration resulted in improved attitudes of white children toward black children, which suggests a basis for improving racial relations through school integration.

Peer Group Effects on the Individual Child

Group Norms and Conformity

The norms of a group guide its members in the tasks of the group. One of the earliest studies of the formation of group norms was conducted by Merei (1949) who observed 12 groups of 4 children each in a day-care situation. Although the children varied in age from 4 to 11 years, Merei reported no age differences in norm formation. He did report that groups developed norms dealing with a wide variety of behavior, such as seating order, rights of possession, game sequences, and verbal expressions. Although this study provides clear evidence for the formation of group

Conformity is expressed in dress codes, language, and personal values. (Cary Wolinsky/Stock, Boston)

norms, the extent to which the structured atmosphere of the situation—including the presence of adults—influenced the formation and the types of norms is not known.

Closely allied to the study of the formation of norms in a peer group is the study of group **conformity,** that is, the extent to which the individual behaves in ways deemed appropriate by members of the group. Unlike the paucity of theory and research on norm formation in children's peer groups, there is a lot of research and theorizing on conformity in children, most of it within the framework of imitation and social-learning theory (see Chapter 10). One notion advanced to explain conformity in group behavior is generalized imitation (Gewirtz, 1969). According to social-learning theory, conformity to the behavior of peers should vary with the reinforcement of conforming responses. Since social-learning theories are non-developmental, however, they yield no predictions about age trends in conformity. At best, they can be used to argue that if conformity is increasingly reinforced during part of the life span of the individual, then conforming behavior should also increase during this time.

PIAGET'S THEORY. Piaget (1932) has discussed children's conformity to peers within the context of learning the rules of social behavior. Piaget postulated a sequence of 3 stages in the development of the understanding of social rules, particularly the rules of games. In the first or *egocentric* stage, the child has no clear idea of social rules. Whatever rules the child does follow are laid down by parents. During this stage, which lasts until about the age of 6, children may imitate the behavior of others, especially adults, but they have little if any understanding of the reasons for that behavior. During the second stage, *extreme conformity*, which lasts from about

A child belongs to a number of different peer groups that may not overlap at all in membership. (Jerry Berndt/Stock, Boston)

age 6 to age 11, children increasingly interact with peers and conform to social standards of behavior. They begin to follow rules, such as those of games, but they view these rules as coming from outside forces, mainly adults, and as being inflexible and unalterable. At about age 11, the child's conception of rules begins to change once again. During this third stage, *variant rule application*, the child interprets rules as the result of agreement among people rather than coming from some outside source. The child now considers rules as flexible and open to change by group consensus. This understanding of rules leads to a decline in peer conformity because of the flexibility now attributed to rules.

Piaget suggests that conformity to peers should increase during childhood and then gradually decline as the adolescent gains an adult perspective on rules. These changes in conformity result from the developing cognitive abilities that allow for different interpretations of norms as these cognitive abilities mature. Unlike social-learning theory, Piaget's theory does enable us to make predictions about age changes and differences in conformity as a result of changes in the developing child's intellect.

Research findings lend support to the predictions based on Piaget's theory and thus lend credence to the notion that conforming behavior in children is in part a function of their cognitive abilities. One classic investigation was carried out by

Berenda (1950). Conformity to peers was assessed by the child's aggreement with peers' inaccurate estimates of the length of a line drawn on a card. One experiment compared a group of 7- to 10-year-olds with a group of 11- to 13-year olds. The child was exposed to incorrect judgments presumably made by the 8 brightest children in the child's class. Conformity was measured by the number of times the child agreed with the peer group and gave an inaccurate estimate of line length. Although the younger children conformed to the false judgments more than the older children, the difference was not statistically significant. For both age groups, the number of incorrect answers was greater when the child was exposed to incorrect peer responses than when the child gave judgments alone, indicating conformity to peer group pressure. On the basis of similar experiments, Berenda (1950) reported significant age differences in conformity to peer judgments between 7- to 10-year-olds and 11- to 13-year-olds only when the members of the peer group gave false, nonuniform overestimates of line length. When the peer overestimates were all uniform, no significant age differences in conformity occurred.

CONFORMITY AND CULTURE.   Iscoe, Williams, and Harvey (1963, 1964) performed 2 experiments that indicated that conformity to peer norms was not only a function of age differences in cognitive ability but also was open to cultural influences, in this case, race. The first experiment was conducted with white children and the second with black children. In both cases the subjects were 7, 9, 12, and 15 years of age. Their task was to count metronome clicks. Each child was told that 3 other children were also participating in the experiment and was given incorrect information about the number of clicks these other subjects reported. Conformity was assessed by the number of times the subject reported an incorrect number of the clicks.

Although the shape of the curve relating conformity to age was the same for the white and the black children, the peak age of conformity occurred earlier for the black than the white children. For the white children, conformity increased between the 9- and 12-year-olds and then decreased. The black subjects showed increased conformity between the 7- and 9-year-olds and then decreased. The white children generally conformed more than the black children. These racial differences are consistent with Piaget's analysis of children's conformity as affected by their interactions with peers. Since black children are exposed to stronger peer interactions earlier than most white children (Hartup, 1970), they may reach an earlier peak in conformity. Hartup also suggests that the black peer culture encourages greater independence and tolerates less conformity than the white peer culture, which may account for the generally lower conformity found for the black children. The above results, then, are consistent with Piaget's theory.

CONFORMITY AND AMBIGUOUS SITUATIONS.   Conformity in children is also influenced by the situation (Hoving, Hamm & Galvin, 1969; Costanzo & Shaw, 1966; Bixenstine, DeCorte & Bixenstine, 1976). Conformity to peers increases with task

FIGURE 14-3   *Children's Mean Corrected Agreement Scores on Tasks of Varying Ambiguity*

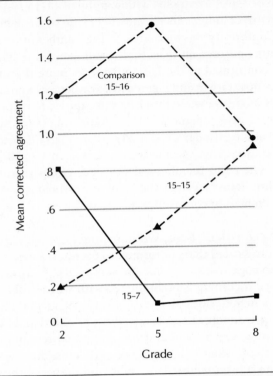

SOURCE: Hoving, K. L., Hamm, N., and Galvin, P. Social influence as a function of stimulus ambiguity at three age levels. *Developmental Psychology*, 1969, *1*, pp. 631–636.

ambiguity. Ambiguous tasks require the child to make a difficult decision, as in counting clicks, estimating line length, or counting dots (see below). In unambiguous situations conformity decreases as age increases. This was clearly shown by Hoving, Hamm, and Galvin (1969), who had children in grades 2, 5, and 8 judge whether the right- or left-hand side of a slide image had more dots on it. One set of slides had an equal number on each side (15–15), and 2 sets had an unequal number (15–16 or 15–7). A system of lights informed the child how his "classmates" had rated the slide. Figure 14-3 shows the level of conformity for each grade level. For the ambiguous task (15–15), conformity increased with age, but for the unambiguous task (15–7) it decreased.

These developmental trends in conformity to the peer group seem to reflect changes in the need for peer approval and a growing awareness of and need to be correct (Bixenstine et al., 1976; Hoving et al., 1969). These two motives are thought to vary with age and the ambiguity of the task. Hence, Hoving et al. (1976, p. 636) note the following:

In unambiguous tasks, the subject's need to be correct and need for peer approval are placed in direct conflict. If the subject agrees with the group to gain peer approval, he fails to satisfy his need to be correct. In the younger subjects neither need is great but apparently peer approval can be gained at this age by agreeing with the group even if the group's choice is obviously incorrect. This, when coupled with minimal opposition from the need to be correct, results in relatively large amounts of conformity at younger age levels. In older subjects we find a much stronger need to be correct coupled with the subject's presumed inability to gain peer approval for agreement when the apparent choice of the group is obviously incorrect. Hence the minimal conformity at older ages on unambiguous tasks.

The positive relationship between age and conformity on ambiguous tasks is also thought to be due to the increasing need to be correct and to gain peer approval, which occurs with age. The child's past history of reinforcement is presumed to result in his agreeing with the choices of others when in doubt as to the correct answer. Optimal satisfaction of both motivational systems occurs if the subject agrees with the choices of others in ambiguous situations. This optimizes his chances of being correct and produces maximal peer approval.

This research indicates clear age differences in the degree of children's conformity to the peer group. As we have noted, social-learning theories cannot easily account for the relation between age and conformity. The general trend of the age differences in conformity, however, can be predicted from Piaget's theorizing about the child's understanding of social rules and lends support to the notion that as the child's cognitive abilities change, so does the child's understanding of social rules. This developing understanding of social rules, in turn, is related to conformity. The evidence strongly suggests that cognitive factors play an important role in peer group influences on social behavior.

Factors Affecting Popularity Among Peers

Popularity among peers has been assessed with a number of sociometric measures, for example, the **Guess Who technique,** preferences for play partners, and best friends. Most investigators correlate sociometric ratings of popularity with scores from personality or cognitive tests, social class, or physical factors to assess the relation of popularity and individual difference variables. Because the resulting data are correlational, however, the direction of causality in the relationship may be unclear. And some unmeasured variable, for example, may be the underlying cause of the relationship found. For example, assume we find a positive correlation between grades in school and ratings of popularity with peers. It is just as likely that being popular causes one to do better in school—perhaps by making one more relaxed and comfortable in the school setting—as it is that doing well in school causes one to be popular. Or perhaps children with high IQs do better in school and also are more popular. Because such correlational data are difficult to interpret, we must be cautious in making inferences about the causes of popularity.

Popularity is usually considered to reflect the desire of a child's peers to seek contact with him. But a low popularity rating by one's peers may not mean rejection or avoidance by them. Unpopular children may simply be ignored by their peers. In other words, popularity and rejection are not the end points of a single dimension (Moore & Updegraff, 1964).

STABILITY OF PEER POPULARITY.   It is commonly believed that friendship patterns in early childhood fluctuate quickly because of day-to-day encounters. This presumably results in a low level of stability in peer popularity. Empirical investigations of the stability of popularity, however, provide evidence to the contrary (e.g., Hartup, Glazer & Charlesworth, 1967; Gronlund, 1955; Moore & Updegraff, 1964).

McCandless and Marshall (1957) found that stability correlations for popularity ranged from +.41 to +.76 for nursery school children over an interval of 20 days. Hartup et al. (1967) found a stability coefficient of +.68 over a 5-month interval, thus showing considerable consistency in peer-group popularity. Although other investigators have reported somewhat lower correlations (see Witryol & Thompson, 1953, for a review of the earlier work in this area), the general consensus of the research is that popularity is reasonably stable in early childhood.

Friendship patterns during adolescence seem to fluctuate even less (e.g., Horrocks & Thompson, 1946; Thompson & Horrocks, 1947). These investigators found that over a 2-week period, popularity was more stable for older (16- to 18-year-olds) than younger (11- to 15-year-olds) adolescents. These data thus indicate an age trend in the stability of popularity—friendships are more stable with increasing age.

These data indicate that popularity is a fairly stable trait, thereby making it *reasonable* to study its antecedents. The data are also sufficiently reliable (consistent) to measure popularity, thereby making it *possible* to study its antecedents.

PHYSICAL ATTRACTIVENESS.   One well-documented contributor to popularity is physical attractiveness (Dibiase & Hjelle, 1968; Lerner & Gellert, 1969; Kleck, Richardson, & Ronald, 1974). The obese, the physically disabled, and those who do not have what is considered a normal and pleasant physical appearance tend to be less well accepted socially. Even children as young as kindergarten age show an aversion to some physical characteristics (obesity, for example) and are able to correctly indentify their own physical shape (Lerner & Gellert, 1969). It has been suggested that appearance is particularly important in the first phases of social interaction but becomes less important with time and a fuller acquaintance with the individual's personality (Kleck et al., 1974). We have, however, very little information on the truth of this assertion (Richardson, 1969).

Kleck and his co-workers assessed the degree to which close contact with peers was associated with popularity and the degree to which popularity was a function of physical attractiveness. Boys aged 9 to 14 who were attending a summer camp rated the social acceptability of their peers, whom they had known for 2 weeks. In the next camp session, a new group of boys rated photos of the earlier boys by saying which one of each of 5 pairs of photos they would like to have as a friend. Each pair of photos contained a well-liked peer and one who was not well liked, according to the ratings of the previous group. The results indicated that preferences based on the photos alone (that is, the preferences of the second group of campers) were closely related to popularity ratings by the first group. A picture of a highly accepted boy was chosen about 64 percent of the time over a picture of a less socially accepted boy. This finding was replicated in a second study by the same authors and has been demonstrated by other researchers (e.g., Bersheid & Walster, 1974). Contrary to the popular notion, physical attractiveness, particularly head and facial attributes, is important not only in initial interactions but also as a predictor of long-term social acceptance.

IQ AND ACHIEVEMENT. Early investigations of the relation between IQ and peer popularity focused on the correlation between IQ scores and sociometric ratings of popularity. This correlation is positive and ranges from a low (about $+.20$) to a moderate (about $+.65$) level (Davis, 1957; Hill, 1963; Wardlow & Greene, 1952). But these findings are difficult to interpret because of the positive correlation between IQ and social class. As a result, it is unclear whether the positive correlations are due to IQ or social class.

An experiment by Roff and Sells (1965) helps clarify the issue. A total of 2,800 fourth-grade students were divided into 4 social-class levels on the basis of their parents' income and education. IQ information was also available for all the children. In each class the children were asked to make choices of the 4 best-liked and 2 least-liked peers, with boys picking boys and girls picking girls (because of the importance of same-sex peer groups at this age). Each child was then assigned a popularity score based on the number of times he or she was chosen as a most- or least-liked peer. The data are presented in Figure 14-4. For both boys and girls at each socioeconomic level, the highly popular children had higher IQ scores than the children low in popularity. These data demonstrate a close relationship between IQ and popularity, independent of social class.

Since IQ and scholastic achievement are positively correlated, it is reasonable to expect that popularity should also be related to scholastic achievement. Several investigations have proven this to be the case. Sells and Roff (1967), for example, reported that for fourth- through seventh-graders, school marks and popularity correlated $+.33$, with higher correlations in the earlier grades and lower ones in the later grades.

COGNITIVE DEVELOPMENT. Working within a Piagetian framework, Rardin and Moan (1971) recently studied the relationship between popularity and cognitive development in kindergarten through third grade. These investigators tested Piaget's

FIGURE 14-4 *The IQ and Choice Status of (a) Girls and (b) Boys in Relation to Socioeconomic Background*

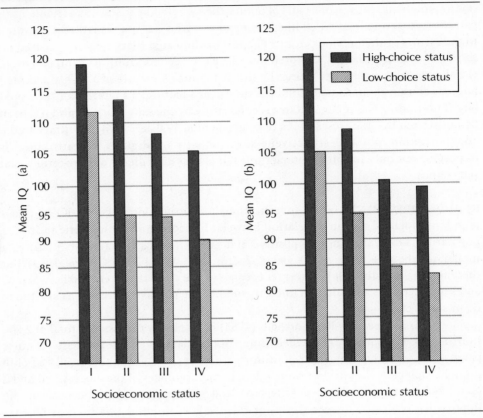

SOURCE: Roff, M., and Sells, S. Relations between intelligence and sociometric status in groups differing in sex and socioeconomic background. *Psychological Reports*, 1965, 16, pp. 511–516.

idea that peer interaction is a major factor in the change from preoperational thinking to concrete operations and that social development parallels cognitive development. Piaget's theory implies that cognitive development varies directly with the quality of peer relationships. To assess cognitive development, all 81 children were given tests of conservation and classification/class inclusion. Then each child identified his or her 3 best-liked classmates. Correlational analyses revealed that the child's cognitive development was only weakly associated with the quality of peer relations. Measures of popularity (derived from the child's reasons given for picking best friends, the stability of friendships over a 6-week period, and other measures) indicated that its course ran parallel to cognitive development since both types of measures showed developmental increases across grade levels. Popularity and cognitive development, however, were only slightly related, thus supporting Piaget's contention that the two types of development run parallel but independently. The researchers concluded that peer interaction has only a minor effect on cognitive development.

More recent studies of the relation between popularity and cognition have focused on the role of the child's egocentricity in communication (e.g., Deutsch, 1974; Rubin, 1972). Piaget (1926) has suggested that one important aspect of popularity is the ability to take someone else's point of view into account during communication. Peers who can do this, that is, peers who are less egocentric in their communication, will be more popular. This does seem to be the case for children in kindergarten and second grade, but not for older children (Deutsch, 1974; Rubin, 1972). Although the exact reasons for this relationship are unknown, it may be due to the child's willingness to decenter and to engage in mutual intellectual give-and-take with peers (Miller & Brownell, 1975). The inability or unwillingness of the less cognitively advanced child to decenter may lead to frustration in relations with more cognitively advanced peers, creating strained relations with them and a low popularity rating.

Less bright students, then, are not as popular as their brighter and scholastically more successful peers. The Roff and Sells study suggests that intellectual level or scholastic achievement causes the greater popularity rather than the reverse.

SOCIAL CLASS MEMBERSHIP.   We have already noted that within a social class, IQ and popularity are positively correlated, but we did not discuss the possibility of an independent relation between social class and popularity. What little research has been done on this question suggests that the lower-class child is less popular than the middle- or upper-class child. To determine the relation between social class and popularity, we must ensure that IQ is not a confounding factor, for the same reasons that we must not confound the relation of popularity to IQ without social class as a contaminating variable. In a study of sixth-graders divided into 3 IQ levels, Wrighter (1948) reported a positive relation between father's social class, based on occupation, and a child's popularity. It appears that social class and popularity are correlated in much the same manner as IQ and popularity. The higher the child's social class, the higher his popularity rating by peers.

Since measures of social class are so global, there are many possible explanations for its relation to popularity. The results of a study by Feinberg, Smith, and Schmidt (1958), conducted with male adolescents from the lower, middle, and upper classes (defined by family income) suggest that the different values held by children from different social classes may account for the greater popularity of children coming from the middle and upper classes. At all levels, the popular peers were characterized as intelligent, fair, athletic, good company, honest, and so on. At the lower- and middle-class levels, the boys also stressed common interests, minding one's own business, and the ability to talk well as important qualities of popular peers. The boys from the high-income group stressed leadership, scholarship, cooperativeness, and participation in activities as critical for peer acceptance. These data strongly suggest that friendship patterns are related to social class and that this relation is based on differences in the values of children from different social classes. In spite of the agreement of children from all social classes on certain values, there are also differences in values that are important in selecting friends. Since values are learned from parents, directly or by modeling them, it is important to discuss child-rearing practices related to popularity.

CHILD-REARING PRACTICES. An examination of child-rearing practices may be fruitful for explaining how IQ and social class come to be related to popularity. The findings of what little research has been done in this area point to disciplinary techniques as the most important effect of child-rearing on popularity (e.g., Hoffman, 1961; Winder & Rau 1962). Winder and Rau reported that the parents of highly popular boys used very little physical punishment, preferring love-withdrawal and the withholding of privileges as the primary means of discipline. Both of these latter techniques lead to low physical aggressiveness in children, one of the correlates of popularity. The parents of popular children were also well adjusted and felt their children were competent. Moreover, they communicated this confidence to their offspring.

Popular children expressed more satisfaction with their home life, felt a stronger family bond, and were generally happier than less popular children (Elkins, 1958). This security and stability felt by the parents were communicated to their children and reflected in the children's psychological adjustment.

The picture we get from this research is of a child who is happy, competent, comes from a cohesive home, has a secure self-concept, has parents with high self-concepts and who do not teach the use of physical aggression. Not surprisingly, these are the traits children ascribe to popular peers. Child-rearing techniques thus very likely have an influence on the child's popularity with his or her peers.

Peers as
Socialization Agents

The reader now should have a fairly clear picture of age differences in the formation of peer groups and of the effects of the peer group on the individual child, particularly such determinants of peer-group membership as conformity to group norms and popularity within the group. In this section we examine research on more specific ways in which peers act as agents for the socialization of the child's behavior. Anyone familiar with children knows that peers play an important role in socializing the child. The more interesting questions concern how this takes place, what behavior is socialized, and what are the relative contributions of peers and adults to the child's socialization.

Peers act as models for and reinforcers of each other's behavior. (Jim Harrison)

For a general view of the importance of peers in the child's socialization, we need only think about the social world of the growing child. The first encounters with peers are likely to be with children in the neighborhood. Later, in nursery or elementary school, the child encounters large numbers of peers with whom long-term contact is forced, such as in school. In these forced associations, the child must adjust his or her wishes, desires, and behavior to suit those of others with whom interaction is taking place. This adjustment may entail the learning of new modes of interaction or the changing of old habits. The child must learn to share with others, to understand that others may have different purposes, and to deal with the conflicts that inevitably arise. Difficulties experienced in this task stem, in part, from the child's background and upbringing. The greatest difficulty in adjusting to peers probably occurs when there are large differences in these rearing characteristics. It is also likely that socialization by peers will be strongest in these instances.

Peers undoubtedly reinforce some of the child's social skills, but not others. Peers also act as new models for social behavior, both acceptable and unacceptable. As the child encounters these new models for imitation and identification, he or she must choose those best suited to his or her needs. Finally, the child encounters peers whose views and behavior differ from those the parents have taught. This contrast in ideals often produces conflict between the peers and the child and also between the child and the parents. The child must learn to deal with this conflict in such a way as to maintain workable relations with both peers and parents.

Peers as Reinforcing Agents

Research on peer reinforcement effects has of necessity focused on social reinforcement from peers, because peers typically have no other reinforcers (such as food) to dispense. Social reinforcement includes such things as praise, companionship, or a pat on the back. Laboratory research on peer reinforcement has focused on situational factors related to the effects of peer reinforcement on the child's behavior (Hartup, 1970). Observational research, on the other hand, has concentrated on mutual reinforcement among peers (Hartup, 1970). Both kinds of research have been guided primarily by the interests of the individual investigator rather than by theoretical considerations. We must therefore make inferences from quite different research strategies in order to achieve a general picture of the effects of peer reinforcement.

EXPERIMENTAL SITUATIONS.   Although reinforcement did not come from peers, Cohen's (1966) study, "Justin and His Peers," is perhaps the clearest demonstration of the effects of social reinforcement on children's behavior with peers (Hartup, 1970). The experimental situation was cleverly designed so that either cooperative or competitive responses between Justin, a 13-year-old boy, and another person were reinforced. Reinforcement consisted of either candy or pennies. The response required of the subjects was pulling a plunger. Cooperative and competitive responding were studied with Justin and, in turn, each of five other people: his brother (age 16), his sister (age 14), a friend (age 13), a male stranger (age 14), and his mother. Justin was placed in one room, his "partner" in another. Cooperative behavior was defined as a response (plunger pull) by one of the two participants followed within a .5-second interval by a response from the other. Both were reinforced. Reinforcement for cooperative behavior was studied as was reinforcement for leadership behavior, for example, Justin's response being followed by his partner's, or vice-versa.

Table 14-1 summarizes the results of the experiment shown in acquisition curves for the reinforced behavior. Cohen interpreted these findings according to Justin's relations to the various partners. For example, Justin assumed the role of leader with partners he was accustomed to leading—his brother and his friend—and took the role of follower with those people he usually followed. This experimental technique proved useful in describing the child's social behavior within the context of environmental events, namely, reinforcement contingencies and previous history of interaction with the partner.

Several recent experiments have studied the relation between peer reinforcement and previous relations with peers, particularly those who were liked or disliked. The research of Hartup and his co-workers is especially enlightening in this regard. To investigate the effectiveness of social reinforcement by peers, Hartup (1964) tested 4- to 5-year-olds in a simple marble-dropping task. Following a baseline period in which the subjects dropped marbles but received no reinforcement, there was a 6-minute experimental period during which marble dropping was periodically

TABLE 14-1   Justin's Social Profile

| TEAM | UNCONTROLLED LEADERSHIP | CONTROLLED LEADERSHIP | | UNCONTROLLED COMPETITION |
		JUSTIN LEADS	OTHER LEADS	
Justin and . . .				
Brother	Justin leads. Long acquisition Individual responses	Long acquisition Brother persists in leading.	Shorter acquisition Justin slow to follow.	
Friend	Justin leads; halts friend's attempts to lead.	Rapid acquisition	Rapid acquisition Justin slow to follow.	Alternation of leadership
Stranger	Stranger leads strongly.			Unstable competition becomes alternation of leadership.
Sister	Sister leads strongly.	Rapid acquisition Bursts of responding		Competition
Mother	Mother leads strongly.	Rapid acquisition Bursts of mother responding	Rapid acquisition	Alternation of leadership

SOURCE: Cohen, D. J. Justin and his peers: an experimental analysis of a child's social world. *Child Development.* 1962, 33, pp. 697–717.
NOTE: No entry-condition not used.

reinforced with verbal approval by a liked or a disliked peer. The results given in Figure 14-5 show the change in the rate of marble dropping from the baseline to the experimental period. Both the 4- and 5-year-olds responded at a higher rate when a disliked peer delivered the reinforcement. In their replication of this experiment, Tiktin and Hartup (1965) reported similar findings for second- and fifth-graders. Performance improved when a disliked peer delivered the reinforcement, decreased when a liked peer delivered the reinforcement (perhaps because the liked peer was more distracting), and remained stable when a neutral peer delivered the reinforcement.

Hartup (1970) has suggested that these unexpected results may be due to anxiety, aroused because the child did not expect positive reinforcement from a disliked peer. The increased anxiety is evidenced in higher rates of response in the marble-dropping task. This cognitive-motivational hypothesis suggests that the peer-reinforcement effects are due to the child's expectations about the behavior of peers. The cognitive (expectancy) and motivational (anxiety) components interact, and both must be taken into account to predict the effects of peer reinforcement on behavior.

These studies show that within the confines of the experimental situation —well-defined behavior, specific tasks, and so forth—peers may alter a child's behavior by dispensing reinforcement. This suggests that it may be valuable to examine the effects of peer reinforcement in childrens' natural groups.

FIGURE 14-5   *Mean Change in Rate of Marble Dropping by Four- and Five-Year-Olds for Liked and Disliked Peers*

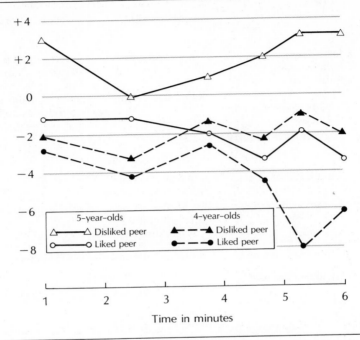

SOURCE: Hartup, W. Friendship status and the effectiveness of peers as reinforcing agents. *Journal of Experimental Child Psychology*, 1964, *1*, pp. 154–162.

NATURAL SITUATIONS.   Patterson, Littman, and Bricker (1967) studied the reactions of a peer group to aggressive behavior in a nursery school. These researchers observed and coded 2,583 aggressive responses in 62½-hour sessions. These responses took the form of bodily attacks, attacks with an object, or verbal/symbolic attacks. The responses of the child to whom the aggressive act was directed were coded as passive, cries, defensive posture, telling the teacher, recovering property, or retaliation. The hypothesis of Patterson et al. was that social reinforcement dispensed by peers would increase aggressive behavior because it would usually produce a desirable result for the aggressive child. They also hypothesized that the victim's counteraggression would cause the aggressing child to suppress his behavior or to choose another victim.

Table 14-2 presents the data, which show that the peer group reinforced aggressive responses between 71 percent and 89 percent of the time. The children clearly, though not intentionally, reinforced aggressive behavior in their peers, thus supporting the first hypothesis. The second hypothesis also received support since counteraggression by a victim resulted in a change in victim, a change in response, or both. Finally, victims who counteraggressed and were reinforced for doing so showed an increase in aggression. Children who were not victims or whose counteraggression was not successful showed no increase in aggression. These data demonstrate that the peer group can shape aggressive behavior in children.

The results of this study are important for a number of reasons. First, they clearly support the laboratory research discussed above. Second, they demonstrate that peer reinforcement in natural settings does alter children's behavior—either increasing or decreasing it. Third, they suggest that the behavior of the peer group may explain changes in childrens' behavior after they begin school. Parents often complain that their children's behavior changes after they begin school, for example, they often become more aggressive. One plausible explanation is that children learn these new behavior patterns through reinforcement by their peers. Finally, an extrapolation from the results of Patterson et al. is that peers can effectively serve as agents of behavioral change, perhaps as confederates of parents or teachers, since their behaviors act as positive or negative reinforcers of children's behavior.

Peers as Models

In Chapter 10 we discussed the theoretical basis of the importance of modeling (imitative learning), through which new behaviors are learned without reinforcement; the behavior of the model also may inhibit or disinhibit the observer's behavior. Such observational learning from peers is an important feature of

---

TABLE 14-2   Descriptive Data of Assertive Behaviors

	BLOCKS OF TIME				
VARIABLES	I	II	III	IV	V
Nursery School C:					
Frequency, total assertions per hour	11.7	17.7	18.2	14.5	12.2
Proportion positive reinforcements	.89	.86	.78	.71	.76
Number *Ss* with 3 or more assertive responses per hour	3	3	5	4	3
Number of bursts per hour	1.2	1.6	1.2	.7	1.1
Nursery School P:					
Frequency, total assertions per hour	13.0	20.4	28.2	40.0	13.2
Proportion positive reinforcements	.76	.83	.82	.85	.73
Number *Ss* with 3 or more assertive responses per hour	2	5	4	5	3
Number of bursts per hour	.2	.6	1.4	6.0	.4

SOURCE: Patterson, G. R., Littlman, R. A., and Bricker, W. Assertive behavior in children: a step toward a theory of aggression. *Monographs of the Society for Research in Child Development,* 1967, *32,* p. 113.

socialization, since the child spends more time with peers than with parents. In addition, a careful consideration of the conclusions of Patterson et al. (1967), discussed above, suggests that children may learn aggressive behavior from observation of aggressive peers.

INFLUENCE OF PEERS VERSUS ADULTS.   Research clearly shows that children do imitate peer models (Cheyne, 1971; Ross, 1971). Hicks (1965) investigated two aspects of imitation. First, he compared the imitation of peers with the imitation of adults to see which would be more influential. Second, he tested for imitation just after the subjects had observed the model, and again 6 months later. The second time the subjects were not given another exposure to the models, thus making this test one of retention. The subjects, 30 boys and 30 girls from about 4 to 6 years of age, were divided into 4 experimental groups and 1 control group. Different groups were exposed to different models—an adult male, an adult female, a male peer, or a female peer. The control group had no model. Films showed the model aggressing on a bobo doll, for example, hitting it with a bat, striking it with a mallet, and throwing plastic balls at it. The children were then taken to a room containing the same toys as those the model had. For the next 20 minutes, the children's imitative behavior was recorded. About 6 months later, the children were again placed in the same room and their behavior recorded.

Table 14-3 shows the results for the initial assessment of imitation and for the 6-month retest. All 4 experimental conditions produced significantly more aggressive behavior than the control condition. Children viewing the male peer model produced significantly more aggressive behavior than did children viewing the adult

TABLE 14-3   Mean Imitative Aggression Scores

| RESPONSE CATEGORY | EXPERIMENTAL CONDITIONS | | | | |
	ADULT MALE	ADULT FEMALE	PEER MALE	PEER FEMALE	CONTROL
Immediate Test					
Imitative Aggression	9.58	16.33	22.75	13.42	.00
Boys	14.60	27.50	24.83	20.33	.00
Girls	5.17	5.17	15.67	6.50	.00
Posttest					
Imitative Aggression	8.92	3.92	6.42	4.33	.33
Boys	7.33	7.17	5.17	6.50	.67
Girls	10.50	.67	7.67	2.17	.00

SOURCE: Hicks, D. J. Imitation and retention of film-mediated aggressive peer and adult models. *Journal of Personality and Social Psychology*, 1965, 2, pp. 97–100.

A bully is reinforced by the peer group and acts as a model for aggressive behavior.
(Jim Harrison)

male model or the female peer model. Analysis of the 6-month posttest data revealed no significant differences. These findings indicate that peers may be more effective models than adults for shaping children's behavior. However, the long-term effects of differential reactions to peer or adult models remains an open question.

IMITATIVE AGGRESSION.   Hick's findings about the importance of peer models in the acquisition of aggressive behavior by children have been replicated (Dubanoski & Parten, 1971). These investigators also demonstrated that the aggressive responses learned by children observing aggressive models are probably situation-specific. Here, the model seems to enhance the acquisition of *imitative* aggression, perhaps by calling attention to this behavior, but does not lead to more general aggression by the subjects. In other words, the children's aggressive behaviors in these experiments were limited to those exhibited by the model. Thus, we must be cautious in extrapolating from the effects of observational learning because the behavior may be specific to the situation and may not generalize beyond the experimental conditions.

MODELING WITH REINFORCEMENT.   Hartup and Coates (1967) studied the effects of peer models on the imitative behavior of 4½-year-old children in connection with the child's history of reinforcement by the peer group. The children were divided into 2 groups: those receiving a high frequency of reinforcement from their nursery school peers and those receiving a low frequency of reinforcement from their classmates. These 2 groups were further divided into 2 groups, one observing a model who was a rewarding peer, and the other observing a model who was a nonrewarding peer. A fifth group observed no model. Both the child and the model performed some simple maze tasks. On completion of each of the 10 mazes, the child and the model were rewarded with 6 trinkets which they could either put into a bowl and keep, or distribute between their bowl and that of a fictitious child. In the experimental session, the model performed the 10 mazes and then gave away 5 trinkets to the fictitious child, keeping only one for himself. Then the subject performed on the 10 mazes. His distribution of the trinkets to himself and the fictitious child was recorded.

The subjects in the experimental groups shared more (behaved altruistically) than the subjects in the control group. The children who were frequently reinforced by their peers imitated the model's altruistic behavior to a greater extent when the model was a reinforcing peer than when the model was a child who did not normally reinforce the child. The opposite was true for children in the group with the low frequency of reinforcement. These children imitated the altruistic behavior of the model to a greater extent when the model was a child who did not normally reinforce the subject. This experiment shows the importance of identifying the characteristics of peer models that are relevant to the socializing influence of peers. Not all peers are effective models for all children. The data here suggest that children will imitate peer models when they see themselves as similar to the peer model, but not when they see themselves as different from the model.

MODELING AND SELF-REWARDING.   Other studies have been carried out with peers as models. Bandura and Kupers (1964), for example, investigated self-rewarding by children aged 7 to 9 years. Half the subjects saw a model perform in a bowling game and set a very high standard of performance as a criterion for self-reward; the other half observed a model with a low criterion of performance for self-reward. The patterns of self-reward adopted by the children when they performed the same task matched those of the model they had observed. Thus, peer models influence assessments of the quality of performance, an important variable in our culture. In a similar study, Stein and Bryan (1972) exposed third- and fourth-grade girls to either a peer who verbalized and practiced a rule for self-reward in a bowling game or to a peer model who verbalized but violated the rule. Following exposure to the model, the subjects' self-reward behavior was observed while they played the bowling game. Subjects who had watched a model who conformed to the rule followed it more closely than those who had seen a model who violated the rule.

PRACTICAL IMPORTANCE OF MODELING.   A recent experiment by Keller and Carlson (1974) provides an excellent example of the practical importance of the study of peer modeling. They applied the modeling procedure to changing the isolate behavior of preschool children aged 3 to 5. Isolated children spend significant amounts of time alone, not interacting with the staff or the other children—behavior which is undesirable as it is inconsistent with the development of the social skills needed to interact appropriately with peers and adults. The children in the experimental group were exposed to 4 videotapes showing children imitating, smiling and laughing, giving objects to others, and initiating physical contact with others. A 5-minute film was shown to the isolate children on each of 4 consecutive days. The isolates were observed before their exposure to the models, just following the treatment, and 3 weeks later. The treatment proved effective in increasing the social behavior of the isolates, both immediately after the exposure to the models and, to a slightly lesser degree, 3 weeks later. The results of this study indicate that these experimental procedures can be used to teach social behavior.

SUMMARY

We have presented evidence that peers play an important role in socialization. The research we have discussed here also provides insights into the psychological processes in the formation of peer groups, their effects on the child, and the mechanisms of reinforcement and modeling by which the peer group exerts its socializing influence. One important feature of norm-following and conformity to the peer group is the child's developing cognitive competence. As noted in our discussion of prosocial (Chapter 13) and moral development (Chapter 12), the child's developing conception of rules allows for a more flexible reinterpretation of the social order with the result that the child may interact with social influences in ways not previously possible.

We do not claim that cognition mediates all the influences of the peer group. The research of the effects of peer reinforcement, however lacking in depth, suggests that the application of the principles of learning theory to the role played by peers in socialization allows us to explain the influence of peers without recourse to cognition. Other examples of social differences, such as the antecedents of popularity, seem to be free of a cognitive base. By considering both the cognitive and noncognitive determinants of peer interaction, we can assemble a picture of the effects of the peer group on the child that permits an explanation of both developmental changes and nondevelopmental influences. We can thus apply research findings from areas as disparate as operant conditioning and cognitive theory to the activities and influences of children's peer groups.

CHAPTER 15

ADOLESCENCE: THE TRANSITION TO ADULTHOOD

THE TRANSITIONS in cognitive, biological, and social development discussed in previous chapters continue during the period we call adolescence. The importance of these changes, however, sets off adolescence as a distinct period in development, one of transition from child to adult.

In this chapter our discussion concentrates on the continuities that extend from childhood to maturity. In a complex society such as ours, adolescence is a critical time for adjusting to adulthood roles.

Definition

The term **adolescence** comes from the Latin verb *adolescere,* which means "to grow up" or "to grow to maturity." Psychologists use the term to refer to physiological and social development during the transition from childhood to adulthood. Investigations of adolescence, then, focus on the physical, cognitive, and social changes taking place during this period, as well as their contribution to learning mature behavior appropriate to the particular society.

Psychologists agree that adolescence begins with the physiological changes accompanying pubescence and ends with the achievement of full adult status as measured by economic, social, and physical maturity. Although these criteria may not be met at the same time, they are sufficiently objective for the purposes of psychologists.

We have not used chronological age in the definition of adolescence, since age alone is of little help in marking off developmental periods. Pubescence begins at various ages, and adult status is attained at different times in life for different individuals.

There are several explanations for the emergence and formalization of adolescence as a distinct period of development within the society. They can be conveniently grouped into 4 categories.

SOCIETAL VIEW.   A societal view of adolescence holds that this period is important because of the individual's need to become an effective adult in the society. The adolescent needs time to adjust to the adult world and to acquire the skills required to function effectively as a grown-up (Campbell, 1969; Emmerich, 1973). In less complex, nonindustrialized societies, this adjustment is less difficult (Mead, 1950, 1953; Benedict, 1938). Puberty rites formalize a rapid transition in roles from childhood to adulthood. These ceremonies are possible because many less industrialized societies have very similar role expectations for children and adults (Benedict, 1938; Mead, 1970). In complex societies such as ours, however, the numerous vaguely defined roles an adult is expected to play require learning new and often very different skills. Adolescents are expected to pursue vocational training (Mayer, 1971; Wolfbein, 1964) and learn other adult roles—marital, parental, civic, and spiritual (Martineau, 1966). The relatively long period of adolescence allowed in our society reflects both the complexities involved in acquiring these capabilities and the earlier onset of puberty. Adolescence is both a luxury, because the society can afford to give this time to an individual, and a necessity, because the individual has to have this time to become an effective adult.

DEVELOPMENTAL PSYCHOLOGY VIEW.   A developmental psychology view of adolescence describes this period as a time to experiment with various adult roles. In so

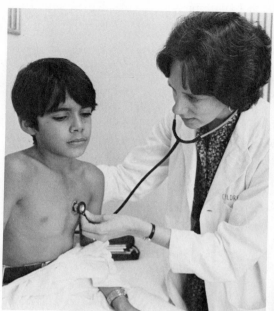

Every adult has to learn a complexity of roles.
(Judith Sedwick)

doing, the adolescent gradually develops a comfortable, stable sense of self (Campbell, 1969; Emmerich, 1973; Ahammar, 1973). He or she learns to be a leader or a follower, an athlete or passive observer, and a host of other personality traits. It is no wonder, then, that adolescence is a time of questioning, "Who am I?" The cognitive advances undergone during adolescence give rise to this question and allow the individual to experiment with answers without having to accept the entire adult responsibilty for a specific solution.

BIOLOGICAL PERSPECTIVE. Adolescence is a time of massive, rapid biological change. Height and weight soar, and reproductive capability begins. These changes are important in their own right, but they also signal that maturity is imminent. One important feature of these changes is their timing. Being an early or a late maturer appears to have some permanent psychological effects. Since girls reach physical maturity 1½ years earlier than boys, these biological changes may be important for understanding sex differences in the behavior of adolescents. These biological changes relate to social changes in the individual's behavior as well as in the behavior of others toward the individual.

INTELLECTUAL PERSPECTIVE.   Adolescence is a time during which the individual learns to cope with formal-operational thinking and its consequences for social development and conceptions of the self (Elkind, 1967 a, 1968; Looft, 1972; Flavell, 1977). IQ scores are more stable during adolescence (Honzik, Macfarlane, & Allen, 1948) than childhood. Researchers are emphasizing qualitative changes in intellect during adolescent development (Flavell, 1977), among them the achievement of formal operations (see Chapter 6). Adolescent changes in intellect allow for new interpretations of the social environment, which make possible new forms of behavior. For example, without competence in formal-operational thought, an individual's thinking about morality or sex roles would be very limited.

Developmental Tasks of Adolescence

The adolescent has to learn a good deal. Robert Havighurst (1951, 1972) spelled out the practical importance of adolescence as a developmental period bridging childhood and adulthood in very concrete terms. He coined the term **developmental tasks** to refer to the individual's accomplishing certain social tasks related to passing from one stage of development to the next. These tasks— viewed as the skills, knowledge, functions, and attitudes one must acquire to adjust to the difficult roles that lie ahead—are carried out through physical maturation, social fulfillment, and personal effort.

Havighurst has noted 9 major tasks of adolescence:

1. Accepting one's physical make-up and acquiring a masculine or feminine sex role
2. Developing appropriate relations with agemates of both sexes
3. Becoming emotionally independent of parents and other adults
4. Achieving the assurance that one will become economically independent
5. Deciding on, preparing for, and entering a vocation
6. Developing the cognitive skills and concepts necessary for social competence
7. Understanding and achieving socially responsible behavior
8. Preparing for marriage and family
9. Acquiring values that are harmonious with an appropriate scientific world picture

However eclectic, these tasks point up several important aspects of adolescent development. This list also focuses our attention on specific problems encountered by the adolescent. The time spent in adolescence provides the individual with the experiences needed to accomplish these tasks and to enter adulthood as a well-adjusted person.

Theories of
Adolescence

Theories of adolescent development may be divided, somewhat arbitrarily, into those that emphasize biological changes, those that emphasize social-cultural factors, and those that are biocultural, that is, emphasize both biological and social changes. This breakdown highlights the major historical themes in the study of adolescent development.

Biological (Maturational) Theories

G. S. HALL'S BIOGENETIC THEORY.   The scientific study of adolescence may be traced back to the pioneering work of G. Stanley Hall, who published his two-volume text *Adolescence* in 1904. Although a number of hypotheses based on his theory have been disproven, Hall's thinking had a shaping influence on the field for many years.

According to Hall's concept of **recapitulation**—an extrapolation from Darwin's *Origin of Species* (1859)—The experiential history of the species becomes part of the genetic structure of the individual organism and is therefore passed on from one generation to the next. Thus, the development of the individual organism mirrored the development of the species—that is, it went through a series of stages corresponding to those mankind had passed through in its development. Hence, the often-heard phrase "**Ontogeny** [the development of the individual organism] recapitualtes **phylogeny** [the development of the species]." Although Hall paid lip service to cultural and situational influences on behavior, his major thesis was that the development of the organism was controlled by genetic factors. Maturation was assumed to occur no matter what its environmental or sociocultural context.

Hall viewed adolescence as a period of storm and stress (*Sturm und Drang*), corresponding to the period of human development when people were in a turbulent, transitional stage. Popular current conceptions of adolescence still cling to this view of adolescence as a transient, disturbed period.

More recent evidence, however, suggests that adolescence is not a period of storm and stress. IQ-test reliability remains stable, and there is no strong evidence for emotional instability or of rapid changes in personality or social relations. While some changes in these areas do take place, they are slow and represent continuities in development. Some adolescents may experience periods of storm and stress, and some may experience significant stress, but most do not.

Hall also believed that in adolescence the personality underwent rapid change and a different person emerged. In other words, he believed that development from childhood through adolescence was discontinuous. The evidence on this issue is somewhat more in Hall's favor. Some adolescent changes are quite different from

Adolescents spend considerable time thinking about the question, Who am I? (Jean-Claude Lejeune)

the processes that prevail in childhood. Physical growth and its psychological concomitants, for example, undergo marked changes. Because this growth is visible and rapid, it has been generalized to other aspects of adolescent development. For example, at about the age of 12, the choice of cross-sex friendships begins to rise. Changes in cognition, such as formal-operational thinking, are another example of developmental changes in adolescence that have implications for personality development, particularly egocentric behavior. On the other hand, most developmental changes are continuous and gradual rather than discontinuous and abrupt. Perhaps the adolescent's rapid physical growth tempts us to believe that the psychological changes are equally rapid and discontinuous, but they are not. Those who study adolescent development must constantly check their own biases to ensure that they do not obstruct the objective interpretation of the nature of adolescent change.

PSYCHOANALYTIC THEORY.   Anna Freud (1948), the daughter of Sigmund Freud, has described some of the dynamics of the psychoanalytic view of adolescent development. Like Hall, she postulates a discontinuity in development owing to the biological changes that pubescence brings and that, she felt, result in an upsurge of sexuality. The adolescent's increased sexuality causes a recurrence of the Oedipal situation, which must be resolved by developing appropriate heterosexual relationships, as with developing opposite-sex friendships. Anna Freud, too, believes the adolescent lives in a state of constant stress that needs defenses. The psychoanalytic theory of adolescent development, then, emphasizes the relationship between **defense mechanisms** against stress or anxiety and behavior. These defenses may lead to either abnormal or appropriate social development.

Examples of defense mechanisms are repression (keeping anxiety-producing impulses from consciousness), denial (insisting that some aspects of psychological reality do not exist), sublimation (redirecting impulses from a sexual object to a social one), and withdrawal (mental or physical flight from unpleasant situations). Adolescents most often use the mechanisms of **asceticism** and **intellectualism.** The former refers to attempts to deny the existence of instinctual drives, such as sex, so as not to "give in" to them. "Intellectualism" refers to an abstract, impersonal treatment of issues in a way that implies they are not central conflicts. Hence, discussions of free love, the existence of God, and the like *may* represent the adolescent's attempt to deal with deep-seated personal conflicts.

The psychoanalytic view is that the individual must develop a set of defense mechanisms that allow healthy adaptation to the maturational changes taking place during adolescence. Maturational theories tend to rely heavily on stress and discontinuities in development to explain adolescent behavior. Environmental and cultural influences are presumed to play a secondary role. Hence, this point of view is focused on the relation between physiological development, particularly physical growth and hormonal effects, and psychological behavior.

Cultural Theories

The work of Hall, Freud, and others who consider biological change the major impetus in adolescent development is challenged by the cultural anthropologists, who point out that the developmental patterns found in industrialized Western society have been found to be absent in other cultures, which use other practices for socializing the adolescent. Thus, cultural anthropolgists view environmental and cultural factors to be of primary importance and genetically determined physical growth factors as secondary.

Margaret Mead and Ruth Benedict are perhaps the two most influential cultural anthropologists who have written about adolescent development. Mead's *Coming of Age in Samoa* (1950) and *Growing Up in New Guinea* (1953) are field studies of the effect of culture on adolescent development. Although hers is not a formalized theory, Mead believes that to understand the development of human behavior, we must look at the role of cultural institutions in shaping that behavior. Studies of the influence of culture on development have yielded two concepts: **cultural determinism** and **cultural relativism.** Cultures determine development which, in turn, reflects cultural differences—different cultures produce different kinds of personalities (cultural relativism). The universality of biological changes is of no significance unless cultures incorporate these changes into their fabric.

Ruth Benedict (1938) has more clearly spelled out ways in which cultures affect development by focusing on the mediation of cultural influences through differences or similarities in the roles of childhood and adulthood. While in some cultures children and adults play much the same roles, in others, such as ours, children's and adults' roles differ markedly. Benedict's thesis is that cultures vary in the continuity between childhood and adulthood roles and thus in the transition from one stage to the other. If the transition is socially and legally well defined and discontinuous, such as the one we have, the specific transitions are different from those of cultures without such discontinuities.

Benedict (1938) notes that Western cultures contain several discontinuities that force children to unlearn childhood behavior during the transition to adulthood. In other societies, such as the Samoan culture, children and adults have similar roles, so that adolescents need not unlearn childhood behavior. A smooth, gradual, and stress-free transition to adulthood is the role. On the other hand, conflict and frustration arising from the redefinition and confusion of roles can make adolescence a very difficult period.

A good example of these two forms of transition is the socialization of sexual behavior. In Western cultures, sexuality in childhood, adolescence, and adulthood has a very different role than it does in many other cultures. In the United States, the traditional view has been that young people must wait until they are married before engaging in sexual intercourse, but in some other cultures, children as well as adolescents are allowed and may even be encouraged to engage in sexual behavior. Other cultures socialize sexual behavior in still other ways, for example, allowing sex play among children but not adolescents. Cultural practices and attitudes about sexuality show wide variations, both in industrialized and nonindustrialized societies. In the United States, a good deal of conflict about sexuality occurs during adolescence, but such conflicts are virtually unknown in some other cultures. These cultural differences occur despite the universality of the biological changes accompanying adolescence. It is not the biological conditions alone that create conflict, but **cultural conditioning,** according to the cultural anthropologists' view of adolescence.

Cultural anthropology has its psychological counterpart in social-learning theory, which explains development on the basis of S-R learning, imitation, and modeling. Cultural factors are assumed to shape social development through the reinforcement of desired behavior and through models of appropriate role behavior. Gewirtz (1969) and Bandura (1969a) have written extensively about development from this point of view. In addition, Bandura and Walters (1959, 1963) have discussed the implications of this theory for adolescent development. Since we have already discussed social-learning theory in detail (Chapter 10), we need only remind the reader that the individual can acquire new behavior and a knowledge of the conditions under which to use it appropriately by direct teaching and by observing others. Social-learning theorists explain the behavior of adolescents by cultural conditioning and social expectations. The behavior of adolescents is assumed to be the consequence of child-rearing that teaches specific roles, with deviant or aberrant development stemming from a failure of socialization during early childhood. Development is thus continuous and represents the product of socialization rather than maturation.

Biocultural Theories

By far most theories of adolescent development take neither of these extreme views. Most psychologists studying adolescence prefer biocultural theories that explain adolescent development as resulting from the interaction between biological and cultural influences.

AUSUBEL'S DRIVE THEORY. Ausubel (1954) noted two aspects of change in adolescence. First, there is biological change, most notably the new sex drive. There is a sharp discontinuity between the pre- and postpubescent sex drive and related attitudes and behavior. Ausubel also notes that this is the first drive since infancy that needs to be socialized. Second, there is pyschosocial change including the achievement of independence from adults. Adolescents must learn to function on their own, apart from their caretakers, and to become their "own person."

Psychobiological development refers to the psychological consequences of biological change. For example, the complex psychological reactions to pubescence include physical (e.g., sex drive) as well as psychological (e.g., attitudes toward sexuality) changes. The physical changes of pubescence have psychological concomitants. Perhaps the most well-known example in America involves the effects of early versus late maturity, which is discussed later in this chapter. The psychobiological aspects of development are also universal, occurring in all cultures. Specific cultural practices, however, determine the manner in which the psychobiological aspects of development emerge at adolescence. The effects of rate of maturity are not evident in many societies, for example. "Psychosocial change" refers to any changes owing to cultural factors. These changes are more specific, such as changes in sexual behavior from pre- to postadolescence. Ausubel has attempted to provide an integrated picture of these two kinds of influences, especially as they affect the individual's developing notions of self, including strivings for independence and coming to view oneself as a sexual being.

ERIKSON'S THEORY. Like Ausubel, Erikson (1963) has attempted to integrate anthropological evidence about cultural influences on personality development with psychoanalytic theory. He believes that the primary adolescent crisis is one of ego identity—the person's sense of who he is, what he is, and his evaluation of himself. Erikson's theory gives greater prominence to cultural determinants of behavior than does classic Freudian theory.

The crisis of adolescence—identity versus identity diffusion—must be dealt with successfully for the individual to become an effective adult. To the degree that the individual can resolve this conflict in adolescence, the greater the ease with which he or she can resolve adult conflicts. The individual acquires an identity through his or her efforts to define who and what he or she is. Cultural (sex roles, for example) and social (child-rearing practices and peer relations) factors play an important part in the answers to this question. Moreover, the "fit" of the various roles (leader or follower, for example) tried out by the adolescent help define the self. Physical maturation is also important in determining how the individual answers these questions, since these growth factors form part of the self-concept, particularly through notions of physical capabilities, rates of growth relative to peers, and comparison with peers.

As Lewin (1935, 1939) wrote, the adolescent is a marginal person, neither child nor adult. The adolescent's role is not well defined; adults treat the adolescent sometimes like a child and sometimes like an adult. This inconsistency leads to confusion about who and what one is. The conflict in roles and expectations makes it difficult to develop stable notions of the self and contributes to the adolescent's identity confusion.

Thus far, we have emphasized the differences among the cultural, biological, and biocultural theories of adolescent development. There are, of course, similarities. All the theorists mentioned are aware of endocrinological and other physical

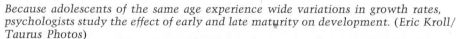

Because adolescents of the same age experience wide variations in growth rates, psychologists study the effect of early and late maturity on development. (Eric Kroll/ Taurus Photos)

changes affecting growth, although they differ in the developmental importance they attach to these changes. Similarly, all these theorists view adolescence as a transition between childhood and adulthood. One does not simply leave childhood and enter adulthood. Even the most primitive of cultures usually have a rite of passage, a formal ceremony, that marks the transition from childhood to adulthood. In Western civilizations, this transition is more informal but is built into the society through the role of adolescence.

We have discussed these theories for several reasons. First, they point out the difficulty of explaining adolescent growth and development. Second, they provide ways of viewing adolescence as a transition between childhood and adulthood. Third, they suggest areas in which research remains to be done: physiological development and its relation to changes in behavior; personality development, particularly the self-concept; changes in social roles and role expectations, relations between parents and adolescents, the influence of peer groups, and changes in cognition and the relation between cognition and social behavior.

Biological Changes

The most obvious changes in adolescence take place during the growth spurt. These changes are important for a number of reasons. First, they signal puberty and the concomitant capability of reproduction. Correlated with this change is an increase in the sex drive, which must be socialized. Second, the physical changes during the growth spurt signal the individual's approaching maturity. Both the adolescent and others with whom he or she interacts change their behavior. Third, these physical changes require that one's physical appearance be integrated with the notion of the self and its capabilities. The timing of these physical changes—particularly if one is an early or a late maturer—has important psychological effects. Finally, differences between the sexes in the onset of pubescence are important for understanding differences in social expectations about the behavior of adolescent males and females.

Physical Changes

Pubescence is a general term referring to the physical changes in the adolescent—the various morphological (shape and size) and physiological changes occurring throughout the body over an extended period of time. **Puberty** is more specific, referring to the attainment of sexual maturity, the capacity to reproduce. In boys, the pubescent growth spurt may begin as early as $10\frac{1}{2}$ years or as late as 16 years (Tanner, 1970). In girls, it starts as early as $7\frac{1}{2}$ years of age or as late as $11\frac{1}{2}$ (Tanner,

1970). Figure 15-1 illustrates these growth rates for height. Girls enter the growth spurt about 1½ to 2 years before boys, and reach full adult height several years before boys do. On the other hand, boys grow more during the growth spurt; their full adult height is several inches greater than that of females.

These changes in height, along with other physical changes during adolescence, are due to hormonal changes, particularly those controlled by the pituitary gland. Hormones secreted by the pituitary gland trigger hormonal secretions by other endocrine glands, such as the sex glands, that bring about maturation of the sexual characteristics. Hormones such as HGH (Human Growth Hormone) have three main functions, of which **morphogenesis,** the determination of organ growth

FIGURE 15-1 *Average Height Gain per Year for Boys and Girls*

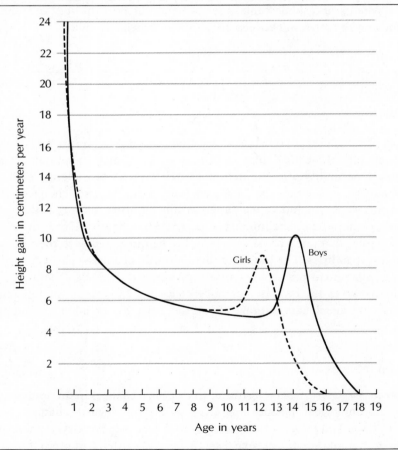

SOURCE: Tanner, J. M., Whitehouse, R. H., and Takaishi, M. Standards from birth to maturity for height, weight, height velocity, and weight velocity: British children, 1965. *Archives of Disease in Childhood*, 1966, 41, pp. 455–471.

TABLE 15-1 Chronology of Pubertal Growth Changes

AGE	FEMALE	AGE	MALE
10–12	Critical phase in internal organ structural growth; equivocal morphology	12–13	Critical phase in internal organ structural growth; equivocal morphology
11–12	Initial development of breast and pelvis	13–14	Initial pubic hair growth, juvenile type
12–13	Initial pubic hair growth; juvenile type	14–15	Intensification of thoracic and muscular development
13–14	Initial axillary hair growth	14–15	Initial axillary growth
13–14	Menarche	14–16	Increase in size of genital organs
15–18	Completion of definitive female shape and psyche	16–18	Beginning of frank facial hair growth
		19–22	Completion of male shape and psyche

SOURCE: Botella-Llusia, J. Endocrinology of woman. Philadelphia: W. B. Saunders, 1973, p. 342.

and size, is the most germane to this discussion. This hormone changes the shape and structure of the body (bone and skeletal structure, for example), as well as the shape and size of the secondary sex characteristics. Because hormonal changes are related all of the changes that occur during the growth spurt are interrelated. Table 15-1 shows the approximate chronological sequence of growth during puberty. We need simply look at a seventh- or eighth-grade class to see the difference, both within and between sexes, in the rate of development.

The correlation between prepubertal and postpubertal height is about +.80; the short tend to stay short and the tall to remain tall. Those who enter the growth spurt earlier tend to be somewhat taller than those who enter it later, whether males or females. In turn, those who enter the growth spurt later are likely to be somewhat shorter as they finish the growth spurt.

Body physique during adolescence is important because it affects the way the individual views the self and the way that others act toward the individual. Between 10 percent and 15 percent of adolescents are obese, as defined by measures of subcutaneous fat. Obesity is an abnormal state characterized by excessive deposits of fat throughout the body. A poor diet, lack of exercise, and excessive eating contribute to obesity. Endocrine imbalances can also cause one to be obese.

EFFECT OF PHYSICAL CHANGES. The rapid changes in height and weight during the growth spurt have a significant effect on the adolescent's body sense. The individual's reactions to these changes can affect personality development (Tanner, 1970; Sheldon, 1940, 1942; Lindzey, 1965). Sheldon classified personality types according to body type—**endomorph, mesomorph,** and **ectomorph.** The mesomorph was exemplified by the athlete, the ectomorph by the scholar, and the endomorph by the gourmand. This simplistic approach to personality types is limited and probably doomed to failure (Lindzey, 1965). On the other hand, the notion that body type is related to personality is certainly not entirely false. The individual's evaluation of his or her body, which becomes possible with formal-operational thinking, probably causes the individual to behave in certain ways and to develop the traits, likes, and dislikes that enter into one's personality. The importance of body type and rates of maturation lies also in the behavior of others toward the adolescent and in the adolescent's own self-concept. This is shown perhaps most clearly in Chapter 13; peers are more attracted to pleasant-looking children. The same is true of adolescents (Dusek, 1977; McCandless, 1970).

Other physiological changes take place during the growth spurt. Increases occur in muscle strength and tolerance, lung capacity, skeletal size, and bone ossification (the replacement of cartilage with bone tissue). These changes are closely interrelated because they result from a common set of hormonal changes. As bone ossification becomes complete in females, menarche is likely to occur. Similarly, bone ossification is closely related to the appearance of secondary sexual characteristics in boys. Hence, measures of bone ossification, sometimes called skeletal age, have been used as indices of maturity in studies of the relation between maturity level and, for example, social relations and personality development.

Psychological Aspects of Physical Growth and Development

Changes in physiological growth have a twofold importance. First, everyone, peers and adults, can see them. They may disrupt the individual's sense of self-consistency and identity and may require a reevaluation of the self. This is true not only for the obvious changes in height and weight but also for more subtle changes in reproductive capabilities and sex drive. These changes may confuse the adolescent, for they can affect his or her relations with other people.

These physiological changes can also have long-term effects on the development of the individual's personality. The reactions of others, especially parents and peers, toward the individual become critical in mediating the effects of early or late maturation.

EARLY VERSUS LATE MATURITY.   Much of the research on the interaction of physical growth and personality development in adolescents comes from the Berkeley Growth Studies (Mussen & Jones, 1957; Jones & Mussen, 1958). Although most of this research was done with males, we do have some data on the effects of early and late maturity for girls. The typical research design compared a group of adolescents of the same age, but different levels of physical maturity (usually the top and bottom 20 percent of a sample). The index of physical maturity was skeletal age. The social, emotional, and intellectual adjustment of these 2 groups was then assessed and compared.

Among males, the early maturers were taller, heavier, more muscular, more advanced in the development of secondary sex characteristics, and sexually more mature (Mussen & Jones, 1957). Late maturers were characteristically long-legged, slender, weaker, and somewhat less well adjusted. Because of their precocious physical and sexual maturity, the early maturers had the advantage of greater size, strength, and masculinity. These advantages are particularly important in sports, because of accelerated metabolism, more oxygen-carrying red blood cells, and sheer bulk that contribute to athletic prowess. The late maturer is less successful in sports. Since high school athletes tend to be more popular than nonathletes, we can see some of the advantages of being an early maturer.

Early maturing boys are perceived as having more positive attributes by both themselves and their peers. Adults who rated male adolescents consistently found late maturers less physically attractive, less masculine, less well groomed, more childish, more attention seeking, more tense, and less mature than early maturers. Peers rated late maturers as more restless, talkative, bossy, less self-assured, and less popular than their early maturing classmates (Jones & Mussen, 1957). These studies suggest that the extent of physical maturity readily elicits personality judgments from people.

The influence of early versus late maturity in girls has different consequences (Jones & Mussen, 1958), partly because the girls begin maturing earlier than boys. Unlike the early maturing boy, the early maturing girl is initially at a social and emotional disadvantage (Frisk, Tenhunen, Widholm, & Hortling, 1966). She is out of phase with most of her peers and may even be ostracized by them (Frisk et al., 1966). She may have few peers with whom to share her new-found maturity. As her peers "catch up" with her, these social disadvantages disappear, and she may even become the object of envy and a source of advice and guidance (Frisk et al., 1966).

It should come as no surprise that the personality judgments of others carry over to the individual's self-assessment. The Berkeley Growth Studies revealed significant differences between early and late maturers in their self-evaluations. In projective tests, late maturers consistently saw the central figures/heroes as imbeciles or weaklings, scorned by their parents or the authorities. They viewed the hero as incapable of solving his problems and needing the help of others. The themes of the early maturers' stories centered on potency, aggression, and positive self-attribution (Jones & Mussen, 1958). Late maturers were more likely to have negative and derogatory self-concepts, probably because of frustration in their strivings to be potent and strong. For both men and women, this sense of inferiority carried over into adulthood. Early maturing females, however, may be more disadvantaged than late maturers, because, at least initially, they are as out of synchrony with normal development as the late maturing males.

SOME CONCLUSIONS.   These data show that physical maturity influences societal expectations about an adolescent's behavior. Adults may expect the more mature adolescent to behave in a more adult way, probably because the early maturer has a more adult physique. Even the early maturer, however, lacks the cognitive and social maturity of an adult and may not be able to live up to these high expectations. The resulting conflicts between what is expected and what is possible may cause harm to the early maturer's self-esteem. For example, the early maturing boy who is elected class president may have the same youthful exuberance as his classmates, but since he is expected to conduct himself with more decorum, he may bear the onus for class pranks because school authorities expected more from him than from his younger-appearing classmates.

On the other hand, late maturers may be expected to behave immaturely, no matter what their cognitive and social competence. The late-maturing 14-year-old girl who is forced by her parents to wear younger clothes when she wants to dress like her more mature agemates is an example. Societal expectations may be incongruent with the competence of the individual. Adults may locate the source of conflict and confusion in the adolescent when in fact it may lie in adults' expectations that are out of phase with the adolescent's level of development.

Although being an early maturer can have some disadvantages, the assets usually outweight them, particularly for males. There is the possibility of sexual activities with girls of the same age. There is the possibility of engaging in sports, and matching prowess with older boys, as well as achieving a stable identity as an athlete.

Early maturing girls find themselves in a quite different situation. They are at the lower end of the growth spurt, which may be a very lonely place. The early maturing girl faces changes that her peers have not yet undergone, for example, menarche, which may add to her loneliness. Girls who mature very early on may even be ostracized by their agemates because their development is so out of phase (Bardwick, 1971; Frisk, Tenhunen, Widholm & Hortling, 1966). The early maturing girl may be as much as 5 to 6 years ahead of boys her age and as much as 2 to 3 years ahead of her same-sexed peers. She, therefore, finds herself with few peers with whom to share her experiences and may feel lonely, confused, and emotionally deprived (Frisk et al., 1966).

The late maturing boy may have similar bad experiences because of his extreme position at the end of the age-range for reaching physical maturity. He is often treated as a "kid" and denied responsibility and leadership, which may prove detrimental to his self-concept and self-esteem. His lack of physical development may hamper him in the classroom, in the locker room, and in sports. He may feel himself lacking in capability and in the desire to compete. He may seek attention through inappropriate means, which can land him in trouble with teachers or parents. He may also have bad relations with his peers, particularly in heterosexual relations. In general, he may come to feel he just cannot measure up to any standard. Research has shown that the treatment of the late maturing male may have detrimental effects that last up to 20 years (Jones & Mussen, 1958). As adults, late maturing males were less often leaders, executives, or in positions of power than early maturers. On the positive side, however, late maturers tended to have more successful marriages.

The late maturing girl is less handicapped, probably because she enters pubescence two years ahead of boys. Indeed, the late maturing girl may have the best of both worlds, for she enjoys a prolonged childhood and enters pubescence at the same time as boys her age. She can date boys her own age, which may explain why she does not run as high a risk of pregnancy as early maturing girls.

The most difficult adjustments to biological change must be made by the early maturing girl and the late maturing boy because both are at the extremes of the physical maturity continuum. All adolescents, however, experience some problems with development, and all must adjust to the changes in their physical self. We have emphasized two points. First, growth and the rate of development clearly have psychological effects, which may have long-term consequences for psychological adjustment. Second, individuals differ greatly in rates of maturation, both within and between sexes. Both adults and adolescents need to be aware of these individual differences and adapt their expectations accordingly.

BIOLOGY AND SOCIAL BEHAVIOR.   Physical growth has some other implications for socialization. First, generational differences in the rate of biological maturation have important consequences for socialization (e.g., Tanner, 1970; Meredith, 1963, 1969a, 1969b). During the past 4 to 5 generations, adolescents have been reaching maturity earlier than ever before. This is called the **secular trend.** In other words, 13- and 14-year-old boys or girls of several generations back were not as physically mature as contemporary 13- or 14-year-olds. In the past 75 to 100 years, the average age for reaching full growth has gone down from age 25 to age 18 or 19. The average age of menarche has declined by about 4 months every 10 years since 1850 (Tanner, 1970). As a result, those who socialize today's adolescents come from a generation who underwent a different growth rate. They may be out of tune with the degree to which adolescents are now capable of handling certain social responsibilities and may treat adolescents as younger than they really are.

Second, the biological changes in adolescence have important implications for differences between the sexes. Girls are likely to be treated as older than they are, and boys as younger. Consequently, girls tend to date boys who are older than themselves and may thus learn different social patterns than boys their age, who tend to date younger girls. Girls are also more likely than boys to be treated as grown-ups, especially during early adolescence. Although this treatment has certain advantages, it may cause problems because adults, particularly parents, may expect more from the girl than she is capable of, particularly in the way of social behavior. She may not have had the experience, or have the cognitive capabilities, to allow the behavior expected (Flavell, 1977).

Intellectual Changes

We have emphasized that the changes occurring in adolescence are continually evaluated by the adolescent in forming and changing judgments about the self and its place in society. Clearly, this requires a degree of cognitive competence not available to the child. It is no accident that adolescents ask "Who am I?" and come up with more substantive answers than children might give. These changes in response to the question seem to be related to changes in cognition, particularly the acquisition of abstract thinking encompassed by formal operations (see Chapter 6).

Elkind (1967a) has summarized Inhelder and Piaget's (1958; Piaget & Inhelder, 1969) discussion of the cognitive structures of adolescence. First, the adolescent is capable of dealing with combinatorial logic, in which many factors operate simultaneously, either singly or in interaction. Second, the adolescent can use abstract systems that make thought more flexible. Third, the adolescent can deal with the possible as well as the real. This is the highest form of cognition. It epitomizes adolescent thought and has important consequences for adolescent behavior and personality development. The abstract thinking that appears with adolescence is used to evaluate the reactions of others to the individual and the individual's reactions to physical growth and behavior. We can better understand developmental changes in relations with parents and peers, in moral thinking, and so forth, when we consider them in conjunction with adolescent cognitive competence.

Cognition and Adolescent Personality Development

The adolescent's cognitive development involves changes in ego identity, the self-concept, and egocentrism (Elkind, 1967a, 1967b, 1968, 1970; Looft, 1971). Because the onset of formal operations increases the ability to introspect, the adolescent becomes capable of thinking about himself objectively for the first time. As a result, he or she becomes concerned about others' reaction toward the self, and about the discrepancy between the ideal and the real self.

As Elkind has noted, the adolescent becomes capable of thinking one thing and saying another, that is, of hiding his thoughts from others. It is at adolescence that one becomes capable of showing tact in social encounters and of being willfully deceitful and exploitative. In adolescence one may for the first time become—in the broadest sense—a politician.

EGOCENTRISM.   Perhaps the most important feature of adolescent cognition in relation to personality development is **egocentrism.** The adolescent becomes deeply embroiled in a concern over the self. The adolescent is capable of thinking about not only his or her own thought but also the thought of others. "It is this capacity to take account of other people's thought, however, which is the crux of adolescent egocentrism" (Elkind, 1967b, p. 1029). Adolescent egocentrism, then, represents a failure to distinguish one's own thoughts and the events they are about from the thoughts of others (Elkind, 1967b; Looft, 1971). Since the adolescent is absorbed with thoughts about the self, he or she thinks others must be, too. For example, adolescents consumed with concerns of acne, physical size, or identity will often attribute these same concerns about themselves to their parents, siblings, teachers, and friends.

One consequence of this egocentrism is that adolescents feel "on stage," with all attention focused on them. The adolescent plays to what Elkind (1967b) calls an "imaginary audience." "Because he believes he is of importance to so many people, the imaginary audience, he comes to regard himself, and particularly his feelings, as something special and unique" (Elkind, 1967b, p. 1031).

Decentering comes about through social interaction and objective scrutiny of one's own thoughts. Discussions with peers reveal different interpretations of life, as well as the strengths and weaknesses of one's own position. By establishing relations of intimacy, the adolescent develops genuine interpersonal relations (Piaget, 1967; Looft, 1971; Elkind, 1967b). Taking up a vocation and entering the social world of adults combines thought and action and thus promotes decentering (Inhelder & Piaget, 1958). These processes, then, help the adolescent develop the thinking characteristic of adults.

MORAL THINKING.   In our discussion of moral development (Chapter 12), we noted that according to Kohlberg's (1963, 1969) theory, the adolescent reaches the most advanced stage of moral thinking. The content-free formal operations, and the logical abstract thinking reflected in them, are applied to moral situations. The result is a greater capability for dealing with intricate moral issues, thus showing the value of the hypothetico-deductive thinking that develops in adolescence. Adolescents can think of many possible solutions to a problem and devise ways of logically testing the feasibility of each solution, much in the same way a scientist goes about testing a hypothesis in an experiment.

With the advent of formal-operational thinking, the adolescent becomes a moral philosopher, capable of abstract reasoning about moral issues. Psychologists view morality and moral thinking as thinking about and behaving within the constraints of the social order (see Chapter 12). That is, morality relates to the use of rules and the development and questioning of social regulations. As a result, religious and political views undergo changes during adolescence.

Religious development during adolescence revolves around questions of the nature and purpose of life, the values by which one can live, and issues about the nature of religion itself. Adolescents' questioning of religion represents a search for an answer to the question "Who am I?" (Stewart, 1967). Contrary to popular belief, most adolescents do not experience a religious reawakening (Harris, 1959; Kuhlen & Arnold, 1944), although their religious beliefs do become more mature and religion becomes more personal (Kuhlen & Arnold, 1944). While the adolescent's views on religion become more abstract, there is no evidence for a general repudiation of religious belief.

POLITICAL THINKING.   Similar changes occur in the adolescent's political thinking, which also becomes more abstract (Adelson, 1971; Adelson & O'Neil, 1966). During early adolescence, political thinking tends to be concrete and personalized—politics is made up exclusively of specific people or governmental agencies. The mid- to late-adolescent comes to view political institutions as existing to protect people's rights and as governed by rules. Solutions to social problems emerge from cooperation and the interdependence of people and social institutions. Older adolescents can examine the ramifications of decisions made about laws and governing bodies. They demonstrate a reasoned view of the nature of political systems. This emergence of political ideology closely parallels the cognitive changes that take place in adolescence. The notions of justice revealed in Kohlberg's research can be translated into views about political systems.

In contrast to the youthful political activists of the late 1960s and early 1970s (Dusek, 1977), adolescents in the late seventies seem politically conservative. Although this change is not well documented, it is evident in both political polls and the classroom. Perhaps it relates to the absence of an overriding political issue, such as the Viet Nam war or Watergate, which divided the country and polarized opinions. Were such an issue to surface today, we might well see youth again more politically active and socially concerned.

Cognition and Adolescent Social Relationships

Elkind (1967a, 1968, 1970), and more recently Flavell (1977), have noted that the dynamics of formal-operational thinking provides us with insights into much of the social behavior of adolescents, including their relations with their parents and peers. Formal-operational thinking allows the adolescent to realize various alternatives in meeting parental demands because of an increased ability to imagine alternatives to parental views and wishes. As a result adolescents can take exception to parental views—for example, about smoking "pot"—whereas children cannot and must follow parental dictates. Adolescent rebellion comes from an awareness of differences between the possible and the real (Elkind, 1968).

The disparity between the ideal world of adolescents and the real world in which adolescents live can be a source of conflict between parents and their adolescent children. As the adolescent takes on a vocation, however, and joins the adult world with its various roles and responsibilities, he or she achieves a broader un-

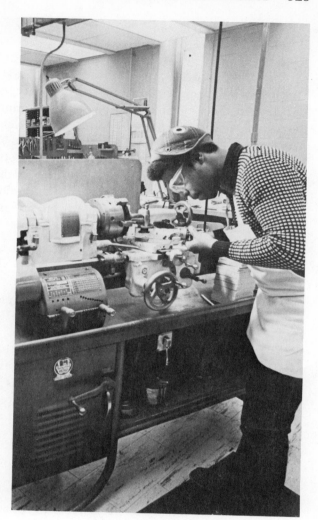

When adolescents take a job they are more able to understand the demands on adults. (Eric Roth/The Picture Cube)

derstanding of the many factors that come together in making decisions. As a result, the relatively pure cognitive approach to understanding parents' decisions is replaced with a more well-rounded perspective. The adolescent thus takes a less militant view, with the result that he or she can assume a more positive stance toward society.

Similar phenomena occur in peer relations. Adolescent friendships become more realistic, because the adolescent learns to tolerate differences of opinion and judges friends as cohorts rather than simply as people to be around and do things with.

The Developing Self

One important feature of adolescent development concerns the changing view of the self, particularly in response to the question "Who am I?" and "What am I all about?" Discussions of the self-concept have pervaded psychological theorizing since William James (1890), who devoted an entire chapter of *The Principles of Psychology* to the development of the self. More recently, Allport (1950), Erikson (1963, 1968), and others have suggested that the self-concept lies at the core of personality development, particularly in the adolescent years. Conceptions of adolescence as a time of questioning and confusion about identity are prevalent in both popular literature and scientific writing.

Definition of the Self-Concept

Definitions of the **self-concept** vary from what the pronouns "I," "me," and "mine" mean (Cooley, 1902; Mead, 1934; Coopersmith, 1967) to complex evalutations of the human organism (James, 1910). For our purposes, the self-concept refers to the individual's evaluation of his or her physical, emotional, social, and cognitive competence. An understanding of the self-concept thus requires familiarity with the cognitive changes taking place in adolescence as well as the many social and biological changes. Hence, we use the term "self-concept" to denote an evaluation of the self as affected by social interactions as well as by the evaluation of past development.

Stability of the Self-Concept

Erikson (1963) has argued that the major crisis in adolescence concerns the identity of the self. The self-concept undergoes dramatic, critical changes during adolescence.

Several studies have examined stability of the adolescent's self-concept. Engel (1959), for example, studied the self-concepts of 172 eighth- and tenth-grade students, and retested them 2 years later. Their self-concepts remained stable, with a test-retest correlation of +.78 over the 2-year interval. No differences in stability due to IQ, sex, or age appeared.

Carlson (1965) also did a longitudinal study of the self-concepts of 49 high school students, 16 males and 33 females. Girls showed some increase in personal orientation, but there were no differences between boys and girls in the stability, which was high, of the self-concept.

Constantinople (1969) has conducted the most ambitious longitudinal study to date of adolescent self-concept; 952 students in the freshman-to-senior levels of college were included in the study. The stability correlations for the self-concept ranged from +.45 to +.81 on the subscales of the test. The median correlation was +.70, indicating a high degree of stability over the 6 weeks of the study.

Recent research (Dusek, 1978) has been concerned with changes in the self-concept of students in grades 5-10. Self-concept was intially measured in 1975. The adolescents were retested in 1976 and 1977. Analyses of the data over the 3-year period revealed no changes in self-concept.

These studies all agree that, during adolescence, the self-concept is quite stable and does not show the broad, sweeping changes suggested by many theorists. Several cross-sectional studies (e.g., Bohan, 1973; Katz & Zigler, 1967) also indicate no significant differences in the self-concept during the adolescent years.

Data such as these suggest that adolescence is *not* a time of upheaval in views of the self, although adolescents may well be concerned with answers to the question "Who am I?" At the present time we can only conclude that perhaps some adolescents go through changes in the self-concept, but that for most of them, the changes are gradual and do not reflect discontinuities in development.

Structure of the Self-Concept

It may be that global measures of the self-concept indicate little change during adolescence but that measures of more specific components of the self-concept do reveal certain changes (Monge, 1973). Monge had 2,062 adolescents in grades 6 through 12 fill out a **semantic-differential scale.** They were asked to rate themselves on a 7-point scale with 21 bipolar pairs of adjectives: for example, smart versus dumb, friendly versus unfriendly, stable versus unstable, and strong versus weak. **Factor analysis** was performed, and 4 factors emerged: (1) achievement-leadership (2) congeniality-sociability (3) adjustment, and (4) sex-appropriateness of the self-concept. As Figure 15-2 shows, there were significant age and sex differences in the self-concept. In every grade, boys ranked themselves higher in achievement and leadership than girls did. These ratings showed an increase over the years, while the girls' ratings showed a moderate increase up to the seventh grade and a decline thereafter. At every level, girls rated themselves as more congenial and sociable than boys did. Both of these effects are in line with traditional stereotypes of the male and female sex roles, which seem to have remained unchanged in recent years (Rosenkrantz, Vogel, Bee, Broverman & Broverman, 1968; Broverman, Vogel, Broverman, Clarkson & Rosenkrantz, 1972). Both sexes showed a decline in adjustment from the sixth to the tenth grade, but at every grade level boys rated themselves higher in adjustment than girls did. Monge suggests that this result may be due to the difficulty adolescents have in living within the social system and, hence, their decline in general adjustment during mid- to late-adolescence. Finally, males seem to solidify their role from grades 6 through 9 and maintain the stereotype of the male through grade 12, but girls seem to react in the opposite way. Perhaps this is because girls face

FIGURE 15-2 *Mean Factor Score for Each Grade Level and Sex Subgroup*

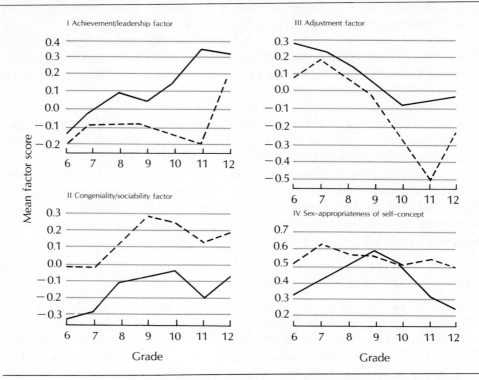

SOURCE: Monge, R. H. Developmental Trends in factors of adolescent self-concept. *Developmental Psychology*, 1973, 8, pp. 382–393.

other decisions about their sex role, or perhaps because the female sex role is not as clearly defined or valued as the male sex role (Maccoby & Jacklin, 1974).

SOME CONCLUSIONS. Monge's data reveal several structural aspects of the adolescent's self-concept and point up the value of examining its components to get a better picture of the whole of it. Unlike the longitudinal data, Monge's results indicate changes in the self-concept during adolescence. But, as Monge notes, the data reveal no broad, sweeping changes, only a rather modest restructuring.

The data on age differences do not support the notion of a widespread reorganization of the self-concept during adolescence; nor do they suggest that it is a time of storm and stress. Rather, the structure of the self-concept changes gradually, like most other features of development (Gecas, 1971; Combs & Snygg, 1959).

The popular stereotypes about adolescence have once again been shown to be false. Adolescents successfully integrate parental influences, physiological changes, and peer relations in a way that allows them to maintain the continuity of the self-identity in spite of dramatic changes in these aspects of development.

Vocational Development

One of the adolescent's most important decisions concerns choice of vocation. The maturity that marks the end of adolescence is often defined as the attainment of psychological and economic independence from the family, and this is largely a matter of embarking on a career. Although we might expect adolescents to give a lot of thought to vocational choice, over 50 percent of them spend little time thinking about their vocational plans (Remmers & Radler, 1967). Counselors in high school are usually more concerned with college-bound students than with those who need other kinds of training or who are seeking other vocational outlets. Hence, many adolescents choose vocations almost at random (Elder, 1968). This phenomenon is nothing less than amazing when we consider the years of schooling, pressures from parents and friends, and the expectations of the adult world, all of which would seem to force the adolescent to give long, serious thought to this important decision.

As Havighurst (1964, 1972) has noted, the choice of a vocation is an extremely important decision for the adolescent. It involves the identification of behavior that will allow for a rational choice one can live with for years to come. Borow (1966, 1976) emphasizes this point in his discussion of the importance of a vocation for a satisfying adult life-style. Yet, as important as decisions about a vocation are, few adolescents take account of all the aspects of making a rational choice.

Conceptualizations of Vocational Decision Making

We have very little theory or data about the adolescent's choice of vocation. Eli Ginzberg and his associates (Ginzberg, 1972; Ginzberg, Ginzberg, Axelrad & Herman, 1951) have described this decision as involving a series of choices about what is wished for and what is possible. Individuals first make vocational choices on the basis of fantasy and wish fulfillment—such as wanting to be a jet pilot, a lawyer, or a doctor—and only later come to make realistic choices based on their actual competencies. We know little, however, of adolescent decision making about vocations, and most of what little information we have is purely descriptive.

A more informative theory has been offered by Super (1957, 1959, 1969) and his colleagues (Super, Crites, Hummel, Moser, Overstreet & Warnaph, 1975), who view vocational choice as a continuous process of decision making in relation to the individual's conception of the self. Vocational choices are made in such a way as to allow for the greatest opportunity for the expression of the self-concept. In its early stages, the self-concept is less well developed, with the result that vocational choices are less rational than in later stages of development. As the self-concept matures, the individual perceives more possibilities for potential vocations. With appropriate guidance, a vocation can be chosen more rationally. One will, or should, pick a vocation that allows the fullest possible expression of the self-concept. By tentatively selecting some occupation and trying it out, one can determine the degree to which the self-concept may be implemented. Although this theory is still largely descriptive, it does suggest that vocational guidance should help the individual understand the self.

Determinants of Vocational Choice

One factor in vocational decision making is physical competence. The professional athlete, for example, has exceptional physical skills. Intellectual capability is also relevant to vocational choice. Some vocations require greater cognitive skills than others, and personality is also clearly important to vocational choice.

Although there has been little research that explains exactly how these factors interact in vocational decision making, they are important and the theories hold promise for helping us to understand how adolescents go about making vocational choices. The role of socioeconomic status and its correlated child-rearing practices and other background influences, sex differences, and intellectual competence become more clearly focused and integrated from this developmental perspective. All of these factors have an impact on the adolescent faced with a decision about a vocation.

SUMMARY

The factors influencing development in childhood continue to operate during the adolescent years. Some, such as biological development, become more important, both in their own right and indirectly, as they influence the reactions of others to the individual. Development does not stop with the end of childhood but goes through a transition, adolescence, on its way to adulthood. Hence, to understand the importance of child development and its long-term consequences, it is instructive to study adolescent development.

Adolescence begins with pubescence, which occurs about 2 years earlier in girls than in boys. Changes in height, weight, and body proportion signal the transition from childhood to maturity. These changes and their rate of occurrence affect social expectations about adolescent behavior. Several long-term effects of being an early versus a late maturer have been identified, especially for boys. Late maturing boys are not as well liked, are seen as less attractive, and are viewed as less mature than early developers. Late maturing boys have less prestigious jobs as adults, but they do have more successful marriages. Late maturing girls do not suffer these experiences, probably because they still mature earlier than most boys.

Another important aspect of development during adolescence is the cognitive change brought about by formal-operational thinking. These changes are related to the new view of the self that emerges during adolescence and also to changes in personality. Interactions with parents and peers are also better understood within the framework of the adolescent's emerging cognitive competence.

Adolescent self-concepts do not change in a dramatic way, but rather are gradual and continuous in development. There are, however, age and sex differences in changes in the self-concept. Global views of the self may not change during adolescence, but various aspects of the self-concept do change.

Vocational choices among adolescents are poorly understood. These choices are often made haphazardly but still reflect the individual's attempt to find a vocation that satisfies the basic needs of the self. Since entering a vocation is one criterion for achieving adulthood, it is important to gain further understanding of this aspect of adolescence.

CHAPTER 16

(David Burnett/Stock, Boston)

ADOLESCENCE: TRANSITIONS IN SOCIAL RELATIONS

JUST AS THERE ARE TRANSITIONS in the development of the individual from child to adolescent, so, too, there are transitions in social relations. Relations with parents and with peers change during adolescence. Although we usually think of child-rearing practices as affecting the development of the child, the evidence indicates that they are important in adolescence as well. The function of the peer group also changes, taking on an added importance because of its similarity to adult peer groups.

Our discussion of these social transitions focuses on two other aspects of development—sexuality and delinquency. First, the adolescent's emerging sexuality requires new adjustments. The child has little experience of the stringent sanctions on sexual behavior that the adolescent must face. Second, we discuss juvenile delinquency, which although it arises mainly in adolescence, may have its roots in childhood.

Parent Influences
on Adolescent Socialization

Changes in the nature and structure of the family are important for explaining the influence of the parents on the adolescent. Whereas at the turn of the century, approximately two-thirds of American families lived in rural areas only a third do so today. The family unit has also changed, reduced in size from the **extended family** (parents, children, and other relatives) to the **nuclear family** (parents and children) and providing adolescents with fewer adult models than their parents had, as well as a very different family atmosphere. As Mead (1970) has pointed out, this change in family structure has resulted in developmental differences between generations that contribute to a lack of communication between them. Adults find it difficult to understand what it is to be an adolescent today because the experiences of contemporary adolescents are so different from their own as adolescents. As a result, we can expect some conflict because of differences in values and orientations between parents and their adolescent offspring (Campbell, 1969; Mead, 1970).

Intergenerational Differences in Development

The expression "generation gap" refers to the differences in values, morals, behavior, and philosophies of life between people who grow up in different generations (Mead, 1970). Much has been made of this notion of a cultural generation gap (Conger, 1971; Munns, 1971; Prugh, 1969), born in the wake of the recent, rapid changes in life-styles and the new values and interests brought about by these changes. We might then expect that the values and orientations of adolescents and their parents would differ significantly.

Surprisingly, research on the extent of the generation gap has not shown consistent differences between the values and life orientations of the two generations. Meissmer (1965), for example, reported that for 13- to 18-year-old boys, 89 percent were happy in their homes and that 84 percent spent more than half of their leisure time at home. Seventy-four percent were proud of their parents and did not hesitate to have their parents meet their friends. Meisels and Cantor (1971) reported that college students, both male and female, perceived their values and orientations as closer to those of their parents than to those of their peers. Finally, Douvan and Adelson (1966) found that 14- to 18-year-olds reported few if any serious disagreements with their parents on social issues.

A more extensive survey of intergenerational differences was conducted by Yankelovitch (1969). Some two-thirds of the adolescents suggested that there was a generation gap but that it had been exaggerated, and about 70 percent of their parents agreed with this view. About three-quarters of the adolescents said that they have about the same values as their parents and that the differences in values were rather

Most adolescents feel they and their parents have similar values. (Paul S. Conklin/ Monkmeyer)

unimportant. This held true for the values of work, independence, and other "establishment" values supposed to be sources of conflict between the generations.

Where, then, do we find intergenerational differences? Many researchers (e.g., Yankelovitch, 1969; Munns, 1971; Conger, 1971; Weiner, 1971; Meisels & Cantor, 1971) suggest that intergenerational conflict revolves around music, art, social injustice, sexual behavior, and specific issues concerning the broad cultural changes taking place within our society. Adolescents' views tend to be more liberal than those of their parents on these issues, but the popular conception of the magnitude of the differences between parental and adolescent values is exaggerated. It is also true that adults disagree among themselves about these issues.

Studies such as these suggest that research reporting large intergenerational differences in values and orientations is misleading. Conger (1973) claims that the explanation for these research results lies in (1) the select samples tested—campus activists or highly liberal adolescents, for example—that are not representative of the majority of adolescents, (2) inappropriate statistical analyses that highlight differences, and (3) small differences between parents and their adolescent children that get blown out of proportion. The evidence thus indicates that the generation gap is there, but it is not as wide as many would have us believe.

This evidence is not surprising. The values and orientations of adolescents should be similar to those of their parents because their parents have spent a good deal of time rearing them, exemplifying those values, and providing opportunities for their children to acquire those values through imitative learning and direct teaching. As a result, the more ingrained personality characteristics and orientations are likely to be more similar to those of parents. Differences between parents and children are likely to be superficial, such as differences in music, art, and slang.

Child-Rearing Techniques and Adolescent Independence Strivings

Parental influences on the socialization of the adolescent do not begin in adolescence but represent a continuation of influences that began earlier in childhood. One important feature of parents' influence on socialization concerns their understanding of what being an adolescent means. Parents must socialize their adolescents differently from the way they did their younger children, allowing them to learn new social behavior; adolescents must in turn help their parents "grow up" in order to accomplish this (Bell, 1968; Rheingold, 1969). Examples of adolescent parent rearing are: demanding independence, participation in the establishment of rules, and being assertive about how to be treated. These new demands require considerable flexibility of the parents and other adults.

The issue with the greatest potential conflict between adolescents and their parents concerns the struggle for independence. It is both necessary and desirable that the adolescent become independent, but gaining this independence from the parents often proves difficult for everyone concerned (Douvan & Adelson, 1966; Elder, 1968). Part of the reason for this difficulty is that a whole social system of expectations, values, interactions, and identities must be changed (Campbell, 1969). Parents must stop dealing with their adolescent offspring on a power basis (e.g., Smith, 1970) and allow the adolescent to gain gradual control over decisions. Important conflict over adolescent strivings for independence is usually due to either of two factors: (1) societal restrictions on independence, such as laws defining adult status for jobs, voting, drinking, and the like; or (2) parental models for independence coupled with child-rearing practices that may deter obtaining independence.

CULTURAL VARIATION IN INDEPENDENCE TRAINING.   A number of societies have formal **rites of passage** that mark the transition from childhood to adulthood (e.g., Mead, 1950, 1953, 1970). In some of these societies, training for independence—teaching the child to accept responsibility, to make decisions, and to rely increasingly on oneself without adult direction—begins as soon as the child is capable of contributing to the society. As a result, there is a greater continuity between the roles of childhood and adulthood, and independence training begins sooner and ends earlier than it does in our culture (Benedict, 1938). These rites of passage clearly define independence. Hence, transitions in development are accomplished smoothly and without the conflict that often occurs in a society that lacks these rites. It is expected that the individual will gain independence, and societal support for this task is built into cultural traditions.

American society today has no such formalized system. Youth are expected to remain dependent on the family, for example, economically and socially, even while they are being taught that independence is desirable. It is not surprising, therefore, that conflict about independence is likely to arise between the adolescent and the socializing agents. Parents and adolescents disagree about the timing and nature of the independence to be won. And there are no universal guidelines that structure independence attainment.

The legal system may add to the confusion, for it considers the individual an adult at the age of 18. The rest of society may not grant adult status until a later age. This disparity can create confusion and difficulties in the attainment of independence; the adolscent may want more than the society or the parents are willing to give.

Horrocks (1962) has pointed out that adolescents want and need autonomy and independence, but only in gradually increasing amounts. They want to have an autonomy they can deal with successfully. Autonomy granted too suddenly (or too slowly) will be unacceptable. Gold and Douvan (1969) investigated autonomy in girls ranging in age from 11 to 18. Their results, presented in Table 16-1, support Horrocks' suggestion. There is growth in both behavioral and emotional autonomy from the family. This growth takes place over a 7-year period, with many of the increases being only minor ones. Gold and Douvan suggest that most transitions in independence are smooth and that most adolescents do not experience significant conflicts about it.

CHILD-REARING AND ATTAINMENT OF INDEPENDENCE. Glenn Elder (1962, 1963, 1968, 1971) has extensively investigated the effects of child-rearing practices on

TABLE 16-1   Indices of Behavioral and Emotional Autonomy for Adolescent Girls

ITEM	CHANGE IN GIRLS FROM 11 TO 18	
	(N = 206) FROM %	(N = 148) TO %
Behavioral Autonomy		
S dates or goes steady.	4	94
S has job outside home.	34	60
S spends most of free time with		
friends	22	46
family.	68	44
Emotional Autonomy		
S thinks friendships can be as		
close as family relationships.	53	71
S chooses adult ideals		
outside the family	22	48
within the family.	66	52
S chooses as confidant		
a friend	5	33
one, both parents.	67	36

SOURCE: Adapted from Gold, M., and Douvan, E. Adolescent development. Boston: Allyn and Bacon, 1969.

TABLE 16-2 Description of Parental Types

TYPE	DESCRIPTION
Autocratic	Parent tells the adolescent just what to do and allows little initiative or assertiveness.
Authoritarian	Parent tells the adolescent what to do but listens to adolescent's point of view.
Democratic	Parent allows ample opportunity for adolescents to make their own decisions but retains final authority.
Equalitarian	Parents and adolescents are involved equally in making decisions about the adolescent's behavior.
Permissive	Adolescent makes his own decisions, but parents like to be heard and have input.
Laissez-faire	Adolescent makes his own decisions and need not listen to the parent.
Ignoring	Adolescents make their own decisions, and the parents don't care what the decision is.

SOURCE: Adapted from Dusek, J. *Adolescent development and behavior.* Palo Alto, Cal.: Science Research Associates, Inc., 1977.

adolescent striving for independence. In a study of some 7,350 adolescents in grades 7-12, Elder identified 7 types of parents based on the subjects' ratings of their parents' styles of child-rearing. These types are listed in Table 16-2, and range from "autocratic" to "ignoring." Since Elder's sample included individuals from different social classes, family sizes, and parental education, these types are fairly representative of the ways adolescents view their parents as child-rearers.

As Table 16-3 shows, the adolescents rate their fathers as more autocratic and authoritarian than their mothers (35 percent versus 22 percent). In addition, parents of large families were rated as more autocratic and authoritarian than were parents of smaller families. Parents with more education tended to be more permissive, although this depended on the age and sex of the adolescent.

The adolescents reacted differently to the various parental types. The respondents were asked, "Do you think (mother's-father's) ideals, rules, or principles about how you should behave are good and reasonable, or wrong and unreasonable?" The statistics summarizing the answers to this question are presented in Table 16-4. The democratic and equalitarian parents were rated as fairer than autocratic or authoritarian parents, with ratings of permissive parents falling between these 2 groups. The authoritarian father was rated as fairer than the authoritarian mother. But the permissive mother was rated as fairer than the permissive father. These data indicate that sex roles affect adolescents' perceptions of their parents.

These differences in the adolescents' ratings of the parents held up even when sex and social class were taken into account. The father can be controlling so long as he is willing to listen to the adolescent's point of view (the authoritarian father), but not when he makes demands without allowing expression of the adolescent's point

TABLE 16-3   Types of Child-Rearing Structures by Parent

PERCENTAGE OF ADOLESCENTS BY TYPES OF CHILD-REARING STRUCTURES

PARENT	N	AUTOCRATIC	AUTHORITARIAN	DEMOCRATIC	EQUALITARIAN	PERMISSIVE	LAISSEZ-FAIRE	IGNORING	TOTAL %
Mother	7359	9.1	12.9	35.5	17.7	23.8	.6	.4	100
Father	7356	17.9	17.1	31.4	. 14.4	17.4	.8	1.0	100

SOURCE: Elder, G. H. Structural variations in the child-rearing relationship. *Sociometry*, 1962, 25, pp. 241–262.

of view (the autocratic father). Communication, then, is critical in judging fairness (Elder, 1962). We might also point out that about 10 percent of the adolescents who characterized their parents as democratic, equalitarian, or permissive indicated that they felt unwanted by their parents, but that 40 percent of the children of autocratic or ignoring parents felt unwanted; this result again suggests that child-rearing practices produce differences in the way adolescents feel about their parents.

Elder (1963) also studied the relationship between autocratic, democratic, and permissive parent types and adolescent strivings for independence. He further studied patterns of communication between parent and adolescent and their relation to independence strivings by dividing each of these groups of parents into those who explained the rules they laid down and those who did not. Elder hypothesized that independence would be most evident in adolescents whose parents were permissive, less autocratic, *and* who explained the reasons for their rules. Autonomy was measured by the individuals' confidence in their own values and by their independence.

The pertinent results are presented in Table 16-5. Adolescent autonomy and independence were highest for democratic and permissive parents *and* for parents who explained their rules. Autocratic parents and those who rarely gave explanations for the conduct they demanded had children with less self-confidence and

TABLE 16-4   The Fairness of Parental Child-Rearing Policy as Related to Types of Child-Rearing Structures

PERCENTAGE OF ADOLESCENTS BY TYPES OF CHILD-REARING STRUCTURES

PARENT	AUTOCRATIC	AUTHORITARIAN	DEMOCRATIC	EQUALITARIAN	PERMISSIVE
Mother	55.1 (367)	58.9 (667)	85.5 (2237)	82.8 (1081)	80.4 (1471)
Father	50.7 (668)	74.9 (942)	85.1 (1966)	77.1 (817)	74.6 (1051)

SOURCE: Elder, G. H. Structural variations in the child-rearing relationship. *Sociometry*, 1962, 25, pp. 241–262.

TABLE 16-5 Levels of Parental Power and Frequency of Explanations in Relation to
Types of Adolescent Dependence-Independence Behavior

| LEVEL OF PARENTAL POWER | PARENTAL EXPLANA-TIONS | N | TYPES OF ADOLESCENT DEPENDENCE-INDEPENDENCE BEHAVIOR | | | | TOTAL PERCENT-AGE |
| | | | LACK OF CONFIDENCE | | CONFIDENCE | | |
			DEPENDENT	INDEPENDENT	DEPENDENT	INDEPENDENT	
Autocratic	Frequent	139	27.3	6.5	37.4	28.8	100
	Infrequent	231	34.2	14.7	20.3	30.3	100
Democratic	Frequent	1233	10.5	6.7	37.6	45.2	100
	Infrequent	194	22.7	9.8	35.6	31.9	100
Permissive	Frequent	729	13.2	7.2	29.8	49.8	100
	Infrequent	177	28.2	13.6	24.9	33.3	100

SOURCE: Elder, G. H. Parental power legitimation and its effect on the adolescent. *Sociometry*, 1963, 26, pp. 50–65.

NOTE: The degree of self-confidence in personal ideas and values was measured by the following item: How confident are you that your own ideas and opinions about what you should do and believe are right and best for you? Lack of Confidence: (1) Not at all confident, (2) Not very confident, (3) I'm a little confident. Confidence: (4) I'm quite confident, (5) I'm completely confident.

Self-reliance in problem solving and decision making was measured by the following item: When you have a very important decision to make, about yourself and your future, do you make it on your own, or do you like to get help on it? Dependent: (1) I'd rather let someone else decide for me, (2) I depend a lot upon other people's advice, (3) I like to get some help. Independent: (4) Get other ideas then make up my own mind, (5) Make up my own mind without any help.

independence. Coopersmith (1967) and Rosenberg (1963, 1965) reported similar findings for adolescents who viewed their parents as showing interest in their opinions and activities and as encouraging independence.

Data such as these, which are extremely rare in the study of adolescent development, demonstrate that similar phenomena exert an influence on the development of adolescents and children. Research such as Elder's suggests that child-rearing patterns may have long-lasting effects on such issues as strivings for independence.

Elder's research and that of others suggest that at least some conflict between generations is due to the ways parents interact with their children and to adolescents' perceptions of these child-rearing practices. Therefore, they support Mead's contention that both broad social influences and personality types are related to conflicts that occur when adolescents seek out independence from the parents.

Transitions in Interactions with Parents

It would be trite to say that adolescents interact differently with their parents than do younger children. We all know this from personal experience. The nature and causes of these differences are, however, less obvious. The transitions are mainly a matter of degree—children behave independently of their parents, but adolescents do so to a greater degree. These transitions are important in order to allow the adolescent to gain independence and autonomy, and to learn how to deal with the adult world in all its complexity. For those adolescents who do not make this transition success in the adult world may be limited, and failure may become a reality. As Horrocks (1962) has suggested, the time and degree of the transitions may be critical. Expecting too much, too soon, or allowing too little, too late may damage the development of the personality and harm self-esteem in adulthood. As a result, the individual may become an ineffectual adult.

Transitions in Peer Interactions

As a child, and then as an adolescent, the individual lives in a world increasingly dominated by the peer group. The almost complete control of adults over development during early childhood yields to the increasing influence of the adolescent's peer groups. The function and importance of the peer group changes from childhood to adolescence. In addition, patterns of friendship and the structure of peer groups—for example, membership in mixed-sex peer groups—change during adolescence to make the peer group quite different from that of childhood. Adolescent peer groups are more similar to adult groups than to childhood groups.

There are also changes in the interactions with members of the peer group. Dating and cross-sex friendships develop, and some adolescents even get married. All of these transitions can have an impact on the adolescent's self-perception, as well as on the orientation of the adolescent to the peer group.

There can be no debate that these transitions in relations with peers are important for the development of the individual. However, popular conceptions would have us believe that the peer group is the most important influence on adolescent social development. This is not so. The peer group's influence remains secondary to that of the parents, just as it was in childhood.

Importance of Adolescent Peer Relations

Adolescent peer groups are worth studying for several reasons. First, as adolescents become emancipated from their parents, they spend more and more time with their peers. This promotes interaction with agemates who share similar problems, conflicts, likes and dislikes, and slowly takes the adolescent away from the influence of the parents. This interaction helps the adolescent adjust to people with different values (Wagner, 1971; Thornburg, 1971). As a result, the adolescent may encounter conflict between the values of the parents and those of peers (e.g., Brittain, 1968, 1969; Conger, 1971; Douvan & Adelson, 1966). Although many of these conflicts are

The adolescent peer group is a training ground for adult social interactions. (George W. Gardner)

superficial and unimportant, the adolescent is becoming increasingly susceptible to peer influences, and some conflict between peer values and parent values may result (Allen & Newtson, 1972; Costanzo, 1970; Brownstone & Willis, 1971).

A second reason for studying the influence of adolescent peer groups is to study similarities as well as differences in the developmental influence of the peer group. In many ways, peer groups in childhood and adolescence have similar functions, but the differences are important. Because the adolescent peer group is more similar to the adult peer group, it becomes a training ground for adult social interactions. This long-term function of the adolescent peer group is quite different from any function of the childhood peer group.

Peer-Group Formation and Function in Adolescence

Adolescents belong to several peer groups. The adolescent moves beyond strictly neighborhood acquaintances and schoolmates and becomes involved with friends from a wider sphere of social and economic backgrounds.

Dunphy (1963) has extensively studied the formation of adolescent peer groups and has noted the structural changes they undergo. He discovered that the adolescent belongs to 2 groups, the crowd and the clique. The crowd, the larger group, is composed of a collection of cliques. The smaller group, the clique, ranges in size from 3 to 9 members. It is thus more intimate and perhaps more important in fostering development.

The evolution of peer groups shows a developmental sequence (Dunphy, 1963). First comes a precrowd stage composed of unisexual cliques that do not interact to any significant degree. This form of peer-group organization is characteristic of late childhood and early adolescence. In the second stage, these cliques interact. The unisexual clique provides the security that promotes interaction with members of the opposite sex. Sexually mixed cliques begin to develop in the third stage, during which the individual maintains affiliations with both mixed and unisexual cliques. In the fourth stage, mixed cliques form a fully developed crowd in which the boys are somewhat (about 10 months) older than the girls (Dunphy, 1963). In the fifth and final stage, the crowd disintegrates into loosely associated groups of couples. The individuals have developed the interpersonal skills to build confident preferences for interaction with members of the opposite sex.

FACTORS AFFECTING GROUP MEMBERSHIP.   Not all adolescents choose to belong to cliques, and some are even rejected by their peers. It is the rare adolescent, however, who does not belong to a clique of some sort (Horrocks & Benimoff, 1967). One factor that determines the group to which an adolescent may belong is social class; groups seldom cut across class lines (Coleman, 1961; Keislar, 1954; Phelps & Horrocks, 1958). This is particularly true of girls, who have more exclusive criteria for group membership. Common ethnic backgrounds, interests, and hobbies, as well as age, provide a basis for friendship and are also important determinants of group membership.

Adolescent Friendship Patterns

Children first form groups and friendships with members of the same sex. The child chooses friends as people to do things with, and these friendships typically involve little emotional involvement. During adolescence, friendship patterns change dramatically, becoming much more important and intimate, often involving intense feelings and emotions. In the adolescent's strivings for independence from parents and family, emotional support comes from the peer group and friends.

Fluctuations in friendships decreases during adolescence (Berenda, 1950; Iscoe, Williams and Harvey, 1963, 1964). In one interesting study, Skorepa, Horrocks, and Thompson (1963) investigated fluctuations in friendship across ages 5 through 21. The authors found that friendships in childhood fluctuated considerably but that this fluctuation then gradually decreased until age 12 or 13—the onset of puberty—when fluctuation increased slightly and then declined until age 18. After 18, the fluctuation again increased, probably because of new situations and friends available to the college student or working adolescent. Girls' friendships fluctuated somewhat more than boys'.

Aside from the obvious reasons of loss of contact with old schoolmates and the making of new friends on the job or at college, this fluctuation may have several causes. One of these is the degree to which the friend is thought to be loyal and trustful (Douvan & Adelson, 1966; Osterrieth, 1969). Close friendships are highly charged emotionally because of the loyality and trust demanded of the friend. When this trust and loyalty are violated, the friendship is often dissolved. When someone sees an incident as a betrayal of trust, the friendship becomes strained and it may be dissolved. These factors may be most important around the onset of puberty and of graduation from high school, two particularly stressful experiences.

As this suggests, one function of adolescent friendship is to share concerns and distresses with someone else who is experiencing similar emotions (Douvan & Adelson, 1966). By sharing their innermost feelings with someone else, adolescents can come to a better realization of who and what they are and can discover that changes in the self are possible. The childhood peer group or friendship does not have this function. As a result, however, adolescent friendships can be very devastating. A former friend might ridicule an adolescent and inform others of that person's innermost feelings.

During the later adolescent years, friendships become less intense, passionate, and selfish; they are based more on individual characteristics of people. The late adolescent begins to appreciate the value of people who are different, and to realize that he or she can be accepted by people with differing beliefs and values (Douvan & Gold, 1966). The declining dependence on peers for support, and greater practice with independence no doubt contribute to this trend.

PEER POPULARITY AND ACCEPTANCE IN ADOLESCENCE.   Acceptance by the adolescent peer group depends upon a number of personal qualities (Coleman, 1961; Bonney, 1946; Hartup, 1970; Horrocks & Benimoff, 1967; Kahanna, 1960; Horowitz, 1967). Well-liked peers are good looking, neat, well groomed, fun, outgoing, and possess the social skills appropriate to their age level. They make others feel accepted. Disliked peers are viewed as homely, sloppy, shy, withdrawn, childish, inconsiderate, and irresponsible. They make others feel uncomfortable. In general, adolescents like peers who are similar to themselves and who hold values similar to their own (e.g., Cavoir & Dokecki, 1973). Peers with very different values or from very different backgrounds tend to be disliked. Adolescents also prefer peers who come from the culturally dominant group in the society (Hallworth, Davis, & Gamston, 1965; Peck & Gellini, 1962).

One important influence on the formation of peer groups is similarity of social class. Most adolescent peer groups are composed of individuals from the same social class. A middle-class group is less likely to accept members from the lower classes than others from the middle or upper social classes. There is, however, some evidence that friendship choices across class lines have been increasing in recent years (Hraba & Grant, 1970; Proshansky & Newton, 1968).

One important criterion for being liked or included in the adolescent peer group is physical attractiveness. Cavoir and Dokecki (1973) investigated this phenomenon in fifth- and eleventh-graders who rated photographs of boys and girls in their own grade level according to their attractiveness. They also rated the degree to which they liked the people pictured in the photos. Physical attractiveness was more strongly related to popularity for fifth- than for eleventh-graders. Even so, for both groups, physical attractiveness was an important determinant of peer acceptance and popularity. Other research (Gronlund & Anderson, 1967; Kuhlen & Lee, 1943) indicates that the personality traits of physically attractive or unattractive adolescents may account for the relation between popularity and physical attractiveness. Popular adolescents were viewed as likeable, enthusiastic, and friendly, while unpopular adolescents were viewed as attracting attention and behaving childishly.

These findings indicate some of the differences between peer groups in childhood and in adolescence. Children pay little attention to personality traits and physical characteristics in their choice of friends. Adolescents, on the other hand, with their growing appreciation for differences among individuals, do take note of these traits and make judgments about how well they can interact with individuals with different personalities. Although we have no data, we suspect that the adolescents' changing cognitive competence allows this sort of interchange to occur. Formal-operational competencies (see Chapters 6 and 15) give the adolescent the skill to role play and to take another's perspective. These are important to the adolescent's changing view of social interaction, part of social cognition (Flavell, 1977). Hence, the formation of adolescent peer groups may be intimately related to cognitive development, much in line with the ideas about social cognition discussed at the end of this chapter.

ADOLESCENT CONFORMITY.   It is popularly believed that adolescents are creatures of conformity. The data on this issue, however, indicate that conformity increases during early adolescence, peaks in midadolescence, and then declines (e.g., Brownstone & Willis, 1971; Costanzo, 1970). Individuals differ widely in the strength of conformity at all ages (e.g., Conger, 1971; Berenda, 1950). Furthermore, these developmental trends have not changed in recent years.

There is certainly no doubt that adolescents conform to fads in dress and music (Munns, 1972) and in their strivings for independence. Their basic values, however, remain closer to those of their parents than to their peers (Conger, 1971; Floyd & South, 1972). Adolescents view their conformity more as an expression of individuality than of conformity (Conger, 1971; Douvan & Adelson, 1966). In other words, they view their conformity as maintaining a difference between them and adults, a barrier that helps them define what they are and removes the stigma of being "marginal." This conformity reflects the way adolescents can maintain a distinct role from that of adults, including norms and values that are somewhat, but not radically, different from those of adults.

Adolescent Heterosexual Peer Interactions

Cross-sex friendships gradually develop during midadolescence (Dunphy, 1963). While these friendships are often awkward and even antagonistic (Douvan & Adelson, 1966; Douvan & Gold, 1966), they do provide the opportunity to adjust to individuals of the opposite sex. Mixed-group activities allow the comfort and security of a same-sex peer group but also allow for interactions with opposite-sex peer groups. As the individual gains familiarity and confidence with opposite-sex peers, he or she becomes capable of interacting with the opposite sex without the support of a same-sex group. A major impetus for this is the practice of dating.

A number of researchers (Broderick, 1966; Broderick & Fowler, 1961; Meyer, 1959; Kuhlen & Houlihan, 1965) have investigated the course of friendships and relations with the opposite sex. There appears to have been an increase over the years 1942–1962 in the choice of opposite-sex friends (Kuhlen & Houlihan, 1965). The percentage of boys choosing girls, and girls choosing boys, as seating partners, for playing games with, studying with, as well as other activities, rose significantly between grades 6 and 12 and has increased significantly for all adolescents during the years 1942–1962.

The most comprehensive study of cross-sex friendships was done by Broderick (1966). Approximately 1,000 middle- to upper-middle-class adolescents between the ages of 10 and 17 served as subjects. For 10- and 11-year-olds, most friendships were with members of the same sex, and cross-sex relations were one-sided. The 12-year-olds, and to only a slightly lesser degree, the 13-year-olds showed the strictest sexual segregation. When cross-sex choices were made, girls tended to pick older boy friends, and boys tended to pick younger girl friends. The 14- and 17-year-olds broke down the sex barrier. Opposite-sex friendships were preferred for dating or going for walks, but there was still a reluctance for the companionship of the opposite sex in activities with large groups, as in taking meals in the cafeteria. Finally, the 16 to 17-year-olds were capable of developing relations of trust and a sense of security with members of the opposite sex. In general, their interactions with the opposite sex closely resembled those of adults.

The findings on cross-sex friendships reveals both intergenerational (between different generations) as well as intragenerational (within one generation) developmental sequences. Heterosexual relationships are acceptable at an earlier age than they previously were. And, with increasing age, cross-sex friendships increase in frequency. They are clearly different from friendships in childhood. Unfortunately, the data on friendship with members of the opposite sex tell us little about why these patterns change as they do.

One study (Meyer, 1959) that sheds some light on this issue investigated the role of reinforcement in cross-sex friendships in a sample of boys and girls in grades 5 through 12. Each subject rated, and was rated by, every other subject on the degree to which the child provided succorance (sympathy) or playmirth (fun). Both the boys and the girls rated same-sexed peers higher than opposite-sexed peers, indicating that same-sexed peers met social needs better than opposite-sexed peers. Moreover, there were no changes in this pattern over grade levels. The data clearly indicate that interaction with peers of the same sex was more reinforcing than with peers of the opposite sex. One developmental trend did appear at about the eighth grade, with boys picking girls, and vice-versa, for playmirth, a measure of who is sought out for fun and good times.

Meyer's (1959) results are consistent with the social-learning view of the development of peer relations. As social encounters lead to reinforcing affiliations

Heterosexual friendships increase during adolescence. (Erika Stone)

with the opposite sex, cross-sex friendships increase. This leads to changes in adolescent groups and cliques. Ultimately, couples find themselves mutually reinforcing and seek out other couples who meet their social needs.

DATING PATTERNS.   The most popular form of interaction between the sexes in adolescence is dating. The earliest age for dating is 10 to 11, when about 25 percent of boys and girls have had a date (Broderick 1966). In the 12- to 13-year-old bracket, dating shows a sharp increase with about 50 percent of the boys and 60 percent of the girls having had a date by age 12 and about 75 percent of both sexes having had a date by age 13. By 14 or 15 years of age, more than 80 percent of adolescents were dating, and dating became more frequent, with about 25 percent of adolescents dating once a week. Finally, by 16 or 17 years of age, 95 percent or more of the boys and girls were dating. In addition, the number of dating partners increased dramatically.

Although dating may lead to courtship and marriage, most adolescents view it as a social experience (Grinder, 1966; Skipper & Nass, 1966; Husbands, 1970; Douvan & Adelson, 1966; Douvan & Gold, 1966). Dating may serve any one or more of the following functions: socialization, learning to interact with the opposite sex, recreation, status seeking—particularly when one is associated with the "in group"—the assertion of independence from the family, companionship, as well as courtship and marriage.

Although dating seems to have the primary function of learning to interact with members of the opposite sex, it can also lead to superficial and empty relationships because the role playing involved is somewhat artificial (Husbands, 1970; Place, 1975). The artificial manners, rules of the game, sex-typed role playing, and the like all contribute to the superficial nature of dating which may foster the development of shallow interpersonal relations. Beginning to date too early or too late may hamper the development of heterosexual relations.

Perhaps the greatest difficulties in dating are encountered by those adolescents for whom its main purpose is courtship and mate selection. Some adolescents rush into marriage as soon as they think they have found the right mate. Although most problems encountered in adolescent marriages are similar to those found in adult marriages—for example, financial difficulties or simply adjustments to living with another person—they tend to be more intense. For most adolescents, the adjustment to marriage is more difficult than for adults because of the unsettled nature of their personality and because of desires for higher education (Burchinal, 1960, 1965; Sebald, 1968). Coping with unwanted pregnancy, a major factor in adolescent marriage, as well as with restrictions on freedom, make adolescent marriages highly unstable and lead to an extremely high divorce rate. Those who marry during adolescence tend to find their marriages less satisfactory and less satisfying than those who marry later.

SOME CONCLUSIONS. The peer group plays a special role in the adolescent's development. Although many of its functions are not very different from those of childhood peer groups, there are several key differences that are important for adolescent socialization. The role of the adolescent peer group has a more long-lasting importance to development than does the childhood peer group. The influence of the adolescent peer group is still subservient, however, to the influence of the parents. Recall that adolescents rated their values and ideals as closer to their parents than to their peers. We must keep this balance in mind so as not to exaggerate the effects of the peer group on development. In addition, we noted above that adolescents choose friends with similar values and backgrounds, who, in effect, reinforce the values the parents taught the adolescent.

Although there is little experimental evidence, it appears that changes in the function of the adolescent peer group may be influenced by cognitive growth. Certainly, involvement in a peer group requires an evaluation of friends and of the role the peer group can play in one's life. This seems to be especially true of the development of the self-concept, on which the peer group has a great influence by providing an accepting sounding board for expressions of the developing self, by sharing similar feelings, and by providing alternate modes of behavior.

Sexual Attitudes and Behaviors

Virtually every textbook and theoretical article on adolescent development gives a major role to the adolescent's emerging sexuality. This is probably the one area of development in which society as a whole and parents in particular judge that a high degree of socialization is needed for proper development. The changes in cultural attitudes toward sexuality that began in the late 1960s make this aspect of development even more important. Indeed, many adults believe that adolescents engage in sexual behavior more than they do themselves. Moreover, many adults feel there is little they can teach adolescents about sexual behaviors because young people have experienced it all. The sterotypic notion is that sexuality dominantes adolescent development to the near exclusion of other interests.

Society has constantly struggled with the problem of how the socialization of sexuality should be accomplished. Cultures differ widely in their handling of sexual behavior, making its study both more interesting and more difficult. Compounding the problem are differences between the sexes in attitudes toward sexuality. Some psychologists (Douvan & Adelson, 1966) have suggested that boys have a much more intense sex drive than girls and that in boys this drive is clearly directed toward sexual activity; girls' sex drive is held to be more diffuse, more readily sublimated, and less directly tied to sexual behavior. These differences may not be universal but may represent one outcome of socialization; males and females may be taught different views about sexual behavior.

It is clear that both males and females increase their sexual activity during adolescence and that attitudes about sexuality become more mature and integrated into an understanding of how sexuality fits within the life of the individual. Hence, views of sexuality change from childhood—where they are virtually nonexistent —to adolescence. Although some researchers (e.g., Brecher, 1971) have suggested that hormonal balances may underlie expressions of sexuality, we concentrate on the socialization of sexual behavior because it seems clearer and may prove more important for understanding differences between the sexes and differences among cultures.

Attitudes Toward Sexuality

Cross-cultural comparisons yield the most obvious examples of cultural influences on sexual attitudes. These comparisons show that cultures vary widely in their attitudes toward sexuality. Some cultures deliberately train sexuality, allowing and even encouraging sex play among children and adolescents. Other cultures, such as our own, stress prohibitions on sexuality, with individuals being taught not to engage in sexual behavior until they are married. At that time, they are expected to become fully functioning sexual partners, having had little if any sexual experience. This discontinuity in behavior often causes problems in adjustment for both adolescents and adults (Benedict, 1938).

Research has brought to light a number of interesting findings about adolescent views on when it is and is not appropriate to engage in sexual behavior. Many researchers (e.g., Reiss, 1960, 1966, 1967, 1970; Schofield, 1965; Kaats & Davis, 1970; Luckey & Nass, 1969) have investigated this issue and agree that adolescent views about the permissibility of various sexual acts vary with the relationship between the people involved and with the age of the individual making the judgment. Kaats and

Davis, for example, studied standards of sexual permissiveness in 319 women and 239 men, all freshmen or sophomores in college. The men's attitudes were more permissive than the women's, but both sexes thought that petting and sexual intercourse were more appropriate for people in love or those who were engaged than it was for those who did not have a particularly affectionate relationship.

The most extensive study of views about the acceptability of sexual behavior was conducted by Luckey and Nass. The sample consisted of high school and college students who were asked about the kind of relationship that should exist before a male and female should consider coitus as personally and socially reasonable. First, most students approved of premarital sexual relations among people who were engaged. Second, there were definite age trends—older students, both male and female, thought that premarital sexual intercourse was more legitimate for those who were engaged, tentatively engaged, or even for people going steady than did younger students. It appears, then, that age strongly affects adolescent sexual standards. Adolescents impose limits on sexual freedom, depending on the relationship between the two individuals and on the age of the individual. It seems that age can compensate for quality of the relationship. The older students thought that sexual intercourse was appropriate even when the relationship was less intimate. For both the younger and the older adolescents, traditional standards—such a sexual behavior outside the bonds of marriage—were less important than the personal relationships involved.

CHANGES IN ATTITUDES.   There is some indication that these views are changing for college females. Bell and Chaskes (1970) compared sexual behavior of college coeds in 1958 and 1968. In 1958, 10 percent of coeds said they had intercourse while dating, 15 percent while going steady, and 31 percent while engaged. The corresponding percentages for the 1968 sample were: 23 percent, 28 percent, and 39 percent, respectively. Although the percentages increased, the same pattern of attitudes was still clear; the quality of the relationship was considered important.

SEX EDUCATION.   These changing attitudes are related to the findings of some interesting studies of sex-education programs in the public schools. These programs have become a source of heated controversy among teachers, adolescents, parents, and school administrators. Many parents think that sex education belongs not in the public schools, but rather in the home or church. When they do approve of such programs in the schools, they want their own values taught, particularly prohibitions on sexuality (Libby, 1970).

The proponents of sex-education programs argue that they are desirable and necessary for preventing pregnancy and reducing venereal disease among adolescents (Gordon, 1973; Reichelt & Werley, 1974). Adolescents are poorly informed about birth control (Osofsky, 1970) and in fact most often do not use it (Settlage, Sheldon, & Cooper, 1974; Lewis, 1972; Gordon, 1973; Zelnick & Kantner, 1974). They are also ignorant about venereal disease. Advocates of sex education argue that

Adolescents in a high school sex education class (Mimi Forsyth/Monkmeyer)

adolescents will learn about sexuality anyway and that the adequacy of the information they receive about sex ought to be controlled (e.g., Gagnon & Simon, 1969; Kirkendall, 1965; Kirkendall & Miles, 1968).

Surveys show that most adolescents want to have sex education taught in the schools, in coeducational classes specifically devoted to it (Hunt, 1970; Harris, 1971). Adolescents think that they would get correct and valuable information, and the opportunity to talk with knowledgeable teachers about sex would be personally profitable and help them develop mature views on the subject. They do not think that classroom discussions of sexuality would provoke increases in sexual behavior, and they believe it would be less embarrassing to discuss sex in a classroom than it would be to talk it over with their parents.

Moreover, a recent survey (Hunt, 1970) of adolescent girls aged 13 to 19 revealed that although sexual physiology was worth knowing, the girls also wanted to learn something of the meaning of sexuality, both as a personal value and a part of a life-style. In effect, these girls were asking for what are traditionally considered moral judgments to be taught in the classroom. These are, of course, much more difficult aspects of sexuality to deal with, but they are perhaps more important in integrating sexuality in one's life.

Finally, Monge, Dusek, and Lawless (1977) reported an evaluation of a sex-education program for ninth-grade students who did in fact learn the information taught. This information concerned not only the biological side of sexuality but also its social and psychological aspects. This study clearly demonstrated that students do learn the information taught in the classroom and will, therefore, acquire important knowledge.

SOME CONCLUSIONS. Adolescents' attitudes toward sexuality tend to be more liberal than those of their parents, who tend to be more conservative and traditional on this issue. Adolescents want to take a more open and honest approach to sexuality, whereas many parents want it to remain a mystery and a taboo topic. Here we have a clear difference between generations. Finally, the current attitudes of adolescents indicate that sexuality should be treated as a personal decision between two people and is not the business of the broader society. The parents' generation, on the other hand, seems to think that social guidelines and sanctions are more important in deciding on the appropriateness of sexuality.

Data such as these suggest a sexual revolution. A more careful examination, however, shows that this is not so. Gagnon (1967) and Conger (1971) have argued that if we are undergoing a sexual revolution, it began several generations ago, and that today's adolescents are continuing a trend that began around the turn of the century.

Sexual Behavior

The Kinsey surveys (Kinsey, Pomeroy, Martin & Gebhard, 1953; Kinsey, Pomeroy & Martin, 1948) were the first serious investigations of sexual behavior. Approximately 55 percent of males had engaged in sexual intercourse by age 15, with more highly educated males engaging in premarital intercourse less frequently than did less well educated males. Similar findings held for the females in the sample. More recent information (Eastman, 1972; Sorenson, 1973; Robinson, King & Balswick, 1972) on reported rate of sexual activity shows little change from that reported by Kinsey and his co-workers. In the Eastman study, 55 percent of males and 49 percent of females had had sexual intercourse before marriage. Men tend to have their first intercourse earlier than women, with nearly 89 percent having their first intercourse between the ages of 16 and 19. The girls were approximately 2 years behind, with over 72 percent having their first sexual intercourse between the ages of 18 and 21.

Some information suggests that the rate of premarital intercourse has increased (Bell & Chaskes, 1970; Robinson et al., 1972). Robinson et al. reported the percentage of male and female college students having had premarital intercourse in 1965 were 65 percent and 29 percent, respectively. These figures agree quite well with Kinsey's data. In 1970, 65 percent of the males and 37 percent of females had engaged in premarital intercourse. It thus appears that sexual intercourse is increasing among college students and perhaps in the adolescent population generally, but these increases seem to be due to changes in female rather than male sexual behavior. If we are undergoing a sexual revolution among adolescents, it is more evident among females than males.

Satisfaction Versus Guilt in Adolescent Premarital Intercourse

One interesting question is how much adolescent sexual experiences are satisfying or guilt-provoking. The 1970 Playboy survey of 7,300 college students indicated that 82 percent of males and 51 percent of females engaged in premarital sexual intercourse. The 1971 *Playboy* survey of 3,000 college students suggested that over 90 percent of college students find their sexual experiences satisfying and over 80 percent of males and 70 percent of females have no guilt about engaging in coitus. This information suggests a redefinition of the role of sexuality by adolescents. It no longer produces guilt but rather satisfaction.

These changes are particularly pronounced for female college students (Luckey & Nass, 1969; Robinson et al., 1972), who have shown dramatic increases in premarital intercourse; between 50 percent and 60 percent of them have engaged in premarital intercourse. This increase is not, however, associated with promiscuity (Luckey & Nass, 1969, *Playboy*, 1971; Schofield, 1965). More than 70 percent of both males and females engage in premarital intercourse with someone they are deeply involved with. Very few females admit to one-night affairs, in contrast to the males who do so much more frequently (Luckey & Nass, 1969; *Playboy*, 1971).

Personal relationships play a significant role in determining whether sexual intercourse will take place between adolescents. The information on promiscuity suggests that adolescents do not engage in sexual behavior for its own sake, but rather view it as an expression of their emotional involvement with someone. The increase in sexual behavior among females suggests that the sexual behavior of adolescents reflects recent changes in attitudes (e.g., Schultz, 1972; Godenne, 1974).

SEXUAL REVOLUTION.   It should be easier, now, to understand our suggestion that no sexual revolution has occurred recently. The percentage of adolescents engaging in sexual intercourse is not dramatically different from that of a generation ago. Godenne (1974) has claimed that today's youth talk more openly about sex, although they probably have not had more sexual experience than did the previous generation. The two generations are probably quite close in sexual experiences. The study by Robinson et al. (1972) suggests that this is the case, but that females' sexual behavior may be more widespread than in the previous generation. This finding, however, does not suggest a dramatic change, and therefore not a revolution. In fact, the generations are similar in many ways, as noted by Harris (1971), whose survey showed that 44 percent of high school and college students agreed that it was not acceptable to enjoy sex simply for its own sake, while 40 percent of high school students and 53 percent of college students believed that it was acceptable to engage in premarital intercourse.

If a revolution is taking place, it seems to concern the attitudes of the two generations toward sexual behavior. Today's adolescents are progressing toward a mature form of sexuality that Ausubel (1954) calls "psychoaffectional sexuality." This may be especially true for girls, who seem somewhat more inclined than boys to engage in sexual behavior only with those for whom they feel a strong affection. Sex is becoming related to the quality of a relationship, independent of marriage. This trend seems to be increasing among adults also. This may be a revolution in attitudes, but it is not necessarily a revolution in behavior.

TABLE 16-6   Correspondence Between Sexual Standards and Sexual Behaviors

CURRENT STANDARD	MOST EXTREME CURRENT BEHAVIOR		
	KISSING	PETTING	COITUS
Kissing	64% (n = 16)	32% (n = 8)	4% (n = 1)
Petting	15% (n = 21)	78% (n = 108)	7% (n = 10)
Coitus	5% (n = 4)	31% (n = 26)	64% (n = 54)

SOURCE: Adapted from Reiss, I. L. The social context of premarital sexual permissiveness. New York: Holt, Rinehart & Winston, 1967, p. 117.

One issue, then, is how much adolescents today engage in sexual behavior consistent with their attitudes. Reiss's (1967) information on this issue (see Table 16-6) indicates a high degree of consistency. The behavior of the 248 individuals corresponds quite well, albeit not perfectly, with their attitudes about what was or was not acceptable.

Deviant Development

The bulk of information collected by psychologists, teachers, and others concerned with adolescent development deals with normal development. Although most adolescents experience development within the wide range we consider normal, there are abnormalities in adolescence, including many of the kinds that we discussed in children. For example, the development of an abnormal self-concept and abnormal intellectual and physical development are not uncommon during the adolescent years.

Aside from clinical case studies of abnormal personality development, the most widely studied form of deviant development in adolescence is juvenile delinquency. "Juvenile delinquency" is an expression applied to the criminal behavior of those under 16 or, depending upon the state, 18 years of age. Hence, "delinquent" is a legal term used to denote lawbreaking by those who are not considered adults and refers to behavior that conflicts with the norms of society, but which may be common within a particular social class or ethnic subgroup. Delinquency thus has both a legal and a cultural basis and may be viewed as a conflict between the norms of society and the behavior of the individual. The behavior of the adolescent may violate the norms of the society but may be reinforced by the norms of a particular peer group or subculture.

A host of variables, including child-rearing practices, peer-group interactions, and subculture membership, are related to the incidence of delinquency and also make for different kinds of delinquents (Johnson, 1959; Quay, 1964, 1965). For example, Johnson has identified two types of delinquents, the individual and the sociologic. The **sociologic delinquent** is the product of deliberate teaching by community and home influences that are directly opposed to the predominant social order. The **individual delinquent** seems to be produced by poor relations with parents, such as belittling of the child's competence. Child-rearing practices and the individual's own evaluation of competence and satisfactions from life seem to be more important in causing this form of delinquency.

Incidence of Juvenile Delinquency

The incidence of reported juvenile delinquency began to increase dramatically after 1948 and is still growing (see Figure 16-1). This increase is partly a result of the increase in the population of 10- to 17-year-olds and partly a result of more complete reporting of delinquent acts; nevertheless, the increase in the adolescent population is considerably less than the increase in cases of delinquency. These data indicate that increasing percentages of adolescents are involved in juvenile delinquency. Estimates are that 3 percent to 4 percent of young people between 10 and 17 years of age appear before the juvenile courts, and that up to 15 percent of all children and adolescents become delinquent before they reach adult legal status.

Boys have a higher rate of delinquency than girls; historically, male juvenile offenses have outnumbered those of females by 4 or 5 to 1 (Gold, 1970). Recent evidence, such as that in the Juvenile Court Statistics (1970), indicates that the disparity between the sexes in delinquency rates is growing smaller. The *Uniform Crime Report of 1967* shows the increasing rate of female delinquency between 1960 and 1967. While delinquency among boys increased about 40 percent during this period, delinquency among girls increased by nearly 76 percent in arrests for burglary, for example. Arrests for larceny increased 141 percent for girls, compared with only 54 percent for boys. Clearly, the disparity between the sexes is narrowing, at least in the number of arrests. Although delinquency rates for girls may have been underestimated previously (Wise, 1967)—perhaps because girls are less likely to repeat an illegal act and run another risk of getting caught—there remains a clear increase in delinquency by females.

The sexes tend to become involved in different kinds of delinquent behavior. Boys most frequently engage in burglary, larceny, theft, and other crimes involving aggression (Gold, 1970). Girls are more likely to be reported as incorrigible for engaging in illicit sexual behavior, or for running away from home. The difference between the sexes corresponds roughly to differences in their sex roles and are not completely unexpected. It may in fact be that the increase in juvenile delinquency for girls reflects changes in social standards and in sex roles, with their antisocial behavior reflecting the greater degree of assertiveness allowed females.

According to official statistics, the rate of delinquency for adolescents with a low socioeconomic status is higher than for middle-class adolescents (Conger, Miller & Walsmith, 1965; Cressey & Ward, 1969; Glueck & Glueck, 1950; Gold, 1970). This is partly because lower-class adolescents are more likely to get caught and prosecuted. However, there is still more delinquency among lower-class than middle-class adolescents (Wax, 1972; Polk, 1969; Kelley, 1972; Gold, 1970). Social class is not, however, the sole determinant of delinquency. Data on delinquency among middle-class youth indicate that poverty and poor living conditions are not such strong determinants of delinquency as we might expect (Sebald, 1968; Pine, 1966; Vaz, 1969). While lower-class adolescent boys engage in more delinquency than do upper-middle, lower-middle, or upper-lower-class boys, the same delinquent

FIGURE 16-1   *Trend in Juvenile-Court Delinquency Cases and Child Population 10–17 Years of Age, 1958–1970 (Semilogarithmic Scale)*

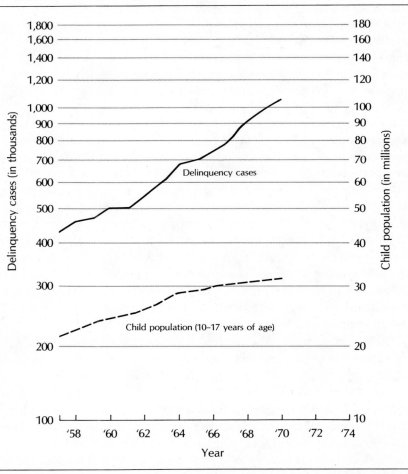

SOURCE: *Juvenile Court Statistics 1970.* National Center for Social Statistics, U.S. Department of Health, Education, and Welfare.

behavior occurs in all 4 groups. These data, when coupled with the fact that middle-class juvenile delinquency is often hushed up, suggest that social class and delinquency are not as closely associated as once was thought (Pine, 1966).

RELIABILITY OF THE DATA. One problem in interpreting data on juvenile delinquency is that the statistics are questionable. Both male and female adolescents commit crimes that are never reported. Hence, rates of delinquency appear lower than they actually are. Also, many adolescents who commit crimes are never caught. Some 80 percent of adolescents think that they have a better than even chance of not getting caught when committing a crime (Gold, 1970). This belief is true. About 33 percent of adolescents who engage in a high degree of juvenile delinquency are caught, but only 19 percent of those who engage in a medium amount of delinquency are caught (Gold, 1970). In addition, the probability of getting caught and convicted varies with social class (e.g., Pine, 1966). Those who live in ghetto areas or the inner cities are more likely to get caught because of the higher concentration of police in these areas than are those who live in the suburbs, where there is less police observation. Moreover, middle-class adolescents have a greater opportunity for being released or not convicted.

Causes of Delinquency

No single cause leads the adolescent to commit crime. For any causal factor we can identify, we can find some adolescents who have that characteristic and are delinquent, and some who have it but are not delinquent. Hence, we must examine a broad spectrum of potential causes of adolescent delinquency.

THE PEER GROUP. For some adolescents, the gang acts as a substitute for the family (Hardy & Cull, 1975; Whyte, 1943) and supports antisocial and delinquent behavior. The gang can conjure up excuses and justifications for delinquency and thus, psychologically, allow the adolescent to deny engaging in delinquent acts. For example, the gang may appeal to the individual's loyalty to the group rather than to the law. This appeal allows the individual to claim that the crime was committed out of loyalty and not out of disrespect for social rules.

After an extensive study of gang delinquency, Miller (1957; 1966) has concluded that the urge to commit violence or to do harm to people are not primary motives for the formation of adolescent gangs. Rather, membership in the gang confers status, masculinity, and honor, which the members may be unable to secure in any other way. Gang members can thus rationalize antisocial behavior as the only way they can gain respect and may not think they are having a bad effect on society.

Other evidence (Eisenthal & Udin, 1972) suggests that both boys and girls think that pressure from peers has a strong effect on their engaging in certain illegal or antisocial behavior, such as the use of alcohol or drugs. Fear of rejection by the peer group, for example, was an important motive for using drugs, whereas chastisement was not. The strong reinforcement value of the peer group makes it difficult to change delinquent behavior, especially when we consider the various times during adolescence when conformity is at a high point. While the adolescent's need for companionship and support from the peer group forces him or her into delinquent acts, simply belonging to a gang does not enable us to predict delinquency.

SOCIAL STRUCTURE.   One of the historically popular views of the causes of delinquency centers on the frustrating conditions engendered in lower-class and minority-group adolescents who grow up in a crime-ridden atmosphere. This view lays great stress on the individual and places the weight of the responsibility for delinquency on the individual's personality. A naive inference from this view is that if the poverty could be alleviated, there would be less delinquency. A growing literature, however, reveals that juvenile delinquency is increasing more in the suburbs than in inner-city or ghetto areas (Conger, 1971; Sebald, 1968). Moreover, delinquency is also on the rise in rural areas (Moore, 1974). One contributing cause of these rises in the rates of juvenile delinquency is the great mobility of today's adolescent and the weakening of family ties to the community (Pine, 1965, 1966). The relation between poverty and delinquency, then, is neither as direct nor as strong as it was once believed to be.

Several researchers have suggested that one important cause of delinquency is the mismatch between the values esteemed in our society and the means available to the individual for realizing these values (Cloward, 1968; Cloward & Ohlin, 1966; Merton, 1966; Seeman, 1959; Caplan, 1974). These writers have also stressed the importance of the individual's estimate of the chances of obtaining what society says is valuable, and the perception of the available opportunities for achieving these goals. Using this perspective, Cloward and Ohlin suggest that deviant behavior depends on a discrepancy between the aspirations the community approves of and the means open to the individual to realize these aspirations. Successful communities offer **legitimate opportunities** to engage in behavior that leads to fulfillment of these aspirations. The unsuccessful community does not provide these legitimate opportunities, and this lack leads to a rise in delinquency. In other words, for lack of legitimate opportunities, youth will seize illegitimate opportunities to gain prestige, status, and success. This complex argument suggests that at times society presents youth with no other way out. Were legitimate opportunities available, delinquency would decline. Hence, the structure of society seems to be one cause of delinquency.

CHILD-REARING.   The single best predictor of adolescent delinquency, particularly for boys, is the relationship to the parents (Ahlstrom & Havighurst, 1971; Conger & Miller, 1966). The better the relationship, the less likely the boy is to commit a crime. The more strained, hostile, and rejecting the relationship, the more likely he is to become delinquent. This conclusion is based on considerable research on patterns of child-rearing and family relations in homes with delinquent and nondelinquent adolescents. The research has demonstrated that the disciplinary techniques used by parents of future delinquents are eratic, overly strict, based on physical punishment with a high degree of hostility toward the child, and no use of induction (explaining rules of conduct) (Medinnus, 1967; Bandura & Walters, 1959; Freeman & Sevastano, 1970; Hardy & Cull 1975; Duncan, 1971). Delinquents often come from homes with a high degree of parental rejection and a low degree of family cohesiveness compared with the home atmosphere of nondelinquents (Monahan, 1966; Ramsey, 1967; Blakely, Stephenson & Nichol, 1974; Wirt & Briggs, 1959).

It is not surprising, then, that the parents of delinquent children have low aspirations about what their offspring should become, express little interest in their schooling, and display a host of personality and adjustment problems of their own (Duncan, 1971; Ahlstrom & Havighurst, 1971; Blakely, et al., 1974). As we noted in our discussion of parent-child interactions (see Chapter 11), it may be that the child's behavior is the cause of the parents' behavior. Pinpointing the causes of social interaction patterns of this sort is at best difficult. Even so, the pattern of interaction described here does enable us to predict delinquency. The most plausible interpretation of this relationship may be that parents act as hostile, antisocial models for their children to imitate.

The relationship between the father and the adolescent makes up one important component of this linkage between child-rearing and delinquency. The absence of the father, for example, is positively correlated with delinquency (Lynn & Saurey, 1959; Kelley & Baer, 1969), perhaps because it may produce an overcompensating personality in the adolescent male. This relationship is especially strong if the father leaves the home before the child reaches the age of 5 (Lynn & Saurey, 1959). The fathers of delinquent adolescents also tend to be cruel, neglecting, and less warm and affectionate than the fathers of nondelinquent adolescents (Bandura & Walters, 1959; Glueck & Glueck, 1950, 1970), providing a poor model for the adolescent.

In our discussion of social-learning theories (Chapter 10), we pointed out the importance of adult models for children learning how to get along in the world. It is not surprising to find out, then, that the parents of delinquents often have police records themselves; the adolescent may be imitating behavior that leads to delinquency.

Somewhat less research has been done on the mother's role in the development of adolescent delinquency. The evidence suggests that the mothers of delinquents are careless in child-rearing, indifferent or hostile toward their offspring, and show little affection or love for their children (McCord & Zola, 1959). Other evidence indicates that these mothers are also domineering and aggressive (Ackerly, 1933; MacDonald, 1938).

In general, delinquents seem to come from homes that are very different from those of nondelinquents (Duncan, 1971). In addition, Duncan suggests that differences in homes may give rise to different types of delinquency. The parents of delinquents tend to be unstable and inconsistent in their feelings toward the child

Delinquency does not begin in adolescence but, in varying degrees, from early childhood. Delinquency is unlikely to occur where father and son have enjoyed a positive relationship. (Joel Gordon)

and each other and present poor role models. In addition, the mothers seem to dominate the fathers, who, in turn, are unable to be authoritative. Finally, Duncan suggests that communication within the home is virtually nonexistent, particularly about unpleasant or embarrassing matters. Other delinquents seem to come from homes where parents are more equal, but with the father demanding conformity to his values, no matter how they conflict with those of society. In effect, the father may demand conformity to antisocial values and thus teach his offspring to behave antisocially.

SOME CONCLUSIONS.   Adolescent delinquents report hostility toward their parents and tend to have very poor relations with them. Elder's (1962, 1963, 1968, 1971) findings support this generalization and provide further evidence that early child-rearing practices may have effects that last through adolescence and adulthood. Given the delinquent's home atmosphere, we should not be surprised that many delinquents have poor self-concepts—having poor opinions of themselves (Fitts & Hammer, 1969). They think that society views them in much the same way. Thus, the self-concepts of delinquent adolescents are uncertain, confused, and highly variable in contrast to the self-concepts of nondelinquent adolescents who tend to have more positive and less conflicting opinions of themselves (e.g., Fitts & Hammer, 1969).

It also comes as no surprise to learn that delinquency does not begin in adolescence but for the most part occurs in increasing degrees from early childhood to about the age of 12 or 13, when it tends to level off (Lerman, 1968). Delinquent acts of a minor nature, such as stealing candy, incorrigibility, breaking city curfews, and the like are among the common delinquent acts of children. In other words, the constellation of factors that produces adolescent delinquency has significant effects on the child's personality development and behavior (Conger & Miller, 1966; Conger, Miller & Walsmith, 1965). The conflicts between the child and parent begin early in life and, in effect, the parent rears an offspring prone to antisocial behavior.

Although our discussion has barely scratched the surface of juvenile delinquency, it should be clear that its causes are extremely complex and that delinquency may be learned because of societal structure and from the parents. It has negative effects on personality development and on views of the self. In effect, the delinquent is likely to be an extremely unhappy individual who cannot find appropriate ways to gain the satisfaction and self-respect we all want to have.

Treating and Preventing Delinquency

The main approach to dealing wih the problem of delinquency has been to treat individuals who are already delinquent (Schur, 1973, Stephens, 1973). Traditionally, this treatment has been with adjudicated adolescents, and other adolescents have been ignored. Unfortunately, little has been done to prevent children from turning into juvenile delinquents, although this approach would be the most socially beneficial.

Treatments for delinquents fall into two main categories: psychoanalytic and therapeutic treatments, and programs of behavior modification. The various therapeutic programs have not had very great success (Steele, Rosenblood & Mirels, 1971), especially once therapy sessions are completed. Although the rate of recidivism goes down during therapy, it tends to jump back up when the therapy ends; few adolescents go through permanent changes in behavior. Behavior-modification programs encounter similar problems (Davidson & Seidman, 1974). The problem with many of the learning-theory approaches is their emphasis on changes in overt behavior and a corresponding soft-pedaling of the internalization of appropriate skills. One promising approach to alleviating this problem is the use of structured-learning therapy (Goldstein, 1973), which not only uses modeling and role playing but also teaches perspective-taking and understanding of the situation and another person's point of view. By training cognitive skills, structured-learning therapy may go far toward promoting generalizability of treatment for delinquents. At present, however, the treatment of delinquency is still a doubtful course of action for reducing delinquency.

SUMMARY

In this chapter, we have traced the course of several important aspects of the social development of adolescents. In each case, development began in childhood and continued in adolescence. Relationships with parents have some conflict, particularly with respect to independence strivings, but most adolescents have harmonious relations with their parents. There does not seem to be a large generation gap for most adolescents. And, for the most part, the gap entails rather superficial differences in language, dress, music tastes, and the like. Adolescents share the same basic values as their parents.

The importance of child-rearing practices for explaining adolescent behavior is shown in their striving for independence and in juvenile delinquency. The adolescent needs autonomy, but only in doses that he can cope with. Parental influences on development begin in childhood and carry over into adolescence. Parents who are hostile, cold, users of physical punishment, and uninterested in their offspring's future tend to have children who grow up with a predilection toward delinquency. Autocratic parents have children who have trouble in their search for independence.

The influence of peers on adolescent social development is extensive and important, but for the adolescent's long-term values and ideals it is secondary to the influence of the parents. The structure and importance of the peer group changes in adolescence, as do patterns of friendship and relations with the opposite sex. Peers of the opposite sex are chosen as friends with increasing frequency during adolescence. Sexual intercourse among adolescents is based on the intensity of the relationships between people and is seen as a matter of individual choice, not social sanction. This view of sexuality contrasts with that of the parents. In spite of this difference, there is no evidence of a sexual revolution. Females may engage in sexual intercourse more than they did in previous generations, but males probably do not.

The increase in juvenile delinquency in the current generation of adolescents probably reflects both more adequate reporting of delinquency and a genuine increase in delinquency beyond the increase in the juvenile population. This increase may be due to the increasing delinquency in middle-class adolescents and females. Rates of delinquency among males seem to have remained unchanged in recent years.

APPENDIX: STATISTICS AND RESEARCH DESIGN

THE MAJOR GOAL of any scientific discipline is to delineate the cause(s) of some event, i.e., to describe those conditions which bring about some event. Although the events of interest may differ among the various scientific disciplines the major goal is the same. In psychology the event of interest is the behavior of living organisms. The question is, What are the causes of some specified piece of behavior? This question may be symbolically represented as follows:

$$B = f (C_1, C_2, \ldots, C_n)$$

where B is the behavior of interest, f means "is a function of," and the C's are potential causes of the behavior. The job of psychology, then, is to fill in the formula by specifying the C's for a given piece of behavior.

In order to determine why a given behavior occurs, or how it develops, psychologists take observations and measurements. Sometimes this is done in a naturalistic setting, e.g., observing parent-child interactions in the home or child-child interactions in the play situation. At times behavior is observed in experimental situations in order to allow greater control over extraneous influences. Examples of observations in the experimental setting may be found throughout this book. Whether observations are made in the naturalistic setting or the experimental situation they must be translated into categories, numbers, and so forth, before very much meaning can be attributed to them. This process of *data compression* entails the use of **descriptive statistics.** If the observations were conducted in order to test some particular hypothesis a second branch of statistics, **inferential statistics,** would also be employed.

Descriptive Statistics

Descriptive statistics are used to summarize data and communicate findings. To illustrate this point consider the data in Table A-1. These data represent the number of child-initiated contacts with the mother when both are in a familiar room and when both are in a strange room. There are 5 mother-child pairs; observations occurred during a 10-minute interval. One way to present the data from this hypothetical experiment is to simply list the scores, as was done in Table A-1. Although all the data are presented in such a listing it is difficult to determine exactly what transpired during the course of observation. In order to better communicate what occurred during observation of the mother-child pairs certain descriptive statistics are useful (see Table A-2).

Measures of Central Tendency

One way to accurately and meaningfully present the data is through a measure reflecting central tendency. There are several such measures, each reflecting a way in which the scores tend to be similar. One such measure, the most commonly used by psychologists, is the arithmetic average, the **mean,** of the scores, which is the sum of the scores divided by the number of the scores. The mean number of contacts initiated in the familiar and strange rooms for the data in Table A-1 is 3.0 and 8.0, respectively.

Two other measures of central tendency, the median and the mode, are also frequently used by psychologists. The **median** of a distribution of scores is the midpoint, that is, the point above and below which 50 percent of the scores occur. The medians for the data in Table A-1 are 3 and 8 for the familiar and strange rooms,

TABLE A-1 Number of Child-Initiated Contacts in a
Hypothetical Study of Mother-Child Interactions

MOTHER-CHILD PAIR	CHILD-INITIATED CONTACTS IN:	
	FAMILIAR ROOM	STRANGE ROOM
1	5	8
2	2	10
3	0	6
4	3	7
5	5	9

TABLE A-2   Table of Basic Statistical Terms

DESCRIPTIVE[a]	INFERENTIAL[b]
Number of subjects or scores (N)	
Mean ($\overline{X}$)	t-test (t)
Median (Mdn)	F-test (F)
Mode (Mode)	Chi square (χ^2)
Range	Probability (p)
Standard deviation (s)	
Correlation Coefficient (r)	

[a]Descriptive—no cause-effect relationships.
[b]Inferential—delineate causes of behavior.

respectively. The **mode** of a distribution of scores is the most frequently occurring score. For the distributions in Table A-1 the mode is 5 for the familiar room. For the strange room there is no mode—each score occurs equally frequently. Each of these measures compresses the data in such a way as to allow meaningful and efficient communication of the observations. Which might be employed depends upon the purposes of the investigator and which measure of central tendency might best represent the distribution.

Measures of Variability

Just as measures of central tendency describe in one sense or another a "typical" score, or the sameness of the scores, measures of variablility describe the differences among the scores of a distribution. One measure of variability is the *range* of the scores—the lowest to the highest score. For the data in Table A-1 the ranges are 0–5 and 6–10 for the familiar and strange rooms, respectively.

A second measure of the variability of the scores in a distribution is the **standard deviation** (s or SD) of the scores The square of the SD is called the **variance** of the distribution. The importance of the standard deviation is that, as illustrated in Figure A-1, in any distribution of scores approximately 68 percent of the scores fall within $+1$ and -1 SD of the mean, and 95 percent of the scores fall within $+2$ and -2 SD of the mean. In other words, by knowing an individual score and the mean and standard deviation of the distribution one can tell the *relative* highness or lowness of the score. For the distribution of contacts in the familiar room in Table A-1 the SD is 1.9. Since the mean is 3, the score of 5 is approximately 1 SD above the mean. This sort of knowledge is particularly useful in comparing several distributions. For example, in Table A-1 the SD of the distribution of contacts in the strange room is approximately 1.4. The score of 9 is slightly less than 1 SD above the mean. In

FIGURE A-1   *Percentage of Scores Falling in Each SD Range in a Distribution of Scores*

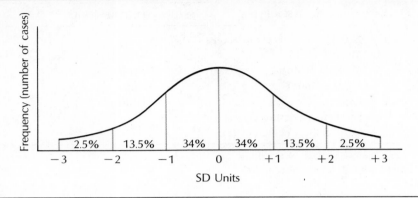

other words, the score of 5 for the familiar room and the score of 9 for the strange room are both *relatively* high (above the mean) and represent nearly identical performance *relative* to their respective distributions.

These measures of variability reflect differences in the scores of a distribution, just as the measures of central tendency reflect similarities. Clearly, use of these measures allows one to communicate information about observations in a manner more efficient than the presentation of all the individual scores. This efficiency of presentation of data, it should be kept in mind, causes the loss of some information, i.e., knowledge of the individual scores.

A Measure of Association

In our example in Table A-1 there are 2 scores for each mother-child pair. One is for performance in the familiar room and one is for performance in the strange room. When 2 scores are available on the same sample one may ask how well the 2 scores go together, i.e., whether each person's pair of scores tend to fall in the same order on each measure. The *correlation coefficient*, denoted by *r*, is a measure of this association. The numerical value of *r* may range from − 1 through zero to + 1, depending upon the strength of the relationship. If *r* = 0 then the 2 scores are not related, which means that knowing one of the scores does not help you predict the other score; if *r* is positive then there is a relationship such that high scores on *X* go with high scores on *Y*, and low scores on *X* with low scores on *Y* for the pairs of scores; if *r* is negative then high scores on *X* tend to go with low scores on *Y*, and low scores on *X* tend to go with high scores on *Y*. The relationships discussed above are graphically presented in Figure A-2. In these instances knowing one of the scores allows some knowledge of the other. In fact, it is possible to write an equation that

FIGURE A-2   *Scatter Plots for Zero, Positive, and Negative Correlations*

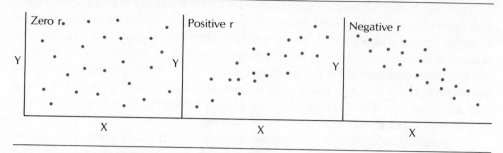

will predict *Y* given knowledge of *X* and the correlation between *X* and *Y*. Although this is beyond the scope of our presentation, you should be aware of these possibilities, as some of the research discussed in the text will draw on these principles.

The **scatter plot** for the data in Table A-1 is shown in Figure A-3. The correlation is +.44, indicating a moderate degree of relationship such that if a child makes a high number of contacts in the familiar room he also has a tendency to make a high number of contacts in the strange room.

FIGURE A–3   *Scatter Plot for Child-Initiated Contacts*

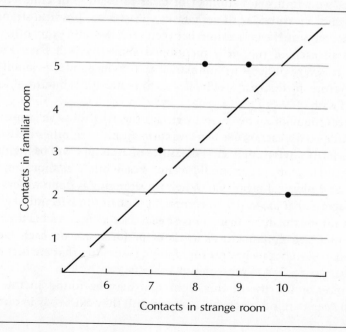

Several words of caution about interpretation of the correlation coefficient are in order. First, care must be taken *not* to infer that because 2 scores are correlated one causes the other. Correlations are not measures of causation but simple reflections of relationships. Indeed, some third unmeasured variable may cause both scores. Second, the absolute value of a correlation coefficient determines the strength of the correlation, not the sign associated with the numerical value. It should be understood, then, that a correlation of −.6 denotes just as strong a relationship as a correlation of +.6. The 2 relationships are equally strong but in opposite directions (see above explanation).

It should be clear that descriptive statistics allow the data from observations to be summarized in terms of the "typical" score, the variability of the scores, as well as the degree of relationship among the scores. Although this is an extremely efficient way to present data, keep in mind that some information is always lost, i.e., the individuality of the scores. However, these data compression techniques are necessary if we are to comprehend our data and test theories of development. Either of these tasks would be extremely difficult, if not impossible, without the use of descriptive techniques.

Factor Analysis

Factor analysis is a statistical tool that is used to derive a relatively small number of factors that may describe a relatively large number of correlations. Suppose, for example, that we adminster a number of tasks to a group of children—language tasks, intelligence measures, arithmetic tasks, measures of physical strength, and so forth. We can compute the correlation between each task and every other task. If we have 4 tasks in each of the areas mentioned above we will have 120 different correlations. It is very difficult to summarize and understand this amount of information. Therefore, factor analysis enables us to reduce the amount of information we must deal with.

The technique of factor analysis groups together those measures that show high correlations with each other but low correlations with other measures. In our example, it is fairly obvious that the 4 measures of each type will be highly related to each other—language measures should relate to each other, as should mathematics, intelligence, and physical measures. When the grouping is done we have a smaller number of factors that are easier to comprehend than the large number of correlations. By examining the items that compose each factor we can label the factor. And, we can examine age differences in levels of performance on each factor. Factor analysis, then, is simply a technique for grouping measures that are highly related to each other but not related to measures on other factors.

Examples of the use of this technique may be found in the book. It is important to keep in mind that factors are not real; they exist only in our data. They are convenient because they allow us to understand vast amounts of information that would otherwise be very difficult to comprehend.

Inferential Statistics

Although descriptive statistics allow the efficient presentation of data, they do not usually represent tests of hypotheses; the exception is the correlation coefficient, since one might hypothesize no relationship or a positive or negative association between 2 measures on the same subjects. The use of inferential statistics allows us to go beyond the mere description of data and infer cause-effect relationships. Although a detailed account of inferential statistics is not called for here, an example based on the data in Table A-3 will prove instructive. These data are identical to that presented in Table A-1, except the scores are now depicted as representing 10 rather than 5 mother-child pairs. Five mother-child pairs were observed in the familiar room (the **control group**) and 5 in the strange room (the **experimental group**—the group upon which the experimental manipulation was conducted). In both groups the same dependent variable was measured—number of mother-child contacts. This simple experiment follows the prototype of all experiments of a manipulative sort in that there is an experimental manipulation with a control and an experimental group in which the same dependent variable is measured.

The logic of the experimental approach is simple. Assume that each mother-child pair was randomly selected from a very large pool of applicants who wished to participate in the experiment. Assume, further, that all applicants had an equal chance of being selected to participate. Our sample of 10 mother-child pairs, then, represents a **random sample** from the population of mother-child pairs, i.e., a

TABLE A-3   Number of Child-Initiated Contacts for Two Groups of Mother-Child Pairs

MOTHER-CHILD PAIR	FAMILIAR ROOM	MOTHER-CHILD PAIR	STRANGE ROOM
1	5	6	8
2	2	7	10
3	0	8	6
4	3	9	9
5	5	10	7

sample picked with no biases. The larger a random sample the more it is representative of the population. Because our sample is random we may assume it accurately represents or reflects all characteristics of the population. When we divided 10 mother-child pairs randomly into 2 groups of 5 mother-child pairs we could assume each was representative of the population and equivalent to the other at the start of the experiment. Therefore, *any difference between the groups at the conclusion of the experiment must be due to the experimental manipulation.* Moreover, the findings of the experiment may be generalized back to the larger population, since the groups involved in the experiment were representative of the larger population.

For the data presented in Table A-2 one may ask whether children initiated more contacts with the mother in the strange (experimental group) or in the familiar room (control group). Certain theories would allow the prediction, or hypothesis, that contacts would be greater in the strange room. Although the difference between the two means is 5, with contacts in the strange room being greater, merely calculating the mean difference is not sufficient for testing hypotheses. Psychologists use inferential statistics, e.g., the **t-test** or the **F-test,** to determine (infer) the likelihood that differences between group means in an experiment might be due to chance. If the difference between group means is so large it would occur by chance a relatively small percentage of the time, it is deemed **statistically significant.** By convention, if the difference between 2 means is so large it would occur by chance less than 5 percent of the time, then the difference is attributed to the experimental manipulation. In other words, if the experimental manipulation really had no effect, a difference between means that was that large would occur by chance about 5 percent of the time or less. This probability relating the statistical significance of the difference between the control and experimental groups is denoted by *p.*

For the data in Table A-2 the *t*-test was employed to see if the experimental manipulation, placing infants in a strange environment, produced significantly more contacts with the mother. The obtained value of *t* was 6.78. This value, when looked up in an appropriate table, indicates that the difference in the means would occur by chance less than 1 percent of the time. In other words, the data support the hypothesis that our experimental manipulation, strange versus familiar room, *caused* the children to initiate more contacts with their mothers. A difference this large or larger would be obtained less than 1 percent of the time if our manipulation actually had no effect on the children's contact seeking. Since it is very unlikely that a difference this large would be obtained by chance, i.e., if the manipulation really had no effect, we attribute it to our experimental manipulation.

The important point to understand is that by manipulating the potential causes of behavior and then demonstrating that the manipulation did affect the observed behavior, we are able to determine what the actual causes of behavior are. We are also able to determine which variables have no effect on behavior, i.e., which variables are not related to determining some behavior.

Hypothesis Testing
and Theory Building

Hypotheses are almost always derived from theories about behavioral phenomena. When tested by observation in naturalistic or experimental situations the hypothesis either gains support or does not. If the data support the hypothesis, the theory from which it was generated also receives support. As more and more hypotheses generated by a theory receive support, the theory gains in stature as being a better approximation to the "truth." That is, the theory allows us to better understand and explain behavioral phenomena. If the hypotheses generated by a theory do not receive support from relevant observations, then the theory loses in truth value. That is, the ability of the theory to lend better understanding and explanation of phenomena comes under serious question, even to the extent that the theory may no longer be considered tenable. In order to support or refute a theory or to test hypotheses based on alternate theories, data must be collected. That is, only the experimental approach, in all of its various forms, allows us to begin to understand, explain, and predict behavior by providing evidence about the utility of theories. Therein lies the value of the experimental approach and the utility of data collection. Although our intent is not to make the reader an expert in research design and statistical analyses, the few principles presented here should help you to better understand the implications of the research and theory, and their interrelationship, presented in this text.

GLOSSARY

Accommodation   The mental operation whereby knowledge of the environment (structure) is modified to incorporate new objects or experiences.

Active-organism model   *See* organismic model.

Adaptiveness   A concept of evolution theory; species and individuals survive environments when their innate structures are suitable.

Adolescence   The developmental period beginning with puberty and ending with the attainment of adulthood.

Adrenalin   A substance secreted by the adrenal medulla, which activates physiological responses.

Affection   Behaviors that express a positive feeling toward others.

Affiliative behaviors   Distal responses to the parent, such as looking and smiling.

Aggression   The infliction of pain, or the threat to do so, in order to achieve a goal.

Alleles   Gene pairs comprised of one gene from the mother and one from the father.

Altruism   Behavior that results in no gain, and perhaps a loss, for the actor.

Anaclitic identification   Identification that results from the child's fear of loss of the mother's love. Freud felt it was especially important for girls.

Androgen   Male sex hormone produced by the gonads.

Androgyny   The ability to display both male and female traits.

Anger   An involuntary emotional response accompanied by a physiological readiness to cause harm to a person, an object, or oneself.

Animism   Attributing life to inanimate objects.

Anoxia   A state where a baby fails to obtain sufficient oxygen to survive.

Anxiety   A fear-like state sometimes involving intensive reactions where the source of fear is not always clearly defined; also a temperament characteristic.

Anxious emotional involvement vs. calm detachment   *See* dimensions of child rearing.

Apgar ratings   A technique for assessing the physical status of newborn babies developed by Dr. Virginia Apgar.

Apnea   A state where a baby fails to breathe; often occurs at birth and is thought to be associated with later learning problems.

Aptitude   A person's ability on some measurable attribute (e.g., verbal, motor).

Asceticism   A defense mechanism which enables a person to resist instinctual drives because they have been defined as nonexistent.

Assimilation   The mental operation whereby a new object or experience is incorporated into existing knowledge (structure).

Associated play   Play that involves interaction with other children and the sharing of play materials. (*See also* solitary, parallel, cooperative, and fantasy play.)

Associative learning   A type of learning where a stimulus is associated with a response; a form of conditioned learning.

Attachment   A social relationship between the child and other people or objects of affection; viewed as a precursor of later social interactions.

Attachment behaviors   Proximal responses to the parent such as touching, clinging, and seeking to be picked up.

Attentional behavior   A behavioral manifestation of the orienting reflex.

Autonomic nervous system   The sympathetic and parasympathetic nerve systems associated with an emotional episode.

Base rate   The initial rate of response of some behavior of interest.

Behaviorism   A school of psychology that stresses learning theory in explaining development.

Behavior modification   The use of learning theory principles of reinforcement to alter an individual's behavior.

Biased sample   A sample that is selected to represent a particular subgroup or that is composed of people having a specific trait. (*See also* random sample.)

Birth cry   The human sound frequently regarded as a protest against leaving the womb, but most likely a reflexive response as air rushes across the vocal system.

Canalization (homeorhesis)   The phenomenon of accelerated growth rate following a period of depressed growth rate (due to illness); acceleration is maintained until normal growth status is achieved.

Carpal age   An index of development based on bone density; rate of bone ossification.

Case study   The systematic study of one person over time.

Cathexis   The psychoanalytic term used to denote the investment of libidinal energy in an object choice.

Centration   The tendency of preoperational children to focus on single attributes of stimuli rather than on the several possible attributes; reduces the ability to perform multiple classifications.

Cephalocaudal trend   The greater development of the head at birth in relation to the hind part of the body.

Chromosomes   Threadlike chemical substances that carry genes and transmit hereditary information.

Classical conditioning   The repeated pairing of a neutral stimulus and a stimulus capable of causing a reflex response, with the object of making the neutral stimulus cause the reflex response.

Clinical method   A method that involves unsystematic exploration of behavior and that is used to examine the psychological meaning of cognitive development; very difficult to reproduce by other investigators.

Cognitive-developmental model   According to this model, which is based on the organismic model, cognitive development underlies development in other areas, such as moral thinking or social development.

Cognitive structures   *See* structure.

Cognitive style   An individual's characteristic manner in approaching and solving problems.

Cohort   The group of people born in the same year.

Competence   The capacity or ability of the individual with respect to some behavior, only imperfectly reflected in performance; also, an abstraction referring to the knowledge of grammatical rules that enables a native speaker to relate sound to meaning.

Conceptual phase   The first phase of the preoperational stage, beginning at 2 years and ending at 4 years, mainly characterized by the onset and elaboration of language and parallel emergence of representational skills.

Concrete operations   Piaget's third stage, in which complex mental operations emerge. This stage lasts until about 11 years of age.

Conditioned stimulus (CS)   An originally neutral stimulus which, when paired with an unconditioned stimulus, activates a conditioned response.

Conformity   Making one's judgments, feelings, dress, and attitudes agree with those of friends or peer groups.

Confound(ed)   Two or more variables in an experiment are confounded when it is not possible to clearly attribute the results to one or the other variable.

Conservation   The mental operation based on the principle that objects maintain their basic physical properties (mass, volume) regardless of appearances; measured by a series of tasks.

Contiguity   Simultaneously occurring events, as in the pairing of a conditioned and unconditioned stimulus.

Contralateral   Controlling certain functions with the opposite cerebral hemisphere.

Control deficiency   The inability to apply a verbal label or statement in solving a problem such as the reversal shift.

Control group   The group of subjects in an experiment on which no experimental manipulation is conducted, so that the performance of this group can serve as a standard against which the performance of the subjects in the experimental group is evaluated. (*See also* experimental group.)

Control (restrictive) vs. autonomy (permissive)   *See* dimensions of childrearing.

Cooperative play   Play that involves games with rules and in which interaction occurs. (*See also* solitary, parallel, associated, and fantasy play.)

Corpus callosum   A bundle of nerve fibers connecting the two major brain hemispheres.

Correlation coefficient   A statistic (denoted by *r*) indicating the strength and direction of the relationship between two measures taken on a single group of subjects. The value ranges between $+1$ and -1. The greater the absolute value of the correlation, the stronger the relationship. If $r = 0$, there is no relationship.

Correlation matrix   A matrix consisting of the correlations of each entry with all other entries; the basis for factor analyses.

Cortisone   A synthetic male hormone.

Co-twin method   An experimental design using genetically identical twins to test for training effects or to determine the heritability of various characteristics.

Counterconditioning   A procedure by which a stimulus arousing a negative response is conditioned to arouse a positive response.

Crawling   A mode of movement in which only the arms are used, while the legs drag along.

Creeping   A mode of movement in which both the arms and legs are used.

Critical period   A period of time when exposure to certain sign stimuli produces permanent learning. The time period is very short among animals but may be extensive for humans.

Crossing-over   A random process whereby genes located on a segment of one chromosome are exchanged with genes from a segment of another chromosome; the process changes genetic characteristics.

Cross-modal transfer   The ability to receive sensory input in one modality and translate it to another modality, for example, touching a cube and then visually selecting it from among other geometric forms.

Cross-sectional experiment   An experiment in which several independent groups of subjects, often representing different age levels, are tested.

Cultural conditioning   Learning based on broad aspects of the culture or subculture; differences in the structures of cultures result in differences in culturally conditioned responses.

Cultural determinism   An anthropological concept denoting the influence of cultural factors on development. (*See also* cultural relativism.)

Cultural relativism   An anthropological concept used to indicate differences in the types of personalities produced by different cultures. (*See also* cultural determinism.)

Décalage horizontale A mental operation by which children incorporate new objects and events into existing structures.

Décalage verticale A transition from one stage to another, higher stage; vertical development.

Deep structure An abstract aspect of syntactic description concerned with meaning.

Defense mechanisms Psychological means of reducing stress or anxiety. (*See* asceticism, intellectualism.)

Delight A positive emotion that is highly generalized in its manifestations.

Denotative meaning The use of words to communicate a generic idea or concept as opposed to something specific.

Deoxyribonucleic acid (DNA) A complex molecule carrying information for cell reproduction.

Dependency Behavior that indicates people, as people, are satisfying and rewarding.

Dependent variable The variable measured in an experiment. (*See also* independent variable.)

Deprivation strategy A scientific method for studying the effects of environment on development. The organisms, almost always animals, are deprived of an experience (sensory deprivation) for a period of time, and effects are noted.

Depth perception The ability to discriminate depth, generally considered innate.

Descriptive statistics Statistics used to summarize and communicate data from an experiment. (*See also* inferential statistics, mean, median, mode, standard deviation, correlation coefficient.)

Desensitization A therapeutic procedure, similar to counterconditioning, where a person learns to cope with a situation by learning to cope with a hierarchy of related situations, beginning with the least negative and progressing to the actual situation.

Detection theory The theory that with development there occurs an increasing ability to discriminate objects and to learn what features of objects are invariant.

Developmental quotient An index of relative developmental status, usually used in tests of infants.

Developmental tasks A term coined by Havighurst to denote possible accomplishments during each stage of development. These include achievements in the social, emotional, and cognitive areas.

Differentiation A component of orthogenesis in which generalized responses (behavioral sequences) become more differentiated but also fuse with other systems to form more integrated patterns.

Dimensions of child-rearing   Dimensions defined by behaviors of parents toward their children and used as bases for classification. There are three major dimensions: (1) *Love* (*warmth*) *vs. hostility* is defined by acceptance and approval and the use of praise vs. use of physical punishment and dislike for the child; (2) *Control* (*restrictive*) *vs. autonomy* (*permissive*) is defined by requiring a rigid adherence to parental rules and demands vs. allowing freedom of choice; (3) *Anxious emotional involvement vs. calm detachment* is defined by babying and overprotectiveness vs. viewing the child's development objectively.

Disinhibitory effect   *See* inhibition/disinhibition effect.

Distancing hypothesis   A concept similar to representation: reality can be represented at some distance from its reference (e.g., object, picture of the object, a word).

Distress   A general undifferentiated emotional state of displeasure from which other negative emotions are derived.

Dizygotic twins   Twins developed from different ova and spermatozoa.

Ectomorph   A body type denoting a thin, slightly muscled, and high-metabolic physique. (*See also* endomorph and mesomorph.)

Efficient cause   Stimulus conditions, represented by the independent variables in an experiment, that cause development or change. (*See also* material, formal and final causes.)

Ego   In Freudian theory that part of the personality responsible for organized behavior; it represents the person's feelings about the self.

Egocentric thinking   The inability of the preoperational child to take another person's viewpoint.

Egocentrism   *See* egocentric thinking.

Elation   A behavioral response more differentiated than delight but less elaborate than the behaviors associated with joy.

Embryo   Unborn organism, in the human from about the tenth day of conception through the third month of pregnancy.

Emotion   A complex physiological and psychological response that is both innate and learned.

Empathy   A vicarious affective response to another's feelings.

Empiricism   The theoretical view that perception is a product of specific learning.

Enactive stage   A first stage of cognitive development in which infants acquire knowledge about the world from repetitive motor activities with objects.

Endomorph   A body type denoted by underdeveloped bones and muscles and a predisposition toward softness and flabbiness. (*See also* mesomorph and ectomorph.)

Engrams Specialized neural systems sensitive to specific stimuli such as language; also called structures.

Epistemology The study of the origins of human knowledge.

Estrogen Female sex hormone produced by the ovaries.

Ethologists Scientists who study the behavior of organisms in their natural environments and are primarily interested in innate behavior patterns.

Experimental group In an experiment, the group of subjects on which some manipulation is conducted. (*See also* control group.)

Expiatory justice *See* retributive justice.

Extended family The nuclear family plus other family members. (*See also* nuclear family.)

Factor analysis A statistical technique for reducing the number of different measures to be considered by grouping those that have high correlations with each other and low correlations with all other measures. Each group of highly correlated variables forms a factor; the number of factors will be less than the number of measures. (*See also* correlation coefficient.)

Fantasy play Play in which the child pretends he or other objects are other than they are, or in which roles, feelings, and other attributes are accepted as part of the child or object. (*See also* solitary, parallel, cooperative, and associated play.)

Fear An involuntary emotional response accompanied by physiological readiness for flight or self-protection.

Fetal period In humans, the period from the tenth day of conception to the end of pregnancy, approximately in the ninth month.

Final cause A teleological (end state directed) view of human development that conceives of humans as motivated to reach the highest levels of development possible. (*See also* efficient, material, and formal causes.)

Fixed Action Patterns (FAP) Stereotyped behaviors that occur in a species even though not previously observed.

Follow-Through Program A federally sponsored program designed to continue helping poor children when they begin elementary school.

Formal cause The view that the human organism is in a continual state of change with the result that the whole is greater than the sum of its parts. Hence, the causes of development are located in the nature of the organism. (*See also* efficient, material, and final cause.)

Formal operations Piaget's final stage, characterized by an ease in abstract thinking and the use of formal logic.

Frustration-aggression hypothesis The view that frustration causes aggression and that all aggression presupposes frustration.

F-test An inferential statistical technique for assessing the statistical significance of the differences in performance between three or more groups in an experiment. (*See also t*-test, statistical significance.)

Functors Words not always necessary to communicate meaning (e.g., prepositions, conjunctions, articles).

Galvanic skin response An involuntary response indicative of an emotional reaction as reflected by an increase in electrical conduction of the skin.

Gender roles The culturally prescribed behavioral differences between males and females.

General intellectual ability (g) Spearman's concept that intelligence is a unitary trait.

Generalizability of Research Findings The extent to which research findings can be applied to understanding the development of subjects other than those in the experiment.

Generalized imitation A learned disposition to imitate models which is the result of reinforcement for imitating. Also, emitting a model's responses in a variety of situations.

Genes Located on chromosomes, genes carry specific hereditary information.

Grade equivalent score An index of relative position in which performance on some measure is compared to the average performance of the individual's grade level.

Grammar The rules used to generate correct, but not incorrect, sentences.

Group factors In terms of intelligence, a set of traits or abilities usually regarded as independent.

"Guess who" technique A sociometric technique in which the child is asked to indicate who in the classroom or peer group is most likely to fit a characteristic.

Guilt Feelings of self-disapproval and self-dissatisfaction for having done something inappropriate.

Habituation The reduction in attending behavior following repeated exposure to and examination of a stimulus.

Haptic perception The ability to identify an object by manual exploration.

Headstart A federally sponsored preschool program developed in the sixties to provide poor children with the skills required in elementary school.

Hedonistic Pleasure-seeking and avoiding discomfort.

Heritability index An index which estimates the contribution of genetic factors to characteristics such as temperament and intelligence.

Hermaphrodite   A person having both male and female reproductive organs.

Heteronomous interactions   One-sided interactions—most typically, parent-child interactions.

Hierarchic organization   The development of advanced integrated systems so that they dominate less sophisticated systems and form a qualitatively distinct system.

Holophrastic sentences   One-word sentences which appear to convey meaning beyond the scope of the word.

Homologous points   Corresponding areas in the two brain hemispheres where, presumably, the dominant side inhibits the nondominant point.

Hormones   Glandular secretions that regulate body growth and function.

Hypothalamus   A lower brain center that can activate the anterior pituitary gland.

Hypotheses   "Best guesses," derived from theories, about the development of psychological functions. They are tested by experimentation.

Id   In Freudian theory the component of personality that seeks pleasure.

Identification   The process by which the individual comes to act, feel, and think like some other person. (*See also* anaclitic identification, identification with the aggressor.)

Identification with the aggressor   Identification that results from fear of the more powerful father. Freud felt it was especially important for boys.

Ikonic stage   The second stage of cognitive development, during which children rely increasingly on imagery or representations of objects and events in the world. Knowledge development involves concepts.

Imitation   Acting and behaving like some other person. It is a performance measure that to a degree indexes observational learning and an activity that promotes cognitive growth.

Imminent justice   The belief that God punishes people for their misdeeds.

Imprinting   A response acquired shortly after birth. The process does not follow learning principles, but is an explanation of how species-appropriate behavior occurs.

Incidental learning   Learning of the kind found in an experiment in which children can attend to either a central or peripheral stimulus, or both. Older children attend to the central stimulus, younger children to both.

Independent variable   The variable that is manipulated in an experiment. It represents a potential (efficient) cause of the behavior under investigation. (*See also* dependent variable.)

Individual delinquent   An adolescent who is delinquent as a reaction to poor parent-child relations. (*See also* sociologic delinquent.)

Induction   *See* nonpower assertive discipline.

Inferential statistics   Statistics used to test the statistical significance of the collected data. (*See also* *t*-test, *F*-test, descriptive statistics, and statistical significance.)

Inflections   The ways in which the basic forms of words are changed to the plural or the past tense.

Inhibition/disinhibition effect   The consequences of inhibiting or disinhibiting the observer from performing the same or similar responses. (*See also* modeling effect, response facilitation.)

Inhibitory effect   *See* inhibition/disinhibition effect.

Inhibitory mechanisms   Presumed physiological and psychological systems that inhibit mental and motoric responses.

Innate releasing mechanisms   Receptor systems that are sensitive to specific stimuli or patterns of stimuli.

Instrumental conditioning   A type of learning where a correct response is required before a reinforcer is received; similar to operant conditioning.

Intellectualism   A defense mechanism evidenced by abstract and impersonal treatment of issues to avoid conflicts.

Intelligence quotient (IQ)   An index of relative performance derived from test scores.

Internalization of schemas   The cognitive ability to manipulate symbols and to have mental representations of cognitive events, which occurs during the sixth and final stage of sensorimotor intelligence (18–24 months).

Intersensory development   *See* cross-modal transfer.

Interval scale   A measurement scale with an arbitrarily defined zero point (on a centigrade scale, zero is the point where water freezes) from which a scale with equal units can be derived.

Introspectionism   A psychological method in which individuals describe their feelings and the descriptions are treated as data.

Intuitive phase   The second phase of the preoperational stage during which children evidence adaptive intelligence by reorganizing structures to solve unique problems (4–7 years).

Inventory   A questionnaire which asks the respondent questions about himself.

Jealousy   An emotional response that appears to be acquired; probably not a true emotion but some combination of fear and anger directed toward a person perceived as a threat.

Joy   A positive response reflecting happiness and having more specific properties than delight.

Kinesthetic perception   The ability to identify an object after making movements (guided by a second party) outlining it.

Klinefelters syndrome   Abnormal sex cells containing an extra X chromosome; associated with mental retardation and incomplete sexual development.

Language Acquisition Device (LAD)   An abstraction proposing a uniquely human system sensitive to linguistic features from which language rules are generated.

Laterality   The phenomenon which dictates that one side of the body controls certain skills and the other side other skills.

Learning   A basic process in which behavior changes as a function of environmental experiences and practice.

Learning theory model   A model of psychological development based on the principles of learning theory and derived from the mechanistic model.

Legitimate opportunities   Acceptable means of obtaining what is esteemed by the community.

Limbic system   A set of structures located in the brain which are activated during an emotional state.

Linguistic rules   The knowledge of a language; also called competence.

Linguistics   The study of language as a system.

Logical positivism   A philosophy of science which stresses that a theory should be based only on concepts that can be directly measured or observed; the philosophical basis of learning theory and behaviorism.

Longitudinal study (experiment)   An experiment in which a sample of subjects is repeatedly tested at regular time intervals.

Love   An emotional response, not very well understood, involving feelings of affection and warmth for another.

Love (warmth) vs. hostility   *See* dimensions of child-rearing.

Love withdrawal   *See* nonpower assertive discipline.

Marasmus   A behavioral state of lethargy and general illness as a consequence of severe malnutrition.

Material cause   The neurological, physiological, or genetic factors that cause development or change. (*See also* efficient, formal, and final causes.)

Maturation   A basic process in which physiological and behavioral changes occur, largely by innate predispositions and minimally by environmental stimulation.

Mean   Arithmetic average of a group of scores.

Mean length of utterance (MLU)   The average length of a speech utterance used to designate levels of language development.

Means-end behavior   An awareness that one's actions on objects have predictable outcomes; becomes apparent between 8 and 12 months.

Mechanistic model   A philosophical view of human development that stresses quantitative developmental change. (*See also* learning theory model.)

Median   The score above and below which half the scores in a distribution fall.

Mediation hypothesis   A mental operation in which verbal labeling of stimuli serves as a basis for grouping, once believed crucial for solution of the reversal shift problem.

Meiosis   The division of sex cells.

Memory   The ability to recall previously exposed objects or events. *Episodic memory* refers to a specific object or event; *semantic memory* is more cognitive, requiring some form of mnemonic strategy for solution.

Mental age (MA)   An index of relative position on an intelligence scale where an individual's performance is compared with individuals of similar chronological age.

Mesomorph   A body type denoted by a hard, firm athletic build, with highly developed bone and muscle structure. (*See also* endomorph and ectomorph.)

Mitosis   The division of somatic cells to produce new cells.

Mode   The most frequently occurring score in a distribution.

Modeling   Imitating the behavior of another person.

Modeling effect   Learning a *new* response by observing a model. (*See also* inhibition/disinhibition effect, response facilitation.)

Model's nurturance   Warm and friendly interactions with a child prior to an experiment.

Model's power   The degree to which the model controls reinforcers and punishments.

Monozygotic twins   Identical twins developed from a single ovum and sperm.

Morality   The system of rules designed to guide social behavior; some of the rules are formalized as laws, others are not.

Morality of constraint   In Piaget's theory, the early stage during which rules are obeyed because they are seen as rigid and unalterable.

Morality of cooperation   In Piaget's theory, the view that rules are determined by reciprocal agreements and depend upon social circumstances.

Moral realism   *See* morality of constraint.

Moro reflex   A startle response pattern which changes during the infancy period. The immature response involves a spreading of the arms and the body forming a bow as the hands approach each other.

Morphemes   The smallest linguistic units of speech which have meaning.

Morphogenesis   Changes in body organ shape and size as a result of the influence of hormones.

Motor copy theory   Learning to identify objects by coordinating manual and visual sensory inputs.

Multiple classification tasks   Tasks designed to measure the ability to use more than one stimulus dimension in classifying objects (e.g., tall-cubes, short-pyramids).

Mutation   A spontaneous change in a gene, usually lethal but sometimes adaptive.

Myelinization   The process whereby nerve fibers in the central nervous system become covered by a white fatty substance called myelin which increases the speed of nerve impulses.

Nativism   The view that perception is largely determined by innate systems requiring external stimulation to be activated.

Negative accelerated curve   A curve which is initially rapid and accelerates at a decreasing rate.

Nonpower assertive discipline   Discipline that does not involve power assertion; often called psychological discipline. There are two types: (1) *Love withdrawal* involves nonphysical expressions of anger or disapproval, such as ignoring the child; (2) *Induction* involves explaining the consequences of some undesired behavior and why it should not be done.

Nonreversal shift   An experimental condition in which a simple stimulus response association is sufficient for learning.

Normative data   Information describing the typical course of development, including norms which summarize average development or behavior for specific ages.

Nuclear family   A family composed of a mother, father, and their children. (*See also* extended family.)

Nurturance   The term used to describe a loving warm acceptance of a child.

Objective moral orientation   Moral judgments made solely on the basis of damage done.

Object permanence   Cognitive awareness that objects not directly visible continue to exist; emerges after 8 months of age.

Observational learning   Learning that occurs as a result of observing a model. (*See also* modeling effect, inhibition/disinhibition effect, response facilitation.)

Oedipal complex   In Freudian theory, the allegorical description of the boy's incestuous desire to possess his mother.

Ogive curve   An S-shaped, positively accelerated curve where initial rate of development is slow, then becomes rapid, and finally slows down again.

Ontogenetic behaviors   Behaviors that may or may not be acquired by an individual; greatly influenced by environmental experiences (e.g., roller skating, skiing).

Ontogeny   The relatively unique development, both prenatal and postnatal, of the individual organism. Also, the study of behavioral changes of individuals over time, reflecting the interaction of individuals and their environments.

Open environment   The educational philosophy in which children provide their own structure rather than having it imposed on them.

Open words   Words that occur with pivot words.

Operant conditioning   A type of learning similar to instrumental conditioning where either a correct response, a specific number of correct responses, or a specific rate of responding, is required before a reinforcer is received.

Operational definition   Defining a concept by the means used to measure it.

Operationalism   A philosophy which insists that all abstract concepts (intelligence) must be defined by a set of operations or behaviors.

Opinionnaire   A questionnaire which asks the respondent to give personal opinions.

Organismic (organic) model   A philosophical view of human development that stresses continual growth and cbange, often conceptualized as occurring in a sequence of stages representing the qualitative nature of development. (*See also* cognitive-developmental model.)

Orienting reflex   An unlearned response in which the infant gives full attention to a stimulus complex.

Orthogenesis   A fundamental principle of development in which there is progressive differentiation of behaviors and at the same time an integration of behaviors and concepts where each higher level incorporates earlier levels.

Orthogonal   A term used in factor analysis and meaning independent.

Overregularization   Misapplication of a grammatical rule (e.g., using -*ed* for the past tense of an irregular verb).

Palmar reflex   Automatic closing of the fingers when the palm of the hand is stroked; occurs in infants until 4 months.

Parallel play   Play behavior of two or more children engaged in the same or highly similar activities, but with no interaction. (*See also* solitary, cooperative, associated, and fantasy play.)

Parasympathetic nervous system   One of two components of the autonomic nervous system, apparently associated with anger.

Peer group   The informal groups of friends to which the child belongs, including neighborhood, school, and sport groups.

Performance   An individual's behavior in a particular task or situation; an imperfect measure of competence.

Phenylketenuria (PKU)   An inherited deficiency in which phenylalanine is not converted to tyrosine; can attack the central nervous system causing mental retardation but can be treated by dietary restrictions.

Phonemes   The smallest units of speech that can be discriminated from another speech unit.

Phonology   The study of sound, in relation to language systems.

Phylogenetic behaviors   Behaviors that are characteristic of a species and whose development is relatively independent of environmental experiences (e.g., creeping, crawling, walking).

Phylogeny   The evolutionary development of a species of organism. Also, the study of behavioral and structural changes in populations over extended periods of time.

Phyone   A product of the anterior lobe of the pituitary gland essential for growth.

Pituitary gland   An endocrine gland consisting of anterior and posterior lobes. The anterior lobes influence physical growth, metabolic processes, and other glands.

Pivot words   For small children, a few words that occur with great frequency in two-word utterances; can be in either the first or second position.

Placebo   The crucial variable given the control group (in drug research, an injection of saline solution).

Placenta   An organ that connects the fetus to the mother, providing nutrients and a system for disposal of waste material.

Plantar reflex   Automatic fanning of the toes in response to stimulation of the sole (plantar surface) of the foot. After about two years the response changes to a curling of the toes. Also known as the Babinski response.

Play   An activity indicative of representational ability and held to be a crucial aspect of cognitive development.

Pneumograph   A device for recording breathing rate.

Power assertion   A disciplinary technique involving the use of physical punishment, the deprivation of privileges, or the threat of these.

Preconcrete operations   In Piaget's theory, the second stage, during which symbolic skills become more elaborate (18 months–7 years).

Predictive ability   The degree to which a test (e.g., intelligence) predicts performance on some other behavior, indexed by validity.

Prelinguistic period   A period prior to actual language production consisting of sounds that become increasingly similar to the native language.

Primary circular reactions   The second stage of the sensorimotor period during which reflexive schemas are repeatedly practiced and become integrated with other schemas.

Privileges of occurrence   A learning theory concept of language acquisition referring to the specific place in a sentence of certain types of words.

Production deficiency   The inability to generate the verbal label required for problem solution.

Productive language   Speech sounds and words produced.

Progesterone   A female sex hormone.

Prosocial behavior   Voluntary behavior aimed at benefiting others, perhaps at a cost to the individual performing them and for which no reward is expected.

Psychobiological development   The development of psychological factors that are the consequences of biological factors.

Puberty   The first phase of adolescence marked by the emergence of sexual maturity and the ability to reproduce the species. (*See also* pubescence.)

Pubescence   The period of approximately two years during which primary and secondary sex characteristics develop and there is a growth spurt. (*See* also puberty.)

Punishment by reciprocity   *See* retributive justice.

Random sample   A sample of subjects drawn from a specified population in such a way that each member of the population has an equal chance of being selected. (*See also* biased sample.)

Reactive organism   A view, derived from the mechanistic model, that human behavior results primarily from people's reactions to environmental stimuli.

Readiness   A physiological and behavioral state when training will be effective; often used in terms of reading.

Recapitulation   In G. S. Hall's theory, the development of the individual in a sequence of stages reflecting human evolutionary development.

Receptive language   The perception of speech sounds that are understood, usually more extensive than productive language.

Reciprocal altruism   In sociobiology, the concept that a person is altruistic because he expects others to be altruistic in return.

Reciprocity (Reciprocal interactions)   The term used to describe mutual give and take among children.

Referential meaning   The highly specific and context-bound reference of a word to particular events, objects, or relationships.

Reflexive stage   The first stage of sensorimotor intelligence consisting of innate reflexive movements.

Reinforcer   Any stimulus that strengthens a response, including the cessation of a painful stimulus.

Relative position   In intelligence testing, an index indicating how much above or below average a person may be; one hundred (100) is usually the average.

Releaser mechanism A stimulus that acts to cause a spontaneous response.

Reliability An index of the degree to which a measure reproduces the same outcome.

Representational ability The cognitive competence, similar to symbolic manipulation, to have mental images of objects and events.

Representational space An understanding of an object and what an object consists of; measured by the ability to draw the object.

Resistance to temptation The ability to resist doing something that would violate a standard when the chances of getting caught are remote.

Response facilitation The action of the model's behavior becomes a discriminative stimulus for the observer to emit a behavior already in his repertoire. (*See also* modeling effect, inhibition/disinhibition effect.)

Reticular formation A system of nerve tissue located in the brain and spinal cord associated with alertness.

Retributive justice In Piaget's theory, two ways children feel justice should be meted out: (1) *Expiatory justice* demands that the severity of the punishment should be in direct proportion to the magnitude of the offense; (2) *Punishment by reciprocity* demands that punishment should be logically related to the misdeed to show the consequences.

Reversal shift An experimental condition requiring the application of a principle rather than a simple stimulus-response association.

Reversibility A mental operation in which the person understands that objects can be transformed from one form to another and back again.

Ribonucleic acid (RNA) Carries DNA information to outer cells.

Rites of passage A formal ceremony, usually found in more primitive, less industrialized societies, marking the individual's acceptance into adulthood.

Role taking Playing the part of another to get a better understanding of the other's perspective.

Rorschach Test The ink blot test used for personality analysis.

Scanning strategies The sequences used in examining stimuli, including eye movement patterns—called saccades—and fixations.

Scatter plot A graphical representation of a correlation in which pairs of scores are plotted on a chart with one variable indicated on the X axis and the other on the Y axis. (*See also* correlation coefficient.)

Schema A psychological concept representing knowledge of a stimulus, stimulus complex, or an abstraction.

Scooting A form of locomotion in which the child remains in a sitting position and pushes himself forward with arms and legs.

Secondary circular reactions In the third stage of sensorimotor intelligence, infants begin to show an awareness of the consequences of their actions (4 months–8 months).

Secular trend The increase in rate of growth over successive generations, as indexed by greater height, earlier age at onset of puberty, and earlier age of reaching full maturity.

Self-concept The attitudes and beliefs an individual holds about himself; an integrated system of beliefs the individual uses to define personal competence.

Semantic differential scale A technique used for measuring the self-concept. Two bipolar adjectives are written at the ends of a line, and the subject places a mark on the line to indicate his feelings about himself with respect to the two adjectives. By repeating this for a number of adjective pairs a broad view of the self-concept may be obtained.

Semantics A system for understanding a word, a phrase, or a sentence.

Sensorimotor intelligence In Piaget's theory, the first cognitive stage, when the child develops from reliance on motor actions to more symbolic operations (birth to 24 months.)

Separation anxiety Anxiety felt by the child separated from an attached person or object.

Serial habituation hypothesis The idea that concepts are learned by attending to various stimulus attributes following some sequential order of relevance.

Seriation The mental operation where stimuli are arranged to reflect an ordering principle; occurs during the concrete operations stage.

Sex role Personality traits and behavioral patterns associated with conceptions of masculinity and femininity in a culture.

Sex role transcendence The ability to behave as a situation demands without being limited to culturally prescribed sex-typed responses.

Sex-typing The processes by which psychological sex differences are learned.

Shape constancy The ability to recognize that a form maintains its shape regardless of its orientation in space; present during infancy.

Sign stimuli Stimuli that release or activate fixed action patterns.

Size constancy The ability to understand the relationship between size and distance and that objects maintain their size regardless of distance; present at birth or shortly thereafter.

Social cognition The ability to mentally characterize others and infer their thoughts, emotions, viewpoints, and feelings.

Socialization The process of acquiring the knowledge and skills to participate as an effective member of society.

Sociologic delinquent An adolescent who learns delinquency and crime as a way of life because what is taught in the home and community is opposed to the predominant social order. (*See also* individual delinquent.)

Sociometric techniques   A variety of techniques for assessing peer popularity, friendship patterns, and the like.

Solitary play   Play behavior in which the child is immersed in his or her own activity without the participation of other children; highly characteristic of very young children. (*See also* parallel, cooperative, associated, and fantasy play.)

Spatial representation   The ability to visualize the relationship of one's self in regard to the environment and the ability to draw a map showing the self in space (mapping).

Specific factors   In terms of intelligence, factors associated with individuals.

Spirality principle   The concept that as a child advances toward some new level of maturity, there will at times be temporary regressions to an earlier level.

Stabilimeter   A criblike device sensitive to movement.

Stages   A term that incorporates an integrated network of conceptualizations concerning a level of functioning such as cognitive stages; it should not be synonymous with age.

Standard deviation   A measure of the dispersion of scores in a distribution. It is the square root of the variance. In a normal (bell-shaped) distribution, 68% of the scores lie within $+1$ and -1 standard deviations of the mean. (*See also* variance.)

Standard score   A statistical procedure in which scores on different measures or scores on the same test for different age groups are made equivalent.

Statistical significance   A measure of the probability that the results of an experiment are due to chance as opposed to the experimental manipulations. A result is considered statistically significant, and not due to chance, if it reaches the .05 level or better; that is, if it could have occurred by chance 5 times out of 100 or less. (*See also* t-test, and F-test.)

Stepping reflex   The walking response of an infant (until about 8 weeks of age) when placed, with support, on his feet.

Stimulus generalization   The ability of stimuli different from the conditioned stimulus to arouse the same response as the conditioned stimulus.

Stimulus orientation   The position of a stimulus in space; the angle of vision.

Strange situation   An experimental setting and course of procedures designed by Ainsworth and her colleagues to assess the development of infant attachment.

Structure   The organization of knowledge about objects, events, and relationships.

Subcortical nuclei Neural structures, theoretically located at a level below the cortex, which are claimed to control neonatal behaviors, including the reflexes.

Subjective moral orientation Making moral judgments on the basis of the transgressor's intentions.

Superego In psychoanalytic theory, the conscience; an internalization of society's codes of moral behavior.

Surface structure The ways in which the constituent parts of sentences are arranged.

Swimming reflex An infant response to being placed on the abdomen; can effect movement in water.

Symbolic operations Any set of mental operations or manipulations that involve acting on and with symbols.

Symbolic stage In Bruner's theory, the maximum stage (enactive, ikonic) where symbolic representation is expressed through language.

Sympathetic nervous system The system of nerves associated with emotional reactions; one of two components of the autonomic nervous system.

Syntax The rules governing the component structures of sentences.

Synthetic theory A concept that views behavior as an integral part of evolutionary change; particularly important in the realm of mate selection.

Tachistoscope A high-speed versatile system for presenting visual stimuli.

Telegraphic sentences Sentence-like utterances containing the key words to communicate meaning but missing other word-types such as conjunctions.

Temperament Predispositions toward behaving in consistent ways that are peculiar to the individual and involve likes and dislikes in terms of social interactions; refers to a behavioristic style, to how one behaves, rather than to specific behaviors; assumed to be largely inherited.

Testosterone A male sex hormone.

Thematic Apperception Test A test for personality analysis; persons tell stories in response to a series of pictures.

Theory A statement or a group of statements, as in axioms and postulates, spelling out the conditions under which a particular event will occur.

Tonic-neck-reflex (TNR) A reflex occurring in newborns, characterized by the extension of extremities on one side of the body and flexion of the extremities on the other side (contralateral) of the body.

Trait A characteristic of an individual and, like temperament, probably innate.

Transductive reasoning The cognitive inability to apply a principle across situations; reasoning that is applied independently from one situation to another.

Transformational rules The rules by which the surface structures (arrangement of words) can be changed.

Transitivity A mental operation requiring the ability to manipulate the ordering of three or more objects when one is implicit. (e.g., John is taller than Bill, Bill is taller than Henry. Who is tallest?).

Transposition A task requiring the learner to understand the relationship between two objects and to apply that principle regardless of the absolute magnitude of the stimulus pairs.

Truth value of a theory Tbe degree to which a theory is an accurate representation of why some event or behavior occurs. When a theory generates hypotheses that are supported by research findings it gains truth value, i.e., our confidence increases that it is a good model of why a behavior occurs.

t-**Test** An inferential statistic, indicating the degree of statistical significance of the difference in the performance of two groups in an experiment. (*See also* F-test, statistical significance.)

Turner's syndrome An incomplete sex cell containing a single sex chromosome (XO).

Unconditioned response (UCR) A response that occurs without previous learning or experience.

Unconditioned stimulus (UCS) A stimulus that causes a response without any previous learning (e.g., food powder causes a hungry dog to salivate).

Unitary trait According to Spearman, the concept that intelligence consists of a general intellectual ability.

Validity An index of the degree to which a measure (e.g., an intelligence test) predicts performance on some other behavior (e.g., mathematics achievement).

Variance A descriptive statistic representing the average amount a group deviates on some variable from the average value for the group as a whole. (*See also* standard deviation.)

Visceral reactions Internal responses that accompany an emotional response involving the autonomic nervous system.

Visual cliff A device for determining the presence of depth perception in infants.

Zygote A fertilized egg prior to differentiation; the first ten days in the human embryo.

REFERENCES

Ackerly, S. Rebellion and its relation to delinquency and neurosis in 60 adolescents. *American Journal of Orthopsychiatry*, 1933, *3*, 147–160.

Adelson, J. The political imagination of the young adolescent. *Daedalus*, 1971, Fall, 1013–1050.

Adelson, J., and O'Neil, R. The development of political thought in adolescence: A sense of community. *Journal of Personality and Social Psychology*, 1966, *4*, 295–308.

Ahammer, I. M. Social-learning theory as a framework for the study of adult personality development. In P. B. Baltes and K. W. Schaie (Eds.), *Life-span developmental psychology: Personality and socialization.* New York: Academic Press, 1973.

Ahlstrom, W. M., and Havighurst, R. J. *400 Losers.* San Francisco: Jossey-Bass, 1971.

Ainsworth, M. D. S. Anxious attachments and defensive reactions in a strange situation and their relationship to behavior at home. Paper presented at the biennial meetings of the Society for Research in Child Development, Philadelphia, Pa., April 1973.

Ainsworth, M. D. S. The development of infant-mother interaction among the Ganda. In B. M. Foss (Ed.), *Determinants of infant behavior.* Vol. 2. New York: Wiley, 1963.

Ainsworth M. D. S. Patterns of attachment behavior shown by the infant in interaction with his mother. *Merrill-Palmer Quarterly*, 1964, *10*, 51–58.

Ainsworth, M. D. S., and Bell, S. M. Some contemporary patterns of mother-infant interaction in the feeding situation. In J. A. Ambrose (Ed.), *Stimulation in early infancy.* London: Academic Press, 1969.

Ainsworth, M. D. S., Bell, S. M., and Stayton, D. J. Individual differences in strange situation behavior of 1 year olds. In H. R. Schaffer (Ed.), *The origins of human social relations.* London: Academic Press, 1971.

Ainsworth, M. D. S., and Wittig, B. A. Attachment and exploratory behavior of one year olds in a strange situation. In B. M. Foss (Ed.), *Determinants of infant behavior.* London: Methuen, 1969.

Alberts, E., and Ehrenfruend, D. Transposition in children as a function of age. *Journal of Experimental Psychology*, 1951, *41*, 30–38.

Allen, V. L., and Newtson, D. Development of conformity and independence. *Journal of Personality and Social Psychology*, 1972, *22*, 18–30.

Allport, Gordon W. *Becoming: Basic considerations for a psychology of personality.* New Haven: Yale University Press, 1950.

Ambron, S. R., and Irwin, D. M. Role taking and moral judgment in five- and seven-year-olds. *Developmental Psychology*, 1975, *11*, 102.

American Psychological Association, Committee on Ethical Standards in Psychological Research. Ethical standards for research with human subjects. American Psychological Association *Monitor*, 1972 (May).

Ames, L. B. The sequential patterning of prone progression in the human infant. *Genetic Psychology Monographs*, 1937, *19*, 409–460.

Apgar, V. A proposal for a new method of evaluation of the newborn infant. *Anesthesia and Analgesia*, 1953, *32*, 260–267.

Arbuthnot, J. Modification of moral judgment through role playing. *Developmental Psychology*, 1975, *11*, 319–324.

Arnold, M. B. (Ed.), *Feelings and emotions.* New York: Academic Press, 1970.

Arnold, M. B. Perennial problems in the field of emotion. In M. B. Arnold (Ed.), *Feelings and emotions.* New York: Academic Press, 1970, 169–185.

Aronfreed, J. The concept of internalization. In D. Goslin (Ed.), *Handbook of socialization theory and research.* Chicago: Rand McNally, 1969, 263–323.

Aronfreed, J. *Conduct and conscience: The socialization of internalized control over behavior.* New York: Academic Press, 1968.

Aronfreed, J. The internalization of social control through punishment: Experimental studies of the role of conditioning and the second signal system in the development of conscience. *Proceedings of the XVIIIth International Congress of Psychology,* Moscow, USSR, August, 1966.

Aronfreed, J. Moral development from the standpoint of a general psychological theory. In T. Lickona (Ed.), *Moral development and behavior: Theory, research, and social issues.* New York: Holt, Rinehart, and Winston, 1976.

Aronfreed, J., and Reber, A. Internalized behavioral suppression and the timing of social punishment. *Journal of Personality and Social Psychology,* 1965, 1, 3–16.

Atkinson, R. C., Bower, G. H., and Crothers, E. J. *Introduction to mathematical learning theory.* New York: Wiley, 1965.

Austin, V. D., Ruble, D. N., and Trabasso, T. Recall and order effects as factors in children's moral judgments. *Child Development,* 1977, 48, 470–474.

Ausubel, D. P. *Theory and problems of adolescent development.* New York: Grune and Stratton, 1954.

Ayres, A. J. *Sensory integration and learning disorders.* Los Angeles: Western Psychological Services, 1972.

Baldwin, A. L. Changes in parent behavior during pregnancy: An experiment in longitudinal analysis. *Child Development,* 1947, 18, 29–39.

Baldwin, A. L. *Theories of child development.* New York: Wiley, 1967.

Bandura, A. Influence of model's reinforcement contingencies on the acquisition of imitative responses. *Journal of Personality and Social Psychology,* 1965, 1, 589–595.

Bandura, A. *Principles of behavior modification.* New York: Holt, Rinehart, and Winston, 1969 (a).

Bandura, A. Social learning theory of identificatory processes. In D. Goslin (Ed.), *Handbook of socialization theory and research.* Chicago: Rand McNally, 1969, pp. 213–262 (b).

Bandura, A., Grusec, J. E., and Menlove, F. L. Vicarious extinction of avoidance behavior. *Journal of Personality and Social Psychology,* 1967, 5, 16–23.

Bandura, A., and Kupers, C. J. Transmission of patterns of self-reinforcement through modeling. *Journal of Abnormal and Social Psychology,* 1964, 69, 1–9.

Bandura, A., and MacDonald, F. J. Influence of social reinforcement and the behavior of models in shaping children's moral judgments. *Journal of Abnormal and Social Psychology,* 1963, 67, 274–281.

Bandura, A., and Mischel, W. Modification and self-imposed delay of reward through exposure to live and symbolic models. *Journal of Personality and Social Psychology,* 1965, 2, 698–705.

Bandura, A., Ross, D., and Ross, S. A. A comparative test of the status envy, social power, and secondary reinforcement theories of identificatory learning. *Journal of Abnormal and Social Psychology,* 1963b, 67, 527–534.

Bandura, A., Ross, D., and Ross, S. A. Imitation of film-mediated aggressive models. *Journal of Abnormal and Social Psychology,* 1963a, 66, 3–11.

Bandura, A., and Walters, R. H. *Adolescent aggression.* New York: Ronald Press, 1959.

Bandura, A., and Walters, R. H. *Social learning and personality development.* New York: Holt, Rinehart, and Winston, 1963.

Bandura, A., and Whalen, C. The influence of antecedent reinforcement and divergent modeling cues on patterns of self-reward. *Journal of Personality and Social Psychology*, 1966, 3, 373–382.

Bardwick, J. M. *The psychology of women: A study of bio-cultural conflicts.* New York: Harper and Row, 1971.

Barkley, R. A., Ullman, D. G., Otto, L., and Brecht, J. M. The effects of sex typing and sex appropriateness of modeled behavior on children's imitation. *Child Development*, 1977, 48, 721–725.

Barrett, D. E., and Yarrow, M. R. Prosocial behavior, social interential ability, and assertiveness in children. *Child Development*, 1977, 48, 475–481.

Barry, H., III, Bacon, M. K., and Child, I. L. Cultural survey of some sex differences in socialization. *Journal of Abnormal and Social Psychology*, 1957, 3, 327–332.

Bar-Tal, D. *Prosocial behavior: Theory and research.* New York: Wiley, 1976.

Bayley, N. The development of motor abilities during the first three years. *Monographs of the Society for Research in Child Development*, 1935, No. 1.

Bayley, N. Individual patterns of development. *Child Development*, 1956, 27, 45–74.

Beach, F. A. Neural and chemical regulation of behavior. In H. F. Harlow and C. N. Wolsey (Eds.), *Biological and biochemical bases of behavior.* Madison, Wisconsin: The University of Wisconsin Press, 1958.

Becker, W. C. Consequences of different kinds of parental discipline. In M. L. Hoffman and L. W. Hoffman (Eds.), *Review of child development research.* New York: Russell Sage Foundation, 1964.

Becker, W. C., and Krug, R. S. A circumplex model for social behavior in children. *Child Development*, 1964, 35, 371–396.

Beckwith, L. Relationships between infants' social behavior and their mothers' behavior. *Child Development*, 1972, 43, 397–411.

Beilin, H. Constructing cognitive operations linguistically. In H. W. Reese (Ed.), *Advances in child development and behavior*, Vol. 11. New York: Academic Press, 1976.

Bell, R. Q. A reinterpretation of the direction of effects in studies of socialization. *Psychological Review*, 1968, 75, 84–88.

Bell, R. R., and Chaskes, J. B. Premarital sexual experience among coeds, 1958 and 1968. *Journal of Marriage and the Family*, 1970, 32, 81–84.

Bem, S. L. The measurement of psychological androgyny. *Journal of Consulting and Clinical Psychology*, 1974, 42, 153–162.

Bem, S. L. Sex role adaptability: One consequence of psychological androgyny. *Journal of Personality and Social Psychology*, 1975, 31, 134–143.

Bem, S. L. On the utility of alternative procedures for assessing psychological androgyny. *Journal of Consulting and Clinical Psychology*, 1977, 45, 196–205.

Bender, L. A visual motor Gestalt test and its clinical use. *American Orthopsychiatry Association Research Monographs*, 1938, No. 3.

Bender, L., and Schilder, P. Aggressiveness in children. *Genetic Psychology Monographs*, 1936, 18, 410–425.

Benedict, R. Continuities and discontinuities in cultural conditioning. *Psychiatry*, 1938, 1, 161–167.

Bennett, E. M., and Cohen, L. R. Men and women: Personality patterns and contrasts. *Genetic Psychology Monographics*, 1959, 59, 101–155.

Benson, D. F., and Geschwind, N. Cerebral dominance and its disturbances. *Pediatric Clinics of North America*, 1968, 15, 759–769.

Bereiter, C., and Englemann, S. *Teaching disadvantaged children in the preschool.* Englewood Cliffs, N.J.: Prentice-Hall, 1966.

Berenda, R. W. *The influence of the group on the judgments of children.* New York: King's Crown Press, 1950.

Berg-Cross, L. G. Intentionality, degree of damage, and moral judgments. *Child Development,* 1975, *46,* 397–406.

Berko, J. The child's learning of English morphology. *Word,* 1958, *4,* 150–177.

Berndt, T. J., and Berndt, E. G. Children's use of motives and intentionality in person perception and moral judgment. *Child Development,* 1975, *46,* 904–912.

Bernstein, B. Language and social class. *British Journal of Sociology,* 1960, *11,* 271–276.

Berscheid, E., and Walster, E. Physical attractiveness. In L. Berkowitz (Ed.), *Advances in experimental social psychology.* New York: Academic Press, 1974.

Bijou, S. W., and Baer, D. M. *Child development I: A systematic and empirical theory.* New York: Appleton-Century-Crofts, 1961.

Bijou, S. W., and Baer, D. M. *Child development II: Universal stage of infancy.* New York: Appleton-Century-Crofts, 1965.

Biller, H. B. *Father, child and sex role.* Lexington, Mass.: Heath Lexington Books, 1971.

Binet, A., and Simon, T. *The development of intelligence in children* (Translated by E. S. Kite). Baltimore, Md.: Williams and Wilkins, 1916.

Birch, H. G., and Bitterman, M. E. Sensory integration and cognitive theory. *Psychological Review,* 1951, *58,* 355–361.

Birch, H. G., and Gussow, J. D. *Disadvantaged children. Health, nutrition and school failure.* New York: Grune and Stratton, 1970.

Birch, H. G., and Lefford, A. Intersensory development. *Monographs of the Society for Research in Child Development,* 1963, *28* (5, Serial No. 89).

Bixenstine, V. E., DeCorte, M. S., and Bixenstine, B. A. Conformity to peer-sponsored misconduct at four grade levels. *Developmental Psychology,* 1976, *12,* 226–236.

Blakely, B., Stephenson, P. S., and Nichol, H. Social factors compared in a random sample of juvenile delinquents and controls. *International Journal of Social Psychiatry,* 1974, *20,* 203–217.

Blehar, M. C., Lieberman, A. F., and Ainsworth, M. D. S. Early face-to-face interaction and its relation to later infant-mother attachment. *Child Development,* 1977, *48,* 182–194.

Block, J. Conceptions of sex role: Some cross-cultural and longitudinal perspectives. *American Psychologist,* 1973, *28,* 512–527.

Block, J. H. Issues, problems, and pitfalls in assessing sex differences: A critical review of *The Psychology of Sex Differences. Merrill-Palmer Quarterly,* 1976, *22,* 283–308.

Bloom, L. *Language development: Form and function in emerging grammars.* Cambridge, Mass.: MIT Press, 1970.

Bloom, L. Language development review. In E. M. Hetherington (Ed.), *Review of child development research.* Chicago: University of Chicago Press, 1975.

Bloom, L. *One word at a time: The use of single word utterances before syntax.* The Hague: Mouton, 1973.

Bloom, L., Lightbown, P., and Hood, L. Structure and variation in child language. *Monographs of the Society for Research in Child Development,* 1975, *40* (2, Serial No. 160).

Bohan, J. Age and sex differences in self-concept. *Adolescence,* 1973, *8,* (31), 379.

Bohannon, J. N. III. Normal and scrambled grammar in discrimination, imitating, and comprehension. *Child Development,* 1976, *47,* 669–681.

Bonney, M. E. A sociometric study of some factors relating to mutual friendships on the elementary, secondary and college levels. *Sociometry,* 1946, *9,* 21–47.

Borke, H. The development of empathy in Chinese and American children between three and six years of age: A cross-culture study. *Developmental Psychology,* 1973, *9,* 102–108.

Borke, H. Interpersonal perception of young children: Egocentrism or empathy? *Developmental Psychology*, 1971, 5, 263–269.

Borow, H. Career development. In J. F. Adams (Ed.), *Understanding adolescence: Current developments in adolescent psychology*. Boston: Allyn and Bacon, 1976.

Borow, H. Development of occupational motives and roles. In L. W. Hoffman and M. L. Hoffman (Eds.), *Review of child development research* (Vol. 2). New York: Russell Sage Foundation, 1966.

Bower, T. G. R. Stimulus variables determining space perception in infants. *Science*, 1965, 149, 88–89.

Bower, T. G. R. The visual world of infants. *Scientific American*, 1966, 215, 80–92.

Bowerman, M. *Early syntactic development: A cross-linguistic study with special reference to Finnish*. Cambridge, England: Cambridge University Press, 1973.

Bowlby, J. *Attachment and loss: Attachment*. New York: Basic Books, 1969.

Bowlby, J. *Attachment and loss: Separation*. New York: Basic Books, 1973.

Bowlby, J. The nature of the child's tie to his mother. *International Journal of Psychoanalysis*, 1958, 39, 35.

Bowlby, J. Symposium on "psychoanalysis and ethology". II. Ethology and the development of object relations. *International Journal of Psychoanalysis*, 1960, 41, 313.

Brackett, C. W. Laughing and crying of preschool children. *Child Development Monographs*, 1934, No. 14.

Brady, J. V. Emotion: Some conceptual problems and psychophysiological experiments. In M. B. Arnold (Ed.), *Feelings and emotions*. New York: Academic Press, 1970, 69–100.

Brain, M. D. S. Children's first word combinations. *Monographs of the Society for Research in Child Development*, 1976, 41, (1, Serial No. 164).

Brain, M. D. S. On learning grammatical order of words. *Psychological Review*, 1963, 70, 328–348.

Brain, M. D. S. The ontogeny of English phrase structure: The first phase. *Language*, 1963, 39, 1–13.

Brazelton, T. B. *Neonatal behavioral assessment scale*. Suffolk: Lavenham; Philadelphia: Lippincott, 1973.

Brecher, E. M. *The sex researchers*. New York: New American Library, 1971.

Brian, C. R., and Goodenough, F. L. The relative potency of idea and form perception at various ages. *Journal of Experimental Psychology*, 1929, 12, 197–213.

Bridger, W. H. Sensory habituation and discrimination in the neonate. *American Journal of Psychiatry*, 1961, 117, 991–996.

Bridges-Banham, K. Emotional development in early infancy. *Child Development*, 1932, 3, 324–341.

Bridges-Banham, K. A genetic theory of the emotions. *Journal of Genetic Psychology*, 1930, 37, 514–527.

Brim, O. G. Family structure and sex role learning by children: A further analysis of Helen Koch's data. *Sociometry*, 1958, 21, 1–16.

Brim, O. G., Jr. Socialization through the life cycle. In O. G. Brim, Jr., and S. Wheeler, *Socialization after childhood*. New York: Wiley, 1966.

Brittain, C. V. A comparison of rural and urban adolescents with respect to peer vs. parent compliance. *Adolescence*, 1969, 4, 59–68.

Brittain, C. V. An exploration of the bases of peer-compliance and parent-compliance in adolescence. *Adolescence*, 1968, 2, 445–458.

Broderick, C. B. Socio-sexual development in a suburban community. *Journal of Sex Research*, 1966, 2, 1–24.

Broderick, C. B., and Fowler, S. E. New patterns of relationships between the sexes among preadolescents. *Marriage and Family Living*, 1961, *23*, 27–30.

Bronfenbrenner, U. Freudian theories of identification and their derivatives. *Child Development*, 1960, *31*, 15–40.

Bronfenbrenner, U. Toward an experimental ecology of human development. *American Psychologist*, 1977, *32*, 513–531.

Bronshtein, A. J., and Petrova, E. P. Issledovanie zvukovogo analizatora novorozhdennykh i detei rannego grudnogo vozrasta (An investigation of the auditory analysis in neonates and young infants) Translated and reprinted in Y. Brackbill and G. G. Thompson (Eds.), *Behavior in infancy and early childhood: A book of readings.* New York: Free Press, 1952.

Bronson, A. W. Infants' reactions to unfamiliar persons and novel objects. *Monographs of the Society for Research in Child Development*, 1972, *37*, (Serial No. 148).

Brooks, F. D. *Child psychology.* Boston: Houghton Mifflin, 1937.

Broverman, I. K., Broverman, D. M., Clarkson, F., Rosenkrantz, P. S., and Vogel, S. R. Sex-role stereotypes and clinical judgments of mental health. *Journal of Consulting and Clinical Psychology*, 1970, *34*, 1–7.

Broverman, I. K., Vogel, S. R., Broverman, D. M., Clarkson, F. E., and Rosenkrantz, P. S. Sex-role stereotypes: A current appraisal. *Journal of Social Issues*, 1972, *28*, 59–78.

Brown, A. L. The development of memory: Knowing, knowing about knowing, and knowing how to know. In H. W. Reese (Ed.), *Advances in child development and behavior.* Vol. 10. New York: Academic Press, 1975.

Brown, R. *A first language: The early stages.* Cambridge, Mass.: Harvard University Press, 1973.

Brown, R. How shall a thing be called? *Psychological Review*, 1958, *65*, 14–21.

Brown, R., Cazden, C., and Bellugi, U. The child's grammar from I to III. In J. P. Hill (Ed.), *Minnesota Symposium on Child Psychology.* Minneapolis, Minn.: University of Minnesota Press, 1969.

Brown, R., and Fraser, C. The acquisition of syntax. In C. Cofer and B. Musgrave (Eds.), *Verbal behavior and learning: Problems and processes.* New York: McGraw-Hill, 1963.

Brownstone, J. R. and Willis, R. H. Conformity in early and late adolescence. *Developmental Psychology*, 1971, *4*, 334–337.

Bruner, J. S. On cognitive growth. In J. S. Bruner, R. R. Olver, and P. M. Greenfield (Eds.), *Studies in cognitive growth.* New York: Wiley, 1956.

Bruner, J. S., Olver, R. R., and Greenfield, P. *Studies in cognitive growth.* New York: Wiley, 1966.

Bryan, J. H. Children's cooperation and helping behaviors. In E. M. Hetherington (Ed.), *Review of child development research.* Vol. 5. Chicago: University of Chicago Press, 1975.

Bryan, J. H., and London, P. Altruistic behavior by children. *Psychological Bulletin*, 1970, *73*, 200–211.

Bryan, J. H., Redfield, J., and Mader, S. Words and deeds about altruism and the subsequent reinforcement power of the model. *Child Development*, 1971, *42*, 1501–1508.

Bryan, J. H., and Walbek, N. H. The impact of words and deeds concerning altruism upon children. *Child Development*, 1970(b), *41*, 747–757.

Bryan, J. H., and Walbek, N. H. Preaching and practicing generosity: Children's actions and reactions. *Child Development*, 1970(a), *41*, 329–353.

Bryden, M. P. Laterality effects in dichotic listening: Relations with handedness and reading ability in children. *Neuropsychologia*, 1970, *8*, 443–450.

Buchanan, J. P., and Thompson, S. K. A quantitative methodology to examine the development of moral judgment. *Child Development*, 1973, *44*, 186–189.

Buffery, A. W. H. An automated technique for the study of the development of cerebral mechanisms subserving linguistic skill. *Proceedings of the Royal Society of Medicine*, 1971, *64*, 191–192.

Buffery, A. W. H. Sex differences in the development of hemispheric asymmetry of function in the human brain. *Brain Research*, 1971, *31*, 364–365.

Burchinal, L. G. School policies and school age marriages. *Family Life Coordinator*, 1960, *8*, 45–46.

Burchinal, L. G. Trends and prospects for young marriages in the U.S. *Journal of Marriage and the Family*, 1965, *27*, 243–254.

Burton, R. V. The generality of honesty reconsidered. *Psychological Review*, 1963, *70*, 481–499.

Burton, R. V. Honesty and dishonesty. In T. Lickona (Ed.), *Moral development and behavior: Theory, research, and social issues*. New York: Holt, Rinehart, and Winston, 1976.

Bushell, D., Jr., and Brigham, T. A. Classroom token systems as technology. *Educational Technology*, 1971, *11*, 14–17.

Buss, A. *The psychology of aggression*. New York: Wiley, 1961.

Calder, N. *The mind of man*. New York: Viking, 1970.

Caldwell, B. M. The usefulness of the critical period hypothesis in the study of filiative behavior. *Merrill-Palmer Quarterly*, 1962, *8*, 219–242.

Caldwell, B. M., Wright, C., Honig, R., and Tannenbaum, J. Infant day care and attachment. *American Journal of Orthopsychiatry*, 1970, *40*, 397–412.

Campbell, D. T. On the conflicts between biological and social evolution and between psychology and moral tradition. *American Psychologist*, 1975, *30*, 1103–1126.

Campbell, E. Q. Adolescent socialization. In D. A. Goslin (Ed.), *Handbook of socialization theory and research*. Chicago: Rand McNally, 1969.

Campbell, J. D. Peer relations in childhood. In M. L. Hoffman and L. W. Hoffman (Eds.), *Review of Child Development Research*. Vol. 1. New York: Russell Sage Foundation, 1964.

Campos, J. J., Langer, A., and Krowitz, A. Cardiac responses on the visual cliff in prelocomotor infants. *Science*, 1970, *170*, 196–197.

Cannon, W. B. *Bodily changes in pain, hunger, fear, and rage*. 2nd Edition. New York: Appleton, 1929.

Caplan, N. Delinquency and the perceived chances for conventional achievement. Department of HEW: National Institute of Education, 1974.

Carlson, R. Stability and change in the adolescent's self-image. *Child Development*, 1965, *36*, 659–666.

Carmichael, L. The development of behavior in a vertebrate experimentally removed from the influences of external stimulation. *Psychological Review*, 1926, *33*, 51–58.

Carmichael, L. *Manual of child psychology*, 2nd edition. New York: Wiley, 1954.

Carroll, J. B. Language development. *Encyclopedia of Educational Research*. 3rd Edition. New York: Macmillan, 1960.

Casler, H. Perceptual deprivation in institutional settings. In G. Merton and S. Levine (Eds.), *Early experience and behavior*. New York: Springer, 1967.

Castañeda, A., McCandless, B. R., and Palumo, D. S. The children's form of the Manifest Anxiety Scale. *Child Development*, 1956, *27*, 317–326.

Cattell, P. *The measurement of intelligence of infants and young children*. New York: Psychological Corp., 1940.

Cattell, R. B. The multiple abstract variance analysis equations and solutions: For nature-nurture research on continuous variables. *Psychological Review*, 1960, 67, 353–372.

Cavoir, N., and Dokecki, P. R. Physical attractiveness, perceived attitude similarity, and academic achievement as contributors to interpersonal attraction among adolescents. *Developmental Psychology*, 1973, 9, 44–54.

Cazden, C. Environmental assistance to the child's acquisition of grammar. Doctoral Dissertation, Harvard University, 1965.

Chandler, M. J., and Greenspan, S. Ersatz egocentrism: A reply to H. Borke. *Developmental Psychology*, 1972, 7, 104–106.

Chandler, M. J., Greenspan, S., Barenboim, C. Judgments of intentionality in response to videotaped and verbally presented moral dilemmas: The medium is the message. *Child Development*, 1973, 44, 315–320.

Chase, W. P. Color vision in infants. *Journal of Experimental Psychology*, 1937, 20, 203–222.

Cheyne, J. Effects of imitation of different reinforcement combinations to a model. *Journal of Experimental Child Psychology*, 1971, 12, 258–269.

Chomsky, N. *Aspects of the theory of syntax.* Cambridge, Mass.: MIT Press, 1965.

Chomsky, N. *Syntactic structures.* The Hague: Mouton, 1957.

Clarke-Stewart, K. A. Interactions between mothers and their young children: characteristics and consequences. *Monographs of the Society for Research in Child Development*, 1973, 38, No. 153.

Cleary, T. A., Humphreys, L. G., Kendrick, S. A., and Wesman, A. Educational uses of tests with disadvantaged students. *American Psychologist*, 1975, 30, 15–41.

Cloward, R. Illegitimate means, anomie, and deviant behavior. In J. Short (Ed.), *Gang delinquency and delinquent subcultures.* New York: Harper and Row, 1968.

Cloward, R., and Ohlin, L. Illegitimate means, differential opportunity and delinquent subcultures. In R. Giallombardo (Ed.), *Juvenile delinquency: A book of readings.* New York: Wiley, 1966.

Cohen, D. J. Justin and his peers: An experimental analysis of a child's social world. *Child Development*, 1962, 33, 697–717.

Cohen, L. B. Observing responses, visual preferences and habituation to visual stimuli in infants. *Journal of Experimental Child Psychology*, 1969, 7, 419–433.

Cohen, L. J., and Campos, J. J. Father, mother, and stranger as elicitors of attachment behaviors in infancy. *Developmental Psychology*, 1974, 10, 146–154.

Coleman, J. S. *The adolescent society.* New York: Free Press, 1961.

Combs, A. W., and Snygg, D. *Individual behavior.* New York: Harper, 1959.

Conger, J. J. *Adolescence and youth: Psychological development in a changing world.* New York: Harper and Row, 1973.

Conger, J. J. A world they never knew: The family and social change. *Daedalus*, 1971, Fall, 1105–1138.

Conger, J. J., and Miller, W. C. *Personality, social class, and delinquency.* New York: Wiley, 1966.

Conger, J. J., Miller, W. C., and Walsmith, C. R. Antecedents of delinquency, personality, social class and intelligence. In P. H. Mussen, J. J. Conger, and J. Kagan (Eds.), *Readings in child development and personality.* New York: Harper and Row, 1965.

Connell, D. B. Individual differences in attachment behavior: Long term stability and relationships to language development. Doctoral Dissertation, Syracuse University, 1977.

Connell, D. B. Individual differences in infant attachment behavior: Relationships to response to redundant and novel stimuli. Master's Thesis, Syracuse University, 1974.

Constantinople, A. An Eriksonian measure of personality development in college students. *Developmental Psychology*, 1969, 1, 357–372.

Cook, H., and Stingle, S. Cooperative behavior in children. *Psychological Bulletin*, 1974, *81*, 918–933.

Cooley, C. H. *Human nature and the social order*. New York: Scribner's, 1902.

Cooley, C. H. *Social organization*. New York: Scribner's, 1909.

Coopersmith, S. *The Antecedents of self-esteem*. San Francisco: W. H. Freeman, 1967.

Corballis, M. C., and Beale, I. L. Bilateral symmetry and behavior. *Psychological Review*, 1970, *77*, 451–464.

Corballis, M. C., and Beale, I. L. Interocular transfer following simultaneous discrimination of mirror-image stimuli. *Psychonomic Science*, 1967, *9*, 605–606.

Corballis, M. C., and Beale, I. L. On telling left from right. *Scientific American*, 1971, *224*, 96–104.

Corter, C., and Bow, J. The mother's response to separation as a function of her infant's sex and vocal distress. *Child Development*, 1976, *47*, 872–876.

Costanzo, P. R. Conformity development as a function of self-blame. *Journal of Personality and Social Psychology*, 1970, *14*, 366–374.

Costanzo, P. R., Coie, J. D., Grument, J. F., and Farnill, D. A re-examination of the effects of intent and consequence on children's moral judgments. *Child Development*, 1973, *44*, 154–161.

Costanzo, P. R., and Shaw, M. E. Conformity as a function of age level. *Child Development*, 1966, *37*, 967–975.

Cowan, P. A., Langer, J., Heavenrich, J., and Nathanson, M. Social learning and Piaget's cognitive theory of moral development. *Journal of Personality and Social Psychology*, 1969, *11*, 261–274.

Cressey, D. R., and Ward, D. A. *Delinquency, crime and social process*. New York: Harper and Row, 1969.

Crowley, P. M. Effect of training upon objectivity of moral development in grade-school children. *Journal of Personality and Social Psychology*, 1968, *8*, 228–233.

Cruickshank, W. M., and Hallahan, D. P. (Eds.), *Perceptual and learning disabilities in children. Vol. I: Psychoeducational practices*. Syracuse: Syracuse University Press, 1975a.

Cruickshank, W. M., and Hallahan, D. P. (Eds.), *Perceptual and learning disabilities in children. Vol. II: Research and theory*. Syracuse: Syracuse University Press, 1975b.

Cruze, W. W. Maturation and learning in chicks. *Journal of Comparative Psychology*, 1935, *19*, 371–409.

Darwin, C. R. *On the origin of species by means of natural selection*. London: J. Murray, 1859.

Davidson, H. P. A study of the confusing letters B, D, P, and Q. *Journal of Genetic Psychology*, 1935, *47*, 458–468.

Davidson, W. S., II, and Seidman, E. Studies of behavior modification and juvenile delinquency: A review, methodological critique, and social perspective. *Psychological Bulletin*, 1974, *18*, (12), 998–1011.

Davis, E. A. The form and function of children's questions. *Child Development*, 1932, *3*, 57–74.

Davis, J. A. Correlates of sociometric status among peers. *Journal of Educational Research*, 1957, *50*, 561–569.

Davitz, J. The effects of previous training on post-frustration behavior. *Journal of Abnormal and Social Psychology*, 1952, *47*, 309–315.

Dearborn, W. F., and Rathney, J. W. M. *Predicting the child's development*. 2nd Edition. Cambridge, Mass.: Sci-Art, 1963.

Dennis, W. Causes of retardation among institutional children: Iran. *Journal of Genetic Psychology*, 1960, *96*, 47–59.

Dennis, W. Infant reaction to restraint: An evaluation of Watson's theory. *Transactions of New York Academy of Science*, 1940, *2*, 202–218.

Dennis, W., and Dennis, M. C. The effect of cradling practices upon the onset of walking in Hopi children. *Journal of Genetic Psychology*, 1940, *56*, 77–86.

Dennis, W., and Najarian, P. Infant development under environmental handicap. *Psychological Monographs*, 1957, *71*, (7, Whole No. 436).

Deutsch, F. Observational and sociometric measures of peer popularity and their relationship to egocentric communication in female preschoolers. *Developmental Psychology*, 1974, *10*, 745–747.

Dibiase, W. J., and Hjelle, L. A. Body-image stereotypes and body-type preferences among male college students. *Perceptual and Motor Skills*, 1968, *27*, 1143–1146.

Dobzhansky, T. On types, genotypes and the genetic diversity in population. In J. N. Spukler (Ed.), *Genetic diversity and human behavior*. Chicago: Aldine Press, 1967.

Dollard, L., Doob, L., Miller, N., Mowrer, O. H., and Sears, R. *Frustration and aggression*. New Haven, Conn.: Yale University Press, 1939.

Douvan, E. Employment and the adolescent. In F. I. Nye and L. W. Hoffman (Eds.), *The employed mother in America*. Chicago: Rand McNally, 1963.

Douvan, E., and Adelson, J. *The adolescent experience*. New York: Wiley, 1966.

Douvan, E., and Gold, M. Modal patterns in American adolescence. In L. W. Hoffman and M. L. Hoffman (Eds.), *Review of child development research*. Vol. 2. New York: Russell Sage Foundation, 1966.

Drucker, J. F., and Hagen, J. W. Developmental trends in the processing of task-relevant and task-irrelevant information. *Child Development*, 1969, *40*, 371–382.

Dubanoski, R. A., and Parton, D. A. Effect of the presence of a human model on imitative behavior in children. *Developmental Psychology*, 1971, *4*, 463–468.

Duncan, P. Parental attitudes and interactions in delinquency. *Child Development*, 1971, *42*, 1751–1765.

Dunphy, D. C. The social structure of urban adolescent peer groups. *Sociometry*, 1963, *26*, 230–246.

Dusek, J. B. *Adolescent development and behavior*. Palo Alto, Cal.: Science Research Associates, 1977.

Dusek, J. B. The development of the self-concept during adolescence. Final report for Grant No. HD 09094, United States Department of Health, Education and Welfare, NICHD, July, 1978.

Dusek, J. B. Experimenter bias in performance of children at a simple motor task. *Developmental Psychology*, 1971, *4*, 55–62.

Dusek, J. B., Kermis, M. D., and Mergler, N. L. Information processing in low and high-test anxious children as a function of grade level and verbal labeling. *Developmental Psychology*, 1975, *11*, 651–652.

Dusek, J. B., Mergler, N. L., and Kermis, M. D. Attention, encoding, and information processing in low- and high-test anxious children. *Child Development*, 1976, *47*, 201–207.

Dusek, J. B., and O'Connell, E. J. The bases of teachers' expectations for students' performance. Unpublished manuscript, Syracuse University, 1976.

Eastman, W. F. First intercourse. *Sexual Behavior*, 1972, *2* (3), 22–27.

Eckerman, C. O., Whatley, J. L., and Katz, S. L. Growth of social play with peers during the second year of life. *Developmental Psychology*, 1975, *11*, 42–49.

Ehrhardt, A. A., and Baker, S. W. Hormonal aberrations and their implications for the understanding of normal sex differentiation. Paper presented at the biennial meeting of the Society for Research in Child Development, Philadelphia, 1973.

Eichorn, D. H. Physiological development. In P. H. Mussen (Ed.), *Carmichael's manual of child psychology*. New York: Wiley, 1970.

Eimas, P. D., Siqueland, E. R., Jusezyk, P., and Vigorito, J. Speech perception in infants. *Science*, 1971, *171*, 303–306.

Eisenberg, R. B., Coursin, D. O., and Rupp, H. R. Habituation to an acoustic pattern as an index of differences among human neonates. *Journal of Auditory Research*, 1966, *6*, 239–248.

Eisenthal, S., and Udin, H. Psychological factors associated with drug and alcohol usage among neighborhood youth corps enrollees. *Developmental Psychology*, 1972, *7* (2), 119–123.

Elder, G. H., Jr. Achievement motivation and intelligence in occupational mobility: A longitudinal analysis. *Sociometry*, 1968, *31*, 327–354.

Elder, G. H., Jr. *Adolescent socialization and personality development*. Chicago: Rand McNally, 1971.

Elder, G. H., Jr. Parental power legitimation and its effects on the adolescent. *Sociometry*, 1963, *26*, 50–65.

Elder, G. H., Jr. Structural variations in the child-rearing relationship. *Sociometry*, 1962, *25*, 241–262.

Elkind, D. *Children and adolescents: Interpretive essays on Jean Piaget*. New York: Oxford University Press, 1970.

Elkind, D. Cognitive development in adolescence. In J. F. Adams (Ed.), *Understanding adolescence*. Boston: Allyn and Bacon, 1968.

Elkind, D. Cognitive structure and adolescent experience. *Adolescence*, 1967a, *2* (8), 427–434.

Elkind, D. Developmental studies of figurative perception. In L. P. Lipsitt and H. W. Reese (Eds.), *Advances in child development and behavior*. Vol. 4. New York: Academic Press, 1969.

Elkind, D. Egocentrism in adolescence. *Child Development*, 1967b, *38*, 1025–1034.

Elkins, D. Some factors related to the choice status of ninety eighth-grade children in a school society. *Genetic Psychology Monographs*, 1958, *58*, 207–272.

Emmerich, W. Socialization and sex-role development. In P. B. Baltes and K. W. Schaie (Eds.), *Life-span developmental psychology: Personality and socialization*. New York: Academic Press, 1973.

Engel, M. The stability of the self-concept in adolescence. *Journal of Abnormal and Social Psychology*, 1959, *58*, 211–215.

Engen, T., Lipsitt, L. P., and Kaye, H. Olfactory responses and adaptation in the human neonate. *Journal of Comparative and Physiological Psychology*, 1963, *56*, 73–77.

Erikson, E. H. *Childhood and society*. New York: Norton, 1950.

Erikson, E. H. *Childhood and society*. 2nd Edition. New York: Norton, 1963.

Erikson, E. H. *Identity, youth, and crisis*. New York: Norton, 1968.

Erlenmeyer-Kimling, L., and Jarvik, L. F. Genetics and intelligence: A review. *Science*, 1963, *51*, 593–602.

Ervin, S. Imitation and structural change in children's language. In E. H. Lenneberg (Ed.), *New directions in the study of language*. Cambridge: MIT Press, 1964.

Ervin, S., and Miller, W. Language development. In H. Stevenson (Ed.), *Child psychology*. Sixty-second Yearbook of the National Society for the Study of Education, Part I. Chicago: University of Chicago Press, 1963.

Ethical standards for research with children. Society for Research in Child Development, *Newsletter*, 1973, (Winter).

Eysenck, H. J. The biology of morality. In T. Lickona (Ed.), *Moral development and behavior: Theory, research, and social issues.* New York: Holt, Rinehart, and Winston, 1976.

Eysenck, H. J. *Dimensions of personality.* London: Routledge and Kegan Paul, 1947.

Eysenck, H. J. The inheritance of extraversion-introversion. *Acta Psychologica,* 1956, *12,* 95–110.

Eysenck, H. J. *The IQ argument, race, intelligence, and education.* New York: Library Press, 1971.

Fantz, R. L. The origin of form perception. *Scientific American,* 1961, *204,* 66–72.

Fantz, R. L. Pattern vision in newborn infants. *Science,* 1963, *140,* 296–297.

Fein, G. G. A transformational analysis of pretending. *Developmental Psychology,* 1975, *11,* 291–296.

Fein, G., Johnson, D., Kosson, N., Stork, L., and Wasserman, L. Sex stereotypes and preferences in the toy choices of 20-month-old boys and girls. *Developmental Psychology,* 1975, *11,* 527–528.

Feinberg, M. R., Smith, M., and Schmidt, R. An analysis of expressions used by adolescents of varying economic levels to describe accepted and rejected peers. *Journal of Genetic Psychology,* 1958, *93,* 133–148.

Feitelson, D., and Ross, G. The neglected factor: Play. *Human Development,* 1973, *16,* 202–223.

Feitelson, D., Weintraub, S., and Michaeli, O. Social interactions in heterogeneous preschools in Israel. *Child Development,* 1972, *43,* 1249–1259.

Feldman, N. S., Klosson, E. C., Parsons, J. E., Rholes, W. S., and Ruble, D. N. Order of information presentation and children's moral judgments. *Child Development,* 1976, *47,* 556–559.

Feldman, S. S., and Ingham, M. E. Attachment behavior: A validation study in two age groups. *Child Development,* 1975, *46,* 319–330.

Feshbach, N. D., and Feshback, S. The relationship between empathy and aggression in two age groups. *Developmental Psychology,* 1969, *1,* 102–107.

Feshbach, S. Aggression. In P. H. Mussen (Ed.), *Carmichael's manual of child psychology,* New York: Wiley, 1970.

Feshbach, S. The catharsis hypothesis and some consequences of interaction with aggressive and neutral play objects. *Journal of Personality,* 1956, *24,* 449–464.

Fitts, W. H., and Hammer, W. T. *The self-concept and delinquency.* Nashville, Tenn.: Nashville Mental Health Center (Research Monograph No. 1), 1969.

Flavell, J. H. An analysis of cognitive-developmental sequences. *Genetic Psychology Monographs,* 1972, *86,* 279–350.

Flavell, J. H. *Cognitive development.* Englewood Cliffs, N.J.: Prentice-Hall, 1977.

Flavell, J. H. *The developmental psychology of Jean Piaget.* New York: Van Nostrand, 1963.

Flavell, J. H. Developmental studies of mediated memory. In H. W. Reese and L. P. Lipsitt (Eds.), *Advances in child development and behavior.* Vol. 5. New York: Academic Press, 1970.

Flavell, J. H., Beach, D. H., and Chinsky, J. M. Spontaneous verbal rehearsal in a memory task as a function of age. *Child Development,* 1966, *37,* 283–299.

Flavell, J. H., Botkin, P. T., Fry, C. L., Wright, J. C., and Jarvis, P. E. *The development of roletaking and communication skills in children.* New York: Wiley, 1968.

Flavell, J. H., and Wellman, H. M. Metamemory. In R. V. Kail and J. W. Hagen (Eds.), *Memory in cognitive development.* Hillsdale, N. J.: Lawrence Erlbaum Associates, 1976.

Flerx, V. C., Fidler, D. S., and Rogers, R. W. Sex role stereotypes: Developmental aspects of early intervention. *Child Development,* 1976, *47,* 998–1007.

Floyd, H. H., Jr., and South, D. R. Dilemma of youth: The choice of parents or peers as a frame of reference for behavior. *Journal of Marriage and the Family*, 1972, *34* (4), 627–634.

Fontana, V. J., and Besharov, D. J. *The maltreated child*. Springfield, Ill.: Charles C. Thomas, 1977.

Fraser, C., Bellugi, U., and Brown, R. Control of grammar in imitation, comprehension, and production. *Journal of Verbal Learning and Verbal Behavior*, 1963, *2*, 121–135.

Freedman, D. G. The infant's fear of strangers and the flight response. *Journal of Child Psychology and Psychiatry*, 1961, *4*, 242–248.

Freedman, D. G. Personality development in infancy: A biological approach. In Y. Brackbill (Ed.), *Infancy and early childhood*. New York: Free Press, 1967, pp. 429–502.

Freedman, D. G. Smiling in blind infants and the issue of innate vs. acquired. *Journal of Child Psychology and Psychiatry*, 1964, *5*, 171–184.

Freedman, D. G., and Keller, B. Inheritance of behavior in infants. *Science*, 1963, *140*, 196–198.

Freeman, B., and Sevastano, G. The affluent youthful offender. *Crime and Delinquency*, 1970, *16* (3), 264–272.

French, D. C., Brownell, C. A., Graziano, W. G., and Hartup, W. W. Effects of cooperative, competitive, and individualistic sets on performance in children's groups. *Journal of Experimental Child Psychology*, 1977, *24*, 1–10.

Freud, A. *The ego and the mechanisms of defense* (Translated by C. Baines). New York: International Universities Press, 1948.

Freud, S. *Collected papers*. Vols. I, II, III, IV. New York: Basic Books, 1959.

Freud, S. *The ego and the id*. London: Hogarth Press, 1950.

Freud, S. *A general introduction to psychoanalysis*. New York: Liveright, 1935.

Freud, S. *An outline of psychoanalysis*, New York: Norton, 1949.

Freud, S. The passing of the Oedipal Complex. In *Collected Papers*. Vol. II. London: Hogarth Press, 1924.

Freud, S. *Three contributions to the theory of sex*. New York: Nervous and Mental Disease Publishing Co., 1930.

Friedlander, B. Z. Receptive language development in infancy: Issues and problems. *Merrill-Palmer Quarterly*, 1970, *16*, 7–51.

Friedrich, L. K., and Stein, A. H. Aggressive and prosocial television programs and the natural behavior of preschool children. *Monographs of the Society for Research in Child Development*, 1973, *38*, No. 151.

Friedrich, L. K., and Stein, A. H. Prosocial television and young children: The effects of verbal labeling and role playing on learning and behavior. *Child Development*, 1975, *46*, 27–38.

Frisk, M., Tenhunen, T., Widholm, O., and Hortling, H. Psychological problems in adolescents showing advanced or delayed physical maturation. *Adolescence*, 1966, *1* (2), 126–140.

Fry, P. S. Success, failure, and resistance to temptation. *Developmental Psychology*, 1977, *13*, 519–520.

Fuller, J. L. and Thompson, W. R. *Behavior genetics*. New York: Wiley, 1960.

Furth, H. On language and knowing in Piaget's developmental theory. *Human Development*, 1970, *13*, 241–257.

Gagnon, J. H. There is no sex revolution. *Herald-Telephone*, Bloomington, Indiana, January 19, 1967.

Gagnon, J. H., and Simon, W. They're going to learn in the street anyway. *Psychology Today*, 1969, *3*, 46–47.

Gardner, H. *Developmental psychology*. Boston: Little, Brown, 1977.

Garrett, C. S., Ein, P. L., and Tremaine, L. The development of gender stereotyping of adult occupations in elementary school children. *Child Development*, 1977, *48*, 507–512.

Gazzaniga, M. S. *The bisected brain*. New York: Appleton-Century-Crofts, 1970.

Gazzaniga, M. S. Cerebral dominance and lateral specialization. Paper presented at the meeting of the American Psychological Association, 1968.

Gecas, V. Parental behavior and dimensions of adolescent self-evaluation. *Sociometry*, 1971, *34*, 466–482.

Gelman, R. Conservation acquisition: A problem of learning to attend to relevant attributes. *Journal of Experimental Child Psychology*, 1969, *7*, 167–187.

Gesell, A. L. *Infancy and human growth*. New York: Macmillan, 1928.

Gesell, A. L. The ontogenesis of infant behavior. In L. Carmichael (Ed.), *Manual of Child Psychology*. 2nd Edition. New York: Wiley, 1954.

Gesell, A. L. *Studies in child development*. New York: Harper and Row, 1948.

Gesell, A. L., and Ames, L. B. The development of handedness. *Journal of Genetic Psychology*, 1947, *70*, 155–175.

Gesell, A. L., and Ames, L. B. The ontogenetic organization of prone behavior in human infancy. *Journal of Genetic Psychology*, 1940, *56*, 247–263.

Gesell, A. L., and Ilg, F. L. *The child from five to ten*. New York: Harper and Row, 1946.

Gewirtz, J. L. Mechanisms of social learning: Some roles of stimulation and behavior in early human development. In D. Goslin (Ed.), *Handbook of socialization theory and research*. Chicago: Rand McNally, 1969, pp. 57–212.

Ghent-Braine, L. Age changes in the mode of perceiving geometric forms. *Psychonomic Science*, 1965, *2*, 155–156.

Gibson, E. J. *Principles of perceptual learning and development*. New York: Appleton-Century-Crofts, 1969.

Gibson, E. J., Gibson, J. J., Pick, A. D., and Osser, H. A. A developmental study of the discrimination of letter-like forms. *Journal of Comparative and Physiological Psychology*, 1962, *55*, 897–906.

Gibson, E. J., and Walk, R. D. The "visual cliff". *Scientific American*, 1960, *202*, 2–9.

Ginsburg, H., and Opper, S. *Piaget's theory of intellectual development: An introduction*. Englewood Cliffs, N.J.: Prentice-Hall, 1969.

Ginzburg, E. Toward a theory of occupational choice: A restatement. *Vocational Guidance Quarterly*, 1972, *20*, 169–176.

Ginzburg, E., Ginzburg, S. W., Axelrod, S., and Herman, S. L. *Occupational choice*. New York: Columbia University Press, 1951.

Glucksberg, S., Krauss, R., and Higgin, E. T. The development of referential communication skills. In F. Horowitz (Ed.), *Review of child development research*. Vol. 4. Chicago: University of Chicago Press, 1975.

Glueck, S., and Glueck, E. T. *Toward a typology of juvenile offenders*. New York: Grune and Stratton, 1970.

Glueck, S., and Glueck, E. T. *Unraveling juvenile delinquency*. Cambridge, Mass.: Harvard University Press, 1950.

Godenne, G. D. Sex and today's youth. *Adolescence*, 1974, *9* (33), 67–72.

Gold, M. *Delinquent behavior in an American city*. Belmont, Cal.: Brooks/Cole, 1970.

Gold, M., and Douvan, E. *Adolescent development*. Boston: Allyn and Bacon, 1969.

Goldfarb, W. Rorschach test differences between family-reared, institution-reared, and schizophrenic children. *American Journal of Orthopsychiatry*, 1949, *19*, 625–633.

Goldstein, A. P. *Structured learning therapy: Toward a psychotherapy for the poor*. New York: Academic Press, 1973.

Goldstein, D., Meyer, W. J., and Egeland, B. Cognitive performance and competence charac- teristics of lower- and middle-class preschool children. *Journal of Genetic Psychology,* 1978, *132,* 177–183.

Goldstein, J. H., Suls, J. M., and Anthony, S. Enjoyment of specific types of human content: Motivation or salience? In J. H. Goldstein and P. E. McGhee (Eds.), *The psychology of humor: Theoretical perspectives and empirical issues.* New York: Academic Press, 1972.

Goodenough, F. L. *Anger in young children.* Minneapolis, Minn.: University of Minnesota Press, 1931.

Goodnow, J. J. Problems in research in culture and thought. In D. Elkind and J. Flavell (Eds.), *Studies in cognitive development: Essays in honor of Jean Piaget.* New York: Oxford University Press, 1969.

Gordon, S. *Facts about sex for today's youth.* New York: John Day, 1973.

Goslin, D. Introduction. In D. Goslin (Ed.), *Handbook of socialization theory and research.* Chicago: Rand McNally, 1969, pp. 1–21.

Gottesman, I. I. Genetic variance in adaptive personality traits. *Journal of Child Psychology, Psychiatry, and Allied Disciplines,* 1966, *7,* 199–208.

Gottesman, I. I. Heritability of personality: A demonstration. *Psychological Monographs,* 1963, *77* (Whole No. 572).

Gould, S. J. Biological potential vs. biological determinism. *Natural History,* 1976, *85,* 12–22.

Green, F. P., and Schneider, F. W. Age differences in the behavior of boys on three measures of altruism. *Child Development,* 1974, *45,* 248–251.

Greenfield, P. M. and Smith, J. *The structure of communication in early language develop- ment.* New York: Academic Press, 1976.

Grinder, R. E. Relations of social dating attractions to academic orientation and peer rela- tions. *Journal of Educational Psychology,* 1966, *57,* 17–34.

Gronlund, N. E. The relative stability of classroom social status with unweighted sociometric choices. *Journal of Educational Psychology,* 1955, *46,* 345–354.

Gronlund, N. E., and Anderson, L. Personality characteristics of socially accepted, socially neglected, and socially rejected junior high school pupils. *Educational Administra- tion and Supervision,* 1957, *43,* 329–338.

Grossman, B., and Wrighter, J. The relationship between selection-rejection and intelligence, social status, and personality among sixth-grade children. *Sociometry,* 1948, *11,* 346–355.

Gruelich, W. W. A comparison of the physical growth and development of American-born and native Japanese children. *American Journal of Physical Anthropology,* 1957, *15,* 489–515.

Grusec, J. E. Power and the internalization of self-denial. *Child Development,* 1971, *42,* 93–105.

Grusec, J. E., and Brinker, D. B. Reinforcement for imitation as a social learning determinant with implications for sex-role development. *Journal of Personality and Social Psy- chology,* 1972, *21,* 149–158.

Guthrie, E. R. *The psychology of learning.* New York: Harper and Row, 1935.

Haff, R. A., and Bell, R. Q. A facial dimension in visual discrimination by human infants. *Child Development,* 1967, *38,* 893–899.

Hagen, J. W. The effects of distraction on selective attention. *Child Development,* 1967, *38,* 685–694.

Hagen, J. W., and Sabo, R. A developmental study of selective attention. *Merrill-Palmer Quarterly,* 1967, *38,* 685–694.

Haith, M. M., and Campos, J. J. Human infancy. In M. R. Rosenzweig, and L. W. Porter (Eds.), *Annual Review of Psychology*, 1977, *28*, 251–293.

Hall, G. S. *Adolescence* (2 vols.). New York: Appleton, 1904.

Hallworth, H. J., Davis, H., and Gamston, C. Some adolescents' perceptions of adolescent personality. *Journal of Social and Clinical Psychology*, 1965, *4*, 81–91.

Halverson, H. M. An experimental study of prehension in infants by means of systematic cinema records. *Genetic Psychology Monographs*, 1931, *10*, 107–286.

Hardy, R. E., and Cull, J. G. Juvenile delinquent and his environment. In R. E. Hardy and J. G. Cull (Eds.), *Fundamentals of juvenile criminal behavior and drug abuse*. Springfield, Ill.: Charles Thomas, 1975.

Harlow, H. F., and Zimmerman, R. R. Affectional responses in the infant monkey. *Science*, 1959, *130*, 421–432.

Harris, D. Sex differences in the life problems and interest of adolescents. *Child Development*, 1959, *30*, 453–459.

Harris, L. Change, yes—upheaval, no. *Life*, 1971, *70*, 22–27.

Harris, M. B., and Siebel, C. E. Affect, aggression, and altruism. *Developmental Psychology*, 1975, *11*, 623–627.

Harris, S., Mussen, P., and Rutherford, E. Some cognitive, behavioral, and personality correlates of maturity of moral judgment. *Journal of Genetic Psychology*, 1976, *128*, 123–135.

Hartley, R. E. Children's concepts of male and female roles. *Merrill-Palmer Quarterly*, 1960, *6*, 83–91.

Hartley, R. E. What aspects of child behavior should be studied in relation to maternal employment? In A. E. Siegel (Ed.), *Research issues related to the effects of maternal employment on children*. University Park, Pa.: Social Science Research Center, 1961.

Hartley, R. E., and Hardesty, F. P. Children's perception of sex-roles in childhood. *Journal of Genetic Psychology*, 1964, *105*, 43–51.

Hartshorne, H., and May, M. S. Studies in the nature of character: *Vol. I*, Studies in deceit; *Vol. II*, Studies in self-control; *Vol. III*, Studies in the organization of character. New York: Macmillan, 1928–1930.

Hartshorne, H., May, M. A., et al. *Testing the knowledge of right and wrong*. New York: Religious Education Association, 1927.

Hartup, W. W. Dependence and independence. In H. W. Stevenson (Ed.), *Child psychology*, National Society for the Study of Education Yearbook, 1. Chicago: University of Chicago Press, 1963.

Hartup, W. W. Friendship status and the effectiveness of peers as reinforcing agents. *Journal of Experimental Child Psychology*, 1964, *1*, 154–162.

Hartup, W. W. Peer interaction and social organization. In P. H. Mussen (Ed.), *Carmichael's manual of child psychology*. Vol. 1. New York: Wiley, 1970.

Hartup, W. W., and Coates, B. Imitation of a peer as a function of reinforcement from the peer group and rewardingness of the model. *Child Development*, 1967, *38*, 1003–1016.

Hartup, W. W., Glazer, J. A., and Charlesworth, R. Peer reinforcement and sociometric status. *Child Development*, 1967, *38*, 1017–1024.

Hartup, W. W., and Keller, E. D. Nurturance in preschool children and its relation to dependency. *Child Development*, 1960, *31*, 681–689.

Hartup, W. W., and Zook, E. A. Sex role preferences in three- and four-year-old children. *Journal of Consulting Psychology*, 1960, *24*, 420–426.

Hatfield, J. S., Ferguson, P. E., Rau, L., and Alpert, R. Mother-child interaction and the socialization process. *Child Development*, 1967, *38*, 365–414.

Hattwick, L. A., and Sanders, M. K. Age differences in behavior at the nursery school level. *Child Development*, 1938, 9, 27–47.

Havighurst, R. J. *Developmental tasks and education*. New York: Longmans, Green, 1951.

Havighurst, R. J. *Developmental tasks and education*. 3rd Edition. New York: McKay, 1972.

Havighurst, R. J. Youth in exploration and man emergent. In H. Borrow (Ed.), *Man in a world at work*. Boston: Houghton Mifflin, 1964.

Heathers, G. Emotional dependence and independence in nursery school play. *Journal of Genetic Psychology*, 1955, 87, 37–57.

Hebb, D. V. *The organization of behavior: A neuropsychological theory*. New York: Wiley, 1949.

Hefner, R., Rebecca, M., and Oleshansky, B. Development of sex-role transcendence. *Human Development*, 1975, 18, 143–158.

Heilbrun, A. B. Measurement of masculine and feminine sex role identities as independent dimensions. *Journal of Consulting and Clinical Psychology*, 1976, 44, 183–190.

Herron, R. E., and Sutton-Smith, B. *Child's play*. New York: Wiley, 1971.

Hershenson, M., Kessen, W., and Munsinger, H. Pattern perception in the human newborn: A close look at some positive and negative results. In W. Walthen-Dunn (Ed.), *Models for the perception of speech and visual form*. Cambridge, Mass.: MIT. Press, 1967, pp. 282–290.

Hertzig, M. E., Birch, H. G., Thomas, A., and Mendez, O. A. Class and ethnic differences in the responsiveness of preschool children to cognitive demands. *Monographs of the Society for Research in Child Development*, 1968, 33 (1, Serial No. 117).

Herzog, E., and Sudia, C. E. Children in fatherless families. In B. M. Caldwell and H. M. Ricciuti (Eds.), *Review of child development research*. Vol. 3. Chicago: University of Chicago Press, 1973.

Hess, E. H. Ethology and developmental psychology. In P. H. Mussen (Ed.), *Carmichael's manual of child psychology*. New York: Wiley, 1970.

Hess, E. H. Imprinting. *Science*, 1959, 130, 133–141.

Hess, E. H. Imprinting in birds. *Science*, 1964, 146, 1129–1139.

Hess, R. D. Maternal influences upon early learning: The cognitive environments of urban pre-school children. In R. D. Hess and R. M. Bear (Eds.), *Early education: Current theory, research, and action*. Chicago: Aldine, 1968.

Hetherington, E. M. Effects of father absence on personality development in adolescent daughters. *Developmental Psychology*, 1972, 7, 313–326.

Hetherington, E. M. Effects of paternal absence on sex-typed behaviors in Negro and White preadolescent males. *Journal of Personality and Social Psychology*, 1966, 4, 87–91.

Hetherington, E. M., and Parke, R. D. *Child psychology*. New York: McGraw-Hill, 1975.

Hewitt, L. S. The effects of provocation, intentions, and consequences on children's moral judgments. *Child Development*, 1975, 46, 540–544.

Hicks, D. J. Imitation and retention of film-mediated aggressive peer and adult models. *Journal of Personality and Social Psychology*, 1965, 2, 97–100.

Hildreth, G. The development and training of hand dominance: I. Characteristics of handedness. *Journal of Genetic Psychology*, 1949a, 75, 197–220.

Hildreth, G. The development and training of hand dominance: II. Developmental tendencies in handedness. *Journal of Genetic Psychology*, 1949b, 75, 221–254.

Hildreth, G. The development and training of hand dominance: III. Origins of handedness and lateral dominance. *Journal of Genetic Psychology*, 1949c, 75, 255–275.

Hill, K. T. Relation of test anxiety, defensiveness, and intelligence to sociometric status. *Child Development*, 1963, 34, 767–776.

Hirsch, J. Behavior genetics and individuality understood. *Science*, 1963, *142*, 1436–1442.

Hoffman, L. W. Changes in family roles, socialization, and sex differences. *American Psychologist*, 1977, *32*, 644–657.

Hoffman, L. W. Effects of maternal employment on the child—A review of the research. *Developmental Psychology*, 1974, *10*, 204–228.

Hoffman, L. W. The father's role in the family and the child's peer group adjustment. *Merrill-Palmer Quarterly*, 1961, *7*, 97–105.

Hoffman, L. W. Mothers' enjoyment of work and effects on the child. *Child Development*, 1961, *32*, 187–197.

Hoffman, L. W., and Nye, F. I. *Working mothers*. San Francisco: Jossey-Bass, 1974.

Hoffman, M. L. Altruistic behavior and the parent-child relationship. *Journal of Personality and Social Psychology*, 1975b, *31*, 937–943.

Hoffman, M. L. Developmental synthesis of affect and cognition and its implications for altruistic motivation. *Developmental Psychology*, 1975a, *11*, 607–622.

Hoffman, M. L. Empathy, role taking, guilt, and development of altruistic motives. In T. Lickona, (Ed.), *Moral development and behavior: Theory, research, and social issues*. New York: Holt, Rinehart, and Winston, 1976.

Hoffman, M. L. Moral development. In P. H. Mussen (Ed.), *Carmichael's manual of child psychology*. New York: Wiley, 1970.

Hoffman, M. L. Parent discipline and the child's consideration for others. *Child Development*, 1963, *34*, 573–588.

Hoffman, M. L. Personality and social development. *Annual Review of Psychology*, 1977, *28*, 295–321.

Hoffman, M. L. Sex differences in empathy and related behaviors. *Psychological Bulletin*, 1977, *84*, 712–722.

Hoffman, M. L. Sex differences in moral internalization and values. *Journal of Personality and Social Psychology*, 1975c, *32*, 720–729.

Hoffman, M. L., and Saltzstein, H. D. Parent discipline and the child's moral development. *Journal of Personality and Social Psychology*, 1967, *5*, 45–57.

Hofstaetter, P. R. The changing composition of "intelligence": A study in T-technique. *Journal of Genetic Psychology*, 1954, *85*, 159–164.

Hogan, R. Moral conduct and moral character: A psychological perspective. *Psychological Bulletin*, 1973, *79*, 217–232.

Honzik, M. P. Developmental studies of parent-child resemblances in intelligence. *Child Development*, 1957, *28*, 215–228.

Honzik, M. P. A sex difference in the age of onset of the parent-child resemblance in intelligence. *Journal of Educational Psychology*, 1963, *54*, 231–237.

Honzik, M. P., Macfarlane, J. W., and Allen, L. The stability of mental test performance between two and eighteen years. *Journal of Experimental Education*, 1948, *17*, 309–324.

Horner, M. S. Toward an understanding of achievement-related conflicts in women. *Journal of Social Issues*, 1972, *28*, 157–175.

Horowitz, F. Infant attention and discrimination: Methodological and substantive causes. In F. Horowitz (Ed.), Visual attention, auditory stimulation, and language discrimination in young infants. *Monographs of the Society for Research in Child Development*, 1975, *39* (5–6), Serial No. 158.

Horowitz, F. D., Paden, L. Y., Bhana, K., Aitchison, R., and Self, P. A. Developmental changes in infants' visual fixation to differing complexity levels among cross-sectionally and longitudinally studied infants. *Developmental Psychology*, 1972, *7*, 88–89.

Horowitz, H. Prediction of adolescent popularity and rejection from achievement and interest tests. *Journal of Educational Psychology*, 1967, *58*, 170–174.

Horrocks, J. E. *The psychology of adolescence*. Boston: Houghton Mifflin, 1962.

Horrocks, J. E., and Benimoff, M. Isolation from the peer group during adolescence. *Adolescence*, 1967, *2*, 41–52.

Horrocks, J. E., and Thompson, G. A. A study of the friendship fluctuations of rural boys and girls. *Journal of Genetic Psychology*, 1946, *69*, 189–198.

Hoving, K. L., Hamm, N., and Galvin, P. Social influence as a function of stimulus ambiguity at three age levels. *Developmental Psychology*, 1969, *1*, 631–636.

Hraba, J., and Grant, G. Black is beautiful: A reexamination of racial preference and identification. *Journal of Personality and Social Psychology*, 1970, *16*, 398–402.

Hull, C. L. *Principles of behavior*. New York: Appleton, 1943.

Hunt, J. M. *Intelligence and experience*. New York: Ronald Press, 1961.

Hunt, M. Special sex education survey. *Seventeen*, 1970, July, 94ff.

Husbands, C. T. Some social and psychological consequences of the American dating system. *Adolescence*, 1970, *5*, 451–462.

Huttenlocher, J. Children's ability to orient and order objects. *Child Development*, 1967, *38*, 1169–1176.

Iannotti, R. J. The many faces of empathy: An analysis of the definition and evaluation of empathy in children. Paper presented at the biennial meeting of the Society for Research in Child Development, Denver. April, 1975.

Imamoglu, E. O. Children's awareness and usage of intention cues. *Child Development*, 1975, *46*, 39–45.

Ingram, D. Cerebral speech lateralization in young children. *Neuropsychologia*, 1975, *13*, 103–105.

Inhelder, B., and Piaget, J. *The growth of logical thinking from childhood to adolescence*. New York: Basic Books, 1958.

Irwin, O. C. Infant speech: Consonantal sounds according to manner of articulation. *Journal of Speech Disorders*, 1947, *12*, 402–404.

Irwin, O. C. Infant speech: Consonantal sounds according to place of articulation. *Journal of Speech Disorders*, 1947, *12*, 397–401.

Irwin, O. C., and Weiss, L. A. The effect of clothing on the general and vocal activity of the newborn infant. *University of Iowa Studies of Child Welfare*, 1934, *9*, No. 4, 149–162.

Iscoe, I., Williams, M., and Harvey, J. Age, intelligence, and sex as variables in the conformity behavior of Negro and white children. *Child Development*, 1964, *35*, 451–460.

Iscoe, I., Williams, M., and Harvey, J. Modification of children's judgments by a simulated group technique: A normative developmental study. *Child Development*, 1963, *34*, 963–978.

Isen, A. M., Horn, N., and Rosenhan, D. L. Effects of success and failure on children's generosity. *Journal of Personality and Social Psychology*, 1973, *27*, 239–247.

Jacobs, B. S., and Moss, H. A. Birth order and sex of sibling as determinants of mother-infant interaction. *Child Development*, 1976, *47*, 315–322.

James, W. *The principles of psychology*. New York: Holt, 1890.

James, W. *Psychology: The briefer course*. New York: Holt, 1910.

Jeffrey, W. The orienting reflex and attention in cognitive development. *Psychological Review*, 1968, *75*, 323–334.

Jeffrey, W. Variables in early discrimination learning: I. Motor responses in the training of left-right discrimination. *Child Development*, 1958, *29*, 269–275.

Jeffrey, W., and Cohen, L. B. Habituation in the human infant. In H. W. Reese (Ed.), *Advances in child development and behavior*. New York: Academic Press, 1971.

Jennings, S. A. Effects of sex typing in children's stories on preference and recall. *Child Development*, 1975, 46, 220–223.

Jensen, A. R. How much can we boost IQ and scholastic achievement? *Harvard Educational Review*, 1969, 39, 1–123.

Jersild, A. T. Emotional development. In L. Carmichael (Ed.), *Manual of Child Psychology*, New York: Wiley, 1954, 833–917.

Jersild, A. T., and Holmes, F. B. Children's fears. *Child Development Monographs* 1935(b), No. 20.

Jersild, A. T., and Holmes, F. B. Some factors in the development of children's fears. *Journal of Experimental Education*, 1935a, 4, 133–141.

Jersild, A. T., and Markey, F. V. Conflicts between preschool children. *Child Development Monographs*, 1935, No. 21.

Jersild, A. T., Markey, F. V., and Jersild, A. R. Children's fears, dreams, wishes, daydreams, likes, dislikes, pleasant and unpleasant memories. *Child Development Monographs*, 1933, No. 12.

Johnson, A. M. Juvenile delinquency. In S. Arieti (Ed.), *American handbook of psychiatry*. Vol. 1. New York: Basic Books, 1959.

Jones, H. E. The galvanic skin reflex in infancy. *Child Development*, 1930, 1, 106–110.

Jones, H. E. The galvanic skin reflex as related to overt emotional expression. *American Journal of Psychology*, 1935, 47, 241–251.

Jones, H. E., and Conrad, H. S. The growth and decline of intelligence: A study of a homogeneous group between the ages of ten to sixty. *Genetic Psychology Monographs*, 1933, 13, 223–298.

Jones, H. E., and Jones, M. C. A study of fears. *Childhood Education*, 1928, 5, 136–143.

Jones, M. C. The later careers of boys who were early or late maturing. *Child Development*, 1957, 28, 113–128.

Jones, M. C., and Bayley, N. Physical maturing among boys as related to behavior. *Journal of Educational Psychology*, 1950, 41, 129–148.

Jones, M. C., and Mussen, P. H. Self-conceptions, motivations and interpersonal attitudes of early and late maturing girls. *Child Development*, 1958, 29, 491–501.

Jost, H., and Sontag, L. W. The genetic factor in autonomic nervous system function. *Psychosomatic Medicine*, 1944, 6, 303–310.

Justin, F. A genetic study of laughter provoking stimuli. *Child Development*, 1932, 3, 114–136.

Juvenile Court Statistics 1970. Washington: National Center for Social Statistics, U.S. Department of Health, Education, and Welfare, 1972.

Kaats, G. R., and Davis, K. E. The dynamics of sexual behavior of college students. *Journal of Marriage and the Family*, 1970, 32 (3), 390–399.

Kagan, J. The concept of identification. *Psychological Review*, 1958, 65, 296–305.

Kagan, J. Disenpany, temperament, and infant distress. In M. M. Lewis and L. A. Rosenblum (Eds.), *The origins of fear*. New York: Academic Press, 1974.

Kagan, J., Henker, B. A., Hen-Tov, A., Levine, J., and Lewis, M. Infants' differential reactions to familiar and distorted faces. *Child Development*, 1966, 37, 519–532.

Kagan, J., and Klein, R. E. Cross-cultural perspectives on early development. *American Psychologist*, 1973, 28, 947–961.

Kagan, J., and Moss, H. A. *Birth to maturity: A study in psychological development*. New York: Wiley, 1962.

Kagan, J., Rosman, B. L., Day, D., Albert, J., and Phillips, W. Information processing in the child: Significance of analytic and reflective attitudes. *Psychological Monographs,* 1964, (Whole No. 578).

Kagan, J., Sontag, L. W., Baker, C. T., and Nelson, V. L. Personality and IQ Change. *Journal of Abnormal and Social Psychology,* 1958, 56, 261–266.

Kagan, S., and Madsen, M. C. Cooperation and competition of Mexican, Mexican-American, and Anglo-American children of two ages under four instructional sets. *Developmental Psychology,* 1971, 5, 32–39.

Kagan, S., and Madsen, M. C. Experimental analyses of cooperation and competition of Anglo-American and Mexican children. *Developmental Psychology,* 1972a, 6, 49–59.

Kagan, S., and Madsen, M. C. Rivalry in Anglo-American and Mexican children of two ages. *Journal of Personality and Social Psychology,* 1972b, 24, 214–220.

Kappel, B. E., and Lambert, R. D. Self-worth among the children of working mothers. Unpublished manuscript, University of Waterloo, 1972. (Reported in Hoffman, 1974.)

Katz, P., and Zigler, E. Self-image disparity: A developmental approach. *Journal of Personal and Social Psychology,* 1967, 5, 186–195.

Keasey, C. B. Social participation as a factor in the moral development of preadolescents. *Developmental Psychology,* 1971, 5, 216–220.

Keasey, C. B. Young children's attribution of intentionality to themselves and others. *Child Development,* 1977, 48, 261–264.

Keislar, E. R. Differences among adolescent social clubs in terms of members' characteristics. *Journal of Educational Research,* 1954, 48, 297–303.

Keller, M. F., and Carlson, P. M. The use of symbolic modeling to promote social skills in preschool children with low levels of social responsiveness. *Child Development,* 1974, 45, 912–919.

Kelley, D. H. Social origins and adolescent success patterns. *Education and Urban Society,* 1972, 4 (3), 351.

Kelly, F. J., and Baer, D. J. Age of male delinquents when father left home and recidivism. *Psychological Reports,* 1969, 25 (3), 719–724.

Kendler, H. H., and Kendler, T. S. Vertical and horizontal processes in problem solving. *Psychological Review,* 1962, 69, 1–16.

Keogh, B. K. Pattern copying under 3 conditions of an expanded visual field. *Developmental Psychology,* 1971, 4, 25–31.

Keogh, B. K. Pattern walking under three conditions of available visual cues. *American Journal of Mental Deficiency,* 1969, 74, 376–381.

Keogh, B. K., and Keogh, J. Pattern walking: A dimension of visuomotor performance. *Exceptional Children,* 1968, 34, 617–618.

Kephart, N. C. *The brain injured child in the classroom.* Chicago: National Society for Crippled Children and Adults, 1963.

Kessen, W. *The child.* New York: Wiley, 1965.

Kessen, W. 'Stage' and 'structure' in the study of children. *Monographs of the Society for Research in Child Development,* 1962, 27, (2, Serial No. 83), 65–82.

Khanna, A. A study of friendship in adolescent boys and girls. *Manus,* 1960, 7, Delhi, 3–18.

Kimura, D. The asymmetry of the human brain. *Scientific American,* 1973, 288, 70–78.

Kimura, D. Functional asymmetry of the brain in dichotic listening. *Cortex,* 1967, 3, 163–178.

Kimura, D. Spatial localization in left and right visual fields. *Canadian Journal of Psychology,* 1969, 23, 445–458.

Kinsbourne, M. The cerebral basis of lateral asymmetries in attention. *Acta Psychology,* 1970, 33, 193–201.

Kinsey, A. C., Pomeroy, W. B., and Martin, C. E. *Sexual behavior in the human male.* Philadelphia: W. B. Saunders, 1948.

Kinsey, A. C., Pomeroy, W. B., Martin, C. E., and Gebhard, P. H. *Sexual behavior in the human female.* Philadelphia: W. B. Saunders, 1953.

Kirkendall, L. Sex education: A reappraisal. *Humanist*, 1965, 1–7.

Kirkendall, L., and Miles, G. Sex education research. *Review of Educational Research*, 1968, 35, 528–544.

Klaus, R. A., and Gray, S. W. The early training project for disadvantaged children: A report after five years. *Monographs of the Society for Research in Child Development*, 1968, 33, (4 Serial No. 120).

Kleck, R. E., Richardson, S. A., and Ronald, L. Physical appearance cues and interpersonal attraction in children. *Child Development*, 1974, 45, 305–310.

Knox, C., and Kimura, D. Cerebral processing of nonverbal sounds in boys and girls. *Neuropsychologia*, 1970, 8, 227–237.

Kohlberg, L. A cognitive-developmental analysis of children's sex-role concepts and attitudes. In E. E. Maccoby (Ed.), *The development of sex differences.* Stanford: Stanford University Press, 1966, pp. 82–173.

Kohlberg, L. Continuities in childhood and adult moral development revisited. In P. B. Baltes and K. W. Schaie (Eds.), *Life-span developmental psychology: Personality and socialization.* New York: Academic Press, 1973.

Kohlberg, L. The development of children's orientations toward a moral order: I. Sequence in the development of moral thought. *Vita Humanitas*, 1963b, 6, 11–33.

Kohlberg, L. Moral development and identification. In H. W. Stevenson (Ed.), *Child Psychology.* 62nd Yearbook of the National Society for the Study of Education. Chicago: University of Chicago Press, 1963a.

Kohlberg, L. Moral stages and moralization. In T. Lickona (Ed.), *Moral development and behavior: Theory, research, and social issues.* New York: Holt, Rinehart, and Winston, 1976.

Kohlberg, L. Sex differences in morality. In E. E. Maccoby (Ed.), *Sex role development.* New York: Social Science Research Council, 1964.

Kohlberg, L. Stage and sequence: The cognitive-developmental approach to socialization. In D. A. Goslin (Ed.), *Handbook of Socialization Theory and Research.* New York: Rand McNally, 1969.

Koppitz, E. M. *The Bender Gestalt Test for children.* New York: Grune and Stratton, 1964.

Kotelchuk, M., Zelazo, P., Kagan, J., and Spelke, E. Infant reaction to parental separation when left with familiar and unfamiliar adults. *Journal of Genetic Psychology*, 1975, 126, 255–262.

Kuenne-Harlow, M. Experimental investigation of the relation of language to transposition behavior in young children. *Journal of Experimental Psychology*, 1946, 36, 171–490.

Kuhlen, R. G., and Arnold, M. Age differences in religious beliefs and problems during adolescence. *Journal of Genetic Psychology*, 1944, 65, 291–300.

Kuhlen, R. G., and Houlihan, N. B. Adolescent heterosexual interest in 1942 and 1963. *Child Development*, 1965, 36, 1049–1052.

Kuhlen, R. G., and Lee, B. J. Personality characteristics and social acceptability in adolescence. *Journal of Educational Psychology*, 1943, 34, 321–340.

Kuo, Z. Y. Ontogeny of embryonic behavior in Aves: IV. The influence of embryonic movements upon the behavior after hatching. *Journal of Comparative Psychology*, 1932, 14, 109–122.

Kurtines, W., and Greit, B. The development of moral thought: Review and evaluation of Kohlberg's approach. *Psychological Bulletin*, 1974, 81, 453–470.

Lamb, M. E. Effects of stress and cohort on mother- and father-infant interaction. *Developmental Psychology*, 1976a, *12*, 435–443.

Lamb, M. E. Fathers: Forgotten contributors to child development. *Human Development*, 1975, *18*, 245–266.

Lamb, M. E. Father-infant and mother-infant interaction in the first year of life. *Child Development*, 1977, *48*, 167–181.

Lamb, M. E. *The role of the father in child development.* New York: Wiley, 1976b.

Lamb, M. E. Twelve-month-olds and their parents: Interaction in a laboratory playroom. *Developmental Psychology*, 1976c, *12*, 237–244.

Langer, J. *Theories of development.* New York: Holt, Rinehart, and Winston, 1969.

Langer, J. Werner's comparative-organismic theory. In P. Mussen (Ed.), *Carmichael's manual of child psychology.* New York: Wiley, 1970.

Larsen, G. Y., and Kellogg, J. A developmental study of the relation between conservation and sharing behavior. *Child Development*, 1974, *45*, 849–851.

LaVoie, J. C. Type of punishment as a determinant of resistance to deviation. *Developmental Psychology*, 1974, *10* (2), 181–189.

Lazarus, R. S., Averill, S. R., and Opten, E. M., Jr. Towards a cognitive theory of emotion. In M. Arnold (Ed.), *Feelings and emotion*, New York: Academic Press, 1970, pp. 207–232.

LeCorgne, L. L., and Laosa, L. M. Father absence in low-income Mexican-American Families: Children's social adjustment and conceptual differentiation of sex role attributes. *Developmental Psychology*, 1976, *12*, 470–471.

Lee, L. C. The concomitant development of cognitive and moral modes of thought: A test of selected deductions from Piaget's theory. *Genetic Psychology Monographs*, 1971, *83*, 93–146.

Leeper, R. W. The motivational and perceptual properties of emotions as indicating their fundamental character and role. In M. Arnold (Ed.), *Feelings and emotions.* New York: Academic Press, 1970, pp. 151–168.

Le Furgy, W. G., and Woloshin, G. W. Immediate and long-term effects of experimentally induced social influence in the modification of adolescents' moral judgments. *Journal of Abnormal Social Psychology*, 1969, *12*, 104–110.

Leizer, J. I., and Rogers, R. W. Effects of method of discipline, timing of punishment, and timing of test on resistance to temptation. *Child Development*, 1974, *45*, 790–793.

Lenneberg, E. *Biological foundations of language.* New York: Wiley, 1967.

Lenneberg, E. H. Of language knowledge, apes, and brains. *Journal of Psycholinguistic Research*, 1971, *1*, 1–29.

Lerman, P. Individual values, peer values, and subcultural delinquency. *American Sociological Review*, 1968, *33*, 219–229.

Lerner, R. M., and Gellert, E. Body build identification, preference, and aversion in children. *Developmental Psychology*, 1969, *1*, 456–462.

Lesser, G. S., Fifer, G., and Clark, D. H. Mental abilities of children from different social class and cultural groups. *Monographs of the Society for Research in Child Development*, 1965, *30*, (4, Serial No. 102), 1–115.

Leuba, C. An experimental study of rivalry in young children. *Journal of Comparative Psychology*, 1933, *16*, 367–378.

Levine, L. E., and Hoffman, M. L. Empathy and cooperation in 4-year-olds. *Developmental Psychology*, 1975, *11*, 533–534.

Levy, D. M. Hostility patterns in sibling rivalry experiments. *American Journal of Orthopsychology*, 1936, *6*, 183–257.

Lewin, K. *A dynamic theory of personality.* New York: McGraw-Hill, 1935.

Lewin, K. Field theory and experiment in social psychology: Concepts and methods. *American Journal of Sociology*, 1939, 44, 868–897.

Lewis, M., and Brooks, J. Self, other, and fear: Infants' reactions to people. In M. Lewis and L. A. Rosenblum (Eds.), *The origins of fear*. New York: Wiley, 1974.

Lewis, M., and Rosenblum, L. *Friendship and peer relations*. New York: Wiley, 1975.

Lewis, T. Birth control for teenagers. *Sexual Behavior*, 1972, 1, 83–94.

Libby, R. Parental attitudes toward high school sex education programs. *The Family Coordinator*, 1970, 19, 234–247.

Lickona, T. Critical issues in the study of moral development and behavior. In T. Lickona (Ed.), *Moral development and behavior: Theory, research, and social issues*. New York: Holt, Rinehart, and Winston, 1976a.

Lickona, T. *Moral development and behavior: Theory, research and social issues*. New York: Holt, Rinehart, and Winston, 1976b.

Lickona, T. Research on Piaget's theory of moral development. In T. Lickona (Ed.), *Moral development and behavior: Theory, research and social issues*. New York: Holt, Rinehart, and Winston, 1976c.

Liebert, R. M., Sprafkin, J. N., and Poulos, R. W. Selling cooperation to children. In W. S. Hale (Ed.), *Proceedings of the 20th annual conference of the Advertising Research Foundation*. New York: Advertising Research Foundation, 1975.

Light, R. Abused and neglected children in America: A study of alternative policies. *Harvard Educational Review*, 1973, 43, 556–598.

Lindzey, G. Morphology and behavior. In G. Lindzey and C. S. Hall (Eds.), *Theories of personality*. New York: Wiley, 1965.

Lipsitt, L. Learning in the first year of life. In L. P. Lipsitt and C. C. Spiker (Eds.), *Advances in child development and behavior*. Vol. 1. New York: Academic Press, 1963, 147–195.

Loehlin, J. C. Psychological genetics. In R. B. Cattell (Ed.), *Handbook of modern personality theory*. Chicago: Aldine, 1969.

London, P. The rescuers: Motivational hypotheses about Christians who saved Jews from the Nazis. In J. Macaulay and L. Berkowitz (Eds.), *Altruism and helping behavior*. New York: Academic Press, 1970.

Looft, W. R. Egocentrism and social interaction in adolescence. *Adolescence*, 1971, 6 (24), 485–494.

Looft, W. R. Egocentrism and social interaction across the life span. *Psychological Bulletin*, 1972, 78, 73–92.

Lorenz, K. *Evolution and modification of behavior*. Chicago: University of Chicago Press, 1965.

Lorenz, K. *On aggression*. New York: Harcourt, Brace and Jovanovich, 1966.

Luckey, E., and Nass, G. A comparison of sexual attitudes and behavior in an international sample. *Journal of Marriage and the Family*, 1969, 31, 364–379.

Luria, A. R. *Higher cortical functions in man*. New York: Basic Books, 1966.

Lynn, D. B. *Parental and sex-role identification*. Berkeley: McCutchan, 1969.

Lynn, D. B., and Saurey, W. L. The effects of father-absence on Norwegian boys and girls. *Journal of Abnormal and Social Psychology*, 1959, 59, 258–262.

McCall, R. B. Challenges to a science of developmental psychology. *Child Development*, 1977, 48, 333–344.

McCall, R. B., Appelbaum, M. I., and Hogarty, P. S. Developmental changes in mental performance. *Monographs of the Society for Research in Child Development*, 1973, 38, Serial No. 150.

McCall, R. B., Eichorn, D. H., and Hogarty, P. S. Transitions in early mental development. *Monographs of the Society for Research in Child Development*, 1977, *42*, Serial No. 171.

McCandless, B. R. *Adolescents: Behavior and development.* Hinsdale, Ill.: The Dryden Press, Inc., 1970.

McCandless, B. R., and Marshall, H. R. A picture sociometric technique for preschool children and its relation to teacher judgments of friendship. *Child Development*, 1957, *28*, 139–148.

McCarthy, D. Language development in children In L. Carmichael (Ed.), *Manual of Child Psychology.* New York: John Wiley and Sons, 1954, pp. 492–630.

McCarthy, D. The language development of the preschool child. *Institute of Child Welfare Monograph Series.* Minneapolis, Minn.: University of Minnesota Press, 1930, No. 4.

McCarthy, D. Research in language development: Retrospect and prospect. *Monographs of the Society for Research in Child Development,* 1959, *24* (5, Serial No. 74), 3–24.

McClearn, G. E. Behavioral genetics: An overview. *Merrill-Palmer Quarterly*, 1968, *14*, 9–24.

Maccoby, E. E. The development of moral values and behavior in childhood. In J. A. Clauson (Ed.), *Socialization and society.* Boston: Little, Brown, 1968.

Maccoby, E. E. Sex differences in intellectual functioning. In E. E. Maccoby (Ed.), *The development of sex differences.* Stanford, Cal.: Stanford University Press, 1966.

Maccoby, E. E., and Bee, H. L. Some speculations concerning the lag between perceiving and performing. *Child Development*, 1965, *36*, 367–377.

Maccoby, E. E., and Feldman, S. S. Maternal attachment and stranger reactions in the third year of life. *Monographs of the Society for Research in Child Development*, 1972, *37*, No. 146.

Maccoby, E. E., and Jacklin, C. *The psychology of sex differences.* Stanford, Cal.: Stanford University Press, 1974.

Maccoby, E. E., and Masters, J. C. Attachment and dependency. In P. H. Mussen (Ed.), *Carmichael's manual of child psychology.* New York: Wiley, 1970.

McCord, J., McCord, W., and Thurber, E. Some effects of paternal absence on male children. *Journal of Abnormal and Social Psychology*, 1962, *64*, 361–369.

McCord, W., McCord, J., and Howard, A. Familial correlates of aggression in nondelinquent male children. *Journal of Abnormal and Social Psychology*, 1961, *62*, 79–93.

McCord, W., McCord, J., and Verden, P. Familial and behavioral correlates of dependency in male children. *Child Development*, 1962, *33*, 313–326.

McCord, W., McCord, J., and Zola, I. K. *Origins of crime.* New York: Columbia University Press, 1959.

MacCorquodale, K., and Meehl, P. E. On a distinction between hypothetical constructs and intervening variables. *Psychological Review*, 1948, *55*, 95–107.

MacDonald, M. W. Criminally aggressive behavior in passive effeminate boys. *American Journal of Orthopsychiatry*, 1938, *8*, 70–78.

McDougall, W. *An introduction to social psychology.* London: Methuen, 1908.

McGhee, P. Cognitive mastery in children's humor. *Psychological Bulletin*, 1974, *81*, 721–730.

McGhee, P. E., and Johnson, S. F. The role of fantasy and reality in children's appreciation of incongruity humor. *Merrill-Palmer Quarterly*, 1975, *21*, 19–30.

McGraw, M. B. Development of neuromuscular mechanisms as exemplified in the achievement of erect locomotion. *Journal of Pediatrics*, 1940, *17*, 747–771.

McGraw, M. B. Development of neuromuscular mechanisms as reflected in the crawling and creeping behavior of the human infant. *Journal of Genetic Psychology*, 1941, *58*, 83–111.

McGraw, M. B. *Growth: A study of Johnny and Jimmy.* New York: Appleton-Century-Crofts, 1935.

McGraw, M. B. *The neuromuscular maturation of the human infant.* New York: Columbia University Press, 1943.

Mackworth, N. H., and Bruner, J. S. How adults and children search and recognize pictures. *Human Development,* 1970, *13,* 149–177.

Macnamara, J. Cognitive bases for language learning in infants. *Psychological Review,* 1972, *79,* 1–13.

McNeil, D. The development of language. In P. H. Mussen (Ed.), *Carmichael's handbook of Child Psychology.* New York: Wiley, 1970.

McNemar, Q. *The revision of the Stanford-Binet Scale: An analysis of the standardization data.* Boston: Houghton Mifflin, 1942.

Madsen, M. C., and Shapira, A. Cooperative and competitive behavior of urban Afro-American, Anglo-American, Mexican-American, and Mexican village children. *Developmental Psychology,* 1970, *3,* 16–20.

Mandler, G., and Sarason, S. G. A study of anxiety and learning. *Journal of Abnormal and Social Psychology,* 1952, *47,* 166–173.

Marantz, S. A., and Mansfield, A. F. Maternal employment and the development of sex-role stereotyping in five- to eleven-year-old girls. *Child Development,* 1977, *48,* 668–673.

Maratson, M. Nonegocentric communication abilities in preschool children. *Child Development,* 1973, *44,* 697–700.

Martin, B. Parent-child relations. In F. D. Horowitz (Ed.), *Review of child development research.* Vol. 4. Chicago: University of Chicago Press, 1975.

Martin, W. Singularity and stability of profiles of social behavior. In C. B. Stendler (Ed.), *Readings in Child Behavior and Development.* New York: Harcourt Brace, 1964, 448–466.

Martineau, P. Adulthood in the adolescent perspective. *Adolescence,* 1966, *1,* 272–280.

Masters, J. C., and Wilkinson, A. Consensual and discriminative stereotype of sex-type judgments by parents and children. *Child Development,* 1976, *47,* 208–217.

Mayer, L. A. New questions about the U.S. population. *Fortune,* 1971, February, 82–85. Source: U.S. Census, 1970.

Mead, G. H. *Mind, self, and society.* Chicago: University of Chicago Press, 1934.

Mead, M. *Coming of age in Samoa.* New York: Morrow, 1950.

Mead, M. *Culture and commitment: A study of the generation gap.* New York: Doubleday, 1970.

Mead, M. *Growing up in New Guinea.* New York: Mentor Books, 1953.

Medinnus, G. R. Delinquents' perception of their parents. In G. Medinnus (Ed.), *Readings in the psychology of parent-child relations.* New York: Wiley, 1967.

Meisels, M. M., and Canter, F. M. A note on the generation gap. *Adolescence,* 1971–72, *6,* 523–530.

Meissner, W. W. Parental interaction of the adolescent boy. *Journal of Genetic Psychology,* 1965, *107,* 225–233.

Menyuk, P. *Sentences children use.* Cambridge, Mass.: MIT Press, 1969.

Meredith, H. V. Body size of contemporary groups of eight-year-old children studied in different parts of the world. *Monographs of the Society for Research in Child Development,* 1969a, *34,* no. 1.

Meredith, H. V. Body size of contemporary youth in different parts of the world. *Monographs of the Society for Research in Child Development*, 1969b, *34*, no. 7.

Meredith, H. V. Change in the stature and body weight of North American boys during the last 80 years. In L. P. Lipsitt and C. C. Spiker (Eds.), *Advances in child development and behavior*. Vol. 1. New York: Academic Press, 1963.

Merei, F. Group leadership and institutionalization. *Human Relations*, 1949, *2*, 23–39.

Merton, R. K. Social structure and anomie. In R. Giallombardo (Ed.), *Juvenile delinquency: A book of readings*. New York: Wiley, 1966.

Meyer, W. J. The development of representational competence. In F. J. Monks, W. W. Hartup, and J. deWit (Eds.), *Determinants of behavioral development*. New York: Academic Press, 1972, pp. 527–530.

Meyer, W. J. Relationships between social need strivings and the development of heterosexual affiliations. *Journal of Abnormal and Social Psychology*, 1959, *59*, 51–57.

Meyer, W. J., and Bendig, A. W. A longitudinal study of the Primary Mental Abilities Test. *Journal of Educational Psychology*, 1961, *52*, 50–60.

Meyer, W. J., and Dwyer, M. Eye-movement patterns as a function of age and stimulus orientation. Unpublished manuscript, 1974.

Meyer, W. J., and Offenbach, S. I. Effectiveness of reward and punishment as a function of task complexity. *Journal of Comparative and Physiological Psychology*, 1962, *55*, 532–534.

Midlarsky, E., Bryan, J. H., and Brickman, P. Aversive approval: Interactive effects of modeling and reinforcement on altruistic behavior. *Child Development*, 1973, *44*, 321–328.

Miles, C. C., and Miles, W. R. The correlation of intelligence scores and chronological age from early to late maturity. *American Journal of Psychology*, 1932, *49*, 44–78.

Miller, L. B., and Dyer, J. L. Four preschool programs: Their dimensions and effects. *Monographs of the Society for Research in Child Development*, 1975, *40* (5–6, Serial No. 162), 131.

Miller, S. A., and Brownell, C. A. Peers, persuasion, and Piaget: Dyadic interaction between conservers and nonconservers. *Child Development*, 1975, *46*, 992–997.

Miller, W. B. Lower-class culture as a generating milieu of gang delinquency. *Journal of Social Issues*, 1957, *14*, 5–19.

Miller, W. B. Violent crimes in city gangs. *Annals of the American Academy of Political and Social Science*, 1966, *364*, 96–112.

Mischel, W. Predicting the success of Peace Corps Volunteers in Nigeria. *Journal of Personality and Social Psychology*, 1965, *1*, 510–517.

Mischel, W. Sex-typing and socialization. In P. H. Mussen (Ed.), *Carmichael's manual of child psychology*. New York: Wiley, 1970.

Mischel, W., and Mischel, H. N. A cognitive social-learning approach to morality and self-regulation. In T. Lickona (Ed.), *Moral development and behavior: Theory, research, and social issues*. New York: Holt, Rinehart, and Winston, 1976.

Moffitt, A. R. Consonant cue perception by twenty- to twenty-four-week-old infants. *Child Development*, 1971, *42*, 717–732.

Moir, D. J. Egocentrism and the emergence of conventional morality, in preadolescent girls. *Child Development*, 1974, *45*, 229–304.

Monahan, T. Family status and the delinquent child: A reappraisal and some new findings. In R. Giallombardo (Ed.), *Juvenile delinquency: A book of readings*. New York: Wiley, 1966.

Money, J. Sex hormones and other variables in human eroticisms. In W. C. Young (Ed.), *Sex and internal secretions*. Vol. II. Baltimore: Williams and Wilkins, 1961.

Money, J., and Ehrhardt, A. *Man and woman; boy and girl*. Baltimore: The Johns Hopkins University Press, 1972.

Money, J., Hampson, J. G., and Hampson, J. L. An examination of some basic sexual concepts: The evidence of human hermaphroditism. *Bulletin of Johns Hopkins Hospital*, 1955, 97, 301–319.

Monge, R. H. Developmental trends in factors of adolescent self-concepts. *Developmental Psychology*, 1973, 8, 382–393.

Monge, R. H., Dusek, J. B., and Lawless, J. An evaluation of the acquisition of sexual information through a sex education class. *Journal of Sex Research*, 1977, 13, 170–184.

Montessori, M. *The Montessori Method*. New York: Schocken, 1964.

Moore, B. S., Underwood, B., and Rosenhan, D. L. Affect and altruism. *Developmental Psychology*, 1973, 8, 99–104.

Moore, N. V., Evertson, C. M., and Brophy, J. E. Solitary play: Some functional considerations. *Developmental Psychology*, 1974, 10, 830–834.

Moore, P. Small towns breed delinquents too. *Psychology Today*, 1974, 8, 40.

Moore, S. G., and Updegraff, R. Sociometric status of preschool children as related to age, sex, nurturance-giving, and dependence. *Child Development*, 1964, 35, 519–524.

Morgan, G. A., and Ricciuti, H. Infants' responses to strangers during the first year. In B. M. Foss (Ed.), *Determinants of infant behavior*. Vol. 4. London: Methuen, 1969, 253–272.

Morris, W. N., Marshall, H. M., and Miller, R. S. The effect of vicarious punishment on prosocial behavior in children. *Journal of Experimental Child Psychology*, 1973, 15, 222–236.

Moss, H. A. Sex, age, and state as determinants of mother-infant interaction. *Merrill-Palmer Quarterly*, 1967, 13, 19–36.

Mowrer, O. H. *Learning theory and behavior*. New York: Wiley, 1960a.

Mowrer, O. H. *Learning theory and symbolic processes*. New York: Wiley, 1960b.

Moyer, K. E. The physiology of aggression and the implications for aggression control. In J. L. Singer (Ed.), *The control of aggression and violence*. New York: Academic Press, 1971.

Mueller, E., and Lucas, J. A developmental analysis of peer interaction among toddlers. In M. Lewis and L. Rosenblum (Eds.), *Friendship and peer relations*. New York: Wiley, 1975.

Munn, N. *The evolution and growth of human behavior*. Boston: Houghton Mifflin, 1955.

Munns, M. Is there really a generation gap? *Adolescence*, 1971, 6, 197–206.

Munns, M. The values of adolescents compared with parents and peers. *Adolescence*, 1972, 7, 519–524.

Murphy, L. B. *Social behavior and child personality*. New York: Columbia University Press, 1937.

Mussen, P., and Eisenberg-Berg, N. *Roots of caring, sharing, and helping*. San Francisco: W. H. Freeman, 1977.

Mussen, P., Rutherford, E., Harris, S., and Keasey, C. B. Honesty and altruism among preadolescents. *Developmental Psychology*, 1970, 3, 169–194.

Mussen, P. H. Early sex-role development. In D. A. Goslin (Ed.), *Handbook of socialization theory and research*. Chicago: Rand McNally, 1969.

Mussen, P. H. Some personality and social factors related to changes in children's attitudes toward Negroes. *Journal of Abnormal Social Psychology*, 1950, 45, 423–441.

Mussen, P. H., and Jones, M. C. Self-concepts, motivations, and interpersonal attitudes of late and early maturing boys. *Child Development*, 1957, *28*, 243–256.

Muste, M., and Sharpe, D. Some influential factors in the determination of aggressive behavior in pre-school children. *Child Development*, 1947, *18*, 11–28.

Myklebust, H. R. (Ed.), *Progress in learning disabilities*. Vol. II. New York: Grune and Stratton, 1971.

Neisser, U. *Cognitive psychology*. New York: Appleton-Century-Crofts, 1966.

Nelson, E. A. The effects of reward and punishment of dependency on subsequent dependency. Unpublished manuscript, Stanford University, 1960. (Described in Maccoby and Masters, 1970.)

Nelson, K. Structure and strategy in learning to talk. *Monographs of the Society for Research in Child Development*, 1973, *38*, Serial No. 149.

Nelson, L., and Madsen, M. Cooperation and competition in four-year-olds as a function of reward contingency and subculture. *Developmental Psychology*, 1969, *1*, 340–344.

Newman, H. F., Freeman, F. N., and Holzinger, K. J. *Twins: A study of heredity and environment*. Chicago: University of Chicago Press, 1937.

Nissen, H., Chow, K., and Semmes, J. Effects of restricted opportunity for tactual, kinesthetic, and manipulative experience on the behavior of a chimpanzee. *American Journal of Psychology*, 1951, *64*, 485–507.

O'Bryan, K. G., and Boersma, F. J. Eye movements, perceptual activity, and conservation development. *Journal of Experimental Child Psychology*, 1971, *12*, 157–169.

Oetzel, R. M. Classified summary of research in sex differences. In E. E. Maccoby (Ed.), *The development of sex differences*. Stanford, Cal.: Stanford University Press, 1966.

Olejnik, A. B. The effects of reward-deservedness on children's sharing. *Child Development*, 1976, *47*, 380–385.

Olson, D. R. *Cognitive development: The child's acquisition of diagonality*. New York: Academic Press, 1970.

Oshman, H. P., and Manosevitz, M. Father absence: Effects of stepfathers upon psychosocial development in males. *Developmental Psychology*, 1976, *12*, 479–480.

Osofsky, H. J. Teen-age out-of-wedlock pregnancy: Some preventive considerations. *Adolescence*, 1970, *5*, 151–170.

Osterrieth, P. A. Adolescence: Some psychological aspects. In G. Caplan and S. Lebovici (Eds.), *Adolescence: Psychosocial perspectives*. New York: Basic Books, 1969.

Overton, W. F., and Reese, H. W. Models of development: Methodological implications. In J. R. Nesselroade and H. W. Reese (Eds.), *Life-span developmental psychology: Methodological issues*. New York: Academic Press, 1973.

Palermo, D. Research on language acquisition: Do we know where we are going? In L. R. Goulet and P. B. Baltes (Eds.), *Life-span developmental psychology*. New York: Academic Press, 1970, pp. 401–420.

Palermo, D. S., and Molfese, D. L. Language acquisition from age five onward. *Psychological Bulletin*, 1972, *78*, 409–428.

Papoušek, H. Conditioning during postnatal development. In Y. Brackbill and G. G. Thompson (Eds.), *Behavior in infancy and early childhood: A book of readings*. New York: Free Press, 1967a.

Papoušek, H. Experimental studies of appetional behavior in human newborns. In H. W. Stevenson, E. H. Hess, and H. L. Rheingold (Eds.), *Early behavior: Comparative developmental approaches*. New York: Wiley, 1967b.

Parke, R. D., and Collmer, C. W. Child abuse: An interdisciplinary analysis. In E. M. Hetherington (Ed.), *Review of child development research.* Vol. 5. Chicago: University of Chicago Press, 1975.

Parke, R. D., and Walters, R. H. Some factors influencing the efficacy of punishment training for inducing response inhibition. *Monographs of the Society for Research in Child Development,* 1967, *32* (1, Serial No. 109).

Parsons, T. Family structures and the socialization of the child. In T. Parsons and R. F. Bales (Eds.), *Family, socialization and interaction process.* Glencoe, Ill.: Free Press, 1955.

Parsons, T. *Structure and process in modern societies.* Glencoe, Ill.: Free Press, 1960.

Parten, M. B. Social participation among preschool children. *Journal of Abnormal Social Psychology,* 1932, *27,* 243–269.

Partenan, J., Bruun, K., and Markkanen, T. *Inheritance of drinking behavior.* Helsinki: Finnish Foundation for Alcohol Studies, 1966 (cited in Loehlin, 1969).

Pasamamik, B., and Knoblock, H. Retrospective studies of the epidemiology of reproductive casualty: old and new. *Merrill-Palmer Quarterly,* 1966, *12,* 7–26.

Patterson, G. R., Littman, R. A., and Bricker, W. Assertive behavior in children: A step toward a theory of aggression. *Monographs of the Society Research of Child Development,* 1967, *32* (113).

Pavlov, I. P. *Conditioned reflexes.* London: Oxford University Press, 1927.

Peck, R. F., and Gellini, C. Intelligence, ethnicity and social roles in adolescent society. *Sociometry,* 1962, *25,* 64–72.

Peck, R. F., and Havighurst, R. J. *The psychology of character development.* New York: Wiley, 1960.

Pepper, S. C. *World hypotheses.* Berkeley, Cal.: University of California Press, 1942.

Peterson, C., Peterson, J., and Finley, N. Conflict and moral judgment. *Developmental Psychology,* 1974, *10,* 65–69.

Phelps, H. R., and Horrocks, J. E. Factors influencing informal groups of adolescence. *Child Development,* 1958, *29,* 69–86.

Phillips, J. R. Syntax and vocabulary of mother's speech to young children: Age and sex comparisons. *Child Development,* 1973, *44,* 182–185.

Piaget, J. *The child's conception of the world.* New York: Harcourt, Brace, 1929.

Piaget, J. Intellectual evolution from adolescence to adulthood. *Human Development,* 1972, *15,* 1–12.

Piaget, J. *The language and thought of the child.* New York: World, 1955.

Piaget, J. *The moral judgment of the child.* Glencoe, Ill.: Free Press, 1932.

Piaget, J. *The origins of intelligence in children.* New York: International Universities Press, 1952.

Piaget, J. *Play, dreams, and imitation in childhood.* New York: Norton, 1962.

Piaget, J. *Six psychological studies.* New York: Random House, 1967.

Piaget, J., and Inhelder, B. *The child's conception of space.* London: Routledge and Kegan Paul, 1956.

Piaget, J., and Inhelder, B. *The psychology of the child.* New York: Basic Books, 1969.

Pick, H. L., and Pick, A. D. Sensory and perceptual development. In P. H. Mussen (Ed.), *Carmichael's manual of child psychology.* New York: Wiley, 1970.

Pine, G. The affluent delinquent. *Phi Delta Kappan,* 1966, *48* (4), 138–143.

Pine, G. Social class, social mobility, and delinquent behavior. *Personnel and Guidance Journal,* 1965, *44,* 770–774.

Pinneau, S. R. *Changes in intelligence quotient.* Boston: Houghton Mifflin, 1961.

Place, D. M. The dating experience for adolescent girls. *Adolescence,* 1975, *10,* 157–174.

Playboy student survey (1971). September, 182ff.

Pleck, J. H. Masculinity-femininity: Current and alternative paradigms. *Sex Roles*, 1975, *1*, 161–178.

Polk, K. Class strain and rebellion among adolescents. *Social Problems*, 1969, *17* (2), 214–224.

Porter, D. Preliminary analysis of the grammatical concept 'verb'. Unpublished manuscript, Harvard Graduate School of Education, 1955.

Prader, A., Tanner, J. M., and Von Harnack, G. A. Catch-up growth following illness or starvation. *Journal of Pediatrics*, 1963, *62*, 646–659.

Pratt, K. C., Nelson, A. K., and Sun, K. H. *The behavior of the newborn infant*. Columbus, Ohio: Ohio State University Press, 1930.

Presbie, R. J., and Coiteax, P. F. Learning to be generous or stingy: Imitation of sharing behavior as a function of model generosity and vicarious reinforcement. *Child Development*, 1971, *42*, 1033–1038.

Pressey, S. L., Janney, J. E., and Kuhlen, R. G. *Life: A psychological survey*. New York: Harper, 1939, p. 127.

Proshansky, H., and Newton, P. The nature and meaning of Negro self-identity. In M. Deutsch, J. Katz and A. R. Jensen (Eds.), *Social class, race, and psychological development*. New York: Holt, Rinehart, and Winston, 1968.

Prugh, D. G. Youth's challenge and our response: Are we a sick society? *American Journal of Orthopsychiatry*, 1969, *39*, 548–552.

Quadagno, D. M., Briscoe, R., and Quadagno, J. S. Effect of perinatal gonadal hormones on selected nonsexual behavior patterns: A critical assessment of the nonhuman and human literature. *Psychological Bulletin*, 1977, *84*, 62–80.

Quay, H. C. Dimensions of personality in delinquent boys as inferred from the factor analysis of case history data. *Child Development*, 1964, *35*, 479–484.

Quay, H. C. *Juvenile delinquency*. Princeton: Van Nostrand, 1965.

Ramsey, C. E. *Problems of youth*. Belmont, Cal.: Dickinson, 1967.

Rardin, U. R., and Moan, C. E. Peer interaction and cognitive development. *Child Development*, 1971, *42*, 1685–1699.

Raven, J. C. *Guide to using the colored progressive matrices*. London: H. K. Lewis, 1960.

Razran, G. H. S. Conditioned responses in children: A behavioral and quantitative review of experimental studies. *Archives of Psychology*, 1933, *23*, No. 148.

Reese, H. W. Verbal mediation as a function of age level. *Psychological Bulletin*, 1962, *59*, 502–509.

Reese, H. W., and Lipsitt, L. P. (Eds.). *Experimental child psychology*. New York: Wiley, 1970.

Reese, H. W., and Overton, W. F. Models of development and theories of development. In L. R. Goulet and P. B. Baltes (Eds.), *Life-span developmental psychology: Research and theory*. New York: Academic Press, 1970.

Reichelt, P., and Werley, H. Contraception, abortion, and venereal disease: Teenagers' knowledge and the effect of education. *Family Planning Perspectives*, 1975, *7* (2), 83–88.

Reiss, I. L. Premarital sex as deviant behavior: An application of current approaches to deviance. *American Sociological Review*, 1970, *35* (1), 78–87.

Reiss, I. L. *Premarital sexual standards in America*. New York: Free Press, 1960.

Reiss, I. L. The sexual renaissance: A summary and analysis. *Journal of Social Issues*, 1966, *22*, 123–137.

Reiss, I. L. *The social context of premarital sexual permissiveness*. New York: Holt, Rinehart, and Winston, 1967.

Reitan, R. M., and Boll, T. J. Psychological correlates of minimal brain dysfunction. *Annals of the New York Academy of Science*, 1973, *205*, 65–88.

Remmers, H. H., and Radler, D. H. *The American teenager*. Indianapolis: Bobbs-Merrill, 1957.

Rest, J. R. New approaches in the assessment of moral judgment. In T. Lickona (Ed.), *Moral development and behavior: Theory, research, and social issues*. New York: Holt, Rinehart, and Winston, 1976.

Rheingold, H. L. The modification of social responsiveness in institutional babies. *Monographs of the Society for Research in Child Development*, 1956, *21*, Whole No. 63.

Rheingold, H. The social and socializing infant. In D. A. Goslin (Ed.), *Handbook of socialization theory and research*. Chicago: Rand McNally, 1969, pp. 779–790.

Rheingold, H. L., and Eckerman, C. O. Fear of the stranger: A critical examination. In H. W. Reese (Ed.), *Advances in child development and behavior*. Vol. 8. New York: Academic Press, 1973.

Rheingold, H. L., Hay, D. F., and West, M. J. Sharing in the second year of life. *Child Development*, 1976, *47*, 1148–1158.

Richardson, S. A. The effect of physical disability on the socialization of a child. In D. A. Goslin (Ed.), *Handbook of socialization theory and research*. Chicago: Rand McNally, 1969.

Ricketts, A. F. A study of the behavior of young children in anger. *University of Iowa Studies of Child Welfare*, 1934, *9*, No. 3, 159–171.

Riegel, K. Dialectic operations: The final period of cognitive development. *Human Development*, 1973, *16*, 346–370.

Riesen, A. H. The development of visual perception in man and chimpanzee. *Science*, 1947, *106*, 107–108.

Robinson, I. E., King, K., and Balswick J. O. The premarital sexual revolution among college females. *Family Coordinator*, 1972, *21*, 189–194.

Roff, M., and Sells, S. B. The relation between the status of chooser and chosen in a sociometric situation at the grade school level. *Psychology Schools*, 1967, *4*, 101–111.

Rommelveit, R. *Words, meanings, and messages*. New York: Academic Press, 1968.

Rosecrans, M. A. Imitation in children as a function of perceived similarity to a social model and vicarious reinforcement. *Journal of Personality and Social Psychology*, 1967, *7*, 307–315.

Rosenberg, M. Parental interest and children's self-perceptions. *Sociometry*, 1963, *26*, 35–49.

Rosenberg, M. *Society and the adolescent self-image*. Princeton, N.J.: Princeton University Press, 1965.

Rosenhan, D. L. Learning theory and prosocial behavior. *Journal of Social Issues*, 1972, *28*, 151–163.

Rosenhan, D. L. The natural socialization of altruistic autonomy. In J. Macaulay and L. Berkowitz (Eds.), *Altruism and helping behavior*. New York: Academic Press, 1970.

Rosenhan, D. L., and White, G. M. Observation and rehearsal as determinants of prosocial behavior. *Journal of Personality and Social Psychology*, 1967, *5*, 424–431.

Rosenkrantz, P., Vogel, S., Bee, H., Broverman, I., and Broverman, D. M. Sex-role stereotypes and self-concepts in college students. *Journal of Consulting and Clinical Psychology*, 1968, *32*, 287–295.

Rosenthal, M. K. The generalization of dependency from mother to stranger. *Journal of Child Psychology and Psychiatry*, 1967, *8*, 117–134.

Rosenthal, R. *Experimenter effects in behavioral research*. New York: Appleton-Century-Crofts, 1966.

Rosenzweig, M. R., Bennett, E. L., Diamond, M. C. Brain changes in response to experience. *Scientific American*, 1972, 226 22–29.

Ross, S. A. A test of the generality of the effects of deviant preschool models. *Developmental Psychology*, 1971, 4, 262–267.

Rothman, G. R. The influence of moral reasoning on behavioral choices. *Child Development*, 1976, 47, 397–406.

Rubenstein, J., and Howes, C. The effects of peers on toddler interaction with mother and toys. *Child Development*, 1976, 47, 597–605.

Rubin, K. H. Relationship between egocentric communication and popularity among peers. *Developmental Psychology*, 1972, 7, 364.

Rubin, K. H., Maioni, T. L., and Hornung, M. Free play behaviors in middle- and lower-class preschoolers: Parten and Piaget revisited. *Child Development*, 1976, 47, 414–419.

Rubin, K. H., and Schneider, F. W. The relationship between moral judgment, egocentrism, and altruistic behavior. *Child Development*, 1973, 44, 661–665.

Rubin, K. H., and Trotter, K. T. Kohlberg's moral judgment scale: Some methodological considerations. *Developmental Psychology*, 1977, 13, 535–536.

Rushton, J. P. Generosity in children: Immediate and long-term effects of modeling, preaching, and moral judgment. *Journal of Personality and Social Psychology*, 1975, 31, 459–466.

Rutherford, E., and Mussen, P. Generosity in nursery school boys. *Child Development*, 1968, 39, 755–765.

Salapatek, P., and Kessen, W. Visual scanning of triangles by the human newborn. *Journal of Experimental Child Psychology*, 1966, 3, 155–167.

Saltzstein, H. D. Social influence and moral development: A perspective on the role of parents and peers. In T. Lickona (Ed.), *Moral development and behavior: Theory, research, and social issues.* New York: Holt, Rinehart, and Winston, 1976.

Sander, L. W. Adaptive relationships in early mother-child interaction. *Journal of the American Academy of Child Psychiatry*, 1964, 3, 231–264.

Sanders, K. M., and Harper, L. V. Free-play fantasy behavior in preschool children: Relations among gender, age, season, and location. *Child Development*, 1976, 47, 1182–1185.

Santrock, J. W. Father absence, perceived maternal behavior, and moral development in boys. *Child Development*, 1975, 46, 753–757.

Santrock, J. W. Influence of onset and type of paternal absence on the first four Eriksonian developmental crises. *Developmental Psychology*, 1970, 3, 273–274.

Sarason, S. B., Davidson, K., Lighthall, F., Waite, R., and Ruebush, B. K. *Anxiety in elementary school children: A report of research.* New York: Wiley, 1960.

Scarr, S. Genetic factors in activity motivation. *Child Development*, 1966, 37, 663–673.

Scarr, S. Social introversion-extraversion as a heritable response. *Child Development*, 1969, 40, 823–832.

Scarr, S., and Salapatek, P. Patterns of fear development during infancy. *Merrill-Palmer Quarterly*, 1970, 16, 53–90.

Scarr, S., and Weinberg, R. A. IQ test performance of black children adopted by white families. *American Psychologist*, 1976, 31, 726–739.

Schacter, S. The assumption of identity and peripheralist-centralist controversies in motivation and emotions. In M. Arnold (Ed.), *Feelings and emotions.* New York: Academic Press, 1970, pp. 111–121.

Schacter, S., and Singer, J. E. Cognitive, social and physiological determinants of emotional state. *Psychological Review, 69,* 1962, 379–399.

Schaeffer, E. S. A circumplex model for maternal behavior. *Journal of Abnormal and Social Psychology*, 1959, 59, 226–235.

Schaffer, H. R. Activity level as a constitutional determinant of infantile reaction to deprivation. *Child Development*, 1966, 37, 595–602.

Schaffer, H. R., and Emerson, P. E. The development of social attachments in infancy. *Monographs of the Society for Research in Child Development*, 1964, 29 (Whole No. 94).

Schaie, K. W. A general model for the study of developmental problems. *Psychological Bulletin*, 1965, 64, 92–107.

Schoenfeldt, L. The hereditary component of the Project TALENT two-day test battery. Paper read at the annual meeting of the American Educational Research Association, Chicago, February 1967.

Schofield, M. *The sexual behavior of young people*. Boston: Little, Brown, 1965.

Schultz, D. A. The sexual revolution. In *The changing family*. Englewood Cliffs, N.J.: Prentice-Hall, 1972.

Schur, E. M. *Radical non-intervention: Rethinking the delinquency problem*. Englewood Cliffs, N.J.: Prentice-Hall, 1973.

Sears, P. Doll play aggression in normal young children: Influence of sex, age, sibling status, father's absence. *Psychological Monographs*, 1951, 65, No. 6.

Sears, R. R. Personality. *Annual Review of Psychology*, 1950, 1, 105–118.

Sears, R. R. Your ancients revisited: A history of child development. In E. M. Hetherington (Ed.), *Review of child development research*. Vol. 5. Chicago: University of Chicago Press, 1975.

Sears, R. R., Maccoby, E. E., and Levin, H. *Patterns of child rearing*. New York: Harper and Row, 1957.

Sears, R. R., Rau, L., and Alpert, R. *Identification and child rearing*. Stanford, Cal.: Stanford University Press, 1965.

Sears, R. R., Whiting, J. W. M., Nowlis, V., and Sears, P. S. Some child rearing antecedents of dependency and aggression in young children. *Genetic Psychology Monographs*, 1953, 47, 135–234.

Sebald, H. *Adolescence: A sociological analysis*. New York: Appleton-Century-Crofts, 1968.

Seeman, M. On the meaning of alienation. *American Sociological Review*, 1959, 24, 783–791.

Sekuler, R. W., Rosenblith, J. F. Discrimination of direction of line and the effects of stimulus alignment (Translated by P. Heath). *Psychonomic Science*, 1964, 1, 143–144.

Sells, S. B., and Roff, M. Peer acceptance-rejection and personality development. Final Report, Project No. OE 5-0417, United States Department of Health, Education, and Welfare, 1967.

Selman, R. L. The relation of role taking to the moral development of moral judgment in children. *Child Development*, 1971, 42, 79–91.

Selman, R. L. Social-cognitive understanding: A guide to educational and clinical practice. In T. Lickona (Ed.), *Moral development and behavior: Theory, research, and social issues*. New York: Holt, Rinehart, and Winston, 1976.

Selman, R. L. A structural analysis of the ability to take another's social perspective: Stages in the development of role-taking ability. Paper presented at the meeting of the Society for Research in Child Development, Philadelphia, 1973.

Settlage, D., Baroff, S., and Cooper, D. Sexual experience of younger teen girls seeking contraceptive assistance for the first time. *Perspectives*, 1974, 6, no. 3.

Sewall, M. S. Two studies in sibling rivalry: I. Some causes of jealousy in young children. *Smith College Studies in Social Work*, 1930, 1, 6–22.

Shantz, C. U. The development of social cognition. In E. M. Hetherington (Ed.), *Review of child development research*. Chicago: University of Chicago Press, 1975.

Shapira, A., and Madsen, M. C. Between- and within-group cooperation and competition among kibbutz and nonkibbutz children. *Developmental Psychology*, 1974, *10*, 140–145.

Shapira, A., and Madsen, M. C. Cooperative and competitive behavior of kibbutz and urban children in Israel. *Child Development*, 1969, *40*, 609–617.

Sharin, K. Cognitive and contextual determinants of stranger fear in six- and eleven-month-old infants. *Child Development*, 1977, *48*, 537–544.

Shatz, M., and Gelman, R. The development of communication skills: Modification in the speech of young children as a function of listener. *Monographs of the Society for Research in Child Development*, 1973, *38* (5, Serial No. 152).

Sheldon, W. H. *The varieties of human physique.* New York: Harper and Row, 1940.

Sheldon, W. H. *The varieties of temperament.* New York: Harper and Row, 1942.

Sherif, M., Harvey, O. J., White, B. J., Hood, W. R., and Sherif, C. W. Intergroup conflict and cooperation: the Robbers Cave experiment. Norman, Okla.: University of Oklahoma Press, 1961.

Sherif, M., and Sherif, C. W. *Groups in harmony and tension.* New York: Harper, 1953.

Sherif, M., and Sherif, C. W. *Reference groups.* New York: Harper and Row, 1964.

Sherman, M., and Key, C. B. The intelligence of isolated mountain children. *Child Development*, 1932, *3*, 279–290.

Shirley, M. M. *The first two years: A study of twenty-five babies.* Vol. I. *Postural and locomotor development.* Minneapolis, Minn.: University of Minnesota Press, 1931.

Shuman, M. The differentiation of emotional responses in infants: II. The ability of observers to judge the emotional characteristics of the crying of infants and of the voice of an adult. *Journal of Comparative Psychology*, 1927, *7*, 335–351.

Siegel, A. W., and White, S. H. The development of spatial representations of large-scale environments. In H. W. Reese (Ed.), *Advances in child development and behavior.* Vol. 10. New York: Academic Press, 1975.

Siegelman, E. Reflective and impulsive observing behavior. *Child Development*, 1969, *40*, 1213–1222.

Sigel, I. E., and Olmsted, P. P. Analysis of the object categorization test and the picture categorization test for preschool children. Unpublished manuscript, Merrill-Palmer Institute, 1968.

Simpson, E. L. Moral development research: A case of scientific cultural bias. *Human Development*, 1974, *17*, 81–106.

Simpson, G. The study of evolution: Methods and present status of theory. In A. Roe and G. G. Simpson (Eds.), *Behavior and evolution.* New Haven, Conn.: Yale University Press, 1958, pp. 7–26.

Sinclair-de-Zwart, H. Developmental psycholinguistics. In D. Elkind and S. Flavell (Eds.), *Studies in cognitive development.* New York: Oxford University Press, 1969.

Singer, J. *The child's world of make-believe.* New York: Academic Press, 1973.

Singer, J. L. (Ed.), *The control of aggression and violence.* New York: Academic Press, 1971.

Singer, J. L. Navigating the stream of consciousness: Research in daydreaming and related inner experience. *American Psychologist*, 1975, *30*, 727–738.

Siqueland, E. R., and Lipsitt, L. P. Conditioned head turning in human newborns. *Journal of Experimental Child Psychology*, 1966, *3*, 356–378.

Skeels, H. M. Adult status of children with contrasting early life experiences. *Monographs of the Society for Research in Child Development*, 1966, *31* (3, Serial No. 105).

Skinner, B. F. *Beyond freedom and dignity.* New York: Knopf, 1971.

Skinner, B. F. *Contingencies of reinforcement: A theoretical analysis.* New York: Appleton-Century-Crofts, 1969.

Skinner, B. F. The phylogeny and ontogeny of behavior. *Science,* 1966, *153,* 1205–1213.

Skinner, B. F. *Science and human behavior.* New York: Macmillan, 1953.

Skinner, B. F. *Verbal behavior.* New York: Appleton-Century-Crofts, 1957.

Skipper, J. K., Jr., and Nass, G. Dating behavior: A framework for analysis and an illustration. *Journal of Marriage and the Family,* 1946, 28, 412–420.

Skodak, M., and Skeels, H. M. A final followup study of one hundred adopted children. *Journal of Genetic Psychology,* 1949, 75, 85–125.

Skorepa, C. A., Horrocks, J. E., and Thompson, G. G. A study of friendship fluctuations of college students. *Journal of Genetic Psychology,* 1963, *102,* 151–157.

Slaby, R. G., and Crowley, C. G. Modification of cooperation and aggression through teacher attention to children's speech. *Journal of Experimental Child Psychology,* 1977, 23, 442–458.

Slaby, R. G., and Frey, K. S. Development of gender constancy and selective attention to same-sex models. *Child Development,* 1975, 46, 849–856.

Slaby, R. G., and Parke, R. D. Effect of resistance to deviation of observing a model's affective reaction to response consequences. *Developmental Psychology,* 1971, 5, 40–47.

Smalley, R. E. Two studies in sibling rivalry: II. The influence of differences in age, sex, and intelligence in determining the attitudes of siblings toward each other. *Smith College Studies in Social Work,* 1930(31), *1,* 23–40.

Smilansky, S. *The effects of sociodramatic play on disadvantaged children: Preschool children.* New York: Wiley, 1968.

Smiley, S. S. Optional shift behavior as a function of dimensional preferences and relative arc similarity. *Journal of Experimental Child Psychology,* 1972, *14,* 13–22.

Smith, M. E. An investigation of the development of the sentence and the extent of vocabulary in young children. *University of Iowa Studies of Child Welfare,* 1926, 3 (no. 5).

Smith, T. E. Some bases for parental influence upon late adolescents: An application of a social power model. *Adolescence,* 1970, 5, 323–338.

Smothergill, D. W. Accuracy and variability in the localization of spatial targets at three age levels. *Developmental Psychology,* 1973, 8, 62–66.

Sokolov, Y. N. *Perception and the conditioned reflex.* New York: Pergamon Press, 1963.

Sorensen, R. C. *Adolescent sexuality in contemporary America.* New York: World, 1973.

Spearman, C. *The abilities of man.* New York: MacMillan, 1927.

Spears, W. C., and Hohle, R. H. Sensory and perceptual processes in infants. In Y. Brackbill (Ed.), *Infancy and early childhood.* New York: Free Press, 1967, pp. 51–119.

Spence, K. W. *Behavior theory and conditioning.* New Haven, Conn.: Yale University Press, 1956.

Sperry, R. W. Left-brain, right-brain. *Saturday Review,* 1975, pp. 30–33.

Sperry, R. W. Mechanisms of neural maturation. In S. S. Stevens (Ed.), *Handbook of experimental psychology.* New York: Wiley, 1951, pp. 236–258.

Spiker, C. C., and McCandless, B. R. The concept of intelligence and the philosophy of science. *Psychological Review,* 1954, *61,* 255–266.

Spinetta, J. J., and Rigler, D. The child-abusing parent: A psychological review. *Psychological Bulletin,* 1972, 77, 296–304.

Spitz, R. *The first year of life.* New York: International Universities Press, 1965.

Sroufe, L. A. Wariness of strangers and the study of infant development. *Child Development,* 1977, *48,* 731–746.

Sroufe, L. A., Waters, E., and Matas, L. Contextual determinants of infant affection responses.

In M. Lewis and L. A. Rosenblum (Eds.), *The origins of fear.* New York: Wiley, 1974.

Staats, A. Linguistic-mentalistic theory versus an explanatory S-R learning theory of language development. In D. I. Slobin (Ed.), *The ontogenesis of grammar.* New York: Academic Press, 1971, pp. 103–150.

Stanley, J. C. (Ed.), *Preschool programs for the disadvantaged.* Baltimore: The Johns Hopkins University Press, 1972.

Stark, R., and McEvoy, J. Middle-class violence. *Psychology Today,* 1970, *4,* 52–65.

Staub, E. A child in distress: The effects of age and number of witnesses on children's attempts to help. *Journal of Personality and Social Psychology,* 1970a, *14,* 130–140.

Staub, E. A child in distress: The effects of focusing responsibility on children on their attempts to help. *Developmental Psychology,* 1970b, *2,* 152–154.

Staub, E. A child in distress: The influence of nurturance and modeling on children's attempts to help. *Developmental Psychology,* 1971b, *5,* 124–132.

Staub, E. Instigation to goodness: The role of social norms and interpersonal influence. *Journal of Social Issues,* 1972, *28,* 131–149.

Staub, E. The use of role playing and induction in children's learning of helping and sharing behavior. *Child Development,* 1971a, *42,* 805–816.

Steckler, G. A longitudinal follow-up of neonatal apnea. *Child Development,* 1964, *35,* 333–348.

Steele, C. M., Rosenblood, L. K., and Mirels, H. L. Modification of delinquent behavior. *Journal of Applied Social Psychology,* 1971, *1,* 2, 118–136.

Stein, A. H. The effects of maternal employment and educational attainment on the sex-typed attributes of college females. *Social Behavior and Personality,* 1973, *1,* 111–114.

Stein, A. H., and Friedrich, L. K. Impact of television on children and youth. In E. M. Hetherington (Ed.), *Review of child development research.* Vol. 5. Chicago: University of Chicago Press, 1975.

Stein, G. M., and Bryan, J. H. The effect of a television model upon rule adoption behavior of children. *Child Development,* 1972, *43,* 268–273.

Steinschneider, A. Developmental psychophysiology. In Y. Brackbill (Ed.), *Infancy and early childhood.* New York: Free Press, 1967, pp. 3–47.

Stern, G. G., Caldwell, B. M., Hersher, L., Lipton, E. L., and Richmond, J. B. A factor analytic study of the mother infant dyad. *Child Development,* 1969, *40,* 163–181.

Stevens, S. S. Psychology and the science of science. *Psychological Bulletin,* 1939, *36,* 221–263.

Stevenson, H. Social reinforcement with children as a function of CA, Sex of E, and Sex of S. *Journal of Abnormal and Social Psychology,* 1961, *63,* 147–154.

Stevenson, H. W. Developmental psychology. In D. L. Sills (Ed.), *International encyclopedia of the social sciences.* New York: Macmillan, 1968, pp. 136–140.

Stewart, C. W. *Adolescent religion.* New York: Abingdon Press, 1967.

Subirana, A. Handedness and cerebral dominance. In P. J. Vinckan and G. W. Buryn (Eds.), *Handbook of clinical neurology.* Amsterdam: North Holland: 1969, pp. 248–272.

Suchman, R. G., and Trabasso, T. Stimulus preferences and cue function in young children's concept attainment. *Journal of Experimental Child Psychology,* 1966, *3,* 188–198.

Super, D. E. *The psychology of careers.* New York: Harper and Row, 1957.

Super, D. E. A theory of vocational development. *American Psychologist,* 1953, *8,* 185–190.

Super, D. E. Vocational development theory: Persons, positions, and processes. *Counseling Psychologist,* 1969, *1,* 2–9.

Super, D. E., Crites, J., Hummel, R., Moser, H., Overstreet, P., and Warnath, C. *Vocational development: A framework for research.* New York: Teachers College, Columbia University, 1957.

Tannenbaum, P. H., and Gaer, E. P. Mood changes as a function of stress of protagonist and degree of identification in a film-viewing situation. *Journal of Personality and Social Psychology*, 1965, *2*, 612–616.

Tanner, J. M. Physical growth. In P. H. Mussen (Ed.), *Carmichael's manual of child psychology*. New York: Wiley, 1970.

Tanner, J. M. The regulation of human growth. *Child Development*, 1963, *34*, 817–848.

Tanner, J. M., Whitehouse, R. H., and Takaishi, M. Standards from birth to maturity for height, weight, height velocity and weight velocity: British children. *Archives Diseases of Childhood*, 1966, *41*, 454–471, 613–635.

Taylor, J. H. Innate emotional responses in infants. *Ohio State University Studies*, 1934, No. 12, 69–81.

Templin, M. *Certain language skills in children*. Minneapolis, Minn.: University of Minnesota Press, 1957.

Terman, L. M. et al. *Genetic studies of genius: I. Mental and physical traits of a thousand gifted children*. Stanford, Cal.: Stanford University Press, 1925.

Terman, L. M., and Oden, M. H. *Genetic studies of genius: IV. The gifted child grows up*. Stanford, Cal.: Stanford University Press, 1947.

Terman, L. M., and Oden, M. H. *The gifted group at mid-life: Thirty five years' follow-up on the superior child*. Stanford, Cal.: Stanford, University Press, 1959.

Thelen, M., and Fryreur, J. Effect of observer and model race on the imitation of standards of self-reward. *Developmental Psychology*, 1971, 133–135.

Thomas, A., and Chess, S. *Temperament and development*. New York: Brunner/Mazel, 1977.

Thomas, A., Chess, S., and Birch, H. G. *Temperament and behavior disorders in children*. New York: New York University Press, 1968.

Thomas, A., Chess, S., Birch, H. G., Hertzig, M. E., and Korn, S. *Behavioral individuality in early childhood*. New York University Press, 1963.

Thomas, D. R. Cooperation and competition among Polynesian and European children. *Child Development*, 1975, *46*, 948–953.

Thompson, G. G. *Child psychology*. Boston: Houghton Mifflin, 1962.

Thompson, G. G. Review of McGraw's "The neuromuscular maturation of the human infant." *Journal of Genetic Psychology*, 1946, *68*, 137–143.

Thompson, G. G., and Horrocks, J. E. A study of the friendship fluctuations of urban boys and girls. *Journal of Genetic Psychology*, 1947, *70*, 53–63.

Thompson, S. K. Gender labels and early sex-role development. *Child Development*, 1975, *46*, 339–347.

Thornburg, H. Peers: Three distinct groups. *Adolescence*, 1971, *6*, 59–76.

Thorndike, E. L. A theory of the action of the after-effects of a connection upon it. *Psychological Review*, 1933, *40*, 434–439.

Thurstone, L. L. *The differential growth of mental ability*. Chapel Hill, N.C.: University of North Carolina, The Psychometric Laboratory, 1955.

Thurstone, L. L. Theories of intelligence. *Scientific Monthly*, 1946, *62*, 101–112.

Thurstone, L. L., and Acherson, L. The mental growth curve for the Binet tests. *Journal of Educational Psychology*, 1929, *20*, 569–583.

Tinbergen, N. *The study of instinct*. London: Oxford University Press, 1951.

Tiktin, S., and Hartup, W. W. Sociometric status and the reinforcing effectiveness of children's peers. *Journal of Experimental Child Psychology*, 1965, *2*, 306–315.

Tolman, E. C. *Purposive behavior in animals and men*. New York: Appleton-Century-Crofts, 1932.

Tomlinson-Keasey, C., and Keasey, C. B. The mediating role of cognitive development in moral judgment. *Child Development*, 1974, *45*, 291–298.

Touwen, B. C. L. Laterality and dominance. *Developmental Medicine and Child Neurology,* 1972, *14,* 747–755.

Tuddenham, R. D. The constancy of personality ratings over two decades. *Genetic Psychology Monographs,* 1959, *60,* 3–29.

Turiel, E. Developmental processes in the child's moral thinking. In P. Mussen, J. Langer, and M. Covington (Eds.), *New directions in developmental psychology.* New York: Holt, Rinehart, and Winston, 1969.

Turiel, E. An experimental test of the sequentiality of developmental stages in the child's moral judgments. *Journal of Personality and Social Psychology,* 1966, *3,* 611–618.

Turiel, E., and Rothman, R. The influence of reasoning on behavioral choices at different stages of moral development. *Child Development,* 1972, *43,* 741–756.

Underwood, B. J. *Psychological research.* New York: Appleton-Century-Crofts, 1957.

United States Department of Health, Education and Welfare. *Child abuse and neglect: The problem and its management.* Vol. 1. 1976.

Urberg, K. A., and LaBouvie-Vief, G. Conceptualizations of sex roles: A life span developmental study. *Developmental Psychology,* 1976, *12,* 15–23.

Uzgiris, I. C. Organization of sensorimotor intelligence. In M. Lewis (Ed.), *Origins of intelligence.* New York: Plenum, 1976.

Vandenberg, S. G. Contributions of twin research to psychology. *Psychological Bulletin,* 1966, *66,* 327–352.

Vandenberg, S. G. The hereditary abilities study: Hereditary components in a psychological test battery. *American Journal of Human Genetics,* 1962, *14,* 220–237.

Vandenberg, S. G. Hereditary factors in normal personality traits (as measured by inventories). In J. Wortis (Ed.), *Recent advances in biological psychiatry.* Vol. 9. New York: Plenum, 1967.

Vaz, E. W. Delinquency and the youth culture: Upper- and middle-class boys. *Journal of Criminal Law, Criminology, and Police Science,* 1969, *60* (1), 33–46.

Vernon, P. E. *The structure of human abilities.* London: Methuen, 1960.

Vincent-Smith, L., Bricker, D., and Bricker, W. Acquisition of receptive vocabulary in the toddler-age child. *Child Development,* 1974, *45,* 189–193.

Vurpillot, E. The development of scanning strategies and their relation to visual differentiation. *Journal of Experimental Child Psychology,* 1968, *6,* 632–650.

Waddington, C. H. *The strategy of the genes: A discussion of some aspects of theoretical biology.* London: Allen and Unwin, 1957.

Wagner, H. The increasing importance of the peer group during adolescence. *Adolescence,* 1971, *6,* 53–58.

Wake, F. R. Changes of fear with age. Unpublished doctoral dissertation, McGill University, 1950.

Waldrop, M. F., and Halverson, C. F. Intensive and extensive peer behavior: Longitudinal and cross-sectional analyses. *Child Development,* 1975, *46,* 19–26.

Walk, R. D. The development of depth perception in animals and human infants. *Monographs of the Society for Research in Child Development,* 1966, *31* (5, Serial No. 107), 82–108.

Walters, J., Pearce, D., and Dahms, L. Affectional and aggressive behaviors in preschool children. *Child Development,* 1957, *28,* 15–26.

Walters, R. H., Leat, M., and Mezei, L. Inhibition and disinhibition of responses through empathetic learning. *Canadian Journal of Psychology,* 1963, *17,* 235–243.

Walters, R. H., and Parke, R. D. Emotional arousal, isolation, and discrimination learning in children. *Journal of Experimental Child Psychology,* 1964, *1,* 163–173.

Walters, R. H., Parke, R. D., and Cane, V. A. Timing of punishment and the observation of consequences to others as determinants of response inhibition. *Journal of Experimental Child Psychology*, 1965, *2*, 10–30.

Wardlow, M. E., and Greene, J. E. An exploratory sociometric study of peer status among adolescent girls. *Sociometry*, 1952, *15*, 311–318.

Washburn, R. W. A study of the smiling and laughing of infants in the first year of life. *Genetic Psychology Monographs*, 1929, *6*, 397–537.

Washburn, S. L. Biological versus social evolution. *American Psychologist*, 1976, *31*, 353–355.

Watson, J. B. *Psychology from the standpoint of a behaviorist*. Philadelphia: Lippincott, 1924.

Watson, J. B., and Rayner, M. Conditioned emotional reactions. *Journal of Experimental Psychology*, 1920, *3*, 1–14.

Watson, J. D., and Crick, F. H. C. Molecular structure of nucleic acids—a structure for deoxyribose nucleic acid. *Nature*, 1953, *171*, 737–738.

Wax, D. E. Social class, race, and juvenile delinquency: A review of the literature. *Child Psychiatry and Human Development*, 1972, *3*, 36–49.

Wechsler, D. *The measurement and appraisal of adult intelligence*. Baltimore, Md.: Williams and Wilkins, 1937, 1958.

Weikart, D. P. Relationships of curriculum, teaching, and learning in preschool education. In J. C. Stanley (Ed.), *Preschool programs for the disadvantaged*. Baltimore, Md.: The Johns Hopkins University Press, 1972, pp. 22–66.

Weiner, I. B. The generation gap—fact or fancy. *Adolescence*, 1971, *6*, 155–166.

Wellman, H. M., and Lemer, J. D. The naturalistic communicative abilities of two-year-olds. *Child Development*, 1977, *48*, 1052–1057.

Wetstone, H. S., and Friedlander, H. Z. The effect of word order on young children's responses to simple questions and commands. *Child Development*, 1973, *44*, 734–740.

Wheeler, R. J., and Dusek, J. B. The effects of attentional and cognitive factors on children's incidental learning. *Child Development*, 1973, *44*, 253–258.

White, G. M., and Burnam, M. A. Socially cued altruism effects of modeling instructions and age on public and private donations. *Child Development*, 1975, *46*, 559–563.

White, S. Evidence for a hierarchical arrangement of learning processes. In L. P. Lipsitt and C. C. Spiker (Eds.), *Advances in child behavior and development*. Vol. 2. New York: Academic Press, 1965.

White, S. H. The learning theory tradition and child psychology. In P. H. Mussen (Ed.), *Carmichael's manual of child psychology*. New York: Wiley, 1970.

Whyte, W. E. *Street corner society*. Chicago: University of Chicago Press, 1943.

Willemsen, E., Flaherty, D., Heaton, C., and Ritchey, D. Attachment behavior in one-year-olds as a function of mother vs. father, sex of child, session, and toys. *Genetic Psychology Monographs*, 1974, *90*, 305–324.

Williams, J. E., Bennett, S. M., and Best, D. L. Awareness and expression of sex stereotypes in young children. *Developmental Psychology*, 1975, *11*, 635–642.

Wilson, E. O. *Sociobology: The new synthesis*. Cambridge, Mass.: Belknap Press, 1975.

Winder, C. L., and Rau, L. Parental attitudes associated with social deviance in preadolescent boys. *Journal of Abnormal Social Psychology*, 1962, *64*, 418–424.

Wine, J. Test anxiety and direction of attention. *Psychological Bulletin*, 1971, *76*, 92–104.

Wirt, R. D., and Briggs, P. F. Personality and environmental factors in the development of delinquency. *Psychological Monographs*, 1959, *73*, 1–47.

Wise, N. B. Juvenile delinquency among middle-class girls. In E. W. Vaz (Ed.), *Middle-class juvenile delinquency*. New York: Harper and Row, 1967.

Wispé, L. G. Positive forms of social behavior: An overview. *Journal of Social Issues*, 1972, *28*, 1–19.

Witryol, S. L., and Thompson, G. G. A critical review of the stability of social acceptability scores obtained with the partial-rank-order and the paired-comparison scales. *Genetic Psychology Monographs*, 1953, *48*, 221–260.

Wohlwill, J. F. *The study of behavioral development*. New York: Academic Press, 1973.

Wolf, P. H. The causes, controls, and organization of behavior in the neonate. *Psychological Issues*, 1966, *15*, 17.

Wolfbein, S. L. Labor trends, manpower, and automation. In H. Borow (Ed.), *Man in a world at work*. Boston: Houghton Mifflin, 1964.

Wolpe, P. *The practice of behavior therapy*. New York: Pergamon Press, 1969.

Yankelovich, D. *Generations apart*. New York: Columbia Broadcasting System, 1969.

Yarrow, L. J. Separation from parents during early childhood. In M. Hoffman and L. Hoffman (Eds.), *Review of child development research*. Vol. 1. New York: Russell Sage Foundation, 1964, 89–136.

Yarrow, M. R., Campbell, J. D., and Burton, R. V. *Child rearing*. San Francisco: Jossey-Bass, 1968.

Yarrow, M. R., Campbell, J. D., and Yarrow, L. J. Acquisition of new norms: A study of racial desegregation. *Journal of Social Issues*, 1958, *14*, 8–28.

Yarrow, M. R., Scott, P. M., and Waxler, C. Z. Learning concern for others. *Developmental Psychology*, 1973, *8*, 240–260.

Yarrow, M. R., Waxler, C. Z., et al. Dimensions and correlates of prosocial behavior in young children. *Child Development*, 1976, *47*, 118–125.

Zahn-Waxler, C., Radke-Yarrow, M., Brady-Smith, J. Perspective-taking and prosocial behavior. *Developmental Psychology*, 1977, *13*, 87–88.

Zangwill, O. L. *Cerebral dominance and its relation to psychological function*. London: Oliver and Boyd, 1960.

Zaporozhets, A. V. The development of perception in the preschool child. In P. Mussen (Ed.), European Research in cognitive development. *Monographs of the Society for Research in Child Development*, 1965, *30* (2, Serial No. 100).

Zaporozhets, A. V., and Zinchenko, V. Development of perceptual activity and formation of a sensory image in the child. In A. Leontyen, A. Luria, and A. Smernov (Eds.), *Psychological research in the U.S.S.R.* Moscow: Progress Publishers, 1966, pp. 393–421.

Zeaman, D., and House, B. J. The role of attention in retardate discrimination learning. In N. R. Ellis (Ed.), *Handbook of mental deficiency*. New York: McGraw-Hill, 1963.

Zelnicker, T., and Jeffrey, W. E. Reflective and impulsive children: Strategies of information processing underlying differences in problem solving. *Monographs of the Society for Research in Child Development*, 1976, *41* (5, Serial No. 168).

Zelnik, M., and Kantner, J. F. The resolution of teenage first pregnancies. *Family Planning Perspectives*, 1974, *6* (3).

Zigler, E. Metatheoretical issues in developmental psychology. In M. H. Marx (Ed.), *Theories in contemporary psychology*. New York: Macmillan, 1963.

Zigler, E., Abelson, W. D., and Seitz, V. Motivational factors in the performance of economically disadvantaged children on the Peabody Picture Vocabulary Test. *Child Development*, 1973, *44*, 294–303.

Zigler, E., and Butterfield, E. C. Motivational aspects of changes in IQ test performances of culturally deprived nursery school children. *Child Development*, 1968, *39*, 1–14.

Zigler, E., Levine, J., and Gould, L. Cognitive processes in the development of children's appreciation of humor. *Child Development*, 1966, *37*, 507–518.

Zinchenko, V. P., Chzhi-Tsin, V., and Tarakanov, V. V. The formation and development of perceptual activity. *Soviet Psychology and Psychiatry*, 1963, *1*, 3–12.

Zubek, J. P., and Solberg, P. A. *Human development*. New York: McGraw-Hill, 1954.

NAME INDEX

SUBJECT INDEX